The Secret Anglo-French War in the Middle East

The role of intelligence in colonialism and decolonization is a rapidly expanding field of study. The premise of *The Secret Anglo-French War in the Middle East* is that intelligence statecraft is the "missing dimension" in the established historiography of the Middle East during and after World War II.

Arguing that intelligence, especially covert political action and clandestine diplomacy, played a key role in Britain's Middle East policy, this book examines new archival sources in order to demonstrate that despite World War II and the Cold War, the traditional rivalry between Britain and France in the Middle East continued unabated, assuming the form of a little-known secret war. This shadow war strongly influenced decolonization of the region as each Power sought to undermine the other; Britain exploited France's defeat to evict it from its mandated territories in Syria and Lebanon and incorporate them in its own sphere of influence; while France's successful use of intelligence enabled it to undermine Britain's position in Palestine, Egypt, Saudi Arabia and Iraq.

Providing a fresh perspective on decolonization in the Middle East, this book is essential reading for scholars with an interest in the political history of the Middle East, decolonization, international relations and intelligence studies.

Meir Zamir teaches at Ben-Gurion University of the Negev in Israel. He studies the role of British and French intelligence in the Middle East in the 1940s and the decolonization of the region. He is the author of *The Formation of Modern Lebanon, 1918-1926*, and *Lebanon's Quest: The Road to Statehood, 1926-1939*.

Routledge Studies in Middle Eastern History

The region's history from the earliest times to the present is catered for by this series made up of the very latest research. Books include political, social, cultural, religious and economic history.

The Secret Anglo-French War in the Middle East

Intelligence and Decolonization, 1940-1948

Meir Zamir

Routledge
Taylor & Francis Group

LONDON AND NEW YORK

First published 2015
by Routledge
2 Park Square, Milton Park, Abingdon, Oxon OX14 4RN

and by Routledge
711 Third Avenue, New York, NY 10017

Routledge is an imprint of the Taylor & Francis Group, an informa business

British Library Cataloguing in Publication Data
A catalogue record for this book is available from the British Library

Library of Congress Cataloging in Publication Data
Zamir, Meir.
The secret Anglo-French war in the Middle East : intelligence and decolonization, 1940-1948 / Meir Zamir.
pages cm. -- (Routledge studies in Middle Eastern history ; 17)
Includes bibliographical references and index.
1. Middle East--Foreign relations--Great Britain. 2. Middle East--Foreign relations--France. 3. Great Britain--Foreign relations--Middle East.
4. France--Foreign relations--Middle East. 5. Espionage, British--Middle East--History--20th century. 6. Espionage, French--Middle East--History--20th century. 7. Military intelligence--Middle East--History--20th century. 8. Middle East--Politics and government--20th century. 9. Decolonization--Middle East--History--20th century. I. Title.
DS63.2.G7Z36 2015
956'.03--dc23
2014022483

ISBN: 978-1-138-78781-0 (hbk)
ISBN: 978-1-315-76542-6 (ebk)

Typeset in Times New Roman
by Taylor and Francis Books

In memory of my father
Na'im Zamir
(1917-2012)
and
my father-in-law
Alexander G.S. James
(1911-2004)

Contents

Preface

This book, a long time in the making, involved repeated research trips to France to locate the whereabouts of, and receive the necessary authorization to view, the Syrian documents on which it is based. Scholars who research intelligence records know that archival authorities tend to be extra cautious when it comes to releasing material.

After publishing two books on the history of Lebanon under the French mandate (1918-1939), I initially intended to write the third volume of a planned trilogy. That volume was to examine the political, social and economic changes in Lebanon against the backdrop of World War II and the Anglo-French rivalry in the Levant (1939-1946).

I worked in archives in France and Britain, obtained material from American sources and examined Lebanese and other Arab resources. I was expecting to write the volume without encountering any specific problems as the war years were well documented. However, during my research, I noticed some unexplained discrepancies between the French documents and those from British, Lebanese and American sources, discrepancies that could not be explained merely by different interpretations of events or the traditional French animosity towards "Perfidious Albion." From my research on the previous two volumes, I was well aware of the capacity of the French High Commission and its intelligence services to monitor local politics, and could not ignore the repeated accusations of British duplicity, or explain them merely as part of the traditional Anglo-French colonial rivalry.

After two years' work and the completion of a significant portion of the manuscript, I decided to return to the archives to reconsider my approach. The result was an article, "*An Intimate Alliance: The Joint Struggle of General Edward Spears and Riad al-Sulh to Oust France from Lebanon, 1942-1944*," published in 2005, in which I laid emphasis on the secret collaboration between Spears and Sulh in the Lebanese constitutional crisis of 1943. While researching that article I became convinced of the need to reexamine de Gaulle's allegations that Britain was behind France's eviction from its mandated territories of Syria and Lebanon. When I looked more closely at General de Gaulle's role in the Lebanese crisis, I became aware of certain "Syrian documents."

In a volume of de Gaulle's letters (*Lettres, notes et carnets, Juin 1943–Mai 1945*), I came across a note he sent on October 19, 1944 to Georges Bidault, then serving as Foreign Minister in the Provisional Government, in which he referred to an annexed exchange of letters between Syrian President Shukri al-Quwatli and King Ibn Sa'ud concerning Greater Syria. The letters themselves were not attached, but a footnote mentioned that they had been obtained by the French intelligence services in Beirut. I subsequently published an article in 2007 titled *"De Gaulle and the Question of Syria and Lebanon During the Second World War."* This was the first of two articles in which I planned to reexamine de Gaulle's role in the Anglo-French rivalry in the Levant. Several research trips to France, during which I began to look for those Syrian documents, followed. After failing to find the trace of any such documents in the archives in which I was working, I decided to focus on de Gaulle's and Bidault's papers in the Archives Nationales in Paris, but many of their files had not yet been made available to researchers. The breakthrough came at the end of 2007, when I discovered French translations of hundreds of Syrian and British documents in Bidault's papers. These included top-secret reports on the covert activities of British agents, and private and official correspondence between the Syrian leaders and other Arab heads of state, together with documents from the files of the Syrian Ministry of Foreign Affairs.

These documents provide new insight into the history of the Middle East during the formative years of the 1940s. Historians can now examine the role of the British intelligence services in the region and, with access to uncensored Arab documents, they can study the Arab point of view directly rather than through Western archives, memoirs or newspapers. In 2008, I spent a sabbatical in Paris during which I was granted access to de Gaulle's papers on Syria and Lebanon; these shed light on his troubled relations with Churchill in the Levant. As a result, I redirected my research to the role of the British and French intelligence agencies in the Middle East in the 1940s and the secret Anglo-French war and its impact on the decolonization of the region.

In de Gaulle's and Bidault's papers I also came across reports on Franco-Zionist intelligence collaboration, indicating that David Ben-Gurion, Moshe Shertok and a small number of their assistants had access to French intelligence sources. I therefore extended my research to Israeli archives looking for evidence that the French intelligence agencies had shared information with the Haganah's secret services. In light of the importance of the Syrian documents I uncovered, I revealed some of my findings in Israeli newspapers. In 2010, I published an article addressing Franco-Zionist collaboration and looking at France's role in the Altalena affair. In another article, titled *"The 'Missing Dimension': Britain's Secret War Against France in Syria and Lebanon, 1942-45,"* I looked at the role of British secret agents in orchestrating the Syrian crisis of 1945. In this article I included over one hundred Syrian and British documents.

The present study, based primarily on the secret British and Syrian documents and French intelligence reports and diplomatic correspondence, exposes the role played by the British secret services in shaping their country's Middle East policy. It unveils details of their little-known modus operandi, especially in co-opting "agents of influence" – prominent Arab leaders, politicians, senior military officers, businessmen, civil servants and journalists who shaped Arab public opinion. These included the Syrian and Lebanese presidents and prime ministers whom they helped to power, as well as ministers and members of parliament. It highlights the use made by British intelligence personnel of covert political action (employing political intelligence for control and subversion) and clandestine diplomacy, and argues that their role in Arab politics and diplomacy comprises the "missing dimension" in the existing historiography of the Middle East. The book claims that Britain conducted a dual policy in the region – that of Whitehall in London, details of which can be found in British archives, and a tacit policy implemented by intelligence agents, military officers and diplomats in the field, which is little documented. Despite decolonization, these "agents in the field," many of whom were Arabists, employed controversial methods to ensure their country's dominance in the post-war Middle East, often without the knowledge or sanction of their government.

Another premise of the book is that a clandestine war took place between Britain and France in the Middle East in the 1940s. Despite collaboration between Britain and Free France during the war, and between Britain and France in post-war Europe, the long-standing rivalry between the two declining colonial Powers continued unabated in the region. After its eviction from the Levant in 1945, France successfully conducted a secret war against Britain in the Middle East due in no small part to the achievements of its intelligence services. The French secret services honed their ability to monitor the British agents' Special Political Operations, study their modi operandi and uncover their ties with their Arab collaborators. This information, available in French, but not British, archives is essential for an understanding of the covert policy pursued by the British secret agents in the Arab-Jewish conflict in 1947-48. The French undercover operations against Britain culminated in the Franco-Zionist intelligence collaboration in the 1948 war in Palestine.

The book comprises two parts; the first presents the role of the British secret services in the clandestine Anglo-French war in the Middle East in 1940-1948. It also briefly examines the Franco-Zionist intelligence collaboration against Britain. The first chapter looks at the modus operandi of the British intelligence services in the Middle East in that period and profiles some of the main protagonists. The second chapter deals with the secret Anglo-French war in the Levant in the early war years under both Vichy and Free France. The third focuses on the role of British agents in engineering the Lebanese crisis in 1943 and the Syrian crisis in 1945, and describes the covert French counter-action. The Epilogue brings to light new findings from the French archives on the part played by the British secret agents in inflaming the Arab-Jewish confrontation in 1947-48 and in provoking the armed Arab invasion of the newly established State of Israel.

The second part of the book comprises close to 400 documents selected from the large number of Syrian documents uncovered in the French archives and translated from French to English for the purposes of this book. The documents aim to sustain the assertions made in the first part, and there are direct references to specific documents within the text. They are also intended to serve as a resource for historians studying the period.

This book is dedicated to my father and my father-in-law. My father, Na'im Zamir, was born in Baghdad in 1917, the year that British forces occupied the city. For three decades he lived under British and Iraqi rule. A member of the long-established Jewish community in Baghdad, after 1948 he became a victim of the Arab-Jewish conflict in Palestine. He left Iraq in 1951 and immigrated to Israel with his family, but spoke fondly of the British officials whom he had met while working in his father-in-law's printing press. My father-in-law, Alexander James, was born in Nairobi to a British family serving in the colonial administration. As an adult, he enlisted in the RAF and served in the Middle East during the 1930s. At a later stage he left England and came to live in Israel. Their experiences – of living under the British Empire – inspired me when writing this book.

Acknowledgements

This book, the result of extensive research in archives in France, Britain and Israel, could not have been completed without the help of a number of colleagues and institutions, and I am happy to thank them all. I am greatly indebted to the Israel Science Foundation, whose financial support helped me to cover costs involved in researching the book, as well as the French Embassy in Tel Aviv for grants that facilitated repeated research trips to France. I would like to thank the archivists and library staff in the various archives, who were always willing to help, especially those in the Archives Nationales in Paris, who pointed me in the right direction in my search for the Syrian documents.

I am deeply grateful to Helen Kedourie for her help in translating the documents and patiently going through the manuscript. I would also like to thank Rosie Demezieux in Paris who, apart from assisting me with my research in the archives, became a good friend. Ilan Shdema, Ezra Nishry and Michal Dratler helped me with my research in archives in Israel. My sincere thanks go to Sylvia Kedourie, Israel Gershoni and Haggai Erlich for their sound advice and insight whenever I needed it.

Finally, I would like to acknowledge Joe Whiting, Kathryn Rylance and Stacey Carter at Routledge for their patience and understanding while I was preparing the final manuscript. My thanks also to Kate McIntosh for preparing the index.

My deepest gratitude goes to my wife, Angela, who accompanied me throughout this project. I could not have accomplished it without her constant support.

Abbreviations

Abwehr	German military intelligence
AN	Archives nationales, Paris
BCR	Bureau central de renseignements
BCRA	Bureau central de renseignements et d'action
BMEO	British Middle East Office
BOAC	British Overseas Airways Corporation
BSM	British Security Mission
CA	Covert Action
CD	Clandestine Diplomacy
CFLN	Comité Français de Libération nationale
CIA	United States Central Intelligence Agency, successor of the OSS
CBME	Combined Bureau Middle East, a regional section of the GC&CS
CICI	Combined Intelligence Centre Iraq
CID	Criminal Investigation Department
COS	Chiefs of Staff
CPA	Covert Political Action
CRPO	Combined Research and Planning Office
DDMI	Deputy Director of Military Intelligence
DMI	Director of Military Intelligence
D Section	SIS sabotage and covert action section
DSO	Defense Security Officer
EMA	Etat-major de l'armée
FSS	Field Security Service
GC&CS	Government Code and Cipher School
GCHQ	Government Communications Headquarters
GHQME	General Headquarters, Middle East
Haganah	Jewish Defense Force
Humint	Human Intelligence
Imint	Imagery Intelligence
IPC	Iraq Petroleum Company
IZL	Irgun Zvai Leumi (National Military Organization)

ISLD	Inter-Services Liaison Department
JIC	Joint Intelligence Committee
JICME	Joint Intelligence Committee Middle East
LEHI	Lohamei Herut Yisrael (Freedom Fighters of Israel)
MAE	Ministère des Affaires étrangères
MECAS	Middle East Centre for Arab Studies
MEHQ	Middle East Headquarters
MEIC	Middle East Intelligence Centre
MESC	Middle East Supply Centre
MEWC	Middle East War Council
MI5	Military Intelligence 5 – UK Security Service
MI6	Military Intelligence 6 – Secret Intelligence Service
MI(R)	Military Intelligence (Research)
NCFL	Comité français de Libération nationale
OSS	United States Office of Strategic Services, forerunner of the CIA
PHPS	British Post-Hostilities Planning Staff
PICME	Political Intelligence Centre Middle East
PWE	Political Warfare Executive
RAF	Royal Air Force
SCR	Section de centralisation de renseignements
SDECE	Service de documentation extérieure et de contre-espionnage
SEL	Section d'études du Levant
SG	Sûreté générale
SGA	Sûreté générale de l'armée
SHAY	Haganah Intelligence Service
SHD/DAT	Service historique de la Défense, direction de l'armée de terre
Sigint	Signals Intelligence
SIME	Security Intelligence Middle East
SIS	Secret Intelligence Service
SOE	Special Operations Executive
SR	Service de renseignement
SSO	Special Service Officers
TNA	The National Archives, London

Part I

1 Great Britain's covert political action in the Middle East during and after World War II

On October 19, 1944, General Charles de Gaulle, head of the French Provisional Government, sent Georges Bidault, his Foreign Minister, a note together with several secret British and Syrian documents obtained by the French intelligence services in Beirut and Damascus. The documents revealed that British agents were secretly scheming to evict France from the Levant and incorporate its mandated territories of Syria and Lebanon into Great Britain's sphere of influence. The documents related to attempts by General Edward Spears, the British Minister in Syria and Lebanon, to pressure Shukri al-Quwatli, the Syrian President, into upholding secret pledges he had made two years earlier to integrate Syria into a Hashemite Greater Syria under Britain's hegemony.[1] This plot had been hatched in August, just before the Arab Preparatory Conference was due to convene in Alexandria. Authorized by Lord Moyne, the British Minister of State resident in the Middle East, it was implemented by Brigadier Iltyd Clayton, his adviser on Arab affairs and head of the Political Intelligence Centre Middle East (PICME) in Cairo, who traveled to Beirut to put it into effect. Their scheme was in sharp contrast to negotiations taking place in London between Anthony Eden, the British Foreign Secretary, and René Massigli, the Commissioner for Foreign Affairs on the French Committee, in which Eden reiterated that his government had no ambitions over Syria and Lebanon and reaffirmed Britain's recognition of France's right to conclude treaties with the two Levant states, similar to its own treaty with Iraq. During the negotiations, Massigli was informed that General Spears, France's bitter opponent, would be ending his term in December that year.[2]

De Gaulle viewed the British and Syrian documents as confirmation of allegations he had been making since July 1941 – when British and Free French forces had taken Syria and Lebanon from Vichy – of Britain's duplicity towards France in the Levant despite his agreement with Oliver Lyttelton, the Minister of State in Cairo at the time. Although Winston Churchill and Eden acknowledged Free France's predominance in the Levant, de Gaulle believed that the British leaders and their representatives in the Middle East were exploiting France's weakness after its defeat in June 1940 to realize their old ambitions of forcing it out of the Levant and dominating the entire

Middle East. He was convinced that General Spears, who was leading the campaign to evict France from Syria and Lebanon, had received the tacit approval of his mentor and friend, Churchill himself. Churchill's ultimatum on May 30, 1945, at the height of the Syrian crisis, and his secret instructions to General Sir Bernard Paget, Commander of the Allied Forces in the Middle East – obtained by the French intelligence services (docs.97-9) – convinced de Gaulle that Churchill was seeking not only to oust France from the Levant, but also to humiliate him personally and force him to resign as head of the French provisional government.[3] Paradoxically, less than two months later, Churchill was defeated by the Labour Party in the general election, while de Gaulle won the French general election in October, only to resign three months later.

Despite de Gaulle's allegations, Bidault made a clear distinction between the policies applied from London by Eden, and later on by Ernest Bevin, and that of the British establishment in the Middle East. He argued that securing Britain's support for the restoration of France's status in Europe was crucial and therefore it should refrain from a confrontation in the Middle East. But he too was unwilling to relinquish France's traditional position there, deeming it essential for its control of North Africa. He sought an Anglo-French agreement to ensure his country's standing in the Levant, especially in Lebanon. But his efforts were only partly successful, as British agents continued and even intensified their subversive activities against France in the Middle East and North Africa. While serving as Prime Minister and Foreign Minister in the Fourth Republic in the second half of the 1940s, Bidault fought Britain with its own weapon – covert action.[4]

The decade of World War II and the early years of the Cold War (1939-1949) was a formative period for the Middle East. The struggle by local nationalist movements for independence from Britain and France intensified as the two colonial Powers sought to retain their standing. Britain initially faced a military threat from the Axis Powers, followed by Soviet attempts to penetrate the region, as well as an economic challenge from the United States. Syria and Lebanon finally secured independence from France; Egypt resumed its long struggle to force Britain to abide by pledges made during the war to revise the 1936 treaty, withdraw its forces and unite Egypt with Sudan; and Saudi Arabia solidified its economic and strategic ties with the United States. The inter-Arab system took shape and in March 1945 the Arab League was formed. But the Arab world was deeply divided over Iraq's and Transjordan's attempts to integrate Syria in a Greater Syria and an Iraqi-led Hashemite confederation. The state of Israel was established following a bitter struggle by the Zionist movement that brought an end to the British Mandate in Palestine, and after the ensuing war against the Palestinians and the Arab states. World War II also hastened social and economic change, as a new generation of radical Arab nationalists seeking social and political reforms began to take over, initially in Syria, where army officers deposed the old nationalist elites in several coups in 1949, and then in Egypt in 1952.

It is therefore understandable why this period in the history of the modern Middle East is one of the most studied. Yet the full facts on Britain's policy in the region are lacking and major issues remain controversial. Britain's part in evicting France from Syria and Lebanon has only recently been elucidated with the discovery of secret Syrian and British documents in French archives, but its role in the formation of the Arab League, the Greater Syria and Fertile Crescent schemes and the 1948 war in Palestine remains unresolved. Scholars studying Britain's retreat from the Middle East continue to debate the causes of its rapid decline despite emerging from the war as the dominant power in the region. Various explanations have been put forward, including Britain's post-war economic weakness, the Labour government's decolonization policy, the intense opposition of local nationalist movements, the Soviet strategic challenge and the failure of its policy in Palestine. Historians describe Britain's Middle East policy in those years as suffering from a lack of coherency and consistency, exacerbated by disagreement between the Labour government and its Chiefs of Staff (COS) against the backdrop of the escalating Cold War. Although these factors did play a part, the premise of this study is that British vacillation was also the result of a "parallel policy" when, alongside Whitehall's Middle East policy applied from London, a more secretive "regional" policy was implemented in the field by a small but influential group of British Arabists serving as diplomats, intelligence agents and military officers, who used controversial methods to retain their country's hegemony in the Middle East. But while Whitehall policy is well documented, there are few traces in the archives of this region-based secretive and controversial strategy. In this regard it is worth quoting Jon Kimche, a British journalist and one of the more critical and shrewd observers of Britain's Arab Middle East policy:

> The decisive feature of these years was the existence of this close cooperation, this "Club" of the British Middle East: it embraced officials at the Foreign Office, the Middle East embassies and legations and most of their staff, the Palestine Government, the oil companies and especially ex-officials and ex-officers who had served in the Middle East from Lawrence onward; they, with a select list of travelers, explorers, writers and journalists, constituted "The Club." It was "The Club" that created the political and press climate in the Middle East and in London; it fathered, formed and sponsored British policy in the Middle East. And in the years that followed the war, from 1945 until 1949, it was "The Club" that prepared the ground for a series of unexampled and humiliating defeats for British policy and the frustration of many sincere hopes in British leadership. The members of "The Club" were, in the event, as blinkered as any monk of the Middle Ages, who sought to blot out ancient truths with blobs of ink and prejudice.[5]

Kimche was not alone in making such claims concerning the role of the "experts" or "Arabists" – the "people in the field" – in shaping Britain's

Middle East policy during and after World War II. William Roger Louis, in his seminal study of Britain's Middle East policy under the Labour government, described Brigadier Iltyd Clayton, a prominent member of "The Club," as the "eminence grise of British imperialism in the Middle East."[6] Elie Kedourie, who examined the influence wielded by the Royal Institute for International Affairs (Chatham House) and its director, Arnold Toynbee, on Britain's pan-Arab policy during and after the war, pointed out the close ties between the Institute in London and its branch in Cairo headed by Clayton.[7] The role of General Spears, another notorious member of "The Club," in ousting France from Syria and Lebanon and exacerbating the tension between Churchill and de Gaulle in the Levant has been examined in numerous studies.[8]

An analysis of the role of the "agents in the field," especially Arabist intelligence officers, in shaping Britain's Middle East policy in the two world wars reveals that while there is extensive research on the role of individuals such as T.E. Lawrence, Mark Sykes, Gertrude Bell and Gilbert Clayton, as well as the Arab Bureau during and after World War I, few studies explore the role of intelligence officers and secret services on its policy there during and after World War II. Yet at this time, intelligence agents and organizations and a small group of British Arabists turned the Middle East into a playground for British covert operations using intelligence, especially covert political action (CPA) and clandestine diplomacy (CD), to conduct regional-based policy, often without London's knowledge or sanction. In fact, they followed their World War I and inter-war predecessors, as Priya Satia observed: "The Middle East was now a land in which British diplomats, technocrats, administrators and academics were the ubiquitous minions of covert empire; they could do as they pleased."[9] But unlike their colorful World War I colleagues, they acted mainly in the shadows and hence their role is less known. Moreover, after the failure of their policy in 1948, they became involved in a large scale cover-up and the writing of an alternative historiography.[10]

The term "Arabists" used in this work is more limited than Kimche's definition of "The Club," and refers to a smaller group of British officials who were using covert intelligence methods. Some were veterans of World War I, who now held high-ranking positions in the British administration, the military and intelligence systems. Others had fought with Lawrence in the Arab Revolt and returned to active duty when the new war broke out. There were intelligence officers, such as Brigadier Iltyd Clayton, Lieutenant-Colonel Walter Stirling and Dame Freya Stark; diplomats, such as Sir Kinahan Cornwallis, the Ambassador in Iraq, Sir Alec Kirkbride, the Minister in Amman and Sir Walter Smart, the Oriental Secretary in the British Embassy in Cairo; and military officers such as Brigadier John Bagot Glubb. Although they cannot be regarded as Arabists, General Spears and Miles Lampson (later Lord Killearn), Ambassador to Egypt, are included in this group. Another category comprised retired officials, such as Colonel Stewart Newcombe and Sir Ronald Storrs, the former governor of Jerusalem, who continued to be active in the Arabist lobby in London. Only with the discovery of the British and Syrian documents have their methods of influencing policy makers in London and Cairo become apparent.[11]

Leslie McLoughlin, a former instructor in the Foreign Office's Middle East Centre for Arab Studies (MECAS), or the "spy school," as it was better known in Lebanon – one of whose founders was Brigadier Clayton – defines "Arabist" as "anyone with the knowledge of Arabic which is relevant to his or her principal activities and, which, to a greater or lesser extent, defines the individual's identity."[12] McLoughlin's definition, based on language knowledge, is somewhat limited for our purposes. General Spears, for example, had no command of Arabic language or culture, yet his goals and the methods he used to attain them made him a leading member of the Arabist circles. Furthermore, understanding language and culture did not necessarily imply, as McLoughlin claims, love and respect for that particular culture. Arab leaders who were in touch with British Arabists often complained of their rude and arrogant behavior (doc.340). In this regard, it is worth quoting Kaplan's observation:

> Whatever the individual traits of the British Arabists, they all operated against a backdrop of imperialism. It was the advantages of power and privilege that imperialism offered that allowed these British men and women to work out their personalities and fantasies upon such an exotic stage. Their myriad eccentricities notwithstanding ... [they] were ... British government agents, and thus it was the mechanics of imperial power that primarily concerned them.[13]

In the 1940s, most of the Arabists, especially the veterans of World War I, lived in the past, in the heyday of British imperialism in the Middle East, overlooking the radical social and political changes that had taken place in the quarter century since then, the rising nationalism and the growing challenge from the two new Great Powers. With an imperial cast of mind, they were committed to ensuring the survival of the British Empire in the region, either formally or informally. Churchill's love for and commitment to the idea of the British Empire served as justification for them to commit unacceptable and morally questionable acts against any forces they considered a threat to the Empire, whether friend or foe. This was particularly true of General Spears, Churchill's admirer, who wholeheartedly adopted the Arabists' agenda of the importance of the Middle East for Britain as a Great Power. In this regard, their wartime efforts to safeguard the Empire reinforced Britain's reluctant post-war decolonization of the Middle East. They could not come to terms with the painful reality that, despite its remarkable victory against the Axis Powers, post-war Britain was no longer a Great Power, but a weak, economically exhausted, declining empire, unable to compete with the United States and the Soviet Union. They regarded their country's control of the Middle East as vital for its strategic interests, for maintaining the Empire, and for post-war economic recovery, and were determined to prevent it from slipping away from Britain's grip. Neither the hostility of the Arab nationalists, the repugnance of the international community, led by the United States, to British imperialism, nor the Labour government's declared decolonization, swayed them from their imperial designs. Quite the opposite – they intended, as the British and Syrian documents attest, to exploit the defeats of France and Italy, Britain's two rival colonial Powers, in order to expand their country's holdings to include the French and Italian territories in Syria and Lebanon as well as in Libya and French North Africa (docs.376, 384, 387). They were influential in shaping Britain's post-war Middle East policy and enjoyed the backing of the strong military establishment, intelligence organizations, business circles in the City of London and the influential Chatham House. The members of this lobby, who voiced their views in *The Times* and *The Economist*, came from military and civilian circles, each with their own interests, but all tried to pressure the government and mobilize public opinion to ensure that Britain would continue to hold the Middle East.[14]

It should be noted that the terms "Arabists," "the Arab lobby" and "the Camel Corps," as they were known in the Foreign Office, are somewhat misleading, as their members did not necessarily support the Arab cause, but, as British agents had done in World War I, exploited it to secure Britain's hegemony over the Middle East. They cynically inflamed Arab-Muslim fears of France, international Communism, Zionism and American capitalism, and presented their country as the only Power defending the Arab cause. Their influence was based on long experience of serving in the region and on personal ties with many of the Arab leaders. They acted as intermediaries between those leaders and the British decision-makers in Cairo and London. They were "specialists," "experts on the Arab mentality," familiar with the language and local culture and able to read the "Arab mind" – the holders of what can be defined as an "institutional tradition," a set of well-established beliefs and concepts, some dating back to World War I. Moreover, veteran Arabists such as Kinahan Cornwallis, Stirling, Alec Kirkbride and Clayton, who enjoyed the unique status of having fought with Lawrence of Arabia, used their prestige and reputation to influence those posted to the Middle East after 1939. These Arabists believed that the new war offered an opportunity to rectify what they regarded as the mistakes of Lloyd George's World War I Cabinet, especially the signing of the Sykes-Picot Agreement that had installed a hostile France in Syria and Lebanon and divided the Fertile Crescent into four weak, non-viable Arab states, and the Balfour Declaration, which had imposed an alien Jewish entity in Palestine, thereby antagonizing the Arabs and undermining Britain's efforts to secure the goodwill of the Arab-Muslim world. They were determined to prevent the politicians in London from repeating those mistakes. They regarded the ousting of France from the two Levant states as a first step towards establishing, under Britain's tutelage, a loyal, Hashemite Greater Syrian monarchy comprising Syria, Lebanon, Transjordan and Palestine, united in federal or confederal ties with

Iraq. This was to remain their ultimate goal throughout the 1940s, making Syria central to their plans. The British and Syrian documents afford us unique insight into the myriad intrigues and schemes of both the British Arabists and the Hashemites in pursuit of this goal, as well as the measures taken by their opponents – whether Syria, Saudi Arabia, Egypt, France, the Soviet Union or the United States – to frustrate British-Hashemite designs. A decade after the war, Britain had lost its "moment" in the Middle East, but the Arabists who were behind one of the most devastating failures in Britain's decolonization were never held to account.[15]

To understand the Arabists' strong influence on policy makers in London and Cairo in the post-war years, the effect of the Cold War on Britain's Middle East policy must be taken into account. The issue of the secret Anglo-Soviet war in the Middle East in the final year of World War II and the post-war period, as revealed in the British and Syrian documents, is discussed in detail in Chapter 3. It suffices to emphasize here that by 1944 the British strategic planners regarded the Soviet Union as the main adversary and assumed that the Middle East would be the first area where a confrontation would erupt. Indeed, Churchill's decision at the end of May 1945 to allow General Paget to secretly oust France from Syria and Lebanon was partly provoked by his fear that de Gaulle could not be trusted in the event of a conflict with the Soviet Union in the Middle East. Moreover, under the Labour government, Britain's strategic concept, promoted by the COS, was that in any future war with the Soviet Union, Britain would respond with an air offensive from bases in the Middle East. Prime Minister Clement Attlee, however, questioned this concept and proposed East Africa as an alternative. Bevin, on the other hand, backed the COS's view that the Middle East was strategically important, believing that Anglo-Arab cooperation could be achieved, even with Egypt, which was insisting on the evacuation of the British forces from their bases along the Suez Canal.[16]

The gap between scholars of political history and intelligence studies is more noticeable with regard to World War II, in which British intelligence, particularly political intelligence, was important for controlling the region. Scholars of intelligence studies were the first to emphasize the need to examine the role of intelligence in fields other than the traditional military-strategic areas. Since David Dilks and Christopher Andrew published their ground-breaking work on intelligence in international relations, termed by them the "missing dimension," intelligence studies as an academic discipline has expanded to include other areas such as colonialism and decolonization. The paucity of primary sources has been partly overcome in the last two decades as the archives of British intelligence agencies have been made available to scholars. French archives, as demonstrated in the present study, are also useful, as French intelligence was deeply involved in the clandestine wars in the Middle East during the 1940s.[17]

The role of British intelligence agencies in post-war decolonization is increasingly attracting the attention of historians. Calder Walton and

Christopher Andrew argue that despite the vast, available decolonization literature, the role of intelligence in this process is noticeably absent, and that although considerable progress has recently been made in the study of intelligence, it remains a "missing dimension" in British decolonization. Others scholars maintain that, contrary to the notion that Britain's "retreat from the Empire" was haphazard but liberal, it was in fact more organized and brutal than we have been led to believe. Britain violently suppressed nationalist insurgencies in parts of its former colonies, such as Malaysia, Ghana and Kenya, to safeguard its economic and military interests.[18] Richard Aldrich describes the close ties between intelligence officers and the British business community in the Far East and their attempts to restore the British Empire in that region after World War II. Such tactics were prevalent in the Middle East, but apart from the joint operation of MI6 (formally known as the Secret Intelligence Service (SIS)) and the Central Intelligence Agency (CIA) in the early 1950s to overthrow Mohammad Mussadeq's democratically-elected nationalist government and install the Shah in Iran, the role of British intelligence in decolonizing the Middle East is still shrouded in secrecy. Aldrich maintains that the "SIS was largely concerned with the politics of Britain's informal empire," while Stephen Dorril claims that in the 1950s, intelligence services in the Middle East often assumed the role of guardians of the British Empire, stepping into the vacuum left by the politicians.[19] Keith Jeffery rightly points out that the political agenda of the intelligence services reflected that of the "privileged class," which certainly also included retaining the Empire.[20] Although in recent years more studies have been published, especially on the role of the British intelligence agencies in their clandestine war against underground Zionist movements, they have been hampered by limited access to official documentation, especially that of SIS.[21] In this regard, the British and Syrian documents shed new light on the role of the British and French secret services in the decolonization of the Middle East. Paradoxically, while British and French intelligence agents spearheaded efforts to retain their countries' influence in the region, their clandestine war undercut their positions and accelerated decolonization. This decolonization of the Middle East by the two colonial Powers was thus the result, not only of their own weakness or the strength of the local nationalist movements, but of the secret war between them.

   The premise underlying this study is that intelligence statecraft is the "missing dimension" in the established historiography of the Middle East during and after World War II, and that examining it may settle some of the more controversial issues. The hypothesis is that intelligence, especially covert political action and clandestine diplomacy, played a key role in Britain's Middle East policy at the time, and that Britain conducted a "parallel policy" in the region: Whitehall policy, details of which can be found in British archives, ran alongside a covert policy implemented by Arabists, intelligence agents, senior military officers, diplomats and colonial officials "in the field," of which there is scant evidence in official documentation. The study argues that British intelligence agencies wielded considerable influence, first in ensuring control over the Middle East during the war, and later when seeking to create a "covert empire" to protect their country's strategic and economic interests in the region despite decolonization. In a way, they were the muscle behind the traditional diplomats, assuming the role of guardians of a British Empire in the Middle East. Another premise is that, despite World War II and the Cold War, the traditional rivalry between Britain and France in the Middle East continued unabated, assuming the form of a little-known secret war. As each Power sought to undermine the other, this shadow war strongly influenced decolonization of the region. Britain exploited France's defeat to evict it from its mandated territories in Syria and Lebanon and incorporate them in its own sphere of influence, while France used its success in its war of intelligence to undermine Britain's position in Palestine, Egypt, Saudi Arabia and Iraq. France's intelligence collaborations, initially with the Zionist movement and later with the state of Israel against Britain and the Arab states between 1945 and 1948, played a part in Britain's failure to reorganize the region under its hegemony. These premises can now be examined with the help of the British and Syrian documents.[22]

Intelligence activities, covert operations and secret diplomacy, like conspiracy theories, have always been endemic in the Middle East. There is much popular, journalistic literature on intelligence, but few academic studies. Scholars have tended to shy away from the subject, mainly because of the dearth of official documentation. But the paucity of academic studies does not mean that Britain and France did not utilize intelligence in their decolonization of the Middle East and North Africa. On the contrary, the Middle East was strategically and economically important, especially for Britain, when the region became a major arena for confrontation with the Soviet Union. It can therefore be maintained that all the Powers involved used intelligence and covert operations to retain their influence or undermine that of their rivals.[23]

The British and Syrian documents

The secret British and Syrian documents uncovered by the author in French archives reveal one of the greatest successes of French intelligence in its clandestine war against British intelligence in the Middle East. In the summer of 1944, the French secret services in Syria and Lebanon recruited an agent in the archives of the British Legation in Beirut, a major center of British diplomatic and intelligence activities in the region. At the same time it recruited an agent who had access to the offices of the Syrian President, Prime Minister and the Syrian Foreign Ministry. Over the following years these agents provided thousands of photographs of secret British and Syrian and other Arab documents. From August 1944 until his resignation in January 1946, de Gaulle received, nearly every week via couriers, scores of documents translated into French from General Paul Beynet, the Délégué Général in Syria and Lebanon. French intelligence in Beirut continued to provide such documents to the leaders of the Fourth Republic, particularly to Georges Bidault, who served in the second half of the 1940s as Foreign Minister or Prime Minister. It should be noted that the documents seen so far by the author are those sent to General de Gaulle, and later to Bidault, in Paris, documents deemed relevant to the formulation of French policy towards Britain and the Arab countries in the Middle East. Other documents considered less relevant, or that dealt with sensitive operative issues, were held in Beirut. Only on rare occasions were operative documents sent to Paris, for example when they involved prominent Syrian and Lebanese politicians who were collaborating with the British secret services.

The documents now available cover the period from early 1941 to November 1947.[24] There is, however, indirect evidence that the flow of documents from Syrian sources continued until 1948. It has not been possible to accurately establish how long the French intelligence services continued their operation in the British Legation in Beirut. But French intelligence officers did have access to documents from the Legation's files in January 1948 after its archives were seized by the Haganah, the Jewish defense forces in Palestine, in a secret operation in December 1947 while the British Army was moving them from Beirut to the port of Haifa in order to ship them to England.[25]

The documents annexed to this volume have been selected from the large number discovered, and, together with over one hundred documents already published, they bring a new perspective to the history of the Middle East in those critical years. The original documents were in Arabic or English, but access has been possible only to the French version.[26] For the purpose of this book, the annexed documents were translated from French into English. The documents originating from the files of the British Legation are termed "British," and those from Syrian sources are defined as "Syrian."

The "British" documents are either original British documents or documents obtained by British intelligence agencies in the Middle East. The former include reports on the activities of British diplomats and secret agents in Syria and Lebanon or ciphered correspondence between Beirut and either London or Cairo, the seat of the Minister in Residence in the Middle East. They contain, for example, instructions from Churchill and the Foreign Office to General Sir Bernard Paget, Commander-in-Chief of the Allied Forces in the Middle East in early June 1945 at the height of the Syrian crisis, as well as details of the clandestine diplomacy conducted by British diplomats, the recruitment of agents, payments to Arab politicians and intelligence reports from Arab agents to their British controllers. Such sensitive operative documents may have been kept by the British intelligence agencies in Syria and Lebanon in the Beirut Legation archives for security considerations, and hence the ability of the French agents to access them.

Other "British" documents include private letters of Arab leaders and documents obtained by the British secret services throughout the Middle East and sent to Beirut for information purposes. This was part of the British intelligence community's policy in the Middle East in order to maintain the flow of relevant information to their various customers in the region. For example, intelligence reports concerning Saudi Arabia were sent to Beirut because of King Ibn Sa'ud's close ties with President Shukri al-Quwatli and his involvement in Syrian affairs. These documents include minutes of the Saudi King's meetings with President Roosevelt, King Faruq and President Quwatli, as well as reports from Ibn Sa'ud's private physician to his British controller in Cairo. As Syria became the focus of Arab unity plans and the Saudi-Hashemite confrontation, intelligence raw material was also sent to Beirut from the headquarters of intelligence agencies in Cairo, and from agencies and diplomats in Riyadh, Baghdad and Amman. This material included copies of Quwatli's secret agreements with the Hashemite leaders in July 1942 and February 1943; private correspondence between Emir Abdullah of Transjordan and his nephew, Emir Abd al-Ilah, the Iraqi regent; and a letter from Crown-Prince Emir Talal, visiting Beirut, to his father, Emir Abdullah (docs.3-4, 41, 45, 68).

The "Syrian" documents originated from the archives of the Syrian Foreign Ministry, as well as from the offices of the President and the Prime Minister. It appears that French agents photographed the entire archives of the Syrian Foreign Ministry. It is impossible to present the entire range of these documents, but the annexed appendices give a picture of their scope and importance. The documents shed light on Syria's foreign policy as it was fighting for independence and becoming a major arena for regional and international rivalries. They include correspondence between the President, Prime Ministers and Foreign Ministers and British, French, American and Soviet representatives in Damascus, as well as reports from Syrian diplomats in London, Paris, Washington, Moscow, Cairo, Baghdad and Ankara. There are also copies of President Quwatli's private correspondence with Arab leaders, including Kings Ibn Sa'ud and Faruq, Emir Abdullah, Abd al-Ilah, Nuri al-Sa'id and the Secretary of the Arab League, Abd al-Rahman al-Azzam, as well as private correspondence between Syrian and Lebanese leaders and detailed protocols of their meetings. The documents provide a glimpse of the covert aspects of the inter-Arab rivalry and the lesser-known politics behind the formation of the Arab League. Some secret reports prepared by President Quwatli were not sent to the Syrian Foreign Minister, indicating that the French had an informer in his office, and reflecting Quwatli's lack of trust in Jamil Mardam Bey, who held that position between 1943 and 1945. Apart from using trusted couriers, President Quwatli made use of the cipher facilities in the Saudi consulates in Damascus and Paris to correspond with Kings Ibn Sa'ud and Faruq, presumably to conceal correspondence from British agents. Of particular interest are exchanges between the Syrian leaders and British officials in Damascus and Beirut, and the reports by Najib al-Armanazi, the Syrian Minister in London. They offer insight into the secret aspects of Britain's Arab policy when British agents were struggling to expel France from the Levant and to incorporate Syria in a Hashemite federation. The documents also reveal how British agents used Syria and the Arab League to destabilize France's position in North Africa. Other documents contain secret Cabinet decisions, correspondence between various ministers and reports by the Syrian Deuxième Bureau (doc.202).

The British and Syrian documents provide a breakthrough in the study of the historiography of the Middle East in the 1940s, challenging some well-established records of that period. They touch on diverse research fields: political history, international relations, decolonization and intelligence studies. They indicate a lack of knowledge of those years, and reveal the importance of covert political action, clandestine diplomacy and the role of the "people in the field" in shaping Britain's Arab policy. Details are exposed of the secret agents' role in manipulating and obstructing Foreign Office policy, as was revealed by their opposition to Eden's and Bevin's attempts to reach an understanding with France in the Levant. In this regard, the documents add a previously hidden dimension to the traditional Anglo-French rivalry and to Churchill's open clashes with de Gaulle in Syria and Lebanon. Moreover, they provide scholars with direct and uncensored access to Arab diplomatic archives, thereby closing the gap in the study of Arab and inter-Arab politics and shedding light on the secret inter-Arab war, of which little is known.

The covert aspects of the British officials' attitude towards the Zionists' aspirations for a Jewish state in Palestine is revealed through informal and uncensored discussions with Arab leaders. New details emerge of the Arab stand towards a Jewish state through private exchanges and secret agreements between the leaders, as well as from Arab correspondence with British, American, French and Soviet diplomats. The documents highlight the need to study the Arab-Zionist conflict in the context of the Anglo-Arab and inter-Arab rivalries[27] rather than as just Anglo-Jewish or Arab-Jewish confrontations. For example, they reveal the British agents' use of the Zionists' aspirations in their scare tactics to coerce Arab leaders into acquiescing to Britain's military presence in the region, and that the question of Palestine had become deeply entangled in the Saudi-Hashemite confrontation.

Another contribution is to our understanding of the roles of intelligence and secret diplomacy in the Great Powers' rivalry in the Middle East in the early years of the Cold War. Anglo-Soviet rivalry in the region had already begun in 1944, when the war in Europe was far from over. Both Powers spied on the activities of the other and made use of propaganda, CD and covert operations to undermine each other's positions. Their struggle, much of it conducted in the dark, rapidly escalated and surfaced after the war. The British and Syrian documents offer a clear view of this struggle, as Syria became a major arena for Anglo-Soviet confrontation in the Middle East following Britain's attempts to integrate it in an anti-Soviet, Iraqi-Turkish regional defense alliance. Another issue the documents help to elucidate is the hidden aspect of the Anglo-American economic rivalry in the region, especially over oil, as well as American officials' deep distrust of Britain's policy in Palestine as expressed to Syrian diplomats in Washington (docs.163, 174, 188, 248).

   The importance of the British and Syrian documents has been demonstrated in recently published studies. For example, it has been revealed that British intelligence agents, diplomats and senior military officers were involved in orchestrating the Syrian crisis in the summer of 1945 and that de Gaulle's accusations that Churchill and the British government had been deeply involved in the eviction of France from Syria and Lebanon were well-founded. The established history of Syria's and Lebanon's independence has to be re-examined following disclosure of the secret collaboration between Britain and the nationalist leaders Shukri al-Quwatli, Jamil Mardam and Riyad al-Sulh during and after the war, and their tacit agreement to place their countries under British hegemony.[28]

   The British and Syrian documents reveal the various types of covert action (CA), including CPA, CD, propaganda and psychological warfare employed by the British secret agents, diplomats and military officers to ensure their country's dominance in the region. These methods were used in events such as the orchestrating of the Lebanese constitutional crisis in November 1943 and the Syrian crisis in May–June 1945, which brought an end to France's influence in both of its mandated countries; the establishment of the Arab League; Britain's attempts to form a Greater Syria as part of its larger endeavor to reorganize the Middle East under its hegemony; its struggle after the war to create a regional defense alliance comprising Turkey, Iraq and Syria against the Soviet Union; the efforts to foil Zionist ambitions for a Jewish state in Palestine; and the first two coups in Syria in 1949.

   CA, widely used during the Cold War, represents the more aggressive measures of intelligence activities in international relations. American scholars regard it as a hidden tool in managing foreign policy and refer to it as "the quiet option" or "the third option" between diplomacy and open warfare.[29] British intelligence organizations termed it "special political action," while British scholars highlight its use in their country's colonial and post-colonial era.[30] The literature on the use of CA in international relations examines moral and ethical issues and its authorization and control in liberal democracies.[31] A National Security directive defines a covert action as:

> An activity or activities of the United States government to influence political, economic or military conditions abroad, where it is intended that the role of the United States government will not be apparent or acknowledged publicly.[32]

According to this definition, CA provides policy makers with a range of foreign policy tools supplementing traditional diplomacy or direct military intervention. The use of CA is based on the assumption that secret means are useful to secure desired ends or specific policy goals. Covert warfare can be effective while under wraps; if uncovered, the initiator can deny responsibility. During the period under study, British governments and their officials in the Middle East often resorted to this practice to counter French allegations. For example, General Spears, who played a key role in orchestrating the 1943 Lebanese crisis, strongly denied any involvement. Similarly, in a speech in the House of Commons in early June 1945, Churchill refuted de Gaulle's accusations of Britain's complicity in the Syrian crisis. But the use of CA can backfire if the intended target becomes cognizant of it. De Gaulle's discovery of Britain's betrayal in the Levant poisoned his relations with London. Although he failed to prevent his country's eviction from Syria and Lebanon, he exploited the information obtained by his intelligence services to fight his own clandestine war against Britain in the Middle East.

The use of CA in international relations became a controversial topic in the United States, especially in the 1990s following the Iran-Contra affair. Increasing demands were made in Congress to ensure strict control of CA and to integrate moral and ethical considerations into American foreign policy. Some argued that strict codes of behavior should be imposed on the secret agents in the field, especially as it had been repeatedly proven that intelligence agencies and their agents often concealed corrupt and immoral action under the guise of patriotism. Others believed that as secret agents seek to defend national interests, they should be immune to moral scrutiny. Such views are more common in a time of war or international tension when the defense of the nation's interests has high priority.[33]

The principal categories of CA fall in the spheres of politics, the economy, propaganda – often defined as psychological warfare – and paramilitary insurgency. Covert Political Action, the main category, frequently encompasses the other three. Its successful use can ensure essential strategic-economic interests for its initiator without the need for direct intervention, as happened in Iran in 1953. The initiating state can deploy a wide range of methods to affect the balance of political power in the target country or coerce its leaders into advancing a particular foreign policy or carrying out certain acts. Political and financial inducements are employed to recruit politicians and place them as front men in positions of power, to gain control over political parties, or to manipulate elections and public opinion. CPA is also exploited by international corporations to further their economic interests. British agents in the Middle East used CPA not only on behalf of their country, but also independently, without government knowledge or sanction. In this regard, a distinction should be made between the use of CPA in international relations, when its target is an independent and sovereign state, and by a colonial power in countries under its direct or indirect control, as was the case with Britain in the Middle East during and after World War II.[34]

British agents in the Middle East took pains to stress to Arab leaders the advantages of collaborating with Britain on both personal and national levels, but the two sides understood that these were asymmetric relations and that Britain's interests would always have higher priority, as President Quwatli was to discover. On one occasion he complained to a British interlocutor that he had not expected Britain to help expel France from Syria only to replace one colonial power with another. Quwatli's claim is questionable, for he surely knew the price of his secret agreement with the British agents.

The use of covert, or special, political action – "dirty tricks," as British secret agents often termed such tactics – was widespread in the Middle East during and after World War II. This term conceals a more sinister side than its name implies. CPA became a key tool in the modus operandi of British intelligence agents, diplomats and military officers in the region, and the historian must display uncommon ingenuity in tracking its use. Great Britain had long experience of using CPA for controlling the Arab world, dating back to the inter-war years, as was the case in the crowning of Faisal I as King of Iraq in 1921. Political and financial bribery to buy "agents of influence" – politicians and other individuals capable of manipulating the government, public opinion and the business community – became the trademark of its rule in the Middle East. In World War II, however, CPA developed into a far more effective and sophisticated tool of control, providing the British agents in the field with the needed flexibility to implement their policies without antagonizing local elites or public opinion. It allowed them to conceal their goals, contain strong nationalist opposition, balance the pressure for decolonization and the need to retain control, overcome international opposition, especially American anti-colonial sentiments and fight the Soviet Union in the post-war years. Such activities came under the various guises of subversion, manipulation and intimidation, including co-opting and corrupting local political elites, promoting friendly politicians to high positions, intervening in elections and using propaganda and psychological warfare to sway local public opinion. The paucity of studies on Britain's use of CPA in the Middle East during the 1940s is understandable, given the British tradition of total secrecy, especially where unsavory and controversial activities are involved. CPA continued to play an important role in Britain's Middle East policy after the war as it sought to retain its strategic and economic interests in the region in the face of the growing threat from the Zionist movement, the Arab countries' demands for full independence and the evacuation of its forces, France's continued subversion, the Soviet Union's strategic threat and the economic challenge from the United States. Methods used to fight the Axis Powers in the Middle East were soon employed by Britain against its own allies, especially Free France and the Zionist movement. It was precisely because of the need to conceal their controversial activities against their allies that British agents resorted to "dirty tricks."

British intelligence officers in the Middle East were particularly efficient in using CPA to recruit "agents of influence," to promote them to prominent political positions and to ensure their collaboration. Such agents were usually in positions that allowed them not only to provide high-grade political information, but to carry out policies in tandem with Britain's own interests. The British and Syrian documents offer unique insight into the complex nature of the relations between the British agents and the Arab leaders whom they helped to attain high political positions. In many cases, the British agents would discover that once those politicians were in power, it was difficult to ensure their collaboration and loyalty without resorting to various CPA methods, including political and financial bribery, pressure, intimidation and extortion. A striking example was Shukri al-Quwatli who, after being elected President of Syria in August 1943 with British help, began to pursue an independent stand and reneged on promises he had made. The annexed documents reveal his complex relations with the British agents from April 1942 until 1947. These relations continued until he was ousted in March 1949 in Husni Za'im's coup. Riyad al-Sulh was another leading politician who was helped by the British agents to be twice "elected" as Lebanese Prime Minister (1943 and 1946). In August 1944 he advised Sa'adallah al-Jabiri, his father-in-law, to refrain from confronting the British authorities, but three years later he tried to act independently, provoking Spears to warn him that "Great Britain is not powerless" (doc.393). Jamil Mardam, who served during most of the 1940s as Foreign Minister or Prime Minister in Syria, was more loyal to the British and in most cases he tacitly collaborated with Colonel Stirling, the main SIS agent in Syria. In this group can be included other Arab leaders who were helped by the British to attain power but who were not necessarily "collaborators," such as Bishara al-Khuri, the Lebanese President, Mustafa al-Nahhas, while serving as the Egyptian Prime Minister from 1942-44, and Abd al-Rahman al-Azzam, the Arab League Secretary General.[35]

The British and Syrian documents, especially the correspondence between Syrian and British officials in Damascus, London and Cairo, highlight the wide use made of clandestine diplomacy – covert and non-diplomatic activities – by British diplomats and intelligence agents. They are a "missing dimension," as there are few traces of them in British archives. Contrary to the use of CA in the management of foreign policy, of which the intended target is unaware, CD entails conscious cooperation with the adversary or ally and disclosure of the diplomat involved. CD allows greater flexibility in conveying informal and controversial messages, airing ideas or advising on policies that may contradict the official position.[36] Such exchanges, often off record, or personal conversations, played an important role in the dealings of British officials with their Arab counterparts. They are exposed only because they were recorded by Arab leaders and diplomats. Significantly, such practices were used by British diplomats, not only to provoke the Syrian leaders against France, the Soviet Union, the United States and the Zionist movement, but even against their own government's policy. For example, Terence Shone and General Paget, who opposed Bevin's agreement with Bidault over the Levant in December 1945, advised Sa'adallah al-Jabiri, the Syrian Prime Minister, to use force if necessary to prevent the implementation of the "new Sykes-Picot" agreement. Spears, in London, proposed that the Syrian leaders improve their relations with the other Powers in order to pressure and blackmail the Labour government (docs.147, 265, 292). Such discreet messages, in contradiction to the Labour government's Middle East policy, were also conveyed by other British officials in Cairo and London, leaving the Syrian leaders confused. In this case, as in others, they chose to follow the personal and informal advice of British agents "on the spot" rather than the Foreign Secretary's assurances. These cases, which come to light in the Syrian documents, provide insight into how British Arabists in the region used their positions to manipulate both their own government and the Arab leaders. In more extreme cases, British representatives tacitly collaborated with the latter to manipulate and present the Cabinet in London with a fait accompli. Such was the case in the 1943 Lebanese crisis, when Spears forged an intimate alliance with Riyad al-Sulh, the Lebanese Prime Minister, against Free France and the Foreign Office in London.[37]

British intelligence in the Middle East in World War II

World War II was the golden age of British intelligence. Innovative methods and technologies transformed it into one of the best in the world, with new, efficient organizations. Its critical role in the Allies' victory became apparent only years later when details were published of Bletchley Park's role in deciphering the German Enigma code. In the Middle East, British security and secret services, with their plethora of civilian and military organizations, successfully countered the Axis Powers' subversion and propaganda and were paramount in enabling Britain to retain control of the region in the face of the German and Italian attacks. Most of the Arab leaders collaborated with Britain, which effectively exploited the region's strategic assets, manpower and natural resources, especially oil, in its war efforts. Intelligence organizations played an important role in this success, closely monitoring opposition groups and using various means to control and manipulate public opinion and win the collaboration of political leaders and officials in key positions. Apart from Rashid Ali al-Gaylani's revolt in Iraq in the spring of 1941 and the Abdeen incident involving King Faruq in February 1942, Britain did not need to use military force to suppress local insurgencies. These accomplishments should be seen in light of the events of 1936-39, when Britain needed to amass 100,000 soldiers to suppress the Arab revolt in Palestine.[38]

British intelligence achievements in the Middle East in World War II were built on solid foundations laid down during the inter-war years. Recent studies have demonstrated the intelligence organizations' vital role in Britain's control of the region. During the 1920s, Britain developed a new method of colonial air control that integrated Royal Air Force (RAF) surveillance from a network of airports with that from political officers – Special Service Officers (SSO) – on the ground. This system, first implemented in Iraq and later in Transjordan, Palestine and other parts of the Middle East under British rule, provided a cheap and efficient means of maintaining colonial control while keeping friction with the indigenous population to a minimum.[39] Intelligence, especially political intelligence, was paramount, as the system was based on indirect rule through local politicians and various "agents of influence." It involved the widespread use of political and financial bribery to buy the loyalty of the political elites and tribal leaders. An essential element was the establishment of efficient security agencies to closely monitor large sectors of the population, particularly nomadic tribes, minority communities, the educated young urban class and local military officers. The security agencies also made use of the local secret police, as they had in Iraq and Egypt. But the system of indirect rule, in which intelligence agencies played a vital part, had its drawbacks. When armed uprisings broke out, such as in Palestine (1936-39) and Iraq (1941), the British authorities were caught unprepared and had to rush in armed forces to suppress them. The use of financial and political bribery corrupted the local elites but seldom ensured loyalty. The British and Syrian documents demonstrate this reality in the case of Shukri al-Quwatli who reneged on his promises and attempted to foil Britain's schemes to form a Hashemite Greater Syria. In addition, reliance on political elites meant that British officials failed to take note of the rapid political and social changes transforming Arab society in the 1930s and 1940s, especially the emergence of a young, educated, radical nationalist generation that became the driving force for political, social and economic reforms and demands for complete sovereignty from Britain.

The system of indirect rule, or "covert empire,"[40] as defined by Satia, became entrenched in the 1930s, when treaties were concluded with Iraq in 1930, Egypt in 1936, and later with Transjordan in 1946. It enabled Britain to preserve its strategic and economic interests in the Arab countries under its rule while granting them "independence." But reliance on the Hashemite family and Nahhas Pasha in Egypt after 1942 was to come at a price. After expulsion from Syria in 1920 by the French and from the Hejaz in 1925 by King Ibn Sa'ud, the two branches of the Hashemite family – in Iraq and Transjordan – rose up against the status quo in the Arab world. Their attempts to take over Syria led to a long struggle with France and Kings Ibn Sa'ud and Faruq, in which Britain became entangled. While most of the British representatives in the Middle East were more than ready to use the Hashemites to oust France from Syria and Lebanon, the bitter rivalry between the Hashemite and Saudi monarchies drove them to side with the former during the war. This proved to be a costly miscalculation, as King Ibn Sa'ud became one of Britain's most accomplished opponents, who strove to jeopardize its efforts to incorporate Syria in a Hashemite Greater Syria. It also antagonized the United States, Ibn Sa'ud's sponsor, and provided French intelligence with the opportunity to expose Britain's double game to the Saudi monarch and the American administration. In Egypt, the brutal methods used by Lord Killearn in the Abdeen incident to impose Nahhas Pasha as Prime Minister on King Faruq, turned the latter into a bitter enemy of Britain. In February 1945, Faruq forged a secret alliance with King Ibn Sa'ud in Radwa (doc.24) against the Hashemites and Britain.

By the mid-1930s Britain, with the help of its intelligence agencies, had gained a large measure of control over Arab and inter-Arab politics in the Middle East. But the rapid deterioration of international order and the threat of a new war in Europe forced it to reorganize its intelligence agencies in the region. The Arab revolt in Palestine served as a timely warning to allocate additional manpower and financial resources and to bolster security agencies in order to monitor local agitation and growing Italian and German subversion. On the eve of the war, existing intelligence organizations were rapidly expanded and two new intelligence-coordinating agencies were established: Security Intelligence Middle East (SIME), which became the main counter-espionage organization responsible for security in the entire region;[41] and the Middle East Intelligence Centre (MEIC), which served as a collation, assessment and coordination organization.[42]

World War II saw the rapid expansion of British intelligence in the Middle East, growing from a collection of colonial intelligence organizations into a modern, innovative intelligence community. It contributed to the British Army's victory in the Western Desert against the invading Axis forces, helped to ensure Britain's control of the region, and played a part in its taking Syria from France. The physical distance and the difficulty in controlling them from London allowed these intelligence organizations a large degree of freedom to experiment and innovate. Brigadier Dudley Clarke's "A" Force (deception organization), Colonel Sir Archibald David Stirling's Special Air Service (SAS), the Long Range Desert Group (LRDG) and Dame Freya Stark's oral propaganda methods were developed and tried out in the Middle East before being adopted on other fronts. With the outbreak of war, the British military and civilian authorities in the Middle East rushed to expand their intelligence capabilities. Substantial resources were allocated to existing organizations, including the CID (Committee of Imperial Defence), the MI5 Defence Security Officer (DSO) and SIS, while new organizations, such as the Special Operations Executive (SOE) and the Political Warfare Executive (PWE) were formed in London and expanded their operations to the Middle East. Since the region had become an active war zone, the army, navy and air force intelligence organizations were expanded in size, as were the areas they covered. Contrary to the rivalry that plagued intelligence agencies in London, especially between MI5 and SIS, in the Middle East a large measure of cooperation was achieved after initial inter-service competition and jealousy. The Joint Intelligence Committee Middle East (JICME), as well as the Middle East War Council (MEWC) and the office of the Minister of State, ensured that the various military and civilian authorities and intelligence organizations would act together to promote the strategic and political goals set out in London or Cairo.[43]

During the war, Cairo became a meeting place for political leaders, military officers, intelligence agents and civilian officials serving in the region, as well as a hub for cultural activities. Churchill and Eden visited, as did other heads of state. It also became an important intelligence center in charge of the Middle East, the Eastern Mediterranean, the Balkans and North Africa. The command centers of all the intelligence agencies and the offices of the Middle East Supply Centre (MESC) were located there, close to the headquarters of the Chief of Staff and the office of the Minister of State in Cairo. The emergence of Cairo as the capital of the entire Middle East during the war reinforced the notion of the region as a single area among British officials.[44]

In the aftermath of El Alamein, and as the threat of war in the Middle East receded, the main concern of the British intelligence agencies was to ensure their country's control of the region after the war. Increased attention was paid to obtaining political intelligence, while covert political operations were stepped up and post-hostility plans were debated. As the volume of ciphered diplomatic traffic in the Middle East multiplied, Government Communications Headquarters (GCHQ) sigint intercept stations in the region were able to provide a higher grade of political information to policy makers. The station in Sarafand near Ramleh in Palestine was especially important as it monitored traffic in Arabic, Hebrew, French, Russian and other languages. Telephone conversations and correspondence between Arab leaders and politicians were routinely monitored. By 1943, the British intelligence community had established an information network that ensured the steady flow of political intelligence between the relevant officials throughout the Middle East. The higher priority given to political intelligence and the need to deal with its growing volume and complexity led in July 1943 to the decision to replace the MEIC with the new PICME, which was to operate as a regional collation and assessment center. All valuable political intelligence was sent to the center, and its director, Brigadier Iltyd Clayton, became the main adviser on Arab affairs to the Minister of State in Cairo.[45]

As deliberations on post-war plans for organizing the Middle East intensified, the use of CPA and CD was stepped up. The British and Syrian documents help to clarify the extent of their use by British secret agencies in the Middle East. They reveal details of recruitment methods, bribery payments, names of agents and their controllers and methods of political espionage, as well as confidential assessments and policy recommendations. Successful or failed special operations, and the agents and methods employed, can be studied. Although British diplomats, military officers and agents from other intelligence organizations were often involved, two organizations – SIS and SOE – spearheaded those operations in the Middle East. While SIS agents specialized mainly in espionage and recruitment, SOE was involved in more aggressive operations, including bribery and extortion. During the war SIS, traditionally in charge of foreign espionage and responsible to the Foreign Secretary, worked in the Middle East under the name of Inter-Services Liaison Department (ISLD). From December 1945 it operated under a new cover – the Combined Research and Planning Office (CRPO) – but its agents also acted under the cover of the British Middle East Office (BMEO) in Cairo. Before the war it had stations in Cairo, Jerusalem, Istanbul and Aden, but during the war more were added in Beirut, Damascus, Baghdad and Tehran. SIS scored major successes against German and Italian forces in the Western Desert, and also helped to control local opposition groups. For example, in April 1941 its agents gave advanced warning of the planned military coup in Iraq, thus allowing the British authorities in Iraq to smuggle the royal family, the Regent and Nuri al-Sa'id out of Baghdad. SIS informants, many of whom held key positions, provided up-to-date political information, while its officers were adept at recruiting Arab political elites and agents of influence.[46]

High-grade political intelligence and the collaboration of top Arab leaders were important in the success of Britain's covert policy in the Middle East. The tacit cooperation of Arab nationalist leaders, such as Jamil Mardam, Riyad al-Sulh, Bishara al-Khuri, Mustafa al-Nahhas and Abd al-Rahman al-Azzam, together with Nuri al-Sa'id and the Hashemite family and many other politicians in high positions, enabled the Arabist secret agents to operate behind the scenes, promoting controversial policies often directed against their own allies. SIS, as the British and Syrian documents demonstrate, established a ring of informers around each prominent Arab leader. The list of Arab politicians, top officials, journalists and businessmen recruited by SIS officers is extensive, but few have been exposed. Some of the collaborators recruited by SIS include Hasanin Pasha, King Faruq's influential adviser; Muhsin al-Barazi, President Quwatli's adviser; Mikha'il Ilyan, a deputy in the Syrian parliament who served as Syrian Foreign Secretary in the 1940s and 1950s; Fa'iz al-Khuri, the Syrian Minister to Moscow; Khair al-Din al-Zirkali, Ibn Sa'ud's adviser; Midhat Sheikh al-Ard, Ibn Sa'ud's personal physician; and Camille Chamoun, the Lebanese Minister of the Interior and its first Ambassador to London. SIS also recruited informants in Vichy and Free France in the Levant, as well as in the Zionist movement.[47] French intelligence reports give details of the identities and activities of SIS officers in Syria and Lebanon, many of whom wore army uniforms or served in the local diplomatic mission, such as Sir Charles Dundas, head of the Beirut and Damascus stations, and his assistant, Michael Ionides. SIS officers in the Middle East often exploited commercial companies to conceal their identities. For instance, Colonel Brigadier Stephen Longrigg, an SIS officer, had been employed before the war by the Iraq Petroleum Company (IPC).[48] In the 1940s, SIS continued to use the IPC as a cover for its agents, some of whom were stationed in the company's offices in Beirut and Tripoli, leading the French authorities to protest its use as a cover for British spies. Another company operating in the Levant and used by SIS agents was the British Overseas Airways Corporation (BOAC), for which Major General Sir Edward Spears obtained concessions for operating in Syria and Lebanon. In 1946 SIS formed its own company in Syria – the Anglo-Syrian Trading Company – headed by General Frère and Colonel Hutchinson, who had previously served in the Ninth Army. Colonel Stirling, who by then had "retired from military service," was one of its advisers. Such activities are revealing, as in the 1940s commercial and finance companies in the City of London lobbied to secure Britain's economic hegemony in Syria and Lebanon.[49]

SOE was founded by Winston Churchill in June 1940 to act against Nazi Germany in Europe. Shortly after its formation, it extended its activities to the Balkans and the Middle East, where it became one of the most active British intelligence agencies. Created by combining two subdivisions of existing organizations – Section D of SIS and MI(R) from the Military Intelligence – its goals were to carry out special operations, including sabotage, subversion, black propaganda and psychological warfare. One of the first regions in which SOE was tested was the Balkans, but after their occupation by the German Army in the spring of 1941, it moved its agents to Turkey and the Middle East. Between July 1940 and July 1941, its agents took part in large scale subversion and propaganda campaigns against Vichy in Syria and Lebanon with the aid of the "Friends" – agents of the Haganah's secret service.[50] As part of its propaganda war against radio broadcasts by the Axis Powers to the Arab-Muslim world, SOE founded Sharq al-Adna (Near East Broadcasting Station) in 1941 in Jaffa; this became Britain's most influential Arabic radio station. After the war, the station was moved to Cyprus and was run by SIS. Once the PWE was formed in 1942 to coordinate the propaganda war, SOE focused more on special operations. It was a new, bold agency that infused its agents with a spirit of audacity and innovation. With its headquarters in Cairo, its officers operated throughout the region. It competed with existing intelligence organizations, especially SIS, for resources and prestige. In 1941 and 1942 it faced intense opposition from both the military and civilian authorities in Cairo, which resented its large resources and freedom of action and sought to limit its size and to control it.[51]

Until the end of 1942, SOE in the Middle East was largely involved in military activities against the Axis forces and in putting together the Stay Behind Plans – a Fifth Column intended to operate against German forces in the event of invasion from the Western Desert or the Caucasus and which entailed mobilizing local groups. These ties would become invaluable in later years. After the German Army's defeats at El Alamein and Stalingrad, which removed the threat of a German invasion of the Middle East, SOE became increasingly engaged in special political operations. Its agents did the dirty work of paying off politicians and other officials in high places, or used more aggressive means, such as intimidation and extortion, when necessary. However, few details of these activities are known, as most of its operational documents were destroyed immediately after the war, leaving only general reports. Once again, the British and Syrian documents can be helpful, for instance in providing details of the activities of Colonel Stirling, who was an SOE officer in Syria and Lebanon from 1942 to 1945. Indirect evidence of the role played by SOE agents in political subversion in the Middle East can be garnered from letters sent by its commander, Major General Sir Colin Gubbins, in June 1945 to Shone and Lord Killearn, the British representatives in Damascus and Cairo, respectively, in which he highlights the assistance provided by the organization to their diplomatic missions and requests their support. This initiative took place after the war while discussions on dismantling the SOE were being held in London. Although some diplomats in the Middle East, including Lord Killearn, were initially wary of SOE's unconventional methods, they soon learned to use its agents to facilitate their tasks. General Spears had no such qualms, making early extensive use of the organization, thus turning it into an important tool of subversion against Free France in Syria and Lebanon. SOE was eventually disbanded in early 1946 and integrated with SIS, bringing in new agents and a much-needed spirit of innovation and aggressiveness.[52]

By 1944, Cairo had become a major center in defining Britain's post-war Middle East policy.[53] The views of the military and civilian authorities there were of crucial importance and neither Churchill nor Eden, and certainly not Attlee or Bevin, could ignore them. In theory, the overall Middle East policy was to be formulated by the Cabinet in London. In practice, this was not always the case; in the early war years, geographical distance and rapid developments in the region afforded the Middle East establishment, especially the office of the Minister of State in Cairo and the MEWC, considerable influence in policy making. After its formation in July 1941, the office of the Minister of State played an important role in defining Britain's policy in the region. The Minister of State was a member of Churchill's War Cabinet and its representative in the Middle East, but apart from Oliver Lyttelton, the first minister, the subsequent three ministers, Richard Casey, Lord Moyne and Sir Edward Grigg (Baron Altrincham), voiced the views of the British establishment in the Middle East and protected it against the Foreign Office. This was clearly evident with regard to Casey, who defended General Spears against Eden's criticism and de Gaulle's accusations. His backing of Spears in the Lebanese constitutional crisis in 1943 allowed the latter to withstand Foreign Office pressure and thus end the crisis with a clear victory. Lord Moyne too adopted his advisers' recommendations, including their Greater Syria scheme. In August 1944, while Eden was negotiating with Massigli in London on an Anglo-French agreement in the Levant, he authorized Clayton and Spears to tacitly pressure President Quwatli into concluding a secret agreement to incorporate Syria in a Hashemite Greater Syria under British influence. In practice, the plan involved the eviction of France from the Levant. Edward Grigg, who was appointed after Lord Moyne's assassination, adopted an even more hostile stand towards France's presence in the Levant and Zionist demands for a Jewish state.[54]

The premise that Britain implemented a two-track policy in the Middle East during the 1940s, and that a small group of Arabists serving as intelligence agents, military officers, diplomats and colonial officials pursued their own policies, can now be substantiated with the help of the British and Syrian documents. But the question remains as to whether this two-fold policy was not merely a convenient way for Whitehall to conduct a flexible policy – allowing its agents to carry out covert operations while denying responsibility. It can be argued that Churchill, known for his passion for intelligence operations, tacitly gave the green light to General Spears to humiliate de Gaulle during the 1943 Lebanese constitutional crisis after the latter's dismissal of General Henri Giraud, President Roosevelt's man on the French

Committee. Similarly, Churchill's decision to issue an ultimatum to de Gaulle in the 1945 Syrian crisis was the result of the tense relations between them, and his conviction that the French leader could not be trusted in the event of a war with the Soviet Union in the Middle East. But even if that were the case, Churchill's negative perception of de Gaulle was clearly reinforced by the intense smear campaign conducted against him by Spears and other British officials. The British and Syrian documents reveal further examples of how the British Arabists in the region conducted their own policy in contradiction of Churchill's and Eden's positions and used covert tactics to pressure them to revise their views. For example, Churchill did not trust the Hashemite family in Iraq and Transjordan and pursued an agreement with King Ibn Sa'ud (doc.6). In March 1944 he promised Ibn Sa'ud not to support a change of regime, or the political or geographic status of Syria and Lebanon in the event of a French withdrawal. Later, in conversations with Ibn Sa'ud and the Syrian President in Cairo in February 1945 (doc.28), Churchill made it clear that the British government did not intend to endorse a Greater Syria or Spears' pledge to oppose a treaty with France. Churchill was also known to support the establishment of a separate Jewish state in Palestine, which was anathema to the Arabists and the British establishment in both London and the Middle East.

The Arabists, despite their Prime Minister's opposition, continued to promote their Hashemite Greater Syria scheme, resorting to covert tactics to force their government to revise its Middle East policy. For example, after the Eden-Massigli agreement in August 1944, Churchill's decision to dismiss Spears, and his celebrated visit to Paris with Eden to mark the liberation of Paris, the Arabists were wary of Churchill reaching an understanding with the French leader over the Middle East and sought to foil any such move. In January 1945, Brigadier Clayton and Colonel Stirling goaded Mardam, the strongman in the Syrian government, into provoking large scale anti-French demonstrations and acts of violence against their government's intention to impose a Franco-Syrian treaty. In early May, General Paget sent a brigade from Palestine into Lebanon for "training," leading Churchill to complain that such a step, which affected high policy, had been taken without Cabinet agreement. This did indeed undermine Churchill's attempt to allay de Gaulle's fears at a particularly critical stage of the Syrian crisis.

Under the Labour government, neither Attlee nor Bevin enjoyed the same authority or prestige as Churchill and Eden among the senior military officers, intelligence agents and Arabists in the Middle East, many of whom belonged to the upper echelons of British society and supported the Conservative Party. They detested and distrusted the socialist government, opposed Labour's declared decolonization policy, and continued to advocate the retention of Britain's imperial hegemony in the Middle East. Bevin, initially confident of his ability to replace Britain's old imperial relationship with the Arab world with a new form of genuine "partnership" was to learn, the hard way, that he could not introduce policies unacceptable to most Arab nationalist leaders, and certainly not through the old British Middle East establishment or the military cast in Cairo.[55]

Bevin's complex relations with the secret services and the Arabists are essential to our understanding of the contradictions and inconsistencies in Britain's post-war Middle East policy. Britain's position during and after the war has been examined in numerous studies, but the present research aims to underline Bevin's troubled relations with the intelligence agencies in the Middle East, especially with SIS, which was formally under the auspices of the Foreign Secretary. This issue is not sufficiently addressed in the existing historiography. For intelligence organizations, top military officers and diplomats to secretly undermine their elected government's policy is an extreme act of disloyalty, hence the scant evidence to be found in official documentation.[56] The British and Syrian documents and French intelligence reports suggest that under Bevin, the Arabists not only stepped up attempts to implement their own policies in the region but also deliberately undermined those of their Foreign Secretary (docs.146-7, 187, 192, 291, 296).

In June 1946, after Bidault complained to Bevin that British intelligence agents were plotting against France in North Africa, the Foreign Secretary strongly castigated his secret services, which were "costing a large amount of money to do more harm than good." He announced his intention to weaken them and strengthen diplomatic posts.[57] In fact, Bevin faced opposition not only from his secret services, but also from the COS and Arabist diplomats in the Foreign Office and the Middle East. A few months earlier he had been confronted by Lord Killearn, Britain's powerful Ambassador in Cairo, who shared the COS' strong opposition to his intention to negotiate with the Egyptian government on the withdrawal of British forces from Egypt.[58] The Arabists and the military authorities also tried to undermine Bevin's attempts to settle the conflict with France in the Levant and coordinate Britain's Middle East policy, especially over Palestine, with that of the United States. In their meetings with Syrian leaders, British officials accused the United States of supporting the Zionist cause for its own domestic considerations and presented Britain as the only Power capable of defending the Arab cause in Palestine. Shone tacitly collaborated with Jabiri to exploit American support for Zionist demands in Palestine in order to provoke the Saudi King into acting against American oil concessions in Saudi Arabia. After sending letters in this vein urging Ibn Sa'ud to penalize the United States, Jabiri sent copies of them to Shone together with the King's political adviser's reply (docs.242-4).

Telegrams from Syrian diplomats in Washington to the Foreign Ministry in Damascus concerning their meetings with senior officials in the State Department disclose that the latter knew of the Arabists' attempts to exploit American support for the Zionists in order to undermine the economic interests of the United States in the Middle East. American diplomats repeatedly warned their Syrian counterparts that Britain was exploiting the question of Palestine to strengthen its hold over the Middle East. Syrian diplomatic reports from Washington also reveal that President Truman and officials in the State Department were well aware that Britain had been behind France's eviction from the Levant and knew of its attempts to secure tacit hegemony over Syria. Bevin, often kept in the dark, learned the extent of the British agents' intrigues only after the Syrian Minister in London approached the Foreign Office to clarify contradictions in British policy (docs.46, 143, 163, 192).

Bevin's inability to control the British intelligence services in the Middle East in 1946-48 was revealed in the continued subversion by British agents, led by Brigadier Clayton, against French positions in North Africa, even as he was pursuing a rapprochement with France. The French learned of this subversion from their Syrian sources. It can be claimed that Bevin was conducting a "two-track" policy – reassuring Bidault that he would put an end to such subversion while tacitly allowing his agents to continue their anti-French activities – in order to punish the French government for its tacit support of the Zionist movement against Britain. But this assumption is contentious, as an alliance with France, which was to culminate in the Anglo-French Treaty of Alliance in March 1947, the Brussels Pact of March 1948, and ultimately the North Atlantic Treaty Organization (NATO), was at the center of Bevin's European policy.[59] Armanazi's reports from London confirm that Bevin's troubles with the British intelligence services in the Middle East continued in 1947. The conflict between Bevin and the secret services and military authorities in the Middle East lasted until the end of his tenure. While Britain was facing the most serious challenges to its position in the Middle East posed by the escalation of the Cold War, the violent confrontation with the Zionist movement, and radicalization in the Arab world, its Middle East policy became deeply divided between that of Whitehall and the "people in the field."

Uncertainty over the future of its Egyptian bases heightened Britain's need for an alternative, thereby reinforcing Iraq's strategic role as a center for an anti-Soviet northern defense alliance. Clayton, Stirling and other Arabists, together with Nuri al-Sa'id, stepped up their joint covert operations in Syria, inter-Arab politics and the question of Palestine, often without informing their Foreign Secretary. Syria continued to play a pivotal role in their schemes, becoming once again the main arena for British and Iraqi covert political operations. The country was deemed essential in a regional defense alliance with Iraq and Turkey; for the formation of a Hashemite Greater Syria united with Iraq, thus overcoming the Iraqi Kingdom's inherent vulnerability; and for solving the intractable problem of Palestine. The British and Syrian documents shed light on the covert Anglo-Iraqi operations and the clandestine diplomacy employed to ensure Syria's incorporation in a regional defense alliance, including the revision of Syrian-Turkish borders to settle the dispute over Alexandretta. Between October 1946 and February 1947, British intelligence officers, led by Brigadier Clayton, took part in negotiations between Ismet Inönü, the Turkish President, Nuri al-Sa'id, the Iraqi Prime Minister, and King Abdullah on forming a Hashemite Greater

Syrian monarchy under the Jordanian King, comprising Syria, Lebanon, Transjordan and part of Palestine. This was part of a more elaborate plan devised by Arabist intelligence agents. The first step, orchestrated by Colonel Stirling and implemented at the end of 1946, entailed the removal of the anti-Hashemite and anti-Turkish Syrian Prime Minister, Sa'adallah al-Jabiri, and his replacement by Jamil Mardam, Britain's own man.

The string-pullers

George Lenczowski, who served in the Middle East in the 1940s, described the officials behind Britain's Middle East policy thus:

> From 1941 onward British action was consistent and purposeful, and it was well synchronized with the action of the Arabs themselves. In this work, British interests were served by a powerful team of experienced Arabists such as Sir Kinahan Cornwallis, Ambassador to Iraq; Brigadier [E].I. H. Clayton, brother of the late Sir Gilbert Clayton, and a man who over a quarter of a century had come to know more living Arab states-men than any other Westerner; Brigadier Glubb Pasha, commander of the Arab Legion; Sir Walter Smart, Oriental Secretary (and later minister) at the British Embassy in Cairo, who was married to an Egyptian lady of a prominent family; Lord Moyne, British Minister of State for the Middle East who replaced Richard Casey in 1944; and General Edward Spears, chief of the British mission to the Levant. General Spears in particular did his best to remove the French influence from Syria and to establish friendly relations with Shukri al-Quwatli's National Bloc Party. Neither the de Gaulle-Lyttelton agreement nor official British denials could con-ceal the fact that, having to choose between Free French or Arab friend-ship, the British chose the latter. The situation was somewhat analogous to that prevailing in British-Zionist relations; the French, like the Zionists, could not bargain; they could only protest.[60]

Wars provide an opportunity for determined and committed individuals to place their mark on events far greater than their formal position permits. The British and Syrian documents and French intelligence reports allow us to examine the covert methods employed by a small group of well-placed British officials in pursuing their own course of action in the Middle East, which often contradicted that of their government. General Spears, Brigadier Clayton, Colonel Stirling, Smart and Cornwallis best represent such officials who wielded great influence on their government's Middle East policy. Spears and Stirling spearheaded the campaign to expel France from Syria and Lebanon from 1943 through 1945; Clayton and Cornwallis orchestrated the efforts to reorganize the Arab states under British hegemony centered around an Iraqi-Greater Syrian union; while Smart represented the Pan-Arabist-Egyptian orientation in Britain's Arab policy. Spears, Clayton, Smart and Cornwallis blended diplomacy and covert action, while Stirling was an intelligence field-officer involved in special political operations. Apart from Smart, all were World War I veterans with experience in intelligence. Spears had served as a liaison and intelligence officer on the French General Staff on the Western Front; Stirling and Cornwallis had fought with Lawrence in the Arab Revolt; Clayton had been a political officer in Damascus in 1919-20. Cornwallis, Clayton and Stirling, as well as Glubb and Kirkbride, had witnessed the backlash that Britain faced in Syria, Iraq and Egypt after the previous war and were determined to prevent it after this one. They had all been involved, directly or indirectly, in SIS activities: Clayton and Stirling served in the organization, Spears took part in its anti-Bolshevist operations in the 1920s and its anti-French activities in Syria and Lebanon in the 1940s, while Smart and Cornwallis worked closely with the organization. The five continued to be involved in British covert operations in the Middle East in the post-war years. After ending his term as British Minister in Syria and Lebanon in December 1944, Spears became a prominent member of the Arab and anti-Zionist "Arab lobby" in London that campaigned for British hegemony over the Middle East and against an independent Jewish state. Stirling remained in Syria as an SIS officer and was involved in the first and second military coups of 1949. Clayton became Britain's Chief Intelligence Officer in the region. Smart officially retired in 1947 from his influential position as Oriental Secretary in the British Embassy in Cairo, but remained in office for several more months. Cornwallis was forced to retire from his position as British Ambassador to Baghdad in 1945 due to ill health, but continued to promote Britain's interests in the Middle East. Although Iraqi Prime Minister Nuri al-Sa'id was an Arab politician, he has been included in this group as he was a key figure in the Arabists' clandestine diplomacy and covert operations, in both the Middle East and London.

General Edward Spears

The role of General Spears in evicting France from Syria and Lebanon and in exacerbating relations between Churchill and de Gaulle over the Levant has been well studied, but the British and Syrian documents illuminate his covert activities while serving in the Levant and later in London as a paid adviser to the Syrian government and as a key figure in the British Arab lobby; his controversial business conduct in Syria and Lebanon; and his opposition to the Labour government's Middle East policy. Spears was a newcomer to the Middle East, who wholeheartedly adopted the Arabists' views, becoming their ally and spokesman. A politician with military and intelligence experience, as well as a businessman, he exploited his position and close ties with financial and commercial circles in the City to promote his and their business interests in Syria and Lebanon. He was the first to effectively employ large scale CPA in the 1943 Lebanese crisis, which led the Maronites in Lebanon to sever their longstanding ties with France, their traditional protector – a pre-condition for dislodging France from the Levant. His success in Lebanon served as a precedent and encouraged British officials to use similar tactics in the Syrian crisis in the summer of 1945. Spears had gained much experience in covert operations as an intelligence and liaison officer in the French General Staff during World War I. In the early 1920s, he took part in Churchill's secret campaign against the Bolsheviks in Russia. In these activities, in which he collaborated with the famous spy Sidney Riley, he had already combined special operations with private business interests. He met Churchill on the Western Front in France in World War I, and, for the next four decades, remained loyal to the man who became his mentor.[61]

Shortly after forming his Cabinet in May 1940, Churchill sent Spears, whom he regarded as an authority on French affairs, to Paris as a personal envoy to Paul Reynaud's government. Spears, who later published two volumes on those chaotic weeks of French capitulation, took part in the last-minute smuggling of de Gaulle to London on June 17. He was proposed as a candidate to head the newly-established SOE, and although he did not receive the position, he was to use the organization against de Gaulle's Free France in the Levant.[62] After the taking of Syria and Lebanon from Vichy in July 1941, Spears was transformed from a passionate supporter of de Gaulle into one of his most bitter enemies. This came about partly as a result of a clash between two powerful personalities, together with Spears's disappointment with French defeatism and his conviction that France could no longer be restored to its pre-war status as a Great Power. He wholeheartedly endorsed the Syrian and Lebanese struggles for independence from France and strongly advocated their incorporation in Britain's sphere of influence. He saw himself as the new Lawrence who would succeed where Lawrence had failed – uniting the Arab world under Britain's hegemony. He became a powerful ally of the Arabists, who used him to convey their views directly to Churchill, thereby sidestepping the Foreign Office. Although he presented himself as a champion of Syrian and Lebanese independence, he was, like many other British officials in the region, an imperialist who saw France's defeat as an opportunity for Britain to take over the Levant.[63]

The Spears Mission, which competed with the French High Commission, comprised by 1944 more than a hundred political and intelligence officers stationed throughout Syria and Lebanon. The Mission dealt with civilian, economic and political issues, becoming an effective tool for Spears to undermine France's position and mobilize Lebanese and Syrian nationalists against it. It had a large budget, used partly for subversion and propaganda warfare, and many of its political officers were in fact intelligence agents. It closely collaborated with other British intelligence agencies in Syria and Lebanon, especially SOE, which became an efficient tool for CPA. SOE had already taken part in subversion and propaganda warfare against Vichy in Syria and Lebanon in 1940-41, although the Balkans were its main operative arena. But after the occupation of Greece by German forces in spring 1941, SOE withdrew its agents to Istanbul, Jerusalem and Cairo. The occupation of

Syria and Lebanon gave Spears the opportunity to recruit many of these agents as political and intelligence officers in his Mission. Moreover, his tense relations with the Foreign Office had affected his ties with SIS, which was officially under its supervision. On the other hand, the SOE was a new organization, whose command in the Middle East was seeking to demonstrate its usefulness and thus was more than willing to collaborate with him. Whereas in France SOE had joined forces with Free France and the Resistance against German occupation, in Syria and Lebanon it took part in covert operations against its Free French allies.[64]

At the end of February 1945, Jamil Mardam, the Acting Prime Minister and Foreign Minister, met with Najib al-Armanazi, who was to become the Syrian Minister in London, and instructed him to follow Spears' advice. Spears, who had returned to London a month before after four years in the Levant, became an adviser and lobbyist on behalf of the Syrian government.[65] He was paid and granted lucrative commercial contracts for his personal business interests and the British companies he represented. The annexed documents, especially Armanazi's reports, give details of Spears' controversial political and business dealings, and reveal how his private business interests affected his political views (docs.64-5, 69). The documents disclose that in London, Spears continued to be intimately involved in Syrian and Lebanese politics, and that the Arabists, the army and SIS used his personal ties with President Quwatli, whom he had helped come to power in 1943, to persuade him to acquiesce in the British demands (docs.84, 172, 187, 364, 369). For example, Spears played a part in Stirling's efforts at the end of May 1945 to coerce President Quwatli into signing a secret agreement with Britain placing Syria under its tacit hegemony (doc.84). In September that year he was also involved in General Paget's attempts to pressure the Syrian government into allowing the British Army to retain forces in Syria, contrary to the Labour government's plan to withdraw them from Syria and Lebanon. Spears continued to play a role in SIS operations in the region, including its attempt in April 1945 to engineer the election of Camille Chamoun as Lebanon's President by exploiting President Bishara al-Khuri's illness (doc.75). That plot also involved the return of Riyad al-Sulh as Prime Minister. Chamoun, who was serving as the Lebanese Minister in London and was Spears' business partner, was in fact an SIS agent. But the plot failed after General Beynet informed President Khuri of the intentions of Chamoun and the British secret services.

Churchill's defeat in the general elections in July and Spears' failure to be re-elected to parliament weakened Spears' standing in Beirut and Damascus. Spears tried to compensate for his waning prestige by stepping up his anti-French and anti-Zionist rhetoric. He exploited the Bevin-Bidault agreement of December 1945 to provoke the Syrian government against the Labour government. Even though Bevin opposed Spears' meddling in British policy in Syria and Lebanon, SIS continued to use his services. In October 1946, Spears went on a well-publicized tour of the Middle East to promote British

interests. At a meeting with Quwatli and Jabiri, in which Clayton participated, he attempted, unsuccessfully, to persuade the Syrian leaders to join
Iraq and Turkey in an anti-Soviet defense alliance. The meeting was followed
by angry exchanges between Jabiri and Spears, with the Syrian Prime Minister threatening to bring an end to Spears' business interests in Syria (docs.194,
239, 322). But Jabiri's threats came to nothing, and in May the following year
Spears had the audacity to protest to Quwatli that a former Syrian minister
was helping American companies seeking to invest in Syria. Armanazi, who
had long before been disillusioned with Spears, wrote to Damascus after the
latter failed to take action against Colonel Stirling's subversion that "all the
efforts made by General Spears are fruitless, even harmful" (doc.145).

Lieutenant-Colonel Walter Stirling

The World War I career of Lieutenant-Colonel Walter Stirling, when he
fought alongside Lawrence in the Arab Revolt, is well known, but far less
known is his role in Britain's special political operations in Syria during and
after World War II. Only after the uncovering of the British and Syrian
documents has his prominent role in Britain's covert political policy in Syria
in 1944-49 become apparent. The French regarded him as their most dangerous enemy and closely monitored his activities, while the Foreign Office,
under both Eden and Bevin, could not control him. Stirling was the chief SIS
officer in Syria – a country that was vital for Britain's strategic designs in the
Middle East. His part in covert operations was decisive in shaping Syria's
political reality at that time. He was instrumental in provoking the Syrian
crisis in the summer of 1945 and in orchestrating Jabiri's resignation and his
replacement by Jamil Mardam at the end of 1946. Three years later, he was
involved in Husni al-Za'im's and Sami al-Hinnawi's military coups, which
almost cost him his life.[66]

Colonel Stirling is the best example of the veteran Arabist intelligence
officer whose views and modus operandi were shaped by his experiences in
World War I. He never forgot his entry into Damascus in early October 1918
together with Lawrence and Emir Faisal's Arab forces, only to see his government reneging on its pledges to the Arabs a year later and handing Syria
over to France. He returned to active duty in the Middle East in World War
II and was determined to do his utmost to prevent the politicians in Whitehall
from compromising Britain's vital interests in the region once again. In 1939
he was recruited to Section D in SIS and sent to Albania – a country he knew
well – to carry out subversive operations. After the integration of Section D
into SOE, he became an intelligence officer in the new organization. Following the German occupation of the Balkans in spring 1941, he moved to
Istanbul and from there to Jerusalem. Shortly afterwards, Spears enlisted him
as a political officer, posting him to Aleppo and the Upper Jazira as a liaison
officer to the Bedouin tribes. It is not clear if this position was a cover for his
true role as an SOE operator or an SIS officer. He continued to value the

loyalty of the Hashemites in Iraq and Transjordan, regarding them as the best way for Britain to retain its influence in the post-war Arab world. Throughout his service in Syria he dedicated his efforts to expelling France and integrating Syria in a Hashemite Greater Syria federation. In July 1944, he was transferred to Damascus under the guise of a liaison officer of the Ninth Army to President Quwatli. For the next two months he was involved, together with Spears, Clayton, Mardam and Nuri al-Sa'id, in the failed attempt to coerce Quwatli into concluding a secret agreement with Britain; in May the following year he finally succeeded in attaining this goal.[67]

Stirling is a prime example of how British Arabist intelligence agents used CPA to control Arab and inter-Arab politics. He exploited his intimate knowledge of Syrian politics and society and his close ties with Syrian leaders, some of whom were his informants and agents, to steer events in accordance with Britain's interests. He took advantage of Syrian politicians' opportunism and ambitions, using financial and political inducements and extortion when necessary to manipulate them into following his "advice." He fueled the fears of Quwatli and ministers of France, Communist Russia, the Zionists and even his own government. He wielded much influence over prominent Syrian leaders, especially Jamil Mardam, in addition to a large number of deputies in the Syrian parliament who owed their election to his support. He spoke fluent Arabic and had excellent ties with the heads of the powerful Bedouin tribes in the Euphrates region and the Syrian Desert, whose loyalty he bought with gold coins, as Lawrence had done in World War I (doc.202). His work there brought him into confrontation with Ibn Sa'ud's emissaries, who were mobilizing support against Emir Abdullah. Muhsin al-Barazi's reports to Stirling, his controller, during the weeks prior to the Syrian crisis provide unique insight into the methods used by Stirling and Mardam to manipulate President Quwatli and his ministers into confronting France. Al-Barazi, who four years later served as Prime Minister in Husni al-Za'im's administration, was to pay with his life for betraying the British secret services. Prime Minister Jabiri, who withstood Stirling's pressure to incorporate Syria in a Hashemite Greater Syrian federation, was more fortunate, as he paid only with his political career.[68]

Stirling was formally a political officer in the Spears Mission, but he also acted through a network of British secret agents who were serving under various guises. French intelligence reports paid particular attention to the activities of Colonel Nur al-Din Marsack and Major Ernest Altounyan. Both Nur al-Din Marsack and his brother, Shams al-Din, had converted to Islam and were involved in British special operations in the Middle East. Nur al-Din served in Damascus as a liaison officer to the Syrian press, while Shams al-Din headed the radio station Sharq al-Adna. Nur al-Din, who controlled many of the Syrian newspapers and journalists, was able to manipulate Syrian public opinion against France and, when necessary, against their own government. Altounyan, a physician in Aleppo, had served with Lawrence and Stirling in World War I. The French counter-intelligence authorities had closely monitored his activities throughout the 1930s. He returned to service in World War II as an intelligence officer in the Ninth Army, exploiting his ties with many dignitaries in northern Syria to foment anti-French activities and mobilize support for a Greater Syrian monarchy. He was to save Stirling's life when the latter was shot and seriously wounded in his house in Damascus in November 1949.[69]

Stirling's move to Damascus coincided with the French intelligence services' success in penetrating the British Legation in Beirut and the Syrian Foreign Ministry in Damascus. Colonel Fernand François Oliva Roget, the French delegate to the Syrian government and a senior intelligence officer, led these operations and was thus able to track Stirling's activities and try to thwart his plans (docs. 75, 77, 79-80, 84, 91-2). Between August 1944 and June 1945, a battle of wits took place between the two adversaries, ending in the defeat of Oliva Roget who, after his controversial role in the Syrian crisis, was forced to return, shamed, to Paris. Yet, despite his failure, Oliva Roget's successful operations enabled French intelligence in the following years to conduct an effective clandestine war against Britain in the Middle East, frustrating many of its goals. In early June 1945, after de Gaulle publicly accused "British agents" of instigating the Syrian crisis, and Oliva Roget named Stirling and Marsack as responsible, Stirling was hurriedly summoned to London. In his book, he presents his return as resulting from the need to provide first-hand information to the War and Foreign Offices on the events in Syria. In fact, he was called back to explain his role in the crisis after Massigli, the French Ambassador to London, made detailed accusations against him. Mardam's letter to the Foreign Office refuting the French charges against Stirling, written at Stirling's request, is a prime example of how agents in the field were able to keep the Foreign Office in the dark (docs.109, 145).

The British and Syrian documents offer a glimpse of the deep distrust of the Labour government harbored by SIS agents in the Middle East. Stirling, like many other intelligence and military officers and diplomats in the region, feared that the new government would take a conciliatory stand towards France and thereby compromise the achievements he had helped to secure a few months earlier. The escalation of the Cold War gave a sense of urgency, and both Stirling and Altouniyan openly stated that France could not be trusted in the event of a new world war against the Soviet Union. Despite criticism leveled against him in the Foreign Office and among Labour members, Stirling returned to Syria at the end of August and resumed his intrigues to ensure that President Quwatli did not renege on his secret undertakings. His activities in support of a Hashemite Greater Syria prompted Quwatli to demand Stirling's recall, but to no avail (docs.179, 189, 201-3). Following the Anglo-French agreement of December 13, 1945, Stirling and other Arabist secret officers stepped up their efforts to prevent its implementation, leading General Beynet to warn Bidault that his agreement with Bevin could not be applied while Stirling remained in Syria. In April 1946 Stirling was demobilized but remained in Damascus under the guise of a *Times* reporter. In the following years he continued to lead SIS special political operations in Syria, with the aim of integrating it into a federation with Iraq and an anti-Soviet regional defense alliance. When Prime Minister Jabiri resisted British pressure in October and November 1946, Stirling mobilized a majority in the Syrian parliament, forcing him to resign.[70]

Brigadier Iltyd Clayton

In December 1945, following attempts by British intelligence officers to undermine Bevin's agreement with Bidault, in which Brigadier Iltyd Clayton was deeply involved, Najib Armanazi, the Syrian Minister in London, warned that the "Secret agents ... cannot represent the true direction of the British Government. I was placed before a precise reality: these are the officials of the Intelligence Service who belong to the clan of Conservatives who create political obstacles for the British Labour Government" (doc.291). But in May 1947, he warned that "supporting General Clayton is something which surpasses the imagination; the British Ministry of Foreign Affairs has been completely forced into accepting him because the intelligence services have categorically refused to remove him from Egypt" (doc.389). Armanazi was not alone in finding it difficult to fathom Brigadier Clayton's actual role in formulating Britain's Middle East policy during and after the war. French and Zionist secret services, well aware of his influence, followed him closely. Indeed, Clayton, whom McLoughlin defined as "the greatest mover and shaker in planning Britain's future role in the Arab world," is absent from most of the studies of British policy in those years, with only a few relating to his role in general terms.[71]

Clayton was personally acquainted with all the Arab leaders during his almost thirty years of service in the Middle East. Indeed, during and after the war, from his permanent seat on the terrace of the Shepheard Hotel in Cairo, he met the stream of local and foreign dignitaries passing through the city. There was a common belief among British officials in the Middle East that personal ties with Arab leaders were essential for conducting an effective policy in the Arab world, and Clayton indeed exercised "personal politics" based on his close relations with Arab leaders. Both an intelligence officer with extensive experience in covert operations and a diplomat with intimate knowledge of Arab and inter-Arab politics, he represented the integration of political intelligence and high-level British policy making in the Middle East. Not content with being merely an adviser to military and civilian decision-makers, he sought to shape the course of events in Middle Eastern politics through what can be termed a "policy of machination." He employed such tactics in orchestrating the Lebanese and Syrian crises; the formation of the Arab League; his support for a Greater Syria and an Iraqi-Syrian merger; in the efforts to form a regional defense alliance against the Soviet Union; and in the Arab conferences on Palestine from 1946 to 1948 (docs. 296, 369). The French intelligence services in Syria and Lebanon were well aware of his influence behind the scenes on the British civilian and military authorities in the Middle East, and termed the British scheme to form a regional defense alliance based on an Iraqi-Syrian axis as the "Clayton Plan." He was to play a pivotal part, behind the scenes, in escalating the 1948 war in Palestine.[72]

Iltyd Clayton was the younger brother of General Gilbert Clayton, General Edmund Allenby's Chief Intelligence Officer in the Middle East in World War I. Iltyd Clayton served as a political officer in Damascus in 1919-20 during Faisal's Arab government, and the following year moved to Iraq, where he was appointed as a military adviser to the Iraqi Army, a position he held until 1927. During the inter-war years he was involved in intelligence activities in Iraq and throughout the Middle East. Some details of his covert activities at that time are revealed in French intelligence reports, as he was considered hostile to the French mandate in Syria and Lebanon. After the formation of the MEIC in 1939, he served as its director in the capacity of Deputy Director of Military Intelligence (DDMI) to General Archibald Wavell, Chief Commander of the British forces in the Middle East. His position as head of the MEIC and his close collaboration with General Wavell afforded him much influence. During and after the war he served as an important link between SIS and Military Intelligence, which partly explains his influential role. In the first two years of the war, with the threat of a German invasion looming, he was engaged mainly in immediate necessities, including covert operations against Vichy in Syria and Lebanon (doc.1). He also established secret ties with the SHAY, the Haganah's intelligence organization, especially with Reuven Zaslani, one of its senior officers.[73] In July 1943 he was appointed head of the PICME and became chief adviser on Arab affairs to the Minister Resident in Cairo, a position that enabled him to influence both British Middle East policy and Arab politics. He saw in the fall of France a golden opportunity to evict it from the Levant and bring about an Iraqi-Syrian federation or to forge Iraq and Syria into a single political entity. Between 1943 and 1945 he took part in the planning for a post-war Middle East, and in this capacity he promoted the plans for a Hashemite Greater Syria united with Iraq and a general Arab union (doc.15). He was instrumental in the establishment of MECAS in 1944, an institute that provided the Foreign Office and British intelligence organizations with a steady flow of trained personnel immersed in Arabic language and culture. His role in the 1948 war in Palestine, partly discussed in the epilogue, is yet to be examined.[74]

Clayton was critical of his government's Middle East policy, especially after Lord Moyne's assassination in November 1944, describing it as weak and inconsistent, and argued that ending France's presence in Syria and Lebanon was necessary for Britain to secure its hegemony over the entire Middle East. He maintained close ties with Abd al-Rahman al-Azzam, Secretary General of the Arab League, who, according to French intelligence sources, was collaborating with the British secret services. These ties enabled Clayton to manipulate the Arab League's activities, including its role in Palestine. As the

Cold War in the Middle East escalated, he became deeply involved in securing Britain's strategic interests in the region. His teaming up with General Paget at the end of 1945 and early 1946 to oppose an Anglo-French agreement and his support of the army's demands for a large military presence in the Middle East brought him into conflict with Bevin and some Labour Members of Parliament, who demanded his removal. Bevin, however, was reluctant to confront the powerful intelligence organizations and the military authorities in the Middle East.[75]

In contrast to other Arabists such as Kirkbride, Glubb Pasha and Stirling, Clayton did not write an autobiography and left few private papers attesting to his true role.[76] The British and Syrian documents and French intelligence reports are therefore of special interest as they help uncover his modus operandi, of which there are few traces in official British documentation. They reveal his subversive activities against France in Syria, Lebanon and North Africa, his efforts to form a defense alliance against the Soviet Union, and his deep involvement in Arab politics. He had close ties with Nuri al-Sa'id, frequently collaborating with him in inter-Arab intrigues and vis-à-vis his own government. The Syrian leaders' accounts of their meetings with him reveal his undiplomatic methods, including pressure and threats, to convince them to act in accordance with Britain's strategic and economic interests. When such methods failed, he took harsher measures, as in the case of the forced resignation of Sa'adallah al-Jabiri, the Syrian Prime Minister, at the end of 1946 (doc.340). He opposed an independent Jewish state and together with Nuri al-Sa'id proposed instead a small Jewish entity in part of Palestine within a Greater Syrian federation or a confederation with Iraq. Zionist agents such as Reuven Zaslani, Eliyahu Sasson and Eliyahu Epstein, who were well aware of his anti-Zionist stand and his role in defining British policy, often met with him in an attempt to uncover the British intentions and tried to win him over. His part in instigating the Arab states' decision to wage a war against the newly-established state of Israel in 1948 is described in the epilogue of this study. He had close ties with the influential Chatham House, serving as a deputy in its branch in Cairo, as well as with political and business circles in London that aimed to ensure Britain's interests in a post-war Middle East. He continued his joint intelligence and diplomatic activities in his new role as Britain's envoy to the Arab League, and later as a Minister in the British Embassy in Cairo. He also served as an adviser in the BMEO, which was used as a cover organization for SIS. The fiasco of the Portsmouth Treaty with Iraq in January 1948 was his personal failure and his influence subsequently diminished.[77]

Sir Walter Smart

Whereas Brigadier Clayton was primarily an intelligence officer with close ties to the military and civilian authorities in the Middle East, Walter Smart was a diplomat and intellectual who contributed to the conceptual framework of

Britain's Arab policy. He served as Oriental Secretary in the British Embassy in Cairo under the towering and forceful Lord Killearn and therefore the extent of his part in the formulation of Britain's Arab policy is not always acknowledged. Nevertheless, as Killearn's senior political adviser, he played a central role in shaping British policy in Egypt, a key state for Britain's control of the Middle East. Years later, the Egyptian President, Anwar al-Sadat, referring to the influence of the Oriental Secretary, the position that Smart filled for most of those years, stressed that "In 1956 the British evacuated this country and at last ended the shameful era when the secretary for oriental affairs at the embassy in Cairo was the real ruler of Egypt, fawned upon by the pasha and the party leaders."[78] Smart's views, expressed in many memoranda and dispatches, drew the attention of Eden, Bevin and high officials in the Foreign Office. Although Egypt was his main concern, he was also involved in formulating Britain's pan-Arab policy throughout the Middle East.[79]

Smart spent his entire diplomatic career in the Middle East, initially in the Embassy in Teheran and later as Consul in Aleppo, Beirut and Damascus. In 1926, he was moved to Egypt, and from 1929 until his retirement in 1947, he served in the British Embassy in Cairo. After separating from his first wife he married Amy Nimr, the daughter of Faris Nimr, the owner and editor of the influential *Al Mukatham* newspaper. Smart used his father-in-law's newspaper to promote his pan-Arabist ideas, and many foreign observers, including the French intelligence services, followed *Al Mukatham* closely, assuming that it expressed the British position. During the war, Smart and his wife turned their house into a meeting place for British and foreign visitors to Cairo, including writers, journalists, politicians and military officers. He was well-acquainted with the French language and culture, although politically he was extremely hostile to France's presence in the Middle East.[80]

Apart from his diplomatic role, Smart was involved in covert political activities. Already while serving in Teheran he had taken part in the 1921 military coup by Reza Khan that eventually led to the rise of the Pahlavi dynasty. As Consul in Damascus, he was implicated in anti-French subversion during the Arab-Druze Revolt of 1925-26. The French intelligence services subsequently regarded him as a Francophobe and followed him closely. A French intelligence report from February 1939 notes that the pan-Arabist policy promoted by Smart was criticized by Colonel Sir Gilbert MacKereth, the British Consul in Damascus, who warned that pan-Arabism could be turned against Britain. As Oriental Secretary, Smart maintained ties with local leaders and was the first to receive reports from the security and secret agencies. During and after the war he stepped up his intelligence activities and covert political operations. Together with Killearn, he implemented the system of indirect control of Egyptian politics through a network of high-ranking politicians and civil servants in the palace, government and parliament, including King Faruq's influential Chamberlain, Hasanin Pasha, and Amin Osman from the Wafd Party, who was close to Mustafa al-Nahhas.[81] He also maintained close relations with many Egyptian journalists, which enabled him to manipulate Egyptian public opinion. The British and Syrian documents reveal that he was also engaged in intelligence activities outside Egypt. For example, he ran Ibn Sa'ud's personal physician, who provided information on Ibn Sa'ud's relations with King Faruq (docs.38-9, 284).

Like many Arabists in the Middle East, Smart regarded the war as an opportunity to evict France from Syria and Lebanon (docs.42-4, 271, 292), but unlike Clayton, Cornwallis and Stirling, who had maintained special relations with the Hashemite family since the Arab Revolt, he was less committed to a Hashemite Greater Syria. He believed that safeguarding Britain's dominance in the Middle East was vital for its strategic and economic interests, but accepted the fact that it could no longer rely on a large military presence or one-sided bilateral treaties. He advocated less arbitrary methods for maintaining Britain's influence in the region based on collaboration with moderate nationalist leaders and promoting economic cooperation, from which both Britain and the Arab countries would benefit. Nevertheless, covert and indirect control formed part of the methods he envisaged. Smart argued that a regional, rather than bilateral, policy would provide Britain with greater flexibility. He therefore supported Arab unity, with Egypt playing a dominant role, maintaining that Britain could use pan-Arabism to promote its own interests. Some of his proposals were adopted by Bevin in Egypt in 1946, but the failure of the Sidqi-Bevin Treaty in October 1946 demonstrated that, contrary to Smart's assumption, an agreement could not be reached with moderate Egyptian nationalists. In addition, his belief that Britain could control pan-Arabism was proven untenable when, a decade later, Nasser used it against Britain itself – of which MacKereth had warned two decades previously.[82]

Sir Kinahan Cornwallis

While Smart epitomized the "Egyptian" orientation of certain British Arabists, Sir Kinahan Cornwallis, Ambassador to Iraq, advocated a more "Hashemite-Iraqi" orientation. He expressed his stand in three meetings with President Quwatli in September 1944, when he demanded that the Syrian President agree to a Hashemite Greater Syria controlled by Emir Abdullah or another Hashemite prince, namely an Iraqi monarch.[83] His views were understandable, given his long association with the Hashemite family and Iraq, where he served for most of his career. Cornwallis' views of the Arab world and Britain's position there were forged in World War I, when he headed the Arab Bureau and fought alongside Lawrence in the Arab Revolt.[84] At that time, he established close ties with Emir Faisal, Iraq's future king. In 1920, he was stationed in Iraq and served in its Ministry of the Interior. In fact, he had been King Faisal's political adviser, a position that enabled him to exert considerable influence on Iraqi politics. In 1939, he returned to service, initially in the Ministry of Information, but in April 1941, at the height of the Rashid Ali coup d'etat, he replaced Ambassador Basil

Newton. The Foreign Office's decision to send him to Baghdad resulted from the assessment that Britain required a strong ambassador, well-acquainted with Iraqi politics, to overcome the serious challenges it faced there. Cornwallis indeed used a firm hand against Rashid Ali and the rebelling Iraqi officers and succeeded in restoring the Regent and Nuri al-Sa'id to power. He retired in March 1945 due to ill health.[85]

Like other British Arabist veterans of World War I, Cornwallis regarded the new war as an opportunity to oust France from Syria and Lebanon and thereby open the way for an Iraqi-Syrian union. He was well aware of the inherent weakness of the Iraqi state, of which he considered himself one of the founders, and saw such a union as a means to strengthen it, both politically and economically. He too believed that Britain should pursue a regional policy, but his main goal remained the political unity of the Fertile Crescent in a Hashemite-led confederation under Iraq. He believed that such a confederation did not necessarily negate an Arab union that would be based on economic and cultural ties between all the Arab states, including Egypt. Indeed, he was involved behind the scenes in Nuri al-Sa'id's proposal in December 1942 for Arab unity, but continued to promote a Hashemite Greater Syria joined with Iraq.[86]

Cornwallis had gained considerable experience of CPA and CD in intelligence operations in World War I. During his long service in Iraq, he forged personal relations with many Iraqi dignitaries, including Shiites and Kurds, and these ties played a role in Eden's decision to appoint him as Ambassador to Iraq. He did not rely solely on the existing intelligence agencies, which included the Combined Intelligence Centre Iraq (CICI), established in June 1941, but also ran his own intelligence network. Shortly after his return to Baghdad, he renewed the system of political advisers, stationed throughout Iraq, who served as a source of information and an instrument through which he could conduct his own policies. Nuri al-Sa'id was a key figure in his Iraqi and inter-Arab politics (doc.13). They both used covert operations and clandestine diplomacy to promote joint goals in the Middle East, as well as vis-à-vis London. Cornwallis, like other Arabists, was well aware of Churchill's and Eden's reservations regarding the plans for a Hashemite Greater Syria and Arab unity, and he used Nuri al-Sa'id to conceal his involvement in promoting such plans. In early 1943, he informed Eden that Nuri al-Sa'id was unstoppable in his efforts to promote Arab union, but his meetings with President Quwatli in September 1944, in which he did his utmost to pressure the Syrian President to agree to a Hashemite Greater Syria, revealed that he was personally committed to the idea. His early retirement weakened Nuri al-Sa'id's position in inter-Arab politics (docs.33, 41). His belief that his work would help his country maintain its influence in Iraq proved premature, as it had been in Egypt; Britain was to discover after the war that it was no longer able to control events in the Middle East. The attempts to establish a Hashemite-led confederation in the Fertile Crescent was undermined by Ibn Sa'ud and Faruq, and in January 1948 the plans to transform Iraq into

Britain's main strategic base in the Middle East collapsed when the Iraqi Regent and Nuri al-Sa'id failed to ratify the Portsmouth Agreement.

Nuri al-Sa'id

Although Nuri al-Sa'id, the strongman in Iraqi politics, did not belong to this small group of influential British Arabists, he is included, as he was actively involved in their CPA and CD in the region and vis-à-vis their own government. They appreciated his loyalty to Britain, his discreet behavior and strategic thinking. He was a front man for many of their schemes, including the efforts to supplant France in Syria and Lebanon; in promoting Greater Syria and Arab unity; in the formation of the Arab League; and in their efforts to prevent a separate Jewish state. These were certainly also his own goals, but when his wishes contradicted those of Britain, he backed down. Nevertheless, he saw in Britain a vital ally in promoting his long-cherished dreams of a Hashemite Greater Syria and an Iraqi-Syrian union. Arab leaders and foreign observers followed his actions closely, assuming that they reflected Britain's position. French intelligence tracked him during his numerous visits to Damascus and Beirut. The British and Syrian documents, particularly the Syrian ones, contain details of his political maneuverings in Syria and Lebanon. The French intelligence services also followed the Iraqi Consul General in Beirut, Tahsin al-Kadri, who was intimately involved in Nuri al-Sa'id's intrigues. They received details of his meetings with local leaders from their agents, tapped his telephone conversations and opened Iraqi diplomatic correspondence.[87]

Their intimate collaboration with Nuri al-Sa'id allowed Cornwallis, Clayton, Stirling and other British Arabists to conduct a more flexible policy and conceal their involvement when necessary. For instance, they used him to counter Ibn Sa'ud's influence in Syria; in their attempts in 1946 to persuade the Syrian leaders to settle Syria's disputes with Turkey over Alexandretta and join a regional defense alliance together with Iraq and Turkey; and in conducting propaganda campaigns in London and Washington against Zionist aspirations for a Jewish state. In 1946-48, Nuri al-Sa'id played an important role in the British Arabists' covert efforts to prevent the establishment of a Jewish state. Although he lost some of his influence in the aftermath of the failed Portsmouth Agreement, they continued to regard him as a loyal partner and involved him in their covert political operations. In August 1949 he took part, together with Stirling, in orchestrating Sami al-Hinnawi's coup d'état in Syria against Husni al-Za'im. In the early 1950s he led Britain's efforts to form the Baghdad Pact and confronted Nasser's radical pan-Arabism. In the coup d'état of 1958 he was overthrown, together with the Hashemite King, and was to pay with his life for his many years of service to Britain.

Notes

1 Archives Nationales (AN), Paris, Archives du Général de Gaulle, Papiers des Chefs de l'Etat, (de Gaulle's Papers), 3AG4/13. See also Zamir, Meir, "The

Missing Dimension: Britain's Secret War Against France in Syria and Lebanon, 1942-45 – Part II," *Middle Eastern Studies*, 46 (6) (2010), pp.791-899; de Gaulle, C., *Lettres, Notes et Carnets, Juin 1943–Mai 1945* (Paris: Plon, 1983), pp.343-4; de Gaulle's letter to Bidault, Paris, October 19, 1944.

2 Zamir, "The Missing Dimension," docs.12-13. For additional studies on Anglo-French rivalry in Syria and Lebanon in World War II, see: Gaunson, A.B., *The Anglo-French Clash in Lebanon and Syria, 1940-45* (New York: St. Martin's Press, 1987); Roshwald, Aviel, *Estranged Bedfellows: Britain and France in the Middle East During the Second World War* (Oxford: Oxford University Press, 1990). For a comprehensive study of Churchill's relations with de Gaulle during the war, see Kersaudy, François, *Churchill and de Gaulle* (New York: Atheneum, 1982). For a French version of the events, see Davet, Michel-Christian, *La Double Affaire de Syrie* (Paris: Fayard, 1967).

3 De Gaulle, Charles, *The Complete War Memoirs of Charles de Gaulle* Vol. II, *Unity*, pp.524; Vol.III, *Salvation*, pp.875-94; (New York: Carroll & Graf Publishers, 1998). (The original three volumes in French were published in 1954-1959.) Zamir, "The Missing Dimension," docs.88-90, Churchill to General Paget; Zamir, Meir, "De Gaulle and the Question of Syria and Lebanon During the Second World War," *Middle Eastern Studies*, 43(5), (2007), pp.675-708. See also Kersaudy, pp.408-13; Wilson, John, "The Foreign Office and the Departure of General de Gaulle, June 1945-January 1946," *The Historical Journal,* 25(1) (1982), pp. 209-16.

4 Zamir, Meir, "'BID' for Altalena: France's Covert Action in the 1948 War in Palestine," *Middle Eastern Studies*, 46(1) (2010), pp.17-58; Schillo, Frédérique, *La Politique Française à l'Égard d'Israël, 1946-1959* (Brussels: André Versaille Editeur, 2012), pp.26-42.

5 Kimche, Jon, *Seven Fallen Pillars: The Middle East, 1915-1950* (London: Secker and Warburg, 1950), pp.7-8; Lenczowski, George, *The Middle East in World Affairs* (Ithaca: Cornell University Press, 1958), p.503. For an unofficial version of British policy in World War II, see Kirk, George, *The Middle East in the War* (Oxford: Oxford University Press, 1954). The author was a post-war director of the Foreign Office's Middle East Centre for Arab Studies. See also Monroe, Elizabeth, *Britain's Moment in the Middle East, 1914-1956* (London: University Paperbacks, Methuen & Co., 1965), especially Chapter 7. For a more critical view of Britain's Middle East policy, see: Kedourie, Elie, *The Chatham House Version and Other Middle-Eastern Studies* (London: Weidenfeld and Nicolson, 1970), especially chapters 8 and 12; Keay, John, *Sowing the Wind: The Mismanagement of the Middle East 1900-1960* (London: John Murray, 2003); Cohen, Michael J. and Martin Kolinsky (eds.), *Demise of the British Empire in the Middle East: Britain's Response to Nationalist Movements, 1943-55* (London: Frank Cass, 1998); Louis, Wm. Roger, *The British Empire in the Middle East, 1945-1951* (Oxford: Clarendon Press, 1984).

6 Ibid, p.364.

7 Kedourie, pp.352-3, 390-4. The Royal Institute of International Affairs (Chatham House) under its director, Arnold Toynbee, became an influential organization during the war, advocating the eviction of France from the Levant, rejecting the establishment of a Jewish state and promoting Arab unity. On the role of officials in the region in formulating Britain's policy, see Porath, Yehoshua, *In Search of Arab Unity, 1930-1945* (London: Frank Cass, 1986), pp.303-11.

8 See for example: Egremont, Max, *Under Two Flags: The Life of Major General Sir Edward Spears* (London: Phoenix Giant, 1997); Zamir, Meir, "An Intimate Alliance: The Joint Struggle of General Edward Spears and Riad al-Sulh to Oust France from Lebanon, 1942-1944," *Middle Eastern Studies*, 41(6) (2005), pp.811-32. For Spears' version, see: Spears, Edward, *Fulfilment of a Mission: The Spears Mission to Syria and Lebanon, 1941-1944* (London: Leo Cooper, 1977); Borden,

Mary, *Journey Down a Blind Alley* (London: Hutchinson & Co., 1947). The author was General Spears' wife.

9 Satia, Priya, *Spies in Arabia: The Great War and the Cultural Foundations of Britain's Covert Empire in the Middle East* (New York: Oxford University Press, 2008), p.272; Dorril, Stephen, *MI6: Inside the Covert World of Her Majesty's Secret Intelligence Service* (New York: The Free Press, 2000), pp.531-49.

10 Aldrich, Richard J., *The Hidden Hand: Britain, America and Cold War Secret Intelligence* (New York: The Overlook Press, 2001), pp.1-16; Aldrich, Richard J., "Policing the Past: Official History, Secrecy and British Intelligence since 1945," *English Historical Review*, CXIX(483) (2004), pp.922-53. Other examples of an alternative British historiography can be found in the memoirs of protagonists such as Stirling, Walter F., *Safety Last* (London: Hollis and Carter, 1953); Spears, *Fulfilment of a Mission*; Stark, Freya, *East is West* (London: John Murray, 1945); Stark, Freya, *Dust in the Lion's Paw: Autobiography 1939-1946* (London: John Murray, 1961); Glubb, John B., *A Soldier with the Arabs* (London: Hodder and Stoughton, 1957); Kirk, George, *The Middle East in the War* (Oxford: Oxford University Press, 1954).

11 For a defense of the Arabists by McLoughlin, who was personally acquainted with many of them, see McLoughlin, Leslie, *In a Sea of Knowledge: British Arabists in the Twentieth Century* (Reading: Ithaca Press, 2002), pp.251-62. See Said's comments on Lawrence and what he defines as the "imperial agent," and his discussion of Hamilton Gibb, who during the war worked in the Chatham House, where he took part in preparing policy papers on the Middle East for the Foreign Office, in Said, Edward W., *Orientalism* (London: Penguin Books,1978), pp.237-46, 276-85.

12 McLoughlin, *In a Sea of Knowledge*, p.3

13 Kaplan, Robert D., *The Arabists: The Romance of an American Elite* (New York: The Free Press, 1995), p.8.

14 For recent studies on Britain's use of intelligence in decolonization see: Grob-Fitzgibbon, Benjamin, *Imperial Endgame: Britain's Dirty Wars and the End of Empire* (New York: Palgrave Macmillan, 2011); French, David, *The British Way in Counter-Insurgency, 1945-1967* (Oxford: Oxford University Press, 2011); Walton, Calder, *Empire of Secrets: British Intelligence, the Cold War and the Twilight of Empire* (London: Harper Press, 2013).

15 This term is taken from the title of Elizabeth Monroe's book.

16 For Bevin's Arab policy, see: Monroe, Elizabeth, "Mr Bevin's Arab Policy," in Hourani, Albert (ed.), *Middle Eastern Affairs* (2), St. Antony Papers, No.11 (Carbondale, Illinois: Southern Illinois University Press, 1961); Louis, *The British Empire in the Middle East, 1945-1951*. Louis' introduction is a good summary of the strategic challenges faced by Britain in the post-war Middle East.

17 Andrew, Christopher and David Dilks (eds.), *The Missing Dimension: Governments and Intelligence Communities in the Twentieth Century* (Champaign: University of Illinois Press, 1985). See the introduction by Moran, pp.1-28, and Walton, Calder and Christopher Andrew, "Still the 'Missing Dimension': British Intelligence and the Historiography of British Decolonisation," in Major, Patrick and Christopher R. Moran (eds.), *Spooked: Britain, Empire and Intelligence Since 1945* (Newcastle upon Tyne: Cambridge Scholars Publishing, 2009), pp.73-96.

18 See Grob-Fitzgibbon, pp.80-100; Walton, *Empire of Secrets*, pp.xix–xxxii; Walton and Andrew, pp.73-96.

19 Aldrich, *The Hidden Hand*, p.72; Dorril, pp.542, 562. On the SIS and CIA joint operation "Boot" (Ajax) to overthrow Mussadeq's elected government in Iran in 1953, see pp.558-99.

20 Jeffery, Keith, *MI6: The History of the Secret Intelligence Service, 1909-1949* (London: Bloomsbury, 2010), p.748. The book is an authorized historiography of SIS.

21 On the British intelligence services' operations against the Zionist movement, see: Andrew, Christopher, *The Defence of the Realm: The Authorized History of MI5* (London: Allen Lane, 2009), pp.352-66; Jeffery, pp.689-97; Walton, pp.72-112; Aldrich, *The Hidden Hand*, pp.256-67; Charters, David A., "British Intelligence in the Palestine Campaign, 1945-47," *Intelligence and National Security*, 6(1) (1991), pp.115-40.

22 Zamir, Meir, "'BID' for Altalena"; Zamir, "Espionage and the Zionist Endeavor," *Jerusalem Post*, November 21, 2008; Barr, James, *A Line in the Sand: The Anglo-French Struggle for the Middle East, 1914-1948* (London: W.W. Norton & Co., 2011), pp.320-32.

23 Shelley, Adam, *British Intelligence in the Middle East 1939-1946* (PhD dissertation, University of Cambridge, 2007); Rathmell, Andrew, *Secret War in the Middle East: The Covert Struggle of Syria, 1949-1961* (London: I.B. Tauris, 1995); Bloch, Jonathan and Patrick Fitzgerald, *British Intelligence and Covert Action: Africa, Middle East and Europe since 1945* (Dingle, Co. Kerry: Brandon Books, 1984), pp.109-42. On World War I and the inter-war years: Satia, *Spies in Arabia*; Sheffy, Yigal, *British Military Intelligence in the Palestine Campaign, 1914-1918* (London: Routledge, 1998); Thomas, Martin, *Empires of Intelligence: Security Services and Colonial Disorder after 1914* (Berkeley: University of California Press, 2008).

24 The documents to which I gained access cover only part of 1941-47. The latest Syrian documents seen in the French archives were from November 1947, but French intelligence reports indicate that the agent in Syria continued to send copies of documents throughout 1948. In 1968, the French evacuated the archives of the mandate period from their embassy in Beirut, and in the process destroyed large numbers of documents, though it is not clear whether they also destroyed the original copies in Arabic of secret Syrian documents for security reasons.

25 Zamir, "Bid for Altalena," p.21; Zamir, Meir, "The French Connection," *Haaretz*, June 20, 2008.

26 Archives Nationales (AN), Paris, de Gaulle's Papers, 3AG4/13. Additional documents can be found in the AN, Paris, Papiers de Georges Bidault (Bidault's Papers), 457AP121/122.

27 For the secret war between Ibn Sa'ud and the Hashemites see Chapter 3.

28 Zamir, "The 'Missing Dimension," docs. 88-90; Zamir, Meir, "Against the Tide: The Secret Alliance Between the Syrian National Bloc Leaders and Great Britain, 1941-1942," in Gershoni, Israel (ed.), *Arab Responses to Fascism and Nazism, 1933-1945* (Austin: University of Texas Press, 2014), pp.55-72.

29 Johnson, Loch K. (ed.), *Strategic Intelligence, Vol.3: Covert Action: Behind the Veils of Secret Foreign Policy* (Westport: Praeger Security International, 2007), p.24.

30 Walton, *Empire of Secrets: British Intelligence, the Cold War and the Twilight of Empire*; Shelley, pp.198-219; Davies, Philip H.J., "From Special Operations to Special Political Action: The 'Rump SOE' and SIS Post-War Covert Action Capability 1945-1977," *Intelligence and National Security*, 15(3) (2000), pp.55-76. Dorril's book is especially helpful as he focuses on SIS's covert operations during and after World War II. He lays emphasis on such methods, which were prevalent in the Middle East.

31 See Johnson's five edited volumes on the various aspects of intelligence: *Strategic Intelligence Vol.1: Understanding the Hidden Side of Government; Strategic Intelligence Vol.2: The Intelligence Cycle: The Flow of Secret Information from Overseas to the Highest Councils of Government; Strategic Intelligence Vol.3: Covert Action: Behind the Veils of Secret Foreign Policy; Strategic Intelligence Vol.4: Counterintelligence and Counterterrorism: Defending the Nation against Hostile Forces; Strategic Intelligence Vol.5: Intelligence and Accountability:*

Safeguards Against the Abuse of Power (Westport: Praeger Security International, 2007).

32 National Security Act Sec. 503(e); Johnson, *Strategic Intelligence, Vol.3: Covert Action*, p.30.

33 For the British approach, see Phythian, Mark, "The British Experience with Intelligence Accountability," in Johnson, *Strategic Intelligence Vol.5: Intelligence and Accountability*, pp.67-88.

34 Johnson, *Strategic Intelligence Vol. 3: Covert Action*, pp.36-7.

35 See Chapter 2; Zamir, "The 'Missing Dimension'," doc.16.

36 Wight, Martin, *Power Politics* (London: Penguin Books, 1978), pp.115-7. See also: Andrew, Christopher and Jeremy Noakes (eds.), *Intelligence and International Relations, 1900-1945* (Exeter: University of Exeter Press, 1987); Halliday, Fred, *The Middle East in International Relations: Power, Politics and Ideology* (Cambridge: Cambridge University Press, 2005).

37 For Sulh's ties with Spears, see Zamir, "An Intimate Alliance." The article was written before the discovery of the secret British and Syrian documents. See also Seale, Patrick, *The Struggle for Arab Independence: Riad el-Solh and the Makers of the Modern Middle East* (Cambridge: Cambridge University Press, 2010), Chapters 17-20.

38 Shelley, pp.11-19, 216-9; Hinsley, F.H. and C.A.G. Simkins, *British Intelligence in the Second World War: Volume IV: Security and Counter-Intelligence* (London: HMSO, 1990), pp.162-7, 209-13, 229-31. For the British intelligence secret war against Germany in the Middle East during the war see West, Nigel, *MI6: British Secret Intelligence Operations, 1909-1945* (New York: Random House, 1983), pp.190-201.

39 Satia, *Spies in Arabia*, pp.239-62, and Satia, Priya, "The Defense of Inhumanity: Air Control and the British Idea of Arabia," *The American Historical Review*, 111(1) (2006), pp.16-51.

40 Satia, *Spies in Arabia*, pp.263-80.

41 On the role of SIME in the Middle East, see Shelley, pp.216-9; Hinsley and Simkins, pp.150-3; Dovey, H.O., "Security in Syria, 1941-45," *Intelligence and National Security*, 6(2) (1991), pp.418-46; Magan, William, *Middle Eastern Approaches: Experiences and Travels of an Intelligence Officer, 1939-1948* (Norwich: Michael Russell Publishing, 2001). The author was head of SIME after the war.

42 On MEIC see: Dovey, H.O., "The Middle East Intelligence Centre," *Intelligence and National Security*, 4(4) (1989), pp.800-12; Shelley, pp.80-7.

43 On the various British intelligence services in the war, see Shelley, Chapters 2 and 3. On the "A" Force, see Clarke, Dudley, *Seven Assignments* (London: Jonathan Cape, 1949). See also Mackenzie, W.J.M., *The Secret History of SOE: The Special Operations Executive, 1940-1945* (London: St. Ermin's Press, 2000). Mackenzie's book is an in-house history of SOE written after the war, but only published in 2000. Garnett, David, *The Secret History of PWE: The Political Warfare Executive, 1939-1945* (London: St. Ermin's Press, 2002).

44 MESC was a regional organization responsible for administering the entire economy of the Middle East as a single region. French sources repeatedly claimed that British intelligence agents used it as a cover. Wilmington, Martin W., *The Middle East Supply Centre* (London: University of London Press, 1972).

45 On PICME see Hinsley and Simkins, pp.188-9; Shelley, pp.151-2. See also an analysis of a comprehensive report from November 1943, prepared by PICME and obtained by the French intelligence service, in Chapter 3.

46 Jeffery, *MI6: The History of the Secret Intelligence Service, 1909-1949*; Shelley, pp.201-3; Davies, *MI6 and the Machinery of Spying* (London: Frank Cass, 2004), pp.191-2; Dorril, pp.534, 538-9. Aldrich presents a more critical view of the British intelligence system in the post-war Middle East and claims that it "lived

off its reputation and was in fact very weak." Aldrich, *The Hidden Hand*, p.259. See also pp.71-2.

47 Apart from human intelligence (humint), which was an important source of political intelligence in the Middle East, the British used signals intelligence (sigint) to monitor hostile and friendly politicians as well as diplomatic posts. Sensitive sigint sources were often disguised as humint sources to protect their identities. Arab countries' diplomatic posts in the region, as well as in Europe and the United States, were a good source of intelligence on foreign and inter-Arab relations. Ciphered correspondence between Kings Ibn Sa'ud and Faruq and President Quwatli, and Syrian diplomats' ciphered reports demonstrate the importance of such sources. On an agent named "Volcano" in Catroux's head-quarters, who handed over copies of de Gaulle's and Catroux's correspondence, see Jeffery, pp.434-5. On the British agent in the Jewish Agency, see Harouvi, Eldad, *Palestine Investigated: The Story of the Palestine C.I.D., 1920-1948* (Kochav Yair: Porat Publishing, 2011, in Hebrew), pp.242-4. See also: Dorril, p.538; West, Nigel, *The Sigint Secrets: The Signals Intelligence War, 1900 to Today* (New York: Quill, William Morrow, 1988), p.137; Thomas, Martin, "France in British Signals Intelligence, 1939-1945," *French History*, 14(1) (2000), pp.59-65.

48 See his books: Longrigg, Stephen H., *Syria and Lebanon under French Mandate* (Beirut: Oxford University Press, 1968); Longrigg, Stephen H., *Oil in the Middle East* (Oxford: Oxford University Press, 1961); Longrigg, Stephen H., and Frank Stoakes, *Iraq* (London: Ernest Benn, 1958). See also Dorril, p.569.

49 Ministère des Affaires Etrangères (MAE), Paris, Syrie et Liban, 1944-1952, vol.301, no.301, Damascus, February 1947, Serres to Bidault; Dorril, p.542.

50 Mackenzie, p.171; Chavkin, Jonathan S., *British Intelligence and the Zionist, South African, and Australian Intelligence Communities during and after the Second World War* (PhD dissertation, University of Cambridge, 2009), pp.39-57.

51 On SOE's organization in the Middle East, see Mackenzie, pp.142, 169-90, 507-15; Shelley, pp.51-8. See also Ranfurly, Countess of, *To War with Whitaker: The Wartime Diaries of the Countess of Ranfurly, 1939-1945* (London: Heinemann, 1994). On political warfare in the Middle East see: Garnett, pp.154-61; Kelley, Saul, "A Succession of Crises: SOE in the Middle East, 1940-45," *Intelligence and National Security*, 20(1) (2005), pp.121-46; Sweet-Escott, B., *Baker Street Irregular* (London: Methuen & Co Ltd, 1965), pp.70-99.

52 Mackenzie, Appendix D: Memorandum – Relations between SOE and the Foreign Office, pp.759-62; Davies, "From Special Operations to Special Political Action," pp.55-76; Aldrich, *The Hidden Hand*, pp.76-80; Dorril, pp.19, 534.

53 Cooper, Artemis, *Cairo in the War, 1939-1945* (London: Hamish Hamilton, 1989).

54 Zamir, "The Missing Dimension," docs.17, 24-6. On Greater Syria, see a study prepared by the Research Department in the Foreign Office in The National Archives, London (TNA), FO 371/61497 9137/42/65, "The Greater Syria Movement," London, January 10, 1948. See also Porath, *In Search of Arab Unity*; Dawn, C.E., "The Project of Greater Syria" (unpublished PhD dissertation, Princeton University, 1948). On Hourani's support for a Greater Syria, see Hourani, Albert H., *Syria and Lebanon: A Political Essay* (The Royal Institute of International Affairs, London: Oxford University Press, 1946), pp.269-70. See also Pipes, Daniel, *Greater Syria* (Oxford: Oxford University Press, 1990), pp.3-6. Pipes rightly observes that the Greater Syria movement should be judged not by its failure, but by the critical role it played in Middle East politics after 1918.

55 Bullock, Alan, *Ernest Bevin: Foreign Secretary, 1945-1951* (London: Heinemann, 1983), pp.112-5, 155-6. Dorril questions Alan Bullock's portrayal of Bevin as a powerful foreign secretary, claiming that he was manipulated by his officials in

the Foreign Office: Dorril, p.37. See his criticism of Bullock for ignoring Bevin's relations with the intelligence services, p.805, note 7.

56 Examples of the British security services conspiring against the Labour Party were the faked Zinoviev letter of 1924, which led to the downfall of the first Labour government, as well as their role in the attempt to overthrow Prime Minister Harold Wilson in the 1970s. See: Andrew, *MI5*, pp.148-52, 321, 632-43; Jeffery, pp.619-20. See also Dorril, pp.35-6, 570. American scholars examine the issue of government control of intelligence organizations far more than British scholars. See for example: Johnson, *Strategic Intelligence Vol. 5: Intelligence and Accountability*; Hastedt, Glenn P. (ed.), *Controlling Intelligence* (Abingdon: Frank Cass, 2005).

57 AN, Paris, Bidault's Papers, 457AP78, Foreign Office, June 14, 1946, conversation with Mr Bevin.

58 Louis, pp.48-50; Keay, p.345.

59 On the disagreement between the Foreign Office and SIS concerning the latter's activities in France, see Jeffery, pp. 676-9. See also Bullock, pp.144-7. For post-war Anglo-French economic cooperation see Woodhouse, Roger, *British Policy towards France, 1945-51* (London: Macmillan, 1995).

60 Lenczowski, p.503.

61 Stafford, David, *Churchill and Secret Service* (New York: The Overlook Press, 1998), pp.83-5, 124-6, 150-3; Egremont, pp.97-8.

62 Mackenzie, pp.68-9. See also Spears, Edward, *Assignment to Catastrophe: Vol. 1: Prelude to Dunkirk, July 1939-May 1940*, and *Vol. 2: The Fall of France* (London: William Heinemann Ltd., 1954).

63 Egremont, pp.213-35; Zamir, "De Gaulle and the question of Syria and Lebanon." Catroux devoted a whole chapter to a personal attack on Spears. Catroux, Georges, *Dans la Bataille de Méditerranée* (Paris: René Julliard, 1949), pp.191-8. On the clashes between General Spears and General Wilson and later General Holmes, Commanders of the Ninth Army stationed in Syria and Lebanon, see Wilson, Lord, *Eight Years Overseas, 1939-1947* (London: Hutchinson, 1951), pp.123-4. See also Mott-Radclyffe, Charles, *Foreign Body in the Eye: A Memoir of the Foreign Service Old and New* (London: Leo Cooper, 1975), pp.98-9, 118-20. The author served at the time as an intelligence officer in the Levant.

64 Mackenzie, pp.169-90; Shelley, pp.51-7.

65 In early 1945, Spears repeatedly raised the issue of Syria and Lebanon in Parliament and campaigned for Britain's arming of the Syrian gendarmerie. On Spears' activities in London against the French and the Zionists and in support of the Arab cause, see Miller, Rory, *Divided against Zion; Anti-Zionist Opposition in Britain to a Jewish State in Palestine, 1945-1948* (London: Frank Cass, 2000), pp.23-54.

66 For Stirling's version of his role in the confrontation with the French in the Levant, see Stirling, pp.215-38. For a biography of Stirling by Hart, B.H.L., see the *Oxford Dictionary of National Biography* (Oxford: Oxford University Press, 2004). See also Barr, pp.289-94, pp.354-7.

67 Stirling, pp.193-214; Rubin, Barry, *Istanbul Intrigues* (New York: McGraw-Hill, 1989), pp.90-1.

68 The claim that Stirling was involved in the 1949 coups is based on French archival sources. On the attempt on his life in November 1949, see Lord Kinross' epilogue in Stirling, pp.239-43.

69 Stirling, pp. 217-8, 239-41; Dorril, p.537.

70 Stirling's role in the first and second coups d'état in 1949, together with Nuri al-Sa'id, is beyond the scope of this study; his departure from Syria after the attack on his life in November that year signified the end of Britain's influence in Syria.

71 McLoughlin, *In a Sea of Knowledge*, p.118. This paragraph is based on the British and Syrian documents, as well as French and Zionist/Israeli archival sources. Both French and Zionist sources stress his presence at Arab summits during 1946-48.

See: Kimche, pp.58, 197; Sasson, Eliyahu, *On the Road to Peace: Letters and Conversations* (Tel Aviv: Am Oved, 1978, in Hebrew), pp.360, 395. Abba Eban, the future Israeli Foreign Minister, and Albert Hourani served as Clayton's assistants in Cairo in the early war years. On the role of MEIC and PICME, which Clayton headed, see Hinsley and Simkins, pp.150-1, 188-9. See also: Dovey, "The Middle East Intelligence Centre"; Shelley, pp.141, 151-2, 180-6; Cooper, *Cairo in the War*, pp.243, 310.

72 The "Clayton Plan," a term used by French and Zionist intelligence sources in 1947-48, is discussed in the Epilogue.

73 Eshed, Haggai, *Reuven Shiloah: The Man Behind the Mossad* (London: Frank Cass, 2005). On Clayton's meeting with Zaslani (Shiloah) to coordinate joint operations against Vichy in Syria and Lebanon, and Germany, see pp.47-8, 71-4. See also: Elath (Epstein), Eliyahu, *San Francisco Diary* (Tel Aviv: Dvir, 1971, in Hebrew), pp.60-1; Sasson, pp.360, 395.

74 On Clayton's role in the establishment of MECAS, see McLoughlin, *In a Sea of Knowledge*, pp.118-9; Shelley, pp.180-6.

75 The claim that Clayton closely collaborated with Azzam is based on French archival sources. See Sasson's report on his conversation with Kamil Riyad, King Faruq's special envoy in Paris, on September 23, 1948, in which Riyad accused the British of bribing Azzam to go to war in Palestine, in Zamir, "Espionage and the Zionist Endeavor."

76 See Sir Iltyd Clayton's Collection in the Middle East Centre, St. Antony's College, Oxford, which includes partial memoirs.

77 On Rashid Ali al-Gailani's collaboration with Ibn Sa'ud against the Portsmouth Treaty, see Chapter 3.

78 Quoted in Louis, p.228, note 5.

79 A useful study of Smart's role in defining Britain's policy in Egypt during and after the war and his relations with Lord Killearn, the Foreign Office and local leaders, is Wichart, Stefanie K., *Intervention: Britain, Egypt, and Iraq During World War II* (PhD dissertation, University of Texas at Austin, 2007), especially Chapter 2 on the role of the Oriental Secretary in the British Embassies in Cairo and Baghdad. See also Cooper, *Cairo in the War*, pp.32, 149-50, 155-8, 183.

80 Amy's sister Cathy was married to George Antonius.

81 Dorril, p.538; Wichart, pp. 43-47, 66-9, 173-9, 229, 247, 412.

82 Wichart, pp.366-9, 376-80.

83 Zamir, "The Missing Dimension," docs. 24-6, Cornwallis' conversations with Quwatli from September 21-24, 1944.

84 Lawrence describes Cornwallis as "A man rude to look upon, but apparently forged from one of those incredible metals with a melting-point of thousands of degrees." Lawrence, T.E., *Seven Pillars of Wisdom* (New York: Penguin Books, 1977), p.58. On his role in the Arab Bureau, see Westrate, Bruce, *The Arab Bureau: British Policy in the Middle East, 1916-1920* (Philadelphia: University of Pennsylvania Press, 2003).

85 For Cornwallis' biography by Martin Bunton, see the *Oxford Dictionary of National Biography*. Wichart examines in detail Cornwallis' role in Iraq in World War II and his relations with the Foreign Office and Nuri al-Sa'id. See for example his role in the Rashid Ali revolt and his relations with Nuri al-Sa'id in Wichart, Chapters 4 and 6. On Cornwallis' involvement in Sharq al-Adna, which was run by SIS from Cyprus, see Dorril, pp.539-40.

86 On the collaboration between Cornwallis and Nuri al-Sa'id in the movement for Arab unity, see Wichart, Chapter 10.

87 Birdwood, Lord, *Nuri As-Said: A Study in Arab Leadership* (London: Cassel, 1959), pp.187-91; Kedourie, p.276; Wichart, pp.339-48; Gomaa, Ahmed M., *The Foundation of the League of Arab States* (London: Longman, 1977), pp.66-72.

2   The Anglo-French Clandestine War in Syria and Lebanon, 1940-1942

Oliver Harvey, Anthony Eden's Private Secretary, writing in his diary shortly after the outbreak of the Syrian crisis in June 1945, expressed his dismay at the officials and the military in the Middle East dragging Britain into a dangerous confrontation with France:

> Yet if we oust the French in this way, as they always said we were aiming to do, we raise the most appalling issue which will lie across our relations for generations. And all this is muddled thinking. The P.M., H.M.G. and the British people have no wish to take over Syria. Local pro-Arab officials in subordinate positions are of course working for it. Spears certainly did so in spite of F.O. instructions while he remained there as the protégé of the P.M. carrying out the opposite of the P.M.'s policy. The stupid military mind fell of course for this nonsense, supposing that we should always have troops to waste in this way. Yet this policy is suicidal to British local interests which are identical with those of the French. We are both occupying Arab territory and the Arabs hate us both as Christians and Europeans.[1]

Harvey was not alone in expressing concern over the Arabists' hold on Britain's Middle East policy; Eden and other professional diplomats in the Foreign Office shared similar views. Eden, who since 1941 had sought to reach a compromise with Free France over Syria and Lebanon, could only have looked on with consternation as Churchill and de Gaulle publicly traded insults in the summer of 1945. As was the case after Spears succeeded in provoking the Lebanese crisis in 1943, local officials and high-ranking military officers inflamed Churchill's animosity towards de Gaulle, and Eden was left once again with the unsavory task of managing the fallout and preventing further deterioration in Anglo-French relations. Senior diplomats such as Duff Cooper, the British Ambassador to Paris, Harold Macmillan, Maurice Peterson, who had served before the war as Ambassador to Baghdad and in 1944 as Ambassador to Ankara, R.M.A. Hankey of the Eastern Department and members of Parliament such as Harold Nicolson, had warned all along against the folly of the anti-French stand of the Arabists, who were ignoring

Britain's interests in friendly post-war France. They warned that British support of pan-Arabism and the Arab League could backfire and be turned against Britain itself. Alexander Cadogan, the influential Permanent Under-secretary for Foreign Affairs, was especially critical of Spears' unscrupulous methods to promote the Arabists' goals of evicting France from the Levant. Eden had his own doubts. Admittedly, in his well-known speeches in May 1941 and February 1943 he had endorsed plans for Arab unity, but these were motivated mainly by the need to ensure Arab collaboration during the war. Aware of the inclination of local Arabists to work behind the scenes to advance their own schemes, he made it clear that the Arab leaders themselves, not local British officials, should take the initiative for Arab unity. Eden also shared the doubts of some of his senior diplomats who questioned the wisdom of British support for the Hashemites, which antagonized Kings Ibn Sa'ud and Faruq.[2]

Such views however, were distasteful to most of the Arabists in the Middle East, whether diplomats, intelligence agents or senior military officers who were implementing the policy on the ground. One of the few officials who openly disputed the policy of ejecting France from Syria and Lebanon, pursued by Spears and the Arabists, was Colonel Sir Gilbert MacKereth, who had served before the war as Consul in Damascus. In 1944, MacKereth was appointed to the Spears Mission, where he repeatedly clashed with Spears over his hostile stand towards France, forcing the Foreign Office to recall him to London. He shared his criticism of Spears with French officials, who often quoted him in their reports.[3] But such views, whether in London or the Middle East, failed to influence the course of Britain's anti-French policy in the region during and after the war, and neither Eden, nor Bevin who succeeded him, were able to impose their views on their subordinates there. As Harvey, Peterson and MacKereth had warned, Great Britain was to pay a heavy price for evicting France from the Levant.

On July 15, 1939, Colonel John Teague, head of the Secret Intelligence Service (SIS) station in Jerusalem, wrote to Captain Bernard, head of the Section d'Études du Levant (SEL) in Beirut, proposing that their two organizations communicate directly rather than through the British liaison officer in Beirut. The fact that SIS's major station in the Middle East did not maintain direct contact with the most prominent French intelligence agency in the region – although they were both facing increased German and Italian subversion – testifies to the deep distrust between the British and French intelligence services in the Middle East in the inter-war years. A year earlier, a French double agent informed his French controller that, at a meeting he had attended, the head of SIS in the Middle East stated that the British authorities recognized the drawbacks of their policy in the Levant and that henceforth they would coordinate their policy in the region with France. But SIS's readiness to cooperate more closely with its French counterpart did not result from a local initiative but from the growing cooperation between the two parent organizations in Europe. While SIS agents stepped up their espionage and subversion activities in Syria and Lebanon in the second half of the 1930s, Colonel Stewart Menzies, deputy chief of SIS in London, and its chief from 1939, forged close ties with Colonel Louis Rivet, head of the Service de Renseignement (SR) in Paris in a joint effort to counter the German threat.[4]

Nevertheless, collaboration between the British and French secret services in the Middle East on the eve of World War II, and then with Free France before the taking of Syria and Lebanon from Vichy in the summer of 1941, was temporary. Despite the war against the Axis Powers, they were engaged in their own secret war dating back to the 1920s. Although Anglo-French colonial rivalry and the clashes between Churchill and de Gaulle in the Levant have been thoroughly researched, this clandestine war remains a "missing dimension." The British and Syrian documents shed light on this feud and its repercussions on the Powers' decolonization of the Middle East. British secret agencies for the most part had the upper hand, but the French intelligence services scored major achievements, beating the British secret services at their own game with covert operations and clandestine diplomacy. The French successes were somewhat surprising given that the war and post-war period were the golden years of the British intelligence services. In the Middle East, British intelligence agencies gained much prestige because of their contribution to the war effort against the Germans and Italians in the Western Desert and the securing of their country's control over the region. After the war they enjoyed even greater influence in shaping Britain's Middle East policy, as they were deemed vital for ensuring their country's strategic and economic interests despite decolonization. Moreover, Bevin and the Chiefs of Staff (COS) regarded them as the first line of defense against Soviet attempts to penetrate the region.[5]

In contrast, the war years were a trying period for the French intelligence. Its archives were either set on fire or seized by the Germans and transferred to Berlin, while many of its officers and agents were rounded up and imprisoned. It was split into rival organizations under Vichy and Free France, and even after the war, when it was rebuilt under de Gaulle and the Fourth Republic, it continued to suffer from internal discord and was viewed with deep suspicion by the communist and socialist parties in the government. And yet, in Syria and Lebanon, the French intelligence organizations retained some of their pre-war professional capabilities and successfully waged a clandestine war against their British counterparts. From the summer of 1944 onwards they provided de Gaulle, and later Bidault, with detailed information on the activities of the British intelligence agencies and their anti-French intrigues, thus enabling the French leaders to maintain some of their country's influence, especially in Lebanon, and to take revenge on Britain for their country's eviction from the Levant in 1945. Their success was due in no small part to the tendency of their British rivals to underestimate their capabilities

Although British counter-intelligence agencies, especially Security Intelligence Middle East (SIME), were present in the two Levant states after taking them from Vichy, they failed to detect that a French agent had infiltrated the

British Legation in Beirut and uncovered some of their most sensitive secrets. This failure is perhaps less surprising given the Soviet success in penetrating SIS through Kim Philby and the "Magnificent Five" during and after the war. While the British intelligence services acknowledged the capabilities and professionalism of the Soviet intelligence agencies, its officers in the Middle East held little regard for their French counterparts. Furthermore, during the war, there was a common belief among many British military and intelligence officers, shared by the Americans, that the French were incapable of keeping secrets, a trait they often attributed to Gallic culture. Their reports to London and the memoirs of many Arabists reveal their contempt for the French army, intelligence officers and civilian officials in the former High Commission. Stirling voiced such prejudices:

> Generally speaking, his Gallic temperament does not permit the Frenchman to see the other man's point of view. The French were quite unable to realize how they had failed to govern in the spirit of the mandate or how they had retarded the growth of Syria. Nor would they believe the intensity of feeling they had aroused against themselves. They simply claimed that it was the British who had created this feeling in the hopes of eventually acquiring the country for themselves. They overlooked the fact that we had twice captured Syria by force of arms and twice renounced any claim to it.[6]

Spears played the most damaging role in reinforcing the contempt and animosity of Britons in the region towards France. He derided French politicians for their defeatism, which had left Britain to face Nazi Germany alone. He described the French as weak, decadent and Anglophobic, incapable of rebuilding their country as a Great Power in post-war Europe, and on whom Britain could no longer rely. He claimed that they differed from the French of World War I who had fought heroically under Prime Minister Georges Clemenceau and Marshal Ferdinand Foch alongside Great Britain to defeat Germany. These views were constantly repeated by Spears during and after the war to officials and military and intelligence officers in the Middle East and London, and reinforced prejudice against the French, as it was believed that Spears was an expert on French culture and society and that he was voicing Churchill's view. Vichy's collaboration with Germany further strengthened the resentment of many Britons in the Middle East, who were dismayed by the ferocity and determination with which the French army had fought against British forces in the Levant in the summer of 1941, compared to its dismal performance against the invading German army in France a year earlier. The bitter conflict with de Gaulle in the Middle East only added to the hostility of the British military and officials, who accused him of being ungrateful and Anglophobic. They viewed the French civil servants in Syria and Lebanon as corrupt and inefficient officials who had cynically exploited Syria and Lebanon for personal gain, ignoring the wellbeing of the local populations.[7]

In contrast, British officials and Arabists dwelt on Britain's liberal policy in its own mandated territories which, they alleged, took into consideration the needs and interests of the local inhabitants. Spears often asserted that without Britain's involvement after the liberation of Syria and Lebanon from Vichy, the two countries would have deteriorated into anarchy and faced a famine. The British tendency to take the moral high ground towards the French was also expressed in contentions that Britain had twice occupied Syria and Lebanon and twice renounced any claim to them. Their accusations against the French mandate, which may have been partly justified, overlooked the fact that British control over the Middle East, especially during the war, had been far from liberal, and that most of the British officials there had never intended to allow France to regain its position in Syria and Lebanon. On the contrary, many Arabists saw France's defeat as an opportunity to extend British hegemony over Syria and thereby solve some of the most pressing issues that their country encountered in the Middle East after the war, especially the protracted problem of Palestine. As for claims of French corruption, it was certainly prevalent among French officials in Syria and Lebanon, but British officials and military officers also exploited their positions to further personal interests. For instance, the Syrian documents provide evidence that Spears received bribes from the Syrian government to promote its interests in London and that he also used his position to further his own business interests in the two Levant states (docs. 64, 194, 239, 322).[8]

French intelligence in Syria and Lebanon

In France, unlike Britain, there has been a general lack of interest in intelligence, reinforced by the negative views of many Frenchmen towards their country's secret services, regarding them as a tool used by cynical politicians rather than as a vital line of national defense. The roots of this approach date back to the Dreyfus affair and political scandals under the Third Republic, in which the French secret services were implicated. In the last decade, more research has been undertaken into the French intelligence services, especially their role in the inter-war years and under de Gaulle's Free France. France, however, had a long tradition of using security and secret services for control and surveillance and for tracking internal and external threats. Indeed, French intelligence scored major successes against Germany in World War I and the inter-war years, although its role in the defeat of 1940 is still debated. Its organizational structure was shaped under the Third Republic. At its core were the military intelligence services, especially the Deuxième Bureau, which was part of the French General Staff and charged with assessing external military threats. It controlled the SR, responsible for external espionage, and the Section de Centralisation de Renseignement (SCR), which dealt with counter-espionage. Another security service was the Sûreté générale (which after 1934 became the Sûreté nationale), a civilian agency that served as a security organization under the control of the Minister of the Interior. This organizational structure, which gave priority to military intelligence and counter-espionage, was formed in response to the threat posed by Germany to France's national defense. Unlike the British intelligence services, the French secret services were less involved in political and economic intelligence and played only a limited role in France's foreign relations. In contrast to Britain, where the Foreign Office collaborates with SIS, which is answerable to the Foreign Secretary, in the Quai d'Orsay there was a long tradition of hostility towards the involvement of the intelligence agencies in foreign relations. Like other governmental institutions, the French intelligence services were well structured and heavily bureaucratic, and tended to gather copious amounts of raw data and issue a large number of intelligence reports. It was one of the first to develop a system to grade the accuracy and value of sources and intelligence information according to a combination of letters and numbers. This grading system allows historians to ascertain how intelligence officers at the time evaluated certain reports. The Syrian documents, for example, are rated A1: they were considered original and outstandingly good.[9]

France, like Britain, formed an efficient colonial intelligence system in order to control its colonies with limited military forces. Its intelligence system in Syria and Lebanon was based on that in North Africa, and in the 1920s many of its officers came from Morocco. Recent studies provide detailed descriptions of the organization and methods used by the French security services in Syria and Lebanon in the inter-war years and their role in maintaining control and formulating policy. The challenges they faced were especially demanding, as the French mandate had been forcibly imposed. It was opposed by the largely hostile Muslim Sunni population in the cities and had to contend with restless ethnic minorities and nomadic tribes in peripheral regions as well as with constant subversion from British agents and the Hashemite family in Iraq and Transjordan. The Druze Revolt of 1925-27, which assumed a nationalistic character, demonstrated the vulnerability of the French mandate in Syria. By the 1930s, the French were facing additional threats from Germany, Italy, Turkey and the Soviet Union.[10]

Direct French control over its mandated territories, coupled with intense nationalist opposition, external subversion and limited military forces, led to the formation of a sophisticated security system that closely monitored all sections of the Syrian and Lebanese populations. This system provided copious amounts of information from diverse sources, including a network of thousands of informers and the constant monitoring of the postal, telephone and telegraph services, as well as reports from French delegates and advisers posted to local governments. Like their British counterparts, the French intelligence agencies co-opted "agents of influence" from the local elites, among them politicians, businessmen, religious leaders and journalists who could influence public opinion. They used political bribery, intimidation and extortion, but, unlike the British agents, they made only limited use of financial bribery, arguing that it was a sign of weakness and could not buy allegiance over time. SR officers not only provided information, but were actively involved in formulating policy as advisers to the High Commission or in implementing policy in rural areas. They were also engaged in controlling ethnic minorities and Bedouin tribes in the peripheral regions of Syria. The organizational structure of the French intelligence system in Syria and Lebanon mirrored that of North Africa and Metropolitan France, and was both civilian and military. At its core was the Deuxième Bureau in Beirut, which was directly linked with the Deuxième Bureau in Paris, but came under the supervision of the Commander-in-Chief of the Levant Army. It was dependent on intelligence received from the SR-SCR, the Bureau Central de Renseignements (BCR – regional counter-espionage offices), as well as the Sûreté Générale de l'Armée (SGA) and the Sûreté générale, which served as a major civilian security agency under the control of the High Commission. The police and gendarmerie provided additional sources of information. These overlapping and complex surveillance and security networks provided large amounts of information, and French intelligence officers came under constant pressure to issue intelligence reports.[11]

The system established in Syria and Lebanon in the inter-war years was instrumental in enabling the French intelligence services, under both Vichy and Free France, to contend with the far superior British intelligence agencies. Unlike the secret services in Metropolitan France, which acted under German occupation, and the Bureau Central de Renseignements et d'Action (BCRA), the newly-formed Free French intelligence organization in London, the French intelligence agencies in Syria and Lebanon continued to operate unhampered during and after the war. Despite dramatic changes in France and the Levant, many of the officers, who had acquired a deep knowledge of Syrian and Lebanese society and politics and had long experience in conducting a clandestine war against the British intelligence agencies in the Middle East, remained to serve under Vichy and, later, under Free France and de Gaulle's provisional government. Furthermore, some of their key agents in the Lebanese and Syrian political systems continued to provide high-grade information.[12]

The SR and the SEL were especially active in the clandestine war against the British secret services under both Vichy and Free France. Despite their small numbers, SR officers exercised a strong influence over France's Syrian and Lebanese policies. They saw themselves as defenders of the French empire in the Middle East and were as knowledgeable about Arab Muslim society as their British Arabist counterparts. It was no coincidence that former SR officers played a prominent role in the Vichy and Free French administrations. General Georges Catroux, who served under de Gaulle as Free France's chief representative in the Middle East, had formed the SR in Syria and Lebanon in 1921 and was responsible for its reorganization after the Druze Revolt. General Henri Dentz, the French High Commissioner in Syria and Lebanon under Vichy, had served as the head of the SR during the Druze Revolt. Another former SR officer, Colonel Philibert Collet, had commanded the Circassian Cavalry of the Army of the Levant and rallied to de

Gaulle at a particularly crucial time in the war against Vichy. Colonel Fernand François Oliva (Olive) Roget, another former SR officer, was responsible for the operations in the British Legation in Beirut and the Syrian Foreign Ministry in Damascus. Captain Pierre Rondot, who became a world-renowned scholar on Arab and Muslim affairs, served in the inter-war years as an SR officer. He was remobilized and sent to the Levant before the war and continued to serve under Vichy, conducting some of the more successful operations against British intelligence in the Middle East.[13]

SR-Levant gathered information not only in Syria and Lebanon, but throughout the Middle East. It was particularly active in Hashemite Iraq and Transjordan, which were regarded as hostile to the French mandate. The SR also had a large presence in Egypt, where France had considerable economic interests, including in the Suez Canal Company. Moreover, in the 1930s, Cairo had become a refuge for anti-French North African nationalists. Apart from providing information and ensuring security, SR officers were involved in administrative affairs, especially among the minorities in the peripheral regions. They were active among the Alawites in Jabal Ansarriya, the Druze in Jabal Druze and the Kurds in the Jazira, implementing the French policy of "divide and rule" by cultivating the minorities' loyalty to France and inflaming their fears of a united Syria controlled by the National Bloc in Damascus. The SR stations in Beirut and Damascus were of particular importance, as their officers closely monitored the activities of the National Bloc leadership and the Muslim opposition in Lebanon headed by Riyad al-Sulh. Responsible for providing high-grade political intelligence, they thus became intimately acquainted with Syrian and Lebanese politics. They were also in charge of securing the collaboration of prominent Syrian and Lebanese politicians and other "agents of influence" using various methods of CPA, including extortion and political and financial bribery.[14]

Like the SR-SCR, the SEL in Beirut played a central role in the secret war against British intelligence in the Middle East in the 1930s and later under Vichy and Free France. When it was formed in 1930, one of its main tasks was to counter British-Hashemite subversion in the French mandated territories. It was to provide assessments and information to the counter-espionage agencies on the activities of German and Italian agents. Its main task, however, was to evaluate political and strategic developments in the mandated territories and the Middle East as a whole. Britain's policy in the Middle East therefore featured prominently in its analyses. It reported directly to the General Staff in Paris, but its recommendations figured highly in the formulation of French policy in Syria and Lebanon. It received intelligence from various sources, including reports of the Levant SR-SCR, BCR, SGA, Sûreté générale, the network of French delegates and advisers in the local governments, diplomatic missions in the region, military attachés and liaison officers. By the end of the 1930s, the SEL had become engaged in counter-espionage and regularly issued reports to SR-SCR on foreign intelligence activities in the mandated territories.[15]

The Anglo-French clandestine war in the 1930s

The French 1934-1942 military intelligence files from Syria and Lebanon, found in "Fonds de Moscou," provide unique insight into the modus operandi of the French intelligence agencies in the Middle East, as well as their clandestine war against the British secret services.[16] This information is useful, as many traits of the Anglo-French secret war during the 1930s and under Vichy were to continue under Free France and into the post-war years. The reports of the SEL and SR-SCR provide details on the British secret agencies' operating methods in the Levant and include names of intelligence officers and their local agents. They describe the activities of SIS and SSO officers from Iraq, Transjordan and Palestine in the French mandated territories and those of British diplomats in Beirut, Damascus and Aleppo. SEL reports maintained that British secret agents were working under various guises, for instance as journalists, archeologists or representatives of British commercial companies such as the Iraq Petroleum Company (IPC) and the Nairn Transport Company that operated between Baghdad and Damascus. They also reveal the identities of SIS officers active in Iraq, Transjordan and Palestine. It should be noted that a SEL report from July 1936 to SCR claims in a "façon indiscutable" that, in addition to his role as Commander of the Arab Legion in Transjordan, Glubb Pasha took part in SIS operations. In fact, Glubb had served as an RAF intelligence officer in Iraq in the 1920s and in 1940-41 took part in SOE subversion against Vichy in Jabal Druze and among the Bedouin tribes in the Syrian Desert. SEL reports also reveal the names of local agents in Syria and Lebanon employed by SIS. These included the Kettaneh brothers, owners of one of the largest automobile import companies in the Middle East, the banker Albert Pharaon, and Dr Ernest Altounyan in Aleppo. Apparently French intelligence in the Middle East was still obsessed with what can be termed the "ghost of Lawrence;" its agents closely followed Arnold Lawrence, Lawrence's brother, when he visited Altounyan in Aleppo in July 1937. They also monitored the activities of British Arabists associated with Lawrence, among them Cornwallis, Newcombe, Clayton, Kirkbride and officials known for their hostility towards the French mandate, such as Sir Walter Smart and Glubb Pasha.[17]

In the late 1930s, British intelligence stepped up its surveillance in the French mandated territories following increased Italian and German subversion. German and Italian agents were using Syria and Lebanon to spy and carry out subversive acts in the British mandated territories of Palestine and Iraq. Although the French and British security agencies faced the same Italian and German threats, their mutual distrust meant that they failed to collaborate. Furthermore, in 1936 France concluded treaties with Syria and Lebanon undertaking to grant them independence within three years. This prompted the British and the Hashemites to increase their efforts to secure the support of Syrian politicians for a union with Transjordan and Iraq. The construction of the oil pipeline from Mosul in northern Iraq to Tripoli in

Lebanon and the decision of the IPC to build a refinery in Tripoli added to Britain's interests in Syria and Lebanon. British oil companies sought concessions for oil exploration in the Jazira, which was believed to contain large reserves. French intelligence reports from May 1937 give details of meetings between Colonel Stephen Longrigg, an SIS officer positioned in the IPC offices in Baghdad, and Syrian and Lebanese politicians, aimed at mobilizing support for British oil companies.[18]

The revolt in Palestine from 1936-39 drove the British intelligence agencies to step up their subversive activities in Syria and Lebanon, as they became major hubs for arming and financing the rebels. After fleeing from Palestine in October 1937, the Mufti, Haj Amin al-Husseini, settled near Beirut, from where he directed the revolt against the British forces. Attempts by British diplomats to persuade the French High Commission to curtail the Mufti's activities met with little success. French officials remembered well the assistance provided by British agents to the Syrian and Druze rebels a decade before. Moreover, the British authorities in Egypt had not heeded French requests to act against anti-French North African nationalist refugees in Cairo. British diplomats and secret agents acted unilaterally, recruiting informers and collaborators among Syrian and Lebanese politicians, as well as French officials, to undermine the activities of the Mufti and his local supporters. The British Consulates in Damascus and Beirut became the focus of these efforts. MacKereth, the Consul-General in the Syrian capital, successfully used bribery to win the collaboration of prominent Syrian politicians, including Prime Minister Jamil Mardam.[19]

With the war in Europe becoming inevitable, France was no longer ready to give up direct control over Syria and Lebanon and was unwilling to ratify the 1936 treaties. The War Council reconsidered the strategic role of the two Levant states in the event of war against Germany and Italy in the Eastern Mediterranean and defined a new strategy based on close collaboration with Britain. Syria and Lebanon were to serve as a base for a large military force capable of opening a second front in the Balkans and assisting British forces in the Middle East in defending the Suez Canal. Turkey was expected to be an ally, and the ceding of Alexandretta, completed in July 1939 with British endorsement, was to ensure Turkey's tacit collaboration. Three members of the War Council – General Henri Huntziger, General Maurice Gamelin and General Maxime Weygand – had served previously in the Levant, and this undoubtedly reinforced the military importance of the region in France's overall war strategy.[20]

At the end of August 1939, General Weygand, High Commissioner in Syria and Lebanon from 1923 to 1925, was appointed Commander-in-Chief of the Eastern Mediterranean theater. Immediately upon arrival in Beirut he traveled to Alexandria, where he met General Wavell and Admiral Andrew Cunningham, Commander of the British Navy in the Mediterranean, to coordinate a joint strategy. In the coming months, Weygand and Wavell established close working relations and exchanged visits in Beirut and Cairo.

Weygand also visited Ankara to secure the collaboration of the Turkish High Command. In early 1940, scores of ships transported three divisions of reserve troops from France to Beirut in addition to combat aircraft, tanks, heavy guns and large quantities of ammunition. Work on military projects was accelerated, new port facilities were built in Beirut, an airport was opened in nearby Khaldeh and a communications center was constructed to relay French radio broadcasts in the Middle East. The airport in Rayak was extended, and new barracks and ammunition dumps were constructed in army camps to serve the thousands of French troops arriving in Syria and Lebanon. Fortifications were built along the coast and heavy guns were installed in the mountains above Beirut. Tripoli was also fortified and work on the refinery was speeded up. A civil defense system was organized and 10,000 French soldiers were sent from Lebanon to Syria, where they took up positions around Damascus and other major cities.[21]

After arriving in Beirut in January 1939, Gabriel Puaux, the new High Commissioner, spent the months before the war tightening French control over Syria and Lebanon. France's Middle East policy, like that of Britain, was almost exclusively determined by military and strategic considerations. With war looming in Europe, France was unwilling to allow the National Bloc leaders, whom it had always distrusted, to wield power, preferring instead to rely on the more friendly minorities in Jabal Druze and the Alawite region. Since the end of 1938, SR officers had been inciting Druze and Alawites, as well as Kurds in the Jazira, to demand greater autonomy from Damascus. After the German invasion of Poland, Puaux declared a state of emergency, suspended the Syrian and the Lebanese constitutions and dissolved the governments and parliaments, while the High Commission assumed direct control over the two states.[22]

Reorganization of the intelligence agencies in the two Levant states reflected the increasing importance of the strategic role of the mandated territories. Additional manpower and resources were allocated to the security services, especially the SGA and BCR, while the SEL was given a larger role in coordinating inter-services counter-espionage. Members of radical groups known for their close ties to German and Italian intelligence, such as the Partie Populaire Syrienne (PPS) and the Arab Club, were detained, and in the aftermath of the Ribbentrop-Molotov Pact in August 1939, French security stepped up its monitoring of members of the Syrian Communist Party. The High Commission issued a decree stipulating that all offenders against national security be brought before a French military court, while the Sûreté générale intensified supervision of the thousands of foreign citizens in the mandated territories. Martial law was imposed and control of the postal services and censorship of the press were enforced. Measures were also taken to form an efficient propaganda system, based mainly on "Radio Levant."[23]

France's capitulation in June 1940 after a mere six weeks of war shocked and humiliated the French in Syria and Lebanon. Reports sent from Damascus and Beirut by Haganah agents Eliyahu Sasson and Eliyahu

Epstein vividly described the feelings of demoralization, apprehension, uncertainty and helplessness among the French troops, officials in the High Commission and the large French community in Beirut. Puaux and General Eugène Mittelhauser, who replaced General Weygand, who had been recalled to Paris, were faced with a grueling predicament – to recognize the authority of the new government in Paris under Marshal Philippe Pétain and General Weygand, the new War Minister, or to heed the appeal of the little-known General de Gaulle to continue the war against the Axis Powers. In a desperate attempt to convince General Mittelhauser and Puaux to continue the war, General Wavell traveled to Beirut, but the British naval assault on the French navy in Mers el-Kebir in early July and the failed Anglo-Free French attack on Dakar in September brought an end to any willingness on the part of the French generals in the Levant and North Africa to heed Britain's call to join its war against Nazi Germany. Ironically, France's defeat revived old feelings of Anglophobia and resentment towards Britain among the French military officers and officials in the Levant, many of whom believed the rumors that Britain had abandoned France to fight alone against the invading German forces and that it would surrender within a few months. General de Gaulle was portrayed as a traitor used by Britain to take over parts of the French empire, while officials in the High Commission voiced their fears that Britain would exploit France's defeat to realize its old ambitions in Syria and Lebanon. Nuri al-Sa'id's visit to Damascus in early July, together with Emir Abdullah's declarations that France's defeat had opened the way for the establishment of a Hashemite Greater Syria, only reinforced their suspicions. The French intelligence officers in Syria and Lebanon went through similar experiences of shock, humiliation and uncertainty over the future of their motherland under German occupation. Nevertheless, the French secret and security services were professional organizations; their rank and file, seeing themselves as the first line in defending the French empire in the Middle East against internal and external threats, remained loyal to Marshal Pétain. Their professionalism was put to the test in the face of the growing resentment among Syrian nationalists and the attempts by neighboring states and international Powers to take advantage of the vacuum left by France's defeat to raise claims over Syria and Lebanon. The two countries thus became targets of intense subversion and propaganda campaigns by Germany, Italy, Britain, Free France, Turkey, Iraq, Transjordan and Saudi Arabia.[24]

Documents in the files of the French military intelligence services and the Sûreté générale provide a detailed picture of foreign subversion and the French security agencies' efforts to counter them. Despite the defeat and uncertainty over France's future position in the two Levant states, these agencies continued to function. Their immediate concern was to counter the subversion of the increasing numbers of German and Italian agents in the mandated territories. The arrival of the Italian military mission for disarmament in Beirut in August added to their resentment and humiliation. Its arrival was in accordance with Hitler's recognition of Italy's supremacy in the

Mediterranean and the Middle East. It set up headquarters in the St. George Hotel in Beirut and its first request was for details on the French armed forces in Syria and Lebanon. The French security services closely followed its meetings with Syrian and Lebanese leaders and dignitaries, including Maronite clergy, who saw Italy as a Catholic Power that could replace France as protector of the Christians in Lebanon. Large sums of money were given to politicians and journalists to garner public support for Italy. But the French security services were more concerned with the activities of the German agents. In August, Rudolf Röser, an Abwehr agent, arrived in Beirut, followed by Werner Otto von Hentig, a senior diplomat in the German Foreign Ministry. Röser and von Hentig set up offices in the Hotel Metropole in Beirut, which became a center for German subversion and propaganda. The files of the French military intelligence services and the Sûreté générale give a detailed picture of the German activities, including meetings with Syrian and Lebanese leaders, journalists and dignitaries, as well as the sums of money handed over. The German subversion prompted General Henri Dentz, who replaced Puaux in December 1940, to repeatedly request the Vichy authorities in France to curtail German activities that were aimed directly against the French administration. Indeed, contrary to the existing historiography, which claims that the demonstrations and strikes in Damascus in March 1941 were triggered by food shortages, Dentz accused the German agents and Quwatli of instigating them. He was also concerned about the British reaction to the use of Syria and Lebanon by German agents to spy and carry out subversive acts in the British territories of Palestine, Transjordan and Iraq. The British secret services were well aware that, in some cases, French SR officers were collaborating with German agents. The Germans' endeavors in Syria culminated in April-May 1941 with their use of the French mandated territories to provide military assistance to the anti-British revolt in Iraq.[25]

The Anglo-Vichy secret war in Syria and Lebanon, 1940-1941

World War II sparked a renewed interest in the Middle East, as Arnold Toynbee notes in his introduction to George Kirk's book:

> In an age in which the Middle East had long since ceased to be the most civilized and populous region in the Old World, it had regained its ancient central position in another way. The fall of France and intervention of Italy in the war in the summer of 1940 immediately enhanced the importance of the Middle East theater, and from then on it remained the crucial theater until the completion of the expulsion of the Axis forces from North Africa carried the war back on to the soil of continental Europe from Tunisia via Sicily.[26]

The fall of France and the success of the Pétain government in imposing its control over Syria and Lebanon presented the British High Command in

Cairo with an unexpected military threat and an intelligence vacuum. The well-equipped 100,000 troops of the Levant Army, which was to serve as an expeditionary force against the Axis Powers in southeastern Europe and provide an additional line of defense for the Suez Canal, now threatened the British forces in the Middle East. General Wavell, with limited forces at his disposal and the large theater of operations for which he was responsible, faced a new threat – that Vichy-Levant might allow the Axis forces to launch attacks on Britain's strategic positions in the Middle East from within France's mandated territories. In this event, these forces would be able to attack the Suez Canal, not only from the Western Desert, but also from Syria and Lebanon in the north. The Luftwaffe could use Syrian and Lebanese airports to strike Britain's oil resources in northern Iraq and the Persian Gulf, including the Abadan refinery. Germany, starving for additional supplies of oil, could gain access to the Middle East oil reserves. The Axis forces in the Levant would be able to isolate Turkey and threaten it from both the Balkans in the west and Syria in the south, thereby foiling one of Churchill's major goals – securing Turkey's collaboration with the Allies. Finally, their military presence in Syria and Lebanon might allow Axis agents to step up their subversive operations in Iraq, Transjordan and Palestine, forcing Britain to allocate additional forces to ensure its control over its own territories.[27]

These grave dangers prompted Churchill and the War Cabinet in July 1940 to warn Vichy that if it allowed the Axis Powers to use the Levant, Britain would take over Syria and Lebanon. The arrival in August of the Italian military mission for disarmament and the increasing activities of German secret agents in the French zone added to British anxieties. The German overrun of Yugoslavia and Greece in April 1941 and the defeat of the British expeditionary forces in Greece brought the Axis Powers closer, as the Luftwaffe was now capable of attacking Cyprus, Britain's main strategic hub in the Eastern Mediterranean. Churchill's immediate concern however, was the success of Admiral François Darlan, the influential French Naval Minister, in dragging the Vichy government into a close collaboration with Germany in the Levant and North Africa. The Rashid Ali Revolt in Baghdad, the arrival of German planes in Aleppo in early May and the military assistance provided to the Iraqi rebels by the Vichy authorities in Syria and Lebanon were perceived as the realization of Britain's fears. It should be noted that at this early stage of the war in the Middle East, Spears collaborated with de Gaulle to persuade Churchill to instruct the reluctant General Wavell to occupy Syria and Lebanon – a goal the Arabists in Cairo had been seeking all along.[28]

Vichy's success in retaining control over the Levant posed a serious challenge to the British secret and security services in the Middle East. Following their collaboration in 1939 and early 1940 with French intelligence in Syria and Lebanon, especially on issues of security and counter-espionage, British intelligence agencies increasingly relied on French sources for information on German and Italian subversion in the Levant and elsewhere in the region. But they now faced a vacuum and urgently needed to provide accurate military and political intelligence on the French mandated territories to the British High Command in Cairo. General Wavell, precisely because of the limited military forces under his control, required reliable, up-to-date information on Vichy's intentions. Economic blockades and covert action (CA) became Britain's major means to pressure the Vichy authorities into maintaining neutrality. From July 1940 until July 1941, when the British forces occupied Syria and Lebanon with the aid of Free France, the British intelligence agencies waged a new, secret war against Vichy-Levant, using subversion, clandestine diplomacy, political warfare and especially propaganda. This was the first time since the two Powers had occupied the region in World War I that Britain had conducted this type of warfare against France in the Middle East. Many of these methods would be employed later against Free France in the Levant. Britain had to resort to this mode of warfare in order to refrain from directly confronting Vichy and Free France. In both cases it revised its policies and intervened militarily: against Vichy when its army invaded and occupied Syria and Lebanon in the summer of 1941, and against Free France when General Paget issued his ultimatum to General Beynet on May 30, 1945, during the Syrian crisis.[29]

It was argued previously that war often presents individuals with the opportunity to make their mark on events larger than their formal position permits. This was certainly true of Brigadier Iltyd Clayton's part in the secret war against Vichy-Levant. Clayton, who served as General Wavell's Deputy for Military Intelligence and headed the Middle East Intelligence Centre (MEIC), played a role in World War II similar to that of his elder brother, Brigadier-General Sir Gilbert Clayton, Allenby's Chief Intelligence Officer in World War I. Because of his position and the extensive knowledge that he had acquired on the Middle East during his long service there, Iltyd Clayton was able to influence policy making. He entered the void between the military and civilian authorities and the many intelligence agencies that operated from Cairo. His knowledge, like that of other Arabists, was essential once the Middle East became an active military theater of high strategic importance. He demonstrated his abilities in the clandestine war against Vichy in Syria and Lebanon. This required the unique combination of espionage, subversion, political warfare and CD, as well as assessment and policy implementation. Clayton would gain much experience in all these fields, which he subsequently used to ensure France's eviction from the Levant and to secure his country's strategic and economic interests despite its "retreat" from the Middle East.[30]

The military and political information that the intelligence agencies were required to provide the War Cabinet in London and the Commander-in-Chief in the Middle East was vital for Britain in defining its policy towards Vichy-Levant. The most critical issues were whether and when Vichy would allow the Axis forces to use the Levant; the policy that Britain should follow to deter the Vichy authorities from collaborating militarily with Germany; and the effectiveness of the British economic blockade and propaganda campaigns among the French and local Arab populations. The MEIC was to evaluate whether it was possible to overthrow the Vichy administration using subversion and political warfare, as Catroux suggested, and the extent to which the Levant Army would resist in the event of a British and Gaullist invasion of Syria and Lebanon. Other questions that had to be addressed concerned the future of Syria and Lebanon in the event of a British occupation, and the consequences for Britain's position in the Arab world if Vichy was replaced with a French-Gaullist administration.[31]

The secret war conducted by the British intelligence services against Vichy in the Levant became a laboratory where they gained experience and honed their professional skills. While the British intelligence community in the Middle East demonstrated its ability to provide reliable military and political intelligence under rapidly evolving circumstances, some of its weaknesses surfaced, especially its tendency to underestimate the capabilities of the French intelligence agencies. In fact, numerous details of the British covert operations in Syria and Lebanon can be found in the files of the French military intelligence, which closely monitored them. French counter-espionage sources provide details of the British intelligence agencies that were involved, their subversive operations and the methods they used to recruit French and Arab agents. The experience acquired by these agencies would later be exploited by the Free French secret services to counter their British adversaries.[32]

Apart from humint sources, sigint played an important role in providing essential military and political intelligence on Vichy-Levant, as the Government Code and Cypher School (GC&CS) – Britain's wartime sigint organization – had succeeded in breaking Vichy codes in the early stages of the war. In fact, at the beginning of May 1941, the German intelligence service warned the Vichy authorities that their instructions to General Dentz were reaching the British High Command in Alexandria before Dentz himself received them in Beirut. The German Abwehr was unaware that its own code had been broken by the British later that year. Another important source of political information was Geoffrey Havard, the British Consul-General in Beirut, who remained in the post until May 1941, providing up-to-date intelligence on Vichy and serving as a link to local Syrian and Lebanese nationalist leaders. Indeed, the first direct contact with Riyad al-Sulh in early March 1941 was established by a member of the British Consulate. Political and military information was also provided by the American Consul-General in Beirut, Cornelius V.H. Engert, who served as an intermediary between the British authorities and General Dentz, as well as between them and the Syrian and Lebanese nationalist leaders. An additional source of military and political intelligence were the Haganah agents in Syria and Lebanon, especially during the first months after the fall of France when the British secret services faced an intelligence void in Vichy-Levant. Zionist agents were also used to bribe Druze leaders in the Mount Hermon region. The British received information from the Iraqi and Turkish intelligence services as well, both of which were active in Syria and Lebanon.[33]

The need to deter Vichy from collaborating with Nazi Germany and the belief that it was possible to replace its administration in the Levant with de Gaulle's supporters turned political warfare, especially the dissemination of propaganda, into a major tool in Britain's clandestine war against Vichy-Levant. Two separate propaganda campaigns were conducted – one in French, aimed at winning over French officers and soldiers in the Levant Army, and the other in Arabic, targeting the local population. This latter campaign was also intended to counter the effective German-Arab propaganda. Various agencies and means were employed, including radio broadcasts in French and Arabic from Cairo, Jerusalem and Haifa, in addition to the BBC in London. At the same time, SOE made use of Zionist agents to smuggle large quantities of printed propaganda into the two Levant states. As the military situation deteriorated, airplanes scattered pamphlets in French and Arabic over Syria and Lebanon. The files of the French military intelligence contain detailed descriptions of the British methods together with copies of pamphlets and analyses of the contents of the British broadcasts. Of particular interest are the weekly reports of a special committee for propaganda formed in February 1941 in the High Commission to monitor British propaganda and counter it.[34]

British propaganda aimed at the Syrian and Lebanese population stressed the negative economic and political repercussions of Vichy rule and the great benefits, especially economic, were Britain to administer Syria and Lebanon. It promised that the two states would gain independence and that the blockade would be removed immediately, thereby ending the oil and foodstuffs shortages and the problems of high prices, inflation and unemployment. However, there was an inherent contradiction in Britain's Levant policy, which was reflected in its propaganda. While Britain undertook to grant independence to Syria and Lebanon, it also recognized Free France as the representative of France in the mandated territories that were to be liberated from the illegal Vichy administration. But most Syrians and Lebanese did not distinguish between the two French authorities and were equally hostile to both. Glubb noted this contradiction after the occupation of the two states, when he remarked that while previously the British representatives had tried to provoke the indigenous population of Syria and Lebanon against France-Vichy, they were now attempting to convince them to recognize a new France, both of which they held in contempt.[35]

The close intelligence collaboration with General Catroux and Free France in Cairo against Vichy-Levant was fraught with difficulties and had only limited success. The British military authorities and civilian officials in Cairo expected Free France to exploit Vichy's defeatism and its collaboration with the hated Germany to win support for de Gaulle and counter charges made by Vichy and Axis propaganda that Britain intended to take over Syria and Lebanon. It was hoped that General Catroux, the highest-ranking officer who rallied to de Gaulle, would be able to win the loyalty of French officers in the Levant Army and civilian officials in the High Commission. But it turned out that the Gaullist propaganda was far less effective, and only a small number of French were willing to desert and join de Gaulle. Although Catroux had served as a senior intelligence officer in the Levant in the 1920s, he had lost touch with the current French administration there. His belief in his ability to mobilize support among the French in Syria and Lebanon and undermine the Vichy administration proved to be erroneous. The military and political intelligence provided by his agents was often inaccurate and overly optimistic, reinforcing the unfounded assumption that the Levant Army would only partly resist the invading Allied Forces. Some British officials, especially the old-guard Arabists, justifiably argued that Britain's support of de Gaulle and his movement would not go as planned, as it would provoke Vichy, which regarded de Gaulle as its bitter rival, to do its utmost to resist the British forces. The Americans were to learn this lesson when they excluded Free France's military involvement in the landing in North Africa in Operation Torch. Paradoxically, the secret collaboration between Free France and the Haganah's secret service against Vichy in Syria and Lebanon, promoted by the British intelligence services, would backfire, as five years later the Franco-Zionist intelligence collaboration was directed against the British themselves.[36]

Vichy-Levant's secret war against Britain and Free France

In the wake of France's capitulation, a Syrian journalist voiced the views of many Syrians when he noted that it was insulting for Syria to be controlled by a weak Power who "only knows bravery by name." This statement reflected the reaction of the majority of people in the Middle East, who were baffled by the news of the French Army's defeat. It was first met with astonishment and contempt followed by uncertainty, but also expectation that French rule was about to end. The French in the Levant no longer represented a strong, feared and respected Great Power, but a defeated and subservient nation that was about to end its historic "mission" in the Middle East. The British Arabists anticipated that after France's capitulation, Britain could exploit the entire Middle East for its immediate war needs and restructure it under its hegemony. Syria's neighbors had their own designs. On June 28, Emir Abdullah went to Jerusalem and demanded from High Commissioner Sir Harold MacMichael that Britain use France's defeat to establish a Greater Syrian monarchy under his rule. A few days later, Nuri al-Sa'id arrived in Damascus to drum up the Syrian leaders' support for an Iraqi-Syrian union. Ibn Sa'ud's messengers followed suit in an attempt to counter Hashemite efforts to take over Syria. Building on its success before the war in taking over Alexandretta, Turkey hoped to realize its ambitions to gain control over Aleppo and the northern part of the Jazira. Its agents stepped up their subversive activities among the inhabitants of the two regions to mobilize support for annexation to the Turkish republic. For its part, Italy made it clear that it regarded the Levant as its own sphere of influence and that it intended to replace France as the dominant Catholic Power in Lebanon.[37]

Many Frenchmen in the Levant likened their country to a badly wounded nation over whose assets the "vultures" were already hovering. But despite the expectations that Vichy's control of Syria and Lebanon would shortly be over, it lasted for another year, ending only after an intense war during which the British Army, assisted by Free French forces, invaded and occupied the two Levant states, leaving heavy casualties on both sides. Vichy's success in retaining control over the Levant and most of the French empire was the outcome of its own weakness – the two warring Powers, Britain and Germany, each for its own reasons, preferred that the Vichy regime remain in France. For its part, Vichy strengthened its international standing by pursuing an effective foreign policy that exploited those rivalries and secured American support for its survival. After the initial shock of their country's capitulation, the majority of the French in mainland France and the empire opted to follow Marshal Pétain, a World War I national hero. They desperately believed his undertaking to protect France and its empire through collaboration with Nazi Germany, especially as they deemed Britain's defeat inevitable. The French in the Levant shared those beliefs and expected Axis forces to crush the British Army in Egypt and take over the entire Middle East.[38]

Vichy was anxious to retain control over Syria and Lebanon, where it was particularly vulnerable to British and Gaullist subversion. The fall of the two states to de Gaulle would enhance Free France's prestige and strengthen it both militarily and politically; it might also serve as a precedent for the French in North Africa. Although Vichy propaganda portrayed de Gaulle and his followers as a British tool and his Free France as a marginal movement lacking any real support among the French public, the Pétain government regarded him as a threat, as he represented an alternative to Vichy defeatism and collaboration with the hated Germany. These concerns were underlined during the armistice negotiations in July 1941, when senior Vichy officers made it clear to their British counterparts that, for lack of a better alternative, they would prefer direct British control over Syria and Lebanon to that of Free France. Moreover, General Huntziger, the new Vichy War Minister, was committed to retaining the region. In June–July 1941, after the invasion of the British Army and the Gaullist forces, he instructed Dentz to use all means available to prevent the fall of Syria and Lebanon.[39]

Fortunately for Vichy, several events not directly linked to its rule in the Levant undermined Britain's ability to overthrow its administration there. The British attack on the French navy in Mers el-Kebir in early July 1940, in which 1400 French officers and seamen lost their lives, coupled with the British failure in the Battle of Dakar (Operation Menace), discredited Britain and Free France, and convinced many French serving in the Levant that Vichy's claims of Britain's treachery were justified. Furthermore, General Wavell, engaged in a protracted war against the Axis Powers in the Western Desert and Greece, was unable to allocate sufficient forces to occupy Syria and Lebanon. The Rashid Ali Revolt in Iraq in April 1941 generated strong anti-British feelings in Syria and Lebanon, and undercut Britain's pledges to conduct a more liberal policy if the two Levant states came under its rule. Domestically, the assassination of Abd al-Rahman Shahbandar, a prominent Syrian nationalist leader, in June 1940, in which National Bloc leaders, including Jamil Mardam, were implicated, considerably discredited the nationalists, who were the only political power capable of provoking large-scale demonstrations against the French administration.[40]

From July 1940 until May 1941, French security and secret agencies in the Levant played an important role in Vichy's control over its mandated territories. Their achievement was significant as Puaux, then serving as High Commissioner, was far from loyal to Vichy. Despite personal and organizational rivalries that surfaced after the defeat, the agencies remained intact, continued to function professionally and maintained their loyalty to the legal regime in France. It was precisely under these trying circumstances that their members were infused with a sense of duty to defend the mandated territories against any internal or external threat. The turning point came in September 1940, when the security agencies uncovered a plot engineered by de Gaulle's followers in the mandated territories and General Catroux, who had just arrived in Cairo – to topple the Vichy administration. The plot provoked General Huntziger to instruct the Commander-in Chief of the Levant Army and the High Commissioner to take harsh measures against de Gaulle's supporters. Those implicated were court-martialed and imprisoned. This was followed by the arrival of Colonel Bourget, a former staff officer under Weygand, who was sent to oversee the flushing out of disloyal officials and military officers. The Levant Army and the High Commission were reorganized and those suspected of disloyalty were sent back to France and North Africa, together with thousands of discharged reserve troops who were no longer needed in the Levant. General Dentz, who replaced Puaux in December, adopted a firm stand towards Britain and de Gaulle's Free France. He was well informed about British and Gaullist espionage and subversion in Syria and Lebanon, detailed descriptions of which can be found in the files of the French military intelligence services. For example, French intelligence officers opened the diplomatic bags of the British Consulate in Beirut, photographed their contents and re-sealed them, thereby uncovering the Consul's secret contacts with French officials and Arab politicians who opposed Vichy. Their contents also revealed details of bribery payments, agents' code names and military and political information that the Consulate was required to report back to Jerusalem and Cairo. Vichy's secret agencies penetrated the headquarters of General de Gaulle in London and of General Catroux in Cairo, and their agents sent reports of Free France's anti-Vichy operations and policy deliberations with the British High Command on the joint British-Gaullist campaign against Vichy in the Levant. Another source was the sigint station in Syria that monitored British and Gaullist traffic, including exchanges between de Gaulle and Catroux. French security agencies were well aware of the close collaboration between the SHAY, the Haganah's intelligence organization, and the Gaullists, and were able to uncover and arrest SHAY agents operating in Syria and Lebanon. One of them was Tuvia Arazi, who in 1945 was to play a prominent role in establishing the secret collaboration between the Free France intelligence service and the Haganah against Britain.[41]

SR officers in the Levant led the clandestine war against their British adversaries. In December 1940, Captain Rondot exploited the British secret services' attempts to recruit Syrian politicians and officials, and sent a high-ranking civil servant in the Syrian administration to Cairo under the guise of meeting his Egyptian counterparts. In Cairo, the Syrian agent met with senior SIS officers (Brigadier Clayton, Colonel Longrigg and Colonel Teague), as well as with British diplomats (Killearn, Smart and Frank Ogden, the former Vice-Consul in Damascus), all of whom pressed him to collaborate with Britain. The agent, code-named BYR 87, persuaded Clayton to dictate in detail Britain's aims in Syria and Lebanon, and brought a copy back to Rondot. (doc.1) It is significant that already at that early stage Clayton made it clear that "Britain would not agree to a French presence in Syria in the future."[42]

Propaganda – both printed and radio broadcasts – played a central role in Vichy's war against the British and Gaullists. It aimed to counter their hostile propaganda and win over the allegiance of the large French community in Syria and Lebanon to Marshal Pétain. The main tool was Radio Levant, which broadcast in Arabic and French, and whose contents were determined by the High Commission and the intelligence services. Propaganda in Arabic had little effect on the local population, but Vichy indirectly benefited from the far superior German propaganda emanating from Radio Berlin, whose programs in Arabic were very popular throughout the Middle East. One of its influential broadcasters, the anti-British Shekib Arslan, was particularly popular among Syrian and Lebanese listeners. Vichy propaganda aired on Radio Levant mainly targeted the large French community in the Levant, and intentionally adopted an extremely anti-British line, bordering on Anglophobia. It repeated claims that Britain – "Perfidious Albion" – had a long history of betraying France and fighting its wars with the blood of others, the latest example being in the Battle of France, when the British Expeditionary Army and the Royal Air Force left the French forces to fight alone against the Germans. The British massacre of French seamen in Mers-el-Kebir and the attempt to take over Dakar were further examples of such treachery. Under the shock of the capitulation, the tens of thousands of reserve officers and soldiers in the Levant, many of whom had left their families behind, tended to believe any slander, however wild. Another line repeated in Vichy propaganda was Britain's betrayal of France in the Middle East: since World War I, Britain had been trying to take over France's mandated territories in Syria and Lebanon, and now it was exploiting its temporary weakness to accomplish its old ambitions. To judge from the relentless resistance of the Levant Army to the advancing British forces, this propaganda, which alongside hostility towards Britain, stressed allegiance to Marshal Pétain, patriotism, military honor and the defense of the empire, was effective. Many French, both military and civilian, who were exposed to such Anglophobic campaigns, remained in the Levant under a Free French-British condominium. The contempt with which most of the British in Syria and Lebanon regarded the French – whether former Vichyists or Free French – did little to diminish anti-British feelings among the French in the Levant.[43]

Condominium: The clandestine Anglo-Free French war in Syria and Lebanon, 1941-1942

Historians tend to view the Anglo-French rivalry in the Levant during World War II as the culmination of the long-standing rivalry between the two colonial Powers. This may have been the case, and de Gaulle certainly believed it. But his immediate goal, especially during the dark years of 1940-42, was to secure the Levant as a base for his movement's struggle against Vichy; hence his bitter reaction to the intrigues of British agents against Free France's efforts to establish itself in Syria and Lebanon when it was at its most vulnerable. Moreover, in the face of Vichy's accusations that he was serving Britain and responsible for France losing the Levant, he had to demonstrate to the French public in France and North Africa that he was no less committed to the defense of the empire than Marshal Pétain.[44]

Catroux's background as a senior intelligence officer in the Levant was useful in the reorganization of the French intelligence services under Free France, as well as of the demoralized staff of the Délégation Générale, both of which had been weakened by the internal strife between supporters of Vichy and Free France. It is significant that in his appeal to the intelligence officers and officials who had served under Vichy to join Free France, he stressed the need to protect French interests in the Levant against British incursions. Before leaving for France, General Verdilac, the Commander of the French Levant Army under Vichy, raised a similar argument to persuade the Officiers Spéciaux to remain in Syria and Lebanon. But this was an exception; in most cases the Vichy authorities purposely tried to undermine the Free French secret services. The Vichy decision to move the archives of the Deuxième Bureau and the Sûreté générale to North Africa and France, which left the Free French intelligence services with no organized records, was a severe setback. Another Vichy decision – to transfer to North Africa large sums of money that had accumulated in the budget of the former High Commission from the income of the Common Interests – further weakened the position of those intelligence services, as Free France was unable to provide them with sufficient resources to counter the British agencies. Furthermore, the Free French secret and security agencies were under constant pressure from their British counterparts, who succeeded in recruiting senior members of the Délégation Générale, as well as enticing local Sûreté générale informers, to work for them. Nevertheless, the French services were able to retain most of their informers, as attested to by the thousands of intelligence reports in the files of the Sûreté générale and Deuxième Bureau. Free French control over the telephone network and postal services in Syria and Lebanon gave them access to an important source of information.[45]

French intelligence officers, who closely followed the activities of their British counterparts, became the first line in the defense of their country's interests in Syria and Lebanon against British subversion. Their ingrained hostility towards the British was reinforced by the overbearing and contemptuous attitude of the British officers. But their authority was limited as they were no longer the sole masters in the Levant; they had to contend with the superior British intelligence agencies which had far greater resources. Nonetheless, the French intelligence services had one advantage over the British newcomers – their deep knowledge and long experience with the extremely complex social and political makeup of the two Levant states. In contrast, Syria and Lebanon posed a challenge for most British intelligence officers, even for those who had worked in the Middle East before the war. They had served in Iraq, Transjordan and Palestine, or India, and were not always qualified to deal with the mostly French-educated, sophisticated, feudal and bourgeois elites of Beirut and Damascus. Spears was actually better skilled at dealing with these Levantine elites.

The need to clarify once again Britain's policy towards Free France in the Levant became apparent after the signing of the Armistice of Saint Jean d'Acre with Vichy, in which senior British officers went against their government's pledges to General de Gaulle. On September 1, 1941, two months after taking Syria and Lebanon from Vichy, the Commander-in-Chief of the British forces in the Middle East issued a circular to his officers warning of "the mistaken misconception regarding British policy in Syria and Lebanon." His warning came a few days after Oliver Lyttelton had reached an agreement with General de Gaulle on coordinating the military and civilian control of Syria and Lebanon. The circular quoted Churchill's letter to de Gaulle of August 7, 1940, pledging that "It is the determination of His Majesty's Government, when victory has been gained by the Allied arms, to secure the full restoration of the independence and greatness of France," and stressing that "Since the Vichy Government are not capable of protecting the rights of France, His Majesty's Government have pursued a policy of recognizing General de Gaulle as the trustee of France in such French territories as have been preserved or rescued from German or Italian control." The Commander-in-Chief questioned claims that it would be in Britain's interest to take direct responsibility for Syria and Lebanon. He cautioned his officers not to be impressed by complaints by the local population against the French, as similar complaints were also being directed against Britain by the Arab population in areas under its control. He ended with a warning that:

> There is a tendency for every Englishman who arrives in the Middle East to become his own Foreign Secretary. This temptation should be resisted. Every officer should make himself a champion of British policy and do everything in his power to check opinions and arguments in himself and

others which run counter to it. For it is only if Britain's word is trusted that British policy can hope to succeed amid the difficulties which lie ahead.[46]

The repeated statements by Churchill and Eden that collaboration with Free France was essential for an Allied victory; the Lyttelton-de Gaulle agreement; and the Commander-in-Chief's circular did not impress the well-entrenched British Arabists, diplomats and military and intelligence officers in the region. Spears and other senior officials criticized Lyttelton for "selling" Syria and Lebanon to de Gaulle after the British forces had fought hard to take them from Vichy. The hundreds of dead and thousands of wounded British soldiers sacrificed in the war against Vichy only intensified their resentment. The deep division between Pétain's and de Gaulle's supporters and the corruption and inefficiency of French officials faced by British officers after the occupation added to their contempt for the French. Moreover, de Gaulle's confrontational behavior, his threats and criticism of the British High Command's conduct in the Syrian campaign reinforced ill-feeling towards both the Vichyists, who had fought against them, and the Free French, who had fought alongside them. In fact, as the circular noted, British officers often treated Vichy officers with more respect than their Free French allies.[47]

French sources provide ample details of the subversive activities of the British secret agents, particularly political officers, to foil Free French attempts to take over control of the civilian administration of the two states. They describe the efforts of British officers to coerce Syrian and Lebanese politicians to demand direct British administration by reassuring them that the Lyttelton-de Gaulle agreement did not represent the British policy, which in reality aimed to evict France from the Levant. A memorandum by Colonel Collet in July presents in detail the activities of British agents, especially Glubb, in Jabal Druze, the Houran and the Syrian Desert. His memorandum is noteworthy precisely because it was written by a senior French officer who did not share the Anglophobic sentiments of his colleagues but advocated Anglo-Free French collaboration in Syria and Lebanon. Reports from Zionist agents in Damascus and Beirut confirmed the French claims. For example, Eliyahu Sasson, who had close ties with many Syrian National Bloc leaders, reported that British officers were inciting Syrian politicians to oppose the conclusion of a treaty with Free France and demand a treaty with Britain that would ensure their country's independence and "the political, cultural and economic unity of the Arab world." These activities clearly violated Churchill's statements that Britain had no designs in Syria and Lebanon.[48]

The previous chapter examined the role of the "agents in the field" in implementing British policy in the Middle East contrary to their government's stand. This issue was put to the test after the occupation of the Levant, which was among the first territories to be "liberated" from the control of an Axis-associated Power. The need to make urgent political decisions beyond the immediate conduct of the war efforts highlighted the contradictions in Britain's Middle East policy as decided by the Cabinet in London and what amounted to a "regional government" in Cairo run by "agents in the field." London and Cairo did not see eye to eye on many issues in the Levant, including who would administer Syria and Lebanon in practice; the relations between independent Syria and Free France; and Lebanon's existence as a separate state. Moreover, the occupation of Syria and Lebanon brought plans for a Greater Syria and Arab unity, endorsed by most British officials in the Middle East, closer to reality. After removing the French-Vichy obstacle, these officials opposed replacing it with Free France. In fact, the Arabists tacitly encouraged Hashemite subversion against Free France as well as their efforts to win the Syrian politicians' support for a Greater Syria and an Iraqi-Syrian union.

Britain's stand vis-à-vis the Free French in the Levant was shaped in the period between the occupation of Syria and Lebanon in July 1941 and the victory in El-Alamein at the end of 1942, when the German military threat to the Middle East had receded. Old colonial rivalries resurfaced and new ones emerged as the region became an arena for personal clashes between Spears and Catroux, and Churchill and de Gaulle. British policy towards Free France was conducted on two levels: the Cabinet's formal policy, expressed in repeated assurances by Churchill and Eden that Britain had no intention of supplanting France in Syria and Lebanon, and overt and covert policy conducted jointly by the Arabists and Spears, who sought to evict France and extend Britain's control over the Levant. As these activities often assumed a covert nature, the Cabinet was largely unaware of their extent. Worse still were the biased, inaccurate and misleading reports emanating from the Middle East, especially those sent by Spears to Churchill. The issue was not – as Spears and the Arabists presented it – a choice between Free France and the Arab world, but Britain's exploitation of the Syrian and Lebanese national struggles for independence from France to incorporate the two Levant states under its hegemony.

John Keay, referring to Britain's decolonization of the Middle East during and after the war, observed:

> Decolonization was one thing; disengagement was another. The war handsomely demonstrated how existing linkage could be used to mobilize emerging nations on behalf of their colonial sponsors. The wisdom of retaining some kind of informal influence was thus confirmed and the work of finessing this would continue.[49]

In this regard, it is worth noting Shukri al-Quwatli's remark that the Syrian nationalists did not realize that the price of British support for their struggle for independence would be the replacement of direct French colonial rule with tacit British control. Quwatli made this remark years later, after learning that Britain's aid had entailed a heavy price for the Syrians. The issue under discussion, however, is not the struggle of local nationalist movements for independence, but their use by British agents against France, the Zionists and other Powers which were considered as threats to their country's interests in the Middle East. The aim of the Arabists was not to help the Syrian and Lebanese nationalists obtain independence. Their true goal was more sinister, as the British and Syrian documents reveal: to exploit the struggles of the local nationalist movements to force France out of the Levant and open the way for the integration of Syria and Lebanon in a Hashemite Greater Syria united with Iraq and dominated by Britain. They would therefore do their utmost to undermine Catroux's attempts to conclude treaties with the Syrian and Lebanese leaders, as well as their own Foreign Office's efforts to promote such treaties, while laying the blame for their failure on de Gaulle's intransigence. Hence the dispute over the drafting of the declarations of independence for Syria in September and for Lebanon in November 1941, stoked by Spears, did not in fact involve the independence of the two states, but the future of French influence.

The declaration of Lebanon's independence, which became the focus of a dispute between Catroux and Spears, demonstrates the hidden agenda of the British "agents in the field." Spears and the Arabists recognized that the Christians in Lebanon, especially the Maronites, were the bastion of France's religious, political, cultural and economic influence in the Levant, and that as long as those traditional ties continued, it could not be dislodged. An independent Lebanese Christian state, like a Jewish state, would impede their plans for a Hashemite Greater Syria. Moreover, in the early war years Lebanon, especially Beirut, had become de Gaulle's main base in his war against Vichy, and some Free French had even proposed declaring Lebanon "French territory." Such a notion reinforced the negative views of local British representatives towards Lebanon, many of whom already questioned its right to exist as a separate state within the 1920 borders. Spears and other officials told Lebanese Christian leaders, including the Maronite Patriarch Antoine Arida that as long they continued to demand French protection, Britain would oppose the Lebanese state, stressing that France's defeat demonstrated that it was no longer a Great Power on whose protection they could rely. Their arguments were effective, especially among the members of Bishara al-Khuri's Constitutional Bloc, many of whom would collaborate with Spears.[50]

Spears' insistence that Lebanon's declaration of independence should include neither a reference to its borders nor a treaty with France exposed his true goal: not the independence of the Levant states, but the ousting of France. De Gaulle and Catroux were well aware of the double game being played by Spears and local British officials. They therefore sought Foreign Office support, while reassuring the Lebanese Christians, especially the Maronite Patriarch, that Free France would continue to protect them and the independence of their state in its existing borders. Catroux insisted on including in Syria's declaration of independence, references to "the indivisibility of its borders," aiming to undermine efforts by Emir Abdullah and British agents to detach territories, especially Jabal Druze and the Houran, from Syria and annex them to Transjordan. In the clash over the declaration of Lebanon's independence, Catroux had the upper hand, as it included direct references to Lebanon's existence as a separate state, its 1920 borders and a treaty with France. It was, however, only a temporary victory: Spears managed to transform the dispute over Lebanon into a major Anglo-French confrontation while presenting himself to the local population as a champion of their struggle to free themselves from France. In the next round in Lebanon in 1943, he would score a clear victory. Indeed, Spears' main achievement in the Levant was his success in 1943 in putting an end to the traditional ties between the Maronites and France, thereby opening the way for France's eviction from the Levant.

Although in the 1920s and '30s, and particularly after the outbreak of war, the British intelligence agencies monitored the French mandated territories closely, they remained mostly uncharted regions for the secret and security services, which lacked first-hand experience there. After the occupation, both military and civilian intelligence agencies rapidly expanded their operations. The security agencies faced serious challenges, as Syria and Lebanon had, under Vichy, been used to launch anti-British subversive activities by Axis secret agents. In addition, both Vichy and German secret services left behind fifth-column agents and gave large sums of money and arms to Bedouin tribes in the Syrian Desert and minority groups in the Jazira and the Biqa Valley, inciting them to oppose the British forces. Some French intelligence officers, particularly the Officiers Spéciaux who joined Free France, remained loyal to Vichy. Many Frenchmen who stayed in Syria and Lebanon and joined Free France remained deeply hostile toward their British counterparts, leading Spears and British security officers to accuse officials in the Free France administration of being Vichy supporters and insist on their return to France.[51]

Thus, despite their collaboration with the Free French security agencies in Syria and Lebanon, the British security agencies monitored their allies' activities, especially as the threat of an Axis attack in the Middle East was looming. But the most disruptive issue was the large-scale involvement of British intelligence agencies in secret anti-French activities aimed at weakening their allies' position in Syria and Lebanon. It was precisely because of the need to conceal such controversial activities from their allies, as well as from their own government, that they resorted to CPA. Only after the discovery of the Syrian and British documents have historians been able to gain insight into the more secretive anti-French operations, especially the widespread co-opting of prominent Syrian and Lebanese nationalist leaders against the Free French administration.

As in other regions of the Middle East, the activities of the British military and civilian intelligence agencies in Syria and Lebanon overlapped, providing both military and political information. Although they were all engaged in one form or another in monitoring the Free French military and officials, some, such as the British Security Mission (BSM), were more closely involved in the anti-Free French secret war. The BSM was a civilian security agency with its headquarters in Cairo, but the French suspected that many of its officers were actually political officers in the Spears Mission, and therefore the Deuxième Bureau and the Sûreté générale monitored them closely. Another British intelligence agency active in this secret war was the Ninth Army's Field Security Service (FSS). The FSS was a military security agency responsible for monitoring foreign and local agents suspected of anti-Allied activities. Its officers, stationed throughout Syria and Lebanon, provided useful political information and countered the activities of French officers, especially in Syria's peripheral and minority regions. Other British agencies that expanded their operations in Syria and Lebanon and took part in anti-Free French activities were SIS and SOE. The former engaged in extended efforts to recruit Syrian and Lebanese "agents of influence" as well as French informers and collaborators. SOE, which before the occupation had run subversive operations against Vichy in the Levant, was, until 1942, mainly involved in "stay-behind" activities in the event of an Axis attack on the region. After 1942, SOE officers stepped up their involvement in bribing local tribal and political leaders in addition to anti-Free French CPA.[52]

British propaganda organizations, along with the secret and security agencies, increased their activities in Syria and Lebanon. Considerable effort was invested in countering Axis propaganda and winning the support of the local population. Newspaper owners and journalists were handsomely paid, while new publications were sponsored. Their control over paper, in short supply throughout the war, allowed the British authorities, especially the Spears Mission, to pressure local newspaper owners. As political confrontation with Free France escalated, the well-organized British propaganda machine successfully targeted de Gaulle and his supporters in the Levant, using black propaganda as one of its methods. The British military censorship in force there, which dealt with security issues, was later employed against the Free French to prevent publication of pro-Gaullist reports in the press. Such means were widely used during the Lebanese and Syrian crises.

Free France was only one of the concerns of the British security services in the Middle East, and certainly not the most important. But for Spears and his Mission it was the main target. From 1942 to 1944 Spears used the Mission, which largely duplicated the French Délégation Générale, to undermine France's political and economic influence in Syria and Lebanon. It became an informal tool for controlling the two states, employing over 100 political officers, with its own budget and military, economic, press, propaganda and censorship sections, as well as cipher facilities linking it directly to Cairo and London. The political officers, used by Spears to undermine French influence, were stationed throughout Syria and Lebanon and played a similar role to that of their counterparts in Iraq; they provided political information and acted as links to local leaders. The French security services closely monitored their activities and hence the French archives provide ample details of their and Spears' covert political activities. Spears' experience as a member of the House of Commons was useful for establishing close ties with Syrian and Lebanese politicians. Politics as practiced in Syria and Lebanon, which was dominated by small political and economic elites and was riddled with political and financial bribery, particularly suited his modus operandi. He demonstrated his considerable political skills during the Syrian and Lebanese parliamentary elections in the summer of 1943 and in the nominations of the Syrian and Lebanese Presidents and Prime Ministers.[53]

The Mission's economic and financial section, which worked closely with the Middle East Supply Centre (MESC), which was in charge of coordinating the Allies' economic interests in the Middle East, enabled Spears to forge close ties with the Syrian and Lebanese commercial and financial elites. He had considerable influence over these elites, as the British authorities provided well-paid contracts for the construction of roads, air strips and military barracks, as well as lucrative import and export licenses. Indeed, Bishara al-Khuri's close associates, Michel Chiha and Henri Pharaon, who owned one of the largest and most well-established financial institutions in Beirut – the Pharaon-Chiha Bank – figured among them. The Wheat Office, which Spears established to oversee the food supply and prevent large price increases, became another means to influence politicians and merchants. He would later use his ties with commercial and financial circles in Beirut and Damascus to promote his own business interests. Nevertheless, it is unclear to what extent his financial interests and close ties to financial and commercial circles in the City of London influenced his unrelenting efforts to end the privileges enjoyed by French companies in the two Levant states.[54]

It is not easy to assess Spears' role in provoking Churchill's animosity towards de Gaulle. Other considerations, especially President Franklin D. Roosevelt's enmity towards de Gaulle and Free France, alongside de Gaulle's own intransigence, should be taken into account. But Spears certainly played an important part in reinforcing the tension and suspicion between the two leaders. In a presentation in 1982 at the De Gaulle Institute in Paris, Gaston Palewski, the influential director of de Gaulle's war cabinet, accused Spears of exacerbating relations between them. Palewski's statement is revealing, as he was one of the first in de Gaulle's cabinet to view the British and Syrian documents sent to Paris from Beirut, and witnessed first-hand their effect on de Gaulle's relations with Churchill. Indeed, the role of Spears and the secret services in the Middle East in reinforcing Churchill's animosity towards de Gaulle should be re-examined, as, from the fall of 1944, de Gaulle became directly exposed to British anti-French covert operations in the Middle East.[55]

Palewski's declaration was made more than three decades after the events, but following the occupation of Syria and Lebanon, de Gaulle and Free French officials believed that if Spears' anti-French intrigues were revealed, the British Prime Minister would put an end to them. Thus, in November 1943, in the midst of the Lebanese constitutional crisis, the French liaison officer in Jerusalem told a Jewish Agency official:

> Churchill is a true friend of France and we cannot believe, even for one
> moment, that he would agree to the demands of his advisers who

connived to rob us of our empire and divide it between Britain and the United States. The only culprit is General Spears, who hates de Gaulle, and we hope that Churchill will settle the matter after receiving full information on the situation from French sources.[56]

De Gaulle initially shared these beliefs, as revealed in the records of his meetings with Churchill in 1941-42, in which he attempted to convince him of Spears' anti-French activities and have him recalled to London.[57] But Churchill remained loyal to his old friend and protégé. As his relations with de Gaulle deteriorated, Churchill began to view Spears as a means by which to sanction and control the intransigent French leader. In retrospect, despite Eden's continued efforts, Spears succeeded in reinforcing Churchill's resentment of de Gaulle and convinced him that the French leader was staunchly Anglophobic. Only in August 1944 did Churchill submit to Eden's pressure and recall Spears from the Levant – but by then it was too late; Churchill distrusted de Gaulle, regarding him as an ungrateful anti-British leader, while de Gaulle, who was aware of Spears' intrigues, believed that such action directed against him personally could not have taken place without Churchill's tacit approval.

Although Spears wholeheartedly adopted the anti-French bias of many British Arabists, he added new facets: a personal hatred of de Gaulle and the skill to implement his own policy despite opposition from the Foreign Office. His reports to Churchill harshly criticizing de Gaulle, Catroux and the French administration in the Levant are a prime example of how agents in the field can manipulate decision-makers. Spears was particularly effective, as Churchill trusted him and regarded him as an expert on French affairs. Moreover, his reports reached Churchill directly without undergoing Foreign Office scrutiny. He conducted a successful smear campaign against de Gaulle, portraying him as a dictator and a fascist who could not be trusted, and the French officials in the Levant of being corrupt, inefficient and Vichyist supporters, while portraying himself as one of the few British representatives able to withstand de Gaulle's provocations and defend his country's interests and prestige. Churchill frequently repeated Spears' accusations, which were either unfounded or largely exaggerated, in meetings with de Gaulle and other senior Free French members. An example of Spears' biased reporting to Churchill was his detailed account of de Gaulle's confrontation with Lyttelton in Cairo at the end of July 1941 after learning of the British-Vichy Armistice of Saint Jean d'Acre. While Spears presented de Gaulle's outburst as proof of the latter's Anglophobia, an accusation he later repeated in his memoirs, Lyttelton was far more understanding and even sympathetic towards de Gaulle's predicament.[58]

Co-opting Syrian and Lebanese "agents of influence"

The use of CPA by Spears, the British Arabists and the secret services to dislodge France from the Levant was facilitated by the co-opting in 1941-45 of hundreds of Syrian and Lebanese "agents of influence" from all walks of life. They included political leaders, deputies, senior officials and journalists and tribal chiefs, as well as members of the commercial and financial elites in Beirut and Damascus. Unlike in other Arab states under British control, where they were able to conduct such activities in the dark, the British secret services in Syria and Lebanon were under constant French surveillance. French intelligence agencies followed these efforts, but only after obtaining direct access to British and Syrian documents did they discover the true scope of the British success in co-opting prominent Syrian and Lebanese politicians and helping their "election" to top positions in the parliaments and governments of their respective states. A copy of a document describing the recruitment of Mikha'il Ilyan, a Syrian deputy who later became Foreign Minister, reveals that some agents were required to sign a written undertaking to collaborate with Britain (doc.51). The French also acquired from files in the British Legation copies of receipts of bribes paid to politicians, both directly or indirectly, apparently kept because of budgetary requirements. These were later used by French secret agents to implicate Syrian and Lebanese politicians and officials and force them to become double agents.[59]

The relations of these agents of influence with the British secret agencies and the Spears Mission depended on the type of services they were able to provide. Some, such as Muhsin al-Barazi and Camille Chamoun, were directly involved in intelligence operations, while others provided information, helped further British interests or assisted in influencing local public opinion. Many politicians were elected to the Syrian and Lebanese parliaments or appointed to top positions with British assistance. Of special value were national political leaders in high positions, where they could formulate their country's policies in tandem with British interests. These included the Syrian President, Shukri al-Quwatli (1943-1949); Jamil Mardam, who served as Foreign Minister and later as Prime Minister (1943-1945, 1946-1948); Riyad al-Sulh, the Lebanese Prime Minister (1943-1945, 1946-1951); and Bishara al-Khuri, the Lebanese President (1943-1952). The success of the British secret services in securing the collaboration of these nationalist leaders and helping them rise to power attests not only to the efficiency and professionalism of its intelligence services in the Middle East, but also to the opportunism of many Arab politicians.[60]

The political careers of these four leaders were influenced by the war, as they only rose to power once Britain had become the dominant force in Syria and Lebanon. The relations between Quwatli, Mardam and Sulh, three pro-minent pan-Arabist leaders, and the British secret officers, who helped them attain top positions, demonstrate that once they gained power, control over them became more difficult. Throughout their long political careers, these leaders strongly opposed the French mandate and fought for their countries' independence and sovereignty, but they were also critical of Britain's colonial hold over Arab countries, especially its conduct in Palestine. But this did not deter them from cooperating with Britain, not merely to liberate their countries from France; they were even ready, under the banner of Arab unity, to integrate them in a Hashemite Greater Syria dominated by another colonial Power – Great Britain. Indeed, Nuri al-Sa'id was actively involved in co-opting them.

Shukri al-Quwatli

President Shukri al-Quwatli, like other Syrian nationalist politicians, rarely distinguished between national and personal interests. The British initially accused him of collaborating with the Germans under Vichy, including him in the list drawn up by their security services of suspected pro-German politicians to be arrested. Following the Allied occupation of Damascus he found refuge in the Saudi Consulate and only after mediation by Ibn Sa'ud and Nuri al-Sa'id did the British authorities agree to sponsor him. In February 1942, under British pressure, Catroux allowed him to leave for Baghdad and Riyadh. Nuri al-Sa'id sought to use Quwatli's close ties with Ibn Sa'ud to weaken the latter's opposition to his plan for an Iraqi-Syrian union. In April, while he was in Baghdad, he concluded a secret agreement with Nuri al-Sa'id undertaking to collaborate with Iraq and support the latter's plan for Syrian and Arab unity (doc.3). This agreement, and another concluded in July, was an early version of Nuri al-Sa'id's "Blue Book" that the latter presented to Casey in early 1943 (doc.4). Although Great Britain was not party to the agreement, British diplomats had in fact initiated it and Cornwallis sent a copy to Spears in Beirut. The agreement laid the foundation for Iraqi-Syrian collaboration. Its central focus was Quwatli's agreement that Syria, after winning independence from France, would become part of an Arab federation under the Hashemites. There was no reference to what he would receive in return, but in a conversation with a colleague three years later, he recounted that the British had kept their promises to oust France from Syria and Lebanon and ensure his election as President. The agreement testified to the lengths to which Quwatli, a sworn opponent of the Hashemites, would go to gain British support for obtaining the presidency and ending French rule in Syria.[61]

In February 1943, shortly after the French declared their intention to hold elections in Syria and Lebanon, the Arabists and Nuri al-Sa'id became concerned by the secret negotiations that Quwatli was conducting at that time with Catroux. Distrusting him and suspecting that he would not abide by his undertakings after his election, they pressured him to sign the agreement again (doc.4). The British and Hashemite doubts were justified, as, after attaining the presidency, Quwatli reneged on his promises and in March 1944 concluded a secret agreement with Ibn Sa'ud, his patron, to join forces against the Hashemites (doc.7). His tense relations with the British and the Hashemites and the methods employed by British agents to coerce him into collaborating during 1944-47 are revealed in the British and Syrian documents, which also include hitherto unknown details of his close collaboration with Kings Ibn Sa'ud and Faruq against the Hashemites. In March 1949 he was deposed in a military coup led by Husni al-Za'im, which in its early stages was supported by Iraqi and British secret agents. But Quwatli would take his revenge six years later, when he returned to serve as President, by adopting pro-Nasserist and pro-Soviet policies.[62]

Jamil Mardam

Jamil Mardam was the first to contact British officials and Nuri al-Sa'id after escaping from Damascus to Baghdad in October 1940 following his implication in Shahbandar's assassination. His political career was at its lowest point; the Syrian public held him responsible for the failure of the treaty policy with France, which he had advocated before the war, as well as for the loss of Alexandretta. In Baghdad, he met with Cornwallis and Nuri al-Sa'id and later, in Cairo, with senior British officials including Clayton, Killearn and Smart. Mardam, a sophisticated politician, was well acquainted with the French, with whom he either fought or negotiated throughout the mandate. Determined to take revenge for his humiliation after the French government failed to ratify the 1936 treaty, despite the major concessions he had made, he joined forces with the British Arabists in their covert operations against the French and was a key figure in orchestrating the Syrian crisis. Spears and the British secret agents preferred to deal with him directly on sensitive issues rather than with Quwatli, whom they distrusted. Alongside his anti-French campaign, Mardam contrived to replace Quwatli as President. The Syrian documents reveal that he undertook to help the Hashemites incorporate Syria in a Hashemite Greater Syria in return for his appointment to a prominent position in the future enlarged state (doc.8). The French used his secret agreements with Nuri al-Sa'id in April and September 1944 to discredit him before Faruq and Ibn Sa'ud during the deliberations over forming the Arab League (doc.23). He was paid handsomely by the Hashemites in return for his services (doc.45). French and Zionist sources confirm that he received payments from the British as well. In August 1945, faced with strong opposition (doc.159), partly orchestrated by French agents, he took Shone's advice and resigned (docs.156, 164-5). In the following year he represented Syria in the Arab League headquarters in Cairo, where he was also involved in covert British anti-French operations in North Africa, as well as in Palestine, where he closely coordinated his activities with Brigadier Clayton. The British rewarded him for his services by ensuring his election as Prime Minister at the end of 1946. He continued to be involved in inter-Arab politics in 1947-48, especially in Palestine, while maintaining close ties with Nuri al-Sa'id (doc.359). His loyal service to the British made him a target for French extortion.[63]

Riyad al-Sulh

In early March 1941 Riyad al-Sulh sent Sir Geoffrey Furlonge a message via Marun Arab, an adviser in the British Consulate in Beirut, offering to collaborate with Britain against France (doc.2). Sulh's initiative marked the beginning of his covert collaboration with the British authorities in the Middle East that lasted until his assassination in Amman in July 1951. The covert collaboration between Sulh and British agents, especially Spears, was at the center of the Lebanese constitutional crisis that effectively ended France's hold on Lebanon.[64]

Securing the cooperation of Sulh, an Arab nationalist and prominent Sunni Muslim leader in Lebanon, in their secret operations was a significant achievement for the British intelligence agencies. Sulh, a shrewd opponent of the French mandate, had been involved in anti-French activities for more than two decades. He was discreet and skilled in covert operations, having come under the constant surveillance of the French security agencies. His close ties with leaders of the Syrian National Bloc, of which he was one of the founders, especially with Sa'adallah al-Jabiri, his father-in-law, enabled him to mediate between them and the British authorities. He was trusted by British intelligence officers who used him to convey sensitive messages to the Syrian leaders, and already at the end of 1943 he was told that he would take part in their covert anti-Zionist activities. He established close ties with Brigadier Clayton and throughout the 1940s he collaborated with him in undercover operations, clandestine diplomacy, inter-Arab affairs and the conflict over Palestine. Although the French repeatedly complained to the Foreign Office of Spears' role in Sulh's nomination as Prime Minister, it was only after obtaining the British and Syrian secret documents that they discovered the extent of Sulh's collaboration with the British secret services. They took part in engineering his resignation in January 1945, and five months later forestalled his attempt to regain the premiership with the help of British secret agents. Only in December 1946 did he succeed, with British assistance, in recapturing the premiership.

Sulh's overtures to Britain, when Syria and Lebanon were still under Vichy domination and a British victory was far from guaranteed, testify to his strategic and political foresight. Throughout his political career he believed that only after severing the Gordian knot between the Maronites and France would the Arab nationalists succeed in dislodging the latter from Syria and Lebanon and secure their independence and unity. He realized that only with Britain's help would it be possible to evict France, attain Arab unity and ensure a pro-Arab solution in Palestine. Sulh was a veteran of Faisal's Arab government in Damascus, but he believed that Britain would not repeat its mistake of 1919 when it had sacrificed its ties with the Arab world for the sake of its relations with France and the Zionists. On a personal level he knew that only with British assistance could he rise to a prominent position in Lebanese politics. Like Mardam and other Syrian and Lebanese politicians, Sulh was funded by British secret agents, and British documents confirm that they gave him large sums of money during his election campaign. French sources reveal that he also received substantial financial backing from the governments of Iraq, Egypt and Saudi Arabia. Nevertheless, French intelligence, which was extremely hostile towards Sulh, confirmed that, contrary to Mardam, he used this money to promote national, not personal, interests.[65]

An intriguing issue is Sulh's stance towards Lebanon as a separate state in its 1920 borders after the 1941 Anglo-Free French occupation of Syria and Lebanon. He knew that Syrian National Bloc leaders were hoping to exploit the war to revise Lebanon's borders, especially by the return of the "four districts" and Tripoli to Syria. He also knew that many British officials opposed a separate and enlarged Lebanese state. In meetings with Nuri al-Sa'id during the latter's visit to Beirut and through his close contacts with Tahsin al-Kadri, the Iraqi Consul in Beirut, he expressed willingness to back the British-Hashemite plan for a Greater Syria that would include autonomous Mount Lebanon in its pre-1920 borders. In early August 1944, he was directly involved in the British efforts to persuade Quwatli and Jabiri to support the plan (doc.14). At the Alexandria Congress, Nuri al-Sa'id accused him of reneging on his promise to support a Hashemite Greater Syria (doc.17). Like Quwatli, Sulh apparently changed his political orientation after being elected to the premiership, preferring to serve as a prominent leader in Lebanon rather than play a minor role in a Hashemite Greater Syria. Faced with strong opposition from the Christians to Lebanon's incorporation in a Greater Syria and an Arab confederation, he believed that it would be preferable for Lebanon to be part of a large, loose Arab union, as promoted by Egypt, rather than the political union advocated by the Hashemites (doc.68). From 1945 he began to distance himself from the Hashemites and drew closer to the Egyptian-Saudi axis, while continuing to maintain close ties with British secret officers, especially Brigadier Clayton.[66]

Bishara al-Khuri and the Constitutional Bloc

Spears and the British secret services also sought the collaboration of leading Maronite politicians to evict France from the Levant. Bishara al-Khuri and other members of the Constitutional Bloc, his main political and ideological platform since the 1930s, became their main allies. Like Emile Eddé, his sworn political rival, Khuri had been a prominent politician in Lebanon in the 1920s and '30s. But while Eddé, with whom he had competed for the presidency, was a staunch supporter of France and continued to regard it, despite its defeat, as the protector of the Lebanese Christians, Khuri had, already in the 1930s, been critical of the French mandate and joined forces with the Muslims in Lebanon in the struggle for independence. The French, who distrusted him, barred him from the presidency, regarding him as an opportunistic, weak politician influenced by his family and close friends. Their accusations were to a large extent justified, although they overlooked Khuri's goals in his campaign for Lebanon's independence. After France's defeat and the British-Free French takeover of Syria and Lebanon from Vichy in the summer of 1941, Khuri and other Constitutional Bloc members realized that it was in Lebanon's national interests, as well as their own, to align themselves with Britain – the new master – in order both to ensure Lebanon's independence in its 1920 borders and to attain power. French reports give details of Khuri's attempts to improve his relations with the British officials, as well as with Sulh and Syrian National Bloc leaders. In June 1942, with Spears' tacit mediation, he traveled with Mardam to Cairo, where they discussed plans to form an Arab union with Nahhas. During his stay there he also met with senior British officials, far from French eyes. The following month, Kadri handed him a copy of Nuri al-Sa'id's plan for an Arab confederation that was to include Lebanon. Spears played a key role in securing the presidency for Khuri; part of the deal was Sulh's nomination as Prime Minister. Khuri proved his loyalty to the British and Sulh when he rejected Catroux's offer during the constitutional crisis to reinstate him as President provided that he relinquish Sulh as Prime Minister. He secretly collaborated with Furlonge, as well as with Syrian leaders during and after the Syrian crisis. Indeed, in a letter to President Quwatli, who had questioned some of his policies, Khuri replied: "Since I have concerned myself with public affairs, they [the British] threaten me all the time with taking their help away from me" (doc.357). Despite Khuri's cooperation with them, in their private conversations Quwatli, Mardam and Jabiri continued to voice their distrust of him and other Lebanese Maronite leaders.[67]

The collaboration between Spears and Khuri was also founded on the success of political officers in the Spears Mission and the British secret services in co-opting other members of the Constitutional Bloc, including Camille Chamoun, Hamid Franjieh and Michel Chiha, as well as Henri Pharaon. Of prime importance was the cooperation of Chiha and Pharaon. Chiha, in particular, exerted a strong influence over Khuri, to whom he was related. During Khuri's presidency, Chiha played a central role in shaping Lebanon's political and economic systems. Besides being a banker, he was a politician, journalist and writer who authored many books on Lebanon's political and economic systems. He was a devoted Francophile with little interest in Arabic culture or language, but like many other Lebanese Christians, he changed his opinion following France's defeat, believing that Lebanon should strengthen its ties with Britain and the United States. From the 1930s, Chiha had been editor of *Le Jour*, a French-language newspaper critical of the French mandate and that supported Khuri. At the end of 1941, with the help of the Spears Mission, he established *The Near Eastern*, an English-language newspaper that aired British views. The Spears Mission provided the paper on which it was printed, and Spears himself often defended it against French censorship.[68]

Henri Pharaon, one of the richest businessmen in Beirut, played an important role in Lebanese politics in the 1940s. He was involved, together with members of the Spears Mission, in financing the election campaigns of anti-French and pro-British candidates, including Sulh. Due to his wealth, Pharaon was more immune than other Lebanese politicians to British pressure. In early 1945 he was instrumental in securing the nomination of Sulh's rival, Abd al-Hamid Karameh, as Prime Minister, in whose government he served as Foreign Minister.[69]

After co-opting prominent Syrian and Lebanese nationalist leaders, Spears and the Arabists strove to ensure that pro-British politicians would replace the pro-French Presidents and Prime Ministers appointed by Catroux in 1941. Throughout 1942, Spears pressed Catroux and tried to convince the Foreign Office of the need to hold "democratic" elections in Syria and Lebanon. He rejected Catroux's arguments that holding elections in a time of war would destabilize the two states, claiming that the French refusal was further proof of their disregard for the independence of Syria and Lebanon, which had been guaranteed by Britain. The military victory in the Western Desert and the landing of the American and British forces in North Africa at the end of 1942 enhanced Britain's prestige in the Middle East. As the threat of war in the region receded, Spears resumed pressure to hold elections. In January 1943 the newly-formed Comité Français de Libération Nationale (CFLN) announced its agreement to hold elections. On March 18, Catroux formally declared that they would take place in July. Shortly afterwards, he left for Algiers, where he was to assume the position of Commissioner of Muslim Affairs.

Notes

1 Harvey, John (ed.), *The War Diaries of Oliver Harvey* (London: Collins, 1978), p. 383.
2 Peterson, Maurice, *Both Sides of the Curtain: An Autobiography* (London: Constable and Co., 1950), p.237; Nicolson, Nigel (ed.), *Volume II of the Diaries and Letters of Harold Nicolson: The War Years, 1939-1945* (New York: Atheneum, 1967), p.19; Gaunson, pp.110-11, 128, 131, 137, 158-69; Dilks, David (ed.), *The Diaties of Sir Alexander Cadogan, 1938–1945* (New York: G.P. Putnam's Sons, 1972), pp.468, 475-6, 696.
3 AN, Paris, de Gaulle's Papers, 3AG1/264, no.873, Beirut, August 8, 1944, Beynet to de Gaulle; Egremont, pp.259-61; Fry, Michael G. and Itamar Rabinovich, *Despatches from Damascus: Gilbert MacKereth and British Policy in the Levant, 1933-1939* (Jerusalem: Tel Aviv University, Daf-Chen Press, 1985).
4 Service Historique de l'Armée, Vincennes, (SHA), Série 7NN, Fonds de Moscou (Moscow), 7NN2229, Section d'Etudes du Levant (SEL), Beirut, July 26, 1939, correspondence between Captain Bernard and Colonel Teague; SEL, Report from agent "Lichtenstein," June 30, 1938. See also Jeffery, pp.290-4.
5 Shelley, pp.198-215.
6 Stirling, p.228, and Spears, *Fulfilment of a Mission*, p.93. For a critical view of the French, see Pearse, Richard, *Three Years in the Levant* (London: Macmillan, 1949). The author served in the FSS in the Levant during the war. See also Mockler, Anthony, *Our Enemies the French: Being an Account of the War Fought Between the French and the British, Syria 1941*(London: Leo Cooper, 1976). For a different viewpoint, see Sykes, Christopher, *Four Studies in Loyalty* (London: Collins, 1946), pp.180-224. The author served in SOE in the Middle East during the war. Gaunson, pp.5-10.
7 After the war Spears published an extremely negative account of the French leadership during the traumatic months before France's capitulation in June 1940,

when he served as Churchill's personal envoy to Paul Raynaud's government. See Spears, *Assignment to Catastrophe*, Vols.1 and 2. See also: Egremont, pp.277-9, 284-6; Zamir, "De Gaulle and the Question of Syria and Lebanon," pp.674-5.

8 Egremont, pp.279-83.

9 For a comprehensive study of the French intelligence, see: Forcade, Olivier, *La République Secrète: Histoire des Services Spéciaux Français de 1918 à 1939* (Paris: Nouveau Monde, 2008); Deacon, Richard, *The French Secret Service* (London: Grafton Books, 1990), p.108; Becker, Anja, "The Spy Who Couldn't Possibly be French: Espionage (and) Culture in France," *The Journal of Intelligence History*, 1(1) (2001), pp.66-87. After the war several French intelligence officers published their accounts. See for example Navarre, Henri, *Le Service de Renseignements, 1871-1944* (Paris: Plon, 1978).

10 For a detailed study of the French intelligence in Syria and Lebanon, see: Thomas, *Empires of Intelligence*; Mizrahi, Jean-David, *Genèse de l'Etat Mandataire: Service de Renseignements et Bandes Armées en Syrie at au Liban dans les Années 1920* (Paris: Publications de la Sorbonne, 2003); Thomas, Martin, "French Intelligence-Gathering in the Syrian Mandate, 1920-40," *Middle Eastern Studies*, 38(1) (2002), pp.1-32.

11 Forcade, pp.386-91, 409-10, 534-8; Thomas, *Empires of Intelligence*, pp.186-8, 276-86.

12 For BCRA's role in the war see Marck, David de Young de la, *Free French and British Intelligence Relations, 1940-1944* (PhD dissertation, University of Cambridge, 2000) and his article: "De Gaulle, Colonel Passy and British Intelligence, 1940-42," *Intelligence and National Security*, 18(1) (2003), pp.21-40.

13 Oliva Roget's role in Free France's secret war against the British in Syria and Lebanon is discussed in detail in Chapter 3.

14 Thomas, *Empires of Intelligence*, pp.173-90, 211-9, 276-9.

15 Forcade, pp.410-11.

16 SHA, Moscow, are the French military intelligence archives captured by the Germans in 1940 and transferred to Berlin, but in 1945, these were seized by the Red Army and moved to Moscow. In the 1990s some were returned to France. They include files on the French military intelligence in Syria and Lebanon in 1934-1942. For SEL reports see: SHA, Moscow, 7NN 2229; 7NN 2534; 7NN 2715. See for example its report to SCR in 7NN 2534 on the British Secret Service in the Middle East, July 30, 1936, and in Palestine, December 5, 1936.

17 SHA, Moscow. Based on various reports in carton 7NN 2534. See for example reports on June 30, 1938, Arnold Walter Lawrence's visit; Longrigg's visit to Tripoli, May 4, 1937, and the British secret agencies in the Middle East, a report from July 30, 1936. For Elizabeth Monroe's visit see 7NN 2229, report from June 2, 1937.

18 SHA, Moscow, 7NN 2534, Longrigg's visit to Tripoli, May 4, 1937 and SEL report on Longrigg, August 20, 1936. See also his book: Longrigg, Stephen H., *Oil in the Middle East* (Oxford: Oxford University Press, 1961).

19 SHA, Moscow, 7NN 2534, Syrian nationalists' ties with MacKereth, May 5, 1936, and complaints by British liaison officer in Beirut of the Mufti's anti-British activities, March 11, 1939. See also: Fry, Michael G. and Itamar Rabinovich, *Despatches from Damascus: Gilbert Mackereth and British Policy in the Levant, 1933–1939* (Jerusalem: Tel Aviv University, Daf-Chen Press, Ltd., 1985), pp.40-56; Barr, pp.166-70.

20 Albord, Maurice, *L'Armée Française et les Etats du Levant, 1936-1946* (PhD dissertation, University of Paris X – Nanterre, 1998), pp.84-5; 95-140.

21 SHA, Moscow, 7NN 2534, SEL note 1047 from March 2, 1940. See also Albord, pp.91-95.

22 For his account, see Puaux, Gabriel, *Deux Années au Levant: Souvenir de Syrie et du Liban 1939-1940* (Paris: Hachette, 1952). See also Albord, pp.80-95.

23 SHA, Moscow, 7NN 2229, no.4854, June 6, 1940. On increased security measures, see reports in 7NN 2534. See also: Zamir, Meir, *Lebanon's Quest: The Road to Statehood, 1926-1939* (London: I.B. Tauris, 1997), pp.236-9; Thomas, *Empires of Intelligence*, pp.290-1.

24 AN, Paris, de Gaulle's Papers, 3AG1/263, Cairo, July 24, 1941, de Gaulle to Churchill; Etat de problème Syrien, Cairo, March 31, 1941; Collet's note, a/s de la situation actuelle en Syrie, July 27, 1941; Report on measures to be taken against Axis agents in the Levant, July 14, 1941. Centre des Archives Diplomatique, Nantes (CADN), Syrie et Liban, 2135, Circulaire no.153, September 25, 1940. Ben-Gurion Archives, Sede Boqer (BGA), Correspondence. See reports from Damascus and Beirut by Sasson and Epstein, June 29, July 12, August 14 and August 16, 1940. See also Albord, pp.133-4, 140-5.

25 SHA, Moscow, 7NN 2534, reports on subversion of German and Italian agents before and in the early war years. On German espionage, see report, March 6, 1940, and long report on Italian espionage in the Midddle East in SHA, Levant, 4H386, Note d'Etude sur le S.R. Italien dans le Proche Orient, February 4, 1938. See also Zamir, "Against the Tide."

26 Kirk, p.52.

27 Zamir, "De Gaulle and the Question of Syria and Lebanon," pp.680-6. See also Tamkin, Nicholas, *Britain, Turkey and the Soviet Union, 1940-45: Strategy, Diplomacy and Intelligence in the Eastern Mediterranean* (London: Palgrave Macmillan, 2009), pp.51-5.

28 AN, Paris, Papiers Georges Bidault (Bidault's Papers), 457AP134. The volume includes documents on Darlan's negotiations with German representatives; SHA, Levant, 4H394, Une Triste Histoire – a summary of the French arming of the Iraqi rebels in May 1941. See also Roshwald, pp.16-9, 41-8.

29 SHA, Moscow, 7NN 2534, various reports on the British secret services' subversion in Syria and Lebanon, 1940-1941. For example: no.2388, British activities in the Middle East, November 18, 1940; no.6997, November 18, 1940. See also Roshwald, pp.62-82.

30 SHA, Moscow, 7NN 2534, no.203, by Captain Rondot, December 23, 1940; Dovey, "The Middle East Intelligence Centre," pp.800-12.

31 SHA, Moscow, 7NN 2534, November 26, 1940, note pour 6000, on the contents of the diplomatic bag of the British Vice-Consul in Damascus. See also Shelley, pp.80-7.

32 SHA, Moscow, 7NN 2534, no.1654, October 17, 1940, British activity among the Druze; no. 2388, Novermber 18, 1940; no. 1320, October 14, 1940, British activity in the Middle East; no. 1270, March 16, 1941; no. 792, February 6, 1941, Anglo-Turkish intelligence collaboration in the Levant. See also AN, Paris, Catroux's Papers, 72AJ438, April 5, 1941, report by British agent code-named Romulus.

33 For German warnings to Vichy that its code had been broken by Britain, see AN, Paris, Bidault's Papers, 457AP134, May 4, 1941, German demands concerning Iraq. SHA, Moscow, 7NN 2534, no.2388, November 18, 1940, British activity in the Middle East. For an example of an Iraqi report from Beirut, see FO 371/27321 1483/89, no.244, Cairo, March 18, 1941, Lampson to Eden. See also: West, pp.193-4; Jeffrey, pp.389-98; Thomas, "France in British Signals Intelligence," pp.59-60.

34 SHA, Moscow, 7NN 2534, no.5071, October 17, 1940; no.532, January 17, 1941; no.780, February 9, 1941, on British smuggling of printed propaganda into Syria and Lebanon. On Zionist agents employed by the British Secret Service, no.442, January 11, 1941. See also Gilad, Zrubavel, *Secret Shield: Activities of the Jewish Underground in World War II* (Jerusalem: Jewish Agency Publishing House, 1948, in Hebrew), pp.44-7, 74-88.

35 SHA, Moscow, 7NN 2534, reports analyzing British propaganda and counter-measures, and samples of British and Free French pamphlets in French and Arabic. See for example no.19710, May 25, 1940. See also: Zamir, "Against the Tide"; Barr, p.214.

36 AN, Paris, de Gaulle's Papers, 3AG1/263, Cairo, March 31, 1941, Etat de problème Syrien. For Catroux's account see Catroux, pp. 85-95. SHA, Moscow, 7NN 2534, reports on Vichy counter-espionage. For example, no.6672, October 7, 1940, on Gaullist activities in Palestine. See also Albord, pp.160-80.

37 CADN, Syrie et Liban, carton 2135, Notes, February 26 and March 11, 1941; SHA, Moscow, 7NN 2534, no.5071, October 17, 1940; AN, Paris, de Gaulle's Papers, 3AG1/263, November 1940, Catroux's letter to General Arlabosse, and November 29, 1940, Arlabosse's reply.

38 Ibid. CADN, Syrie et Liban, carton 1039, nos.346-8, Beirut, March 27, 1940, Puaux to the Quai d'Orsay. See also Albord, pp.133-4.

39 AN, Paris, Bidault's Papers, 457AP134, "Armistice syrien – Dossier relative à l'armistice de St Jean d'Acre." For example of Huntziger's instructions to Dentz, see: SHA, Levant, 4H282, no.11.934, Vichy, June 1, 1941; no.680, July 7, 1941; no.709, July 11, 1941; Huntziger's private letter to Dentz, July 3, 1941. See also Albord, pp.280-1.

40 SHA, Moscow, 7NN 2534, Movement Arabe, no.1652, October 25, 1940; Mardam, Salma, *Syria's Quest for Independence* (Reading: Ithaca Press, 1994), pp.18-22.

41 SHA, Moscow, 7NN 2534, no.6997, November 18, 1940, a/s du SR Britannique, note pour 6000; note 442, January 11, 1941; note 2734, January 17, 1941, British attitude towards the French mandated territories; Albord, pp.160-73; Thomas, "France in British Signals Intelligence," p.59.

42 SHA, Moscow, 7NN 2534, note 203, December 23, 1940, report by Captain Rondot. On Rondot's activities in Ankara, see SHA, Levant, 4H393, March 25, 1942, report by the Deuxième Bureau.

43 SHA, Moscow, 7NN 2534, no.19710, March 16, 1941, note 270, enemy propaganda and French counter-propaganda, and May 17, 1941, note 895, British activity in the French mandated territories; CADN, Syrie et Liban, 2135, Note, Beirut, February 18, 1941; carton 783, Beirut, n.d., Note a/s du statut de Radio-Levant; Note no.466, Beirut, April 8, 1941, on how to respond to anti-French propaganda.

44 See for example: Roshwald, pp.vii–ix; Gaunson, pp.1-10.

45 SHA, Moscow, 7NN 2534. See reports by Vichy informers on tension between the Gaullist and British administrations. For example: no.2577, August 30, 1941, Political situation in Syria and Lebanon; no.1271, September 13, 1941, Relations between the British authorities and the Gaullists; no.2794, December 1, 1941, British activity in Syria and Lebanon; no.2849, December 18, 1941, the Gaullist administration in Syria and Lebanon. CADN, Syrie et Liban, 772, no.457, Beirut, October 15, 1941, Note pour les Officiers des Services Spéciaux. There are examples from conversations between Syrian and Lebanese politicians. Sulh was a major target. For the importance of such conversations for French intelligence, see a telephone conversation at the height of the Syrian crisis in which the Iraqi Consulate in Damascus informed Baghdad of Mardam's request for arms and ammunition, in SHA, Levant, 4H309, 105/SP, May 20, 1945, Oliva Roget to Beynet. Albord, pp.336-8.

46 SHA, Levant, 4H382, September 1, 1941, "Political Aspects of the War, Circulated by Order of the Commander-in-Chief."

47 AN, Paris, de Gaulle's Papers, 3AG1/263, August 8, 1941, Lyttelton to General de Gaulle; AN, Paris, Catroux's Papers, 72J438, March 28, 1941, Note pour le Général; SHA, Moscow, 7NN 2534, no.0410, September 23, 1941, Letter from a

British intelligence officer in Syria; Middle East Centre, St. Antony's College, Oxford (MEC), Spears Papers, no.26, Cairo, August 1, 1941, Lampson to FO. See also: Lyttelton, Oliver, *Lord Chandos: An Unexpected View from the Summit* (New York: New American Library, 1963), pp.236-44; Wilson, *Eight Years Overseas*, p.118; Zamir, "De Gaulle and the Question of Syria and Lebanon," pp.684-5.

48 AN, Paris, de Gaulle's Papers, 3AG1/263, July 27, 1941, Collet's note, a/s de la situation actuelle en Syrie; July 1, 1941, Catroux to Colonel Gardner; Ain Sofar, August 2, 1941, Spears to de Gaulle. French officers in Syria and Lebanon regularly reported on British intelligence activities in their respective regions, including names of agencies, officers and local agents. See for example: SHA, Levant, 4H382, no.652/DSL, April 26, 1944, on British intelligence in Lebanon; no.393/SAM, November 27, 1945, Organization of the FSS in Marjayoun, and similar reports from Sidon and Tripoli. See also BGA, Correspondence, Beirut, February 2, 1942, Sasson's report on conditions in Syria.

49 Keay, p.264.

50 CADN, Syrie et Liban, 1366, no.3019, September 10, 1941, Note sur la situation politique au Liban; carton 1365, Note, October 11, 1941; carton 771, Beirut, November 13, 1941, Note pour le Captain O. Lyttelton; AN, Paris, de Gaulle's Papers, 3AG1/263, Cairo, June 21, 1941, Spears to de Gaulle.

51 CADN, Syrie et Liban, 772, Information, March 7, 1944. See also Dovey, "Security in Syria, 1941-45," pp.418-46. Another concern of the British security agencies was that Syria would become a gateway for German and Vichy agents operating from Turkey.

52 SHA, Levant, 4H336, November 14, 1941, British memorandum on Jesuit clergy's suspected collaboration with Vichy; CADN, Syrie et Liban, no.2986bis, Beirut, August 7, 1942, Helleu's memorandum to Casey; SHA, Moscow, 7NN 2534, no.2626, September 24, 1941, British activities. For a general overview of the British security and secret agencies' reorganization in the Middle East in 1942-3 see Shelley, sections 3 and 4. See also Pearse, *Three Years in the Levant*.

53 SHA, Levant, 4H308, Information no.660/SS, Baalbeck, November 17, 1943; CADN, Syrie et Liban, 2419, Paris, December 1944, France's position in the Levant. On the Spears Mission see: Roshwald, pp.85-92; Egremont, p.238.

54 CADN, Syrie et Liban, 2986bis, Beirut, August 7, 1942, Helleu's memorandum to Casey; carton 764, Beirut, August 10, 1944, Note on British intervention in the Syrian and Lebanese economy; Spears, *Fulfilment of a Mission*, pp.173-6, 187-202. For background on MESC see Wilmington, pp.20-8, 90-102. See also Roshwald, pp.100-3.

55 Palewski, Gaston, "De Gaulle, Great Britain and France, 1940-1943," *Espoir*, Revue de l'Institut Charles de Gaulle (Paris: Plon), no.43, June 1983. See also: AN, Paris, de Gaulle's Papers, 3AG1/263, London, July 29, 1942, Minutes of Churchill-de Gaulle meeting; Kersaudy, pp.194-200.

56 Central Zionist Archives, Jerusalem (CZA) S25/6595, Jerusalem, November 23, 1943, Vilensky to Shertok on his conversation with the Free French liaison officer in Jerusalem.

57 AN, Paris, de Gaulle's Papers, 3AG1/263, London, July 29, 1942, Churchill-de Gaulle meeting.

58 AN, Paris, de Gaulle's Papers, 3AG1/263, Cairo, July 24, 1941, Lyttelton-de Gaulle agreement; Beirut, August 7, 1941, Lyttelton to de Gaulle. For Spears' account, see Spears, *Fulfilment of a Mission*, pp.132-47. See also: Wilson, *Eight Years Overseas*, pp.123-4; Kersaudy, pp.140-50; Zamir, "De Gaulle and the Question of Syria and Lebanon," pp.686-7.

59 SHA, Levant, 4H382, list of British agents prepared by SEL; Zamir, "Against the Tide"; Shelley, pp.120-2. See also Murphy, Christopher J., "SOE's Foreign Currency Transactions," *Intelligence and National Security*, 20(1) (2005), pp.191-208.

60 The identities of "agents of influence" recruited by the British secret services are extremely difficult to uncover and are based mainly on Syrian and British documents, as well as references in French intelligence reports. See for example SHA, Levant, 4H382. See also Zamir, "Against the Tide."

61 SHA, Moscow, 7NN 2534, September 25, 1941, Renseignement d'archives; no.3.106, April 2, 1942, Political Situation in Syria. For the co-option of Shukri al-Quwatli, see Zamir, "Against the Tide."

62 French sources claimed that Quwatli was being supported financially by Ibn-Sa'ud. See SHA, Levant, 4H384, no.1561, Saudi influence on Syrian nationalists. See also Freya Stark's account of her conversation with Quwatli in the summer of 1943, in Stark, *East is West*, pp.122-5.

63 SHA, Moscow, 7NN 2534, no.2.577, August 30, 1941, Political situation in Syria; SHA, Levant, 4H384, March 13, 1943, Information; 4H322, Note B/2, March 22, 1942; TNA, FO 226/233 31/42, no.637, Beirut, June 28, 1942, British Legation in Beirut to Minister of State, Cairo. For the co-option of Jamil Mardam, see Zamir, "Against the Tide." A different version is presented by his daughter, Salma Mardam, in *Syria's Quest for Independence*. See for example pp.56-9, 81-2.

64 Zamir, *Lebanon's Quest for Independence*, pp.110-12, 206-11, and "An Intimate Alliance," pp.814-23. See also Seale, *Riad El-Solh*, pp.434-50.

65 SHA, Levant, 4H384, Informations, Beirut, December 4 and 23,1943 and January 14, 1944; Zamir, "Agaist the Tide." On Sulh's role in the war in Palestine, see Epilogue.

66 CADN, Syrie et Liban, 2455, no.330, August 11, 1944; MAE, Paris, Syrie et Liban, 1944-52, vol.279, June 22, 1945, Crise ministérielle au Liban. For details see Chapter 3.

67 CADN, Syrie et Liban, 771, no.95/GB, Beirut, November 6, 1941, Catroux to Spears; carton 1365, no.1181/SP, Beirut, December 17, 1942, report on Lebanese parties, including the Constitutional Bloc, containing a copy of a letter from Khuri to Catroux from October 10, 1941; carton 787, Beirut, December 23, 1942, Note sur la situation politique au Liban. The turning point was Khuri's visit with Mardam to Egypt in June 1942 and his meeting with Nahhas and British officials. The trip had been arranged by Spears. See various French reports on this trip in carton 1086. TNA, FO 226/233 31/42, Beirut, July 31, 1942, Hamilton to Smart.

68 CADN, Syrie et Liban, 782, no.9/602/43, Beirut, September 6, Spears to Helleu, and no.7910, September 8, 1943, Helleu to Spears; no.169/8/43, September 22, Spears to Helleu; carton 1109, December 5, 1943, note by the director of the French Information Service; carton 2457, no.54, Beirut, January 22, 1944, Chataigneau to Massigli.

69 SHAT, Levant, 4H314, November 22, 1943, Le Liban entre 1939 et 1943; CADN, Syrie et Liban, 772, July 19, 1941, Note pour le Général. Receipts obtained by the French intelligence agencies from the files of the British Legation in Beirut give details of large sums of money passed on by Pharaon to Sulh. The Spears Mission was able to channel funds to parliamentary candidates via Pharaon and the Pharaon-Chiha Bank without the scrutiny of the authorities in London and Cairo.

3 Britain's Perfidy – France's Revenge, 1943-1948

Tuvia Arazi, a Haganah intelligence officer who was in Beirut in February 1945 preparing a covert Franco-Zionist campaign against Spears, reported that he had seen scores of files in which the French had detailed Spears' subversive activities. Titled "Sur les agissements de Spears," they revealed the strong anti-British sentiments of French officials and secret service agents there. His report was written shortly after the French intelligence services uncovered the schemes by Spears and British secret agents to oust France from the Levant. Many Frenchmen in Beirut, Algiers and later, Paris, saw this subversion as merely another example of the treachery and duplicity of "Perfidious Albion," which was exploiting France's temporary weakness to rob it of its empire in the Middle East and North Africa. A senior French official accurately predicted the impact of these findings on Anglo-French relations after the war when he told Arazi: "The affairs between us and Britain will be settled; treaties will be signed and a modus vivendi will be reached. On the face of it, things will return to normal, but one thing that is impossible to restore is 'la confiance' of France in Britain."[1]

This chapter examines the clandestine Anglo-French war in the Middle East from 1943 until 1948, presenting both the "perfidy" and the "revenge." These years can be divided into the periods before July 1944 and after, when the French intelligence services carried out successful operations in both the British Legation in Beirut and the Syrian Foreign Ministry in Damascus. During the first period the clandestine war was asymmetric, with the British secret agents having the upper hand. In the second, French decision-makers in Paris and Beirut, with a small number of intelligence officers, exploited the information gleaned from those covert operations to take revenge and undermine Britain's Middle East policy, especially the Arabists' scheme to eject France from the Levant and integrate Syria into a Hashemite Greater Syria united with Iraq.

In 1943 and early 1944, Free France was unable to retaliate. Spears, backed by Casey, and closely coordinating his moves with the Arabists, exploited the fact that de Gaulle and Catroux were tied up in Algiers to conduct effective overt and covert attacks on France's position in the Levant. The French Committee's declaration in January 1943 on holding elections in Syria and

Lebanon resulted from the realization that Free France's priority was now in North Africa, where it desperately needed Britain's support against the hostile American stand. After Operation Torch and the Allies' landing in French North Africa in November 1942, Catroux's main attention turned to Algeria where, throughout the following year, he mediated between Generals de Gaulle and Giraud. Catroux, who deemed it essential to secure France's control of North Africa, feared the effects of a conflict with the Arab Muslims in the Middle East on its position there. Believing that the Arab nationalist politicians in Syria and Lebanon represented a genuine national movement, he was willing to adopt a more liberal policy towards them, even at the price of antagonizing the Lebanese Christians. He argued that in the long run only a "Muslim" policy could guarantee France's position in North Africa. Paradoxically, de Gaulle, who was critical of Catroux's stance, later adopted a similar policy in Algeria in 1958 and in the Arab world in the early 1960s; this became known as his "Arab policy."[2]

In a last-minute effort, Catroux attempted to secure a treaty with the Syrian nationalists before the elections. He offered the presidency to Hashem al-Atasi, the former President, in return for the latter's undertaking to endorse a treaty similar to that of 1936, but Atasi refused. Shukri al-Quwatli, however, had no such reservations, secretly negotiating an agreement with Catroux between January and March. Quwatli also wrote to de Gaulle offering his cooperation. His immediate aim was not only to gain Catroux's support, but to prevent a French veto of his candidacy. He made it clear to Catroux that while Britain backed the Zionists and Turkey, which was harboring territorial designs over northern Syria, France, after regaining its standing as a Great Power, could help to guarantee Syria's independence and territorial integrity. Catroux was obviously unaware of Quwatli's secret undertaking (docs.3-4) to the British authorities and Nuri al-Sa'id to incorporate Syria in a Hashemite Greater Syria and unite it with Iraq.[3]

Quwatli's overtures came as Catroux received from his own intelligence services a copy of an eight-point plan for an Arab union presented to Casey by Nuri al-Sa'id, while Eden was publicly declaring Britain's endorsement of Arab unity. Catroux knew that Quwatli, like many Syrian National Bloc leaders, opposed Emir Abdullah's ambitions for the Syrian crown. He was also aware of Quwatli's close ties with Ibn Sa'ud, the Hashemites' sworn enemy. But there was another reason for his support of Quwatli. In early March, one of Spears' advisers warned the French that Quwatli had informed the British that he had no intention of keeping his promises to them. Seeing this warning as an attempt by Spears to prevent Quwatli from attaining the presidency, Catroux resolved to back him. He also requested that before the elections the British government renew its undertaking to support treaties between France and Syria and Lebanon. But Spears refused, arguing that it was subject to the agreement of future elected parliaments and national governments. Spears obviously knew that the Syrian and Lebanese nationalist leaders, whom he was helping to power, had no intention of concluding treaties with France.[4]

Another move by Catroux designed to strengthen the anti-Hashemite camp in Syria and Lebanon was to facilitate the intervention of Nahhas Pasha, the Egyptian Prime Minister, in Syrian and Lebanese politics as a counter-balance to Nuri al-Sa'id. From January to July 1943 he corresponded with Nahhas through the Egyptian embassy in London, emphasizing the French Committee's intentions to honor its undertaking to grant independence to Syria and Lebanon based on treaties with France. In June, Nahhas became directly embroiled in Lebanese politics when he mediated in the dispute between Christians and Muslims over the distribution of deputies in the elected parliament. His involvement in Syria's and Lebanon's affairs, with Catroux's blessing, helped to transform Egypt into a strong rival of the Hashemites in the Levant. Nevertheless, Catroux's efforts to win over Nahhas backfired: during the Lebanese constitutional crisis, Nahhas led a particularly hostile campaign against the Free French.[5]

Orchestrating the Lebanese constitutional crisis

In 1943, Spears enjoyed considerable freedom of action in Syria and Lebanon as de Gaulle and Catroux turned their attention to French North Africa. The rivalry between de Gaulle and Giraud in 1943 left the Free French in disarray, and Catroux spent most of his time in their new headquarters in Algiers. Despite his intimate knowledge of the Levant, Catroux could barely cope with Spears' intrigues. He was replaced by a weak and naïve Jean Helleu, the former Vichy Ambassador to Ankara, who lacked any understanding of complex Levantine politics. In the months that followed, Helleu was outmaneuvered by Spears and pro-British Syrian and Lebanese politicians. In November 1943, losing his nerve, he overreacted by imprisoning President Khuri and Prime Minister Sulh.[6]

The parliamentary elections in Syria and Lebanon in the summer of 1943 were critical for Spears and the Arabists, especially after Churchill rejected Spears' and Casey's plans to oust France from the Levant. They believed that ensuring the rise to power of nationalist leaders in Syria and Lebanon was the only way to further their policy. Even before the elections, some French officials had warned that Britain's Levant policy was no longer being defined in London but in Beirut and Cairo. The ensuing months proved the accuracy of such warnings: Spears' success in securing the election of many pro-British deputies in the Syrian and Lebanese parliaments and in helping Quwatli, Mardam, Khuri, Sulh and other pro-British politicians to rise to power opened the way for tacit collaboration with the nationalist leaders in staging the crises that ended France's influence in the Levant.[7]

The elections revealed Spears to be an accomplished politician, well-versed in political maneuvering, and exposed the incompetence of the French delegation, headed by Helleu. Spears sent numerous telegrams to London and Cairo accusing the French of rigging the elections, while concealing the role that he and his political officers were playing in determining their outcome.

Spears' political officers and the British secret services were central to the success of anti-French and pro-British candidates in an electoral campaign fraught with petty politics and personal rivalries. The Syrian documents and French sources reveal that the British wielded considerable influence over many of the elected Syrian and Lebanese deputies. Spears and the nationalists succeeded in turning the elections into both a national struggle for independence and sovereignty and a referendum on France's presence in Syria and Lebanon. While this was the Syrian and Lebanese nationalists' primary goal, it was perilous for Britain as a possible precedent for the Arab countries under its own control. Foreign Office officials warned that ousting France from Syria and Lebanon without treaties, as advocated by Spears and the Arabists, would harm Britain's position in Iraq and Egypt. After the Lebanese crisis, Churchill reprimanded Spears, telling him, "We should discourage the throwing of stones since we had greenhouses of our own – acres and acres of them."[8] But Spears, determined to oust France and humiliate de Gaulle, did not heed his Prime Minister's warning.

As expected, the National Bloc won the Syrian elections and many of its members were elected to parliament. With Spears' backing, Quwatli was elected President, Jabiri was nominated Prime Minister, while Mardam was to serve as Foreign Minister. Mardam was the most influential member of the government and until his resignation two years later he secretly collaborated, first with Spears and later with Stirling, to oust France from Syria and Lebanon. In Lebanon, the elections sparked an Anglo-French confrontation in which Spears outmaneuvered the French delegation. Spears, Furlonge, Marun Arab and the British political officers in the five electoral districts were directly involved in securing the election of anti-French and pro-British candidates, notably Riyad al-Sulh and Abd al-Hamid Karameh.[9]

In Lebanon, unlike Syria, the election of the President and the nomination of the Prime Minister were accompanied by political intrigues involving Spears, Helleu and the candidates themselves. Helleu and his officials were outplayed and misled by Spears, as well as by Khuri, who promised his loyalty to France. The meeting between Khuri and Sulh on September 19, 1943 – later the cornerstone of the National Pact that laid the foundation for Christian-Muslim cooperation in independent Lebanon – is an important milestone in Lebanese historiography. At that meeting, Khuri agreed to nominate Sulh as Prime Minister, which had in fact been Spears' main goal and his condition for supporting Khuri's election as President. In dispatches to the Foreign Office, Spears adamantly rejected French charges that he had advanced the nomination of a Prime Minister known for his hostility towards France. But in a "personal and secret" message to Casey after Sulh had formed his government, Spears boasted of his achievement: "The appointment of the Riad Solh Ministry means that everything has ended infinitely more satisfactorily than I ever dared hope for. I have felt all along as if I were building a house of cards and that each additional card was likely to bring down the whole structure. Yet until the last tier was in position nothing had been achieved."[10]

The period between Sulh's inaugural speech in the Lebanese parliament on October 7, which set the stage for a direct confrontation with France, and the release of Khuri and Sulh from French imprisonment on November 22, is one of the most studied in Lebanon's historiography. It is presented as the culmination of the joint Christian-Muslim national struggle for Lebanon's independence and sovereignty from French colonial rule. Spears' part in orchestrating the crisis has been examined, but the uncovering of the secret collaboration of Sulh, Khuri, Mardam and Quwatli with Spears and British Arabist intelligence officers obliges historians to reassess the entire event.[11]

The Lebanese crisis demonstrates the effect of the war on politics in the Middle East. In early September 1943 Italy surrendered, and a month later the Allies occupied Corsica. An Allied invasion of France and its restoration to its former international status appeared imminent. The British establishment in the Middle East, particularly Arabist veterans, were resolved to create a fait accompli and end France's presence in the Levant lest the precedent of 1919 be repeated. In effect, Spears and the Arabists adopted Glubb's proposal of May 1943 to "maneuver" France out of the Levant. This sense of urgency was reinforced by Nahhas's progress in his deliberations with Arab leaders on Arab unity. On October 13, shortly before the Syrian delegation, led by Prime Minister Jabiri, left for Cairo to discuss the convening of an Arab preparatory conference, Clayton and Newcombe arrived in Damascus and met with Quwatli. Two days later Clayton held a meeting with Sulh and Mardam together with the Egyptian Consul in Shtura on the Syro-Lebanese border. Clayton's presence in Shtura when Mardam and Sulh, Britain's most trusted Syrian and Lebanese politicians, were planning their joint move against the French is particularly significant. British and Syrian documents reveal that Clayton's visits to Beirut and Damascus usually coincided with initiatives to promote tacit political goals that were not always in line with Foreign Office policy. It should be noted that Colonel Stirling and Major Altounyan, who were implicated in orchestrating the Syrian crisis in 1945, were in the Syrian capital during the Lebanese crisis. In fact, Colonel Oliva Roget, the French delegate in Damascus, reported that they were involved in provoking anti-French demonstrations in the city.[12]

Unlike Mardam, who closely coordinated his moves against the French with Sulh and Spears, Quwatli, reluctant to confront France directly, took a more cautious stand throughout the Lebanese crisis. Senior French officers who visited him in September and October emphasized that once Italy capitulated, France would be liberated and restored to its pre-war position as a Great Power, alluding to the 300,000 French soldiers in North Africa. Quwatli, for his part, stressed that the Lebanese elections had proved once again that Lebanon was an artificial entity. Quwatli's cautious stand during the Lebanese crisis should have served as a warning to the Arabists and Nuri al-Sa'id; a few months later Quwatli signed a secret agreement with Ibn Sa'ud opposing a Hashemite Greater Syria.[13]

The anti-French campaign in October and early November was carefully orchestrated by Spears and Sulh, apart from two unexpected events initiated by the French themselves, which in fact played into Spears' hands. The first was de Gaulle's move to consolidate his position in the National Committee of French Liberation (NCFL) by removing General Giraud as co-president, and the second was Helleu's imprisonment of President Khuri, Prime Minister Sulh and other ministers and deputies. The removal of Giraud, Roosevelt's man, from the French Committee shortly before Churchill's meeting with the American President in Cairo, infuriated the British Prime Minister. Spears exploited Churchill's rage and the ensuing Lebanese crisis to direct his attacks against de Gaulle, presenting him as an Anglophobe and accusing him of being personally responsible for Helleu's use of force against the democratically elected Lebanese government. Helleu's coup provoked large-scale anti-French demonstrations in Lebanon, Syria and the Arab world, severely undermining de Gaulle's prestige in Britain and the United States.[14]

The pendulum swings back

During the Lebanese crisis, Britain's stand towards France's presence in the Levant veered sharply towards the anti-French policy promoted by Spears and the Arabists. But in the following year, Churchill and Eden tried to restore the balance and improve relations with de Gaulle and the French Committee. The immediate cause of this change was the decision made by the Big Three at the Teheran Conference at the end of November on an Allied invasion of France in the summer of 1944. The cooperation of de Gaulle and the French Committee was deemed essential for the operation's success and for the liberation of France. In London, criticism was leveled against the anti-Free French campaign conducted in the British media during the Lebanese crisis. It was pointed out that the BBC was participating in the campaign while at the same time broadcasting to mainland France to win the support of the French public for the Allies. A directive issued by the Political Warfare Executive (PWE), of which the Free French obtained a copy, reminded officials in the BBC and the British media that the events in Lebanon were marginal to the war in Europe.[15] But apart from the immediate military considerations, Eden and other ministers in the War Cabinet, especially those representing the Labour Party, sensed that Spears had provoked Churchill to adopt an unnecessarily brutal and humiliating stance towards de Gaulle and the French Committee. At the Foreign Office, Duff Cooper, the new envoy to the French Committee in Algiers, Harold MacMillan and senior diplomats in the Western Department argued that a strong France was central to rebuilding Europe after the war. Some Middle East experts in London and Cairo warned that the anti-French campaigns in Egypt and Iraq were assuming a xenophobic character and that if France were evicted from the Middle East, Britain would remain the sole colonial Power in the face of a hostile Arab Muslim world. Reports from Washington warned that attacks in the American media and public opinion against Free France's conduct in Lebanon were turning into criticism of Britain's policy in its colonies, especially India.[16]

In the Cabinet and Foreign Office there was a growing realization of the need to tighten control over Spears and the Arabists in the Middle East to ensure that their policies were in line with those of the Cabinet. Although Eden could not persuade Churchill to recall Spears, in January 1944 Casey, who failed to restrain Spears and was swayed by his Arabist advisers, moved to India. He was replaced by his deputy, Lord Moyne, Churchill's close friend. As a counter-balance to Spears' hard-line anti-French policy, in May the Foreign Office appointed Gilbert MacKereth to the Legation, a former Consul in Damascus who was skilled in Syrian politics and had good relations with the French officials. In December 1943, during his stop-over in Cairo while accompanying Churchill to Teheran, Eden made it clear to local British officials that the Cabinet was not seeking France's eviction and that it supported the French Committee's efforts to secure treaties with the two Levant states. He reiterated this position in parliament and Churchill publicly endorsed it.[17]

The Lebanese crisis was the climax of Spears' anti-Gaullist crusade. Although he continued to serve as Minister in Syria and Lebanon for another year, his ability to provoke Churchill against de Gaulle was diminished. In their meeting in March 1944 in Cairo, Churchill criticized Spears for his anti-French stand, reminding him that it was not the Cabinet's intent to oust France from the Levant. He considered recalling Spears to his parliamentary duties, but decided against it out of political considerations and loyalty to his friend. Even the Arabists in Cairo realized that Spears' aggressive anti-French policy was becoming burdensome, and Smart, Clayton and Killearn all criticized it. However, their criticism did not detract from their recognition of his accomplishment in undermining France's standing in the Levant, thereby opening the way for Britain to promote its plans for reorganizing the Fertile Crescent states. Like Spears, they noted the change in Churchill's attitude towards the French Committee, but assumed it was only temporary, prompted by the war needs. They believed that in the aftermath of the military operations to liberate France, they could reverse their government's policy.[18]

Senior army officers in the Middle East, although wary of Spears' anti-French crusade, shared his and the Arabists' aim of securing Britain's control of the Levant. By the end of 1943 there was growing concern in military circles in London and Cairo that after the war the Soviet Union would pose a threat to Britain's strategic interests in the Middle East. Faced with strong opposition to the presence of large military forces in Egypt, the High Command in Cairo under General Bernard Paget, the new Commander-in-Chief of the Allied Forces in the Middle East, sought to transform Syria into a permanent base for British forces. Already in December 1943, Oliva Roget warned that the goals of the British Army in the Levant were no different than those of Spears and other anti-French British officials. In February 1944 Spears asked Mardam for the Syrian government's agreement to the army's construction of permanent military barracks. In the following months the army began to expand its infrastructure in Syria and Lebanon, reinforcing French suspicions that British forces were intending to remain after the war. The army also took part in Spears' initiative to arm the Syrian Gendarmerie, and senior British officers, especially General Paget, were directly involved in orchestrating the Syrian crisis a year later. Ending France's influence in the Levant was also backed by commercial and financial circles in London, and in early March Spears asked Mardam to grant British companies concessions for oil exploration in Syria. Despite Foreign Office criticism of his role in the Lebanese crisis, he resumed his anti-French campaign and found a willing partner in Jamil Mardam.[19]

The game of Spears and the Arabists backfires

In early December 1943, the French intelligence post in Damascus obtained a copy of a top secret British report on the pan-Arab movement written in Cairo by Colonel William Elphinston, assistant to Brigadier Clayton, head of the Political Intelligence Centre Middle East (PICME). The report was passed on to the French by a "friend" who requested that it be kept in utmost secrecy. A month later, the same post obtained another comprehensive PICME study that examined the positions of Arab and non-Arab states towards Arab unity plans and made policy recommendations. It exposed the way of thinking and modus operandi of many Arabist intelligence officers at the time. The limited number of distributed copies and the list of recipients, which included governors, the main embassies in the Middle East and military and civilian intelligence agencies, attested to its importance. The fact that it was written by the PICME, the main intelligence agency advising the Minister of State in Cairo on policy-making, reinforced its significance.[20]

The report highlights Eden's statement to parliament on February 24, 1943, on Britain's stand towards Arab unity. But while the tenet of Eden's declaration was that the British government would leave it to the Arab countries themselves to advance their unity, the report argues that Britain, and especially its representatives in the Middle East, should undertake to unite the Arab states. It appears that its authors were confident that British agents in the region could overcome the difficulties that lay ahead, including the Arabs' apathy. It sheds light on Britain's role in the formation of the pan-Arab movement and the Arab League, issues still debated by historians, and underscores the grounds for the widespread use of covert political action by the Arabist intelligence officers in their Middle East policy.[21]

The report's authors clearly had intimate knowledge of the Arab leaders' true opinions regarding the Arab unity plans. It details Nuri al-Sa'id's attempts to promote the Fertile Crescent and Greater Syria schemes, Nahhas's efforts on behalf of Arab unity, and the obstacles they encountered throughout 1943. In Iraq, the report notes, there was general apathy towards the pan-Arab movement. The Kurds and Shiites opposed the idea, while the Sunnis displayed little interest. In Syria, the main concern was union with Lebanon rather than Arab unity, and despite his public statements, President Quwatli was strongly opposed to Syria coming under Iraqi or Egyptian domination. The Christians in Lebanon rejected union with Syria and continued to support French protection and "complete separation from the hinterland." The Lebanese Muslims were indifferent to a union with Transjordan or Palestine, but were in favor of reattachment to Syria. The Arabs in Palestine lacked interest in either Arab unity or a Greater Syria and feared that an Arab federation would undermine the White Paper, which they viewed as a guarantee against partition in Palestine. In Transjordan, Emir Abdullah was only concerned with Syria and Palestine and disinterested in Arab unity. (doc.5) The report examines Ibn Sa'ud's hostility towards a Hashemite Greater Syria, an Iraqi-Syrian union or Arab unity under Egypt's leadership, and quotes the Saudi King's remark to the British Minister in Jeddah in April 1943: "Leave the Arabs of each country to take care first of the development in their own countries." Referring to Egypt, the report states: "The country in general is extremely disinterested in the whole idea," stressing that Nahhas was motivated by vanity and personal interests and that his attempts to promote Arab unity were strongly opposed by the Palace and the Egyptian public.[22]

Relating to the non-Arab states' attitudes towards Arab unity plans, the report points out that France believed that Britain was behind those plans and regarded the pan-Arab movement as a threat to its position in the Levant and North Africa. It argues however, that "There is no need to attach too much weight to French protests." It maintains that like Britain, the United States supported regional economic and cultural cooperation and that the Anglo-American disagreement regarding Saudi Arabia and Palestine could be bridged. Turkey, too, suspected that Britain was behind the plans for an Arab federation and preferred that Iraq and Syria remain independent weak states. Nevertheless, the report estimates that Turkey would accept Britain's patronage over an Arab federation, which would "prevent Arab hostility directed against it." It fails to mention, however, that an additional incentive for the Turkish leaders was their belief that Turkey could better promote its territorial ambitions over Aleppo and the northern Jazira if Syria were part of a Hashemite federation. The Syrian documents indeed reveal that British Arabists and Nuri al-Sa'id promoted such a solution in 1946. The report also alleged that Iran, too, preferred a weak neighboring Iraqi state to a large united Arab federation that might claim the region of Khuzistan. It does not relate the Soviet Union's position, but does examine Nazi Germany's attitude towards Arab unity plans. It quotes comments aired on Radio Berlin that "This Unity is a maneuver intended to back British imperialist policy … Nuri Pasha is only an instrument who has allowed England to stretch out its hands …" and "… England has built this masquerade of pan-Arabism because it constitutes a convenient way to seize Syria and Lebanon from the French and place them directly under British domination, and a way of getting rid of American influence in Saudi Arabia."[23]

The report's assessment of the Jewish Agency's and the Zionist movement's position towards Arab unity reflects the Arabists' belief that the formation of a Jewish state was an obstacle to their plans for a Greater Syria. It points to Jewish Agency efforts to reinforce the opposition of the Christian communities and the Kurds to the pan-Arab movement; its attempt to secure the collaboration of Turkey against such plans; and Jewish influence in the United States. It nevertheless highlights the position of moderate Zionist leaders, such as Dr Yehuda Magnes, who were endorsing a solution based on a semi-autonomous Jewish entity incorporated into an Arab federation. It also stresses that, unlike the limited territory of Palestine which could not support a large number of inhabitants, such a solution would facilitate the immigration of millions of Jews. This was indeed proposed by Nuri al-Sa'id in his Blue Book, presented to Casey in early 1943.[24]

Summing up its findings, the report concludes that: "Until the drawing up of this document, (Nov. 43) discussions on the question of Arab Unity were purely informatory and no general progress has been made." And further on, "The Arab leaders recognize that the idea of Arab Unity in 1918 was premature in the face of powerful, well-known regional interests and the dynastic jealousies of the Arabs." It then stresses that: "We have seen that there is very little good sense in the intentions of the Arab states and that the pan-Arab movement corresponds far less to a union of the Arabs themselves than to a cooperation between the Arabs against the outside world." This last sentence came in response to warnings voiced in the Foreign Office and various London circles, as well as by the French and the Zionists, that the pan-Arab movement could become xenophobic. The Arabists obviously had no problem with such a movement being directed against France, the Zionists or the Soviet Union. They were confident, however, of their ability to prevent it from turning against Britain itself, as "the most moderate leaders ... know that they will need for many years the help and protection of any Great Power or a group of Powers," namely Great Britain. But their confidence was ill-placed. The hostility inflamed by British agents among the Arab leaders and the general public during the Lebanese and Syrian crises was soon directed against Britain itself.[25]

While the first part of the report dwells at length on the obstacles, the second part explains the need for Arab unity and regional cooperation, whether encompassing all the Arab countries or smaller regional blocs that would cooperate in a joint federal council.[26] It concludes that Britain ought to undertake the task of promoting inter-Arab cooperation. The key word in the report's conclusions, reflecting the mentality of many Arabists, was the duty of British officials in the Middle East to "guide" the Arab leaders towards regional cooperation and Arab unity, which in fact implied coercing, manipulating or pressuring them into complying with Britain's interests. It was no coincidence that most of the report's recipients were intelligence agencies and that its authors were Arabist intelligence officers, confident in their power to shape local public opinion and maneuver Arab leaders into acquiescing with

Britain's designs. Hence, when referring to Iraqi apathy towards Arab unity, the report emphasizes: "That does not mean that a certain enthusiasm could not be created by the requisite incentives. A wave of xenophobia beginning for whatever reason in another country could be one; substantial concessions to Zionists in Palestine at the expense of the Arabs could be another." Indeed, Nuri al-Sa'id and Iraqi nationalist leaders cultivated pan-Arabism to overcome religious and communal divisions within Iraq. They also stressed Iraq's responsibility to defend the Arab cause, whether in Syria against the French, or in Palestine against the Zionists. As for the Arabists' intentions to consolidate the pan-Arab movement around the Arabs' hatred and fear of the Zionists, the Syrian documents provide ample evidence of attempts by British agents to provoke Arab fears of Jewish ambitions, thereby strengthening Britain's position as defender of the Arab cause. While in 1941-45 France was assigned the role of enemy of the Arabs, in 1946-48 the Zionist movement played this role in British covert operations.

In the following years the Arabists discovered, however, that their ability to advance their Arab unity plans was limited as they became entangled in inter-Arab intrigues. In the face of growing threats, both within the region and from outside Powers, to their country's strategic and economic interests, they resorted to covert political operations and clandestine diplomacy to promote their schemes while their government remained undecided. Anti-Hashemite Arab leaders, as well as France, the Soviet Union, the Zionist movement and occasionally the United States, were involved in a great secret game aimed at frustrating Britain's ambitions of dominating the entire Middle East.

Syria, owing to its strategic position and pivotal role in the Arab unity plans, became once again central to this scheme. It was crucial to the Greater Syria plan that would provide a solution to the Jewish question without establishing a separate, independent Jewish state – anathema to most of the British officials in the region. Union with Iraq would strengthen the latter and allow it direct access to the Mediterranean, thereby securing a stable oil supply. And it was central to Britain's regional defense strategy against the Soviet Union. President Quwatli, however, became a major obstacle to these plans. Confident after his sweeping victory and election as President, he made it clear that Syria had first to secure independence and national sovereignty from France before it would discuss any form of Arab unity. After securing the presidency he moved closer to Ibn Sa'ud, with whom he had maintained close ties since the 1920s. Attempts by Clayton and Newcombe in mid-October to persuade him to back the Anglo-Hashemite unity plans failed. In discussions with Nahhas, Sa'adallah al-Jabiri, who headed the Syrian delegation in the Arab deliberations in Cairo, stated that Syria was willing to endorse the formation of a Greater Syria provided it retained its republican regime and Damascus as its capital. Quwatli and Jabiri were further encouraged by Nahhas's statement that "The [unity] plans between Iraq and Syria could push Egypt aside from its predominant position in the Levant."[27] They therefore adopted the Egyptian formula of a loose Arab union led by Egypt which, together with Saudi Arabia, would defend Syria's independence against Hashemite ambitions. But Nuri al-Sa'id was unwilling to allow Nahhas or Ibn Sa'ud to thwart his designs over Syria. He exploited Quwatli's and Jabiri's opposition to Abdullah's ambitions for the Syrian crown to promote an Iraqi-Syrian union and, together with the Arabists, buttressed Mardam's ambitions for the presidency.[28]

In early March 1944, the British authorities in Cairo, and the Arabists in particular, faced a severe setback when Churchill reassured Ibn Sa'ud that if France withdrew from Syria and Lebanon, Britain would not "favor any change of regime, or the political or geographic status of these countries" (doc.6). This undertaking attested to Churchill's lack of confidence in the Arab Hashemite policy that had been promoted by the Arabists since 1941. Churchill repeated this promise when he met Ibn Sa'ud in Cairo in February 1945. The Saudi monarch and President Quwatli were confident that the policy pursued by Spears and local British officials had not been endorsed by their government in London. Following Churchill's undertaking, Quwatli concluded a secret agreement with Ibn Sa'ud coordinating Syrian-Saudi policy in inter-Arab and international affairs. Oliva Roget commented that his agreement with Ibn Sa'ud reinforced Quwatli's confidence to resist pressure from Spears, Clayton and Nuri al-Sa'id a few months later. Nuri al-Sa'id and Mardam reacted by re-signing their secret agreement to form an Arab Hashemite kingdom including Syria, in which Mardam would play a central role under a designated sovereign (doc.8). Although the agreement left open the question of the future monarch, the crown was in fact assigned to Abd al-Ilah until Faisal II came of age. The two agreements illustrate the deep dissension within the Syrian leadership over their country's orientation. Quwatli was obviously unaware that his Foreign Minister and the Iraqi premier were plotting against him.

The Syrian President demonstrated his newfound confidence when, with tacit French endorsement, he sought to strengthen Syria's international standing by securing recognition of its independence from the Soviet Union and the United States. Quwatli evidently hoped to bolster Syria's independence not only vis-à-vis the Hashemites, but also from Britain itself. In April 1944, Jabiri met with a Russian diplomat in Cairo; shortly afterwards Quwatli sent a personal envoy to the Egyptian capital to negotiate with officials in the Russian Embassy about establishing diplomatic relations. In fact, France was keen to ensure the Soviet Union's recognition of Syria's and Lebanon's independence. The Syrian documents provide full details of the Syrian-Soviet negotiations, in which Khaled Bakdash, head of the Syrian Communist Party, participated (docs.9, 11-2, 21-2). The Soviet diplomats were concerned lest Britain attempt to gain control over Syria, and sought to establish that there was no secret Anglo-Syrian agreement to place Syria under British hegemony. In July, the United States and the Soviet Union officially recognized Syria's and Lebanon's independence and established diplomatic relations with the two states.[29]

The endless intrigues in inter-Arab relations, in which British agents had become fully involved, were overshadowed by the Allied landing in France in June 1944. Since the fall of France in June 1940, Syrian nationalists had been dreading its liberation and return to its pre-war position as a Great European Power. This was the message that de Gaulle and Catroux had conveyed to the Syrian leaders to persuade them to conclude a treaty with France. But with Spears and Arabist agents tacitly encouraging them to reject the French proposal, while reassuring them that Syria could secure national sovereignty without such a treaty, they chose to wait. After the liberation of Paris in August and the formation of de Gaulle's provisional government, Quwatli, Jabiri and Mardam feared that Britain would betray them, as it had done after World War I, and cut its own deal with France. Spears and local British officials further fueled these fears to pressure Quwatli into acquiescing to their demands.

On the eve of D-Day, Spears reached an agreement with Mardam to jointly advance an Anglo-Syrian treaty; the latter acted without the knowledge of his President and Prime Minister (doc.10). Spears' initiative was in sharp contrast to the policy advocated by Eden, who sought an entente with France in the Levant. He also stepped up his anti-French campaign and organized a boycott of the 14th of July celebrations, while Mardam formally requested Britain's protection and aid. Eden reacted sharply, instructing Spears to "refrain from any intervention in local affairs."[30] Eden's plan to negotiate an Anglo-French agreement in the Levant with Massigli; rumors of Churchill's intention to end the Spears Mission in Syria and Lebanon; and the convening of the Arab preparatory conference in Alexandria in September reinforced the sense of urgency among the British authorities in Cairo.

On August 5, Lebanese Prime Minister Riyad al-Sulh traveled to Damascus and handed his counterpart, Sa'adallah al-Jabiri, a proposal for a secret Anglo-Syrian agreement dictated to him in the British Legation in Beirut by Gilbert MacKereth. MacKereth himself opposed the initiative, but was acting on strict orders. The initiative, approved by Lord Moyne and backed by General Paget, had been instigated by the Arabists in Cairo; Brigadier Clayton, Moyne's chief adviser for Arab affairs, arrived in Beirut to implement it (doc.14). The use of Sulh was intended to conceal the move from French officials and lend it an informal character. The Arabists could no longer ignore Quwatli's game to tacitly align Syria with Ibn Sa'ud against their Hashemite allies. Clayton's message, which he repeated to Quwatli when he met him in Damascus, attested to his impatience with the Syrian President's tactics (doc.15). It is noteworthy that apart from undertaking to "protect Syrian independence against any aggression," namely from France, the Arabists used the "Jewish incentive" to lure the Syrian President into acquiescing with the British demands. The proposal stated that "Great Britain pledges to ensure the application of the clauses of the White Paper in Palestine and promises to put a complete stop to Jewish ambitions" (doc.14). Thus, while in London Eden negotiated an Anglo-French entente in the Levant with Massigli, the British authorities in Cairo sought to foil the Foreign Secretary's policy and cut its own deal with the Syrian leaders.[31]

The Syrian documents and French intelligence reports provide details of the various tactics employed by Spears, Clayton and other British agents, as well as Nuri al-Sa'id, to coerce the Syrian President and his Prime Minister into consenting to the proposal conveyed to them by Sulh. Yet neither Quwatli nor Jabiri yielded to the British and Hashemite pressure (docs.16-9). They knew, as Sulh had warned them, that rejecting the British offer would impact heavily on them personally, as well as on their country, which needed Britain's support to free itself from France. They were willing to collaborate with Britain, but on their own terms. They were ready to grant it a privileged strategic and economic status, but not to incorporate their country in a Hashemite-led Greater Syria united with Iraq. Quwatli's observations, after three days of talks with Cornwallis, indicate that he understood the British tactics. He concluded that the British officials were divided over the question of Greater Syria; that Syria could exploit this to retain its republican regime; and that Britain had its own interests in bringing an end to France's presence in the Levant. Ibn Sa'ud's support was essential for Quwatli's resistance to British and Hashemite pressure, as the correspondence between the two leaders before and during the Alexandria Conference attests. It was also indispensable in securing indirect American backing for Syria's independence (docs.26-30).

The British authorities in Cairo, and the Arabists in particular, were ambivalent towards the outcome of the Alexandria Conference. Although they failed to secure Arab support for Nuri al-Sa'id's plans for a Greater Syria and an Iraqi-Syrian union, they succeeded, with Nahhas's collaboration, in promoting the notion of an Arab League as a regional organization that would further inter-Arab cooperation. On the other hand, the anti-Hashemite camp led by Ibn Sa'ud and Quwatli was able, with Nahhas's active support, to steer the conference towards endorsing a loose form of Arab union in which the two Levant states would safeguard their independence. Another concern was the improved relations between Faruq and Ibn Sa'ud – both kings were distrusted by the British officials. Nahhas was the first to pay for his independent stand. Lord Killearn had all along been resisting pressure from King Faruq to replace Nahhas, but in early October he was dismissed by Faruq when Lord Killearn was conveniently on a visit to South Africa. The British administration in Egypt thereby gained another powerful enemy who would not forget their betrayal despite his loyal service during the war. Nahhas's resignation was followed by that of Jabiri and Sulh. British agents were involved behind the scenes in the first, and the French in the second. But British troubles were not over – they now had to confront their old rival. After being outplayed for years by the British secret agencies, the French intelligence services in Syria and Lebanon were now set on revenge. Armed with a new weapon, they waged their own secret war against their British adversaries.[32]

Operation Oliva Roget

At the end of June 1944, documents from the Syrian Foreign Ministry were published in Egyptian and American newspapers. They claimed that efforts to convene an Arab preparatory conference in Alexandria were fraught with difficulties and that the Arab governments had agreed to refrain from raising the question of Palestine. In early July, the Reuters correspondent in Palestine reported that the plan for Greater Syria would be discussed in Alexandria and that a referendum would decide its regime, whether a monarchy or republic. An Arab League would be formed, including Greater Syria and Iraq; Palestine would become part of Greater Syria. The published Syrian documents and press reports stirred intense reactions in the Arab capitals. Muhammad al-Unsi, Emir Abdullah's senior adviser, arrived in Jerusalem and questioned Eliyahu Sasson, head of the Arab Section of the Jewish Agency about whether the Agency was behind the leak, but Sasson denied it. Shortly afterwards, the Egyptian Consul in Beirut notified his Foreign Ministry of his conversation with Mardam in Damascus and gave details of the Iraqi-Syrian summit held in Sofar in which Quwatli, Jabiri, Mardam and Sulh had met with Nuri al-Sa'id and other Iraqi leaders. In his dispatch, of which French intelligence obtained a copy, he also reported that it had been decided at the meeting to form a confederation comprising Iraq, Syria and Lebanon which would coordinate national defense and foreign policy, as well as customs duties, between its members. The Consul warned that the plan's main goal was to exclude Egypt and Saudi Arabia, as the two monarchies were "not going far enough" to realize Arab unity.[33]

The articles in the Egyptian press and the *Palestine Post* provoked an angry reaction in Cairo, while Emir Abdullah, fearing that he would be left out of the proposed Iraqi-Syrian union, declared that Transjordan would be willing to take part in the pan-Arab conference in Alexandria. In Damascus, Prime Minister Jabiri denied the reports and, assuming that British agents were behind the leak, confronted Colonel Nur a-Din Marsack, who was in Damascus with Major Altounyan to promote the Greater Syria plan (doc.14). Sulh, criticized by Christians for jeopardizing Lebanon's independence and by Muslims for his compliance in compromising the Arab cause in Palestine, issued a formal denial. But in a telephone conversation with the Iraqi Consul in Beirut, he claimed that, unlike Jabiri, his denial had been made merely to calm public opinion. In the coming months he reiterated his opposition to Zionist ambitions in Palestine, while his supporters initiated a campaign to boycott Zionist goods.[34]

The press reports in June and July were the first shots by France's new weapon in its secret war against Britain in the Middle East. Colonel Fernand François Oliva Roget, the French delegate in Damascus, was behind this covert operation. In July, Oliva Roget recruited a top Syrian government official in Damascus and an agent in the British Legation in Beirut. The thousands of Syrian and British documents provided by these agents in the coming years were to revise the nature of the Anglo-French secret war in the Middle East. They influenced de Gaulle's relations with Churchill and solidified the clandestine Franco-Zionist collaboration against Britain in Palestine. They can be termed the "missing dimension" in the historiography of the Middle East in the 1940s, as well as in the study of Anglo-French relations.

Colonel Oliva Roget (promoted to the rank of Brigadier-General in March 1945) was behind one of the most successful French undercover operations against the British secret services in the Middle East. He was a tragic figure who died in January 1949, alone and bitter after his humiliating expulsion from Damascus by General Paget for his part in the Syrian crisis. British propaganda portrayed him as an example of the "savagery" of French colonialism in the Levant, while in Paris he was accused of being a Vichy supporter and held responsible for France's loss of Syria and Lebanon. In Syrian history books, as well as British officers' memoirs, he is presented in a highly negative fashion. His request for a trial was rejected by the French military authorities, who were unwilling to expose details of his still ongoing operation. In a desperate attempt to clear his name, he leaked to a journalist a secret report he had written in July 1945 exposing details of the events leading up to the Syrian crisis and accusing British agents and Syrian ministers of purposely provoking the crisis to evict France from the Levant. After his death, his private papers were seized by the French military security services and closed to historians.[35]

Oliva Roget had been an officer in the French Army in World War I. In 1921 he was posted to the Levant, where he remained for the next 24 years apart from short spells in France, Algeria, Morocco and Somalia. He served mainly in the intelligence services and in 1931 headed the Services Spéciaux in Damascus. Unlike other officers who favored working in cosmopolitan Beirut with its easy life, he opted to serve an extended period in Damascus, which afforded him intimate knowledge of Syrian politics. In July 1941 he joined Free France and was posted by Catroux to Jabal Druze, where he successfully upheld the French position against Glubb's and Kirkbride's subversion. Catroux, who recommended his promotion, wrote to Helleu: "If Jabal Druze remained under French influence, it is exclusively as a result of Colonel Oliva Roget's personal action."[36] A sharp observer of the British agents' machinations in Syria, he early on warned Catroux and later Helleu and Beynet of British duplicity and the Arabists' intentions to evict France from the Levant. Reporting in December 1943 on the Syrian leaders' role in the Lebanese crisis, he warned that British agents were using the same methods they had employed against France after World War I:

> Obstacles will be placed before us and we know by whom and we know why. Practices will be repeated like after the other war aimed at the same goal: to make the Syrians dislike the French in Syria. Those who carried this out then, the friends of Lawrence, the Claytons, Newcomb, Elphinston, are the leaders of the game today.[37]

Oliva Roget, already in his fifties when he joined Free France, had far more experience in Levantine politics than the officers who arrived with de Gaulle and Catroux. In his superiors' periodic evaluations he was described as a professional, meticulous, and authoritative but also impulsive, officer. In 1943 he was appointed Délégué Général in Damascus and Commander of the French forces in Damascus and southern Syria. His service in both civilian and military positions brought him into confrontation with General Humboldt, the Commander of the Levant Army. Contrary to the allegations leveled against him, he shared Catroux's liberal policy towards the nationalists and established close ties with many Syrian leaders, in both government and opposition. Examining the conduct of the Syrian leaders during the Lebanese crisis, he noted:

> Syria is led by people whose nature we know. We knew them before we let them come to power. We had contacts with them. We received promises, assurances from them … Can it be said that they misled us or did we mislead ourselves about them? … Events showed that the present hours were neither theirs nor ours. They belonged to England … England has its plan. It might not be to totally eliminate us from here. It is certainly not to leave France in a better position than its own. Its former agreements do not say that. But since those agreements there has been American intervention, competition over oil; there was the Russian advance and its aims in the eastern Mediterranean. England wants to deny entry. An Arab union is first of all that, and putting France aside would now make the operation easier.[38]

In the 1940s, Damascus became a center for Anglo-French and inter-Arab intrigues. Under Oliva Roget's direction, an efficient surveillance network was set up in the city, comprising hundreds of informers, some in senior positions, who reported details of meetings between the Syrian President and his ministers, and British diplomats and intelligence officers and Arab emissaries. The French security services monitored every hotel and knew of the visits of British secret agents and other foreign guests. They also tapped hundreds of telephones, including those of Quwatli, Jabiri and Mardam, as well as the British, American, Saudi and Jordanian Consulates. Oliva Roget often included the contents of those conversations in his reports to Beynet.

Oliva Roget's most successful operation was the recruitment of a senior official in the Syrian government with direct access to the offices of the President, the Prime Minister and Foreign Minister. He is described as someone "well-placed to know what is going on in the presidential palace" and Oliva Roget met with him frequently in his capacity as Délégué Général. In addition to copies of documents from Quwatli's and Mardam's offices, the agent provided high-grade up-to-date information on the Syrian leaders' views and plans, as well on their meetings with British, American and Soviet diplomats and Arab emissaries. This wealth of information enabled Oliva Roget to closely follow the Syrian leaders' most guarded secrets, in particular Mardam's intrigues with Spears, Stirling, Clayton and Nuri al-Sa'id.[39]

The French intelligence service, like other secret organizations, attached great importance to obtaining original confidential documents. In the early stages, the Syrian agent provided only a small number of such documents, but in later years he and other agents recruited by the French secret service supplied thousands more. It appears that almost the entire archive of the Syrian Foreign Ministry and most of Quwatli's personal correspondence were obtained by the Deuxième Bureau in Beirut.

The operation in the British Legation in Beirut was initiated by Oliva Roget and his staff in Damascus. Not much is known about the agent's identity apart from the fact that he was of Arab origin and had direct access to the most confidential files, including top secret operative documents, in the Legation's archives. As part of the strict security precautions, such documents were rarely sent to Paris. The documents allowed the Deuxième Bureau to learn the names of local politicians and agents collaborating with the British secret services, and their modus operandi throughout the Middle East. At a later stage, French intelligence used those details to force senior Syrian and Lebanese politicians and officials to become double agents. No details of those operations are known apart from a remark made by General Gross, Commander of the Levant Army, to an agent of the Jewish Agency during his visit to Palestine in September 1945. General Gross disclosed that the British were bribing Mardam and other Syrian officials, and that the French secret services were exploiting the information to force him and others to collaborate with them. If Mardam, a key figure in British special political operations in Syria, in inter-Arab affairs and in the Arab-Jewish conflict in Palestine, had indeed become a French double agent, it would have seriously compromised Britain's undercover activities in the Middle East in 1945-1948.[40]

Oliva Roget often attached short comments to the Syrian and British documents he sent to Beynet, providing additional details on their immediate context. Beynet then sent his comments and the documents themselves via courier to de Gaulle's office, where they were read and assessed by a young diplomat, Etienne Burin des Roziers, who served as Palewski's assistant. De Gaulle often saw the documents himself and wrote his own comments. Concurrently, Beynet sent de Gaulle private letters in which he analyzed particular documents and proposed policies.[41]

Paying back in kind

In August 1944 Quwatli, Jabiri and Mardam discerned a sharp change in Beynet's and Oliva Roget's attitudes. Their conciliatory policy had been replaced by an uncompromising stand, while allegations were made that they were conspiring to reach a secret agreement with Britain. The Syrian leaders attributed this change to renewed French confidence, now that Paris had been liberated and France was regaining its international status as a Power in

Europe. In fact, the immediate cause was Oliva Roget's operation, which had a profound impact on the senior military and intelligence officers in Beirut and Damascus. Many of the French officers and officials in the Levant were already bitter towards their British counterparts, who had been ignoring them and treating them with contempt. Their feelings of anger, resentment and helplessness were reinforced by Spears' unscrupulous anti-French attacks. The evidence of Britain's scheming to eject France from the Levant reinforced their determination to take revenge.

The Deuxième Bureau in Beirut became a center for anti-British subversion, not only in Syria and Lebanon, but throughout the Middle East. Some of its officers, such as Colonel Alessandri and his "Bureau Noir," waged their own vendetta against the British. In December 1944, the French Embassy in London asked the Delegation in Beirut for its reaction after receiving complaints from the Foreign Office that a certain secret officer – Colonel Alessandri – was assisting anti-British Arab and Jewish terrorist groups in Palestine. Officials in the delegation accused British agents of helping local anti-French elements, but were critical of Alessandri's unilateral activities among the Syrian government's opponents. MacKereth, who attempted to find out if Alessandri was acting with Beynet's tacit permission, received only a vague answer. In fact, Beynet, who had arrived in the Levant in early 1944, was not always in full control of the French intelligence apparatus, which was deeply divided between former Vichy and Free French officers. The Deuxième Bureau in Paris often complained that it was not receiving reports from its office in Beirut. In these circumstances local intelligence officers took the opportunity to act unilaterally. Alessandri and the "Bureau Noir" were an extreme example.[42]

Operation Oliva Roget and the discovery of the extent of British anti-French subversion, coupled with the large quantity of Syrian and British documents received, compelled the French secret services in the Levant to reorganize. New intelligence officers arrived from Algiers, while the Deuxième Bureau in Beirut and Damascus and the secret and security services now closely monitored the British agents directly involved in covert anti-French activities, as well as Syrian and Lebanese politicians collaborating with them. After September 1944, there was an increase in the number of intelligence reports on the activities of these agents, especially Clayton, Stirling, Altounyan and the Marsack brothers, together with Colonel Furlonge, Marun Arab and other political officers in the Spears Mission. Mardam's and Sulh's telephone conversations and their meetings with British officials were also monitored.

The wealth of information gleaned by French intelligence from the Syrian and British documents, and the subsequent use of Syrian and British politicians as double agents, enabled the Deuxième Bureau to conduct effective and extremely damaging undercover operations against Britain's position in the Middle East. The extensive use by the British secret services of special political operations made them particularly vulnerable to French subversion. Moreover, the accurate information received about Britain's covert Middle

East policy and the inter-Arab rivalry enabled de Gaulle and Bidault in Paris, Beynet and Ostrorog in Beirut, and Oliva Roget in Damascus to conduct efficient clandestine diplomacy.

French subversion from September 1944 to May 1948 can be divided into three phases. In the first, from September 1944 until May 1945, the French made cautious use of undercover operations to counter British intrigues and to secure treaties with the two Levant states. In the second phase, from the Syrian crisis in June 1945 until de Gaulle's resignation in January 1946, French covert operations became more vindictive and aggressive. The French intelligence helped known anti-British and anti-Hashemite Arab leaders – Rashid Ali al-Gailani and the ex-Mufti Amin al-Husseini – to undermine British interests in the region, while the Franco-Zionist tacit collaboration against Britain solidified. Nevertheless, despite de Gaulle's ambivalent stand, Bidault continued to seek an Anglo-French entente in the Levant; he exploited Labour's rise to power to reach an agreement with Bevin in December 1945. In the third phase, under Bidault and the Fourth Republic, France's policy in the Middle East mirrored that of Britain. It adopted "parallel" policies: seeking an entente in Europe while allowing the secret war with the British in the Middle East to continue unabated. The most effective anti-British weapon used by the French secret services at this stage was their clandestine collaboration with the Jewish Agency, which culminated in the war of 1948.

Intelligence services maintain the utmost secrecy over their use of CPA because of its controversial nature. The French intelligence officers, familiar with British security and secret service capabilities and the possible repercussions for Anglo-French relations were their anti-British activities discovered, took extreme precautions to conceal them. Nevertheless, the Syrian documents, British messages to the Syrian leaders and indiscreet reports by Beynet, Oliva Roget and other senior military officers, together with British and Zionist sources, provide details of the French undercover operations, which were accompanied by overt and covert diplomacy. Their goal was to counter Britain's anti-French intrigues in the Levant and North Africa while undermining its interests in the Middle East. Syria and Lebanon became the primary arena for French special operations, although they also extended to Palestine, Egypt, Saudi Arabia, Transjordan, Iraq and Yemen. The French secret services scored impressive achievements in this clandestine war, particularly as their British counterparts continued to underestimate their capabilities.

In mid-September 1944, Ostrorog met with Lord Moyne, Brigadier Clayton and other senior British officials in Cairo and urged them to assist France in securing treaties with Syria and Lebanon. Lord Moyne's response that the Syrian and Lebanese leaders opposed such treaties was far from convincing, as Ostrorog well knew that a month earlier Clayton and other British agents had, with Lord Moyne's blessing, tried to force President Quwatli to acquiesce in a secret agreement with Britain. Ostrorog also knew that, contrary to Eden's instructions, Spears was pressing the Syrian and Lebanese governments to reject France's proposals for treaties. In their reports to Paris, Beynet, Ostrorog and Oliva Roget pointed to the disparities between statements made by Churchill and Eden in London that France should retain a privileged position in Syria and Lebanon similar to that of Britain in Iraq – and the anti-French subversive activities of the local British officials. Expectations that such activities would cease after Spears' departure were not met. In London, Spears continued his anti-French campaign, and although the new British Minister in Syria and Lebanon, Ernest Shone, was more amenable, his goals were no different than those of his predecessor.[43]

Although only part of the French covert activities in the period prior to the Syrian crisis is known, it can be ascertained that they took place on four levels: locally in Syria and Lebanon; in inter-Arab relations; vis-à-vis the Zionist movement; and vis-à-vis the Soviet Union. Lebanon became the first region in which the French sought to regain their influence. Emile Eddé and a small number of pro-French, anti-Khurist Maronite leaders were informed of Riyad al-Sulh's and Mardam's intrigues and secret collaboration with British agents against an independent Lebanese state. In fact, Raymond Eddé, Emile Eddé's son, took part in French undercover operations (doc.23). Messages were conveyed to Patriarch Arida and other Maronite bishops, as well as to the Lebanese Phalangist Party on the Anglo-Hashemite conspiracy against Christian Lebanon, in which, it was alleged, Sulh was involved. The outspoken Bishop Mubarak of Beirut, who had previously criticized the French mandate, began to campaign for safeguarding Lebanon's independence under French protection. Pro-French Christian newspapers were urged to warn of the danger inherent in the Arab unity plans and called on President Khuri to defend Lebanon. Under increased Maronite pressure, Sulh was forced to reassure Patriarch Arida that he had no intention of jeopardizing Lebanon's independence in Alexandria. And indeed, during the discussions there, Sulh adopted a cautious stand, leading Nuri al-Sa'id to remark that Lebanon was a "thorn in the Arab nations' side" (doc.17). The French, who continued to view Sulh as a threat to their position in Lebanon, were involved behind the scenes in forcing him out of office in January 1945. His resignation allowed the French delegation to sow discord between Lebanon and Syria more effectively.[44]

From September 1944 until May 1945, Syria became a major arena for French undercover activities to counter British designs to incorporate it into a Greater Syria and unite it with Iraq. After his role in the secret Anglo-Hashemite plans was discovered, Mardam became the main target of French covert operations aimed at discrediting him and forcing his resignation. Reports of his secret agreement with Nuri al-Sa'id were leaked to President Quwatli, Prime Minister Jabiri and his main rival in the government, the Minister of the Interior Sabri al-Asali. The close collaboration between Mardam, and Nuri al-Sa'id and British diplomats during the Alexandria Congress reinforced doubts among his fellow ministers about his loyalty to an independent Syrian republic. Indeed, the agent told Captain Cristofini, Oliva

Roget's deputy, that Mardam had become "more English than the English themselves."[45] The French also leaked copies of Mardam's secret agreement with Nuri al-Sa'id from September 1944 to King Faruq via Raymond Eddé, as well as to King Ibn Sa'ud. Mardam's failure to promote the Greater Syria plan during the discussions in Alexandria and Cairo prompted Emir Abdullah to write to his nephew, the Iraqi Regent Abd al-Ilah, criticizing Nuri al-Sa'id's reliance on Mardam, whom the Hashemites had paid handsomely (docs.36, 45). The French failed, however, to force Mardam's resignation owing to the backing he received from Colonel Stirling and other British agents who pressured President Quwatli to keep him in power. Aware that French agents were conspiring against him, Mardam adopted an even more vindictive attitude.

The French stance towards Quwatli was ambivalent. Oliva Roget regarded him as an opportunistic politician, pointing to his willingness to accord Britain a privileged status in Syria on condition that it gave up its plans for a Hashemite Greater Syria. He also saw him as a weak, frail President, unable to withstand British pressure and Mardam's scheming. Beynet, however, feared that his resignation would open the way for Mardam to gain the presidency. Quwatli's ability to withstand the pressure from Spears and Clayton in August and September enhanced his standing in the General Delegation. Moreover, Quwatli was supported by Ibn Sa'ud, the Hashemites' main opponent. The secret Saudi-Syrian agreement of March 1944 and Quwatli's correspondence with the Saudi King convinced Beynet and Ostrorog that he was the best barrier against British and Hashemite ambitions. His coordination of the Syrian stand in deliberations on the Arab union in Alexandria and Cairo with Ibn Sa'ud and the secret alliance he formed with the Saudi and Egyptian monarchs in February 1945 reinforced the French decision to help him behind the scenes to retain the presidency (doc.27). During their conversations with Quwatli, Beynet and Oliva Roget tried to convince him that France was not Syria's enemy and that an alliance between the two states would protect Syria's independence against Hashemite and Turkish ambitions. Nevertheless, at the moment of truth, Quwatli caved in, as Oliva Roget had warned, and agreed to incorporate Syria into a Greater Syria and place it under tacit British hegemony. From his correspondence with Kings Ibn Sa'ud and Faruq in 1944-1947, and Barazi's reports to Colonel Stirling, Quwatli appears as an ill-fated leader, a victim of his own ambitions, the intrigues of his rivals, especially Mardam, and the inter-Arab and Anglo-French secret wars over Syria (docs.75, 77, 79-80, 91-2). But it was precisely his weakness that helped him to remain in power throughout 1943-49.[46]

Oliva Roget also tried to bolster the government's opponents. After frequent meetings with Bahij al-Khatib, the former Prime Minister, he concluded that the opposition was weak and that its leaders merely expected France to help them regain power. Far more effective were the undercover operations, reinforcing the resistance of the minorities – the Alawis, Druze, Kurds and Christians – to a Sunni-Arab nationalist government. Throughout the inter-war years, the French High Commission implemented a "minorities" policy aimed at strengthening the separatist tendencies of the minority communities against the central government in Damascus. Catroux, who had been advocating an agreement with the Sunni Muslim majority and the nationalists in Damascus since 1941, was willing to relinquish France's close ties with the minorities. But Beynet, after uncovering the collaboration between the nationalists and British secret agents, reverted to the "minorities" policy. The French now began to back the minority groups' demands for greater autonomy, fueling their fears of an Iraqi take-over of Syria.

Oliva Roget used his close relations with prominent families in Jabal Druze, already fearful of government intentions to dismantle their region's administrative autonomy, to strengthen their opposition to Damascus. In the Alawi region, agents of the Officiers Spéciaux backed Suleiman al-Murshid, who led an Alawi religio-political separatist movement. In that region, French officers encountered their British rivals who were attempting to encourage Alawi leaders to collaborate with the central government. The Alawis' rebellious movement ended when Murshid was executed for treason in December 1946. French agents were also active among the Kurds in the Jazira, reinforcing their fears of a Syrian-Iraqi union. Their activities coincided with those of Soviet emissaries, who also sought to toughen Kurdish resistance to an Iraqi-Syrian union dominated by Britain. Christian communities in the Jazira, which included Armenians, Syrian Orthodox, Syrian Catholics and Assyro-Chaldeans, became another target of the French scare campaign. French agents stressed the danger for the Christian minorities of an independent Syrian state, pointing to the fate of the Armenians in Turkey and the Assyrians in Iraq. Of special significance were the relations between Beynet, Ostrorog and Cardinal Ignace Gabriel Tapuni, head of the small Syrian Catholic Church in the Jazira, as the latter was involved in French efforts to mobilize the Holy See's support for France's continued protection of the Christian communities in Syria and Lebanon. Beynet and Ostrorog shared details of the Oliva Roget operation with Cardinal Tapuni and frequently took his advice on policy-making.[47]

Ibn Sa'ud's correspondence with Quwatli, which the French followed closely, reveal his pivotal role in sustaining the Syrian President's opposition to British and Hashemite ambitions over Syria. De Gaulle and Catroux had begun cultivating Free France's relations with the Saudi monarch in 1943, but after the extent of British subversion in Syria became known, secret collaboration with Ibn Sa'ud solidified and played an important part in French policy against the designs of the Hashemites and their British sponsors to take over Syria. The French Mission in Jeddah was upgraded, while Beynet leaked incriminating documents to Saudi officials about Mardam's cooperation with the Hashemites and British secret agents. Oliva Roget and Captain Cristofini met with Saudi emissaries, including Yusuf Yasin, Ibn Sa'ud's Secretary of Foreign Affairs, who often came to Damascus to confer with Quwatli.[48]

The secret Radwa Agreement (doc.24) between Kings Ibn Sa'ud and Faruq in early February 1945 further underscores the Saudi monarch's central role in the anti-Hashemite coalition. Although the agreement was directed against the Hashemites, it was also aimed at Britain's attempts to retain its dominance over the Middle East. Quwatli's visit to Riyadh and his joining the Saudi-Egyptian alliance reinforced the Saudi King's role in sustaining his resistance to the British and Hashemite pressure. The success of this triple alliance in frustrating the designs of British officials and Nuri al-Sa'id to further the Greater Syria plan during deliberations on the formation of the Arab League in Cairo highlights its importance. Ibn Sa'ud's efforts to convince Quwatli to reach an understanding with France added to his credit among French decision-makers in Beirut and Paris. Nevertheless, on May 29, 1945, the Saudi monarch failed to prevent Quwatli from caving in to British pressure. After learning of Quwatli's concessions to Shone and Paget, Ibn Sa'ud stepped up pressure on the Syrian President to renege on his undertakings.

In early March 1945 Beynet left for Paris, where he remained for over two months, to gain time until the war was over and France was better positioned to impose its own terms on Syria. In Paris he established contact with Adnan al-Atasi, the new Syrian Minister Plenipotentiary. He must have been pleased to read Atasi's dispatches to Damascus endorsing an agreement with France. When the Quai d'Orsay learned that Britain had no intention of allowing Syria to take part in the Peace Conference, laying the blame on France, it informed the Syrian government that France did support Syria's participation. After assuring Abdullah that Britain would not back Syria's request to go to San Francisco, the Foreign Office reversed its position, taking credit for its invitation to the Peace Conference, while British diplomats in Cairo and Damascus accused France of claiming credit for an act in which it had taken no part (docs.42-3).

The "missing dimension" in de Gaulle-Churchill relations

One of the perils of providing leaders with raw intelligence material directly is that they may make policy decisions at odds with their assessment agencies. Churchill was known for insisting on receiving raw intelligence information decoded by the Government Code and Cypher School (GC&CS). Unlike Churchill, de Gaulle, who was exposed to the Syrian and British documents, lacked an organized assessment apparatus to place them in their wider context and recommend policy options. He distrusted the Quai d'Orsay, many of whose diplomats had served under Vichy. Bidault, the new Foreign Minister, lacked experience in international affairs and certainly had no knowledge of the complexity of Middle East politics, while Catroux had lost much of his prestige after the discovery of the extent of Britain's anti-French subversive operations. In January 1945, Catroux became the new French Ambassador to Moscow. Beynet, with whom de Gaulle corresponded directly, took part in policy-making, but had limited influence on his leader. From October 1944 until May 1945, de Gaulle alone defined French policy in the Levant. The breakdown of this policy in the Syrian crisis was his personal failure, raising the fundamental question of whether it is always helpful for a decision maker to know of his opponent's intentions. In the Syrian crisis, de Gaulle was aware of the British ploys, yet failed to foil them. In this regard, the results of both crises – the Lebanese in 1943 and the Syrian in 1945 – were the same: a French defeat by superior British forces. It was precisely because he knew about Britain's duplicity that de Gaulle hardened his stance and rejected Bidault's initiative to seek a compromise with Churchill and Eden. His intransigence eventually backfired and France lost its position in the Levant.[49]

There have been many studies of de Gaulle's tense relations with Churchill during World War II. Historians point out that it was in the Levant that the two leaders clashed directly, and often quote de Gaulle's allegations that the British government and its agents in the Middle East purposely provoked the crises in the Levant to oust France. Most of the studies place more emphasis on de Gaulle's strong reactions and his deep suspicion, bordering on Anglophobia, than on British provocations. The British and Syrian documents provide the "missing dimension" in our understanding of de Gaulle's attitude towards Churchill while he was serving as head of the provisional government in Paris. One can imagine his feelings as he read, a few days after Churchill's brutal ultimatum, the British Prime Minister's instructions to General Paget: "The prestige of France in Syria and in Lebanon has annoyed us very much up to now. And it is necessary to abolish it once and for all" (docs.97-9), or Richard Law's instructions to General Paget: "The most interesting point is to make believe that all terror has been inspired by General de Gaulle" (doc.102). In fact, the British propaganda machine carried out these instructions efficiently, and in the weeks following the Syrian crisis, portrayed de Gaulle in the media in London, Paris and Washington as an Anglophobe consumed by an irrational hatred of Britain, whose soldiers had just fought to liberate France from Nazi occupation. De Gaulle, who had always believed that Spears would not have acted without Churchill's tacit approval, found it difficult to grasp that Churchill himself had become victim of a smear campaign orchestrated against him and France by Britain's powerful Middle East establishment.[50]

De Gaulle, like many Frenchmen of his generation, was biased against Britain. But the warm reception accorded him in London by the British government and public after his escape from France in June 1940, and Churchill's support for him and his movement during the dark years, led him to see Britain differently – as a brave, confident nation determined to fight against the odds, that had allocated part of its scarce resources to help his movement liberate France. But in the subsequent years his relations with Churchill deteriorated, especially after Churchill sided with President Roosevelt, who held Free France and de Gaulle in contempt. The conflict in the Levant did not detract from his personal gratitude to the British Prime Minister, as demonstrated during the latter's historic visit to Paris in November 1944, but the Syrian and British documents revived his old belief in Britain's perfidy. References in his personal letters and memoranda reveal the depth of his distrust: "I have no confidence in the English; they take and retain a hypo-critical attitude" and, "the reality and duplicity of the policy in London" or, "the stupid greed of our allies here (in the Levant)."[51]

An intriguing question with as yet no clear answer is how far de Gaulle's uncovering of Britain's subversion against France in the Levant and North Africa influenced his European policy. Could de Gaulle have separated France's national interests, which necessitated collaboration with Britain, from his own feelings after learning that Spears and British officials in the Middle East were targeting him personally? He was greatly disappointed that he had not been invited to the "Big Three" summit in Yalta. Minutes he received from Beynet of President Roosevelt's conversations with Ibn Sa'ud (doc.26) and Faruq, as well as of those between Churchill and Ibn Sa'ud (doc.28) and Faruq and Quwatli in Febuary 1945, reinforced his conviction that the two Anglo-Saxon Powers were seeking to expel France from the Middle East and secure their dominance over the region, especially control of its rich oil resources.[52]

While there is no clear answer regarding the extent to which the operation staged by Oliva Roget affected de Gaulle's European policy, there is no doubt as to its immediate effect on his policy in the Levant. Between October 1944 and May 1945, his Middle East policy was considerably influenced by the information he gleaned from the British and Syrian documents he received from Beynet. Since December 1943 he had reluctantly adopted Catroux's "dual" policy of pursuing a compromise with the Syrian and Lebanese nationalist governments while seeking to circumvent Spears and the locally-based British officials and negotiate directly with Whitehall. But after October 1944, it became apparent that any French concessions in Syria and Lebanon would be exploited by Britain to take over the Levant. In the ensuing months, de Gaulle hardened his position; he insisted on treaties with Syria and Leba-non guaranteeing France's strategic, economic and cultural interests before making any further concessions. He adopted a wait-and-see policy, assuming that when the war was over France would be in a better position to extract concessions from Britain and the two Levant states. The information he received on Syrian resistance to the British-sponsored Greater Syria and the alliance between Ibn Sa'ud and Faruq against the Hashemites reinforced his confidence, especially after he learned of the British failure to implement its schemes for a Hashemite Greater Syria and a Syrian-Iraqi union during the deliberations in Alexandria and Cairo. But de Gaulle was not seeking merely to gain time; he allowed his secret services in Syria and Lebanon to actively carry out undercover operations against Britain's interests in the Middle East. He was personally involved in CD as he sought to strengthen ties with Kings Ibn Sa'ud and Faruq. He communicated directly with the Saudi monarch and, on his way to Moscow at the end of December, stopped in Cairo and met with the Egyptian King. His overtures took place while Beynet was leaking incriminatory documents about the British and Iraqi subversion in Syria to the two monarchs.

De Gaulle's firm stand on the Levant and his attempts to gain time were not without risk. Bidault, who suspected that de Gaulle was too emotionally attached to the region, believed that the provisional government should compromise in Syria and Lebanon, as its relations with Britain in Europe, especially on the German question, were far more important for France's national interests. He therefore advocated a liberal policy towards the two Levant states despite knowing of the British agents' anti-French activities there. De Gaulle's Levant policy was also opposed by members of the Constituent Assembly, as well as the French press, which criticized his clashes with Churchill in Syria and Lebanon when France desperately needed Britain's assistance to rebuild its economy and standing in Europe. Communist and socialist deputies in the Assembly condemned his "reactionary" policy towards the Syrian and Lebanese nationalists who were striving for independence.[53]

Beynet, who was to implement de Gaulle's Levant policy, had his own reservations. At the end of January 1945 he sent de Gaulle a personal letter arguing that France had three options: reach an agreement with Britain; collaborate with the Soviet Union; or strengthen its military presence in Syria and Lebanon. The second option coincided with de Gaulle's attempts at the end of 1944 to bolster France's relations with the Soviet Union as a counterweight to the Anglo-American alliance. But Franco-Soviet collaboration in the Middle East was fraught with danger, as it could provoke Britain's ire. As for Beynet's third option, the British High Command in the Middle East opposed the dispatch of French reinforcements, suspecting that de Gaulle might use military force to restore France's position. Subsequently, de Gaulle's attempts to pressure Britain and improve France's position in the forthcoming negotiations on the Levant backfired. He failed to take into account the ability of the powerful Arabist circles in London and the Middle East, backed by the High Command in Cairo, to win over their vacillating Prime Minister, and convince him that de Gaulle could not be trusted and that Britain ought to bring an end to France's presence in the Levant[54] (docs.95-6).

Orchestrating the Syrian crisis

Addressing officials of the Ministry of Information in Cairo at the end of December 1944 when de Gaulle was meeting with King Faruq, Brigadier Clayton warned of the "shattering effect" that the re-establishment of France in the Levant would have on Britain's standing in the Arab world. As head of PICME, Clayton had been receiving reports from the British secret services and the Beirut and Damascus Legations of increased French subversion against Britain's interests. France, he had learned, was stepping up its covert collaboration with Ibn Sa'ud to undermine British plans for a Hashemite Greater Syria and a Syro-Iraqi union. French agents were also bolstering King Faruq's opposition to the Hashemites. Security and secret agencies were particularly concerned with reports of clandestine cooperation between officers of the Deuxième Bureau and Zionist agents, as well as between French officials and Soviet envoys in the Levant. Information on de Gaulle's intentions to reinforce the French Army in the Levant was worrisome; the unpredictable French leader might use force to impose treaties securing France's strategic and economic position in Syria and Lebanon. Another source of concern for the Arabists and military in Cairo was that following his historic visit to liberated Paris, Churchill had become more disposed to support Eden's conciliatory policy towards France in the Levant. The present British Cabinet, the Arabists feared, was about to repeat the mistake made by Lloyd George's government in 1919.[55]

In contrast to the Foreign Office, which favored an agreement with France in the Levant, the British authorities in the Middle East gave priority to safeguarding their country's strategic and economic interests in the region. The Arab unity plans they had been promoting since 1941 were perceived as a means to retain Britain's supremacy over the Middle East in the face of a growing tide of nationalism in Egypt and Iraq. A Syro-Iraqi union would strengthen two weak Arab states that were vulnerable to external subversion, while a Greater Syria would facilitate a solution to the Jewish question in Palestine without creating an independent Jewish state. Lord Moyne's assassination and the increasing Soviet propaganda and subversion in Iraq and Syria were seen by the Arabists as validation of the policy they had been pursuing all along. As the war was coming to a close, the feeling of urgency intensified among them and the military circles in Cairo; but while France still remained in the Levant it was impossible to implement their plans. Backed by General Paget and the secret service agencies, Arabist intelligence agents began, in the early months of 1945, a covert campaign to undercut Eden's attempts to further a Franco-Syrian agreement and mobilize support for France's eviction. Winning Churchill's endorsement was central to their strategy.[56]

In early January, Brigadier Clayton traveled to Beirut and Damascus to contend with the outcome of Spears' departure. Pro-British Syrian and Lebanese politicians, who had become targets of French subversion, feared that with the government in London seeking an agreement with France, local British officials would no longer be able to help them. President Khuri was the first to sense the change in the Anglo-French balance of power. Under pressure from his own community, he withdrew his support for Prime Minister Sulh, forcing him to resign. Beynet tried to replace Sulh with the pro-French Abdullah al-Yafi, but Khuri, pressed by Clayton and Furlonge, nominated the anti-French Abd al-Hamid Karameh as Lebanon's new Prime Minister. Whether due to the rough treatment by the two British officers or the death of his close friend, Selim Taqla, Khuri suffered a nervous breakdown a few days later and was taken secretly to Haifa for treatment. During his visit to Lebanon, Brigadier Clayton also met with Patriarch Arida and warned him that Britain would not support an independent Lebanese state were it to serve as a base for French influence in the region.[57]

President Quwatli, however, proved to be better able to withstand British pressure than his Lebanese counterpart. After the failure of the August initiative to reach a secret agreement with Syria, Clayton and other British agents saw the Syrian President as the main obstacle to their plans for regional reorganization. They were well aware of Quwatli's secret alliance with Ibn Sa'ud and Faruq, but their scare tactics – intimidating him with an Anglo-French rapprochement or threatening that British forces would not defend Syria if France used force – were no longer effective. Confident of the Saudi sovereign's support, and thus American backing, Quwatli began to view Britain, rather than France, as the main threat to Syria's independence and his own position. In fact, the threat of replacing him with Mardam remained the most efficient British tool for pressuring him.

Mardam, who became Acting Prime Minister in early April, played a central role in the British anti-French undercover operations. He closely coordinated his moves with Colonel Stirling, who had stepped into the vacuum left by Spears' departure. Mardam was required to serve his British masters, as well as the Hashemites, with whom he had concluded a secret deal and from whom he was receiving large sums of money, all the while promoting his own ambitions to replace Quwatli. His immediate goal was to prevent Ibn Sa'ud from persuading Quwatli to negotiate with France. He was criticized in Cabinet by Sabri al-Asali and deputies in parliament and by his ministers in Paris, London and Washington for his over-reliance on British support. But he was undeterred, and while waiting for France to make the first move, he exploited the dispute over the Troupes Spéciales to confront French representatives (docs. 77, 91).

Two weeks after Clayton's visit, Mardam and Stirling instigated large-scale anti-French demonstrations in Damascus and Aleppo. The demonstrators, mostly university and secondary-school students, came out against a treaty with France and demanded the formation of a "National Army," namely the transfer of the Troupes Spéciales to government control. Stirling's and Mardam's immediate goal was to prove to decision-makers in London that the Foreign Office's policy of helping France to impose treaties on the local governments would spark disorder and jeopardize the freedom of action of the British forces in the Levant. Indeed, in their meetings with their French counterparts, British diplomats claimed to have been surprised by the intensity of the opposition to France in Syria and that the local protests proved that France should be more accommodating with regard to its future status in the Levant. In Paris and Beirut, however, where the role of British secret officers in instigating the demonstrations was known, it was seen as further proof of both the British government's inability to control its agents in the field and its duplicity. Oliva Roget, who closely followed Clayton's meetings with Syrian and Lebanese politicians and was well aware of Mardam's and Stirling's role in provoking the protests, defined them as a "project" of the British secret services. President Quwatli apparently shared this belief, as he instructed Mardam to complain to Shone of the British intelligence officers' interference in Syria's affairs. French officials were reassured by Quwatli's reaction and his instructions to the head of police to prevent further anti-French protests. They were also pleased to witness the tension between Wadsworth, the American Minister in Syria and Lebanon, and the British diplomats after British secret agents in northern Syria had instigated anti-American demonstrations against Washington's support for the Zionist cause. It is worth noting Wadsworth's warning to Mardam, which indicates that the American diplomat knew of the British agents' game:

> America does not mean to be treated in this country in the same way as France. If the French receive and swallow insults, the Americans are not inclined to put up with the demonstrators' affronts and insults … . I know that the latest activities are not spontaneous. Various elements took part in organizing them. We know the exact involvement of particular Englishmen, just as we know how far French officials encouraged certain demonstrators in order to deter them from any action against France, but we advise the Syrian Government, if it really wants America's friendship, not to tolerate such demonstrations. (doc.46)

In the post-war years, Britain's reputation in the Middle East often exceeded its true ability to control the region. Even before the war ended, it had been losing ground. What Quwatli and Ibn Sa'ud believed to be sophisticated British ploys intended to pressure Syria frequently resulted from wavering policy. British efforts to deter the Syrian President from teaming up with the Saudi-Egyptian anti-Hashemite alliance backfired. Attempts by Nuri al-Sa'id and Mardam to use the anti-French protests as a pretext for the Iraqi Army to enter Syria prompted Quwatli to appeal for Ibn Sa'ud's intervention. The British also failed to prevent Quwatli's visit to Riyadh. His discussions with Ibn Sa'ud and his subsequent meetings with Kings Faruq and Ibn Sa'ud in Faiyum near Cairo on the eve of the Arab unity congress in Cairo marked his joining the Saudi-Egyptian axis. The Saudi and Egyptian monarchs enhanced their prestige, with Egypt becoming the dominant force in the newly established Arab League. In contrast, Britain's loyal allies, the Hashemites, lost ground. The change in the inter-Arab balance of power was demonstrated in the deliberations on the establishment of the Arab League, when Nuri al-Sa'id, who had initiated the formation of an Arab union, failed to promote his plans for a Greater Syria and an Iraqi-Syrian union (docs.33, 35-6, 41). His failure was also the failure of the British Arabists, who had been promoting these plans. It is therefore not surprising that British officials in Cairo and London were initially ambivalent towards the Arab League, fearing that it could be used against Britain. Only after the Arabists secured the collaboration of its Secretary General, Abd al-Rahman al-Azzam, did the Arab League turn into an expedient tool in their covert Middle East policy. In fact, after 1945 Azzam became, no less than Nuri al-Sa'id, a pivotal partner in their covert operations and clandestine diplomacy in the region.[58]

Quwatli's reports to his Cabinet on his discussions with Ibn Sa'ud highlight the latter's deep suspicion of British intentions. The Saudi monarch was convinced that the Hashemites would not have attempted to take over Syria without British support. Furthermore, he feared that British agents would force him out of the *Hejaz* and from Islam's two holiest cities, over which he had taken control two decades earlier after expelling his Hashemite rivals. He undoubtedly shared his concerns with American diplomats in Riyadh and Jeddah, as well as with President Roosevelt and his successor, Harry Truman, who knew of the British intrigues against their principal Arab ally. From the Saudi minutes of Ibn Sa'ud's meeting with Churchill, and from Quwatli's reports, it is evident that the three Arab leaders were aware of the divergence between the British Cabinet and its agents in the region, which left them uncertain as to who was actually defining Britain's Arab policy. This divergence was apparent in the Greater Syria plan. The minutes of the meeting with Churchill quote the British Prime Minister as stating:

> As far as Greater Syria and Syrian-Lebanese independence are concerned ... It is true ... that at one particular moment there was a question mark over this but England cannot insist on a plan which is, on the one hand, rejected by the Syrian people and, on the other, is considered, by the king, Abd al-Aziz, our close friend, to be prejudicial to him and the interests of his family. As a result, nothing will therefore be done in the way Nuri Said wants. (docs.28-30)

Despite their Prime Minister's undertaking, the Arabists and senior military officers in Cairo were resolute in promoting the Greater Syria and Iraqi-Syrian unity plans. They continued to believe that they could win the support of Churchill and the War Cabinet to eject France from the Levant, thereby opening the way to reorganizing the Fertile Crescent states under Britain's tutelage and solving the Jewish question in Palestine. They found willing partners in Spears, retired Arabist diplomats and officers and financial circles in London.

On January 17, 1945, Spears addressed members of the Royal Empire Society, stressing the strategic and economic importance of the Middle East for the British Empire and arguing that Britain should seek friendly relations with the Arab world. France's presence in the Levant and the Zionist ambitions in Palestine were, in his view, the main obstacles for Britain in securing its interests in the region. In the coming months he led violent anti-French and anti-Zionist campaigns. Reports from the French Embassy in London provide details of his activities, which often assumed a "Gaullephobic" character. Spears was regarded as an "expert" on the Middle East, especially the Levant, and often had the opportunity to air his anti-French views to the British public. He was determined to prove to Churchill that, in contrast to the stance of Eden and Foreign Office diplomats, his warnings of de Gaulle's Anglophobia were justified. As previously mentioned, Spears had become a paid adviser of the Syrian government while promoting his personal business interests in Syria and Lebanon. He continued to be involved in the activities of the British secret services and coordinated his actions with Arabist intelligence officers in the region. Dispatches from Najib al-Armanazi, the Syrian Minister in London, on his meetings with Spears and other British diplomats and businessmen shed light on their views and goals. Armanazi warned that influential British circles continued to promote Greater Syria, pointing to (docs.66, 69, 129) the remark by the editor of the *Economist* that even Mardam, the Syrian Foreign Minister, supported this plan. This must have seemed strange to Armanazi when he reported it to Damascus. From his accounts it also emerges that the Soviet threat to the Middle East was becoming a major source of concern in London.[59]

Despite the undercover activities of the British secret services in the Middle East and the campaigns by Spears and the pro-Arabist lobby groups in London, it was the changing perception of the Soviet Union – from war ally to a threat to the British Empire – that hardened Churchill's attitude towards France's presence in the Levant. After Yalta, France became entangled in the already tense Anglo-Soviet relations. Britain's Middle East strategy and its policy towards France were increasingly determined by its strategic interests in the face of the emerging hostile Soviet Union. This was highlighted in a series of strategic studies by the Post-Hostilities Planning Staff (PHPS) warning that the Soviet Union would launch a general war in 1956. The Middle East was assumed to be one of the first regions to come under direct Soviet attack.[60]

By the end of 1944, the Foreign Office and the Chiefs of Staff (COS) had become divided over the perceived threat that the Soviet Union would pose to Great Britain after the war. Eden did not share the military's alarmist views and rejected the premise that Britain's strategic interests in the Middle East required the ejection of France, which could not be trusted in the event of war with the Soviet Union. After the Yalta summit, Churchill, who had initially shared Eden's views regarding the need for an Anglo-French entente in Europe and the Middle East, began to side with the military and the secret services to end France's presence in the Levant. It can be assumed that de Gaulle's overtures to the Soviet Union and reports of increasing Soviet subversion in the Middle East influenced Churchill's change of heart. His deep suspicion of de Gaulle's claimed Anglophobia and the British secret service reports on French subversion in the Middle East undoubtedly played a part. Already in January 1945, Spears noted in his diary that Churchill had promised that "one day he would fire a last broadside at de Gaulle which ought to settle him; that would be to remind him of the fact that I had brought him out of France. He said the French could obviously not keep their position or indeed remain in the Middle East but we ought not to be the people to push them out."[61] And yet, until the last minute, Churchill sought to avoid a direct clash with de Gaulle. He obviously did not realize that the French leader was aware of the British intrigues and was not about to yield without a show of force. But contrary to de Gaulle's assumption that he would ultimately back down, Churchill took action after his secret services in Syria provided him with the necessary pretext. His assessment that de Gaulle's policy of confronting Britain over the Levant was not popular among French politicians and the public proved accurate.

General Paget played a central role in evicting France from Syria and Lebanon. He sought to transform Syria into a permanent British army base and integrate it in a strategic regional defense organization together with Turkey, Iraq, Transjordan and Palestine. He pursued a more hard-line policy towards the French Army, formally under his command, and aggressively promoted the arming of the Syrian Gendarmerie to counter the Troupes Spéciales under French control. At a meeting with Churchill in Cairo in October 1944 he warned that de Gaulle might attempt to reinforce the French forces in the Levant. And despite Foreign Office opposition, he formed an Anglo-French military committee, thus allowing British officers to intervene in issues that he claimed fell under his military jurisdiction. The Syrian and British documents provide ample examples of Paget's involvement in covert anti-French operations in the months prior to the crisis. His part in the secret negotiations with Quwatli and Mardam in June and July illustrate his key role in expelling France and placing Syria under Britain's tacit control.[62]

On April 1, the Middle East War Council (MEWC), chaired by Sir Edward Grigg, the Resident Minister, convened in Faiyum for a five-day conference to define its policies to the War Cabinet on Britain's Middle East policy. The participants, including top military officers and senior diplomats, addressed key issues, including Britain's stand towards the Arab League, the Soviet threat, the growing American economic competition, and the question of Palestine in the aftermath of Lord Moyne's assassination. With regard to Palestine, Grigg wrote a comprehensive memorandum which Killearn hoped would "kill Partition."[63] Of immediate concern was France's future in Syria and Lebanon. The policy defined by the MEWC in the two Levant states largely reflected Arabist thinking, especially that of the PICME and its director, Brigadier Clayton; it was implemented after Churchill was persuaded to give the go-ahead (doc.56). Article 5 of the MEWC instructions, which Grigg sent to the military and intelligence agencies and senior British officials in the Middle East, reads: "Fight as much as possible against the French intrigues in Syria and Lebanon. Keep secret our fights and do not give any proof of our fighting them." Secret service agents were instructed to undermine French commercial and financial interests in the two Levant states, especially that of the Banque de Syrie et du Liban. The need to keep the anti-French subversion in utmost secrecy was also underlined by Alexander Cadogan, the Permanent Under-Secretary at the Foreign Office. He sent telegrams to Grigg and the British Legation in Beirut stressing that "It is strictly forbidden to give any proof whatsoever that we are against the French," and that they should secretly promote the Greater Syria plan (doc.49). Copies of Grigg's instructions and Cadogan's telegrams were on de Gaulle's desk a week after they reached the British Legation in Beirut.

Following their failure in the formation of the Arab League, Nuri al-Sa'id and Emir Abdullah, with British tacit support, stepped up pressure on Quwatli. Abdullah, seeking to promote his own ambitions in Syria and Lebanon, planned to send his popular son, Crown Prince Talal, on a trip to Damascus and Beirut (docs.50, 68). After Syrian government objections, Talal had to restrict himself to a trip to Beirut. His visit there in mid-April and meetings with Karameh and leading Muslim and Christian politicians aroused deep concern in Damascus. Although Mardam met with Karameh to coordinate a joint Syro-Lebanese response to Abdullah, Quwatli, who distrusted his Acting Prime Minister, wrote to the Lebanese Prime Minister, warning him that "There is a group of Englishmen who, influenced by the Jews, believe that the success of the Emir will be theirs and support his ambitions ... ," and that "In Syria it is impossible for us to tell the people that we oppose the Union of Arab Countries, especially Syria, Transjordan, Palestine and Lebanon; but if we adopt this project, we will find ourselves in a dire situation which will only benefit the French since they will arouse the Lebanese Maronites against us and yourself. We will have made the situation worse instead of improving it." (doc.60)

Reports in early May of de Gaulle's intentions to send reinforcements to Beirut led Iraq to renew its efforts to intervene militarily in Syria, ostensibly against France. Mardam, Chamoun and British intelligence officers in Baghdad were involved in the scheme. The British secret services hoped that an Iraqi operation would save Britain from having to take direct action against the French in Syria. But Ibn Sa'ud, learning of the plot from his attaché in Baghdad, warned Quwatli not to allow the Iraqi Army to enter Syria. Increased pressure by Stirling, Marsack and other British intelligence officers, coupled with Mardam's intrigues to depose him, added to Quwatli's fears. He became increasingly isolated in his presidential palace, a target of scare campaigns conducted by British agents, the Hashemites, Mardam and Barazi. The rapidly rising popularity of his Acting Prime Minister, who enjoyed public support for his nationalist struggle against France, was another concern. Growing numbers of deputies and ministers in the Cabinet sided with his rival. A week before the outbreak of the crisis he suffered an ulcer attack and was forced to remain in bed throughout the critical days when his country was becoming the focus of an international crisis (doc.91).

French archival sources enable the last phase of the crisis, which continued throughout May, to be reconstructed day by day. Developing into an open Anglo-French confrontation, it escalated into a personal clash between Churchill and de Gaulle. The Syrian and British documents reveal the setting up of the trap by the British agents, especially the part played by Stirling, in close collaboration with Mardam, in engineering the crisis. The ploy was accompanied by an effective anti-French propaganda campaign which targeted de Gaulle personally, as illustrated by the instructions from London to General Paget at the height of the crisis (docs.100, 102, 105). And yet, the question still remains of why de Gaulle fell into the British trap despite being aware of it.[64]

While the MEWC was meeting in Faiyum, de Gaulle, Bidault and Beynet met in Paris to discuss France's Syrian policy and the future of the Troupes Spéciales. De Gaulle rejected Bidault's proposal to adopt a more conciliatory stand towards Syria, arguing that France could not give up its military presence in the Levant while a large contingent of British forces remained. Such a policy, Beynet warned, might provoke a confrontation in which the loyalty of the Troupes Spéciales could not be relied upon. He therefore asked for three additional battalions, two of which would serve as reinforcements. De Gaulle seriously misjudged the gravity of the situation when he stated that "Each day it is becoming less likely that serious trouble will erupt in the Levant. The English are now preaching peace and quiet. The neighboring Arab states are less inclined than ever to side with the present leaders in Damascus. The local governments, in fact, thanks to France, have just gained much prestige by forcing their way into San Francisco."[65] He clearly underestimated Churchill's resolve to evict France from the Levant, while overestimating Ibn Sa'ud's influence in sustaining Quwatli's resistance to British pressure (doc.83). His decision to reinforce the French troops in Syria and Lebanon granted Britain the necessary pretext to move into action.

In early May it became clear that France's Syrian policy had reached an impasse: attempts to reach an understanding with Britain had failed, while friendly overtures to the Syrian leaders had produced no result. Even an initiative to negotiate a *Convention Universitaire* was rejected by Mardam. Mardam's letter to Quwatli on his intentions to exploit the negotiations on a cultural agreement to gain time and toy with "those idiot French" increased resentment in Beirut and Paris. Unilateral evacuation of Syria and Lebanon was out of the question, especially as de Gaulle knew that Britain was plotting to expel France in order to take its place. His memoirs, written years later, reflect what he defined at the time as "Britain's policy of intimidation:"

> I had always expected it, for the national ambitions masked by the world conflict included the British plan to dominate the Middle East. How many times had I already confronted this passionate resolve that was prepared to shatter any barrier that stood in its way! With the war's end in Europe, its occasion had come. In an exhausted France, the invasion and its consequences had obliterated our former power. As for the Arabs, a political program as subtle as it was costly had rendered a number of their leaders accessible to British influence.[66]

De Gaulle's decision to reinforce the French troops was a calculated risk intended to convey to the British Cabinet that France was determined to retain its rights in its mandated territories and to force Churchill to reveal Britain's true ambitions or seek an agreement. It was also intended to pressure the Syrian and Lebanese governments before General Beynet returned to Beirut. On May 19, Beynet presented Henri Pharaon and Jamil Mardam, the Lebanese and Syrian Foreign Ministers, with an aide mémoire reiterating the familiar French demands for treaties safeguarding France's interests before turning the Troupes Spéciales over to the local governments. But the French démarche was never taken seriously – Mardam and senior British officers were already preparing for a military showdown. The exact timing depended on whether the French could be provoked into taking the first step and whether Quwatli would succumb to British pressure.

Throughout May, British diplomats and intelligence and military officers sent the Syrian leaders mixed messages regarding their government's intentions if the French forces attacked (docs.87-8). Their policy can be seen as the result of indecision in London, but evidence indicates that it was a well-orchestrated campaign designed to mislead de Gaulle and pressure the Syrian President and his ministers into giving in to British demands. The British charade continued until the last minute as Shone advised moderation while Stirling tacitly worked to provoke a confrontation with the French forces.

Indecision within the Syrian Cabinet ended after Mardam's meeting with General Paget in Damascus on May 22. Mardam reported to his anxious colleagues that General Paget had informed him that a British Division had crossed the border from Palestine into Lebanon for training; that Paget had offered to arm the Syrian Gendarmerie; and that British forces would intervene if necessary to ensure security, but not to protect French positions against Syrian attacks. Paget's stand was viewed by the ministers in Damascus as granting permission to escalate anti-French activities, confident that if the French retaliated, the British Army would intervene in Syria's defense. Following General Paget's visit to Damascus, Stirling secured the collaboration of Sabri al-Asali, Mardam's main rival, who controlled the Gendarmerie and other Syrian security agencies (docs.91-3). With the two prominent members of the government agreeing to forcibly expel the French, other ministers fell in line and approved Mardam's proposal to step up attacks on the French forces.[67]

With Quwatli confined to his sickbed, Mardam handled the conflict during the critical days leading up to the May 29 crisis. Oliva Roget's reports and the Syrian and British documents, especially those of Barazi to Stirling, provide details of his activities. Mardam coordinated his anti-French moves with Stirling, Marsack and Shone. It is unnecessary to describe the entire range of tactics and intrigues they used to discredit the French in Syria. The Syrian documents from June–July provide ample evidence of Mardam's pivotal role in engineering the crisis and ensuring the conclusion of the secret Anglo-Syrian agreements with Shone and Paget.[68]

Although there were contingency plans for a military intervention, the French attack on the parliament and the shelling and bombing of Damascus in the evening of May 29 were not planned operations, but acts of revenge stemming from frustration and anger after Oliva Roget learned from his agent of Quwatli's and Mardam's secret agreement with Shone (doc.94). It provided Churchill with the pretext to issue his humiliating ultimatum to de Gaulle and to instruct General Paget to take action against the French forces (docs.95-6).

The French retaliation also gave the British and Syrian governments an effective weapon in their propaganda war against France, which was to assume a central role in the subsequent weeks.[69]

After the British Army seized Syria and Lebanon from Vichy with the help of de Gaulle's Free French forces, Spears wrote to Churchill that Britain should take the opportunity to oust France from the Levant and reorganize the Middle East under its hegemony. In the summer of 1945, the first goal was finally achieved, opening the way for Britain to establish its "covert empire" in the Middle East. As it turned out, Britain gravely miscalculated. After its humiliating eviction, France escalated its clandestine war against Britain, aiming to exact revenge and prevent Britain from taking control of the Middle East.

The march of folly

In February 1948, Permanent Under-Secretary for Foreign Affairs Sir Orme Sargent, who had replaced Alexander Cadogan, remarked, in the aftermath of the collapse of the Portsmouth Treaty with Iraq:

> Although we can easily make new Treaties with certain friendly politicians or the local King or Regent, when we try to get them ratified we run up against a new force which the ruling classes can no longer control, namely a new Arab nationalism which has come into existence since the war and which it would be foolish to try to ignore. It is not primarily anti-British but it might easily become so if we play our cards clumsily.[70]

But this was not entirely accurate, as less than three years previously Britain had implemented its "Syrian solution" – a tacit agreement with Arab leaders allowing it to extend its rule over the Arab states without the approval of the local parliaments or hostile nationalists. This was in essence the "covert empire" that the British Arabists and military authorities had tried to establish in the Middle East in the post-war years. But they soon discovered that, like its bilateral treaties with Iraq and Egypt, it was difficult to impose this new method of indirect control.

Many British officials in the Middle East "lived in the past," as Muhammad Hussein Heikal, President of the Egyptian Senate, told Eliyahu Sasson. Referring to Britain's determination to hold on to its empire in the Middle East, Glen Balfour-Paul noted: "Habits of mind die hard, habits of practice even harder."[71] In reality, the British diplomats, military officers and secret agents in the Middle East were building castles in the air. Britain's eviction of France and its attempt to take over Syria had been a grave miscalculation that hastened the demise of its Middle East empire. The Syrian leaders celebrated their heroic struggle against French colonialism and their success in securing their country's "independence" and driving out the foreign forces without a treaty. Their victory became a benchmark for the Egyptian and

Iraqi nationalists under Britain's rule; like their brethren in Syria, they were determined to secure complete independence and national sovereignty.[72]

Britain's tacit agreement with the Syrian leaders and its attempt to control Syria became an open secret in Riyadh, Cairo, Moscow and Washington (doc.94). It provoked the Soviet Union to escalate its subversion in the two Levant states in order to undermine Britain's designs to dominate Syria and incorporate it in an anti-Soviet regional defense alliance. It reinforced President Truman's suspicion of British imperialism and hastened American efforts to check Britain's endeavors to control the Middle East economy and integrate Syria in a Hashemite Greater Syria, which might endanger Saudi Arabia. Britain's attempts to bring Syria under Hashemite influence destabilized the inter-Arab balance of power. Ibn Sa'ud, seeing it as a direct threat to his own kingdom, stepped up his secret war against the Hashemites and their British sponsors. The British intrigues in Syria reinforced the fears of King Faruq, who was involved in his own struggle to drive Britain out of Egypt and incorporate Sudan under his crown. Britain's premise that France would submit to its will in the Middle East proved faulty as well. Bitter and vengeful, de Gaulle and a small group of French military and intelligence officers in the Levant embarked on a secret campaign against Britain that would have a devastating effect on its interests in the Middle East.

After taking control over Syria, the British agents hastened to secure their country's strategic and economic predominance there. Plans were made to build a railway directly linking Syria and Iraq and ideas were aired regarding possible ports for Britain on the Syrian and Lebanese coasts in a Greater Syria (doc.126). Nuri al-Sa'id was sent to Ankara to negotiate on behalf of Syria a solution to its dispute with Turkey over Alexandretta. One of the proposals was to turn Alexandretta into a free-trade zone administered jointly by Britain, Turkey and Syria, and thereby transform the city and its port into a strategic British base. Another proposal was to revise the Turkish-Syrian border to compensate Syria for its territorial loss (docs.205, 207, 238, 284, 287). British secret officers in Damascus and Cairo, and diplomats and financial and commercial circles in London vigorously promoted the Greater Syria plan. In early January 1946, Brigadier Clayton presented President Quwatli with an ultimatum: either consent to a Greater Syria that would include Syria, Transjordan and part of Palestine – in which case a plebiscite would be held on the nature of the regime and the choice of king if it became a monarchy – or to an Arab confederation comprising Iraq, Syria, Transjordan and part of Palestine. In the latter case, until Prince Faisal II came of age and became king, Quwatli would serve as ruler in Syria, Abd al-Ilah in Iraq, and Abdullah in Greater Transjordan (doc.296). In February, Nuri al-Sa'id traveled to Damascus to promote an immediate Iraqi-Syrian union. Accompanied by Colonels Stirling and Marsack, he then proceeded to Beirut, where he discussed with Maronite politicians plans to revise Lebanon's borders by annexing to Syria regions with large Muslim populations, notably Tripoli. In August 1947, following the plan for the partition of Palestine, British officials explored the idea of annexing south Lebanon to the northern Arab part of Palestine while compensating Lebanon in the north with the Alawite region of Syria. In Cairo, intelligence and military officers were engaged in expanding Britain's control over Tripolitania, aiming to transform it into a strategic base for British forces in the event of their evacuation from Egypt. British officials proposed that King Faruq extend his rule to Libya in return for his agreement to give up his claims to Sudan (docs.162, 183, 384, 387). Another idea that British officials came up with to solve the Hashemite-Saudi dispute over Syria was that Ibn Sa'ud recognize Hashemite control over the entire Fertile Crescent; in return, the Hashemites would renounce their claims to the Hejaz and Ibn Sa'ud would extend his control over Yemen (doc.355). Another plan devised by the Arabists in 1947 was to tacitly support the Sultan of Morocco in his struggle for independence from France and help him to form a Greater Morocco that would include Algeria in return for his agreement to place the new, enlarged North African state under Britain's influence (doc.376). These ideas may have been unrealistic, but they reveal the frame of mind of those officials who entertained them. Indeed, the Arabists lived in the past, when Britain controlled the Middle East and drew the lines on its map.[73]

While, in Cairo, military planners and Middle East experts drew up charts to secure Britain's strategic and economic interests in the post-war Middle East, in Damascus and Beirut, Paget and Shone were consolidating its hold over Syria. Detailed agreements were concluded to liquidate France's assets in Syria and ensure Britain's military and economic predominance. Accordingly the British Army was to arm the Syrian Army and British officers would advise and train its forces (doc.118). British troops would be allowed to remain in Syria to defend it after the French evacuation, and British companies and banks would enjoy special privileges and be allowed to exploit Syria's oil resources. After his retirement, Stirling took part in establishing a trading company to promote Anglo-Syrian economic cooperation, while Marsack formed an association to further academic exchanges between the two countries.[74]

On July 23 1945, the Labour Party won the general election; Clement Attlee replaced Winston Churchill as Prime Minister and Ernest Bevin became the new Foreign Secretary. In mid-August, reports arrived in Cairo of Bevin's discussions with Massigli, the French Ambassador in London, on the evacuation of the British and French forces from Syria and Lebanon. On August 22, General Paget informed General Beynet that he had received instructions from London to withdraw his forces from the Levant and coordinate a mutual Anglo-French evacuation. Two days later, Bevin notified senior diplomats in the Middle East of his intentions to convene a meeting to discuss "measures of social advancement" and a policy that would "benefit the common people." These were the first signs of discord between the new Foreign Secretary and the Arabists in London and the Middle East, which culminated after Bevin's agreement with Bidault in December that year.[75]

Churchill's defeat and the formation of a Labour government came as a shock to the senior military and intelligence officers and diplomats in the

Middle East. Labour's attitude towards the Empire, especially among the party's more leftist members, and Attlee's intentions to liquidate Britain's overseas assets and withdraw most of the British forces from the Middle East, were seen as the end of Britain's standing as a Great Power. The army and intelligence services were still feeling the traumatic impact of the pre-war years when Britain had been caught unprepared. The Empire had been central to Britain's victory in that war. Faced with the threat of another war, this time against the Soviet Union, with the Middle East the principal arena, they were determined that Britain would not be caught unprepared again. French reports indicate that British military and civilian circles in the Middle East believed that Labour rule was only temporary and that they had a duty to safeguard British interests in the region until the Conservative Party regained power. Paradoxically, their determination to defend the Empire at any cost hastened its demise.[76]

The Arabists, especially the intelligence officers, regarded Bevin's intentions to incorporate a "socialist" approach in Britain's Middle East policy and his proposed "partnership" as naïve and dangerous. British policy in the region since World War I had been based on "agents of influence" from among the ruling classes, whom Britain, either directly or indirectly, controlled. This strategy had proved its efficacy when it enabled Britain to tacitly expand its control over Syria. Its failure in Iraq in January 1948 and Egypt in July 1952 demonstrated that Bevin's ideas were not so naïve after all. As late as 1953 the notion of tacit domination through the ruling elite was implemented in the overthrow of Mussadeq's nationalist government and in the imposition of the Shah in Iran. After the military coup that overthrew the Hashemite monarchy in Iraq in 1958, Harry St John Philby, an Arabist and explorer who had served as an intelligence officer in World War I, converted to Islam and become an adviser to King Ibn Sa'ud, commented on the policy of his former colleagues in Iraq:

> The trouble with Britain was that she was always incapable of cooperating with people of different coloring or culture than her own, except on the basis of her own dominance over them ... blind to the approaching storm in spite of the gusts which swept some of her friends into oblivion ... Her (Britain's) tail feathers were ruffled by the storm ... but she only muzzled her head deeper in the sands.[77]

The Syrian documents reveal the gap between the Labour Government rhetoric on implementing a liberal policy in the Middle East and the high-handed approach of the "agents in the field." They also expose the discord between Bevin and his senior diplomats and the military and secret services in Cairo, which escalated into a power struggle. But in the best British tradition of concealing unsavory details, it was presented as disagreement over policy. In reality, Bevin, known for his domineering personality, was misled and subsequently failed to control his subordinates in the Middle East, who continued to run their own show (docs.258, 265, 267, 282, 289, 291).

Shone's request from the Syrian Prime Minister to convey to the Foreign Office his satisfaction with the British representatives in Syria, attests to the apprehension of many diplomats in the region regarding their future under the Labour Government (doc.317). The departure from Egypt in April 1946 of Lord Killearn, the powerful British Ambassador, took place when Bevin could still throw his weight about and impose his own policy despite the reluctance of the secret services and the Arabist diplomats. But this was a rare instance. His attempts to strengthen the diplomatic missions in the Middle East in order to weaken the role of Secret Intelligence Service (SIS) officers in policy-making were unsuccessful. In August 1945 Colonel Stirling returned to Syria and resumed his undercover operations despite Foreign Office opposition (docs.145, 179, 189, 201-2). During the following year SIS built an influential and sophisticated intelligence network in Syria that continued to control Britain's policy there until 1949. French reports quoted diplomats in the British Legation in Beirut who complained of having little influence on Britain's policy in Syria and Lebanon.[78]

Britain's "parallel policy" in the Middle East – of Whitehall and the "agents in the field" – left Arab leaders confused. Each time Quwatli or Jabiri instructed their Minister in London to raise the issue with the Foreign Office, he was told that the Foreign Secretary alone decided on policy and that "If a British official says the opposite, he is only expressing his personal opinion and not that of his Government ... " (docs.220, 289). At a meeting with Brigadier Clayton in January 1946, Quwatli questioned how his plans for a Greater Syria or an Iraqi-Syrian union were to be implemented, taking into account the accord Britain had concluded with France two weeks earlier. He was told, "This is not under discussion; when you want unity everything will be settled with France." (doc.296). In their meeting in Cairo that month, Ibn Sa'ud and Faruq decided to jointly raise in London the issue of policies pursued by local British officials. And yet in November 1946, Ibn Sa'ud informed Quwatli once again that he had been notified by the Foreign Office "that the relevant British civil servants in the Middle East have not been asked by their Government to bring about the state of Greater Syria, that their action is purely personal and that the British government has given the necessary instructions for them to conform to them and not to embark on scheming which is beyond the scope of their prerogatives." (doc.321). De Gaulle, however, had no such illusions, convinced that under Labour, the military and secret services in the Middle East were continuing to decide Britain's policy.

Referring to the need for Britain to adopt a comprehensive approach to the Middle East, Walter Smart commented: "Syria is part of the Arab world and it is impossible to have all but Syria in the Arab world under our aegis and expect that this anomaly will work without continual friction and economic and political unrest." Citing the great Anglo-French showdown in Africa in the nineteenth century, he acknowledged that this would anger France, but in the long run would be worth the risk: "The French would no doubt treat this as another Fashoda, but it is not inappropriate to remember that, six years after Fashoda, the Anglo-French entente was signed."[79]

Smart wrote this in November 1945 while Bevin was negotiating an agreement in the Levant with Bidault. After the Syrian crisis, British officials in the Middle East believed that France's historical role in the Levant had come to an end. They therefore strongly opposed Bevin's intentions to allow France to regain its influence after they had labored for years to oust it from the region. The military authorities and the secret services, who deeply distrusted France, remembering its capitulation in the war, rejected Bevin's plan to incorporate it in a collective defense system in the Middle East (docs.236, 267, 271, 289). They were also concerned that Bevin's instructions to withdraw British troops from Syria and Lebanon would reinforce Egyptian demands for a similar withdrawal. Indeed, after receiving instructions to prepare for evacuation, General Paget hastened to conclude yet another secret agreement with President Quwatli allowing the British Army to remain in Syria even after the withdrawal of the French forces.[80]

The Syrian documents and French intelligence reports reveal the covert tactics used by the Arabists in the Middle East to undermine their Foreign Secretary's policy to pursue an agreement with France. They warned the Syrian leaders that the Labour Government could not be trusted, that it would allow France to retain its position in Lebanon, and that it might even make concessions to the Zionists in Palestine. Once again they used the old ploy of provoking the Syrians to attack French assets. Another tactic was to provoke the Syrian leaders into playing the American card – a proposal first made by Spears, who had advised the Syrian leaders to improve their country's relations with other Powers in order to put pressure on his own government. Indeed, throughout December and early January, Jabiri negotiated with the Americans on military and financial aid, clearly with Shone's full knowledge. As the negotiations advanced, Jabiri had to put an end to them, leaving the American diplomats resentful of the whole British charade (docs.279-81, 290, 301). For his part, Mardam in Cairo advised Jabiri to play the Soviet card, a proposal probably made with the tacit agreement of Smart and Killearn (doc.271). When the Soviets offered to provide Syria with military and economic aid, neither Jabiri nor Shone, who were fully aware of the Syrian Prime Minister's game, seriously considered the offer; the point was that it was reported in the press for Whitehall to see (docs.298, 304). But the Arabists' most effective tool remained their control of the information passed on to London; they were the experts who interpreted the events in the region, proposed policy and implemented it on the ground – or foiled it when they opposed it.[81]

Settling the score

In a debate in the Consultative Assembly in June 1945 on the Syrian crisis, Bidault told the British Government: "Hodie mihi, cras tibi." (Today it is me, tomorrow it will be you.) Duff Cooper, the British Ambassador, who had met de Gaulle at the height of the crisis, quoted the angry French leader as saying: "We are not, I admit, in a position to open hostilities against you at the present time. But you have insulted France and betrayed the West. This cannot be forgotten." De Gaulle indeed never forgot how he – namely France – was humiliated by Britain in Syria and Lebanon. In self-imposed isolation in Colombey-les-Deux-Eglises, where he wrote his memoirs, he repeated his accusations that "Perfidious Albion" had betrayed France and exploited its temporary weakness to oust it from a region with which it had centuries of religious, cultural, educational and economic ties. De Gaulle, however, was not content with merely expressing his anger in his memoirs, nor did he delay his revenge. He immediately set out to implement the second part of Bidault's statement. Initially under de Gaulle and later under Bidault, French secret agents stepped up their covert anti-British operations. France and its representatives in the Middle East were in a good position to carry out their undercover war against Britain. Weakened by the war and hated in the region, Britain had become highly vulnerable to subversion.[82]

Alongside his desire for revenge, de Gaulle strove to salvage France's interests in the Middle East, while Bidault was concerned with protecting the Christians in Lebanon and safeguarding France's "mission civilisatrice" there. But the main factor that propelled both leaders to continue their secret war against Britain's interests in the Middle East was the subversion by the British secret services against France in North Africa (docs.122, 131, 138, 354, 371, 374). The Syrian documents and French intelligence reports provide ample details of the subversive activities in French North Africa, spearheaded by Brigadier Clayton in Cairo. Clayton, who had been formally nominated as the British envoy to the Arab League, coordinated his anti-French campaign in Tunisia, Algeria and Morocco with Azzam and Mardam, who was serving as Syria's envoy in Cairo. Bevin's attempts to curtail his secret services' subversion against France in North Africa failed. Facing Soviet claims over the former Italian colonies in Libya, senior British officers and secret agents in Cairo repeatedly warned that France might become "red" and allow the Soviet Union direct access to strategically important ports in North Africa. Bidault and Quai d'Orsay diplomats repeatedly complained to Bevin and their British counterparts in the Foreign Office, to no avail. In a meeting attended by high-ranking British and French diplomats and military officers in February 1948 in Paris on strategic coordination between the two countries in the Middle East, the French representatives again complained of Clayton's subversive activities in North Africa, but Bevin was unable to impose his will on his secret services.[83]

In the immediate aftermath of the Syrian crisis, disagreement deepened between de Gaulle and Bidault, who throughout most of the crisis had been representing France in San Francisco. The French Delegation in Beirut was demoralized and General Beynet asked to resign after he and his staff were harshly criticized for their role in the crisis. One of the few counter-activities at this stage was the public naming of British secret agents and diplomats who had participated in engineering the Franco-Syrian confrontation, while details on Churchill's role in the crisis were conveyed to Labour Party members. But the feelings of demoralization and defeat changed dramatically after the Labour victory as French policy towards Britain in the Levant acquired new vigor.[84]

Shortly after the Labour victory was announced, de Gaulle wrote to Beynet: "Churchill's defeat and the arrival of the Labour will introduce flexibility in British policy," and that [Labour] "would not adopt a brutal attitude towards us."[85] He noted that pressure on Britain in Egypt, Iraq and Palestine would increase and France's presence in the Levant would become of secondary importance. France, he stressed, should not agree to withdraw its troops from Syria if the British Army remained there and should be willing to evacuate the Levant only if Britain withdrew its forces from the neighboring Arab states. But Bidault, who did not share de Gaulle's uncompromising stand, saw the Labour victory as an opportunity to break the deadlock. From August to November he negotiated with Bevin an agreement on a mutual withdrawal of French and British forces from the Levant. He knew that Bevin was facing strong opposition from General Paget and his secret services and diplomats in the Middle East, that the Troupes Spéciales had already disintegrated, and that France had only a small contingent of 1,500 troops in Syria compared to the 40,000-strong Ninth Army. But despite de Gaulle's criticism, the agreement he reached with Bevin in mid-December was a diplomatic accomplishment that ensured the evacuation of both the French and British forces and Britain's undertaking to include France in a regional defense organization. Although nothing came of the latter, the accord over the Levant paved the way for Anglo-French entente in Europe.[86]

The British military and secret services in the Middle East, determined to undermine the agreement, stepped up their subversive activities in the Levant and French North Africa while French agents paid back in kind. They reckoned that if Britain had exploited Syrian and Lebanese nationalists to force France out of the Levant, France could support the nationalists in Egypt and Iraq, as well as the Arab Palestinians and Zionists. French secret agents in Beirut and Paris began large-scale covert operations against Britain's positions in the Middle East. The difficulty in tracing CPA has been noted, but the Syrian documents, Beynet's letters to de Gaulle and Bidault, French intelligence reports and Zionist sources reveal some of these operations. They included targeting Britain's "agents of influence," sharing information with Britain's opponents and conducting overt and covert propaganda campaigns. The information gleaned from the Syrian documents was central in France's war against Britain in the Middle East, which took place while the two countries were cooperating in Europe.

Targeting Mardam and Quwatli

French agents took steps to counter British efforts to take control over Syria, but after their humiliating defeat that summer, they lost much of their freedom of action. They had to contend with the British secret services' expanded operations, while many formerly pro-French local politicians and officials ceased to collaborate. Nevertheless, their well-placed agent continued to provide high-grade intelligence. They also retained a certain degree of influence over former officers of the Levant Army now serving in the Syrian forces and intelligence organizations. Indeed, the French archives contain Syrian Deuxième Bureau and Sûreté générale reports from 1946 and 1947 (docs.202, 346, 356, 392).

A top priority became the removal of Mardam, who played a key part in Britain's covert policy in Syria and North Africa. Ibn Sa'ud became France's main ally in Syria. His letters to Quwatli and the reports of meetings between Saudi and French agents attest to their close cooperation against Mardam. French agents conducted a smear campaign against him while his opponents in the government, especially Sabri al-Asali, stepped up their attacks. In August 1945, he was forced to resign and was sent to Cairo to represent Syria in the Arab League (docs.159, 164-5). There he became involved in Brigadier Clayton's clandestine diplomacy and covert operations in inter-Arab politics, especially in Palestine and North Africa. As already noted, by that time he may have been forced to collaborate with the French intelligence services, although no details are available. In December 1946, under pressure from Brigadier Clayton, he was appointed Prime Minister by President Quwatli, replacing Sa'adallah al-Jabiri. Although during this term Mardam was more cautious in his dealings with British agents, he remained, as Armanazi believed, loyal to Britain and closely coordinated his policy with Nuri al-Sa'id.[87]

Mardam's resignation in August 1945 bolstered Quwatli's confidence in his dealings with the British diplomats. But Quwatli remained a weak, indecisive leader, whose main priority was to hold on to the presidency. Despite pressure from Ibn Sa'ud, he was reluctant to come out openly against Britain and the Hashemites (docs.148, 197-8, 277). The British rewarded him by not opposing his re-election as President in April 1948, but a year later they had had enough of him and forced him to resign.

Mobilizing the Maronite Church

France had significant political, economic and cultural assets in Lebanon that it was determined to hold on to. Beirut remained a center for the French intelligence services in the Middle East even after the evacuation of French forces at the end of 1946. But in Lebanon, as in Syria, the Deuxième Bureau faced strong competition from its British rivals. Colonel Furlonge, who maintained close ties with President Khuri, the new Prime Minister Sami Sulh, and Foreign Minister Hamid Franjieh, was the key player in Britain's CPA in Lebanon. Khuri continued to tacitly collaborate with the British secret agents, leading his cousin, Bishop Abdullah al-Khuri, to remark that he was "completely in the hands of the British."[88] This was to some extent an exaggeration, as by 1946, Khuri had become more cautious in his dealings with British diplomats and the Syrian government. The French became concerned, when at the end of that year, Riyad al-Sulh, with British backing, resumed the premiership. But this time Sulh, far more confident, pursued an extremely sophisticated policy, leading the director of the Syrian Sûreté générale to comment on the outcome of the Lebanese elections in 1947: "Mr Riad Solh, whose position I cannot define exactly as he is with the English as well as with the Americans, and with the French as well as the Communists, has also succeeded" (doc.392).

Beynet sought to sow discord between Lebanon and Syria and to solidify France's relations with the Christians, especially the Maronite Church. France still enjoyed considerable influence among the Maronites. The Syrian crisis and the evacuation of French forces from Lebanon reinforced the Christians' concern for their country's existence as a separate independent state. It prompted Emile Eddé to renew proposals for revising Lebanon's borders to ensure a Christian majority. But Khuri and the Constitutional Bloc, still determined to retain Lebanon in its current borders and safeguard its independence vis-à-vis Syria or a Hashemite Greater Syria, would not hear of it.

The Christians in Lebanon and Syria became an effective tool in French covert propaganda in the United States. French diplomats used the mistreatment of the Christians in the Jazira to highlight the danger facing Christian minorities after France's withdrawal. They also mobilized the Holy See's support for France's historical role of protecting the Christians in Lebanon, and in March 1946 General Beynet went to Rome to enlist the Pope's support. The French delegation found willing partners in Patriarch Arida, head of the Maronite Church, former Presidents Emile Eddé and Alfred Naqash, and other pro-French Maronite politicians (doc.136). French officials and the Maronite Church coordinated a propaganda campaign in the United States. The French Delegation in Beirut and diplomats in the Quai d'Orsay secretly organized two Maronite propaganda missions to the United States in 1945-46, led by Antoine Aql and Habib Awad, with the tacit collaboration of Zionist agents. The two emissaries mobilized the large Lebanese Christian communities in the United States to campaign for French protection, while warning senior Catholic clergymen, members of Congress and officials in the State Department of the danger facing Christians in Syria and Lebanon. Their activities culminated in an unpublicized meeting with President Truman. De Gaulle paid special attention to Habib Awad's mission and met him personally. Awad, an American citizen, had been involved during the war in the activities of the American Ministry of Information in the Middle East and maintained ties with members of Congress, as well as in the State Department and the Office of Strategic Services (OSS), the precursor of the Central Intelligence Agency (CIA). The activities of Aql and Awad were embarrassing for the Lebanese government, which tried to revoke Aql's Lebanese passport, but backed down under French and American pressure.[89]

King Ibn Sa'ud and operation Rashid Ali al-Gailani

Ibn Sa'ud, together with the Zionists, played an instrumental role in France's secret war against Britain. He was an extremely shrewd and sophisticated leader and Britain was to pay dearly for its support of the Hashemites, his sworn rivals (docs.148, 193, 197-8, 201, 209). Its attempt to place Syria under the Hashemites turned him into a dangerous adversary. He feared that after his death the kingdom he had established would disintegrate and the Hashemites would reclaim the Hejaz. His concerns were reinforced by Britain's viewing of Hashemite Iraq and Transjordan as central partners in its regional defense system and in settling the Jewish problem in Palestine. Britain's recognition of Transjordan's formal independence in March 1946, which Emir Abdullah marked by enthroning himself as king, only added to his concerns. King Abdullah celebrated his new title by publishing his memoirs, which included direct attacks on Ibn Sa'ud, and by stepping up his subversive activities in the Hejaz. The Saudi monarch reacted by intensifying his secret collaboration with France and his anti-British and anti-Hashemite activities in Syria. He also cemented his relations with King Faruq against the Hashemites.[90]

The most successful Franco-Saudi operation against Britain was their use of Rashid Ali al-Gailani against the Hashemites in Iraq. Rashid Ali had, with German support, led the revolt against Britain and the Hashemite monarchy in April 1941. After its failure he fled to Berlin, where he took part in German propaganda against Britain. At the end of the war he found refuge in France. In October 1945, the British press reported that he had escaped to Saudi Arabia with Syrian help. The reports embarrassed the Syrian government, which asked Spears to deny any Syrian involvement. In fact, Rashid Ali's move to Saudi Arabia had been organized by the French secret services together with their Saudi counterparts (docs.239, 249, 255). The Iraqi government, with British support, demanded his extradition, but Ibn Sa'ud, backed by Faruq, refused, invoking the Bedouin tradition of hospitality. In subsequent years Rashid Ali, who retained much of his popularity among the nationalists in Iraq, carried out, with Saudi funding, subversive activities against the Iraqi monarchy and Britain. He was to play a part in undermining the Anglo-Iraqi Portsmouth Treaty in January 1948.[91]

King Faruq and the ex-Mufti Amin al-Husseini

After receiving reports that Syrian agents had been using Egyptian territory to conduct subversive activities against the French in North Africa, King Faruq wrote to President Quwatli in early May 1947 questioning whether the Arabs should come to the assistance of their brethren there if France was merely to be replaced by another foreign Power. He rejected Quwatli's appeal, made on behalf of British diplomats, to curtail France's influence in Egypt following its involvement in Yemen and its support of the Zionists, stating that: "France, in spite of everything, is loved by the Egyptians and it is difficult for us to reproach the French for anything with their current correct attitude." (doc.385). His remarks, which he was unaware the French were privy to, reflected his friendly attitude towards France. He emerges from the Syrian documents as an astute leader who understood Britain's intrigues well and tried to oppose its control of his country. A decade before Nasser fought against the Baghdad Pact, Faruq more effectively opposed Britain's efforts to form a regional defense organization based on a Turkish-Iraqi-Syrian coalition. His alliance with the Saudi monarch in the Radwa pact further solidified after the Syrian crisis and Britain's attempt to incorporate Syria into Hashemite-led Fertile Crescent confederation (docs.193, 304, 315-6, 321). It was marked by his visit to Jeddah in September 1945 and Ibn Sa'ud's reciprocal visit to Cairo in January 1946.[92]

De Gaulle, and later Bidault, attached prime importance to France's relations with King Faruq, as France had extensive economic, cultural and educational interests in Egypt. The French Embassy in Cairo was one of the largest in the region and its military mission was tracking the subversive activities of the British secret services in North Africa. Cairo was also the seat of the Arab League, whose Secretary General led hostile overt and covert campaigns against France's rule in North Africa. The city became a center of anti-French propaganda and subversive activities of nationalist leaders from Morocco, Algeria and Tunisia who found refuge there and were often tacitly supported by the British secret service. In June 1946, French intelligence reciprocated by arranging the "escape" of the ex-Mufti Amin al-Husseini from France to Cairo, where he was welcomed by King Faruq and the Egyptian government. As in the case of Rashid Ali, this operation too extracted a heavy price from Britain and its Hashemite allies.[93]

After the failure of the Rashid Ali coup in Iraq, Amin al-Husseini had fled to Rome and Berlin and taken part in Fascist and Nazi propaganda in the Arab world. His arrival in France after the war coincided with the Anglo-French confrontation in Syria. The French intelligence services sought to use him against Britain, and while he was in Paris, secret agents were involved in dealing with him. In their internal correspondence, French officials admitted that the ex-Mufti could be considered a war criminal and that Britain had a legal case for demanding his extradition. For its part, the British government pursued a contradictory policy – while requesting his extradition, the Foreign Office actually preferred that he remain in France. The Syrian documents describe the repeated attempts by British agents in the Middle East to instigate Arab leaders to demand his release, while the British-sponsored Arab media accused France of mistreating him (docs.110, 113, 221, 250). In fact, after the Rashid Ali fiasco neither the British nor their Hashemite allies wanted the Mufti in the region.[94]

The timing of Amin al-Husseini's "escape" was set to coincide with the publication of the report of the Anglo-American Committee of Inquiry for Palestine and the convening of the Bludan conference. (doc.319) It was coordinated with Faruq's agents in Paris and intended to cause as much damage as possible to Britain's position in the Middle East. Another consideration in opting for Cairo was Amin al-Husseini's undertaking to exert his influence on North African nationalist leaders to moderate their attacks on France. In the summer of 1947 he organized a secret meeting between French diplomats and North African nationalist leaders. While Rashid Ali led the struggle against the monarchy in Iraq, the ex-Mufti targeted King Abdullah and his British patrons, becoming an extremely disruptive force in Britain's policy in Palestine.[95]

Collaborating with the Soviet Union

In July 1944, the Deuxième Bureau in Beirut reported that Spears suspected that the Soviet Union's recognition of Syria's and Lebanon's independence had been secretly coordinated with France. In the following years, senior British officers, intelligence agents and diplomats in the Middle East were convinced that French agents in the Levant were secretly cooperating with their Soviet counterparts against Britain's interests. De Gaulle's initiative to involve the Soviet Union in an international settlement of the Syrian crisis reinforced British suspicions. Armanazi reported from London that certain British officials had cynically remarked that while in the past France had been known as "the elder daughter of the Church," it was now turning into "the eldest daughter of the Soviet Union" (doc.116). Military and intelligence circles in Cairo were convinced that France was becoming "red," especially during the Fourth Republic, when communist and socialist parties were represented in the governments.[96]

In a memorandum to Bidault in June 1946, after Amin al-Husseini's "escape" to Egypt, Beynet remarked: "It is therefore certain that Haj Amin's arrival in the Middle East poses a grave danger to the British in that it compromises the house of cards that they are painstakingly building to their own benefit and against the Soviet Union."[97] Beynet also noted that the Soviet Embassy in Paris knew of Amin al-Husseini's departure. He appended a document which contained Musa al-Alami's report to the Mufti on his secret discussions with Solod, the Soviet Minister in Syria and Lebanon. In referring to a "house of cards," Beynet was alluding to the extensive anti-Soviet propaganda campaigns conducted in Syria and Lebanon by British diplomats and intelligence officers. The clandestine Anglo-Soviet war in Syria and Lebanon in 1945-47 is beyond the scope of this study, but the Syrian documents provide ample details of its extent. Alongside the propaganda war, another war was taking place between the British and Soviet secret services. British agents closely monitored Soviet diplomats and intelligence agents. They followed Solod's visits to northern Syria and the Jazira in the autumn of 1945. That summer Special Operations Executive (SOE) agents, in collaboration with SIS, had broken into the Yugoslav Consulate in Beirut, suspecting that it was being used by Soviet intelligence. The Soviets, for their part, turned their Legation in Beirut into a center for their secret activities in the Levant and it later became their main post in the Middle East. They maintained a large number of secret agents in their Mission in Damascus, leading the French to name the senior Soviet intelligence officer there the "Russian Lawrence of Arabia." Soviet agents also mobilized the Syrian Communist Party, the Kurds in the Jazira, the Greek Orthodox Patriarch and the Armenians to deter the Syrian government from collaborating with Britain.[98]

The Anglo-Soviet rivalry in the Levant was followed closely in Paris and Beirut. After the Syrian crisis, Franco-Soviet collaboration against Britain's dominance over Syria intensified. The Soviet Ambassador in Ankara told his French counterpart "in confidence" that Molotov, the Minister of Foreign Affairs, supported France's position in Syria.[99] Britain's attempt to evict it from the Levant placed France in a unique position – while cooperating with Britain in Europe against the Soviet Union, in the Middle East it often joined forces with the latter against Britain. De Gaulle used his ties with the Soviet Union to pressure Britain into recognizing France's strategic interests in the Levant, while Bidault exploited British concerns over France allying itself with Moscow to extract concessions from Bevin. For its part, the Soviet Union sought to deepen Anglo-French discord. In meetings with Fa'iz al-Khuri, the Syrian Minister in Moscow, and Syrian officials in Damascus, Soviet diplomats repeatedly warned that they had not recognized Syria's independence only to have French rule replaced by British domination (docs.79, 211, 278). When Fa'iz al-Khuri presented his credentials to President Kalinin, the latter remarked: "As long as France competes with Britain for influence and preponderance over your country, you have nothing to fear, and your future in these conditions will be better than at present."[100] Kalinin, who made this remark while Bevin and Bidault were negotiating an accord over the Levant, was referring to the fact that the Syrian President and his Acting Prime Minister had concluded a secret agreement with British officials placing their country under Britain's tacit control. Although the Soviets opposed the Anglo-French attempts to reach an agreement in Syria and Lebanon, they shared French opposition to British attempts to form a Hashemite Greater Syria or an Iraqi-Syrian union.

Beynet and his intelligence officers had to handle the sensitive ties with their Soviet counterparts under the watchful eyes of the British security and secret services. Beynet rarely dealt directly with the Soviet envoys, leaving direct contact with Solod to Ostrorog. French intelligence became, often unwittingly, part of the Anglo-Soviet secret war. It closely followed this war, but was extremely cautious in its dealings with Soviet intelligence officers, and any anti-British collaboration was a closely-guarded secret. Nevertheless, there is evidence that both sides shared information and coordinated their policies towards the Syrian and Lebanese governments. Soviet diplomats often supported the French position in the Middle East and North Africa. It was also apparent that Solod had intimate knowledge of Anglo-Syrian relations, leading Quwatli to warn Mardam that, "All the Ministry of Foreign Affairs' secrets are known to these resourceful Russians" (doc.79). Indeed, after June 1945, there was a recurrent pattern when, shortly after the

Deuxième Bureau received information on the Syrian government's giving in to British pressure, Solod would complain to the Syrian Foreign Ministry.[101]

Reinforcing President Truman's mistrust of Britain's Middle East policy

Kermit Roosevelt, a senior CIA political officer in the Middle East, commented on his British counterparts: "Any American with experience in the Middle East knows of times when British representatives on the spot were, in defiance of London's instructions, doing all in their power to knife their American opposite numbers and make Anglo-American collaboration in the area a strictly one-way proposition. It is, unfortunately, equally true that there have been Americans on the scene whose every act was inspired by a desire to 'do the British in'."[102] Kermit Roosevelt was familiar with his British counterparts' intrigues; in April 1949 he took part in the CIA "hijacking" of Husni Za'im's coup which had been initially engineered by Colonel Stirling.

The Syrian documents describe the tactics used by British diplomats and secret agents to undermine American political and economic interests in the Middle East in the post-war years. American policy towards Britain's attempts to retain its hegemony over the region shifted between strong opposition to its imperialism – and, for that matter, to that of the French and the Dutch – and recognition of the need for its continued influence to counter the growing Soviet threat. In 1945-46, however, American policy was opposed to Britain's supremacy in the Middle East, and only in early 1947, with the escalation of the Cold War and the embracing of the Truman Doctrine, did the United States begin to dampen down its criticism. Even then it continued to oppose Britain's economic dominance in the Middle East, especially over the region's oil resources. Reports from Washington by Qudsi and his deputy, Constantin Zureiq, of their discussions with officials in the State Department, point out that in the immediate post-war years the Americans did not share the British alarmist attitude towards the Soviet Union. They opposed Britain's efforts to form an anti-Soviet "Arab-Islamic bloc" and regarded its plan for a regional defense organization as a pretext to retain its domination over the Middle East (doc.228). They also believed that the British agents were fueling the Arab-Jewish conflict for the same purpose. The American administration was particularly critical of Britain's designs to form a Greater Syria united with Iraq under Hashemite influence, seeing it as a threat to Ibn Sa'ud.

The Syrian documents shed light on how the Syrian leaders became caught up in the Anglo-American rivalry and how British officials tried to exploit them to undermine American economic interests in the region. British diplomats and secret agents opposed the American oil companies' efforts to construct a pipeline linking the oil fields in Saudi Arabia to the Mediterranean through Syria and Lebanon, seeing them as competitors to the IPC (docs.45, 63, 125, 244, 380). They also objected to American plans to build a refinery in Syria or Lebanon and deterred the Syrian government from offering concessions for oil exploration in the Jazira and the Syrian Desert. These

activities testify to the close ties between SIS agents and the British oil companies in the Middle East. British diplomats and military officers foiled the
Syrian government's plans to purchase arms from the United States and were
active in countering attempts by American airlines to expand their operations
in the Middle East. Spears had personal interests, as he was involved with
Lebanese politicians and entrepreneurs in establishing a Lebanese airline
(Middle East Airlines) together with the British Overseas Airways Corporation.

But the most effective tool employed by the British agents to counter
American influence in the Middle East was the latter's support for the Zionist
cause. They used the "Zionist card" to undermine American economic interests in the Arab world; deflect Arab accusations that Britain had been
responsible for the Zionists' ambitions in Palestine; and present their country
as the sole defender of the Arab cause against the American pro-Zionist
ploys. As the United States stepped up its involvement in the escalating conflict over Palestine, British agents intensified their use of the Zionist card
against the Americans. British diplomats attempted to exploit President Truman's statement in August 1945 on the need to allow 100,000 Jewish refugees
from the camps in Europe to enter Palestine to provoke Ibn Sa'ud and Syrian
leaders against the United States (docs.137, 155, 235, 242-4). The secret
decision in Bludan to impose sanctions on American and British oil companies, in which Nuri al-Sa'id played a central part, was aimed primarily at the
American oil companies in Saudi Arabia. In fact, throughout the deliberations, Brigadier Clayton and Colonel Stirling were present in Bludan to
ensure that Britain's interests were not harmed. Officers in the Deuxième
Bureau in Beirut, who closely followed the conference's proceedings, believed
that British agents were fueling Arab opposition to the Anglo-American
Committee on Palestine's report to demonstrate to the American administration and their own government that it would be impossible to implement its
recommendations.[103]

The Anglo-American rivalry in Syria was welcomed in de Gaulle's office.
After the Syrian crisis, France's standing in the United States had sunk to its
lowest point. The American media extensively covered the bombing of
Damascus and the seizure of the Syrian parliament by French troops. A Quai
d'Orsay report of the reaction in the United States to the events in Syria
noted that none of the 331 editorials in American newspapers in the first
week following the crisis were favorable to France. In this crisis, as in the
Lebanese crisis, the French could not compete with the far superior British
propaganda.[104]

The reactions in the United States and the charges made against him personally came at an especially sensitive time for the French leader. Following
his stormy relations with President Roosevelt, de Gaulle was anxious to
establish friendly ties with the new President based on cooperation and trust.
France desperately needed American economic assistance and its support on
the German question. On June 1, in the midst of the Syrian crisis, de Gaulle
informed President Truman that to end the crisis, the French government had

ordered its forces the previous day to cease fire and asked him to instruct his diplomats to advise the Syrian and Lebanese governments to moderate their anti-French stance. He used his trip to Washington in August to reveal to President Truman details of Britain's role in instigating the events in Syria, having in his possession Churchill's instructions and details of Quwatli's secret agreement with Shone and Paget. He knew of Truman's interest in the petroleum industry since he had chaired a Senate committee in June 1944 dealing with American petroleum policy, in which relations with Saudi Arabia played an important part. The information he received from Beynet on British agents' intrigues against Ibn Sa'ud and the American oil companies in Saudi Arabia was thus highly useful.[105]

Before de Gaulle departed for Washington, his office received a copy of a coded telegram sent by the Syrian Minister in Washington highlighting the depth of President Truman's distrust of Britain's Middle East policy. In a conversation with Professor Philip Hitti, head of the Department of Oriental Languages at Princeton University, Truman was quoted as saying that he did not believe that "the current leaders in Syria and Lebanon are working in favor of their countries; they are directly in the service of Great Britain, and are far from their people and their aspirations" (doc.143). The American President had been well informed by his own intelligence services in the Levant, and by Prince Faisal al-Sa'ud, then visiting the United States. Truman resented not only Britain's attempts to expand its empire in the Middle East, but also its conduct in the Levant, which he feared could drive France to ally itself with the Soviet Union.[106]

During August 22-25 de Gaulle held meetings with President Truman. In his memoirs he recounted that the Levant had been extensively discussed. On August 24, Qudsi sent a telegram to Damascus informing the Foreign Minister that he had been urgently summoned to the State Department and that American officials had received word of the Syrian government's agreement to a union with Iraq to form a state under a Hashemite throne, and that it was working with Britain to promote this plan (docs.174, 177). This was one of the immediate results of the incriminating evidence that de Gaulle had passed on to President Truman. A week later Truman sent his famous letter to Prime Minister Attlee in which he formally proposed that Britain allow 100,000 Jewish refugees to enter Palestine. Although it is unknown whether President Truman was affected by the evidence of Britain's role in the Syrian crisis, it can be assumed that it deepened his mistrust of its Middle East policy, which continued in later years despite the Cold War.[107]

The clandestine Franco-Zionist war against Britain

On May 22, 1947, David Ben-Gurion noted in his diary: "If there is a pro-Zionist country in Europe, it is France, but it won't admit it publicly."[108] A memorandum written in early May 1948 by Jacques Boissier, a top adviser to Bidault, provides rare insight into the French modus operandi for securing a

Jewish victory and a Jewish state. Boissier maintained that France's goal in Palestine was to bring about the failure of the Arab League without compromising the French government. He argued that the American retreat from their support for partition and proposed trusteeship would provide the Arab League with a diplomatic victory. But on the military front he maintained that the Arabs would not be able to claim victory, as the Jewish community and the Haganah were mobilizing a fighting force and transforming it into a true army. France, Boissier argued, could exploit this state of affairs to bring about an Arab defeat "which would be all the more humiliating, as it would be achieved by Jewish soldiers." He proposed that France assist the Zionist diplomats in the United Nations by undermining the American proposal for trusteeship, but also warned of "the danger that the joint action of Britain and Palestine's neighboring Arab states might change the military balance such that the Jews will be crushed." He therefore recommended that the French delegation in the UN should try to persuade American diplomats to revert to their endorsement of partition, lest their new policy push the Jews into the Soviet camp, and that French diplomats should attempt to delay a vote on any resolution that could replace the Partition Resolution (UN Resolution 181 from November 29, 1947) until May 16, 1948, when the Jewish Agency was to officially declare a Jewish state, and thus "present the world and especially the Americans with a fait accompli." He also proposed to raise the issue of Jerusalem, which would both be in France's own interests and serve as a delay tactic. Other moves he recommended were to promote an arms embargo under the pretext of ensuring "a peaceful solution to the crisis in Palestine," thereby putting indirect pressure on Britain and benefiting the Jews, as monitoring the coast of Palestine would be more difficult than monitoring its territorial borders with the Arab states; and to refrain from encouraging a Jewish-Arab compromise, as "this would oblige the Jews to make concessions, which would be regarded as a victory for the Arab League."[109]

Alongside tacit diplomatic support for the Zionists in the UN, Boissier recommended that France should provide military aid to enable the Jews to defend themselves against the Arab regular armed forces and secure sufficient territory to establish their state. France should therefore make sure that the Jews were not at a military disadvantage by secretly arming them, "but without compromising its stand vis-à-vis the Arabs." The relevant authorities should be instructed to "turn a blind eye to the arms purchases that the Jews were secretly making in France and to the transit of war equipment across French territory."[110]

The disparity between the Quai d'Orsay's official position and the tacit support that Bidault and his advisers gave to the Zionist movement and the newly established state of Israel is revealed in another memorandum from early June 1948, which in fact argues against formal recognition of the Jewish state. It advocated maintaining the existing policy of covert assistance, citing various examples, including the suspension of arms sales to Syria, notwithstanding signed contracts; preventing the sale of a large consignment of arms by a Swiss company to Ethiopia, which was actually destined for Egypt and Jordan; pressuring Belgium to suspend arms sales to the Arab states; rejecting a British request to allow a squadron of British aircraft to land in France on their way to Transjordan; authorizing Air France to transport military cargo to Tel Aviv; allowing aircraft [carrying arms from Czechoslovakia] to land on French territory in transit to Israel; discreetly giving diplomatic support to Israel in the UN; and permitting two arms shipments to "Nicaragua," that were actually intended for Israel.[111]

And yet, in neither these memoranda, nor others found in the French archives on France's assistance to the Zionist movement from 1945 to 1948, are there any direct references to sharing intelligence gleaned from the Syrian documents with the Jewish Agency. France's aid to the Zionist movement in establishing a Jewish state by providing arms and facilitating illegal immigration has been well documented, but little is known about its help in providing intelligence, as it has only recently emerged that its secret services had succeeded in infiltrating the British Legation in Beirut and the Syrian Government in Damascus. The information given by the French was of great importance for Ben-Gurion in preparing the Jewish community in Palestine to withstand an Arab invasion and allowing him to remain one step ahead of the British secret agents. This intelligence collaboration was one of the most closely-guarded secrets, with few on either side being privy to it. Well aware that the British secret agencies were closely following the clandestine Franco-Zionist cooperation, French intelligence services did their utmost not to compromise its sources.[112]

The SHAY – the Haganah secret intelligence agency – was an effective organization whose agents had acquired much operational experience during the early years of World War II through their association with SIS and SOE. The Jewish Agency's Political Department and its Arab Division had gained ample experience in observing international and inter-Arab affairs, but lacked personnel, and although they had some high-grade sources, they still found it difficult to make accurate assessments of the rapidly developing post-war events in the Middle East. Access to the Syrian documents helped to transform them, especially the Arab Division headed by Eliyahu (Elias) Sasson, into intelligence organizations with broad regional and international outlooks. They now had direct access to ongoing details of the inter-Arab rivalries and the Arab leaders' stance towards the Jewish community in Palestine based on their private correspondence. In addition, officers of the Deuxième Bureau in Beirut had long experience in monitoring the covert political operations and clandestine diplomacy of British diplomats, senior officers and secret agents in the Middle East. They had also acquired detailed information on the making of Britain's Middle East policy, especially the discord between Whitehall and its agents in the field. In fact, contrary to claims that Ben-Gurion and his intelligence advisers failed to accurately assess the British goals or the Arab plans for invasion, Ben-Gurion had received detailed information on both British and Arab intentions. The difficulty in assessing the British strategy, as well as that of the Arab leaders, was due not to lack of information, but to their rapidly evolving positions. The uncertainty was reinforced by the Arabist intelligence officers' extensive use of undercover operations and clandestine diplomacy to manipulate the Arab leaders' stand on Palestine. A comparison between the French and Zionists' assessments, especially Sasson's, indicates similarities, as both sides found it difficult at the end of 1947 and the early months of 1948 to accurately gauge Britain's intentions and hence the Arab leaders' positions. In light of their own experience in the Syrian crisis, French intelligence officers often tended to make grimmer assessments, estimating that the British Cabinet would not be able to impose its will on its secret services and military in the Middle East, including on the question of Palestine.[113]

Apart from political intelligence on British and Arab strategies in Palestine, the Deuxième Bureau had detailed information on the Arab states' armed forces, especially those of Syria, Lebanon and Egypt. It also shared details of Arab plans, often with tacit British assistance, to purchase weapons, enabling the Haganah agents to foil them. After September 1947, the Arab League's political and military committees often convened in Beirut and Damascus, allowing the Deuxième Bureau to obtain accurate information of their most secret decisions (doc.396). This information was vital for Ben-Gurion and his closest advisers during the critical months between September 1947 and May 1948.[114]

Documents in French and Zionist archives reveal the initial stages of the clandestine Franco-Zionist collaboration against Britain – the people involved, the methods used to transfer information and the early joint covert operations. The aid provided by the Haganah agents to Free France in 1940-1941 against Vichy in Syria and Lebanon has been well documented. Brigadier Clayton himself, then head of the MEIC, mediated between the Haganah and the Free French movement. This early assistance laid the foundation for later cooperation against the British themselves. The Franco-Zionist collaboration began at the end of 1944 and was part of General Beynet's counter-measures in the aftermath of the Oliva Roget operation. The early contacts were made with Eliyahu Epstein (Elath) in June and September 1944. In mid-October, Beynet met David Ben-Gurion in Beirut. Ben-Gurion recounts the meeting at length, but refrains from disclosing details of any secret understanding. Nevertheless, on November 23, 1944, he wrote in his diary that he had sent a letter with Captain Blanchard, a Free French intelligence officer, to Paris. In February 1945, Tuvia Arazi became involved in undercover anti-British operations with officers of the Deuxième Bureau in Beirut.[115]

The secret Franco-Zionist cooperation was initially fraught with difficulties owing to differences in expectations and goals on both sides. A report from Beirut by a Zionist agent in July 1945, disguised as a commercial report, describes the Zionists as only "one of the suppliers" and alludes to the cautious attitude of the French officials.[116] Indeed, for Beynet and officers of the

Deuxième Bureau, the Zionists were only one partner in their covert anti-British operations. While they were collaborating with the Jewish Agency, in Paris French secret agents were holding discussions with Amin al-Husseini, the Zionists' bitter enemy. There were also disparities between the modi operandi of the two secret services. The French intelligence service was a structured, bureaucratic organization, with long experience and traditions. The Zionists comprised a small number of individuals who served as both secret agents and diplomats, who took initiatives and were quick to improvise. The French caution was seen by the Zionists as indecision, and, in their internal correspondence, Zionist agents criticized their French counterparts. They frequently adopted a patronizing attitude, provoking resentment among French intelligence officers. On one occasion, Arazi was advised by his superiors to adopt a less assertive attitude in his dealings with his opposite numbers in the Deuxième Bureau.[117]

General Beynet was the true architect of the secret Franco-Zionist alliance. From his arrival in Beirut in March 1944 until his departure in June 1946 he strove to further this partnership. By the time he left it was on solid ground. In a letter to de Gaulle at the end of June 1945, he specified the political benefits for France of collaborating with the Jews in Palestine, especially in exploiting the Jewish Agency's propaganda skills in the United States. He also raised a moral consideration – the suffering of French Jewry under the German occupation (doc.119). Before being nominated as the Délégué Général in Syria and Lebanon, Beynet had served as head of the Free French military mission in Washington, where he was impressed by the extensive ties the Jewish Agency representatives had in the American capital and their skills in public relations. Under his instructions, the Deuxième Bureau expanded its information-gathering on the Jewish community in Palestine. Numerous reports can be found in French files from 1944 to 1948 on the Yishuv's political, economic and social organizations, and especially on the Jewish Agency's relations with the British authorities. The weekly or bi-weekly reports of the French liaison officer in Jerusalem provide detailed information on the military capabilities of the various underground movements and their interrelations. These reports were sent via courier to Beirut and were read by officers of the Deuxième Bureau and occasionally by Beynet himself. French officers and diplomats frequently visited Palestine to gather information.[118]

Beynet's support of Franco-Zionist collaboration was backed by Gaullist military and Deuxième Bureau officers in Beirut. After de Gaulle's resignation, many Gaullist officers retained key positions in the military and intelligence services, especially the newly-formed Service de Documentation Extérieure et de Contre-Espionnage (SDECE), where they continued to help the Zionist struggle against Britain. Nevertheless, other officials, particularly in the Quai d'Orsay, opposed collaboration with the Zionist movement. The Quai d'Orsay was a center of conservative policy with little sympathy for the Zionists, and Jean Chauvel, its influential Secretary General, advocated a cautious policy towards the Jews in Palestine. Officials there frequently warned

Bidault of the possible consequences of a pro-Zionist policy on France's interests in North Africa and the Middle East, while French diplomats in Arab capitals cautioned that such a policy would provoke intense Arab Muslim hostility towards France. René Massigli, the Ambassador to London, and Georges Catroux in Moscow, warned that France's support for a Jewish state would jeopardize its relations with Britain and strengthen anti-French sentiment among the Muslims in North Africa. Yet neither de Gaulle nor Bidault heeded these warnings and continued to provide tacit aid to the Zionist struggle against Britain. Beynet's personal letters to both leaders and the secret documents he sent from Beirut on Britain's duplicity had a greater effect.[119]

De Gaulle valued the Zionists' support for Free France in 1940-1941, but in early 1945 he was wary when Beynet proposed cooperating with the Jewish Agency. Only after the Syrian crisis and the assistance provided by the Jewish Agency's envoys in the United States in facilitating his visit there, did he give the go-ahead to increase tacit collaboration with the Jewish Agency against Britain. Apart from being motivated to pay Britain back, he sought to use the Zionists to improve France's standing in the United States. As American involvement in the question of Palestine intensified and Zionist underground movements stepped up their anti-British operations, de Gaulle became more disposed to support the Zionists.

Bidault has been portrayed by Israeli historians as displaying a reserved attitude towards the pre-state Zionist movement. But his private papers reveal such claims to be simplistic. Bidault distinguished between Europe, where he sought to cooperate with Britain, and the Middle East, where the long-standing Anglo-French rivalry continued, albeit mostly in the dark. Like the military and intelligence officers, he believed that France should help the Jews in Palestine against the Arab states, as an Arab victory in Palestine would strengthen the Arab League's influence and jeopardize France's position in North Africa. Indeed, without his discreet support from 1946 to 1948, it would have been far more difficult for the pro-Zionists in the government, the army and the secret services to provide intelligence and military aid to the Zionist movement.[120]

In the Jewish Agency, only David Ben-Gurion and Moshe Shertok (Sharett) were directly involved in the secret alliance with France. From 1945 to early 1947, Ben-Gurion spent long periods in Paris, which became the center of the Zionists' struggle against Britain. The Jewish Agency was helped by its close relations with many French politicians, especially in the Socialist Party, and sympathy among the French public for the Jewish cause. Ben-Gurion and Sharett circumvented the Quai d'Orsay by dealing directly with Bidault and other members of the French government, while Jewish Agency agents worked with the French secret services. Together with Ben-Gurion and Sharett, four other men played major roles in initiating the Jewish Agency's secret ties with France: Maurice Fischer, Tuvia Arazi, Eliyahu Epstein and Eliyahu Sasson. They had all been involved in helping Free France in 1940-1941 against Vichy in the Levant.[121]

Maurice Fischer immigrated to Palestine from Belgium in 1930, joined Free France in 1941 and for the next five years served as an officer in the Deuxième Bureau and the Sûreté Générale de l'Armée in Beirut. He used his close ties with officers in the Deuxième Bureau to establish secret collaboration between the Jewish Agency's Political Department and French intelligence. At the end of 1945 he was appointed as a secretary in the Jewish Agency offices in Paris and for next three years served as the unofficial liaison officer with the French secret services. After the founding of the state, he became Israel's first ambassador to France.[122] Like Fischer, Tuvia Arazi served as an intelligence agent in Free France. Sent to Syria and Lebanon on espionage missions and undercover operations, he was caught and imprisoned by the Vichy authorities but managed to escape. Officers in the Deuxième Bureau greatly appreciated his service to France, trusted him and allowed him direct access to their secret files.[123] Eliyahu Epstein was the Political Department's envoy to Syria and Lebanon in the 1930s. He used his frequent visits there to forge close ties with officials in the French High Commission and Lebanese Maronite Christian religious and political leaders. In early 1945 he was appointed head of the Jewish Agency office in Washington, where he maintained close ties with the French Embassy. He took part in the secret Franco-Zionist diplomatic collaboration in the UN in 1947-1948.[124]

Eliyahu Sasson, head of the Arab Division in the Political Department and Ben-Gurion's chief adviser on Arab affairs, was a key figure in the secret ties with the French intelligence services. During the critical months between December 1947 and May 1948, he relayed information from French sources directly to Ben-Gurion. Born in Damascus, Sasson joined the Jewish Agency in 1933, and was an entire intelligence organization unto himself. His role in the Franco-Zionist intelligence partnership has yet to be studied, as his activities were conducted in the utmost secrecy. Reports by French officers of their meetings with him provide a glimpse of his clandestine diplomacy and covert operations. He had an intimate knowledge of the complex inter-Arab relations and knew many of the Arab leaders personally. French intelligence officers valued his understanding of Arab affairs and often met him and included his assessments in their reports. From 1946 to 1948 he frequently traveled to Paris, where he had direct access to the Syrian documents. His assessments of the Arab states' strategy towards the Jewish community in Palestine were based on those and other Arab documents he received from the French, as well as from his own sources. His access to those sources allowed him to closely follow the British Arabists' intrigues, not only in inter-Arab relations but in the Jewish-Arab conflict; hence his constant warnings that British agents were provoking the Arab leaders to invade the Jewish state.[125]

The early Franco-Zionist undercover operations were mainly in propaganda. The first, in which Arazi took part, was directed against Spears. It was conducted in Britain and involved the leaking of unsavory details of Spears' secret dealings with the Syrian and other Arab governments, and his misuse of his former position in Syria and Lebanon to promote his private business enterprises. The second operation, in which Arazi in Beirut and Epstein in Washington participated, entailed helping Antoine Aql's and Habib Awad's public relations campaigns in the United States. Both Arazi and Epstein had long-standing relations with the Maronite Church and pro-French Maronite politicians, especially the former Lebanese Presidents Emile Eddé and Alfred Naqash. The Zionist-Maronite alliance, tacitly supported by the French, culminated in a secret agreement between the Jewish Agency and Patriarch Arida in the summer of 1946 (doc.318). This alliance was part of the Jewish Agency's minorities policy that sought to join forces with other minority communities in the Middle East, whether Maronites, Kurds or Druze, against the Muslim majority and Arab nationalism.[126]

The turning point in the tacit Franco-Zionist collaboration came during de Gaulle's visit to the United States in August 1945. De Gaulle was concerned that his visit would provoke anti-French demonstrations following the hostile American media coverage of the French bombardment of Damascus in which Syrian civilians were killed. At the end of June, General Beynet conveyed to de Gaulle the Jewish Agency's offer to collaborate in a public relations campaign in the United States (doc.119). Apparently de Gaulle heeded the Agency's proposal as, in early August, Arazi reported from Paris that he was working with de Gaulle's staff. Jewish Agency representatives and leaders of the Jewish community in the United States mobilized public support to ensure de Gaulle a friendly reception. He was greeted warmly by large crowds in New York and Chicago and his role in liberating France from the Nazi occupation was hailed in the press. The benefit for the Zionist movement was immediately evident, as de Gaulle provided President Truman with detailed information on Britain's devious role in the Syrian crisis as well as in the Palestinian question.[127]

After the Labour Party's electoral victory in July 1945, the information obtained by the French intelligence services on Britain's Middle East policy under Attlee and Bevin, especially the latter's disagreement with the military and secret services, was crucially important to Ben-Gurion and Sharett. On October 7, Ben-Gurion sent his well-known directive from Paris to the Haganah to form a resistance movement together with the Etzel and Lehi, the other Zionist underground organizations, and begin an armed struggle against the British forces in Palestine. The French secret services also had valuable information regarding Truman's distrust of Britain's policy in Palestine, as well as on the Anglo-Soviet rivalry in the Middle East. For example, a report from October 1945, undoubtedly prepared by the Deuxième Bureau in Beirut and passed on to the Political Department, gives accurate details of the Anglo-Soviet rivalry in Syria. The agent who received the report forwarded it on to Jewish Agency envoys in Washington with the recommendation that contact be made with Soviet diplomats. The extensive information that the French intelligence agencies had on inter-Arab rivalry and Britain's Arab policy was essential for Ben-Gurion and Sharett in defining their policy, as the question of Palestine became entangled in Anglo-Arab and inter-Arab relations as well as in the escalating Cold War.[128]

The deterioration into violent clashes between Arabs and Jews in Palestine following the resolution on Partition of November 29, 1947; the formation of the Arab Liberation Army, irregular Arab forces headed by Fawzi al-Qawuqji; the question of whether the Arab states would invade Palestine if a Jewish state was established; and the uncertainty over Britain's policy in Palestine, made the constant flow of political and military information from the French sources even more essential. Moreover, the Arab League's political and military committees on Palestine convened frequently between September 1947 and May 1948 in Damascus, giving French intelligence agents direct access to their most secret decisions. Various channels were established to ensure the rapid transfer of intelligence from French sources in Beirut to Ben-Gurion and his closest advisers who were privy to the secret ties with France. From August 1947 to June 1948, Sasson either visited Paris or met in Jerusalem with the French military attaché from Beirut. Military and political information was also sent directly by Maurice Fischer in Paris or from Beirut via couriers to Tuvia Arazi in Haifa. French diplomats in Washington and New York also passed on information to Eliyahu Epstein. In March 1948, French intelligence proposed that the Haganah should establish a wireless station in Beirut. At the same time, powerful decoding machines were installed in the French Consulate compound in Jerusalem, giving its military attaché direct contact with his Paris headquarters and his counterparts in Beirut and Cairo. An agent of the Political Department maintained daily contact with the Consulate, and the information he received was conveyed to Sasson and Reuven Zaslani, Ben-Gurion's chief intelligence officer. The French also passed on information through Dumarçay, the French Consul General in Amman, who had previously served as an intelligence officer in Lebanon. He frequently came to Jerusalem and met with Sasson. The French information was incorporated into Sasson's assessments and was used by Ben-Gurion in defining his strategy against Britain and the Arab states during the critical months from January to July 1948.[129]

An intriguing question is what the British security and secret services knew about the clandestine Franco-Zionist intelligence collaboration. It is evident that they were aware early on of France's assistance to the Zionist movement in illegal immigration and later military aid. In fact, they followed the contacts between Zionist agents and French officials in Beirut. The British authorities subsequently denied Epstein an entry visa into Lebanon; he was only allowed entry after French intervention. The Syrian documents from 1945 to 1947 reveal that British diplomats used Quwatli, Jabiri and Mardam to solicit the agreement of Kings Faruq and Ibn Sa'ud to sever their ties with France because of its support for the Zionist movement (docs.358, 374, 379, 382, 385, 387). They also disclose that the British secret services were aware that the French Legations in Beirut and Damascus served as meeting points with Zionist agents. For instance, in January 1947 Armanazi reported that the

British security services were closely monitoring the Legations because they were "areas favorable to Jewish activity. The British spy on everything that happens, fearing that the French Consulates, with their money, will come to the aid of the Jewish rabbis but, so far, nothing tangible has confirmed this." (doc.370). It is worth noting Mardam's response that the French Consulate in Damascus was being monitored by the Syrians themselves and that its staff were incapable of acting against Syria.[130] (doc.381)

The British security and secret services' failure to uncover the high-grade information that the French intelligence services were passing on to the Jewish Agency was mainly due to their failure to detect the French infiltration of their Beirut Legation and recruitment of an informer in the Syrian government. Only after the archives of the British Legation in Beirut were seized by the Haganah, in December 1947, did they intensify their tracking of the Franco-Zionist intelligence collaboration. During the Arab Legion's siege of Jerusalem, the French Consulate was constantly bombarded by irregular Arab soldiers, which led to the injury of scores of staff members. The French diplomats were certain that British secret agents had provoked the attacks to force an evacuation of the Consulate compound. Despite repeated protests to the Foreign Office and King Abdullah, the bombardments lasted until July 1948. During this period, the Haganah forces provided basic commodities to its staff.[131]

In a meeting on October 6, 1945 with Marc Jarblum, head of the Zionist Labor Federation in France, de Gaulle remarked: "The Jews in Palestine are the only ones capable of chasing the British out of the Middle East."[132] Three years after the Syrian crisis, de Gaulle had his revenge. Britain's withdrawal from Palestine in May 1948 and the upheaval in the Arab states following their defeat marked the beginning of the demise of Britain's empire in the Middle East.

Notes

1 CZA, S25/7576, Jerusalem, March 1, 1946, Arazi's report on Spears.
2 CZA, S25/6595, Jerusalem, April 24, 1946, Czernovitz to Bernard Joseph; AN, Paris, Bidault's Papers, 457AP125, nos.505-18, Moscow, March 10, 1948, Catroux to Bidault. See also Catroux, pp.429-38; Lerner, Henri, *Catroux*, (Paris: Albin Michel, 1990), pp.223-30. For an overview of Franco-Arab relations, see Brown, L. Carl, and Matthew S. Gordon, (eds.), *Franco-Arab Encounters: Studies in Memory of David C. Gordon* (Beirut: American University of Beirut, 1996), pp.11-13.
3 AN, Paris, Catroux's Papers, 72AJ438, Beirut, March 8, 1943, Note pour le Général.
4 AN, Paris, Catroux's Papers, 72AJ438, Beirut, March 7, 1943, Note pour le Général, and Spears' letter to Catroux, March 16, 1943; CADN, Syrie et Liban, 779, Damascus, March 2, 1943, Information no.687. The information on Nuri al-Sa'id's unity plan had been given to the French intelligence by Fa'iz al-Khuri. TNA, FO 226/241, no.P/1/1/10, Beirut, February 28, 1943, Furlonge to Spears concerning Sulh's report on Quwatli's support for Britain.

5 AN, Paris, Catroux's Papers, 72AJ438, Correspondence between Catroux and Nahhas via the Egyptian Legation in London, January-March 1943; CADN, Syrie et Liban, 787, nos.1714 and 1728, exchange of letters between Catroux and the Egyptian Consul in Beirut, March 18 and 24, 1943; carton 755, no.968, Beirut, October 13, 1944, Beynet to Bidault.

6 MAE, Paris, Massigli's Papers, vol.1468, Helleu's letter to Massigli, Damascus, July 26, 1943; Zamir, "Intimate Alliance," pp.824-6.

7 CADN, Syrie et Liban, no.552/SP, Information, Beirut, May 1943; AN, Paris, Catroux's Papers, 72AJ438, March 16, 1943, Spears' letter to Catroux; Zamir, "Intimate Alliance," pp.820-3.

8 MEC, Spears Papers, on his meeting with Churchill, Cairo, December 9, 1943.

9 CADN, Syrie et Liban, 768, British intervention in the elections, August 1943.

10 Quoted in Zamir, "Intimate Alliance," p.824. See also Furlonge's report to Spears on his conversation with Sulh, pp.827-9.

11 For Khuri's description of those events, see his autobiography, Khuri, Bishara al-, *Haqa'iq lubnaniyya*, Vol.2 (Beirut: 1960), pp.15-52.

12 AN, Paris, de Gaulle's Papers, 3AG 1/265, no.387, December 21, 1943, Oliva Roget's report on the repercussions of the Lebanese crisis in Syria, November–December 1943 and CADN, Syrie et Liban, 1102, Kuneitra, October 21, 1943, Information no.32. See also Roshwald, p.133.

13 AN, Paris, de Gaulle's Papers, 3AG1/265, Oliva Roget's report on the repercussions of the Lebanese crisis in Syria, November-December, 1943; 3AG1/264, Beirut, August 26, 1943, Note pour Monsieur l'Ambassador; AN, Paris, Bidault's Papers, 457AP121, Beirut, February 22, 1945, Beynet's meeting with Quwatli.

14 AN, Paris, de Gaulle's Papers, 3AG1/264, no.1967/8/43, Cairo, December 6, and no. 1984/4/43, December 11, 1943, personal letters to Palewski; CADN, Syrie et Liban, 771, Note on British intervention in Lebanon since the elections, n.d.

15 AN, Paris, de Gaulle's Papers, 3AG1/264, no 2753, Algiers, November 27, 1943, Commissioner of the Interior to General de Gaulle.

16 Roshwald, pp.158-9; Gaunson, pp.140-1.

17 AN, Paris, de Gaulle's Papers, 3AG1/264, no.373, Algiers, October 11, 1943; Egremont, pp.257-61.

18 Gaunson, pp.148-9.

19 Zamir, "The Missing Dimension," docs.4-6. The British army also stepped up its propaganda campaign, stressing its role in defending Syria. In March 1944, the RAF organized "Spitfire Day," which included flypasts over Damascus and an exhibition of airplanes as part of its efforts to raise funds for the purchase of eight Spitfires.

20 SHA, Levant, 4H384, PICME report, November 18, 1943. See also Lieutenant Porte, head of the secret service in Damascus, to Captain Coullet, head of SEL in Beirut, December 2, 1943. The French translation is dated January 10, 1944.

21 PICME report, November 18, 1943.

22 Ibid.

23 Ibid.

24 Ibid. See doc.4.

25 PICME report, November 18, 1943.

26 The report proposed four such blocs – Greater Syria comprising Syria, Transjordan, Lebanon and Palestine; Iraq and the Gulf states; Saudi Arabia, Yemen and the region of Hadhramout; and Egypt and North Africa.

27 Ibid.

28 CADN, Syrie et Liban, 787, August 9, 1943, the Egyptian Consulate in Beirut to the Foreign Ministry in Cairo; AN, Paris, de Gaulle's Papers, 3AG1/265, no.132, Beirut, February 11, 1944, Interviews with Nuri al-Sai'd while he was visiting Damascus. See also Porath, p.279.

29 AN, Paris, de Gaulle's Papers, 3AG1/264, no.748, Beirut, August 8, 1944, Beynet to Massigli; no.6/P.A., August 1, 1944. Khaled Bakdash, head of the Syrian Communist Party, was used to pass messages from Soviet representatives to the Syrian government.

30 Zamir, "The Missing Dimension," doc.11; CADN, Syrie et Liban, 771, no.763, Beirut, July 15, 1944.

31 AN, Paris, de Gaulle's Papers, 3AG4/13, Damascus, September 11, 1944, Note for Captain Cristofini; 3AG1/265, no.664, July 19, 1944, Colonel Stirling's activities, Beynet to Massigli. On MacKereth's disagreement with Spears, see 3AG1/264, no.873, Beirut, August 8, 1944, Beynet to de Gaulle. See also: MAE, Paris, Syrie et Liban, 1944-52, vol. 301, September 20, 1944, Note pour le Secrétaire Général; SHA, Levant, 4H388, Information, August 3, 1944; CADN, Syrie et Liban, 1210, Information no. 304, July 28, 1944; Zamir, "The Missing Dimension," docs.16, 20.

32 AN, Paris, de Gaulle's Papers, 3AG4/13, Damascus, September 11, 1944, Note for Captain Cristofini; CADN, Syrie et Liban, 755, no.968, Beirut, October 13, 1944, Beynet to Bidault, and carton 1142, Note, January 1945; Zamir, "The Missing Dimension," docs.18, 19, 24-7, 29. On the discussions of the Preparatory Committee in Alexandria, see Porath, pp.267-84; Gomaa, pp.191-231.

33 AN, Paris, de Gaulle's Papers, 3AG1/265, no.781, Beirut, August 15, 1944, Beynet to Bidault, including translation of a letter from the Eyptian Legation in Beirut to Cairo; CADN, Syrie et Liban, 2455, Information no.330, Beirut, August 11, 1944; SHA, Levant, 4H319, no. 250, August 10, 1944, on the reaction of Lebanese Christians to the "Mardam-Nuri Pasha" plan.

34 AN, Paris, de Gaulle's Papers, 3AG1/265, no.783, Beirut, August 15, and no.821, August 22, 1944, Beynet to Massigli with a copy to de Gaulle.

35 AN, Paris, de Gaulle's Papers, 3AG4/12, Beirut, June 9, 1945, Grigg's press conference in Beirut attacking Oliva Roget and the latter's response; MAE, Paris, Syrie et Liban, 1944-52, vol.278, London, June 16, 1945, Spears' defense in Parliament of Stirling and Marsack against Oliva Roget's accusations. While expelling Oliva Roget from Damascus, the British secret services seized his belongings and released them only after French protests. See SHA, Oliva Roget's personal files, 13Yd725, no.770, Beirut, June 8, 1945. See also: Stirling, p.230; Kirkbride, Alec S., *A Crackle of Thorns: Experiences in the Middle East* (London: John Murray, 1956), p.151; Mardam, pp.210-20.

36 SHA, Oliva Roget's personal files, 725-13Yd, Catroux's annotations, Beirut, July 4, 1943; no.3494/CC, Damascus, October 13, 1943, Oliva Roget to the commander of the French Army in the Middle East.

37 Ibid.

38 AN, Paris, de Gaulle's Papers, 3AG 1/265, Oliva Roget's report on the repercussions of the Lebanese crisis in Syria, November-December, 1943.

39 AN, Paris, de Gaulle's Papers, 3AG 1/265, Note no.1066/SP, Damascus, August 6, 1944, Oliva Roget to Beynet. The agent's identity is known to the author.

40 CZA, S25/6594, Jerusalem, September 26, 1945, Vilensky to Bernard Joseph. It is unclear if and when the French secret services forced Mardam to collaborate, although evidence from 1947 indicates his odd behavior towards them. The Zionist agent commented that the information received by the Jewish Agency substantiated French claims that British agents were bribing Mardam.

41 AN, Paris, de Gaulle's Papers, 3AG4/13, de Gaulle's hand-written comment on the Anglo-Syrian agreement from May 29, 1945. For Burin des Roziers' comments, see files in 3AG4/12.

42 MAE, Paris, Syrie et Liban, 1944-52, vol.301, no. 1518, London, December 29, 1944, Massigli to Bidault; vol.251, no.180, Beirut, December 15, 1944, unidentified official in the French Delegation to Ostrorog in Paris. See also: Roshwald, p.174; Barr, pp.273-5.

43 AN, Paris, de Gaulle's Papers, 3AG4/12, Ostrorog's report, Beirut, September 17, 1944; Bidault's Papers, 457AP121, Algiers, September 4, 1944, instructions to Beynet following a meeting headed by Catroux; no.940, Beirut, October 3, 1944, Beynet to Bidault; CADN, Syrie et Liban, 755, no.179, Beirut, January 29, 1945, Beynet to Bidault.

44 CADN, Syrie et Liban, 1142, Bulletin no.3, March 26, 1945; carton 755, no.187, Beirut, February 9, 1945, Beynet to Bidault; SHA, Levant, 4H319, Information no.925, Beirut, March 28, 1945; MAE, Paris, Syrie et Liban, 1944-52, vol.311, no.942, Beirut, October 9, and no.1168, December 11, 1944, Beynet to Bidault.

45 AN, Paris, de Gaulle's Papers, 3AG4/13, no. 1267, Damascus, September 13, 1944, Oliva Roget to Beynet; CADN, Syrie et Liban, 755, no.179, Beirut, January 29, 1945, Beynet to Bidault; carton 798, Damascus, January 29, 1945, note no.136/SP, and Beirut, February 23, 1945, no. 247, Beynet to Bidault.

46 CADN, Syrie et Liban, 755, no.316, Beirut, January 8, 1945, Beynet to the Quai d'Orsay; carton 798, Damascus, February 24, 1945, Beynet's meeting with Quwatli. See for example AN, Paris, de Gaulle's Papers, 3AG4/12, Oliva Roget's version of those months in his report, "Les Relations Franco-Syriennes, Les Activités Anglais et les Evénements de Syrie, vus de Damas, de Janvier à Juin 1945," pp.10-51.

47 SHA, Levant, 4H382, no.377, Damascus, March 21, 1945, Note pour Ostrorog; MAE, Paris, Syrie et Liban, 1944-52, vol.301, Beirut, September 17, 1944, Ostrorog to Chauvel; Mardam, pp.193, 195.

48 AN, Paris, de Gaulle's Papers, 3AG4/13, Damascus, September 11, 1944, Note for Captain Cristofini; Bidault's Papers, 457AP122, no.1156, Beirut, October 1, 1945, Beynet to Bidault; SHA, Levant, 4H384, no. 629, Beirut, September 19, 1944, Report on Abd al-Ilah, Abdullah and Ibn Sa'ud, and Anglo-American activities. See also: Zamir, "The Missing Dimension," docs. 27, 29, 34-6; Mardam, pp.168-70.

49 AN, Paris, de Gaulle's Papers, 3AG4/12 and13. Documents in both cartons attest to the considerable time that de Gaulle and his assistants devoted to Franco-British relations in the Levant, when they were facing far more pressing problems in France itself. AN, Paris, Bidault's Papers, 457AP121, October 19, 1944, de Gaulle's letter to Bidault, with the secret Syrian documents explaining Levantine affairs. See also: Beevor, Antony and Artemis Cooper, *Paris after the Liberation, 1944-1949* (London: Hamish Hamilton, 1994), pp.128-9; Zamir, "De Gaulle and the Question of Syria and Lebanon," p.676.

50 AN, Paris, de Gaulle's Papers, 3AG4/12, Paris, May 6, 1945, de Gaulle to Churchill; de Gaulle, *War Memoirs, Salvation*, pp.880-6; Kersaudy, pp.397-412.

51 Bell, Philip M.H., "La Grande-Bretagne, de Gaulle et les Français libres, 1940-1944: Un bienfait oublié?" *Espoir*, no.71, June 1990, p.28.

52 AN, Paris, de Gaulle's Papers, 3AG4/12, no.2707, Paris, February 25, 1945, de Gaulle to Bidault. See also: Cooper, Duff, *Old Men Forget: The Autobiography of Duff Cooper* (London: Rupert Hart-Davis, 1953), pp.344-55; Kersaudy, pp.391-409.

53 At the end of March, members of the Foreign Committee in the Consultative Assembly passed a resolution calling for the government to adopt a more liberal policy towards Syria and Lebanon. See AN, Paris, Bidault's Papers, 457AP121, London, March 7, 1945, Massigli to Chauvel; Paris, March 29, 1945, Vincent Auriol to Bidault; CADN, Syrie et Liban, 1161, no.2, Beirut, June 26, 1945, French press reaction to the Syrian crisis. See also de Gaulle, *War Memoirs, Salvation*, pp. 891-2.

54 CADN, Syrie et Liban, 755, no.179, Beirut, January 29, 1945, Beynet to Bidault; AN, Paris, Bidault's Papers, 457AP121, nos.723-37, Beirut, March 29, 1945, Beynet to Bidault.

55 AN, Paris, Bidault's Papers, 457AP122, no.278, February 6, 1945, British policy in the Middle East, Massigli to Bidault; de Gaulle's Papers, 3AG4/12, "Les Relations Franco-Syriennes," pp.22-36; Roshwald, p.286, note no.3.

56 CADN, Syrie et Liban, 755, no.179, Beirut, January 29, 1945, Beynet to Bidault; carton 1142, Note, January 1945; Note no.193, Cristofini's meeting with Major Altounyan, Damascus, February 10, and Bulletin no.3, February 25, 1945; AN, Paris, Bidault's Papers 457AP122, no.940, Beirut, October 3, 1944, Note on the future of the Middle East, Beynet to Bidault; no.278, London, February 6, 1945, British policy in the Middle East, Massigli to Bidault.

57 CADN, Syrie et Liban, 755, no.187, Beirut, February 9, 1945, Beynet to Bidault. Khuri's nervous breakdown prompted Chamoun to seek a revision of the constitution so that he could be elected as Vice-President, but Henri Pharaon and Michel Chiha also saw themselves as possible candidates. See carton 1142, Bulletin no.2, April 4, 1945. This carton contains many reports concerning Khuri's health and its political repercussions. See also Zisser, Eyal, *Lebanon: The Challenge of Independence* (London: I.B. Tauris, 2000), p.117.

58 AN, Paris, de Gaulle's Papers, 3AG4/12, Beirut, October 22, 1945, Beynet to de Gaulle; Louis, pp.132-3; SHA, Levant, 4H384, no. 629, Beirut, September 19, 1944, Report on Abd al-Ilah, Abdullah and Ibn Sa'ud, and Anglo-American activities.

59 CADN, Syrie et Liban, 798, no.102/SP, Damascus, January 23, 1945, Oliva Roget to Beynet; AN, Paris, Bidault's Papers 457AP122, no.940, Beirut, October 3, 1944, Note on the future of the Middle East, Beynet to Bidault; no.278, London, February 6, 1945, British policy in the Middle East, Massigli to Bidault. See also Zamir, "The Missing Dimension," doc.45.

60 SHA, Série S – Etat-major des armées (EMA), 14S313, no.758, November 20, 1946, Les Anglo-Saxons et l'URSS; Gorst, Anthony, "'We must cut our coat according to our cloth': the making of British defense policy, 1945-48," and Aldrich R.J., and John Zametica, "The rise and decline of a strategic concept: the Middle East, 1945-51," in Aldrich, Richard J. (ed.), *British Intelligence, Strategy and the Cold War, 1945-51* (Abingdon: Routledge, 1992).

61 MEC, Spears Papers, extract from Levant Diary, 1944-45.

62 Roshwald, pp.185, 195-7.

63 Evans, Trefor E. (ed.), *The Killearn Diaries, 1934-1946* (London: Sidgwick & Jackson, 1972), p.337, entry for April 3, 1945.

64 AN, Paris, de Gaulle's Papers, 3AG4/12, Beirut, May 28, 1945, Beynet's personal letter to de Gaulle; 3AG4/12, "Les Relations Franco-Syriennes," pp.83-184.

65 SHA, Levant, 4H309, Paris, April 5, 1945, "Réunion du 5 avril au sujet des affaires du Levant."

66 De Gaulle, *War Memoirs, Salvation,* p.879.

67 AN, Paris, de Gaulle's Papers, 3AG4/12, Paris, May 6, 1945, de Gaulle to Churchill, and Beirut, May 28, 1945, Beynet's personal letter to de Gaulle. See also Zamir, "The Missing Dimension," docs.68, 72-3, 80, 82-3.

68 AN, Paris, de Gaulle's Papers, 3AG4/12, Beirut, May 28, 1945, Beynet's personal letter to de Gaulle; SHA, Levant, 4H309, no.105/SP, Damascus, May 20, 1945; 4H375, Ninth Army Intelligence Summary No.1, June 12, 1945. See also Zamir, "The Missing Dimension," docs.98-124.

69 For Oliva Roget's detailed description of the events in Damascus from May 29–June 3, see AN, Paris, de Gaulle's Papers, 3AG4/12, "Les Relations Franco-Syriennes," 135-84. See also: Salma Mardam, which glorifies her father's role in those events, pp.213-20; Zamir, "The Missing Dimension," pp.812-3.

70 Louis, p.345.

71 BGA, Correspondence, Jerusalem, February 3, 1947, "Conversation with Muhammad Hussein Heikal on January 29, 1947"; Balfour-Paul, Glen, *The End*

of the Empire in the Middle East (Cambridge: Cambridge University Press, 1991), p.9.

72 MAE, Paris, Syrie et Liban, 1944-52, vol.293, no.529, Beirut, April 15, 1946, Ostrorog to Bidault. The volume contains numerous reports on the official ceremonies marking the evacuation of the French and British forces.

73 AN, Paris, de Gaulle's Papers, 3AG4/12, Paris, October 31, 1945, Note for Palewski; SHA, Levant, 4H382, Bulletin d'Information no.11, March 23, 1946; SHA, EMA, 14S321, no.2824, Paris, October 22, 1945, Intelligence report on Britain's policy in the Midde East; MAE, Paris, Syrie et Liban, 1944-52, vol.300, Minutes of a meeting between Nuri al-Sa'id and Sa'adallah al-Jabiri, Damascus, February 6, 1946, published in an Iraqi newspaper in early October 1946; vol.301, no.1278, Beirut, August 27, 1946, du Chayla to Bidault.

74 SHA, Levant, 4H382, no.155, Beirut, May 31, 1946, Cristofini to Beynet, with a copy of an original Syrian document from the Minister of Foreign Affairs to the Minister of the Interior; Renseignements no.123, May 31; no.1620, May 11; no.1632, May 13, 1945; CADN, Syrie et Liban, 798, no.715, Beirut, June 25, 1945, Beynet to Bidault. Zamir, "The Missing Dimension," docs. nos.117-21.

75 AN, Paris, de Gaulle's Papers, 3AG4/12, nos.922-5, Beirut, August 22, 1945, Beynet to de Gaulle; Paris, August 31, 1945, Note to General de Gaulle; AN, Paris, Bidault's Papers, 457AP/121, no.21/8/89, London, September 3, 1945, Bevin to Massigli; September 15, 1945, meeting of Attlee, Bevin and Duff Cooper with Bidault and Massigli.

76 AN, Paris, de Gaulle's Papers, 3AG4/12, Paris, January 3, 1946, Note to Palewski; MAE, Paris, Syrie et Liban, 1944-52, vol.280, no.915, Beirut, August 6, 1945, Beynet to Bidault. See also: Dorril, pp.35-7; Jeffery, pp.619-20.

77 Quoted by Hamdi, Walid M.S., *Rashid Ali Al-Gailani and the Nationalist Movement in Iraq, 1939-1941* (London: Darf Publishers Ltd., 1987), p.196.

78 SHA, Levant, 4H382, no.414, Beirut, April 6, 1946, copy of a note by the British Legation in Beirut obtained by the French intelligence services; no.155, Beirut, May 31, 1946, Cristofini to Beynet, with a copy of an original Syrian document from the Minister of Foreign Affairs to the Minister of the Interior; MAE Paris, Syrie et Liban, 1944-52, vol.301, no.99, Damascus, February 3, 1947, Serres to Bidault. See also Louis, p.49.

79 Wichart, p.375.

80 AN, Paris, de Gaulle's Papers, 3AG4/12, Beirut, January 1, 4 and 14, 1946, Beynet's personal letters to de Gaulle.

81 Another tactic was to arrange for Attlee and Bevin to meet with visiting Arab leaders who shared the Arabists' views, while preventing those who were more critical of their policy, such as President Quwatli, from going to London. See for example, MAE, Paris, Syrie et Liban, 1944-52, vol.300, nos.33-4, Beirut, January 6, 1946, Beynet to de Gaulle.

82 AN, Paris, de Gaulle's Papers, 3AG4/12, Paris, October 27, 1945, Burin des Roziers to Palewski; Kedourie, p.229.

83 AN, Paris, Bidault's Papers, 457AP122, Anglo-French meeting, Paris, February 17-18, 1948; SHA, Levant, 4H382, no.414, Beirut, April 6, 1946, the Deuxième Bureau's translation of a secret document prepared by the British Legation in Beirut summarizing the political situation for the week ending March 5th. A British officer warned that the Soviet Union would try to evict Britain from the Middle East as Britain had evicted France, Information, August 22, 1945; SHA, Série Q – Secrétariat général de la défense nationale (SGDN), 4Q43, Cairo, February 26, 1946, the French military mission in Egypt on Brigadier Clayton and the British secret agencies involved in North Africa.

84 AN, Paris, de Gaulle's Papers, 3AG4/12, Beirut, July 9, 1945, Beynet to de Gaulle; SHA, Levant, 4H373, no.1935, Beirut, June 21, 1945, Oliva Roget to the

Commader-in-Chief of the Levant Army; MAE, Paris, Syrie et Liban, 1944-52, vol.280, Beirut, July 2, 9 and 23, 1945, Ostrorog to Chauvel. Bidault's Papers, 457AP121, Beirut, June 10, 1945, Ostrorog's memorandum, "Reflexions sur notre politique au Levant."

85 AN, Paris, de Gaulle's Papers, 3AG4/12, Paris, August 1, de Gaulle to Beynet, and August 11, 1945, Note for General de Gaulle.

86 MAE, Paris, Syrie et Liban, 1944-52, vol.280, Paris, July 24, 1945, Bidault to Beynet; AN, Paris, Bidault's Papers, 457AP121, Beirut, October 1, 1945, Ostrorog to Chauvel.

87 MAE, Paris, Syrie et Liban, 1944-52, vol.293, no.36, Damascus, August 26, 1946, Serres to Bidault; CADN, Syrie et Liban, 755, no.434, March 25, and no.481, Beirut, April 1, 1946, Beynet to Bidault.

88 AN, Paris, de Gaulle's Papers, 3AG4/12, Beirut, June 25, 1945, Beynet to de Gaulle.

89 AN, Paris, de Gaulle's Papers, 3AG4/12, Bulletin de Renseignements no.481, Paris, November 29, 1945; MAE, Paris, Syrie et Liban, 1944-52, vol.311, no.833, Beirut, July 23, 1945, Beynet to Bidault; no.1822, Washington, November 24, 1945, Henri Bonnet to Bidault.

90 SHA, SGDN, Q51, Paris, March 8, 1949, a comprehensive study on Saudi Arabia prepared by the Deuxième Bureau; SHA, Levant, 4H384, no. 629, Beirut, September 19, 1944, Report on Abd al-Ilah, Abdullah and Ibn Sa'ud, and Anglo-American activities. See also: Graves, Philip. P. (ed.), *Memoirs of King Abdullah of Transjordan* (London: Jonathan Cape, 1950), pp.258-60; King Abdallah of Jordan, *My Memoirs Completed* (London: Longman, 1978), pp. 35-7.

91 SHA, Levant, 4H361, Beirut, Deuxième Bureau's reports for the weeks of January 12-18, and February 1-7, 1946; SHA, SGDN,4Q22, no.559, Paris, February 12, 1948, British policy and diplomacy in the Middle East. On King Faruq's support of Rashid Ali's subversion in Iraq, see Chavkin, Jonathan S., *British Intelligence and the Zionist, South African, and Australian Intelligence Communities during and after the Second World War* (PhD dissertation, University of Cambridge, 2009), pp.112-3.

92 See document no.6, a dispatch from the U.S. Embassy in Cairo, January 23, 1946, on Ambassador Killearn's overbearing attitude during Ibn Sa'ud's visit to Egypt, in Rashid, Ibrahim al- (ed.), *Documents on the History of Saudi Arabia*, Vol.V, Part II (Salisbury, NC: Documentary Publications, 1980). See also Qadi, Atif al-, *Qimmat Radwa* (Yanbu', 2008, in Arabic). The book marks King Faruq's visit to Radwa and King Ibn Sa'ud's reciprocal visit to Cairo. On King Faruq's opposition to Britain's efforts to secure a regional defense agreement, see Doran, Michael, *Pan-Arabism before Nasser: Egyptian Power Politics and the Palestine Question* (Oxford: Oxford University Press, 1999), pp.44-9, 67-71.

93 MAE, Paris, Syrie et Liban, 1944-52, vol.280, Beirut, July 9, 1945, Ostrorog to Chauvel. Improving relations with King Faruq was also intended to counter Azzam's hostility towards France.

94 AN, Paris, de Gaulle's Papers, 3AG4/12, Paris, October 27, 1946, Note to Palewski; Bidault's Papers, 457AP78, London, June 14, 1946, conversation with Bevin. See also attached note. MAE, Paris, Syrie et Liban, 1944-52. The entire volume 30AL concerns the Mufti. See for example reports by Henri Ponsot, the former High Commissioner in Syria and Lebanon, on his five meetings with the Mufti, especially no.10, August 24, 1945 in which the Mufti denies accusations of involvement in the extermination of Jews in Auschwitz. See also no.255, Cairo, June 28, 1946, on the Mufti's arrival in Cairo, and no.484, Paris, July 20, 1946, Bidault to the French Ambassador in Cairo.

95 MAE, Paris, Syrie et Liban, 1944-52, vol.30AL, no.356, Cairo, October 10, 1946; Cairo, June 11, 1947, a report on the Mufti's meeting with North African leaders.

96 AN, Paris, Bidault's Papers, no.940, Beirut, October 3, 1944, Beynet to Bidault; CADN, Syrie et Liban, 755, no.179, Beirut, January 29, 1945, Beynet to Bidault. General Catroux served from February 1945 until April 1948 as Ambassador to Moscow, by which time he had become critical of Britain's Middle East policy after being duped by Spears and other British agents in the Levant. See also, Thomas, "France in British Signals Intelligence," p.64.

97 AN, Paris, Bidault's Papers, 457AP121, Beirut, June 11, 1946, Beynet to Bidault. While in Paris, the Mufti had contacted the Soviet Embassy, which he could not have done without French permission. A SHAY agent reported that the French intelligence were tapping the telephone lines of the Soviet Embassy in Paris. See Haganah Archives Tel Aviv (HA), 14/732, "Yannai," December 11, 1947.

98 AN, Paris, de Gaulle's Papers, 3AG4/12, Bulletin de Renseignements no.M/483/ 2428, Paris, December 6, 1945; SHA, Levant, 4H309, Beirut, May 11, 1945, Report to Beynet; AN, Paris, Bidault's Papers, 457AP122, Note on Russian activity in the Middle East.

99 AN, Paris, Bidault's Papers, 457AP122, no.639, Ankara, June 15, 1945, Maugras to the Quai d'Orsay.

100 AN, Paris, de Gaulle's Papers, 3AG4/12, Paris, August 17, 1945, Note pour le Général.

101 MAE, Paris, Syrie et Liban, 1944-52, vol.290, no.1008, Beirut, August 27, 1945, Beynet to Bidault. Only a small number of the Syrian documents concerning the Anglo-Soviet secret war in Syria have been included in this book.

102 Roosevelt, Kermit, *Arabs, Oil and History: The Story of the Middle East* (London: Victor Gollancz Ltd., 1949), p.249.

103 MAE, Paris, Syrie et Liban, 1944-52, vol.300, no.194, Damascus, December 8, 1946, the French Minister in Damascus to the Quai d'Orsay; SHA, Levant, 4H382, no.1041, Beirut, January 15, 1944, Information; CZA, S25/8004, Cairo, February 1, 1946, Sasson's report on his meeting with Clayton.

104 AN, Paris, Bidault's Papers, 457AP122, August 7, 1945, "Les Etats-Unis, La Crise de Syrie et le Proche Orient."

105 AN, Paris, de Gaulle's Papers, 3AG4/12, June 1, 1945, General de Gaulle to President Truman; August 1, 1945, de Gaulle's letter to Beynet, and Paris 14, 1945, Note for General de Gaulle.

106 AN, Paris, de Gaulle's Papers, 3AG4/12, Paris, August 14; Bidault's Papers, 457AP81, Paris, August 7, 1945, memorandum on the United States and the Middle East. Beynet passed on information on British agents' anti-French intrigues to American diplomats in Beirut before and after the May crisis. See also Andrew, Christopher, *For the President's Eyes Only: Secret Intelligence and the American Presidency from Washington to Bush* (New York: Harper Perennial, 1996), pp.149-98.

107 De Gaulle, *War Memoirs, Salvation*, pp.904-13.

108 Pinkus, Benjamin, *From Ambivalence to a Tacit Alliance: Israel, France and French Jewry, 1947-1957* (Sede Boqer: Ben-Gurion University of the Negev Press, 2005, in Hebrew), p.35.

109 Zamir, "Bid for Altalena," pp.22-24.

110 Ibid.

111 Ibid.

112 For an example of Franco-Zionist intelligence sharing, see MAE, Paris, Syrie et Liban, 1944-52, vol.301, no.89, Beirut, January 26, 1948, the French Minister in Beirut to Bidault. SHA, EMA, 14S349, Beirut, January 26, 1948, French Military Attaché's report to Bidault on his meeting with Sasson in the Eden Hotel, Jerusalem, including an original hand-written summary of Sasson's words. See also Zamir, "Espionage and the Zionist Endeavor."

113 SHA, Levant, 4H386, Beirut, April 1, 1945, Colonel Terrier's report on his visit to Palestine from March 27-31, including the arrangements with Tuvia Arazi on

secret Franco-Zionist collaboration. Zamir, "Espionage and the Zionist Endeavor." See also Lefen, Asa, *The SHAY: The Roots of the Israeli Intelligence Community* (Tel Aviv: Ministry of Defense Publications, 1997, in Hebrew).

114 HA, 105/112, Paris, March 31, 1948, French intelligence bulletin no.6, on the Arab League forces for March 25. See details of the Syrian army in SHA, EMA, 14S363, and of the Egyptian army; SHA, Série T – Etat-major de l'armée de terre (EMAT), 10T789. See also Zamir, "Bid for Altalena," p.22.

115 SHA, Levant, 4H386, Beirut, April 1, 1945, Colonel Terrier's report on his visit to Palestine; Zamir, "Bid for Altalena," pp.18-21, and "Espionage and the Zionist Endeavor."

116 CZA, S25/22395, July 7, 1945, Eran to undisclosed recipients.

117 CZA, S25/22395, June 27, 1945, Nathanael to Hadad. (Hadad was Arazi's code name.)

118 SHA, Levant, 4H485. See confidential correspondence between the French military liaison officer in Jersualem and Beirut from 1943-1946, for example no.9614, Jerusalem, November 2, 1945. File of telegrams from the French Consulate in Jerusalem; AN, Paris, Bidault's Papers, 457AP121, Beirut, October 1, 1945, Ostrorog to Chauvel; CZA, S25/6594, April 12, 1946, Fischer to Sasson.

119 SHA, EMA, 14S348, no.23, Beirut, February 9, 1948, the Military Attaché to the Prime Minister; Zamir, "Bid for Altalena," pp.18-21; Schillo, pp.24-34.

120 Zamir, "Bid for Altalena," pp.18-21. For a detailed description of the Franco-Zionist alliance before May 1948, see Pinkus, Chapters 1-3, and the first part of Schillo's book.

121 Pinkus, pp.55-72; Schillo, pp.35-42.

122 SHA, Levant, 4H382, Beirut, November 29, 1943, letter from Gautier, the former director of the Sûreté générale aux Armées, to Maurice Fischer, attached to no.216/SC, October 8, 1944, in which Major Altounyan commented on the large number of Jewish officers serving in the French army in south Lebanon.

123 CZA, S25/492, Arazi's reports from Paris. For Arazi's secret activities in Syria and Lebanon under Vichy, see Gilad, pp.74-88.

124 CZA, S25/6594, Eliyahu Epstein's report to Ben-Gurion on his conversation with General Beynet on September 8, 1944. See also his book, Elath, *San Francisco Diary*.

125 SHA, EMA, 14S349, Beirut, January 26, 1948, French Military Attaché's report to Bidault on his meeting with Sasson; See Sasson, *On the Road to Peace*. On Sasson's clandestine diplomacy in Paris, see Cohen-Shany, Shmuel, *Paris Operation: Intelligence and Quiet Diplomacy in a New State* (Tel Aviv: Ramot Publishing, Tel Aviv University, 1994, in Hebrew), pp.27-43, 73-96.

126 AN, Paris, de Gaulle's Papers, 3AG4/12, Bulletin de renseignements no.481, November 1945; CADN, Syrie et Liban, 755, no.437, Beirut, March 25, 1946, Beynet to Bidault, including *Al Hayat*'s article from March 22nd criticizing Bishop Mubarak's interview in the *Palestine Post*; SHA, Levant, 4H385, no.8197, Jerusalem, January 15, 1945, report by the French liaison officer; See also Eisenberg, Laura Zittrain, *My Enemy's Enemy: Lebanon in the Early Zionist Imagination, 1900-1948* (Detroit: Wayne State University Press, 1994), pp.126-46.

127 CZA, S25/6594, Arazi's private letter from Paris from early August 1945; For a detailed description of de Gaulle's visit to the United States, see AN, Paris, de Gaulle's Papers, 3AG4/72.

128 CZA, S25/22123, no.31/1/94, November 11, 1945, Uriel Heyd to Dr. Nahum Goldmann and Eliyahu Epstein.

129 Zamir, "Bid for Altalena," pp. 21-2 and "Espionage and the Zionist Endeavor." Intelligence originating from French sources was usually masked, but top secret reports often indicated its French origin, with an added emphasis that "the French reports are usually accurate."

130 CZA, S25/1280, Jerusalem February 13, 1944, Bernard Joseph to le Comte du Chaylard and a hand-written note from Epstein to Joseph; Harouvi, pp.230, 254.
131 AN, Paris, Bidault's Papers, 457AP125, Amman, May 24, 1948, nos.109-10, Dumarçay to the Quai d'Orsay; Zamir, "Bid for Altalena," pp.31-3. See also Jules Moch's report in SHA, SGDN, 1Q31.
132 BGA, Correspondence, October 7, 1945, Jarblum's report on his conversation with de Gaulle.

Epilogue
"Those who pulled the strings and those who pulled the trigger"[1]

On the eve of the meeting of the Political Committee of the Arab League in Sofar, Lebanon, on September 11, 1947, the Lebanese newspaper *l'Orient* published an article entitled, "Bloc Oriental et extension de la Ligue," arguing that, like the Greater Syria plan, the Oriental Bloc (a French term for Britain's planned regional security pact) hung over the independence of the Arab countries and the Arab League like the sword of Damocles, and that its authors were the very same: Nuri al-Sa'id and King Abdullah. On September 20, the Lebanese newspaper *Le Jour* reported that after the Sofar conference, General [Brigadier] Clayton, whom it defined as "head of the British intelligence in the Middle East," had left for Damascus. It quoted a Syrian newspaper speculation on whether his visit was connected to the Greater Syria scheme and the tense relations between Quwatli and Khuri, and King Abdullah, or to events in Palestine.[2]

On February 19, 1948, the Lebanese newspaper *Le Soir* published an article titled "Claytonmade." Based on "Zionist sources," it reported that Brigadier Clayton, "architect" of the Greater Syrian plan, the Oriental Bloc and the bilateral treaties with the Arab states, was now advocating a new scheme for the partition of Palestine, according to which: "Imperialist Lebanon will annex the Western Galilee up to Shavei Zion; Syria the northeastern part of the Galilee and part of its southern region; Egypt will have part of the cake; and Transjordan will swallow up the rest."[3] A month later, the Cairo newspaper *al-Kutla* warned that,

> "British imperialism, with its intrigues, has succeeded in engaging the Arab people and their leaders in the question of Palestine, while in the meantime seeking one-sided treaties to its own benefit. Iraq has managed to save itself from this trap. Egypt objected to the British plan for 'Sudanization,' and yet its leaders were mainly concerned with the Palestinian question, to the neglect of Egypt's essential problems."[4]

Information conveyed by the French intelligence services to the Haganah in the autumn of 1947 indicated that Brigadier Clayton and his assistants were involved in a new initiative to secure Britain's strategic position in the Middle

East, and linked Clayton to the escalating Arab-Jewish conflict in Palestine. The sources also referred to a new partition plan promoted by Clayton that, in contradiction to the UN plan, intended to split Palestine between the neighboring Arab states while limiting the designated territory of the Jewish state to an area on the coast between Atlit, just south of Haifa, and Tel Aviv. The French tied this initiative to renewed British efforts to implement the Morrison-Grady cantonization plan and warned of the danger of an attack on the Yishuv by irregular forces organized by the Arab League. They also warned that an invasion by the Arab regular armies to prevent the establishment of a Jewish state could not be ruled out.[5]

The information passed on by the French after the UN vote on partition on November 29, 1947 was even more alarming. On January 13, 1948, Maurice Fischer reported from Paris, based on "top–certain information" from French sources, that on December 17, 1947, Clayton had reached an understanding with Lebanese Prime Minister Riyad al-Sulh, according to which the British forces would evacuate northern Palestine and give free rein to the irregular forces of the Arab Liberation Army, organized by the Arab League and headed by Fawzi al-Qawuqji, to attack Jewish settlements. The following day two officers from the Deuxième Bureau in Beirut arrived in Haifa and informed the French military attaché that the Syrian Prime Minister, Jamil Mardam, was mobilizing an irregular force of 20,000 volunteers to invade Palestine.[6]

In the second half of August 1947, Sasson was called urgently to Paris, where he remained until mid-September, sending information and instructions to warn King Abdullah and the Egyptian government that British agents were planning to provoke their countries into a war against the Jews in Palestine. Reports in the Haganah Archives from those months, where Clayton's name frequently figures, tie the escalation of the Arab-Jewish conflict to Britain's efforts to secure its strategic position in the Middle East. They too alluded to a new scheme, promoted by the British secret services in Cairo, to divide Palestine between the neighboring Arab states. A Tenne report stated that during the Arab League meeting in Cairo in mid-December 1947, Clayton, Smart and Nuri al-Sa'id proposed that Britain should try to convince the United States to withdraw its support for the establishment of a Jewish state if the Arab leaders agreed to conclude defense treaties with Britain. Another Tenne report noted a change in the secret scheme according to which Egypt, like other Arab states, would receive territory in Palestine adjacent to its own borders. In the early months of 1948 information continued to reach the SHAY on secret British attempts, orchestrated by Brigadier Clayton's "clique" in Cairo, to reconcile between the Arab leaders and convince them to join forces to prevent a Jewish state.[7]

The concern of Ben-Gurion, as well as of Zaslani, Sasson and other Haganah intelligence agents regarding the undercover activities of Brigadier Clayton and Arabist "experts" in the Foreign Office and the Middle East intensified between August 1947 and May 1948. On November 11, 1947 Ben-Gurion sent a former British-Jewish officer to interview Clayton, who was unaware that Ben-Gurion had drafted the questions.[8] The urgency of uncovering the British secret services' intentions prompted Ben-Gurion to approve the aforementioned "Acre" operation, in which the Haganah seized the files of the British Legation in Beirut the following month. On January 11, 1948 Sasson sent King Abdullah a letter warning him of a plot being hatched in London and Cairo, promoted by Clayton, Nuri al-Sa'id and officials in the Foreign Office and Ministry of Colonies against the UN Partition Plan, which aimed to provoke Transjordan into a war against the Yishuv, contrary to his understanding with the Jewish Agency.[9] In February, Zaslani traveled to London to establish whether Britain's failure in Iraq had influenced its stand on Palestine and if there was indeed a British plot to thwart the formation of a Jewish state. He reported that although the Cabinet did not intend to oppose partition, the "experts," arguing that it could not be implemented, were working against it. Among them Zaslani counted Bevin's adviser Harold Bailey, Iltyd Clayton and Gerald de Gaury, a Foreign Office Arabist liaison officer. Zaslani noted that these "experts," who advocated a collective military agreement with the Arab countries, believed that a future Jewish state could not be relied upon. He added that they were reinforcing the Arab side without Cabinet agreement. Nevertheless, he assessed that they would not be able to influence the Cabinet's decision to end the mandate and withdraw the British forces from Palestine, as it was supported by the two highest ranking British officials in Palestine – the High Commissioner Sir Alan Cunningham and GOC Palestine, General Sir Gordon MacMillan. A similar assessment was made by Ben-Gurion in a conversation with a French diplomat in early March.[10] In a March 7 entry in his diary, Ben-Gurion notes that: "Clayton went to Syria; the British want to make Syria their base after failing in Iraq and Egypt. The situation in the Arab world is difficult – riots in Iraq, and Britain is trying to concentrate the Arab thought on Palestine."[11]

The above examples from the Arab press and French and Zionist sources raise intriguing questions. Was there indeed a connection between Britain's efforts to conclude bilateral military treaties with Iraq, Egypt and other Arab states or form a collective regional defense organization, and the alleged attempts by its secret services in Cairo to provoke a Jewish-Arab war in Palestine? Why was Brigadier Clayton associated with a secret scheme to split Palestine between its neighboring Arab states? Why was he implicated in provoking Arab attacks, initially on the Yishuv by irregular forces and, later, on the newly-established Jewish state by the Arab regular armies? Like General de Gaulle, who blamed Britain for conspiring to evict France from the Levant, Ben-Gurion accused it of trying to sabotage the establishment of a Jewish state and secretly provoking an armed invasion by Arab states. The Syrian and British documents uncovered in French archives confirming de Gaulle's accusations also reinforce Ben-Gurion's charges. These documents and French intelligence reports reveal that the British Arabist secret agents, who engineered France's eviction from the Levant in 1945, took similar steps to prevent the formation of a Jewish state in 1947-48.[12]

Before presenting the new findings, it is worth recapping some of this work's main suppositions, as they relate directly to the British secret agents' covert operations in the 1948 war. The study argues that the role of the British secret services in the Middle East during and after World War II comprises the "missing dimension" in the historiography of the region in the 1940s, a premise based on the British and Syrian documents in the French archives. The study contends that during the war, a plethora of British security and secret agencies active in the Middle East formed a close-knit intelligence community. They employed innovative methods to secure their country's hold over the region, exploiting its strategic and economic resources, especially oil, in Britain's war efforts. This community included a small number of intelligence officers, some of whom were World War I veterans. They comprised part of a larger group of "Arabists" or "agents in the field," who wielded considerable influence on Britain's Middle East policy in the 1940s. They sought to take advantage of the new war to rectify what they regarded as two historical errors made by Britain in World War I: the Sykes-Picot Agreement, which allocated the Levant to France; and the Balfour Declaration, which granted Jews a homeland in Palestine. They aspired to exploit France's defeat in World War II to evict it from Syria and Lebanon and prevent the establishment of an independent Jewish state in Palestine, thereby opening the way for a reorganization of the region under Britain's hegemony. They regarded these steps essential for securing their country's dominance in the post-war Middle East and maintaining the Empire and Britain's status as a Great Power. These designs were endorsed by influential lobby groups in London, among them financial and commercial circles. Various schemes – Greater Syria, a confederation of the Fertile Crescent states, and an Arab union – were aired for the reorganization of the region. The Greater Syria plan attracted most attention as it was deemed central to solving the protracted Palestine problem. The Cold War and the threat of a third world war against the Soviet Union, in which the Middle East would become a major arena, turned these schemes into a priority in Britain's regional security strategy. Backed by the powerful military and defense establishments, intelligence agents, military officers and diplomats shouldered the task of securing their country's overt and covert control of the Middle East in the face of the rising tide of pan-Arabism, the struggle of nationalist movements for independence from the colonial Powers and international pressure for decolonization. They were determined that Britain would not, once again, be caught unprepared for war. This strategy, advocated by the Chiefs of Staff (COS) and the High Command in the Middle East, met with opposition from Prime Minister Attlee. Facing an acute domestic economic crisis, he was compelled to reduce the high cost of retaining a large military presence in a region whose strategic importance he doubted.

A central premise of the study is that in the 1940s, Britain conducted a two-track policy in the Middle East – one, a well-documented, official policy defined by Whitehall under both the Conservatives and Labour, and another informal, secretive policy that can be termed "regional," implemented by the "agents in the field," which left few traces in British archives. It was perpetrated by a small, influential group of Arabist secret agents who manipulated the Cabinet in London and implemented their own policies, which deviated from the official position. These agents enjoyed a unique status as intermediaries between Whitehall and local Arab leaders. Either intentionally, or because of deep-seated personal beliefs, they provided biased assessments. They did not merely gather and interpret information and recommend policy, but controlled the flow of information and implemented their own policies while keeping the London decision-makers in the dark. This was demonstrated in their success in engineering the eviction of France from Lebanon in 1943 and from Syria in 1945, as well as in their attempt to undermine the Bevin-Bidault agreement of December 1945 and implement the Greater Syria plan despite Whitehall's opposition. They joined forces with Arab rulers, whom they portrayed as voicing the Arab view, in order to mislead their government. Their tactics, which were backed by senior military officers in Cairo, gathered momentum under the Labour Government and during the crisis in Palestine in 1947-48.

The Arabists' success in implementing their policies was due largely to their use of indirect control, developed and perfected during the war, over local "agents of influence." They employed undercover political operations, clandestine diplomacy and covert propaganda to manipulate local leaders and public opinion – methods already used in the Middle East in the inter-war years, but more widely deployed during World War II. The Syrian and British documents provide unique insight into the modus operandi of the British secret services in co-opting prominent Arab leaders, helping them to positions of power in return for their collaboration. President Quwatli and Prime Minister Mardam in Syria, President Khuri and Prime Minister Sulh in Lebanon; and Secretary General of the Arab League Abd al-Rahman al-Azzam, are prime examples, but there were many others. This is not to say, however, that the British intelligence officers entirely controlled those leaders. Relations were complex and entailed various means of coercion. Apart from political and financial bribery, and when necessary, pressure and extortion, an effective tactic was to convince them that collaborating with Britain was in their own and their country's interests. But such maneuvers, as was the case with President Quwatli, did not always succeed. After the war, as Britain's prestige waned and its military and economic standing diminished, undercover political operations were stepped up, becoming an essential tool for the Arabist secret agents to safeguard their country's strategic and economic interests in the Middle East.

The Arabists exploited their personal ties with Arab leaders and politicians to manipulate policies. Cornwallis had close relations with the Regent Abd al-Ilah, Nuri al-Sa'id and other prominent Iraqi politicians; Stirling with President Quwatli and Prime Minister Mardam; Spears and Furlonge with President Khuri and Prime Minister Sulh; Kirkbride and Glubb with King Abdullah;

and Killearn, Smart and Clayton with King Faruq and other Egyptian leaders. Brigadier Clayton, the senior intelligence officer in the Middle East, had
a unique standing as he held region-oriented positions – as head of Middle
East Intelligence Centre (MEIC) and Political Intelligence Centre Middle
East (PICME) and adviser to the Minister Resident in Cairo; later as an
envoy to the Arab League; and from 1947 as Minister in the British Embassy
in Cairo and an adviser to the British Middle East Office (BMEO). In these
capacities he coordinated policies with the various British authorities and
maintained direct personal contacts with all the Arab leaders, thus being able
to influence Britain's Middle East policy throughout the 1940s. He was
involved in promoting bilateral relations with Egypt and Iraq, while his close
ties with Azzam allowed him to tacitly advance regional policies through the
Arab League.[13]

For the Arabist intelligence officers, the Middle East was a playground in
which they advanced what they perceived to be their country's vital strategic
and economic interests during and after the war. They were well acquainted
with the Arab leaders with whom they were dealing and knew how to exploit
their weaknesses, fears and need for prestige, as well as the rivalry between
them, to coerce them into collaborating or advancing particular policies. They
were not always successful: some Arab rulers were aware of their methods, while
others tried to exploit their ties with them to promote their own goals,
whether personal or national. But in most cases the British agents had the
last word. Their most effective tactic of "divide and rule" played on the enmity
between the Hashemites and their opponents, Kings Ibn Sa'ud and Faruq.
Syria was pivotal in the inter-Arab rivalry, hence the importance of the Syrian
documents. Although they gave priority to Britain's relations with the
Hashemites, they tried to present themselves as neutral, independent arbi-
trators in the inter-Arab squabbling. In reality, they instigated rivalries and
jealousies, only to mediate in accordance with Britain's needs. They exploited
King Abdullah's obsession with the Syrian crown to intimidate President
Quwatli, and his determination to take revenge for his family's expulsion from
the Hejaz to pressure Ibn Sa'ud. The latter took these threats seriously,
knowing well that behind the Hashemites stood Britain's might. Nuri al-Sa'id,
a master schemer and the strong-man of Baghdad, played a key role in the
British agents' regional game while furthering his own ambition to unite the
Fertile Crescent states under Iraq's leadership. He was to take part in the British
secret services' grand scheme in Palestine in the autumn of 1947.

Britain's Middle East policy was both bilateral – towards each Arab state
separately – and region-oriented. Despite playing on the rivalries between
Arab rulers, British agents viewed the Middle East as one single region and
advanced various unity plans. The Arab League, formed in March 1945,
became the main tool in their overt and covert regional policy following the
British secret service's success in co-opting its Secretary General, Abd al-
Rahman al-Azzam. Brigadier Clayton's appointment in 1946 as Britain's
envoy to the Arab League, contrary to the Foreign Office's stand, attests to

the importance the Arabists in Cairo attached to the League as a tool to circumvent the Arab governments. They regarded it as a unifying institution for regional political and economic cooperation and as a safety-valve against Muslim and Arab nationalist extremists. They exploited the question of Palestine and Azzam's ambitions for power and prestige to transform the Arab League from a loose alliance of seven states into a tight organization with authority. In fact, already in 1946, they had tried to persuade the Arab governments to form, alongside their national armies, a joint Arab army to be supervised by the Secretary General and a military committee representing all the states. Those ideas were tested in the war in Palestine. Faced with strong opposition to bilateral military treaties from Egypt and Iraq in 1947 and 1948, British strategists then considered forming a collective defense alliance based on the Arab League, in which Turkey would later be incorporated.[14]

The bitter rivalry between the Arab rulers, their dissension over Palestine and the role assumed by the Arab League on behalf of its Arab inhabitants transformed Azzam into a central figure as the spokesman of the "collective Arab stand" towards Palestine and a champion of the Arab world against the Zionist threat. This enabled Clayton to tacitly collaborate with him against the establishment of an independent Jewish state while advancing Britain's ends. In fact, the Arab-Jewish conflict was intentionally inflamed to further Britain's strategic goals in the Middle East.

Another premise of the study is that a clandestine war took place between Britain and France in the Middle East during and after World War II. Despite collaboration between Britain and Free France during the war, and between Britain and France in post-war Europe, the long-standing rivalry between the two declining colonial Powers continued unabated in the Middle East. After its eviction from the Levant in 1945, France successfully conducted a secret war against Britain in the Middle East due in no small part to the achievements of its intelligence services, especially the Oliva Roget operation. The French secret services honed their ability to monitor the British agents' Special Political Operations, study their modi operandi and uncover their ties with their Arab collaborators. This information, available in French, but not British, archives is essential for an understanding of the covert policy pursued by the British secret agents in the 1948 war.

After its eviction from the Levant, France became concerned with Arab League subversion in North Africa led by Azzam and tacitly supported by the British secret services in Cairo. Subsequently, its intelligence agencies and diplomats in the Middle East closely monitored Azzam's ties with Brigadier Clayton. During an Anglo-French meeting in Paris in mid-February 1948 to coordinate strategy in the Middle East, French officials complained to their British counterparts of Clayton's subversive activities in French North Africa. The French Embassy in Cairo became a center for spying on the British secret services and the Arab League. It had reliable informers in the League's offices who provided information on Azzam's activities, as well as copies of documents and protocols of its meetings and secret decisions on Palestine in

1947-48. This information sheds light on the British agents' role in instigating the war in Palestine.[15]

The hitherto unknown details of the intelligence collaboration between France and the Jewish Agency, presented in the last part of Chapter 3, afforded David Ben-Gurion and a small group of Haganah secret agents and diplomats, led by Eliyahu Sasson, direct access to the Syrian and British documents and the wealth of French intelligence information on inter-Arab politics and the British secret services' modus operandi. This information became crucial between August 1947 and May 1948. It helped Ben-Gurion uncover the British and Arab schemes and prepared the Jewish community in Palestine for an all-out war against the Arab states while obstructing British designs.

The Syrian documents and the war of 1948

A major hurdle when studying the 1948 war is the lack of access to Arab archives. The Syrian documents, which contain uncensored private correspondence and secret agreements between the Arab leaders, as well as diplomatic exchanges, give scholars a closer look at the Arab stand towards a Jewish state in Palestine without having to rely solely on Israeli and Western archives, Arab rulers' inflammatory public rhetoric and memoirs, or articles in newspapers. It is not the intention of this study to argue that the Arab leaders were willing to acquiesce in an independent Jewish state in the heart of the Arab world. The documents reveal, however, that their attitudes towards the Zionists' aspirations derived not only from their hostility towards a Jewish state, but were far more complex, and thus highlight the need for scholars to study the Arab-Zionist conflict in the context of Anglo-Arab and inter-Arab rivalries, rather than merely Anglo-Jewish or Arab-Jewish relations.

The Arab-Jewish conflict became deeply entangled in the inter-Arab rivalries as each ruler advanced his own interests while undermining those of his rivals. The most vehement opposition to a Jewish state came from President Quwatli and King Ibn Sa'ud, who feared that any solution to the problem in Palestine would be to the benefit of their Hashemite opponents. President Quwatli was concerned that in the event of partition, King Abdullah would annex the Palestinian-Arab designated regions to Jordan, thereby bolstering his ambitions to take over Syria, while Ibn Sa'ud was opposed to any British-Hashemite plan to solve the Jewish problem in Palestine within the context of a Greater Syria under King Abdullah or a confederation headed by Iraq. In fact there was a disparity between King Ibn Sa'ud's anti-Zionist and anti-Jewish stand – deeply rooted in his religious beliefs, and which he repeated publicly and in his exchanges with the American Presidents – and his pragmatic approach to the Arab-Jewish conflict. Despite his intense opposition to a Jewish state he did not cut off oil supplies or jeopardize his relations with the United States, but pressed the American administration to intervene primarily to prevent the establishment of a Hashemite Greater Syria that would include Syria and Palestine. Ibn Sa'ud's pragmatism was also revealed by his tacit collaboration with France despite being well aware of its support for the Zionist movement.[16] King Faruq adopted a similarly pragmatic policy towards the United States and France. Both Kings strongly opposed Abdullah's attempt to take over Jerusalem, the third holiest city in Islam after Mecca and Medina. Abdullah wanted Jerusalem, where he had buried his father, as a first step towards restoring his family's religious standing after Ibn Sa'ud had ousted it from Mecca and Medina. But Ibn Sa'ud saw the taking of Jerusalem by Abdullah, whose family descended from the prophet Muhammad, as a threat to his own position as guardian of the two holy cities. King Faruq also harbored designs over Jerusalem since his father had sought the caliphate in the 1920s. The rivalry over Jerusalem between Kings Abdullah and Faruq impacted on their military operations in May 1948. The Arab Legion's attack on Jerusalem was made at King Abdullah's insistence, while the Egyptian military plan was intended to prevent the Jordanian King from taking over the city.[17]

The Syrian and British documents also shed new light on how the Powers used the Arab-Jewish conflict to promote their own interests in the Middle East. Soviet diplomats endorsed the Arab position, reminding the Syrian leaders that it was Britain that had installed the Jews in Palestine. While the French tacitly collaborated with the Zionists, in their propaganda they blamed Britain for being responsible for the Jewish problem in Palestine and warned of a British-Jewish conspiracy. American diplomats, on the other hand, advised the Syrian government to reach a compromise with the Zionist movement. In this regard, it is worth noting a State Department official's warning to Nazim al-Qudsi that it was "in the interest of the Arabs to accept this solution, because it is preferable that some of the Arab countries withdraw in favor of the Jews, rather than leaving the door wide open to Jewish demands" (doc.142).

Informal and uncensored views of British officials and agents regarding the Zionists' aspirations are revealed in their exchanges with Arab leaders. Their views, often not in line with the formal, carefully-worded dispatches sent to London, provide insight into their use of the Zionists, both in their policy of divide and rule and as scare tactics to coerce the Arab leaders into acquiescing to Britain's military and economic dominance over the region. The documents also disclose British attempts to deflect allegations of responsibility for the Jewish problem by laying the blame on the United States, France and the Soviet Union. British agents associated Zionism with communism, while fanning Arab fears of Zionist expansion, and presented Britain as the only Power capable of defending the Arab world against the Zionist threat and preventing the establishment of a Jewish state. But this help would exact a price – Arab willingness to recognize Britain's paramount position in the Middle East.

There is no tangible evidence in the Syrian documents of direct attempts by British secret agents to instigate Arab attacks on the Jewish community in

Palestine.[18] However, the documents seen so far relate only to the first half of 1947, before the Arab-Jewish conflict escalated into violence. French intelligence reports, which clearly relied on the Syrian documents from the end of 1947 and early 1948, and French diplomatic correspondence do contain such evidence. Moreover, French, American and Zionist officials assumed that British agents in the Middle East would have no qualms about provoking an Arab-Jewish confrontation to further their country's interests. French intelligence officers believed that the British agents would not hesitate to use covert operations against the Jews in Palestine similar to those they had employed in evicting France from Syria and Lebanon – a belief shared by American diplomats in Washington. For example, already in November 1945, Constantin Zureiq informed Prime Minister Jabiri of an American warning that "Great Britain wishes to exploit the Arab-Jewish conflict because it is the only way for it to remain in Palestine, to dominate all the Arab countries," and that "The British colonial authorities will do everything to prevent [a settlement], as Great Britain wishes for incidents to worsen in Palestine and for disorder, where blood is spilt, to take place" (doc. 254).

Ben-Gurion and his close advisers were certain that British Arabist agents would not balk at instigating Arab-Jewish violence. Thus when meeting Brigadier Clayton in February 1946, Sasson questioned him directly over whether Britain was provoking an Arab-Jewish confrontation. Iltyd Clayton denied the accusations, noting that his elder brother, General Gilbert Clayton, had, after World War I, sought to bring Jews and Arabs closer, and expressed the hope that he could do the same. But French and Zionist sources from late 1947 and early 1948 point to his key role in instigating the Arab-Jewish conflict in 1948.[19]

The secret British scheme

On May 28, 1947 Armanazi informed Mardam of a confrontation, involving Brigadier Clayton, between the Foreign Office and the secret services, who had "categorically refused to remove him from Egypt." Armanazi noted that support for Clayton "surpasses the imagination," adding that he had been given a "carte blanche to direct the vast program he aims to complete." After conducting an enquiry, Armanazi reported that this program consisted of advancing the Greater Syria plan and securing British control over Libya (doc.389). The same day, Mardam instructed Armanazi to alert officials in the Foreign Office that the Syrian government would forcibly oppose any intervention by King Abdullah in Syrian affairs (doc.388). He had previously notified Armanazi that British agents were inciting the Druze and Bedouin tribes against the Syrian government (doc.381). In early June, Mardam wrote directly to Bevin and complained of the intrigues of the British officers in the Arab Legion against Syria, adding, "What makes the situation even more delicate is that the plot organized against Syria is welcomed by all the British officials in the Near East" (doc.394). He warned that if Syria had no other way to safeguard its independence, it would seek foreign assistance, including from the Soviet Union (docs.391, 394). Reports on increasing subversion by British agents in Syria came during the Syrian parliamentary elections and the escalating tension along the border between Syria and Jordan in the summer of 1947. The deterioration in Syro-Jordanian relations coincided with the Anglo-Iraqi negotiations on a new military agreement to replace the 1930 treaty and as relations between the Iraqi government and King Abdullah were improving. Spears told Armanazi that the Greater Syria plan was being discussed seriously, and offered to mediate between the Syrian leaders and King Abdullah (doc.389). These were the initial steps of the scheme devised by the secret services in Cairo, Amman and Baghdad and implemented between July 1947 and January 1948.[20]

In the summer of 1947, British policy in the Middle East reached an impasse. Egyptian Prime Minister Nuqrashi, backed by King Faruq, insisted that Britain undertake to evacuate its forces before the Egyptian government would agree to proceed with negotiations on an Anglo-Egyptian treaty and the future of Sudan. In July, the Egyptian government went further when it brought its case before the United Nations. British policy in Palestine reached a deadlock as well. After the failure of negotiations with Arab and Zionist representatives in London in early 1947, the British Cabinet declared its intention to return the mandate over Palestine to the United Nations. Britain was losing ground in the propaganda war, especially in the United States, as the Zionists successfully portrayed the conflict in Palestine not as an Arab-Jewish but an Anglo-Jewish conflict between a Zionist liberation movement and a colonial Power. Its harsh measures against the illegal immigration of Holocaust survivors from the refugee camps in Europe to Palestine drew international criticism, which culminated during the Exodus affair. Continued reports of Zionist attacks on British soldiers stirred up intense public resentment and hardened the resolve of the Cabinet to evacuate Palestine. As the economic crisis deepened, Prime Minister Attlee was compelled to cut the expenses involved in retaining considerable armed forces overseas to defend an Empire that Britain was no longer capable of sustaining, either militarily or economically. In June the Cabinet dramatically announced Britain's intention to withdraw unilaterally from India.[21]

Arab rulers closely followed the dramatic events unfolding in London, indicating that Britain's imperial order in the Middle East was beginning to crumble. They saw Britain failing to suppress the Zionist insurgency, gradually losing its grip over the Middle East and being relegated to an inferior position vis-à-vis the United States. President Truman's declaration that the United States would defend Turkey and Greece against the Soviet Union reinforced these beliefs. Britain's plan for a regional security pact was perceived as being less likely; Turkish and Arab leaders were less inclined to be part of it. But President Quwatli heeded Spears' warning that "Britain is not powerless to settle its accounts with anyone at all ... " (doc.393). Well aware of the might of the British secret services and deeply suspicious of their intrigues, he believed that Britain would not give up the Middle East without a struggle. King Faruq shared his fears, telling Mardam that "Great Britain played us all and exploited us in its own interest and won on all fronts simultaneously" (doc.395). The French intelligence service estimated that Britain was far from losing its grip over the Middle East and that "it still had many cards to play."[22]

In the summer of 1947, a shift took place in the Arabists' stand – especially those in the secret services – towards the Labour Cabinet's Middle East policy. Unable to influence their Prime Minister, who was resolved to withdraw a substantial part of the British forces from the region, they "hijacked" Britain's Middle East policy, taking matters into their own hands. They were determined to act against what they perceived as a policy that was endangering their country's vital strategic interests in the face of the Soviet thrust into the region. From June 1947 until May 1948 Britain thus conducted two contradictory policies in the Middle East – one official, carried out by the Cabinet and the Foreign Secretary, and another, unauthorized and secretive, devised by Arabist secret agents in Cairo, Amman and Baghdad. Brigadier Clayton played a key role in coordinating and implementing this covert policy.[23]

The following brief analysis examines only whether the Arabist secret agents intentionally instigated Arab armed attacks against the Jewish community in Palestine and later against the State of Israel without their Cabinet's knowledge or sanction. It does not address the inter-Arab balance of power, which was closely tied to the war in Palestine; the military and diplomatic counter-strategy adopted by Ben-Gurion and his close advisers after learning of the secret British scheme; nor the French or Soviet counter-action in undermining British designs in the Middle East. The analysis is based primarily on French intelligence reports, dispatches sent by French diplomats in the Arab capitals and London, and documents in Israeli archives.

On September 23, 1947, shortly after the Arab League meeting in Sofar, the French Chargé d'Affaires in Baghdad sent a report to Bidault providing details of a secret British scheme to instigate an Arab-Jewish war in Palestine in order to facilitate the implementation of the Greater Syria plan. The report, reproduced in part here, disclosed that the Iraqi Prime Minister's militant stand in Sofar had been coordinated with British agents and "marked a turning point in Britain's Middle East policy."[24]

> It seems, in effect, that the British government, urged on by the young elements in the Foreign Office and the Intelligence Service (a clique opposed to that of General Spears[25]) has decided, after months of hesitation, to undertake a large-scale maneuver that will enable it to consolidate, at little cost, its present wavering position in this part of the world.
>
> The British believe that the UN will no doubt ratify the UNSCOP decisions. Disturbances will thus begin in Palestine. The English will

benefit from the situation to build new positions as advantageous as those they have lost in Egypt. According to information from an English source, the British plan will be as follows:

England will give up its mandate over Palestine as soon as possible and will return it to the UN, which will oversee, if necessary, an international force to reestablish order in this country. A retreat from Palestine of most of the British troops can already be envisaged. In the event of open conflict between Jews and Arabs, the English, under the pretext of not wanting to be attacked from both sides in these hostilities, where it maintains an officially neutral position, will retreat to Transjordan, from where one or two British divisions will be able to immediately intervene if necessary. British agents will now push the Arab countries to intervene to help their brethren in Palestine if they are attacked by the Jews.[26]

The report indicated that Britain would abstain from voting on the final United Nations Special Committee on Palestine (UNSCOP) report, "leaving the Americans and their satellites the responsibility of creating a Jewish state." It provided details of a scheme aimed at provoking Syria into a war against the Jews in Palestine in order to open the way for King Abdullah's Arab Legion and the Iraqi army to advance on Damascus under the pretext of defending Syria against a Zionist attack. "Once there, the King of Transjordan will receive overwhelming support and will attempt to reestablish peace in Palestine while incorporating the Arab part of this country into the new Greater Syria that will be united with Iraq."[27]

But contrary to the French Attaché's account, the Cabinet in London neither knew of nor approved the scheme of their secret agents to instigate an Arab armed invasion of a Jewish state. Prime Minister Attlee, who decided on withdrawal from Palestine despite the objections of his military, would not have taken on the moral responsibility for a plot that could have annihilated the Jews in Palestine only three years after the Holocaust. Moreover, such an act could have jeopardized Britain's international standing and its relations with the United States. Bevin, who still believed in the strategic importance of the Middle East, was caught between his Prime Minister, the COS and the secret services. But it was unlikely that he would have acted against his Prime Minister's decision. The record of his troubled relations with the secret services in the Middle East reinforces the assumption that he too was misled, a victim of his inability to control them.[28] He was led to believe that the hostilities between the Arabs and Jews in Palestine resembled the religious and inter-communal strife in India between Muslims and Hindus following Britain's decision to withdraw. As in India, the violence and loss of life would eventually force the two sides to reach the compromise that Britain had failed to convince them to make. Britain could thus not be held responsible for a partition it had not believed in, and might be called upon to implement a more acceptable solution. While many British politicians and officials shared this belief, neither Bevin nor other Cabinet ministers were aware that their secret services in Cairo and Arabist diplomats in London and the Middle East, supported by the senior military authorities, were determined, contrary to Cabinet decision, to hold on to the Middle East even if it led to an all-out Arab-Jewish war. Many essential issues nevertheless remain unresolved, including the role of senior military officers in London and Cairo; what the members of the Joint Intelligence Committee (JIC) knew; and the part played by Secret Intelligence Service (SIS) headquarters in London and its agents in the Middle East.[29]

While the report from Baghdad focuses on a secret scheme by British agents to provoke an Arab-Jewish war to further Greater Syria and its union with Iraq, other French reports disclose that its immediate goal was to safeguard Britain's strategic position in the Middle East. Another goal was to prevent the establishment of a Jewish state or an Arab Palestinian state based on the UN partition. There were also emergency safety measures – both military and diplomatic – to prevent the Jewish state from expanding its territory if the Arab armies were defeated. In this event, British forces stationed in Transjordan and Egypt would intervene, while British diplomats in the UN Security Council would act to impose a ceasefire. French intelligence sources present the scheme as an attempt by Britain to shuffle its cards in the Middle East and inflame Arab hostility towards a Jewish state in order to secure its dominance in the region. Whether the Arabs won or were defeated, its instigators assumed that Britain would be in a better position than it had been in the summer of 1947. Indeed the Attaché's report concluded that: "The British position, which for some time has appeared precarious, will thus find itself again dominant, all the more so as Egypt's termination of the Anglo-Egyptian treaty will enable the British forces to maintain their position on the Suez Canal."[30]

During deliberations in London and Cairo in the summer and autumn of 1947 on British defense strategy in the Middle East, it was decided that Britain would seek bilateral military treaties with each Arab state, rather than a collective agreement brokered through the Arab League, to replace existing treaties. It was assumed that Britain would be in a better position to conclude bilateral treaties with the friendly Hashemite Iraq and Transjordan and subsequently attain similar ones with other Arab governments, especially that of Syria. A treaty with Egypt remained a high priority for the British High Command. The Foreign Office expected that after failing in the UN, Egypt would be more willing to renew negotiations, thus ensuring Britain's military use of its territory and solving the question of Sudan. But King Faruq and his Prime Minister, as well as President Quwatli, were reluctant to conclude treaties with Britain, a declining colonial Power. They faced an upsurge of nationalist passion among the younger generation, who were demonstrating in the streets for independence and social and economic reforms, and refused to be drawn into a war between the Western Powers and the Soviet Union. As the communist threat became less convincing, British agents believed that they had to come up with more effective leverage to persuade the Arab governments and public that their countries needed Britain's assistance.[31]

Without the knowledge of their Cabinet, from June 1947 until May 1948 British secret agents conducted their own covert policy. Officially they aimed to convince the Arab governments of the importance of concluding defense agreements with Britain in the face of the escalating Soviet threat, while secretly instigating an Arab-Jewish confrontation in Palestine to advance Britain's strategic ends. They sought to use a war in Palestine to deflect the Arab public's attention from the controversial treaty negotiations; as an incentive for the Arab governments to conclude defense treaties with Britain; to demonstrate to the Arab rulers their countries' need for military collaboration; to reinforce the Arab states' military dependence on Britain; while preventing the establishment of a Jewish state or limiting its size. The war in Palestine was also intended to pressure the United States into revising its position on partition. No longer would Zionist propaganda be able to portray the struggle against Britain as that of a national movement fighting to liberate itself from colonial rule. An Arab-Jewish conflict would also validate Britain's long-held position regarding the solution to the Palestinian problem and demonstrate that, despite its good intentions, it was caught in the middle. Moreover, it would help Britain secure its strategic assets in Palestine: namely Haifa, with its port and refineries, and the Negev region in the south.[32]

Brigadier Clayton's frequent visits to the Arab capitals in the last months of 1947 and his behind-the-scenes involvement in the Arab League's meetings in Sofar, Aley and Cairo, were part of the scheme hatched by the Arabist secret agents in Cairo, Baghdad and Amman. Nuri al-Sa'id, Azzam, Mardam and Sulh were used to implement it. King Abdullah was essential for the scheme's success, as he and his Arab Legion were to serve as a means to pressure Quwatli, Ibn Sa'ud and Faruq, while forcing the Zionist leaders to acquiesce to Britain's proposals. The attempts by British agents in Transjordan to intimidate the Syrian President; the Iraqi government's militant stand in Sofar and Aley and its insistence that the Arab League take action in Palestine; and Clayton's proposal to split Palestine between the Arab states were all part of the ploy.[33]

In mid-January 1948 the Arabists' scheme seemed on the verge of succeeding. While the Arab public's attention was focused on the events in Palestine, Britain concluded a defense treaty with Iraq. A similar agreement with Transjordan was to be signed without any hindrance. After failing to persuade Kings Ibn Sa'ud and Faruq to conclude an agreement with Syria against Abdullah, President Quwatli was more predisposed to give in to British pressure, particularly as British agents had undertaken to restrain the Jordanian monarch. He was also anxious to prevent them from jeopardizing his efforts to be elected President for a second term. Prime Minister Sulh, who opposed a Jewish state on Lebanon's border that might reinforce Maronite separatism, secretly collaborated with Clayton and publicly endorsed a treaty with Britain. But when Ronald Campbell, the British Ambassador to Egypt, and Brigadier Clayton proposed to Nuqrashi that Britain prevent the establishment of a Jewish state or limit its territory in return for a treaty, he rejected any attempt to link the conflict in Palestine with Egypt's demands for the evacuation of British forces and unity of the Nile Valley.[34]

Alongside negotiations with the Arab governments on defense treaties, the British secret agents stepped up their efforts to fuel violent Arab-Jewish clashes, urging the Arab leaders to close ranks against the Zionist threat. Between September and December 1947, Brigadier Clayton and other secret agents tacitly collaborated with Azzam, Mardam and Sulh to organize an irregular force – the Arab Liberation Army (ALA) – under Qawuqji's command, to be activated before Britain formally withdrew from Palestine. While Azzam regarded the ALA as a means for the Arab League to intervene in Palestine, Mardam and Sulh, and President Quwatli in particular, saw it more as a means to preempt an attempt by Abdullah's Arab Legion to take over the northern part of Palestine than to help their Palestinian brethren against the Jews. A British military mission under Colonel Fox, an unofficial adviser to the Syrian High Command since 1946, tried to obtain arms and ammunition from British army stocks in Palestine to arm the ALA volunteers in the Katana camp south of Damascus.[35] French intelligence sources reported that British army and police deserters, disguised as Arabs, were to be seen in the streets of Damascus. Scores of IPC employees arrived in the city, leading to Syrian press speculation on why the Syrian capital had suddenly become an attraction for British tourists. British agents also negotiated with the Mufti, initially indirectly through Sulh, and later with his envoy, following his demand to command his own armed forces in Palestine. The ALA entered Palestine in the first half of January 1948; Qawuqji later wrote that the British army hardly hindered the advance of his forces on northern Palestine.[36]

The collapse of the Portsmouth Treaty marked the failure of the bilateral treaty approach. Although Bevin signed a new treaty in London with Jordanian Prime Minister Tawfiq Abd al-Huda, other Arab leaders, including Azzam, Mardam and Sulh, openly declared their opposition to treaties with foreign Powers. British military planners and Arabists in the Foreign Office and the Middle East now had to come up with a new strategy – a collective defense agreement with the Arab states through the Arab League. In March 1948, Azzam and Mardam began a campaign to revise the Arab League pact in order to consolidate ties between its member states against the Zionist threat, an initiative that was tacitly coordinated with the British secret agents. After consulting with King Ibn Sa'ud, King Faruq declared that before any negotiations could take place on a collective defense agreement, Britain had to abrogate its existing bilateral treaties with the Arab states. In their reports to London, the Arabists – and Clayton to a lesser degree – linked the collapse of the Portsmouth Treaty directly to the events in Palestine. Their failure in Iraq increased the likelihood of war in Palestine, as British secret agents became even more determined to provoke an Arab-Jewish conflict. The defeat in April of the ALA irregular forces and of those commanded by Abd al-Qadir al-Husseini, the Mufti's nephew, reinforced their conviction that only the Arab regular armies could prevent the establishment of a Jewish state.[37]

In this brief epilogue it is impossible to detail all the maneuvers and intrigues of the British Arabists in Cairo, Amman and Baghdad to instigate an Arab attack on the Jewish state. Sources in Israeli and French archives shed some light on those intrigues. The British secret agents used almost all the "dirty tricks" in their arsenal – fear, jealousy, greed, false promises, misleading information and playing on inter-Arab rivalries – to provoke the Arab rulers into a war in Palestine. Nuri al-Sa'id until the failure of the Portsmouth Treaty; King Abdullah between June 1947 and May 1948; and Azzam, Mardam Sulh and other co-opted "agents of influence," allowed the British secret services to operate behind the scenes to implement their schemes. King Ibn Sa'ud aptly described the British agents as "master puppeteers." The Arab leaders were trapped between their reluctance to go to war and pressure from their public that they themselves had incited with inflammatory rhetoric on destroying the Jewish state (doc.396). Azzam admitted to a Jewish Agency representative that "We have no choice but to go to war, even if we will be defeated."[38]

Provoking Egypt to join the war in Palestine was central to the British secret strategy. French sources give details of the British agents' tactics – teaming up with Azzam to press King Faruq to instruct his army to join the war despite the opposition of his Prime Minister. They also included an undertaking to supply the Egyptian army with weapons and ammunition from British stocks in the Canal Zone and a deliberate underestimation of the military strength of the Jewish forces. Like other Arab rulers, King Faruq, under public pressure to take action, was vulnerable to British machinations. He could not remain on the sidelines while his rival, King Abdullah, was sending forces to Palestine. The May 11 report from the French Military Attaché in Beirut on the secret discussions of the Arab League's political committee in Damascus reveals that apart from King Abdullah, other Arab leaders were hesitant, seeking a way to delay an invasion of Palestine. It also exposes the British agents' direct intervention in their decisions (doc.396). At the last minute, King Faruq overruled his reluctant Prime Minister and commanded his army to go to war. Although other politicians opposed the King's decision, Isma'il Sidqi, President of the Egyptian Senate, was the only one who came out publicly against Egypt's involvement in the war in Palestine.[39]

The 1948 war swept away the "anciens régimes" and opened the road to power for a young generation of radical Arab nationalist officers determined to avenge their countries' defeat and bring an end to Britain's dominance in the region. The old Arab rulers, victims of British machinations and their own ambitions were to pay dearly. King Abdullah, the Regent Abd al-Ilah, Nuri al-Sa'id, Sulh, Nuqrashi and Barazi lost their lives. King Faruq and President Quwatli were more fortunate, losing only power. Although Mardam failed to realize his aspirations for the Syrian presidency, he retired to Cairo, where he lived comfortably. Despite British assessments that after his death the kingdom he had created would disintegrate, King Ibn Sa'ud lived long enough to bequeath his sons a stable and prosperous state. David Ben-Gurion was to see the country in whose foundation he had played a central part develop into a modern state, but fall short of achieving peace with the Palestinians and its Arab neighbors. The Arabist protagonists – the secret agents, diplomats, military officers and civil servants – retired to Britain, leaving behind the legacy of a divided, violent Middle East in which the states formed by the two colonial Powers after World War I failed to withstand the test of time.

Notes

1 HA, 8/124, Tenne, June 14, 1948, remark by René Neuville, the French Consul in Jerusalem to an Israeli official. (Tenne – basket in Hebrew – was the code name of the SHAY, the Haganah's secret service. It issued top secret daily reports with the directive "to be read and destroyed.") Balay, the French Minister in Baghdad, referring to Britain's attempt in June to secure an immediate ceasefire, remarked: "It inflated the balloon, only to deflate it." AN, Paris, Bidault's Papers, 457AP126, nos.162-3, Baghdad, July 8, 1948, Balay to the Quai d'Orsay.
2 SHA, EMA, 14S349, Bulletin d'Information no.9, September 21, 1947. The Sofar meeting was convened to decide on the Arab response to the UNSCOP report. For the minutes of the meeting and subsequent meetings in Aley, Cairo and Damascus, see Iraqi Parliamentary Committee on the War in Palestine, *Behind the Curtain* (Tel Aviv: Israel Defense Forces Publications, 1954), translated into Hebrew by Shmuel Segev, pp.47-63. See also Kimche, *Seven Pillars*, pp.58, 197.
3 SHA, EMA, 14S349, Bulletins d'Information no.4, February 23, and no.5, Beirut, March 8, 1948.
4 HA, 25/105, Tenne, March 17, 1948.
5 AN, Paris, Bidault's Papers, 457AP125, no.642, London, March 8, 1948, British policy in Palestine, French Chargé d'Affaires to Bidault; HA, 115/58, Tenne, August 26 and October 12, 1947; HA, 105/112, May 13, 1948, report by an agent codenamed "pupil."
6 BGA, Correspondence, Paris, January 8 and 13, 1948, Fischer to the Jewish Agency; HA, 40/115, Tenne, January 14, 1948; HA, 112/115, Operation "Nylon," Paris, September 18, 1948, mentioning Clayton's proposal for unrestricted guerilla warfare. See also SHA, EMA, 14S351, no.114, Beirut, October 7, 1947, Captain de Sèze to the War Minister. De Sèze, the military attaché in Beirut who was in contact with the Haganah, estimated that if the Arab-Jewish conflict remained on a military level, the Jewish forces would win.
7 SHA, EMA, 14S349, Bulletins d'Information no.1, January 12, and no.4, Beirut, February 23, 1948; HA, 25/105, Tenne, 115/58, August 28 and December 12, 1947. See testimony of Haganah intelligence officer Baruch Guriel on the SHAY's belief that the British intelligence and Arabists in Cairo were the nerve center of Britain's Middle East policy and intrigues, in HA, file 139.38, August 20, 1964.
8 Milstein, Uri, *History of the War of Independence: The First Month* (Lanham, MD: University Press of America, 1997), p.159.
9 Sasson's letter to King Abdullah, Jerusalem, January 11, 1948, in Sasson, pp.394-7. The assessment by the heads of the Jewish Agency of British goals in Palestine was relatively accurate. See for example Israel Galili's presentation during the meeting of members of the Haganah's European headquarters in Paris, November 5-8, 1947, in HA, 14/36. Galili served in a position similar to that of Commander-in-Chief of the Haganah. See also Ben-Gurion's conversation with a French diplomat in AN, Paris, Bidault's Papers, 457AP125, no.19, Tel Aviv, March 1, 1948.

10 Israel State Archives, Yogev, Gedalia (ed.), *Political and Diplomatic Documents, vol.1, December 1947-May 1948* (Jerusalem, 1979), doc. no.258, March 7, 1948; AN, Paris, Bidault's Papers, 457AP125, Tel Aviv, March 1, 1948, Ben-Gurion's conversation with a French diplomat. See also: Eshed, pp.105-6; Chavkin, pp.112-3.

11 Rivlin, Gershon and Elhanan Orren (eds.), *Ben-Gurion's War Diary* (Tel Aviv: Ministry of Defense Publishing, 1982), vol.I, pp.282-4.

12 SHA, SGDN, 4Q43/8, Bulletin d'Information no.19, June 1948; carton 14S348, no.24, Beirut, February 13, 1948, the military attaché to the E.M. Défense Nationale, Paris; HA, 40/115, December 17, 1946, discussions in Cairo led by Clayton.

13 SHA, EMA, 14S349, Bulletin d'Information no.6, Beirut, August 11, 1947; AN, Paris, Bidault's Papers, 457AP125, no.11, Tripoli, February 3, 1948, Chambord to the Quai d'Orsay.

14 AN, Paris, Bidault's Papers, 457AP125, no.642, London, March 8, 1948, British policy in Palestine, French Chargé d'Affaires to Bidault.

15 The French secret service in Cairo might have been decoding the Egyptian Foreign Ministry's communications, or had an agent in the Ministry. See SHA, SGDN, 4Q22, no.2260, August 23, 1945, telegram from the Egyptian Ambassador in Moscow to Cairo; 1Q31, Paris, December 20, 1947, La Ligue Arabe et la Question Palestinienne. On coordinating SEDEC operations in Egypt with that of the military attaché, see SHA, EMA, 14S313, telegram no.235, Cairo, February 9, 1948.

16 Referring to the Saudi monarch's efforts to modernize his army with American aid, a French intelligence report concluded that such an army would be "directed against an eventual Greater Syria more than Zionist imperialism." See SHA, SGDN, 4Q43/8, Bulletin d'Information no.19, June 1948. See also Bulletin d'Information no.12, November 1947.

17 Graves, pp.64-73; AN, Paris, Bidault's Papers, 457AP125, nos.107-8, May 22, and nos.112-5, Amman, May 25, 1948, Dumarçay's report on his meeting with Abdullah; See also SHA, SGDN, 4Q43/8, Paris, December 1947, Bulletin d'Information no.13.

18 In discussions with French officers, British officers often spoke of the need to use force to suppress the Jewish uprising. See for example minutes of a conversation with Col. Altounyan, MAE, Paris, Syrie et Liban 1944-52, vol.301, no. 998, Latakiya, October 27, 1945. See also SHA, EMA, 14S349, Beirut, August 11, 1947, Report on the situation in the Middle East.

19 CZA, S25/8004, Cairo, February 1, 1946, Sasson's report on his meeting with Clayton. See BGA, Correspondence, Sasson's report on his meeting with Clayton, September 8, 1946. Brigadier Clayton's code name in the Haganah's secret service was "Clayman."

20 SHA, EMA, 14S351, December 8, 1946, Saudi agent's report on Kirkbride's role in urging King Abdullah to promote the Greater Syria scheme; carton 14S349, no.253, Beirut, August 14, 1947, an Arab intelligence report on the activities of British secret agents in Syria and Egypt. See reports in files on Greater Syria 1946-49, including the Syro-Jordanian confrontation at the end of 1946, in carton 14S351. See also SHA, SDGN, 4Q43, Bulletins d'Information nos.13 and 20; carton 4Q118, Bulletin de Renseignements no.63, September 20, 1947. See Lord Listowel's remarks on Cadogan, whom he presents as a defender of SIS in the Foreign Office and a liaison between the service and the Conservative Party. He also refers to tension between Cadogan and Bevin over policy towards the United States. Lord Listowel was Post Master and spokesman of the Cabinet in the House of Lords. See report in MAE, Paris, 457AP6, Paris, March 5, 1947.

21 SHA, EMA, 14S349, August 14 and September 14, 1947, John Kimche's articles in *l'Orient* on the change in British strategy in the Middle East. See also: SHA,

SGDN, Q50, no.303, Paris, January 31, 1948, British Military and Defense Policy during 1947; Louis, pp.11-5.

22 SHA, SDGN, 4Q22, no.254, Paris, January 21, 1948, note on the situation in Palestine; carton 1Q51, no.4514, Paris, November 26, 1947, Deuxième Bureau report on Anglo-Saxon strategy and diplomacy in the Middle East.

23 The French secret services and the SHAY closely followed Clayton's activities between July 1947 and May 1948, thus many Deuxième Bureau and Haganah intelligence reports refer to him. As part of their secret war, the French intelligence services often leaked reports on his activities to the Agence France-Presse (AFP) or directly to Lebanese newspapers, especially *le Soir* and *l'Orient*. Many can be found in the Bulletins d'Information of those months. Clayton's name frequently crops up in reports by French diplomats and military attachés in Cairo, Damascus and Beirut. He operated through the BMEO, which shared the same compound in Cairo with SIS. See Dorril, pp.541-2. For a top secret BMEO report from February 1948 on a meeting with Azzam, probably written by Clayton, see HA, 352/105. Some intelligence and military circles in the Middle East believed that the Labour Party and Government policy in Palestine was under Jewish influence. See for example the remark by the British military attaché in Beirut that not much could be expected due to the considerable influence of Jews in the House of Commons and the Cabinet, in SHA, EMA, 14S349, Beirut, August 11, 1947, Situation in the Middle East. See also Kimche, Jon and David Kimche, *Both Sides of the Hill: Britain and the Palestine War* (London: Secker & Warburg, 1960), pp.110-6.

24 MAE, Paris, Syrie et Liban 1944-52, vol.37, no 400, Baghdad, September 23, 1947, Chargé d'Affaires to the Foreign Minister. This volume contains numerous reports on the Syro-Jordanian confrontation over King Abdullah's ambitions for Greater Syria.

25 This refers to Spears' longstanding opposition to Hashemite control over Syria, especially by King Abdullah. After the failure of the Portsmouth Treaty, the Arabists in Cairo had become disillusioned with the Hashemites in Iraq. Brigadier Clayton's suggestion to strengthen Syria's position in Britain's regional defense system was opposed by the Arabists in Amman.

26 MAE, Paris, Syrie et Liban 1944-52, vol.37, no 400, Baghdad, September 23, 1947, Chargé d'Affaires to the Foreign Minister. See also copies of telegrams from the Syrian Legation in Jeddah from August 1947 in SHA, EMA, 14S351, no.635, July 10, and no.863, September 18, 1948, and a copy of Abdullah's letter to Quwatli from August 14, 1947. See also Landis, Joshua, "Syria and the Palestine War: Fighting King Abdullah's 'Greater Syrian Plan'," in Rogan, Eugene L. and Avi Shlaim (eds.), *The War for Palestine* (Cambridge: Cambridge University Press, 2007), pp.182-90.

27 MAE, Paris, Syrie et Liban 1944-52, vol.37, no 400, Baghdad, September 23, 1947, Chargé d'affaires to the Foreign Minister.

28 Bevin did not support the Greater Syria plan promoted by certain Arabists in the Foreign Office and secret service agents in the Middle East. On British foreign policy in the Middle East see AN, Paris, Bidault's Papers, 457AP125, no.615, London, March 9, 1948, Chargé d'Affaires to Bidault. French diplomats frequently noted that Bevin appeared to be ill-informed on events in the Middle East. See for example, 457AP125, no.135, Amman, June 3, 1948, Dumarçay to the Quai d'Orsay. See also Harouvi, pp.218, 359-65. On October 18, 1947, Bevin sent instructions to the High Commissioner in Palestine and the ambassadors in the Middle East, Moscow, Washington and the United Nations to deny rumors of any secret agreement between the British Government and Arab states on Arab military moves after Britain's withdrawal from Palestine; see Harouvi, p.352.

29 AN, Paris, Bidault's Papers, 457AP125, no.615, London, March 9, 1948, British policy and Palestinian affairs; SHA, SGDN, 4Q22, no.254, Paris, January 21,

1948, note on the situation in Palestine; HA, 8/124, Tenne, November 12, 1947. On the British Security and Secret Services' covert operations against the Zionist movement, see Jeffery, pp. 649, 689-94, 712; Andrew, *MI5*, pp.352-66; Aldrich, *The Hidden Hand*, pp.256-67. See also Aldrich, Richard J. and John Zametica, "The rise and decline of the strategic concept: the Middle East, 1945-51, in Aldrich (ed.), *British Intelligence, Strategy and the Cold War*, pp.236-74; Chavkin, pp.75-8.

30 MAE, Paris, Syrie et Liban 1944-52, vol.37, no 400, Baghdad, September 23, 1947, Chargé d'Affaires to the Foreign Minister; SHA, SGDN, Q31/2, no.559, Paris, February 12, 1948, Deuxième Bureau report on Britain's policy in the Middle East; carton 4Q22, no.254, Paris, January 21, 1948, note on the situation in Palestine. See also memorandum, "The British Record on Partition as Revealed by British Military Intelligence and Other Official Sources," submitted to the UN by Freda Kirchwey, President of the Nation Associates, in *The Nation*, New York, May 8, 1948. The memorandum was written by the SHAY. See in particular Part XII, "British Smear Campaign Shown by Official Records."

31 SHA, SGDN, Q31/2, Deuxième Bureau report no.751, Paris, February 27, 1948; carton Q50, no.303, Paris, January 31, 1948, British Military and Defense Policy during 1947; SHA, EMA, 14S349, Bulletin d'Information no.2, Beirut, January 26, 1948, especially "Les Projets Britanniques"; MAE, Paris, Syrie et Liban 1944-52, vol.300, no.193, Damascus, February 28, 1948, Serres to Bidault. On the British role in the 1948 war, see presentation by Shalheveth Freier, head of the Haganah's secret service, in HA, 11/117. See also Louis, pp.24-7; Kimche, *Seven Fallen Pillars*, pp.79-82.

32 AN, Paris, Bidault's Papers, 457AP123, 31/714, no.39, Baghdad, January 23, 1948, Balay to Bidault; vol.457AP126, nos.1302-4, Cairo, October 1, 1948, Lucet to Bidault; SHA, EMA, 14S351, no.253, Damascus, June 29, 1948, Serres to Bidault; SHA, SGDN, 4Q118, Algiers, April 15, 1948, Deuxième Bureau Bulletin de Renseignements no.65.

33 SHA, SGDN, 4Q43/8, Bulletins d'Information nos.14 and 15, January and February, 1948; carton 4Q118, Algiers, November 1947, Deuxième Bureau Bulletin de Renseignements no.63. SHA, EMA, 14S351, no.253, Damascus, June 29, 1948, Serres to Bidault; MAE, Paris, Syrie et Liban 1944-52, vol.300, no.193, Damascus, February 28, 1948, Serres to Bidault.

34 AN, Paris, Bidault's Papers, 457AP123, no.8, Cairo, January 3, 1948, Arvengas to Bidault.

35 SHA, EMA, 14S351, no.107, August 3, 1945, note to Serres; carton 14S348, no.382, Beirut, April 14, 1948, du Chayla to the Quai d'Orsay; MAE, Paris, Syrie et Liban 1944-52, vol.293, no, 67, Damascus, May 29, 1948, Serres to Bidault. See also a copy of a telegram from February 21, 1948, from the British Minister in Damascus to the military authorities in Palestine, obtained by the Haganah, in HA, 36/115.

36 MAE, Paris, Syrie et Liban 1944-52, vol.301, no.434, Damascus, May 19, 1948, Serres to Bidault, report on British activities in Syria; vol.30, no.1091, Cairo, August 11, 1947, Arvengas to Bidault; Qawuqji, Fauzi al-, "Memoirs, 1948, Part I," *Journal of Palestinian Studies*, 2(1), 1971, pp.29-31.

37 SHA, EMA, 14S349, Bulletin d'Information no.5, Beirut, March 8, 1948; SHA, SGDN, Q31/2 no.559, Paris, February 12, and no.751, February 27, 1948, Deuxième Bureau report on Britain's policy in the Middle East. See also carton 4Q43/8, Bulletins d'Information nos.15, 17, 1948.

38 Horowitz, David, *State in the Making* (New York: Alfred A. Knopf, 1953), pp.255-7. See also: SHA, EMA, 14S349, no.253, Beirut, August 14, 1947, Arab intelligence report on the activities of British secret agents in Syria and Egypt; Landis, pp.186-7.

39 SHA, SGDN, 4Q43/8, Bulletin d'Information no.19, June 1948; carton 4Q118, Bulletin de Renseignements no.65, Algiers, April 15, 1948.

Part II

List of documents

Documents

1. December 25, 1940   "Operation Rondot"

Text in English conveyed to the agent by General [Brigadier] Clayton himself.
   In light of the agent's hesitation in taking a headed paper, the General dictated to him the following translation:
   The Aims of the English Government

i   For Syria to be peaceful and friendly, all Italian and German propaganda should be strongly opposed.
   The British Government intends to oppose by any means within its power the presence of Italian or German forces in Syria.
ii   It will also oppose the establishment of any Italians in positions of influence or authority in Syria.
   The relations between the English and French governments are correct, but it is understood that the party in France that represents the true spirit of the Anglo-French alliance is Free France.
iii   The creation in Syria of a situation in which it will align itself with the Allies as Equatorial Africa did, will be welcome, and it is certain that General Catroux, who is aiming for this, has the help and support of the English.
iv   In all, Syria should return to the situation it was in before the Armistice.

2. March 14, 1941   Riyad al-Sulh's letter to Marun Arab

Top secret; Beirut,
March 14, 1941

My Dear Brother, Marun Bey Arab,

   I ask you to confirm to HE Mr Furlonge[1] my true desire to reach an understanding with him, as I stated to Mr Jailez[2] when I met him again in the presence of our discerning brother Munir Abu Fadel.

   This understanding, dear brother, will not have a bearing on illusions but on a chosen action which will save us from this hell.

   I hope that he will take a second step following the points we have reached.

   You know that the misunderstanding which arose between you and me in the past does not constitute an obstacle between us and between new

friendship and collaboration, particularly as the work awaiting us demands speed from us, without making a big deal of the past.
Greetings.

Riyad al-Sulh

Notes

1 At this time, Mr Furlonge was HM the King's British Consul in Beirut.
2 Phonetic spelling.

3. April 25, 1942   Secret agreement between Nuri al-Sa'id and Shukri al-Quwatli on Syrian Unity

Baghdad, April 25, 1942
Following is the agreement concluded between Nuri al-Sa'id and Shukri al-Quwatli, which they swore by God to adhere to and make all their efforts to implement.

It is with their faith in Arabism and its glory, in our nation and its virtues, that they concluded it, inspired by God and counting on Him for everything they have decided to work for.

They realize that for centuries the Arab nation has suffered from divisions and separations, and foreigners and infidel intruders established their sovereignty over it.

They acknowledge that the ignorance rife in the Arab countries is the main factor in the humiliation felt by the Arab people and that it is one of the fundamental causes of the despotism and humiliation to which it is subjected.

It is in light of all the above and having considered the issue at length, that the good God inspired them to conclude the following agreement:

1   Nuri al-Sa'id will endeavor in Iraq and wherever it is deemed necessary, to prepare the ground for an absolute and complete Arab Unity. He pledges before God to do this.
2   Shukri al-Quwatli will endeavor in Damascus and wherever it is deemed necessary, to prepare the ground for an absolute and complete Arab Unity. He pledges before God to do this.
3   Each of the two contracting parties is responsible to himself, to his brother and to God for his actions. He is responsible for the desired success and must lead his region to attain it with the agreement of his brother.
4   Each of the two contracting parties undertakes to honestly help his brother like a friend helps a friend and a close friend helps a close friend.
5   Nuri al-Sa'id undertakes to facilitate and morally and materially help his brother Shukri with regard to all foreign authorities. For his part, Shukri undertakes the same with regard to Nuri.
6   Both contracting parties agree that presidencies and thrones do not constitute an obstacle between them. Both of them seek only the Arabs'

interests, whoever the foreign power might be, the goal being the interests of the Arab nation.

That said, both contracting parties recognize the following two facts:

7 The house of the Hashemites benefits from its dominant position in the Arab cause and thus deserves the greatest appreciation and gratitude.

    a Great Britain, which is the largest global power dominating the Near East, is not a hostile obstacle to the Arabs, because the interests of the Arabs necessitate a true friendship and staunch loyalty with regard to this power, and if the Arabs do not gain its friendship of their own accord, the circumstances and events will force them to submit to it by force, which must be avoided by all means.

8 The Unity of Syria with all the regions that were detached is vital for the entire Arab nation. This Unity must be the goal towards which all efforts must be coordinated. It is understood that all these efforts must be made after the understanding between the two brothers who signed this document.

9 The question of Syria and Lebanon must be resolved in accordance with the Arabs' interests in order to remove the foreign colonizer who rules there.

10 The Syrian borders in the north must be modified in order to guarantee the return of the Arabs of Cilicia to the cradle of the motherland.

11 The friends of one of the contracting brothers are the friends of the other and vice versa. Each of the two contracting parties undertakes not to make things easy for and to struggle against the political and personal enemies of his brother.

12 The question of Palestine is sensitive. Neither of the two contracting parties may express a definitive opinion on the subject without consulting with Great Britain.

13 The two contracting brothers undertake to help each other succeed in their respective countries and to collaborate with all the Arabs who are striving towards the goals that they pursue.

14 Each of the two contracting parties will strive, within the limits of its ability, to form a bloc of Arab states which can support each other to facilitate cultural, economic, political and military collaboration between the Arab peoples.

15 Lebanon's situation is special. Each of the contracting parties must apply himself to realizing Lebanese Unity with the other Arab countries, by collaborating on the one hand with our Lebanese brothers and on the other with Great Britain which seeks the annexation of Lebanon to Syria.

16 Turkey and Persia pose a threat to the Arab nation. Iraq and Syria will support each other to ward off these serious threats.

17 France poses a direct threat which we must remove by any means possible. Syria's liberty is necessary in attaining Arab Unity. Deliverance from

the French threat is a basic factor to which all possible help must be rendered in order to remove this threat.

In any event, Nuri al-Sa'id promises that Iraq will not recognize the present Syrian government.

18   The attitude of Iraq and Syria with regard to the House of Sa'ud will be defined by an agreement between the two contracting parties. No guiding principle will be adopted with regard to Ibn Sa'ud before there is complete agreement between Iraq and Syria.

19   This agreement will retain its general form until Shukri al-Quwatli rises to power. The provisions of the agreement will constitute the basis of the agreement on national issues. Drawn up at the present on a personal level, this agreement will then be brought to the national Arab level.

This is our agreement. God is our witness.

Signatures:

Shukri al-Quwatli
Nuri al-Sa'id

4. July 42/February 1943   Quwatli's secret agreement with the Hashemites on Syrian Unity

Top Secret

Plan for Syrian Unity

1   Syria is one geographical unity (*illegible word*) and must regain its unity.
2   Syrian Unity can be realized in stages, but at each stage, the wishes of the peoples of the Syrian regions must be taken into consideration and their interests must be safeguarded.
3   The Syrians, Lebanese, Palestinians and Transjordanians, united from the beginning by their noble traditions, are currently linked by economic interests which are becoming increasingly important.
4   Greater Syria is able to rule elements which may not be purely Arab, but are of noble origin. All hostility is suppressed. The Jews, because of the blood ties between them and the Arabs, will be the object of hostility only if they initiate it.
5   Greater Syria will be a part of the Greater Arab Unity.
6   Each region of [Greater] Syria will retain its distinctiveness and its financial autonomy, while they will all pursue the same common economic and national vision.
7   Autonomy is guaranteed to each region, but Syrian Unity firstly and Arab Unity secondly have one sole aim, which is to find the unique means that will firmly ensure the common interests of each one.
8   The aim of this plan is to create an Arab bloc sufficiently strong to guarantee and protect the Arab culture and way of life in the Islamic East against annihilation and disappearance.

This plan will allow us to collaborate efficiently, according to our traditions, with the Great Powers and not submit ourselves to their will. End.

Each one signed the present document, adding the following remarks:

Emir Abd al-Ilah–
From the bottom of my heart I declare my abidance by this noble plan.

Emir Abdullah –
It is for the realization of this noble ideal that we live, we, members of the Hashemite family.

Nuri al-Sa'id –
I welcome this plan which will rouse the Arabs, which will unite them and create a true friendship between them and their cousins.

Shukri al-Quwatli –
I agree, but we must wait for the right opportunity.

This plan is dated July 1942. It was signed by Shukri al-Quwatli in February 1943. As for the Jews, their agreement or refusal was not mentioned anywhere.

Note by the agent
This plan was authored by Dr Magnessi [*]. It has been approved so far by Emir Abd al-Ilah, Emir Abdullah, Nuri al-Sa'id and Shukri al-Quwatli.

Notes

[*] Phonetic spelling. Probably "Mac Ness"
Author's note: In 1942 Dr Judah Magnes, President of the Hebrew University, headed a group of Jewish intellectuals who advocated a bi-national or autonomous Jewish entity within an Arab Federation. French sources indicate that the above agreement was prepared in four languages, including Hebrew.

5. October 11, 1943   Emir Abdullah to Egyptian Prime Minister Nahhas Pasha

Top secret

The Emirate of Transjordan
Office of the Emir
(See O.R.-7/393)

Personal

Abdullah Bey al-Hussein, Emir of the Emirate of Transjordan
to
His Excellency Mustapha Nahhas Pasha, President of the Egyptian Council

Your Excellency,

Your Excellency knows that His Majesty the King, my late father Hussein Ibn Abdullah, was the first to put the Arab question to the world. He was the first to defend the interests of the Arab nation, regarding as his own the cause of the nation and its community. The Arabs glorify in it. May our prayers and the reverence of humanity be offered to our great prophet and ancestor.

Your Excellency perhaps remembers the great sacrifices His Majesty my father made for his nation and his religion. You know that all this harmed his health, his peace of mind, his reputation and his position. He renounced the throne and the kingdom to please God and to follow his doctrines and his pact.

We praise God that we, Hussein's son, have inherited the heavy burden that our late father carried. We pray to God to keep us alive until we have won the honor of achieving the vow so desired by His Majesty my father.

That is why my emotion was great on learning the noble efforts you are making to bring about the Unity we have always lived for. Tawfiq Pasha, whom I have delegated to you, has told me of your kindness, wisdom and good instincts. Allow me therefore to thank you and to congratulate you on the great and noble qualities you are endowed with.

May I also be allowed to make some suggestions regarding the realization of Arab Unity:

1 The British are firmly decided on achieving Unity on condition that the Arabs work for it and get on with one another.
2 Ibn Sa'ud constitutes a natural obstacle to achieving any Arab Unity. He will create difficulties for us, one after the other, and will be a thorn between us and the desired Unity.
3 The pillars of Arab Unity must be Iraq, Egypt and Syria. As for Yemen and Ibn Sa'ud, they will have to unite with us, but this union requires a great deal of effort and circumstances different to those in which we find ourselves at the moment.
4 Syria in its current situation cannot be part of the Unity for different reasons: the French presence, the existence of Lebanon and the position of the Jews in Palestine.

I have succeeded, thanks be to God, after many attempts with the English, to come to an understanding with them on the following points, relative to Syria and its unification:

a The English show particular sympathy towards the idea of the creation of a united Syrian state to include Syria, Lebanon, Palestine and Transjordan, under the auspices of the undersigned.
b The Maronites in Lebanon will enjoy a special status and administrative, financial and judicial autonomy.

c The Jews in Palestine will enjoy a special status and administrative, financial and judicial autonomy.

d United Syria will conclude with Great Britain a treaty of friendship and mutual aid similar to the Iraqi and Egyptian treaties.

e United Syria will conclude with Egypt and Iraq, on the basis of equality, a treaty of federation or of confederation. These three States will have a federal Council which will reside for one year in Baghdad, one year in Damascus and one year in Cairo on a rolling basis. These three Arab countries will form only one state from the economic, military and diplomatic points of view.

These suggestions I put before Your Excellency deserve to be considered. They are likely to be modified or changed according to the needs of the general interest which we ask for God's help for.

I confirm to Your Excellency that these suggestions have won the formal agreement of the British party which strongly desires to unite the Arabs and which is disposed to do them justice and to grant them their legitimate rights.

With my warm greetings,

October 11, 1943   s/ Abdullah

Registered in the Ministry of Foreign Affairs of the Syrian Republic
No. 162 – Secret documents
Agent's note – This letter was given to President Shukri al-Quwatli by the Egyptian Justice Minister Sabri Abu al-Alami Pasha when he came to Damascus for the Lawyers' Conference of September 1944. It is not known if Sabri Abu al-Alami had received Nahhas Pasha's consent for this secret communication. It must not be forgotten that in Egypt he is an advocate of Ibn Sa'ud.

6. March 2, 1944   Churchill's undertaking to Ibn Sa'ud

Top secret

                Photocopy of a document kept by the Saudi Government

The Prime Minister of the United Kingdom undertakes, if France withdraws from Syria and Lebanon, not to strive, for his part, to maintain (in these two countries) British occupying troops.

He also undertakes not to favor any change of regime, or the political or geographic status of these countries.

Cairo, March 2, 1944

                                            Signed: Winston Churchill

Registered in the Saudi Ministry of Foreign Affairs
No. 277 – Diplomatic documents

7. March 15, 1944   Secret Syro-Saudi agreement

Top Secret

Secret Syro-Saudi Agreement of March 15, 1944

Between

His Royal Highness Emir Sa'ud Ibn Abd al-Aziz, heir to the Arab Saudi Kingdom, and His Excellency Sheikh Yusuf Yasin, head of the political cabinet, acting on behalf of His Majesty Abd al-Aziz Ibn Abd al-Aziz Ibn Abd al-Aziz al-Faisal al-Sa'ud on the one hand,

and

His Excellency Jamil Mardam Bey, Minister of Foreign Affairs of the Syrian Republic, acting on behalf of His Excellency Shukri bey Quwatli, President of the Syrian Republic, on the other.

- - - - - - - - -

Article 1 – The representatives of the two sides have agreed to help each other and consult with each other on anything related to their general interests or that concerns the politics of the two states, both with regard to one or more other Arab states, or one or more foreign states.

The representatives of the two sides have agreed to provide mutual assistance in any dispute, conflict or conciliation that might arise between one of them and another Arab or foreign party.

Article 2 – Anything relating to plans for Arab Unity must be done with complete understanding between the two parties.

The two parties undertake not to adopt, under any circumstances, a stand opposed to the stand adopted by the other.

Article 3 – The government of the Syrian Republic and the government of the Saudi Arabian Kingdom will help each other completely with any matters relating to the interests of the nomadic Bedouin. The two states will pursue a single approach in any dispute or conflict that might arise between the Bedouin under their jurisdiction.

Article 4 – The two governments will help each other on all matters pertaining to the natural resources that have already been exploited or that will be exploited in the Arab states, as well as on matters regarding oil and the companies that have obtained or will obtain concessions.

Each contracting government will approve any measures that the other might take against any operating company or establishment.

Article 5 – This agreement is concluded for a period of five years, tacitly renewable unless one of the signatories requests its modification.

Article 6 – Two copies of this agreement have been made.

Bodet al-Tanhat, March 15, 1944

S/ Yusuf Yasin
S/ Jamil Mardam

The seal of Sa'ud Ibn Abd al-Aziz
Registered in the Syrian Ministry of Foreign Affairs
No. 37 – Documents

8. April 15, 1944   Jamil Mardam's secret agreement with Nuri al-Sa'id

This is a copy of the agreement signed on April 15, 1944 between the former Iraqi Prime Minister, Nuri al-Sa'id Pasha, and the current Minister of National Economy in Syria, Jamil Mardam Bey.

We, Nuri al-Sa'id and Jamil Mardam Bey, have agreed:

a To work together for Syria's liberation from the yoke of the colonizers and for the unity of these countries.
b To strive for the formation of an Arab Hashemite state including Syria.
c The head of the kingdom will be and can only be Jamil Mardam. The latter, who will be the sole leader of the kingdom, will be second in rank after the designated sovereign.
d Nuri Sa'id undertakes to work towards the realization of this plan and to accept the authority of the chosen sovereign.
e The two parties undertake to respect this agreement, which God is the only witness thereof.

Signed: Nuri al-Sa'id and Jamil Mardam

Two copies made
April 15, 1944
Author's note: An identical agreement was signed again on September 15, 1944.

9. May 4, 1944   Negotiations on Soviet recognition of Syria's independence

Top secret

Letter from Deputy Naim Antaki, on mission in Cairo
to Sa'adallah al-Jabiri, President of the Council

HE the President of the Council of Ministers of the
Syrian Republic

Greetings ... I believe that I have fulfilled my mission in the best possible conditions. I will set out the result of my efforts in this report.

Having been in contact with HE the Russian Minister Plenipotentiary, and having expressed to him the desire of the Government of the Syrian Republic for the Government of the Union of Soviet Socialist Republics to recognize our independence and establish diplomatic relations, I had to wait for him to get in touch with his Government to present it with our current wish.

Four days passed in this way. On the fifth day, he invited me to tea. We resumed our conversation in the light of instructions he had received from his Government.

First of all, he asked to be told the circumstances in which Syrian independence had been achieved, the basis on which it rests and if we, the Syrians, believe that our independence is a reality or a "distraction" which the English and the French have tried to give us while waiting, once the war is over, to go back on their actions. The English, for example, he said, have given Egypt and Iraq their independence; but you know better than anyone else the meaning of independence in these countries. With you, we know that General Catroux has published a definitive document. Has this document been obtained through your efforts, that is to say is it your fight that has forced General Catroux to recognize your independence, or was another factor guiding him?

At last he came to the outcome he wanted, saying:

"We find ourselves facing a people, the Syrian people, whose independence has been recognized by Free France; but we are also facing an English authority which is growing stronger and gaining ground by the day. Is this independence you have arrived at emancipation from France and freedom of action given to England? It is true that the circumstances of war are difficult, but we notice, particularly in the mentality of the men in this government, far more haste towards Great Britain than is necessary. From our point of view, this haste bears a meaning and breadth just when we want to recognize the independence of this country. In addition, many of the people who are currently in power have not always been sincere in the Cause of Democracies, or even towards the cause of England. They were Germanophiles, at the extreme, when German influence reigned in your country. All these points must be clarified before we can think about recognizing your independence."

The conversation between us lasted about three hours. I believe that I convinced him completely. My replies were inspired by my way of seeing things. By and large, these replies rested on the following points:

1 We are not puppets of the British, but we regard Great Britain as our friend.
2 The proclamation of independence is the result of our country's spectacular twenty-year struggle.
3 Our independence rests with our people and not with France, which has in reality been forced to recognize this.
4 The men in the current Government are in no way Germanophiles; they are forced, by the interests of our people, to be in touch with foreign groups, whoever they are, but this does not in any way commit them.
5 We wish the Soviet Union to be represented with us in its capacity as a powerful democratic force, and for it to reaffirm its presence so that the other great democratic Powers will not be the only ones in our country.

That is a summary of the conversations. He promised to give me his definitive answer as soon as possible.

Yours sincerely,
Cairo, May 4, 1944

s/ Naim Antaki

Ministry of Foreign Affairs
Document No. 3 – Diplomatic correspondence – the Soviet Union

10. June 5, 1944   Mardam-Spears understanding

Secret and Confidential

Republic of Syria
Ministry of Foreign Affairs
Cabinet, Damascus, June 5, 1944
No. 119/23/S.B.
Verbal Note

His Excellency General E. Spears, Minister Plenipotentiary of His British Majesty's Government, Damascus.

In confirmation of our conversation, I consider it my duty to confirm our ultimate desire to conclude a frank and clear agreement between us.

The proposals that you submitted encourage us to believe that our understanding will ensure the safeguarding of our and your interests.

With deep respect,

Minister of Foreign Affairs
S/Jamil Mardam Bey

11. June 24, 1944   Mardam to Novikov, Head of the Soviet Political Commission

Top secret

Letter from Jamil Mardam Bey, the Syrian Minister of Foreign Affairs
to
Mr Novikov, The President of the Soviet Political Commission, Minister Plenipotentiary

I confirm to you, on the eve of establishing diplomatic relations between us, that independent Syria wishes with all its heart that the Soviet Union will recognize its independence and will exchange diplomatic representatives with it.

In the name of the Government of the Syrian Republic, I declare that we will always know how to show ourselves worthy of the confidence placed in us,
– that we will keep our independence intact and pure,
– that we will not neglect the rights which come to us with this independence,
– that we will never renounce our sovereignty,
– that we will favor public freedoms and parties so that they exert themselves to the benefit of the Syrian people and their interests,
– that we will not fail to ask the Soviet Union for help with everything that could be useful to us,
– and that we will only follow the inspiration of democratic, free principles in our political life.

June 24, 1944   The Syrian Minister of Foreign Affairs
s/ Jamil Mardam Bey

Registered in the Ministry of Foreign Affairs
No. 16 – Diplomatic Correspondence – the Soviet Union

12. June 25, 1944   Mardam's report on diplomatic relations with the Soviet Union

Top secret

Report by Jamil Mardam Bey on the negotiations
which resulted in the establishment of diplomatic relations
between the USSR and Syria

- - -

Summary for the Council of Ministers

- - -

The conversations which took place between the Syrian Ministry of Foreign Affairs and the Members of the Political Mission, representing the Government of the Soviet Union, finished today.

I have the honor of communicating the summary of these conversations to your esteemed Council.

Above all, we kept secret the question of the Commission's presence for fear that negotiations would fail, and that disappointment would be bitter, with unfortunate consequences.

I think it important that the esteemed Council of Ministers should know that Mr Khaled Bakdash, President of the Syrian Communist Party, has made praiseworthy efforts to bring these negotiations to a conclusion. He has shown, in all his actions, a praiseworthy patriotism which deserves thanks and appreciation.

The Soviet Political Commission has asked, above all, for the following:

- information on the history of Syrian independence,
- details on the situation of parliamentary representation in Syria,
- a summary of Franco-Syrian relations, and the conditions in which General Catroux proclaimed Syrian independence,
- precise details on England's degree of participation in consolidating this independence as well as the strength of political relations linking us to Great Britain.

The Commission has tried to find out if a second public or secret agreement exists between us and a foreign power.

It asks for information on:

- The economic and financial situation of Syria with regard to the laws concerning production, taxes and the state of agricultural, industrial and commercial property.

   It is informing itself on ethnic and religious minorities and on their origins. It is enquiring into the government apparatus, its shape and the degree of religious representation at its center.

   It asks for information:
- on the teaching and educational system of the nation
- on mining, and on industrial, agricultural or mineral monopolies

– on the Syrian oil company and on its agreements
– on the reasons for the non-development of Syrian oil and on the attitude of the Syrian Government towards this. Is the Government determined to maintain the status quo or not?

The Commission discussed the financial situation and the Issuing Bank with us. We showed it the Bank of Syria's agreement and concession.

Lastly it asked us for guarantees which we have provided in the name of the Syrian Republic, and a copy has been sent to your esteemed Council.

In reviewing the information which the Commission tried to obtain, it has emerged that this Ministry has had a praiseworthy success in clearly setting out the Syrian position in all its respects, allowing the Commission to pronounce itself satisfied and to recognize, in the name of the Government of the Soviet Union, our independence unconditionally and without reservation.

It is my pleasure to announce this happy news to the esteemed Council of Ministers.

June 25, 1944   S/ Jamil Mardam Bey

Registered in the Ministry of Foreign Affairs
No. 15 – Diplomatic correspondence – the Soviet Union

13. July 22, 1944   Egyptian Consul on his meeting with Emir Abdullah

The Royal Consulate of Egypt in Palestine and Transjordan, Jerusalem
Memorandum of a meeting with HH Emir Abdullah, Prince of Transjordan

Following Ministry despatch No. 6, received before midday on Friday 31st of this month, about the date of the General Arab Congress Preparatory Committee meeting, I contacted Amman by telephone to fix the date when I will have the honor of meeting HH Emir Abdullah, Prince of Transjordan. I had the honor of meeting His Highness that very evening. After HH had read the contents of the despatch he gave me his opinion on it and other matters.

The date of the Preparatory Committee meeting:

I am in agreement with fixing this date for September 25, the date when HE Tawfiq Pasha will be in Egypt. I will talk to him about it and will confirm with you as soon as possible.

If putting back this date is required, I approve this although as far as I am concerned I see no drawback in having to work during Ramadan.

The Arab Union, its practical direction and some characteristic facts

Alongside this, our duty is to reflect more deeply on the practical direction of the Arab Union and some of its characteristics. If one says that there will be Union between Egypt, Transjordan and Iraq, these are acceptable, reasonable words. As for Union with Syria as it currently is, with its troubled situation, and wanting to repulse the French, with Maronite Lebanon like

Syria in the ways I have just mentioned, that is a difficult question. If Greater Syria were to be realized, then the matter would be completely different.

As for Union with Saudi Arabia, with its current rotten regime, this is an impossibility and our family here and in Iraq are seething with anger. We will not calm down unless this rotten Najd regime is chased out of the Hejaz. We are waiting for a chance to chase out these people who, for a long time, have been our enemies and the enemies of Egypt which has fought them and spilled blood and money for that. What surprises me at the moment is seeing certain ministers and important people in Egypt visiting the Hejaz, taking part in these people's debauchery and then flattering and praising them more than common courtesy requires. As for me, I watch them closely to uncover their mistakes. Recently I wrote Mr Churchill a letter, which the High Commissioner had delivered to him, a letter in which I expressed my indignation about the fact that "non-Muslims" were involved in the fight against locusts in the Hejaz. These people have in effect been removed and replaced by Muslims.

Iraq

HH asked me, "Did HE Nahhas Pasha and Prince Abdul talk when the latter was in Egypt?" I replied that I knew nothing. His Highness told me that such negotiations are very good given the current circumstances because there is not a single man in Iraq. You know my opinion on Nuri who is worthless, who is not interested in the general interest but whose whole concern is provoking uproar all around himself. As for al-Pachachi, he is Nuri's double. He is a stupid, empty man. His downfall, like Nuri's, is inevitable. I do not see a single man in Iraq today, now that power rests with the English far more than before Cornwallis (the British Ambassador).

Egypt

We will turn towards Egypt again and again, "which only has to call us for us to accept its invitation." Here HH the Prince authorizes my return to Palestine.

22.7.44
(Signed) the Consul General

14. August 5, 1944 Secret British proposal presented by Riyad al-Sulh to Sa'adallah al-Jabiri

Top Secret
British Proposals Officially Presented by Riyad al-Sulh on August 5, 1944 to Sa'adallah al-Jabiri

----

1 The British Government pledges to effectively and completely and absolutely protect Syrian independence against any aggression or transgressions from any state or group of states that lay claim to Syria's rights.

2 Great Britain pledges to provide the necessary funds to exploit Syria's agricultural and metallurgical resources in the framework of a financial and economic agreement in which Syria's interests will be safeguarded in all ways possible.

3 Great Britain pledges to provide experts and technicians who will freely enter into contracts with the Syrian government and who will be considered its officials.

4 Great Britain will help Syria to set bounds to the direction of Arab Unity. It will occupy itself with unifying financial and economic regulations as well as teaching methods in the Arab states. It will help Syria to attain a prominent position among the Arab states.

5 Great Britain pledges to ensure the application of the clauses of the White Paper in Palestine and promises to put a complete stop to Jewish ambitions.

6 If Syria seeks unification with Transjordan and Palestine, the British Government will not impose the type of regime. If Syria chooses a monarchy, Great Britain will not impose Emir Abdullah as King, but it hopes that the Syrians will choose a Hashemite Arab Emir.

7 In return for all this, Great Britain wishes to be assured:
   a That Syria will finally strive to free itself.
   b That Syria will conclude a treaty with Great Britain only.
   c That Syria will not enter into any pact or international agreement before consulting Great Britain.

Author's note: The proposal was dictated by Colonel MacKereth to Sulh in the British Legation in Beirut.

15. August 5, 1944   Brigadier Clayton to the British Legation in Beirut

Coded
Office of the Minister Resident in the Middle East
Service du Levant
We do not want any intervention in our internal affairs.

This would produce difficulties and complication and the position becomes clearer every day in the following sense:

1 Those people who are governing at present pretend to be with us but they cannot continue with us.

2 We are compelled to make our choice between them and our friends and we cannot change our plan, it being not a question of tactics but a matter of principle.

3 Our proposals so far submitted have been without response. We should not insist on getting an answer. It is up to them to come to us and not up to ourselves to come to them.

4 It is necessary that our behavior be the following:

We are not satisfied with this situation. But we do not intend to undertake anything to change it. It is up to our friends to make up their minds. We are being in two opposite camps. We are wanting to be on good terms with both of them.

Especially it is the international events which are urging us to consolidate our position with one of those camps.

Considering this important question it should be decided upon who is for and who is against us.

All these questions will be studied on the spot as soon as I shall have arrived with you.

Signed: Clayton

16. September 27, 1944   President Quwatli to Jabiri in Alexandria

Top secret

Letter from Shukri al-Quwatli
given to Sa'adallah Jabiri at the Alexandria Conference
by Mazhar Pasha Raslan

- - -

My dear brother Sa'adallah Bey Jabiri,

Greetings from Arabism. I delayed the trip of our brother Mazhar waiting for the reply from HM the King.[1][Ibn Sa'ud] Thank God, this reply arrived.

First, I am happy with the procedure you followed. You knew – may God look favorably on you – how to follow the best route to protect the dignity of His Majesty. The general invitation which you thus threw open does him honor, as it does you and me, and I do not know how to express my pleasure and my thanks to you for this success.

I have received from His Majesty a fairly short note. The delegates will collaborate fully with you. His Majesty did not want to make you bear the responsibility of opposition to Nuri Pasha and his associates. His delegates will take care of the opposition. All that His Majesty expects from you is that you act as an intermediary between him and the others.

As a result, I beg you to stick to the principles we have agreed. I wish you success in whatever we desire and that God has inspired us, so that neither this side nor that can trifle with us.

Here, I believe that we will need to face many difficulties to extricate ourselves from the plans that Nuri Pasha and Emir Abdullah confront us with, but God be praised, His Majesty is firmly decided to deal with them properly. He is convinced that all the threats these people utter are only empty words.

However, there is one thing to fear: the coup the British may engineer against His Majesty. It is for this reason that I ask you to be extremely prudent and reserved, so as to always keep open a way to retreat.

I also call your attention to the fact that the plans for unity presented by our brothers, the Hashemites, will encounter difficulties from the American side. I felt this in my conversations with them. This is useful to us, even if the Jews are more favored by them than we are.

Anyway, our course of action is clear: we support His Majesty's delegates in their objections, and we offer ourselves as intermediaries for the understanding.

I will inform you of anything new that happens. May God protect you and keep you with your brothers.

Wednesday 10 Shawwal 1363[2]

S/ Shukri

Notes

1 King Ibn Sa'ud
2 September 27, 1944

17. October 1, 1944   Jabiri in Alexandria to President Quwatli

Sa'adallah Bey Jabiri to
The President of the Republic of Syria

To His Excellency the most Honorable President,

Greetings from Arabism. Here matters are getting worse and worse. Nuri Pasha has revealed his game to us. They are not content with unifying Transjordan with Palestine, but they are demanding that we create a throne for Abdullah or Abd al-Ilah. They thus judge that the unification of Syria and Iraq, under one king, will serve as a prelude to the realization of the Great Unity of the Arabs.

Our brother, Yusuf Yasin, has taken it upon himself to reply to them. A violent clash among them all resulted from this and the incident ended in a dispute serious enough that only God knows how it will resolve itself.

Our pain has increased because they are pressuring us. They do not want to sign any common declaration on the safeguarding of the independence of Syria and Lebanon. They have themselves declared to brother Riyad that they are not desirous of guaranteeing the independence of Lebanon which today constitutes a thorn in the side of the Arab nation. The delegates from Iraq and Transjordan had harsh words with brother Riyad, calling him inconsistent and a hypocrite and said to him, "You have built your political position and your national reputation on the idea of Syrian unity. What has now happened to you that on no matter what occasion you distance yourself from any unity and attack all those who are working for it?"

I do not believe that the efforts made can result in a real accord. It may be that we will succeed in covering up the situation so that our enemies do not rejoice in it. All that I am asking Your Excellency is to please give me, as a matter of urgency, his opinion on all these matters so that we can be in perfect agreement.

With the sincere respect of your devoted

S/ Sa'adallah al-Jabiri

Sunday October 1, 1944

18. October 2, 1944   President Quwatli to Jabiri in Alexandria

Reply from Shukri Bey Quwatli
to Sa'adallah Bey Jabiri's letter
To my brother Sa'adallah Bey Jabiri, may God protect him.

Greetings from Arabism. What has happened pains me, but the designs and the will of God are unassailable. I do not know where these brothers will lead us, especially as from day to day they incite the English to put pressure on us to make us more pliable and to favor them. I have said to them several times: what profit will you gain from Abdullah or Abd al-Ilah? I am with you as you wish, and we will not neglect anything to satisfy you and assure your interests; but it seems that that cannot satisfy them. They continue to regard us with mistrust, fearing that we will not fall in step with the others. But God knows that I prefer death to favoring a Frenchman.

The situation with us is troubled. It is up to you to arrange things there. You must show them a semblance of agreement, affection and understanding, because our enemies are now working with all their strength. Therefore we must not give our brothers the chance to attack us.

Come to an understanding with them over what is possible. As to the questions to which you have drawn my attention, put off their solution to a time when opportunities will be more favorable to us. Adjournment and a bit of time is all that we hope for at the moment, in order to sort matters out with the English and to try to come to an understanding with them.

I leave everything to your wisdom. You know what needs to be done and a man like you has no need of advice.

My greetings to the brothers.
May God keep you to your brother
S/ Shukri al-Quwatli

Monday October 2, 1944

19. October 4-5, 1944   Jabiri in Alexandria to President Quwatli

Top secret

Letter sent from Alexandria by
Sa'adallah Bey Jabiri to Shukri Bey Quwatli,
and brought by air by Fawzi Tello in an attaché case sealed with
red wax at the same time as other documents.

Your Excellency,

Greetings from Arabism. Our brother, His Excellency Sheikh Yusuf Yasin has today told me what the Political Staff of HM King Abd al-Aziz Ibn Sa'ud received the day before yesterday from the Saudi Minister Plenipotentiary in London, an encoded telegram, about conversations which took place or which are currently taking place between the French and the English about the situation in Syria and Lebanon, and on the eventual agreement that these two foreign countries may reach at our expense.

Sheikh Hafiz[1] bases his report on what he was told by a personal friend of HM King Abd al-Aziz, who is a member of the English aristocracy. This important person enjoys great influence and wishes to catch the attention of the Arabs so that they can be wary of the unfortunate consequences of an agreement which could strike like a bolt from the blue.

Although the principles and terms of this agreement are totally unknown to him, this important person is convinced that it could only be prejudicial to us and he wanted to warn us of the danger threatening us.

Sheikh Hafiz Wahba adds that the English no longer expect the plan for Arab unity to succeed through the forum of the Cairo Congress, especially since they realized that the Arabs are hardly disposed to admit of Great Britain's intentions and to profit from the real advantages they can get from British plans.

For my part, I am not surprised by such a change of direction by the English. I was expecting it from the moment when they felt that we would not favor the plans they wanted to make us keep to. But our interest demands that we make their efforts[2] fail so as not to give the French the chance to hit us once they are certain that a direct agreement with us is impossible.

I am sending you a summary of our activities here and I await your valuable advice.

Night of October 4-5, 1944   S/ Sa'adallah

Notes

1 Saudi Arabian Minister in London
2 Probably the Franco-British agreement

20. October 5, 1944   Jabiri in Alexandria to President Quwatli on the Palestinian question

Top secret

The Palestinian Question
Report sent by Sa'adallah al-Jabiri
to the President of the Syrian Republic

- - -

October 4-5, 1944

The members of the Congress think that the Palestine question is an international question that affects the whole of the Arab world, threatens security in the Middle East and may constitute a source of permanent danger for the close relations between Arab and other nations.

The members of the Congress think that obligations already entered into and promises made up till now do not bind either the Arab nations or Arab governments in the least, because Palestine is an Arab land and no nation other than the Arab nation has the right to make decisions about it.

As a result, the members of the Congress think that Balfour's promise has encroached on the Arab nation's sacred rights. They think that the White Book project cannot be a definitive project, but that it can serve in principle for a new study of the Palestine question.

The Arab nation, represented at this Congress, does not authorize relinquishing a single inch of Palestinian land. However, aware of the need to find a refuge for the Jews currently living in Palestine, it agrees to grant them a limited zone, which cannot, under any circumstances, constitute a third of the land of Palestine, leaving to those who want, the possibility of leaving the country after the reestablishment of peace on condition that no immigration into this zone, filling the empty space thus created, takes place.

This zone would remain under the British Mandate, while the other part of Palestine will be wholly granted to the Jews and given its own independence.

(Here, Nuri Pasha and his associates showed a desire to see this part annexed to Transjordan. We put forward to them as a condition that annexation would only take place if the residents consented to it. A long dispute arose among us, but we will not give our consent to their proposition.)

These are the outlines of the solutions which we have reached on the Palestine question. Please give me your instructions swiftly.

S/ Sa'adallah

21. October 14, 1944   Daniel Solod, the Soviet Minister in Syria and Lebanon, to Mardam

Top secret

From the Soviet Minister to the
Syrian Minister of Foreign Affairs

- - -

Verbal note

In assuring you that my Government will receive with great pleasure the movement for Arab Unity, to which it gives its complete approval, I am charged with asking you if you are sure that this movement will serve the interests of the Arab nations alone and that it will not put the Arab nation as a whole under imperial influence.

I am also charged with asking you if there are any secret appendices to the Alexandria agreement and if these secret appendices contain indications on the adoption of a political position determined with regard to one of the great democracies.

S/ Solod

October 14, 1944
Registered in Foreign Affairs in Syria
No. 20 – Diplomatic correspondence – the Soviet Union

22. October 16, 1944   Mardam to Solod

Top secret

From the Syrian Minister of Foreign Affairs
to the Soviet Minister
Note

The Syrian Council of Ministers has qualified me to confirm to you that the Arab League movement will not act as the instrument of any world Power and that the Arab nation and its interests will not put themselves at the service of any imperial Power.

I have the honor of formally denying the existence of secret clauses which you have alluded to.

October 16, 1944   S/ Jamil Mardam Bey

Registered in Foreign Affairs in Syria
No. 21 – Diplomatic correspondence – the Soviet Union

23. December 1944   Raymond Eddé to King Faruq's adviser

Copy corresponding to a letter sent by Mr Raymond Eddé, son of the ex-President of the Republic of Lebanon, to Mr Gallad Pasha, Director of European Administration in the King's Office

Raymond Eddé
Lawyer to the Court
Beirut
H.E. Gallad Pasha
Royal Adviser, Cairo

My dear Pasha,

Following our last conversation, I am sending you, attached, a copy of a document of unquestionable authenticity and whose importance will not escape you.

I believed that it was my duty to get it to you without delay to confirm what I said to you regarding this matter.

I thank you once again for the friendly welcome you gave me and ask you to believe in my sincere and devout regard.

Signed: illegible

24. February 3, 1945   The Radwa secret agreement between Kings Ibn Sa'ud and Faruq

Radwa Pact

A copy of this document, brought by Shukri al-Quwatli, has been filed in the Syrian Foreign Ministry as number 5 – "Documents"

In the name of the most merciful God.

Faruq I, King of Egypt, in possession of Nubia, Kordofan and Zela by the grace of God and Abd al-Aziz Ibn Abd al-Rahman al-Faisal al-Sa'ud, acting in their own names, and in the names of their children and grandchildren, undertake, in the name of all-powerful God, to establish between themselves an everlasting brotherhood and indissoluble attachment, to consult one another on everything that concerns them, to help each other for mutual benefit and to form a bloc against those who declare their enmity to them.

They have held this blessed reunion (the Radwa reunion), fraternized, and undertaken to support Islam and Arabism and lend each other the support of their governments and their forces.

They have reached a mutual understanding to communicate reciprocally between themselves and their governments all meetings likely to bring about change in Arab countries or states.

The two signatories each consider that the health of his friend's country, the interests of his brother and ally, constitute his own health, that of his family and his country.

God is both witness and guarantor.

S/ Faruq
Seal of Abd al-Aziz

Made in Radwa on 20 Safar 1363 of the Hijra.
Author's note: This should be 1364 of the Hijra, namely February 3, 1945

25. February 9, 1945   Mardam to President Quwatli on Musa al-Alami's secret report

The Syrian Republic
Ministry of Foreign Affairs
Report drawn up by Jamil Mardam Bey
on Friday February 9, 1945

Mr Musa Alami has communicated to me the following information about the Shuneh conference:

The Iraqi Government is convinced that the Syrians will once again assume the same role they assumed with the late King Faisal,

- That following information gathered from the Jews (from Mr Shertok or Ibn Gourbon [Ben-Gurion] in particular), HH Emir Abdullah has become convinced that the Syrians have opted for the need to fight the Hashemite movement in Syria.
- That because of this, the meeting between Kings Faruq and Abd al-Aziz is cloaked with an aspect of seriousness and that each man realizes that it only took place on the back of the Hashemite family.

The efforts made by Abd al-Rahman al-Azzam and the help he received from Khalid al- Kerekni and Bashir Sa'adawi, advisers to the King of the Hejaz, have convinced King Abd al-Aziz and the Egyptian Government that the activities of the representatives of Arab Unity are not directed against them at all, but are in reality in the interest of the Arabs and to combat the following dangers:

1 the Turkish danger,
2 the Communist danger,
3 the French danger,

all the more so as these activities do not include the plan for Greater Syria, because realizing this plan, in the shadow of the Hashemite family, is likely to prejudice the interests of the Egyptian and Saudi dynasties, which is where the understanding between the Egyptians and Saudis comes from.

It is here that Their Highnesses Emirs Abd al-Ilah and Abdullah realized that the Hashemite family is on the point of suffering a setback. It is the Jews, friends of this family, who have felt this setback, and the Shuneh meeting can be regarded as an effective response to the meeting which took place between Kings Abd al-Aziz and Faruq.

During their conversations, the two Emirs reviewed the various problems, but the following are the proposed definitive solutions:

1 Iraq will offer its help to Syria to recognize the degree of the Syrians' willingness to accept this help.
2 To invite the Jews to make serious efforts with Presidents Roosevelt and Churchill so that the question be asked once again with the support of the two Presidents.
3 To sound out the British military authorities to discover if they would oppose the creation of incidents at the border to annoy the Syrian authorities if the Syrians refuse to accept Iraqi-Transjordanian help.
4 To prepare all possible forces in case of incidents which the Saudi Arabians could carry out on the Transjordan and Iraq borders.
5 To support the nationalists of Kuwait to fight against Ibn Sa'ud and his regime. (All this has been carried out.)
6 The two Emirs will enter into contact with the British authorities to indicate to them that some of these authorities are very accommodating with regard to Ibn Sa'ud and that they encourage his latest activities, which is an obstacle to the realization of the program drawn up by the two Emirs in agreement with the English.

Registered as No. 15/945 – "Secret political reports"

26. February 14, 1945   Saudi minutes of King Ibn Sa'ud's conversation with President Roosevelt

Top secret
Summary of conversations between HM the King Abd al-Aziz Ibn Sa'ud
and HE President Roosevelt (February 14, 1945)

The Head of HM the King's Political Staff
Yusuf Yasin

HM the King was warmly received by Mr Roosevelt. The latter told him that, together with Mr Churchill, he had had the honor of inviting His Majesty and had made him suffer the weariness of travel, as he wanted to reach an understanding with him on many matters of interest to them both, as well as the Arab world, to whose service HM the King and his family have devoted themselves.

His Majesty thanked the President for his kind words. The President continued:

"When we met Stalin, we discussed the state of war and all matters of interest to the armed forces, and we broached those of the Middle East. I must confirm to you that we all wish you all the best and want the happiness of your country. It matters to us that you collaborate with us, because in reality we are working now not only to win the war but also to win the peace. The Arab Middle East constitutes one of the main future sticking points. We want to be in perfect agreement with you, so as not to provoke difficulties, now or in the future, likely to cause either of us unpleasantness."

The President explained these problems, saying,

"The World Powers each have bases in the Arab world. Our friends the English have worked for centuries to win the friendship of the Arab world. We too have built schools and hospitals and we take a great interest in the Arabs whom we regard as noble friends. You also know that the Communists are very strongly placed at the moment and that in Syria, Palestine and Iraq their party is quite significant. If these forces were to start fighting among themselves, that would be prejudicial to you and would drag the world into new conflicts which we are trying to avoid by first reaching an understanding with you, and then among ourselves.

"We have reached agreement with Your Majesty in a normal, agreeable way. Thanks to your good intentions and your authority we have been able to benefit from the mineral wealth (of your country). It has been the same for you. We aim for greater development in future. We need this wealth. Mr Churchill, Marshal Stalin and I have agreed that we should have a warm and real agreement with you. The oil in Arab countries cannot belong to all the Allies, just as that of Tehran cannot come only to us and the English. The Russians must have their share. They must also benefit like others from Syria's enormous, unexploited oil resources."

The King replied,

"God gave us the wealth of oil. It is useful to exploit it and share the benefit. It matters to us that our friends benefit, but, as Mr Churchill said, it is important not to build one thing just to pull down another. The President knows better than anyone that the Arab world, in whose name I have the honor of speaking, while thanking him for his good intentions, should ask itself and me what the fate of the Arabs will be if the Jewish plans are achieved."

The President, smiling, said,

"We have come to this painful point, on which I have agreed with Mr Churchill and Marshal Stalin before discussing it frankly with you. We do not want to be dictators, just as we do not want to divide the world into areas to be developed, depriving one nation of its rights to give them to another; but you know the sacrifices we have agreed to and the losses suffered by the American people. You also know that without the help of the Jews, we would not have been able to do much. They have paid dearly for the war and the victory. It is a real pity that they cannot enjoy a small part of the world that would act as a homeland for them."

The King replied,

"We too have made sacrifices and have supported the Allies' cause. I do not want to think that we will constitute the price paid to the Jews. You know very well that we only believe in God and that we obey only his orders. His order on the matter of the Jews is clear: 'They are a people who have provoked the wrath of God and who have been cursed by him.' We do not recognize those who are cursed by God. They have done us evil in the past and we are doing it now. They have often tried to poison our prophet, who said of them, 'No Jew will live with me in the Arab peninsula.' Omar bin al-Khattab has in effect chased them out. So, can we then treat them with more indulgence than the Prophet and Omar?"

"Also, you said that nothing would be done without our agreement. I must remind you that no Arab will accept an agreement on the issue of the Jews which has been imposed on us. We consider them a permanent danger, which, if we cannot make them disappear, we want to limit. We do not want to help them establish themselves in the way you and your opposite number for the presidency have let it be understood in your electoral messages."

The conversation dwelt on this matter for a long time. In short, HM the King reached an agreement with the President on the following point:

"Nothing will be undertaken in future in favor of the Jews of Palestine without complete Arab agreement."

This represents a stunning victory.

The conversation then turned to the situation of the Arab world in general. The President said,

"In my opinion, I see the situation like this: England is in a privileged position which it cannot abandon. Russia, through the use of propaganda or the Communist Party, wants to assert itself in any way possible. France is weakened and we do not make much of it, but we are obliged to keep it happy, if only in part, for fear that it will join the left wing. All these forces are currently at work in the Arab world. To these countries we can add Turkey which, it seems, obtained promises at the Adana Conference, promises which are unrealizable, I believe, because the Arabs in Syria heartily detest the Turks, even though the latter claim that Syrian politicians in general are favorable to them."

"All these forces are rushing to maintain or establish influential positions in the Arab world. America is in last place."

"America, Your Majesty, does not have any colonial ambitions. Although it does not support the British colonial policy followed in Arab lands for a hundred years, it is today constrained not to upset it, because an upset of this kind could benefit the Russians. Generally, we want to interact with you as businessmen and do not want to impose anything on you. We want to buy from and sell you products, while preventing any attempt to pressure you from any direction, made with the aim of competing with us."

His Majesty the King expressed his complete agreement. The two sides agreed that:

"The independence of Arab countries is a matter of interest to America. It matters to this nation that there should be no clash between Jews and Arabs, and in addition to all that, that there should be agreement between the Arabs and the world's Great Powers."

This agreement, called the Egypt Accord, has been initialed by the two parties concerned.

Saudi Arabia dossier in the British Political Bureau in Beirut, no. 155.

27. February 16, 1945   Minutes of conversations between Kings Ibn Sa'ud and Faruq and President Quwatli

Top Secret

A summary of conversations between HM King Abd al-Aziz,
HM King Faruq and
HE President Shukri bey Quwatli [16] (February 1945)
The Head of HM the King's Political Staff
Signed Yusuf Yasin

In accordance with the sincere desire expressed by HM King Faruq,

Wanting to settle the many matters of concern to Muslims in general and the Arabs in particular,

Their Majesties the Saudi and Egyptian Kings have agreed with the President of the Syrian Republic to examine, in addition to issues concerning the Saudi Arabian kingdom, the affairs of the Arab world, that is:

1 the Palestine question;
2 Syrian and Lebanese independence and the Greater Syria plan;
3 the plan regarding Arab unity in general.

Their Majesties and the President agreed that the Palestinian question should be settled on the basis of the White Paper and the ban on emigration. Mr Roosevelt in particular will be asked not to be too zealous in defense of the Jews who were, first, the enemies of the Christian world before being those of the Muslim world.

As for Syrian and Lebanese independence, it will be asked for as a right clearly recognized by the Great Powers. Mr Churchill will be faced with the actual, indivisible, truth; it is in effect impossible to logically conceive of this duplicitous attitude of the British: one group aiding, supporting and promoting Emir Abdullah, and another supporting us.

On this matter, HM thinks that the best solution to this crisis is to maintain the status quo. If it is not possible to unite Syria and Palestine on a sensible basis which is not prejudicial to the Saudi family, let the Republic be maintained as it is in this country while awaiting a different solution.

As for the plan for Arab unity, HM King Abd al-Aziz, although giving it his complete support as promised to the King of Egypt, would, however, like to get Mr Churchill to define the degree of support Great Britain will give this Union.

HM, in thus reaching an understanding with King Faruq and Shukri bey Quwatli, wants all three to be of the same opinion and express the same view, all the more so as he does not seem to believe what he sees and hears from our Egyptian brothers. He is surprised by the great preoccupation they are suddenly showing in favor of Arab unity.

Dossier of Saudi Arabia in the British Political Bureau in Beirut, report No. 153 – which follows No. 152. C.f. document no. 1

28. February 17, 1945   Saudi minutes of King Ibn Sa'ud's conversation with Winston Churchill

Top secret

Summary of conversations between HM the King Abd al-Aziz Ibn Sa'ud, HE Mr Churchill and Mr Eden (date – February 17, 1945).

The Head of HM the King's Political Staff

S/ Yusuf Yasin

After the usual diplomatic niceties, the following political matters were discussed:

1   The question of Saudi lands.

Mr Churchill confirmed that the British Government was determined to maintain its friendship with the King, his children and his family. Under no circumstances would the British Government support the Hashemites against him.

He promises, on his honor, that Great Britain will not undertake anything unpleasant with regard to the Saudis, and that it will work towards making its friends and allies adopt a position similar to its own.

For his part, King Abd al-Aziz promised that he would fight the Axis on this, that he would allow the British to profit from the oil on his lands, on the basis of commercial competition, and that he favors England over any other state in these transactions.

As far as the Communists are concerned, the King confirmed to Mr Churchill that he would not permit them either entry to his lands or the benefit of his oil and mines. Mr Churchill objected to these declarations saying, "We do not want to discuss the details now. We will give you our support from this side, but we beg you not to announce these intentions so plainly."

As for the matters concerning the Muslim Arab nation, Mr Churchill said, on the subject of Palestine, "It is the Americans who are causing us problems at the moment by defending the Jews." He has however assured the King that nothing will happen in Palestine if it is not within the framework of the British White Paper.

As far as Greater Syria and Syrian-Lebanese Independence are concerned, Mr Churchill promised that the problem of Greater Syria would not go Emir Abdullah's way or that of the Hashemite family. "It is true," he said, "that at one particular moment there was a question mark over this but England cannot insist on a plan which is, on the one hand, rejected by the Syrian people and, on the other, is considered, by the King, Abd al-Aziz, our close friend, to be prejudicial to him and the interests of his family." As a result, nothing will therefore be done in the way Nuri al-Sa'id wants.

"As for Syrian independence, it is regrettable that the Syrians absolutely refuse to understand the situation. They do not want to understand that the promises made to them by General Spears cannot in any way bind the British Government because Great Britain, as everyone knows, is compelled to seek friendship with France. The French have accused us for a long time of having taken America, Canada and the Indies from them, and say that we have come to take Syria from them too … France holds the most important position in Syria."

If the Syrians do not know how to take this position into account, he (Mr Churchill) fears that they will not be able to keep their independence, which they won thanks to England's warm support.

As for the plan for Arab Unity, Great Britain wants it, supports it and gives it its blessing. Mr Churchill says that only a strong union of free Arabs can form a strong enough obstacle against the wiles of the extremist Communists in future. He hopes, from the bottom of his heart, that this Union comes into being; it will render a considerable service not only to the Arabs but to the whole world.

By and large, the understanding has been completed. Mr Churchill made the King see the Russians' manifest intentions to meddle in the affairs of the Middle East and the Muslim world in general. He added that he was persuaded that the King, the Muslims and the Arabs would not let themselves be drawn to communism in the future. He promised to give the King all the help needed for any Muslim and Arab country because, he said, "Friendship is the most valuable thing in the world, and the friendship of HM the King continues to be very important to Great Britain."

The conversation once again turned to mineral wealth. He (Mr Churchill) said that he wanted the government of the Saudi King to profit from these riches and to receive a reasonable share; he promised to make sure this came about.

As for the Russian demands, Mr Churchill said that King Abd al-Aziz is the only person competent in this matter, but that he will always find support in this regard from Great Britain.

Returning to Syrian affairs, Mr Churchill promised, acceding to HM the King's request, to meet President Shukri al-Quwatli. He confirmed that he sincerely wanted to help the people of Syria and Lebanon but that his friend General Spears had made too much progress with them and had pretended to forget Great Britain's obligations with regard to its ally (or the country which should be its ally), France.

The meeting ended with a complete and real understanding on both sides.

Dossier of Saudi Arabia in the British Political Bureau in Beirut, No. 154.

29. February 20, 1945   President Quwatli's report on his meeting with Churchill and Eden

Syrian Republic
The President
Report by the President of the Syrian Republic

\- -

The copy of the report drafted on February 20, 1945 was registered under the no. 21/245 – "Secret Political Reports".

\- -

On Saturday, February 17, 1945, Mr Terence Shone, the British Minister Plenipotentiary in Syria, informed me that Mr Churchill could receive me immediately after King Faruq. He accompanied me up to the British Prime Minister's house, where the meeting lasted approximately 45 minutes.

I felt that the atmosphere was chilly and that Mr Churchill was not frank with his replies. From the beginning, I noticed that Mr Eden was not favorable towards us; he listened to what I said with chilliness. Mr Shone had warned me about Mr Eden's chilliness, but it hadn't convinced me.

I explained to Mr Churchill all the stages of the Arab cause and spoke to him about Syria's role. It was unfair, I told him, that the affairs of the Syrian people – who are more mature that the other Arab peoples – are destined to be at the mercy of France, which refuses to recognize our legitimate rights.

Mr Eden then said to me:

"But are you sure you have fulfilled your obligations towards France? I believe that General Catroux' declaration conditioned the end of the mandate on the conclusion of a treaty."

I replied:

"We would like to conclude a treaty with all the Allies, not solely with France. We would like to come to the Peace Conference in the company of other Arab states, free and with no ties."

Mr Churchill's reply, if I understood it correctly, was as follows:

"You can deal with the issue of the Peace Conference only after you are in a state of war with the Axis."

I presented the Syrian problem in detail, saying:

"There are some British diplomats who have understood exactly the Syrian issue."

Mr Eden, cutting me off, said:

"You are referring, perhaps, to General Spears."

"Yes," I replied, "He noted the legitimacy of our claims."

But Mr Eden, maintaining his mood, said to me:

"Mr Spears is a citizen of Damascus and is Lebanese … ."

Finally, Mr Churchill asked me this question:

"What solution do you see to the Syro-Lebanese problems? This question interests the Allies in general, not only Britain. It should not be forgotten that France is our ally and friend and we cannot displease it, seeing that we agree that it has a privileged position."

I replied:

"I speak as a patriot before speaking as the President of the Republic. Syria is not willing to recognize France's privileged position and there is nobody in Syria ready to conclude a treaty with France that would preserve the country's state of slavery. We understand what the French are asking of us in their proposed treaty … . Now our independence is final; it has been recognized by all the Great Powers. We offer our friendship to these reunited states and do not wish to favor one and not the others."

Mr Churchill declared:

"All this may be true, but in any event I would advise you to enter into negotiations with the French. They are logical, and political matters are not a question of character, but of interest."

"It is equally a matter of trust," I replied.

Mr Eden then said:

"May the President of the Syrian Republic allow me to remind him, while appreciating his patriotism and desire for the independence of his country, that His Majesty the King Abd al-Aziz attained the success that we welcome only thanks to the important quality he has which makes him practical."

"But, I said, how do you want us to be practical with France when, for twenty years, we had to put up with it? Our people no longer trust the agreements it enters into. It concluded a treaty with us in 1936 that it annulled. I cannot shoulder the responsibility of new action with France – especially now when the matter does not depend only on us – because Syria is the key to all the Arab countries, and all the Arab states are anxious to deliver Syria from French influence."

Mr Churchill continued the conversation, saying:

"I do not doubt, my friend, your noble patriotic feelings, but as I already said, I am not free to act as I please. I informed King Abd al-Aziz, for whom I have a special respect, about all of this. The Middle East is the object of serious conversations among all the Allies. Mr Stalin raised the question of a clash of European interests in this important region. It is a pity that the Arab nations have not yet attained the necessary state of recovery, and there is no doubt that the main world Powers need to agree on their influence in your country."

"France cannot be chased out of positions it occupies. We do not know what the future holds for us, and Stalin's friendship, despite his communism, requires from us, as you know, oil concessions. Are you willing to do that?"

I replied:

"Who can tell us that our according France a privileged position won't be exploited on behalf of the Soviet Union?"

Shrugging his shoulders and smiling, he said to me:

"Who knows, who knows."

Mr Eden then continued:

"We advise the Syrians to weaken the violence of their demonstrations. We equally advise them not to malign France, like they are doing today. We will serve as an intermediary between the two."

Sensing that the meeting was drawing to a close, I said:

"I will make efforts to begin new negotiations on condition that you help us, but I must remind you that right now Syria does not belong solely to the Syrians, that it is an Arab country, and that all the Arab states are signatories of the Pact of Arab Unity and they share its sorrow."

Mr Eden declared:

"Their Majesties Kings Abd al-Aziz and Faruq have confirmed it. Be sure, Mr President, that we wish to satisfy you as much as possible, but you are not unaware that it doesn't depend only on us."

The moment I left, I realized that Great Britain would like to support us, but that support will depend on what we do to oblige it to help us. This confirms what General Spears repeatedly said to me: "Make Great Britain face the fait accompli so that it will help you."

Cairo, Saturday evening, February 17, 1945

S/ Shukri al-Quwatli

30. February 20, 1945 President Quwatli's report to his Cabinet ministers on his agreement with Kings Faruq and Ibn Sa'ud

Top Secret

Report drawn up by Shukri al-Quwatli,
Filed in the Syrian Ministry of Foreign Affairs, No. 22/945
"Secret Political Reports"

To the Council of Ministers.

I reached an understanding with Their Majesties King Faruq and King Abd al-Aziz al-Sa'ud on the following points:

1 To pursue the army's demands, without allying ourselves by treaty or granting a privileged position. The Great Powers will approve of our point of view when they realize that we are firm in our resolve and that the Arab states support us.

Great Britain's current fluctuating position cannot continue for long; the friends of the Arabs in England will not waver in their support as long as we are united.

For our part, in Syria we will engage in negotiations and will show public opinion worldwide that France does not wish us well from the perspective of our independence, and that, in these negotiations, it only seeks to win time in order to reach an understanding with the other colonial forces against us. King Abd al-Aziz thinks that it is in our interest that there should be no clashes or disorder.

It is important to note that the Arab countries are with us and support us.

2 We reached an agreement to declare war on the Axis, which will give us the moral advantage as well as definite gains.

3 We are all ready to clear up any misunderstandings that have arisen between us, Iraq and Transjordan. Every means will be used to bring about peace and transparency between us after the latest incidents.

4 The plans for Greater Syria have been abandoned. Messrs Churchill and Roosevelt have made a promise on this matter to HM King Abd al-Aziz.

We have decided to hold a meeting as soon as possible between the Arab kings and presidents to agree on the difficulties and dangers surrounding the Arabs. HM King Faruq has been charged with this matter.

5 Mr Roosevelt has openly discussed with HM King Abd al-Aziz Russian ambitions in the Middle East. This king has declared that communism is contrary to Islam and that we will not tolerate any activity of this nature in our lands.

As for Syria, I explained to Their Majesties that the situation did not allow the annihilation of the communists, but when a favorable time arises, I will not fail to liquidate them definitively.

6 HM King Abd al-Aziz is sure that President Roosevelt, with his renewed mandate, will pretend to have forgotten his initial declarations with regard to the Jewish question. His Majesty has shown him the legal case to which we Arabs are attached, and the President replied:

"I was unaware of this side of the question, but be assured that from now on I will no longer be against you, being persuaded that the Arabs are defending a legitimate right."

7 During his conversation with Mr Churchill, HM King Faruq felt an atmosphere of uncertainty about the Arab cause. Mr Roosevelt's words only confirmed this feeling. The two presidents said to the King, in different but analogous ways and with similar intentions:

"At the moment, we are surprised to see current Egyptian policy becoming much more Arab than truly national."

The King replied,

"It has been Arab from the time of my late grandfather Muhammad Ali."

8 The British and Mr Roosevelt think that, as this arises from their conversations with HM King Abd al-Aziz, the regrouping and union of the Arabs will secure them the true strength to find a solution to world affairs at the time of the Peace Congress.

HM King Faruq, relying on President Roosevelt's words, believes that the affairs of the Middle East will no longer be solved by only the English and French, because America has goals and Russia has plans. The Middle East, as the President says, must not become a second Balkan problem where international influences compete with one another; but it is up to the Allies to reach an understanding on everything which has a bearing on their interests and those of the Arab countries.

The regrouping of Arab states will make it possible to reach a firm agreement with the Allies.

Mr Roosevelt thinks that the Arab states, united like America for example, will greatly help the success of peace efforts and will push away the dangers which may result from international competition.

Mr Churchill, for his part, thinks that Great Britain was one of the first to welcome this idea, which it has done much to bring about, but it is concerned to safeguard the interests of its Empire and believes that it is its duty to fulfill its obligations with regard to France.

9 The only effort that can profit us at the moment consists in following the advice of Their Majesties the Arab Kings who have promised us maximum help, that is:

a To pursue the dissolution, one after another, of all institutions and positions which consolidate French presence in Syria: societies, institutions, civil servants and concessions.
b To pursue the propaganda campaign in favor of the army, independence and national prestige.
c To guard against every incident allowing the army to intervene to maintain security.
d To pursue negotiations with France without revealing the wish to cut them off, so that the law will be on our side, not against us.

This is a summary of the matters I agreed with Their Majesties, drawn up so that the Council of Ministers will be aware of them.

February 20, 1945

31. February 21, 1945   Mardam in Cairo to President Quwatli

Private letter sent from Cairo by Jamil Mardam Bey
to the President of the Republic by diplomatic bag

Cairo, February 21, 1945

Your Excellency, the revered President of the Syrian Republic.

Greetings from Arabism. To shed light on the conversation that took place between HE Lord Killearn and myself, I took the opportunity of my meeting with Mr Grigg, the British Minister of State, who confirmed to me the following:

"At the time of the Conference of the three, Stalin asked firmly and force-fully that an end be brought to the troubled situation in the Near and Middle East (Syria and Iran).

It is regrettable that the Great [Powers] should have decided to include France in the final settling of these problems."

However, Mr Grigg states that the solution to all these matters is in our hands, our Arab hands. The better we agree among ourselves, the more we will be able to block all foreign influences on our position, to our interests and in our affairs.

I do not know if, despite all the impartiality displayed by the Russians, I am correct in thinking of seeing them jumping to the defense of French interests at the last minute. I do not know either how far our friends will succeed in defending our point of view.

The only thing that I have been able to sense in the Minister's words is a worrying wind blowing in the future. It will not be possible for us to combat the future dangers which cause Mr Grigg this disquiet except by an under-standing with the Iraqis, despite the attitude they have shown. The under-standing with our Arab brothers will give us new possibilities for action and rapprochement.

Over the course of these two days I will try to approach Nuri Pasha and reach an understanding with him on something. I ask you to decide what we can do.

I will write to you to keep you informed of everything that happens regarding this.

s/ Jamil Mardam Bey

32. February 24, 1945   Mardam's memorandum to President Quwatli on the Soviet warning

Top secret

Memorandum from Jamil Mardam Bey, Minister of Foreign Affairs
HE the President of the Republic
HE the President of the Council of Ministers

I think it is my duty to inform you of the outlook of the Soviet Minister Plenipotentiary here.

In the course of a conversation which took place yesterday between him and me, during the banquet given by the President of the Council, we dis-cussed the future of the Arab League and the question of its support by the Great Democracies. The Minister Plenipotentiary told me, word-for-word, "The English and American democracies will wholly support the realization of your Unity, because they consider it as constituting, after Turkey, the second line of defense of their interests, against the Bear, which is what they call the Soviet Union."

Having tried to get a more precise idea, the Minister said to me,

"My words are clear, my friend. Russia, not very long ago at all, was isolated from Europe, even barred. Now that, despite itself, it has entered the international arena to destroy Hitler and his ideology, it finds itself placed before this English mentality which seeks to maintain British dominance over the countries of the Middle East, and which sees that that is only possible by winning the affection of the people who live there."

Personally, I think that the Minister's words will be far-reaching and I firmly believe that the Russians do not look on our Unity with a favorable eye. They see it as a means offered to their competitors. Anyway, we must not retreat; we have chosen the camp we are going to join; the Soviet camp will only bring us two things: either evil communism or the maintenance here of allied France, and in both cases we will go from danger to danger.

I therefore think that it is not in our interest to appear to forget such reasoning, that we must on the contrary regard it as a source of great peril for us.

The Minister of Foreign Affairs
S/ Jamil Mardam Bey

February 24, 1945
Registered in the Ministry of Foreign Affairs
No. 40 – Diplomatic correspondence – the Soviet Union

33. End of February 1945   Mardam in Cairo to President Quwatli on the quarrel between Nuri al-Sa'id and Yusuf Yasin

Letter from Jamil Mardam Bey
sent from Cairo to the President of the Syrian Republic

- - -

Your Excellency, the revered President of the Syrian Republic,
Blessed greetings.

I shall set out the latest developments in the situation, as I see them.

The tension between Nuri Pasha, Sheikh Yusuf and Mr Zirkali has become bitter. I witnessed an unfortunate incident which took place between them in the home of HE Mahir Pasha.

Nuri Pasha, realizing the failure of his efforts, became extremely angry. Then he made some unworthy remarks to me about which I remained silent or rather I pretended not to hear because it is not in our interest to engage in this kind of dispute at the moment.

This conflict resulted in the abstention of two of those concerned at the Conference meetings. I pretended, for them, that they were ill in order to cover up the incident.

The reasons for the conflict and the circumstances in which it happened are as follows:

When Nuri Pasha arrived at Mahir Pasha's house he shook hands with everyone present, and when he reached Sheikh Yusuf, he said to him,

"Have your efforts been crowned with success?"

"What efforts are you talking about, Pasha?"

"When will you take Faisal al-Sa'ud to Damascus as king?"

"You are not serious," answered Sheikh Yusuf.

"I am indeed," said Nuri al-Sa'id. "I think that the Syrians will pray to God for you many times."

"May his name be praised," replied Sheikh Yusuf.

At that moment Mr Zirkali intervened, saying,

"In reality, I do not understand the meaning of your words, Pasha. Faisal al-Sa'ud and all the Bani Sa'ud in general, will only be able to have what God has granted them. You know that they only want the well-being of the Arabs and all Muslims in general."

Nuri Pasha replied in anger,

"I hope that people are unsparing with their advice to you, now, sir. You are from Damascus, and I know the mentality of the Syrians as I have lived among them and seen them in Iraq. God is my witness, the Syrians have always sullied anything they have been involved in."

Sheikh Yusuf, "Oh, excuse me, Pasha, excuse me."

It seems that the Pasha was inclined to get into a fight. He said,

"What have you done and what has your King done?"

Mr Zirkali, "Our King is not the topic of our conversation now."

"But he is," replied Nuri Pasha, "He is the topic of our whole conversation. We cannot remain silent, us Iraqis, about the actions we see and of which we hear. We have not come here to disperse Arabs, but to unite them. All the efforts you have put in since the start of our Conference have been designed to create obstacles for us or to spoil our work."

Dr Ahmad Mahir Pasha intervened, saying,

"What is it, my brothers. We haven't come here to quarrel."

Then he took Nuri Pasha by the hand and went into a neighboring room, where he stayed with him for an hour. We waited for his return. He came back, and the others left; we stayed together and a conversation took place between us on the reasons for the Pasha's anger and the circumstances in which it would be possible to win his silence and satisfy him.

Nuri Pasha is persuaded that we are putting obstacles in his way and that since the Iraqi Government has told us of its desire to help us, with military force, against France, we have immediately communicated this desire to the Saudi Arabian government; so, instead of collaborating politically and militarily with the Iraqis and the Transjordanians, we feared the Iraqi danger far more than we fear the French danger, which is the reason for your visit to the Hejaz where you set before HM King Abd al-Aziz the position in Syria. Nuri Pasha seems perfectly aware of the conversations which took place between you and His Majesty, he even knows the details. He seems to have eyes and ears in the King's palace, something that should worry us deeply.

Currently he notes that the situation has completely changed, against his interest.

Following on from this, the sovereign of the Hejaz called together all the ministers from America and England and showed them his deep desire to meet Mr Eden or Mr Churchill. He also asked the American Minister to invite Mr Roosevelt in his name to visit the Hejaz. All these stages have been revealed in detail by Nuri Pasha. However, what is definite, as Ahmad Mahir Pasha stated, is that the Iraqi premier knows nothing of all the conversations that took place between Messrs Roosevelt, Churchill, Eden and King Ibn Sa'ud, as well as between you, them and King Faruq; but he knows that everything was contrary to his cause from start to finish.

The possibility that new Jewish efforts could perhaps be used against us in America or in England creates new difficulties for us. Although the understanding between us and the Anglo-Saxons may be real we must still treat these efforts with caution, because it is – as Mahir Pasha said to me – a sensitive and delicate point which could create particular problems for us.

The situation can then be summed up thus:

The plans for Syrian Unity, for Nuri Pasha, have failed. Without this setback he would not have adopted this angry attitude.

Mr Cornwallis's departure has greatly weakened Iraq's position. This has been stated by Nuri Pasha and has been confirmed to me by Dr Mahir Pasha, but Nuri Pasha tells us to be wary of the future: "From now on we will agree," he says, "with the demons against you and we will work to annoy you."

In my opinion, Nuri Pasha thinks of the French who may help him against us. He is probably also thinking of the Turks.

I have set out to you the situation with regard to my Iraqi brothers. The only danger to fear is that Nuri Pasha, by his cunning procedures, reveals to the French the reality of our intentions (on which we reached agreement with the English and concerning the goals we seek with regard to the French) because he is familiar with all the details, as you know.

As for me, I put up with his anger, his insults and curses, and he treated me like a traitor – may God forgive him.

There is nothing else to tell Your Excellency. With the sincerest of wishes from your devoted

Jamil Mardam

34. March 1, 1945   Mardam's report to President Quwatli on his conversation with Nuri al-Sa'id

HE the President of the Republic

I talked to Nuri Pasha Sa'id today and set out the basis of our position to him. I told him that it is impossible for us to adopt the Iraqi position regarding direct Arab intervention in the affairs of Syria, because we fear that foreigners will misconstrue this intervention. I believe that Your Excellency will, during your meeting with HH the Regent, share our stance and will, inshallah, manage to convince him.

I reminded the Pasha today that the question of Syria constitutes the cornerstone of all the Arab efforts. If we, the Syrians, were to manage to rid ourselves of French influence, free from conditions and ties, that would be a useful precedent for all Arab states. Our success will help our brothers, the Egyptians, to alter their treaty with England, and will also help to alter the Anglo-Iraqi treaty, whose consequences, which are getting worse by the day, cause our brothers in Iraq to suffer.

To this we can add that our success will offer the greatest benefit, both from the moral and material points of view, for our Arab brothers in Morocco who, like us, want to free themselves from the despotic yoke of France which has reduced them to almost nothing, as it tried to do with us.

I showed the Pasha that we are currently crossing the most dangerous stage of our lives and our struggle. We Syrians want to rid ourselves of the old regime of colonization which has subjugated us. International plots woven against us by France are only the result of the colonization process which Great Britain and France agreed on after the last world war. Our concerns and aims today consist of cutting through any new agreement at our expense, even if it means relying on the Communists and the Americans.

I believe that the Pasha has begun to come round to my view. I ask you to crown your efforts by an understanding with the Regent.

With my deepest respect,
Cairo, March 1, 1945

S/ Jamil Mardam

Registered in the Ministry of Foreign Affairs
Secret reports – no. 81

35. March 3, 1945   Mardam in Cairo to President Quwatli

His Excellency the President of the Syrian Republic.

Blessed greetings! Our work is nearly finished. The constitution, which has been drawn up, is almost an amalgam of the two plans that were put forward. Fortunately, the agreement was completed based on the matters under discussion. No serious difference was raised, apart from what you know about the attitude of our Iraqi brothers and their opinion concerning the Syrian throne which they covet.

The important point we found ourselves facing during our discussions is that of the Moroccan Arabs. Should they be represented or not in the bosom of the Society of Arab States?

Our attitude was guarded and reticent only from the following point of view: among the main powers granted to the Council of the League in the Alexandria Protocol, is the question of Arab countries and their interests. The reality is that it is impossible for us to do anything likely to provoke campaigns against us by the enemies of Arabism while this Council is not definitively constituted. I have explained to my brothers my opinion, which aims, above all, to free us progressively, not all at once, of French influence.

The second point which held our attention is the guarded position, even the astonishing retreat, shown by Great Britain in the White Paper, of which, up till now, I have been unable to obtain a copy.

This evening I met up with His Excellency Lord Killearn; I tried to engage him in conversation, but he slipped away, saying, "Mr Eden has said enough. For my part, I cannot add anything."

I asked him if, in his opinion, the line followed by Great Britain was favorable to his country. He replied with a strange coarseness, "Despite the White Paper, the French are not satisfied. The French Foreign Minister, when he last visited London, openly stated that he wanted England, a friend, to drop any interest in Syria and Lebanon. Great Britain, which has frequently announced that it does not wish to involve itself in Syrian affairs or to profit from them, cannot contradict itself by words and deeds ... " When I said to him, "But then why did General Spears deceive us?" he replied, "Well, I'm not General Spears."

This sad situation will lead to a dreadful collapse unless we guard against it. I do not believe that it would be possible for us to do anything other than rely on our Arab brothers, who should all show their solidarity with us on this serious matter, even by refusing, if need be, to go to San Francisco to protest against this dreadful despotism which we are the object of, or by trying to raise this matter in the heart of Congress.

I feel today that the English have changed their tone with us and I note that our Arab brothers here think of them before thinking of us. We must not rely too heavily on the sentimental declarations of King Faruq. Deeds are not the same as words. The Iraqis and Transjordanians will do nothing and we should not count on them either. Our position is like the proverb:

"The person in distress who invokes Omar is like the man who calls on the fire to lower the heat."

The minimum they are asking of us is to place ourselves under their authority. As for King Abd al-Aziz, despite the valuable help he has given us and his personal intervention with Mr Churchill, he can do nothing practical to help us, because I believe that Roosevelt and Churchill nobbled him and got out of him everything they wanted in the way of benefits and concessions. It is deeply regrettable to find ourselves facing this White Paper after your conversations with him.

The idea which comes to my mind at the moment has not yet come into sharp focus. I wonder whether we can count on one of the Powers, America or Russia, or if we will find ourselves alone facing pernicious France?

Mr Makram Obeid Pasha says that it is in our interest to get on with the French. I don't know your thoughts, but I believe that we could make fun of these idiots a bit and let them think that we will get on with them and give them privileged positions in order to win some time and to reach a settlement between us and the English, even by admitting to them what we will agree to with the French.

I am writing to Your Excellency while very perplexed about what I should do. I cannot express a formal opinion here. Anyway it seems to me that the only path to follow is pursuing the demand for our total independence and that of our army, making the French position critical and ridding ourselves of all influence from that side. I wish to discuss these questions with you properly when we next meet.

May God preserve you for us.

Cairo, March 3, 1945

S/ Jamil Mardam

Filed in the Ministry of Foreign Affairs
Secret reports – no. 83

36. March 5, 1945   Emir Abdullah to the Iraqi Regent Abd al-Ilah

Top Secret

Supreme Office of the Emirate
Private
Abdullah ben el Husain, Emir, by the grace of God, of Transjordan
to HRH Emir Abd al-Ilah Bey Ali, may God protect him.
Amman,
March 5, 1945

Greetings. You are most certainly aware that we placed our hopes on Jamil Mardam's promises and on his agreement with Nuri Pasha. Today the Prime Minister gave me positive proof of Jamil's treason and double dealing. In reality, he only reached agreement with Nuri Pasha through ruses and hypocrisy. I think that this whole intrigue, from start to finish, is some mischief on the part of General Spears, the British ex-Minister Plenipotentiary in Syria. I am now in possession of enough information to convince me that the General intervened and continues to intervene in the affairs of the Arab countries, with the intention of serving the oil interests we know about and in which he has many shares. All his efforts have been towards this end: exploiting the situation in Syria and Lebanon so that the English can maintain their influence and position there, in order for him to realize his ambitions regarding the oil. He has managed to put Jamil Mardam at his service. Personally, I am now certain that Jamil served him faithfully, played with us and pretended to agree with us in order to consolidate his position at our expense.

In other respects, he used his well-known ploy with Shukri Quwatli and his master Ibn Sa'ud, the man without conscience who does not keep his word. I beg my dear nephew to call Nuri Pasha's attention to this, so that he can make his arrangements, revise his conduct with Jamil and be aware that the plans for an Arab Union are dashed to pieces, God forbid, if they are to be conducted in this way.

That is the aim of my letter. May God protect you.

Your uncle S/ Abdullah

37. March 5, 1945   Mardam to Sir Edward Grigg, the British Minister Resident in the Middle East

The Presidency of the Republic
To His Excellency the honorable President

Yesterday the British Minister Resident, Mr Grigg, asked me if I knew anything about the health of HE the President of the Republic of Lebanon.

"As far as I know," I replied, "He is still ill and receiving treatment."

He said to me,

"Haven't you heard what they are saying about his illness? He is hiding from the French for fear they will poison him like last time."

"I don't believe that," I replied. "His Excellency is not prey to such fears. We do not fear France. We did not fear it when it was powerful, so why should we fear it now that it is collapsing? At this point, I must say that it is not in Great Britain's interest to allow France freedom of action with us, because it will completely undermine all your interests. As you know, Minister, we have adopted an honest position with you and have told you of our wish to link our future to yours, for the British nation has a presence in every Arab country, and Arabs have definitely benefited. Why, then, should we link our future to that of France which has become a minor state which no longer counts internationally?"

"Our fears, Minister, are well placed. France never fails to act against our new independence. Every day it tries to realize its colonial dreams at our expense and to turn our country into a base for its forces, or rather a control center for major worldwide communication lines (which, as you know, are in your hands, and which it wants to oversee). The French, who declared our independence, treat it like a scrap of paper. I would not be surprised to see them use sudden force against us. The information we have proves it. But they do not want to act without being certain of success. However, rest assured that they will no longer succeed and that you will find yourselves forced to intervene to defend the independence of a state which loves you and seeks you out; besides, America and Russia will absolutely not allow such aggression against us, whatever France tries. On our side, we have, already some time ago, taken the necessary steps to defend our prestige and ourselves."

"I can confirm to you, Minister, that, personally, I have never seen people like the French, with whom you don't know how to behave. If you talk reason and logic to them, they reply with vague sentimental thoughts. If you make a play of sentiment and politeness they become evasive. I personally have observed their behavior during negotiations between us. At the moment I behave like them and I have no confidence in any of their proposals."

I talked to the minister for a long time and I succeeded in getting him to repeat what his Russian colleague had made us aware of, that is, "Comrade Stalin welcomed the proposal for the union of Arab countries as well as the great strides taken by the Arab nations towards their independence."

I added that the danger we fear at the moment is the attitude of the Americans.

"In reality, America would not want to see any foreign influence maintain itself here, and would want this country to emancipate itself so that it can deal with it equal to equal; but who can tell us how far the Jews will succeed in their plans? Is America giving them real support or not? The American Minister Plenipotentiary has made promises to us and asks us to be patient, but why be patient if the American Government wants someone to render it a service and won't find anyone more docile than the Jews for that."

"In our country America wants to use the politics of the open door in both political and economic matters. This is, in my opinion, also Russia's wish. The competition these Powers will engage in will by itself deliver us from France."

Then the Minister said to me:

"But this policy which will, in your opinion, deliver you from France, will cause problems for us."

"But we are inclined," I replied to him, "To negotiate agreements with you that will ensure you many advantages."

The conversation was broken off. He promised me to talk about this again after consulting his government.

Mr President, please accept my deep respect,

March 5, 1945   S/ Jamil Mardam

Filed in the Ministry of Foreign Affairs on March 18
No. 112 B.M – Secret Reports

38. March 5, 1945   King Ibn Sa'ud's personal physician Midhat Sheikh al-Ard to his controller Walter Smart

Top secret
Letter probably from Dr Midhat Sheikh al-Ard, personal physician to King Abd al-Aziz Ibn Sa'ud and addressed to an unknown Briton resident in Cairo.

Dear Sir,

Circumstances have not allowed me to follow the discussions which you asked me to find out about. However I am sending you a copy of the report which has come to me. As for the personal conversations you allude to, they are not many for, as you know, HM the King takes and does not give, listens and rarely speaks. Anyway, I have noticed a great change in his situation. He seems to suffer from some disquiet he cannot hide. Perusing the note he wrote after his return and reading between the lines, we know that HM is not happy and that he is aware of the dangers appearing before his very eyes.

HM always said, "My God, make the infidels fight among themselves." Well, he has recently noticed that the infidels are not fighting among themselves but that they are fighting us, the Muslim nation, and that an understanding between them would be made at our expense. In other words, HM thinks that the foreign Powers will reach an understanding among themselves on the basis of sharing out the Muslim Arab world into zones of influence, each Power laying claim to a part.

Although HM has not altered his opinion at all about British friendship which he considers the cornerstone of his current and future policy, he is now beginning to realize that England alone does not constitute the future global factor in Muslim countries. He told us, last night, that we, the Muslims must create ties of friendship, whether we like it or not, not only with the English but also with the Americans and Russians.

The truth which holds the attention more than anything else is that HM always cites France among these Powers. He says that France is still alive and that in the near future it can only figure among the great nations. It is impossible for it to be a secondary Power, either in Europe or in the world. This is how he gave his opinion on the need for an agreement with France to Shukri Bey Quwatli.

Anyway, my personal opinion is that HM the King is suffering from some dark disquiet, and I am unable to discover exactly what it is. I hope to be able to tell you the reason for it soon.

The King's health could be better. The King is beginning to suffer from stomach pains. I have provided him with the necessary care, but I believe that the journey tired him. I hope that his health will improve soon.

Please find attached a copy of the reports drawn up by Sheikh Yusuf.

Yours faithfully,

Signature almost completely illegible (Midhat?) but which is very likely that of Dr Midhat Sheikh al-Ard, personal physician to HM the King Ibn Sa'ud, whom he takes care of and spies on for the British.

NB. – All these documents are part of a bundle which came from Cairo to the Political Bureau of the British Legation in Beirut and were placed in a dossier called "Saudi Arabia." In this dossier, the above report bears the number 152 – the reports. attached to it bear the numbers 153, 154, 155, 156. All are dated 15 Rabi al-Awwal 1364 – and were received in Beirut on March 5, 1945 Author's note: Midhat al-Ard was Mardam's brother-in-law. He might have also reported to Mardam.

39. March 5, 1945   Midhat Sheikh al-Ard to Walter Smart

Top secret

Letter from Dr Midhat Sheikh al-Ard, private physician to Ibn Sa'ud, to Mr Walter Smart of the British Embassy in Cairo

- - -

Dear Mr Smart,

It seems that the American efforts are daily becoming more extensive. I personally have been able to see how HM the King has begun to try to profit, in all senses of the word, from the current situation. He thinks that it is now possible for him to exploit both Great Britain and America, these two Powers both being anxious to count on his collaboration and to have him on their side.

It is possible that this is judicious from the point of view of pure politics, but this behavior greatly threatens our interests. In my opinion, it is the security permanently reigning in the kingdom that allows the King to act in this way.

I cannot currently describe to you in an accurate light the situation here. Our Syrian brothers are playing a serious game. One could say that Shukri Bey Quwatli and Bashir Sa'adawi have a lot of influence with the King who has absolute confidence in them. Shukri Bey has discussed with His Majesty with complete frankness the impossibility of placing, at this critical period, the crown on the head of HRH Emir Faisal, but it will not be impossible immediately after the war.

If it is possible to draw a conclusion at the moment from His Majesty's words, one could say that the King is satisfied by the development of events these last few days. He thinks that his audience with Mr Roosevelt constitutes the overture to an era of understanding and collaboration from which he will pick the best fruits.

In addition, His Majesty shows great concern with regard to France, which he calls "the martyr of democracies." Perhaps he is seeking to win the benevolence of the French in order to be able to ask them one day to give their consent to installing his son as King of Syria. He will thus have satisfied, by an easy route, his best and greatest hopes. As you know, this eventuality is not impossible with a mentality like the French mentality, which is guided by feelings and passions. What will be our position then and what will become of our interests?

In a conversation I had with HH Emir Mansur – you know that he is the cleverest and most understanding of HM's sons – I raised the question of an agreement between His Majesty and France. He replied, "It is possible and useful to both sides."

I believe that it is necessary for you to hold new conversations with His Majesty on this subject. Personally I would imagine that Yusuf Yasin is not aware of all this, and that even Shukri al-Quwatli does not know the King's intentions, but that he is acting in the way he wants and you know that Abd al-Aziz can foresee events long before they happen.

Finally, while he is playing with the French with the intention of realizing his plans sooner or later, we also see him playing with the Americans. I believe that it is he who advised Mr Roosevelt to see Emir Abd al-Ilah, and personally I am more and more astounded by this great man.

As to what concerns us, I believe that it is essential that He does not pretend to forget our existence and that he feels, from time to time, the need to pay attention to our interests. I think that the easiest channel we can use to this effect is that of Imam Yahya who has sworn an implacable and deadly hatred for our King.

Yusuf Yasin's reports do not indicate anything of importance, except that the pact has been agreed. His Majesty the King thinks that it is an illusory plan, a matter of form, and will not end in any practical or important result.

Yours sincerely,

4 Rabi al-Thani 364   S/ Midhat

Letter addressed to Mr Walter Smart of the British Embassy in Cairo.
There is a copy of this document in the Political Bureau of the British Legation in Beirut
No. A.S. 115.B

40. March 15, 1945   Nazim al-Qudsi, the Syrian Minister in Washington, to Mardam

Top secret

Letter from Mr Nazim al-Qudsi, Syrian Minister in the United States
to HE the Minister of Foreign Affairs, Damascus

I have noticed that the atmosphere here is not very favorable to the Arab League plan, because in their opinion, it is an English move, designed to regroup the Arab people according to British interests.

I did not believe that I would find in America such an acute spirit of rancor towards the English. Most of those whom I have been able to contact speak of their mistrust of all the English methods which they consider to be duplicitous. One of the American senators told me, "Great Britain takes our arms and our stock and then gives it to the Germans."

This deep tension no doubt has its reasons, particularly as far as the Arab lands in general and Syria in particular are concerned. The strangest words said to me by the Under-Secretary of State at the Department of State for Foreign Affairs are the following:

"We have consumed the greatest part of our earthly riches and it is our right to claim reparations in nature. That is why we try to exploit and why we will exploit the oil resources of the Middle East, which we will not allow to remain in the hands of the English, who have not suffered as many losses as we have."

What is taking on importance here is that the Arab League plan is designed, according to the politicians' understanding, to unite us Arabs, with the aim of allowing the English to make use of us openly to fight the Jewish movement which, disappointed by Great Britain, has had recourse to American justice. President Roosevelt seems determined to serve the fat Jewish capitalists at our expense, to have them at his side and to continue to be served by them as they have done so far.

As far as Syria is concerned, what makes us happy is that the Americans have resolved not to recognize any position by France there. They state that they will not make war in order to strengthen colonization. These words were spoken to me by the Secretary of the Navy personally. In my view they are confirmed by the press campaign originating from the White House and highlighting the view that America will not leave France with any colonizing position in Indochina.

All this is likely to encourage us, but can also weaken our chances, particularly when the Americans – who are called on to play one of the most important roles on the stage in the future – will see us walking in the furrow

made by the English who will lead us where they want and who will make use of us as they want.
March 15, 1945

Your devoted
Nazim al-Qudsi
Minister Plenipotentiary

Registered in the Syrian Ministry of Foreign Affairs
No. 7 – Reports – American Legation

41. March 16, 1945   The Iraqi Regent Abd al-Ilah to his uncle Emir Abdullah

Top secret

Personal letter from HRH Prince Abdul Ilah, Regent of Iraq
to Emir Abdullah of Transjordan

My revered Uncle,

Affectionate greetings and blessings. Shukri Bey has left us, after we reached an agreement. It is now my duty to inform you of what happened.

The Unity of Syria was the main topic of conversation. Shukri Bey told me that he regretted that the Syrian position had not been understood as it should have been. He maintains that the Unity of Arab lands remains his great dream and his biggest concern, and that he knows that it is not possible to unite the whole Arab nation before one of these countries, Syria, is united.

It is thus that he wants to convince me that the plan for Syrian Unity is their plan, that they will not abandon it and that they will not allow its replacement in any way by another; but he thinks that everything has its time and that success, if easy to win today, will not be easy tomorrow. He is, however, of the view that bringing about Syrian Unity is now detrimental to any plan for Arab Unity, and that the Arab nation would find itself very divided about this plan and would thus lose all the advantages it hopes to win.

It is regrettable, and Shukri Bey confirmed it to me, that the reigning Egyptian family should be hostile to us; that is something we cannot conceive of or imagine. King Faruq confirmed to King Abd al-Aziz, during the Radwa meeting, that he would in no way accept or approve of Syrian Unity if a Hashemite Emir were the beneficiary. Mr Cornwallis then confirmed it to me, saying that he only learned of it some days ago. He expressed his regret regarding the position adopted by the King of Egypt, who has thus shown himself to be a bitter enemy of the Hashemite family without this last having done anything bad to him.

The only interpretation I can give this position is that King Faruq has extended, long-term aspirations which he wants to achieve by way of this unfortunate Arab Unity. I do not know if the dreams of this youngster are his or someone else's, but we must always remember that Faruq has in mind the plans of his ancestors Muhammad Ali, Ibrahim and Isma'il. This Albanian believes that it is possible for him to create, in the future and at our expense, at the expense of us who are descended from true nobility, a vast Arab empire. This could only come about if a powerful Arab family were to succeed in governing in both Damascus and Iraq at the same time.

From this point of view, Faruq is therefore a dangerous enemy for us. We must pay far more attention to this than we have done in the past. The advice given about him by Nuri Pasha and the good intentions he attributes to him constitute one of the Pasha's mistakes, by making us bear the wretched consequences.

In my opinion, this is the reason for the rapprochement between Faruk and Ibn Sa'ud, who have formed a powerful bloc against us.

The important matter in all this is that Shukri Bey thinks that the moment is not currently favorable to the realization of Syrian Unity, because this realization would create a scission among the Arabs. The only logical route today consists of the unification of all the Arab efforts for one sole aim: emancipation of Syria from the colonizing foreigner. As soon as French influence disappears, we will all be placed face to face, and that is when we will appreciate the degree of sincerity of our British allies with regard to our family and our interests – those who promised us so much.

I am astonished that Mr Cornwallis personally received, so it seems, instructions from his Government to convince me to reach an understanding with Shukri al-Quwatli in settling the situation. We have effectively reached an understanding to use all our efforts, individual or collective, for one sole aim: chasing the French out of Syria. I hope that the Council of the Arab League manages to help Syria in its legitimate "jihad." For my part, I will not spare any effort to support the Syrians.

That is a broad-brush picture of what happened. I am letting you know to keep you informed.

> Greetings and God's mercy.

March 16, 1945

> S/ Abd al-Ilah
> Regent

A copy of this document is registered in the British Legation in Beirut
No. IR 312 – Top Secret

42. March 19, 1945   Mardam in Cairo to President Quwatli

Top secret

> Letter from Jamil Mardam Bey sent from Cairo to
> President Quwatli, HE the President of the Syrian Republic

HE Sir Walter Smart, Oriental Adviser to the British Embassy and close friend of the Arabs, visited me today. He confirmed that Great Britain would work towards the two Syrian and Lebanese republics being invited to the San Francisco Congress. He even assured me that the Government of the Syrian Republic could from now on consider that its invitation was definite and that the matter was settled.

HE congratulated us on the admirable position adopted by HE Mr Karameh, saying,

"He has really done the Arabs an honor. If the Lebanese had known twenty years ago how to work as they are working now, using the same skilful and wise methods, French influence would have disappeared from Lebanon a long time ago, but unfortunately they did not know how to hide their feelings. They too openly showed their desire to annex themselves to Syria, just when the Maronites of Lebanon were a plaything in the hands of the French, who did what they wanted with them; but the situation has now taken a new turn: the Arabs are linked to Lebanon, and instead of belonging to the Maronites and the French the country is theirs."

Our invitation to the Congress has become definite. I am telling you this good news. Our work is heading for complete success.

Sunday, March 19, 1945

The Minister of Foreign Affairs
S/ Jamil Mardam Bey

Registered in the Syrian Ministry of Foreign Affairs
No. 186 – Arab League dossier

43. March 19, 1945   Mardam in Cairo to President Quwatli

Top secret

Letter from Jamil Mardam Bey sent
from Cairo to the President of the Syrian Republic
HE the President of the Syrian Republic

Dear Mr President,

When the French realized that the Americans and the English were determined, in keeping with our insistent representations, to invite us to the Congress, they tried to exploit the situation for their benefit, making us understand that it was them we were obliged to for the invitation.

It is not possible at the moment for us to show them a sense of humor, for we find ourselves in a critical position and we fear that it will not happen; or if it does, that harmful obstacles will arise from it. That is why we have pretended to be convinced by the French, whom we will even pretend to thank if necessary.

Duplicity is the only way to go with them. Mr Smart told us,

"France intervened after it learned of your invitation. When you take part in the Congress, you must not forget that there is a chance to rid yourselves of it once and for all, if you know how to defend your cause in a logical and explicit way."

The question of Palestine will be the stumbling block. In my opinion, it is not possible for us to undertake something serious in favor of our brothers in Palestine, for our friends, the English, advise us to show great prudence in making decisions that would stir up the Jews against us.

As a result, it is the second of the formulae to which you have given your agreement that will be adopted as the final formula, the first that we set up, earlier, having been filed.

Our English friends are uneasy with Emir Abd al-Ilah's visit to America.
The Russians are as nervous as the English.
Yours sincerely,

The Minister of Foreign Affairs
s/ Jamil Mardam Bey

March 19, 1945

Registered in the Ministry of Foreign Affairs
No. 315 – General political reports

44. March 19, 1945   Mardam in Cairo to President Quwatli

Top secret
Personal

Letter from Jamil Mardam Bey in Cairo
to the President of the Republic

To His Excellency the President of the Republic

Dear Mr President,

I hope I am not troubling you by telling you what Sir Walter Smart said to
me about our relations with France. His Excellency confirms that the affection and solicitude which King Abd al-Aziz is beginning to show towards
France will not be well received, by the English in particular.

Sir Walter thinks that these feelings (the King's) will not in any way change
French attitudes towards the Syrian Arabs. The French mentality towards
the Arabs showed its true colors in Morocco, Tunisia and Algeria, where
it destroyed all the fundamental features of Arabism. They (the French)
tried to do the same to us, but, thank God, their designs did not meet with
success.

The King will have nothing to gain from all the kindness he shows the
French. They only understand their own interests and seek to reaffirm, in
every way possible, their position in our country. We have achieved great
progress on our road to emancipation from their influence. It is necessary that they feel that they do not have any supporters among the Arab
countries.

I ask you – and Sir Walter, who believes that your friendship towards him
is as strong and vigorous as his despite its length, joins me – to try hard with
King Abd al-Aziz from your side to bring about agreement on all these matters. I have written to you in the past on this matter. I am doing so again at
the request of His Excellency.

With my deepest respect, Mr President,

March 19, 1945

S/ Jamil Mardam Bey
Minister of Foreign Affairs

Original from the Presidency of the Republic
(not filed and not numbered).

45. March 26, 1945   Emir Abdullah to the Regent Abd al-Ilah

Top secret

Personal letter from Emir Abdullah of Transjordan to
Emir Abd al-Ilah, Regent of Iraq
Supreme Office of the Emir

Private

HRH Emir Abd al-Ilah Ibn Ali, Regent of the Iraqi throne, Baghdad

My beloved son,

I would like to give you my opinion and advice on the occasion of the invitation you have received from HE President Roosevelt to visit America. I leave you the job of evaluating them.

HE General Gort asked me to write to you to give you these views. Of course you know my feelings and my opinion and you know that I think it is in the interest of the Arabs in general and of the Hashemite family in particular not to distance ourselves from our great friend, England, and to rely always on its honor and good regard. I believe I have already given you this advice, during those difficult days we got through at the time of the Rashid Ali incident. Experience has shown you how right my point of view was. I repeat it to you today and advise you to avoid slipping into the chasm the Jews and Americans want to throw us into. You know just how well-intentioned I was towards the Jews and how hard I tried to find agreement or understanding with them. When the occasion presented itself to them, they showed zeal toward Shukri al-Quwatli and Jamil Mardam. I am convinced that the latter is still betraying us despite all the money he has taken from us. The Jews today only seek to reach an understanding with all the Arab presidents except me, because they are convinced that I would not work against them. They support them to the Americans, neglecting me, as if my success was not theirs.

In short, my letter is about the Americans. Please learn, as I have learned, that America and Russia talked to Mr Churchill at Yalta, and even before that, about the matter of their participation in the exploitation of oil deposits in Iraq and Syria. *Mr Churchill could only have told them that Syrian affairs do not depend on him, but depended first on France, and that it would not be easy for him to take from the French what they still have.*

As for Iraq, it is up to the independent government of this country to settle. "If you reach an agreement with him," he said, "I would not see any drawbacks." It was then that Stalin asked that no political or diplomatic activity should be employed in favor of one of these parties.

This is a summary of the conversation with General Gort, who asked me to make you aware of Great Britain's precise, current situation. This Power holds fundamental positions in the Middle East, positions it will not cede under any circumstances. It has material interests there which it cannot do without. We, the members of the Hashemite family, are its natural allies, and we cannot abandon our friends, even if they betray us and deceive us. We will neither betray nor deceive, and our reward will be great, God willing. We will stick with Great Britain and we cannot help another Power replace it. On the contrary, we fear the growth of Communist influence in our country, something that would be deadly for us.

I beg you, whether you are in Baghdad or elsewhere, not to become too close to the Americans, not knowing where they will lead us. They are sharing out among themselves profits and kingdoms: Syria to X., Iraq to Y., this country to Z., and if we do not make a show of force, of firmness and honesty, our chance will disappear and we will become the prey of one and all.

That is what I wanted to write to you. May God keep you and protect you.

Your uncle
S/ Abdullah

Beginning of Rabi-al-Thani 1364
Date of receipt: March 26, 1945
A copy of this document is in the Political Bureau of the British Legation in Beirut
No. I.R. 311

46. March 27, 1945 American Minister to Syria and Lebanon George Wadsworth to Mardam

HE the President of the Republic
Report

HE Mr Wadsworth, the American Minister Plenipotentiary, visited me today.

As a friend of the Syrians and the Arabs, HE wants to remind us that the Americans remember seeing their country treated with hostility by the Syrians. They regret seeing certain professional agitators striking blows against the prestige and reputation of their nation in the vile manner used in the last few days.

The American Secretary of State has given HE the duty of making us understand that "America does not mean to be treated in this country in the same way as France. If the French receive and swallow insults, the Americans are not inclined to put up with the demonstrators' affronts and insults. HE added his own thoughts: "I know that the latest activities are not spontaneous. Various elements took part in organizing them. We know the exact involvement of particular Englishmen, just as we know how far French officials encouraged certain demonstrators in order to deter them from any action against France, but we advise the Syrian Government, if it really desires America's friendship, not to tolerate such demonstrations."

I promised him to combat all further activity with the greatest of energy. For his part he promised me that the Americans will work to settle the Palestinian question which is currently exploited against them.
March 27, 1945

The Minister of Foreign Affairs
s/ Jamil Mardam Bey

Registered in the Ministry of Foreign Affairs
No. 322 – Political reports

47. April 2, 1945   General Spears to Geoffrey Furlonge

Colonel Furlonge has received the following letter from General Spears dated
April 2, 1945:

"Mr Chamoun must, I assume, be in Beirut now. I am fully in agreement
with the account he will give you. He will draw up, in agreement with you,
the proposal he will present to President Khuri and the Lebanese Government concerning relations between the Lebanese and the French. I have asked
him to use his energies to stop without fail *the signing of a treaty with France,*
and to persuade the Lebanese in general of the huge advantage in maintaining the current relations with the British. I hope that you will work
actively and do from your side everything necessary for the happiness of
Great Britain."

Paper obtained by our Special Services and communicated by Beynet

48. April 2, 1945   Najib al-Armanazi, the Syrian Minister in London, to Mardam

Top secret

Letter from the Syrian Minister in London
to Jamil Mardam Bey, Syrian Minister of Foreign Affairs

HE the Minister of Foreign Affairs, Damascus

The British Foreign Office does not see any drawback in the question of
Palestine being raised in San Francisco by the Arab delegations.

However, it is thought here that the Americans will try by every means
possible to counteract this intervention, because they want to find a solution
to the problem which is economic in nature and likely to upset the British
position and lead them to accept a settlement in favor of the Jews.

The British are determined to remain within the framework of the White
Paper, although the Jews are not in agreement on that. That is why people
here are convinced that the Americans must be faced with united Arab
demands at the same time as a disunited Jewish front.

There is no doubt that American policy is favorable to the Jews. It is up to
us to work to benefit from the English position on this matter.

Another important matter: I was asked to inform you that it would be
worthwhile for you to enter into contact with the Syrian Legation in Paris to
ask it to win the support of the French if the matter were raised.

April 2, 1945   The Minister Plenipotentiary
                                                s/ Najib al-Armanazi

Registered in the Syrian Ministry of Foreign Affairs
No. 33 – Diplomatic Correspondence – London Legation

49. April 2, 1945 Alexander Cadogan to the British Legation in Beirut

Instructions from Cairo
To the British Legation in Beirut

Coded telegram
Order No. 3.532, dated April 2, 1945

It is strictly forbidden to give any proof whatsoever that we are against the French. Our efforts must be strongly concentrated to show them that we are their friends. This order nevertheless must not prevent the departments occupied with local affairs from annoying the French from time to time.

Our wish to live on good terms with the French must not allow the slightest deviation from our interests.

Signed: Cadogan

50. April 4, 1945 Cadogan to the British Legation in Beirut

Instructions from Cairo
To the British Legation in Beirut

Coded telegram
Order No. 3.533, dated April 4, 1945

Do all in your power – and this most secretly – to promote the plans in favor of Greater Syria. The prince Talal, heir to the crown of Transjordan, will pay a visit to Syria and the Lebanon shortly.
Always help him in his mission.

Signed: Cadogan

51. April 3-4, 1945 The British intelligence recruits the Syrian Deputy Mikha'il Ilyan

Undertaking by the Orthodox Deputy of Aleppo, Mikha'il Ilyan
to the British Government

I pledge on my honor and on everything that is sacred to me, to be a devoted friend of the government of Great Britain, and to strive to safeguard its interests, which I believe are in line with those of my country.

S/Mikha'il Ilyan

Undertaking signed and given to Mr Young from the British delegation in Beirut on the night of Wednesday, April 3-4, 1945.

52. April 5, 1945 Nazim al-Qudsi, the Syrian Minister in Washington to Mardam

Top secret
Coded

Telegram
- - -
His Excellency, the Minister of Foreign Affairs, Damascus

Accompanied by Mr Zureiq, I met today with the Under-Secretary of State for Foreign Affairs, who asked me to notify you of the following:

"The American Government is inclined to furnish the Syrian army with more modern arms if the Syrian government desires it. Moreover, it is prepared to begin negotiations with qualified Syrian delegates."

Please reply quickly.

April 5, 1945

S/ Nazim al-Qudsi
Minister Plenipotentiary

Registered in the Ministry of Foreign Affairs
No. 40 – diplomatic correspondence – American Legation

53. April 5, 1945   Nazim al-Qudsi to Mardam

Top secret

From the Syrian Minister in the United States
Coded telegram
to His Excellency the Minister of Foreign Affairs, Damascus

Following my telegram from yesterday, I was invited again today by the Under-Secretary of State for Foreign Affairs, who asked me to notify you of the following:

"Certain American companies wish to conduct exploration in Syria of mines of category 1, 3 and 4.

They ask the Syrian government to authorize these explorations, and if they prove to be profitable, would allow these companies to present a regular request for operation under the best possible conditions.

Facilities granted in this way would favorably benefit the Syrian Government for obtaining the arms they require."

Please answer quickly.

April 5, 1945

S/ Nazim al-Qudsi
Minister Plenipotentiary

Registered in the Ministry of Foreign Affairs
No. 41 – Diplomatic correspondence – American Legation

54. April 7, 1945   Terence Shone, the British Minister in Syria and Lebanon, to Mardam

Verbal note
HE the Syrian Minister of Foreign Affairs

HE Mr Grigg, the British Minister Resident in the Middle East, has asked me to inform you of the following in reply to the verbal note you gave me:

"HM's Government is not in any way targeting the realization of what is called the plan for Greater Syria, which many newspapers are discussing at the moment."

"Great Britain only wants for the Arabs what the Arabs want for themselves. It does not want to propose to them in any way whatsoever things that do not correspond to their deep desires. It believes that they are far from being subject to pressure of any kind whatsoever regarding the realization of such a plan."

"Therefore I ask the Syrian Government to rest assured with regard to our good intentions."
April 7, 1945

Unsigned

Registered in the Ministry of Foreign Affairs
No. 180/945 – British Legation – Diplomatic correspondence

55. April 7, 1945   President Quwatli to President Roosevelt

Top Secret

HE Mr Franklin Roosevelt, President of the United States,

My dear friend,
In reply to the request conveyed by the Under-Secretary of the American Ministry of Foreign Affairs, transmitted to me by your Minister Plenipotentiary in Damascus, please approve of:
Messrs. Faris al-Khuri, President of the Council of Ministers and Naim Antaki, Minister of Finance, as representatives qualified to discuss our present and future relations. They are equally entitled to negotiate financial and economic interests of our two governments.
I hope you approve them and that they will enjoy your solicitude.

Yours with my profound respect,

your devoted
S/ Shukri al-Quwatli
President of the Syrian Republic

Registered in the Ministry of Foreign Affairs
No. 11 – "Letter of credentials"

56. April 8, 1945   Middle East War Council Decisions in Faiyum near Cairo

Top Secret
The Minister Resident
Cairo
No. 727

After having made a detailed statement about the position of our prestige and our interest.
After having studied the orders No. 84, dated October 9, 1944 and No. 112 dated December 7, 1944, and No. 220 dated December 31, 1944.

The following decisions have been taken:

Political points of view:
The Congress recommends:

1 To put an end to all hesitations which are not in conformity with the realization of Arab Unity in a broader sense. This will bring us both in interior and exterior difficulties.
2 Our politic up to now was too slowly to face the things being always guided by personal factors which are not inspired by our high politic. Now it is necessary more than before to form all possible coalitions against our competitors and to let it not to them to take profit out of it. The future period is such one of competition, that is why we shall have to develop our action secretly.
3 The French, American and Russian designs are seemingly meant to encircle and hinder our interests. They always try annoy our friends who should be helped now more than before.
4 We have to give our full approval to the pact of Cairo.
5 Fight as much as possible against the French intrigues in Syria and in the Lebanon. Keep secret our fights and do not give any proof of our fighting them.
6 Take up the same position against the communists in Syria and in the Lebanon.
7 The American interest in Syria and in the Lebanon do not constitute any danger to our interests.
8 As to Syria, have full confidence in President Quwatli.
9 As to the Lebanon, keep always friendship with the Maronite Patriarch.

For the Congress
Signed: [Edward] Grigg

Received on April 8, 1945
The British Legation in Beirut
Political Bureau and registered under No. 2320 – S.

The Minister Resident
Cairo
No. 989
Top Secret

Extract

The economic and financial position in Syria and in the Lebanon from a general point of view is satisfying. Our interests in both countries have become stabilized, the wealth of Syria, coveted by so many foreign countries and representing for us a necessary element must be exploited by ourselves. This all obliges us to fight in a skilled way in order to attain our aim. The following recommendations are of fundamental importance:

1 It is not necessary that the Syrian Pound must be separated from the French Franc. The separation is useful from a political point of view but from an economic and financial point of view it must be underlined that the connection between the Syrian Pound and the French Franc must be exploited by us in a remarkable way.

2 We cannot under the present circumstances satisfy the necessities of the Syrian market.

3 One must pay attention to the economic and financial activities of America in Syria and in the Lebanon in order not to be surpassed by her.

4 There must be staged an action in a political way against the Banque de Syrie et du Liban, the latter being a French establishment.

5 The politics consisting of inundating the market with gold is wrong, it must not be repeated.

6 The project, presented by the financial authorities of the Iraqi government concerning the unified Arabian Dinar is convenient from another point of view. It must be helped as far as possible.

7 The projects of exploitation of those companies representing our interests should be kept secret from now on. The pacts among those companies and the Syrian Government must be kept secret too, in expectation of more prosperous times. These pacts mentioned above have their permanent value.

Author's note: This and the previous document are extracts of decisions of the MEWC which met in Faiyum in the first week of April 1945. They have the same reference number and the same date in the files of the Political Bureau of the British Legation in Beirut. Received on April 8, 1945 at the British Legation in Beirut – registered under No. 2320 – S. This is the original text found in the archives – apparently provided by the agent.

57. April 10, 1945   Mardam to Qudsi

Top Secret

From the Syrian Minister of Foreign Affairs
to the Minister Plenipotentiary of the United States in Damascus

_____

Your Excellency,

The Council of Ministers has, by special decision, instructed me to request you to ask the noble American Government for the following clarifications:

Is it the intention of the American Government to support the supposed claims of the Jews for the creation of a national home in Palestine in opposition to the natural and sacred rights of the Arab nation?

In his personal conversations with Arab kings, HE Mr Roosevelt formally confirmed his absolute conviction in the right of the Arabs to occupy Palestine, while recognizing the need to help the Jews but not at the expense of the

Arab nation which considers itself to be a natural friend to the democratic and free American State.

Following rumors which have been spreading on this subject, Syrian public opinion is very concerned.

Personally I ask you to reassure me once again that the noble American Government will not alter its point of view as far as the justness of Arab demands is concerned.

With my deepest respect,

April 10, 1945

The Minister of Foreign Affairs
S/ Jamil Mardam Bey

Registered in the Ministry of Foreign Affairs
No. 3425/47 – Diplomatic correspondence – American Legation

58. April 12, 1945   Qudsi to Mardam

Top Secret

Coded Telegram

Reply from the Syrian Minister Plenipotentiary in Washington
to the Syrian Minister of Foreign Affairs

Reply to your letter dated April 7.

The American Government is willing and the economic and financial aid requested is ready. Discussions will be held on the following matters:

1 Civil aviation lines.
2 Research and exploitation of seams and mines.
3 Providing the Syrian army with equipment.
4 Creating a lending bank.
5 Possibility of supporting the Syrian currency with the Dollar.

There are projects studied and ready, which will be submitted to us on very favorable terms.

April 12, 1945

Minister Plenipotentiary
s/ Nazim al-Qudsi

Registered in the Syrian Ministry of Foreign Affairs –
Diplomatic Correspondence – Washington Legation – no. 217a

59. April 12, 1945   Faris al-Khuri to President Quwatli

Top Secret

From the President of the Council Faris al-Khuri
en route to San Francisco

HE the President of the Republic

We have arrived in Beirut and tomorrow, God willing, we will be in Cairo.

The Lebanese Government has decided to collaborate closely with us. It has given its delegates strict instructions not to intervene in any debate and not to present any proposition without consultation and in agreement with the other Arab delegations. It is the outcome we were looking for. This was confirmed to me by HE Sheikh Bishara al-Khuri, HE President Karameh and HE Henri Pharaon.

HE Sheikh Bishara spoke to me about Palestine and asked me to do what I can not to raise the question at the moment, because the British authorities are not in favor of it. For our part, we have nothing against the English on this matter. I would like to hear your advice on this.

Yours etc.,

Night of April 12, 1945 The President of the Council of Ministers
s/ Faris al-Khuri

Registered in the Ministry of Foreign Affairs
No. 15 – San Francisco Congress

60. April 14, 1945   President Quwatli to Lebanese Prime Minister Abd al-Hamid Karameh

Letter from President Quwatli
To His Excellency Abd al-Hamid Karameh, Lebanese Prime Minister

My dear brother,

Greetings and divine blessings. You know, dear brother, like I do, of the intrigues woven around us and the harm wished upon us. May God protect us.

My reason for writing to you is the renewed efforts of HM Emir Abdullah to promote his own plans and his ambitions for the throne. This, I fear, risks leading us all to disaster now that we are striving to unite and regroup.

His Majesty is using the Arab League's project in order to realize his own designs. As you unfortunately know, there is a group of Englishmen who, influenced by the Jews, believe that the success of the Emir will be theirs and support his ambitions.

As His Majesty was unable to come and believes that the Crown Prince is more popular here than he is, he sent him to us in order to mobilize our country's support for him.

You know that in Syria it is impossible for us to tell the people that we oppose the Union of Arab Countries, especially Syria, Transjordan, Palestine and Lebanon; but if we adopt this project, we will find ourselves in a dire situation which will only benefit the French since they will arouse the Lebanese Maronites against us and yourself. We will have made the situation worse instead of improving it.

Having said that, the question involves other points of view:

At the moment, the whole world knows that only Lebanon opposes Unity. So why should we not take advantage of it as much as we can and use it to put an end to the Emir's plan?

I must say that the Emir seems to have perfectly sensed the danger. That is why he has sent his son not to us, but to you. God knows what he will do to convince you if he finds you willing to discuss this thorny subject with him.

My intention with this letter is to remind you that it is neither in our interest nor in the interest of the Arab-Islamic nation, to encourage the Emir; on the contrary, he has at least to feel that the project is not yet ripe and that his fears are unnecessary.

At the present I trust, Your Excellency, that you will see to it that our action will be coordinated, and I have confidence in your fraternity and the influence of your views. I am sure that you will see the situation in its true light like we ourselves see it and that you will not give the Emir's efforts a chance. Our future will depend on our stability and our wise action that will be crowned with success, God willing.

I pray Your Excellency to forgive my raising a subject that he is familiar with more than anyone else.

I remain, Excellency, your ever devoted brother.

Damascus, April 14, 1945   S/Shukri al-Quwatli
(Private – delivered by Issam Inglizi)
The copy of this letter is with Jamil Mardam
Registered in the Foreign Office, but not yet added to the file.

61. April 14, 1945   Adnan Atasi, the Syrian Minister in Paris, to Mardam

Top Secret
Reply from Adnan Atasi, the Syrian Minister in Paris, to a request formulated
by Jamil Mardam Bey following Najib al-Armanazi's letter

To H.E. the Minister of Foreign Affairs, Damascus

I was not able to get the French to give us their support on the Zionist question. We did not satisfy any of their requests. We cannot ask them to back our demands.

The French, because of their nature, cannot accept that American influence is strengthened because of the Jews, the creatures of America. It is therefore useless to address a request on this subject to them.

The essential thing we can be sure of is that France will not support the Jews and that is for two reasons:

First – because the French hate the Jews now; this is plain to see.

Second – those responsible for France's destiny have true Christian leanings. They realize that supporting the Jewish demands at the expense of the Arabs and Muslims would bring them moral prejudice in all Muslim countries where there is French influence. This support would also reinforce American influence at their expense and at the expense of the Muslim and Arab peoples.

I believe that the English, in formulating the request they have made of us, only wanted to create a trap for France in order to push it to adopt a position analogous with their own.

My apologies for broaching these issues.

April 14, 1945

The Minister Plenipotentiary
S/ Adnan al-Atasi

Registered in the Ministry of Foreign Affairs
No. 27A. – Diplomatic Correspondence – Paris Legation

62. April 14, 1945   Armanazi to Mardam

Top secret

From Najib al-Armanazi, Syrian Minister in London,
to the Syrian Minister of Foreign Affairs

Coded telegram

I have undertaken what you asked of me.

The Under-Secretary of the Ministry of Foreign Affairs immediately answered me that the British delegation to the San Francisco Congress had agreed with the Americans that the Palestinian question would not be raised.

As to Syria's claims and their desire to raise the issue of the army, it believes that the British delegation (most notably Mr Eden) is not prepared for such a surprise and that it will even be extremely difficult under the present circumstances to request the arbitration of global public opinion against France.

Even if the British wish to completely free the Syrians is genuine, they think that raising the issue of a Syrian army would not help a settlement but would aggravate the matter.

According to British experts, France is also in no position to exercise a colonial policy, especially as the Syrians are no longer favorable. One thing that will keep France within its limits is to be taken into account: the American interest in intervening in Middle Eastern affairs. This wish would not be at Britain's expense but surely at France's.

The English here are well aware that Russia poses a real danger if there were a true agreement between it and France, but fortunately the communists cannot get along well with anybody.

Thus we advise to wait and not to anticipate events that will take place.

April 14, 1945

The Minister Plenipotentiary
S/ Najib al-Armanazi

Registered in the Ministry of Foreign Affairs
Diplomatic correspondence – London Legation
No. 3452/82

63. April 14, 1945   Qudsi to Mardam

Top secret

Coded Telegram
From Syria's Minister Plenipotentiary in Washington
to Syria's Minister of Foreign Affairs

A delegation including representatives of the Socony company will arrive to investigate the possibilities of exploiting oil and metallurgic resources.

On the surface, this delegation will investigate the possibility of constructing a refinery for Tripoli's oil. It will establish permanent connections which will lay the foundation for discussions that will soon begin between us and the Americans.

I ask you to do everything in your power to facilitate an eventual agreement and enable them to mediate an agreement with the Lebanese Government.
April 14, 1945

Minister Plenipotentiary
s/ Nazim al-Qudsi

Registered in the Syrian Ministry of Foreign Affairs
Diplomatic correspondence – Washington Legation
No. 213/30

64. April 15, 1945   General Spears to President Quwatli

Top secret

From General Spears to the President of the
Republic Shukri Bey Quwatli

- - -

April 15, 1945
My dear friend,

The memory I keep in my heart of you and your noble people cannot be threatened by the passage of time. I repeat to you that my mission in life includes, apart from defending the interests of my country, the rights of the people of Syria of whom I honor myself that I am one of its children.

The rights of Syria cannot be ill-used. Its friends will not fail to defend it and be assured that they are many.

The official position of the British Government, although up to now it remains somewhat obscure and is not clear, will not remain so for long, because circumstances will force Great Britain to support once again your clear right.

The collaboration of Arab states and their mutual support will be the elements which will determine the British Government to intervene in your favor when the circumstances are right. You are anyway on the eve of very delicate circumstances. The end to the period of French silence cannot be put off and I believe that a strong and devastating offensive will be undertaken against you this time; but rest assured that they will fail and you will triumph.

My friend, Mr Chamoun, is bringing some plans beneficial to you and to us, in which I am personally interested. I would ask you to study them with care.

I remain your sincere and devoted friend,

S/ E. Spears

Personal letter which President Quwatli keeps with him.
The Arabic copy was sent by Muhsin Barazi to the British.
It is filed in the Political Bureau of the British Legation in Beirut,
No. S.A.1762
(Copy received in Beirut on May 8, 1945)

65. April 15, 1945   Armanazi to Mardam

Top Secret
> Letter from Najib al-Armanazi, Syrian Minister Plenipotentiary in
> London to the Syrian Minister of Foreign Affairs in Damascus

Mr Camille Chamoun will bring this letter to you.

He carries in his bag a set of plans which may consolidate our economic existence thanks to collaboration with English firms which all have worth and power.

The first of these plans, and the most important, relates to future aerial routes. Personally, I think we must support it.

General Spears – who is what we know – is persuaded that the plans for which Mr Chamoun is currently undertaking the trip must receive our approval for they constitute reasonable solutions for us.

On another level, the Permanent Under-Secretary of State for Foreign Affairs has confirmed to us that under no circumstances should we worry about our independence. Nothing can threaten us and we should not imagine that France wishes us harm because – he thinks – in no case will the French do us wrong despite their current position which is that of someone seeking to win time who puts off solutions while waiting to find his strength once again and to profit from more favorable circumstances.

The most important thing for us, as the Under-Secretary of State says, is not to engage in something it will later be difficult for us get out of.

The Under-Secretary of State for Foreign Affairs shares Mr Chamoun's opinion regarding the unification of Syria. So, as you can see, it is not a joke and I believe that the day when the British Government will officially proclaim its support for this plan prepared by the Jews is not far off.

Here the English are worried about the contact taking place between Ahmed Bey Da'uq, Adnan Bey Atasi and the French. They think that it is not in the interest of Syria or Lebanon that diplomatic representatives allow themselves to get caught up in forgetting the state of affairs.

Maître Chamoun will explain his plans to you. I hope to be able to share my thoughts with you soon.

April 15, 1945   The Minister Plenipotentiary
                                                    S/ Najib al-Armanazi

Registered in the Syrian Ministry of Foreign Affairs
Diplomatic correspondence
London Legation – Personal letters
No. A/54

66. April 16, 1945   Armanazi to Mardam

Coded Telegram
HE the Minister of Foreign Affairs, Damascus

Mr Chamoun's journey to Lebanon is driven by the authorities who are currently working towards the realization of the plan for Greater Syria.

He will play the role of courtier with regard to this project. He will contact the essential people in Egypt and Palestine and reach agreement with them on what to do.

Under the influence of the capitalists, the conservatives here work energetically for the success of their new project.

The success of the plan will not mean the destruction and removal of French influence, as they keep telling us, but will, rather, mark our total destruction.
April 16, 1945

The Minister Plenipotentiary
S/ Najib al-Armanazi

Registered in the Ministry of Foreign Affairs
No. 49 – Diplomatic correspondence – London Legation

67. April 17, 1945   Mardam to Quwatli

Top Secret
Meeting between Jamil Mardam Bey, Syrian Minister of Foreign Affairs, and
Mr Solod, Minister of the USSR in Syria
Report
HE the President of the Republic.

Mr Solod visited me today and I drew the following conclusions from his conversation:

"The Soviet Government is disposed to support unconditionally every Arab measure to combat Zionism (which it considers a movement at the service of capitalism)."

"The Arab states must be represented in the heart of the world Security Council,"

"The Soviet Government's candidate for this position is King Abd al-Aziz."

The most important thing to note is that the Soviet Union is dealing with all these matters, big and small, which have to do with Middle Eastern affairs.

So the Russians think that it is their right, even their duty, not to leave to the English alone the job of dealing with the Suez Canal. Nor do they want to leave the aerial lines of communication to the Americans.

We find ourselves facing serious rivals for everything that interests the Americans and the English.

When I talked to him about the influence France wants to maintain with us, he replied to me word-for-word, "France does not represent a danger for anyone."

I hope all these matters will merit our serious attention.

April 17, 1945   The Minister of Foreign Affairs,
                                                        S/ Jamil Mardam Bey

Registered in the Ministry of Foreign Affairs
No. 723 – Secret Political Reports

68. April 18, 1945   Crown Prince of Transjordan, Emir Talal, to his father, Emir Abdullah

Letter from Emir Talal, Prince and Heir of Transjordan,
to his father, Emir Abdullah

My Dear Father,

Having kissed your hands and asked for divine grace, I can tell you that I am happy with my stay in Beirut. The details which the bearer of my letter will give you will prove to you that the field of action is huge and that God will grant us success.

The large number of parties, personal tendencies and the egoism which reigns here will favor us greatly, inshallah!

The important thing at the moment is to convince the Lebanese politicians to work with us.

I don't think Riyad al-Sulh will be useful to us because he is a man who works for himself. He is egotistical and in perfect agreement with his friends from Damascus. It is in our interest to disregard him. He will come to us, to look after his gains, when he feels that the scales are tipping towards us.

As for Abd al-Hamid Karameh, from what I see he is a crank. He is taken with King Faruq and everything to do with him. It would be interesting to try to win him at any price, but I believe he is difficult to handle and that he can only be got through the medium of his family, the Salams. They, as you know, follow English advice.

As for the Christians who live here, I don't believe they hate us or that they don't want the Hashemite family; in any case, they prefer us to Egypt which of course trails Ibn Sa'ud, the Bedouin boor, behind it.

I think Henri Pharaon may become the man we can count on. If he is with us, Karameh will be too. His intelligence and ability mean that he will be able to do a lot for us.

I don't know how much longer my stay here will last, but I think that it would not be in our interest to finish the trip without my reaching an understanding with the Maronite Patriarch. He is the cornerstone of everything to do with Lebanon. Although he may be dotty and fanatical, I would like to succeed with him, because then, inshallah, our success will be certain!

The hidden action of the English here is huge and powerful, but in reality it is unpopular. In the first instance we must win the nation's confidence, because the men of the Bloc, the Independence Party and the Palestinian group have used every means possible to prejudice our reputation. We must therefore sweep away all the rubbish they have thrown at us.

Generally, I am optimistic, and feel that success is possible if we know how to work calmly and peacefully; but the English need to give us their support indirectly, and facilitate our actions.

I am received here eagerly. I don't think it is only politeness, because I am sure that there is a lot of sincerity and affection.

Beirut, April 18, 1945

Your obedient son
S/ Talal.

A copy of this letter was placed in the British Legation in Beirut by a member of the Prince's entourage. It was filed there in the Political Bureau, No. 1832/67 T.R.

69. April 22, 1945   Armanazi to Mardam

Top secret

Coded Letter
Najib al-Armanazi, Syrian Minister Plenipotentiary in London
to the Syrian Minister of Foreign Affairs in Damascus

I sent you a letter with Mr Camille Chamoun. You should bear in mind that the larger part of that letter was written with the sole aim of pleasing him, if only in appearance.

My real advice is the following:

1 He is undertaking the trip in order to work for the plan for Greater Syria.
2 The economic plans for which he is making propaganda are plans that will bring him a lot personally because he will receive a good commission for each of them.
3 Our interest tells us to be distrustful and not to allow ourselves to be carried away by any agreement whatsoever with a Great Power, because that could be awkward for us in the future.

In my opinion, we must be free of any commitment and we should only enter into conversation with those who will provide us with the best conditions and the greatest advantages.

Mr Chamoun likes to play the role of a skilful politician, but I believe I have really understood him, better than anybody.

There will be no harm in welcoming him with a display of affection, but it is our duty to be deeply wary of him.

April 22, 1945
The Minister Plenipotentiary
S/ Najib al-Armanazi

Registered in the Ministry of Foreign Affairs
Diplomatic correspondence – London Legation
Personal letters – No. A/55

70. April 25, 1945   Solod to Mardam

Top secret

From Mr Daniel Solod, Minister of the Soviet Union in Syria
to the Syrian Minister of Foreign Affairs

I have the honor of informing you that my Government has charged me with the task of notifying you of the following:

The plan for Greater Syria, about which HE the President of the Council issued a denial and which he has recently repudiated publicly in the Syrian Chamber, continues to be, as far as we are aware, a reality. Certain authorities, which the Government of the Syrian Republic considers its friends and advisers, work for and lead a campaign in favor of its realization.

The Government of the Soviet Union, which has unconditionally recognized Syrian independence, does not believe that it would be in independent Syria's interest to throw itself – thoughtlessly or after determined efforts – into an unknown and obscure future.

My Government has asked me to warn you of this. I convey this view to you above all as a friend.

Unsigned

Memorandum presented by Mr Solod on April 25, 1945
Registered in the Syrian Ministry of Foreign Affairs
Diplomatic correspondence from the Soviet Legation
No. 3517/177

71. April 27, 1945   Armanazi to Mardam

Top Secret
Coded

From Najib al-Armanazi, Syrian Minister Plenipotentiary in London
to the Syrian Minister of Foreign Affairs

There is one thing we have to pay attention to when examining Britain's future activities.

England hopes the Americans will take an interest in all matters in the Arab Middle East. This truth has been exposed to me by a consultant in the Soviet embassy. He believes that Great Britain's intention is clear: it's not that the Americans should reap the benefit, but in order to make them oppose the Soviets and the French in case they unite with them until the end.

The friend, whose views I convey to you, believes that the current and future attitude of Great Britain towards the Soviets is the same that they themselves had towards Germany in the past.

Our interest in this matter is obvious. The American and British financial or capitalistic establishments almost merged during the war. Granting oil concessions to an American or English company in an Arab country does not pose, in their opinion, a threat to their interests. They deeply mistrust the Soviet efforts to compete with them and beat them. At the moment it is in the economic sphere, but who knows what will happen tomorrow?

We should therefore not allow ourselves be deceived by the competition between the English and the Americans. I fear that we will be dragged into the wake of one of them and that our real intentions will be revealed to the other.

In writing this, I distrust the English, who must know what we think of them.

April 27, 1945

The Minister Plenipotentiary
S/ Najib al-Armanazi

Registered in the Ministry of Foreign Affairs – Political reports
No. 3538/88

72. April 27, 1945   President Quwatli to Mardam

Top secret

Note from the President of the Republic, Shukri Bey Quwatli
to the Minister of Foreign Affairs

The Russian Minister Plenipotentiary has made known to me his Government's point of view regarding our country.

The Foreign Minister must study our current position in the light of the statements (which he made to me) which I set out below:

"Russia has no colonial ambitions, but it wants to be where (using his words) an imperial influence exists. Whether imperial or communist, Russia, the leader of the Soviet Union, does not forget that its geography imposes on it a policy determined with regard to the countries of the Middle East. Unfortunately, Russia tried to abandon this policy after the last world war, and the current war was one of the consequences of its distancing itself from the world arena, because the field was left free for the play of other Powers."

"As far as Syria is concerned, there is the oil in Arab lands, there is the Suez Canal and the global communication routes. All these matters are the subject of English and American ambitions. As for us, we have not declared war on the Axis in order to foster new ambitions and make them everlasting."

"We have recognized, with no hidden agenda, Syria's independence. Our decision was dictated by our desire to enfranchise small nations. It is for that reason that we find ourselves in complete bewilderment in the face of obscure plans 'which are being realized' now in your country, plans we do not understand and about which you are silent, as if the thing hardly involved you and as if you had no part in it."

The Minister Plenipotentiary gave his conversation the form of a set of recommendations. His Government is determined not to recognize any position or any particular interest of any Power and he therefore thinks that it is his duty to give this advice to a state that does not want to see its policies fail. Our poor country must wait for a violent struggle between the colonizing Europeans who are all busy looking after their own interests. I fear that our country will be affected by this struggle as Iran and other Oriental states, where the Great Powers are competing, have been.

I would like these matters to be examined by your Ministry with all necessary care.

April 27, 1945   S/ Shukri al-Quwatli

Registered in the Ministry of Foreign Affairs
Reports for a secret policy, No. 38

73. April 28, 1945   Mardam to Armanazi

Top secret

From the Syrian Minister of Foreign Affairs
to the Syrian Minister Plenipotentiary in London

Please speak to the qualified authorities about our Palestinian brothers held in concentration camps or in exile, and who are currently in Europe.

People such as Haj Amin al-Husseini, who have acted only for the benefit of their homeland, cannot be considered to be pro-Nazi. If the British Government does not want to change its opinion about this person, Syria is disposed to act as guarantor and to receive him here.

This is the President of the Republic's personal desire, a desire which I ask you to use all your efforts to bring about.

I received the letter you sent me through Mr Chamoun. I hope that God favors us.

April 28, 1945   The Minister of Foreign Affairs
                                               s/ Jamil Mardam Bey

Registered in the Syrian Ministry of Foreign Affairs
No. 3553/8 – Diplomatic correspondence – London Legation

74. May 1, 1945   Syro-Lebanese meeting held in Chtaura

Top Secret

Syro-Lebanese meeting held in Chtaura on May 1, 1945

Verbal statement

HE Abd al-Hamid Karameh, President of the Lebanese Council of Ministers, and HE Jamil Mardam Bey, Acting President of the Syrian Council of Ministers, met today, Tuesday, May 1, 1945.

After the exchange of information that was acquired and was founded on:

- a report by the leaders of the Syrian General Security
- a report by the Syrian Commissioner of Information
- a report by the special intelligence service

as well as indications of the Syrian government regarding the French attitude in the preparation of decisive incidents intended to overturn the current power and to reach the foundations of the Syrian constitutional regime:

It has been established that the French are currently encouraging their supporters and agents under their orders by secretly distributing funds. Moreover they are effectively bringing into Lebanon, under cover of "relief," new contingents intended to increase their military forces.

Official reports by the security services and Syrian intelligence reveal that the French are trying to gather sufficient troops to destroy the independence of this wretched fatherland.

After exposing their views and after each party was convinced of the accuracy of the facts reported by the other, it was decided:

1 To put an end to all movement that might weaken Lebanon's national unity. The Syrian government will try to convince their Lebanese brothers not to exceed the limits of patriotism and honest nationalism in those critical circumstances that require complete unity.
2 To reappraise the situation, each party according to its abilities, its means of action and the circumstances.
3 To meet again a second time next Friday in Damascus.

May 1, 1945

S/ Abd al-Hamid Karameh
S/ Jamil Mardam Bey

Registered in the Syrian Ministry of Foreign Affairs
No. 422 – Documents

75. May 2, 1945   Muhsin al-Barazi, Secretary General in the Syrian President's Office, to his controller Colonel Walter Stirling

Top secret

Report presented by no. 325
Drawn up in Arabic with an English translation
A copy of this document is filed in the Political Bureau of
the British Legation in Beirut, no. 1750/S

The author of this report is not known to the informant who believes, however, that that he is Dr Muhsin Barazi, Secretary General to the Presidency of the Syrian Republic

Damascus, May 2, 1945

Mr Chamoun brought HE the President a letter from Mr Najib al-Armanazi and another from General Spears. I will send you the copy of these letters as soon as I have them.

The conversation between the President and Maître Chamoun centered on two points:

1 the question of Palestine
2 that of Lebanon

As far as Lebanon is concerned, Mr Chamoun stated that his initial aim was to re-enter public life after having distanced himself from it. As the President, Sheikh Bishara, was unable to do anything to bring about unity among the Lebanese, he found himself forced, by pressing circumstances, to intervene and bring about an improvement in relations between his brothers, whose friendship he values. He is not worried about Karameh or Riyad al-Sulh. Both are well-disposed towards this meeting, in preparation for which they have already successfully made great progress, but the only danger he perceives comes from Henri Pharaon.

At this point, Mr Chamoun, whose face displayed anger, said, "Henri believes that because of his wealth he has the right to be President of the Republic; but wealth isn't everything. The President must represent the nation. But at the moment the Lebanese nation refuses to put at its head a man who does not represent its precise Arab orientation. The hesitation which the world has recently felt in Lebanon's attitude is due on the one hand to Henri Pharaon and on the other to the weakness of Sheikh Bishara."

For the first time in a long time, I realized that Mr Chamoun has not stopped thinking passionately about the Presidency of the Republic. This time, he is seeking the confidence of everyone in order to succeed Sheikh Bishara.

Our President assured him that the Syrians will not fail to lend him their support so that his efforts may succeed, and have even promised him to send Lutfi Bey Haffar to Beirut to come to a detailed understanding with Mr Karameh, such questions only being capable of discussion between two people who understand each other perfectly.

Mr Chamoun seems to be reassured by the absolute support of the British authorities, at the very least the enquiry departments. I know through our President that using the DSO, BSM and FSS will support Mr Chamoun in every effort he makes. It seems that this support is due to the recommendations of General Spears, who appears up till now to enjoy a position of strong influence with them.

HE our President has not hidden from Mr Chamoun his feelings about the danger from the French which hovers over our country. He is expecting the French to launch an "anti-Government coup." In his opinion, "the British Government, in the official support it gives to the French position, will not be able to undertake anything publicly in favor of our country. It is therefore up to the Syrians and the Lebanese to create incidents, before the French do so, with the sole aim of showing the world that the French are the aggressors."

The natural solution the President sees is "a sharp and violent crisis arising in Lebanon before exploding in Syria. The Allies will be forced to remedy the situation, and the Lebanese as well. It is then that they will carry him (Camille Chamoun) to the presidential seat, as he is the only Christian politician who enjoys the confidence of all the Lebanese politicians, or at least of the majority. If we, the Syrians, guarantee him that we will separate Abd al-Hamid Karameh and Henri Pharaon and if we obtain the support of Karameh and his people for him, the balance will swing towards him and the way to success will be open to him: the presidency which has escaped him in the past will not escape him any longer."

"For his part, Mr Chamoun and his followers, both Lebanese and British, will have to take it upon themselves to create incidents they deem necessary to prepare the overthrow for which Syrians and Lebanese must work together."

Mr Chamoun confirms that, "he is not thinking either of Lebanon or only of bringing about Syrian unity, but of achieving Arab unity. If he becomes President of the Republic, he will bear this burden not for himself but for the Arab nation. It is in order to realize his principles and to attain his ideal, and to conform to the desires of his friends, the English, who are genuine friends of the Arab nation thinking only of its good, that he will take on this task."

Then turning to the question of Palestine, he states that he thinks the plan for the unification of natural Syria is worth looking at, and that there is no need for changes to be made. It is unnecessary, in his opinion, to worry from now about the designation of the King of Greater Syria: "despite being King, it will not be he who governs, but it will be us."

"As for the Jews, their legal position has been defined by the White Paper."

This is a summary of the conversation that took place between HE the President and Mr Chamoun. I am sure that the President agreed and showed enthusiasm for everything Mr Chamoun said. Is it the personality of the latter which influenced him or General Spears's letter? I don't know, but what I do know is that Mr Chamoun speaks in a way that shows that he is almost certain of his success, given the authorities supporting him. Personally, I don't know the true situation. I am just reporting the meeting between these two people for you. With the information you have, you will know the value of this activity. Is it taking place with your knowledge?

S/ Illegible
No. 325

76. May 4, 1945   Armanazi to Mardam

Top Secret
  From Najib al-Armanazi, the Syrian Minister Plenipotentiary in London
          to the Syrian Minister of Foreign Affairs in Damascus
  I am sending you General Spears's words in writing.
  Having asked him if he had any news of Mr Chamoun and the date of his return, the General said to me,
  "I believe that he is in good spirits and is not coming back."
  Then, smiling slightly, he added,
  "Who knows, perhaps he will soon become the President of the Republic of Lebanon."
  Over the course of the conversation he also said to me,
  "Mr Chamoun is very popular. He is trusted by the Arabs as well as the Jews. You know that the Arabs and Jews constitute the two poles of life in the Middle East."
  This is how the conversation with the General came to an end.
  I am sending you this in writing for your information.

May 4, 1945   The Minister Plenipotentiary
                                                    S/ Najib al-Armanazi

Registered in the Ministry of Foreign Affairs
Diplomatic correspondence originating from the London Legation, No. 3592/84

77. May 5, 1945   Barazi to Stirling

Top Secret
                        Report presented by No. 325
                  Drawn up in Arabic with an English translation

            A copy of this document is filed in the Political Bureau
                of the British Legation in Beirut, No. 1752/S

            The informant confirms that the author of this report
                    for the English is Dr Muhsin al-Barazi
Damascus, May 5, 1945

  I can now talk with some accuracy about Maître Chamoun and his contact with the President of the Republic and the Foreign Secretary.
  The President of the Republic is more than convinced that Mr Chamoun is working in agreement with a large number of notable British people in favor of the recently changed plan for Greater Syria. His efforts are naturally supported by a large number of Syrian and Lebanese politicians; he also enjoys much support from groups of Jews worldwide.
  Having consulted them, the President of the Republic reached an agreement with Mssrs Jamil Mardam and Sabri Asali that the Syrians will play around with Mr Camille Chamoun instead of letting themselves be played by him.

The essential part of our behavior with him will consist in totally approving, despite discussions, his political and economic plans (which all have an aspect of exploiting the Jews), then to put off their realization.

Jamil Mardam Bey was not of this opinion. He thought that there were grounds for granting some support to the plan for Syrian Unity (but Sabri Asali revealed some doubts and said, "We didn't want to believe that you were with Nuri al-Sa'id against us").

The Syrian government's opinion with respect to Mr Chamoun's plans is therefore that there is no need to hurry, and that he should be left to work. If he succeeds, we will be able to benefit from his success and if he fails, the consequences will not be attributed to us.

What comes out of all this is that we need to convince Mr Abd al-Hamid Karameh to flatter Mr Chamoun and to support him, even by risking strengthening Riyad al-Sulh and his people.

Riyad Bey no longer appears to enjoy the complete sympathy of our President of the Republic. This is because of his attitude with regard to Karameh and the anxieties he created for him in an unreasonable and undignified manner.

The members of the Syrian government (the President of the Republic and his entourage) are not sure that it is English officials who work in favor of the plan for Greater Syria. In their opinion, there are only British civil servants and politicians who, resorting to their own interest or under Jewish influence, seek to make it end in the enthronement of a Hashemite king; but one asks oneself how far they will dare to go.

The accession of Mr Chamoun, a sincere and trusty friend, to the Presidency of the Republic, will not, on the one hand, be prejudicial to the situation, but it will not improve it either.

Sheikh Bishara is not "the strong ruler and governor." His weakness allows a number of people to plot according to their interests and ambitions, or in the direction desired by their leaders, French as much as Russian; a republic presided over by Camille Chamoun will soon put a stop to all that.

But if Mr Chamoun's accession to power is good from this point of view, it will be detrimental to the Syria plan.

Those responsible (the President and his collaborators) have agreed the following points:

1 To appear to support Mr Chamoun
2 To do what they can with Mr Karameh so that he also supports him on the same terms.
3 To awaken his enthusiasm to work as much as he can against the French.
4 To delay discussion of financial and economic plans he brings, on the pretext of needing to study them closely.

It seems that Mr Chamoun and his friends in Lebanon will not delay in acting. We believe here that their first acts will be directed not against Mr Karameh (unity of rank being necessary), but against the French, which will allow

Chamoun to re-establish a populist position; this is how they act here: every time politicians feel their positions becoming precarious, they direct their thoughts against France.

I now believe that Mr Chamoun has completely failed with our President and that all the expressions of sympathy, kindness and support shown to him do not prove anything.

S/ Unreadable

78. May 6, 1945   Mardam to Quwatli

Top secret
Report from Jamil Mardam Bey, the Syrian Minister of Foreign Affairs
to the President of the Syrian Republic

Your Excellency, the President of the Republic,
To summarize the position after the statements of protest you sent on the arrival of the French armed forces, I believe that, at the moment, we are not justified in relying heavily on Russian help, because the Russians do not want to intervene in matters between Syria and France.

Mr Solod told me that the French troops are not the only Allied troops in Syria. "If France is present here, then so is England. You do not observe the English troops and their movements, so why do you observe the French troops and their movements?"

The Americans do not talk in this tone, but I believe that it is not possible to expect from them moral support which goes beyond the usual.

I therefore believe that at the present time it is not possible for us to count only on our Arab brothers.

Damascus, May 6, 1945

The Minister of Foreign Affairs
S/ Jamil Mardam

Registered in the Syrian Ministry of Foreign Affairs – Reports

79. May 7, 1945   Barazi to Stirling

Top secret
Handwritten: May 7, 1945

Report by Muhsin al-Barazi, Secretary General of the Presidency of the
Republic, British agent No. 325
to Colonel Stirling
- - -

Today the President saw Mr Solod in my presence and that of Messrs Sa'adallah Jabiri and Jamil Mardam Bey.

After the usual polite words, the President said:

"Syria wants to know how far the Government of the Soviet Union will back Syrian independence."

The conversation was long, but the reply finally made by Mr Solod is that the Soviet Union will support Syrian independence in any case, on condition that it exerts itself in favor of Syria and its people and not in favor of Anglo-American imperialism.

Mr Solod in his turn asked questions about certain correspondence exchanged between the Syrian Minister of Foreign Affairs and the British Minister Plenipotentiary about the Liwa of Alexandretta. Jamil Bey denied the existence of such correspondence. He said he had not discussed this matter with the English and had not been asked to by them.

Then Mr Solod asked:

"What is the current situation between you and the French?"

The President replied:

"We await the arrival of General Beynet. Be assured, Minister, that Syrian opinion generally can no longer bear the French who make fun of us."

"I do not believe," said the Minister, "that the French make fun of you. Although we do not support any colonizing ambitions or attempts at exploitation, I believe that the French are correct from one point of view, because they do not want to give their place up to others."

"And who are these others?" Jamil Bey asked.

"You know that better than me," replied Mr Solod, "those to whom you grant privileges and with whom you reach agreements which no one knows anything about. Completely secret things."

President Quwatli then showed his surprise about these secret things, saying that he knew nothing about them.

Mr Solod said:

"The agreement over oil for example, the agreement over the pipeline installation, the agreement on monetary unification using the standard of the pound sterling, and the civil and commercial aviation project. All these things are more dangerous and more threatening to your independence than the Mandate Charter itself."

The banquet of honor was thus transformed into a battlefield between the two parties. The Soviet Minister tried to convince the President and his companions that they were setting little store by the rights of the country, and that just at the moment they were trying to emancipate themselves from the French yoke, it was to throw themselves into the arms of the English; that if his government did not want the French colonizers to stay in Syria, neither did he, categorically, want the English to stay here to replace them.

The meeting ended on a not very cordial note. The two parties have bitterness in their hearts.

After the Minister's departure, the President reproached Jamil Mardam Bey and said to him,

"All the Ministry of Foreign Affairs' secrets are known to these resourceful Russians."

From all this, Sa'adallah Bey concluded that duty demanded that all parties now in existence be suppressed and that all their members be arrested.

I believe that the Russians will quite soon make a show of a lot of activity and that this activity will cause us a lot of trouble.

Monday, May 7, 1945   S/ Muhsin

Report addressed to Colonel Stirling.
Copy filed in the Political Bureau of the British Legation in Beirut, No. S 1754

80. May 9, 1945   Barazi to Stirling

Top secret
>Report by Muhsin al-Barazi, Secretary General of the Presidency of the
>Republic, British agent no. 325
>to Colonel Stirling

The Syrian Government and the President of the Republic are certain that the incidents that occurred in Beirut are the work of Riyad Bey and Maître Camille Chamoun.

Sa'adallah Bey Jabiri discussed this yesterday with HE our President and said to him,

"I never doubted what people said to me about Riyad and what he is capable of doing. I have always been certain that he would follow his words by deeds. He said that he could create all the disorder he wanted and he has done so."

Our President imagines that these incidents will have consequences and cannot remain without repercussions; but the lesson to be learned is that the Lebanese, after their current disputes, will unite and form a single front before the French.

It is regrettable that the President, Sa'adallah Bey and Jamil Bey should all be persuaded that it is you (the English) who are at the source of these incidents and that Camille Chamoun acts, not on his own initiative, but at the suggestion of his British friends. They all believe today that British policy has two faces: an official one favoring France and the other, real one, showing us its solicitude. It is this that inspired the recent troubles. All this does not prevent our Lebanese brothers from exploiting these incidents, prepared out of nothing, and to lay them at the door of the French.

May 9, 1945   S/ Muhsin al-Barazi
                                                                     No. 325

Report addressed to Colonel Stirling.
Copy filed in the British Political Bureau in Beirut, No. S 1755

81. May 17, 1945   Solod to the Syrian Ministry of Foreign Affairs

Top secret
>From Mr Solod, Soviet Minister to Syria and Lebanon
>to the Syrian Ministry of Foreign Affairs
>Memorandum

Translation of the Arabic text attached to the Russian original

I confirm to you once again that the Government of the Soviet Union is determined to recognize and support your independence.

As for the French troops currently here and those that will come, they are not, just as I recently told you, the only Allied troops in Syria; the French are not the only ones to bring black soldiers, others besides them also have these black military men. We are surprised to see you judging that your independence is threatened by an army of very feeble manpower while another army, with numbers twice as high as the first, which is getting stronger and stronger, does not cause you disquiet.

By alerting you to all this we do not want to defend the French colonizers but the proper interests of Syria.

As to what we can do for you if there is aggression on the part of the French, we remind you:

- first: that the latter will not resort to aggression
- second: we are persuaded that responsibility for this crisis rests with you and not with them.

Rest assured that we do not behave in the same way with the French as with you. We are not disposed to help them against you, because so far you, as a government, represent the Syrian people and we cannot allow the encouragement of any state against this people whom we respect.

The only help we can give you is to advise you to fundamentally revise your attitude. If you realized that it was in your interest not to flee one danger in order to encounter a worse one, we could do something and even highly favorable to you.

May 17, 1945   initialed: S.

Registered in the Ministry of Foreign Affairs
No. 430 – Documents

82. May 18, 1945   Karameh to Mardam

Handwritten: May 18, 1945
Top Secret

From Abd al-Hamid Karameh, President of the Lebanese Council
to
Jamil Mardam Bey, Syrian Minister of Foreign Affairs

- - -

Colonel Furlonge, head of the Political Bureau of the British Legation, today visited HE the Foreign Minister.

The British are aware of the situation and, it seems, know the French propositions.

The long conversation which took place between the Colonel and the Minister centered on these propositions. Mr Furlonge said that Great Britain would not intervene in the dispute except as a friend of both parties, because it wanted an agreement between France and Lebanon to be reached. The French propositions must not be considered final, but they can be used as the basis for discussion. In clearer terms, he does not encourage us to break off negotiations with the French, and is, rather, persuaded that they must be pursued. Nor does he advise us to strike and believes that it would be good if we acted calmly, without giving rise to deeds that would inflame the situation and render it unfavorable to our interests.

We no longer understand the mentality of these English people. I remember that this very colonel was one of those who most forcefully incited us against France. And so, today, now that the fruit is ripe and must be picked, they ask us to show proof of reason and wisdom, in other words, by cowardice and evasion.

May 18, 1945   S/Abd al-Hamid Karameh
Letter written on Friday May 18, at
5 o'clock in the evening and sent to Damascus.

Not yet filed in the Syrian Ministry of Foreign Affairs.

83. May 18, 1945   King Ibn Sa'ud to President Quwatli

From HM the King Ibn Sa'ud
to
President Shukri Bey Quwatli

In accordance with your wish, we have given instructions to our son, Faisal. We would always prefer it if you leaned towards peace. If you accept our mediation, we offer it with good heart. Or all the Arab nations and their governments can offer their mediation if you so wish.

6 Jumada al-Thani 1364
(May 18, 1945)

S/ Abd al-Aziz

As of May 19, 1945, not yet registered in the Ministry of Foreign Affairs

84. May 20, 1945   General Spears to President Quwatli

My dear friend,

We all admire you. The people of Syria will mark an important, happy memory on the page of glory. Your heroic struggle cannot fail. Triumph will constitute everything, or just part of what you deserve. In my name, and in the name of my comrades who love you and who only wish your country prosperity and success, we can only confirm, in these critical moments, that we are with you and we will remain so until the shadow of the last colonizing Frenchman leaves your land.

It is regrettable that France, which we have freed with our blood, can only be ungrateful and can only fight the question of liberty; but every man or every nation which has tried to destroy liberty has destroyed itself. What, then, if it tries to enslave a people which has taught others the meaning of liberty and has given humanity this huge heritage of ideas, convictions and religions?

The House of Commons, without any party distinction, shows its concern towards your cause, but you know that here, they greatly appreciate the advantages and I must not hide from you that there are many who would not hesitate in sacrificing you for the success of France. But, my friends and I completely reject that a courageous people should be the object of affront on the part of a despotic and ridiculous nation like France. The only solution I can see is that the crisis will get worse, will become bitter and reach a degree of seriousness allowing us to profit from events which will dictate our direction, which only seeks real independence for Syria.

All our friends have received precise instructions to help you. I hope that Mr Shone will maintain the best of relations with you.

Your sincere friend,
Spears

London, May 20, 1945

This letter, addressed to Shukri al-Quwatli, arrived through the intermediary of Colonel Stirling
Not registered

85. May 20, 1945   Wadsworth to Mardam

HE the Foreign Minister of the Syrian Republic, Damascus

Dear Minister,

In accordance with your wish to convey your request to my government, I can now, after authorization by my superiors, confirm to you the following once again:

The Government of the Republic of the United States has unconditionally recognized the independence of Syria. It does not support and does not even admit that the sovereignty and independence of Syria should be prejudiced in any way or by anyone.

With my deepest sincerity and respect.
Damascus, May 20, 1945

The Minister Plenipotentiary of the Government of the United States
s/ Wadsworth

Registered in the Ministry of Foreign Affairs
No. 2433 – Documents

86. May 21, 1945   Egyptian Prime Minister Muhammad Fahmi al-Nuqrashi to Mardam

Telegram

HE the Minister of Foreign Affairs, Damascus

The Royal Egyptian Government will exercise its mediation in a wise and skilful manner, in order to settle the situation in Syria and to arrive at an understanding between you and the French.

HM the King thinks that it is necessary to use all means possible to settle our difficulties in peace. If this proves impossible on the part of others we will have recourse to the only means possible: force.

This Ministry has given the necessary instructions to all the Egyptian diplomatic representatives, as well as to the Egyptian Delegation in San Francisco, to make contacts with this in mind, with the aim of arriving at the end we aspire to, which is bringing about the independence and total sovereignty of Syria.

May 21, 1945

The President of the Council of Ministers
S/ Muhammad Fahmi al-Nuqrashi

Registered in the Ministry of Foreign Affairs
No. 3888/116 – Diplomatic correspondence

87. May 22, 1945   Karameh to Mardam

HE the President of the Council of Ministers, Damascus

General Paget, accompanied by his adjutants, visited me today and notified me of the following:

"I regret to notify you that the British military authorities will intervene directly to safeguard security if armed aggression is committed against elements of the British Army, or against what is considered as forming part of military property."

When I asked him if they would intervene in the case of conflict between peaceable people and French forces who attack peaceable citizens, he replied, "No."

The conversation between us lasted three-quarters of an hour. In reality I did not understand the aim of this visit. Is it to make us understand that they will intervene? Will their intervention be in our favor or in favor of the French? Or in favor of our interest and that of the French, or perhaps in favor only of their own interest?

Mr Shone visited me later. He repeated to me almost the same statements as General Paget. Having tried to ask him for details he said to me that he was charged with notifying me. He added, "At the moment we are only acting in your favor."

This report has been made to keep you up to date with what is happening.

May 22, 1945

The President of the Council of Ministers
S/ Abd al-Hamid Karameh

Letter written in Abd al-Hamid Karameh's hand
Registered in the Syrian Ministry of Foreign Affairs
No. 3709/35 – Diplomatic correspondence

88. May 22, 1945   Armanazi to Mardam

Coded

HE the Minister of Foreign Affairs, Damascus

A reliable authority led me to understand today that Great Britain does not seek and will never seek to occupy Syria and that it has no ambitions over this country.

The French, in the arguments they use, maintain that the armed forces transported to Syria do not represent the tenth of the English armed forces which have recently entered the country.

This same source led me to understand the following:

"The British armed forces which have entered Syria have been transferred from Palestine, the only aim being training and exercises.

"Great Britain is disposed to make a declaration regarding its good intentions; the mission of the British armed forces is only to safeguard security and prevent any possible trouble which may result from a Syro-French misunderstanding. In these circumstances, the English army's mission is thus a mission aimed at weighting the scales when unpleasant things happen. The English army is minded to withdraw when difficulties hanging directly over France and Syria have been settled."

So, it will seem to you that these proposals give the appearance of being attractive, but I believe that they represent great danger.

London, May 22, 1945

The Minister Plenipotentiary
s/ Najib al-Armanazi

Registered in the Ministry of Foreign Affairs
No. 3704/1OL – Diplomatic correspondence – London Legation

89. May 22, 1945   Mardam to Shone

HE the Minister Plenipotentiary of Great Britain, Damascus

The Syrian Government regrets to inform you of the following:

"Our humanitarian conscience is tearing itself apart with sorrow on seeing evidence of the atrocities and savagery the French armed forces are committing on the territory of independent Syria's homeland."

"You have noted on your tour of duty, how Syrian land has been calm and peaceful, but the repeated attacks by the French armed forces against a peaceful people have roused the hearts and woken the emotions of Syrians who have been and who continue to be generous hosts, but they can no longer put up with insults and attacks on their rights."

"In asking you in the name of the Syrian Republic's Government to inform your Government of the reality of the situation in Syria, I ask you particularly to inform it of our sincere desire for swift British intervention to stop the French attacks which can no longer be tolerated."

"I am sorry to have to repeat to you that the Government of the Syrian Republic can no longer be held responsible for foreign victims who will suffer from the majority of the assaults by the French armed forces."
May 22, 1945

The Minister of Foreign Affairs
s/ Jamil Mardam Bey

Registered in the Ministry of Foreign Affairs
No. 3710/170 – Diplomatic correspondence – British Legation Damascus

90. May 22, 1945   Mardam to the Lebanese Minister of Foreign Affairs

HE the Lebanese Foreign Minister, Beirut

I have been authorized by the Council of Ministers to give my full approval to the measures you have taken.

We recognize, as you do, that the situation in Lebanon is different from that in Syria. The Maronites in Lebanon and the Armenians, who unfortunately have strange tendencies, cannot, under any circumstances, persist for long with the strike.

That is why the Syrian Government agrees to the resistance measures you have adopted and which we consider sufficient to support us in the current circumstances.

I am convinced, Your Excellency, that the success of our victorious struggle will be your success and that our failure, God forbid, will be your failure.

Yours sincerely,
May 22, 1945

The Acting President of the Council of Ministers
s/ Jamil Mardam Bey

Registered in the Syrian Ministry of Foreign Affairs
No. 3708/34 – Diplomatic correspondence

91. May 22, 1945   Barazi to Stirling

The President's illness has definitely provoked worry and uncertainty. We greatly fear that his illness will get worse because the others will not be able to agree about the presidency. It goes without saying that Jamil Mardam is pre-paring to succeed him. The President knew it, which was an important factor in increasing his suffering.

Mr Wadsworth visited the President today and confirmed to him again, on a piece of paper he left him, that America will support Syria in its struggle to shake off the colonialist yoke. The President believes that America is now the best possible friend for all the Arabs because the American people are a trading people, honest in business and as good businessmen, act honestly with customers, which means that they profit from it and make others profit too.

In this respect he alluded to the English who are very egotistical and fickle and cannot be counted on for an extended period of time. They change with their changing interests which take on a new color every day.

The President's illness has not changed anything fundamental in the situa-tion. He has placed everything in the hands of Sabri Bey and asked him to watch Jamil Mardam closely. His doubts grow by the day and he cannot forget that Jamil Mardam Bey is fickle.

Personally, I believe that this latter is trying to prove to the President that he will not deviate from his will under any circumstances, but all this seems pointless, because all the President's friends hate Jamil. The question pre-occupying everyone is stopping Jamil within a reasonable limit, because his influence has begun to make itself felt and is increasing rapidly these days.
May 22, 1945

s/ Muhsin 325

Sent by Stirling to the British Political Bureau in Beirut
registered under no. 1790

92. May 23, 1945   Barazi to Stirling

Yesterday, Ministers were overcome by weakness and fear, but the letters of national support from the President of the Council of Ministers of Egypt and Iraq have strengthened their nerves and today they find themselves in fine fettle for the fight. They will not retreat under any circumstances and will enter into combat against France until the last breath.

The leaders of the movement are Jamil Bey and Sabri Bey and the two are resolved to make France finally disappear. They collaborate together in an astonishing way, despite the differences that separated them in the past.

Jamil Bey believes that if he does not succeed in his plan, he will not be able to live in Syria any more. He is openly gambling with his life and will not retreat.

As for Sabri Bey, his enthusiasm is due to the way in which you knew how to take him and come to an understanding with him, but you must be wary lest this plan does not finally turn against you, because people here can no longer contain their aroused feelings against foreigners and the crowd can no longer conceive of the presence of French or English foreigners on Syrian soil.

The situation has greatly improved and the Ministers' desire to pursue the struggle instead of weakening has greatly increased. They believe that Egyptian and Iraqi military aid will not be slow to arrive.
May 23, 1945 in the morning

S/ Muhsin al-Barazi

Copy sent to the British Political Bureau in Beirut which received it on May 25, 1945
No. 1792 S

93. May 23, 1945   Mardam to the Syrian Cabinet

Top secret

Memorandum
To the honorable Council of Ministers

General Paget, Commander-in-Chief of the Allied Forces in the Middle East, visited me today and told me of his arrangements to withdraw the military sent by British command from Palestine to Syria for training, with the aim of not giving rise to tendentious interpretations about the intentions of the British Government with regard to us.

He also told me that the British security forces will exert themselves not to intervene in current events in Syria but they will see themselves forced to intervene if necessary to safeguard security in an important military zone with regard to the communication routes of armies warring with Japan.

I thanked him for the first part and formulated to him my strong opposition regarding the second part of the matter.

For my part I told him that the Syrian Government is constrained to use force against those who, in the name of force, commit acts of aggression against it and its civil servants.

He promised me once again that he will not tire himself over such questions and that he will not take on the defense of elements of the French army.
May 23, 1945

The President of the Council, for information
s/ Jamil Mardam Bey

(Not yet registered in the Ministry)

94. May 29, 1945   The Quwatli-Shone secret agreement

Secret

Exchange of letters no. 1
I, the undersigned, Shukri al-Quwatli, President of the Republic of Syria, pledge on my honor, in my name, and in the name of the Syrian nation that has honored me by making me its President, to make the utmost effort to realize the unity of Syria in its natural borders, that is, from the Taurus to the desert, to Egypt and to the Mediterranean Sea.

I promise to do my utmost to realize the unity of Bar al-Sham[1] and to be a soldier in the struggle for Syria's absolute unity, a natural step towards complete Arab Unity.

This is our agreement, and God is our witness.
Damascus, May 29, 1945

S/ Shukri al-Quwatli
Approved by the President of the Republic
S/ Jamil Mardam Bey

This document was provided by he who drew it up and who served as secretary.

- - -

Secret

Exchange of letters no. 2

I, the undersigned, Shukri al-Quwatli, President of the Republic of Syria, pledge on my honor, in my name, and in the name of the Syrian nation that has honored me by making me its President, to accept, when necessary, the Agreement of the Syrian Oil Company, to grant it a legal and judicial status and to obtain the Syrian Parliament's vote in its favor.

God be my witness.
Damascus, May 29, 1945

S/ Shukri al-Quwatli
Approved by the President of the Republic
S/ Jamil Mardam Bey

Not delivered to the Ministry of Foreign Affairs.
This document was provided by he who drew it up and who served as secretary.

- - -

Secret

Exchange of letters no. 3

I, the undersigned, Shukri al-Quwatli, President of the Republic of Syria, pledge on my honor, in my name, and in the name of the Syrian nation which has honored me by making me its President, to grant Great Britain a privileged position in all spheres in Syria, in the clearest of terms, namely, to grant it all privileges that are possible to grant to a friendly state, bound with an everlasting friendship.

I am prepared to obtain from Parliament a vote in favor of providing Great Britain with all possible economic, financial and political facilities.
Damascus, May 29, 1945

S/ Shukri al-Quwatli
Approved by the President of the Republic
S/ Jamil Mardam Bey

Not delivered to the Ministry of Foreign Affairs.
This document was provided by he who drew it up and who served as secretary.

- - -

Secret

Exchange of letters no. 4

I, the undersigned, Shukri al-Quwatli, President of the Republic of Syria, pledge on my honor, in my name, and in the name of the Syrian nation that has honored me by making me its President, that the Syrian Government's policies will always be consistent with British policy, we being two friendly states, and that Syria will never turn to another international bloc without the knowledge and agreement of Great Britain.

Damascus, May 29, 1945

S/ Shukri al-Quwatli
Approved by the President of the Republic
S/ Jamil Mardam Bey

Not delivered to the Ministry of Foreign Affairs.
This document was provided by he who drew it up and who served as secretary.

- - -

Secret

Exchange of letters no. 5

I, the undersigned, Shukri al-Quwatli, President of the Republic of Syria, pledge on my honor, in my name, and in the name of the Syrian nation that has honored me by making me its President, that the future Syrian army will be an Arab army that will adopt the most sincere attitude toward the British people and the Government of His Majesty the King.

Its instructors, trainers and guides will preferably be British.

It will depend on Britain's noble assistance for its arming and equipping.

Damascus, May 29, 1945

S/ Shukri al-Quwatli
Approved by the President of the Republic
S/ Jamil Mardam Bey

Not delivered to the Ministry of Foreign Affairs.
This document was provided by he who drew it up and who served as secretary.

- - -

Secret

To His Excellency the President of the Syrian Republic,

I have been authorized by my Government to promise you formally and on my honor, to maintain the secrecy of the text of the letter – a declaration made by Your Excellency regarding Syrian Unity.

Damascus, May 29, 1945

S/ Shone

Not delivered to the Ministry of Foreign Affairs.

- - -

Secret

To His Excellency the President of the Syrian Republic,

My Government has authorized me to formally promise that it will retain the secrecy of the letters nos. 2, 3, 4 and 5 – dated from this day. It hopes, however, that all their contents will, if necessary, assume the form of a treaty linking Great Britain and Syria in eternal friendship.

Damascus, May 29, 1945

Your obedient servant
S/ T. Shone

Not delivered to the Ministry of Foreign Affairs.

Note

1 Translator's note: literally, "Desert of Damascus," an expression denoting geographical Syria. Not delivered to the Ministry of Foreign Affairs.

95. May 31, 1945   Winston Churchill's ultimatum to General de Gaulle

May 31, 1945

"In view of the grave situation which has arisen between your troops and the Levant States and the severe fighting which has broken out, we have with profound regret ordered the Commander-in-Chief, Middle East, to intervene to prevent the further effusion of blood in the interests of the security of the whole of the Middle East, which involves communications for the war against Japan. In order to avoid collision between British and French forces we request you immediately to order the French troops to cease fire and to withdraw to their barracks. Once firing has ceased, and order has been restored, we shall be prepared to begin tripartite discussions in London."

96. June 1, 1945   General Sir Bernard Paget's ultimatum to General Paul Beynet

Army General Beynet
Delegate-General and French Minister Plenipotentiary in the Levant

Owing to the grave situation which has arisen in the Levant States I have, as Supreme Commander in the Middle East theater, been ordered by my Government to assume command in Syria and the Lebanon.

My aim is to restore order as quickly as possible and to do this I require that the following orders shall be carried forthwith:

a Instructions will be issued by French Military, Naval and Air headquarters that all orders and instructions issued by me on my behalf as Supreme Commander will be obeyed without question by all ranks of the French Military, Naval and Air Forces. All firing will cease except in self defense.

b All French troops and troupes spéciales will withdraw to their permanent barracks, except such troops as are guarding vulnerable points who will continue to do so until relieved by British troops.

c All French Military, Naval and Air Forces will remain within the limits of their barracks or establishments except when on such duties as may be arranged between British and French Headquarters.

d All French aircraft in the Levant will remain grounded.

e All French men-of-war will remain in harbor. Supplies for French forces including troupes spéciales will be arranged by my staff in conjunction with the French military authorities. In this respect I shall require the use of French transports which will be made available as needed.

I am concerned lest there should be incidents between the local population and isolated French families. The question of their protection will be discussed between British and French staffs. In any case I require that all French men and women be warned to be in their houses by nightfall.

In conclusion, I hope I may be assured of your cooperation in order to terminate as quickly as possible a state of affairs which we both of us deplore.

I am directed to inform you by my Government that as soon as firing has ceased and order has been restored it is proposed that discussions shall be held in London between the French and British Governments which the Government of the United States will attend.

Signed: General Paget
Commander-in-Chief, Middle East Force

June 1, 1945

97. June 1, 1945 Churchill's order to General Paget

Order

The re-establishment of order has to be performed on a large scale. Put your hands on all and everything. Anyway try to isolate the French.

Signed: Churchill

Political Department
Nr. 3.759/792
June 1, 1945

98. June 2, 1945 Churchill's order to General Paget

Order

There is nothing to be done in Lebanon as long as the affairs in Syria are not completely terminated.

Once order has been reestablished in Syria you may undertake the necessary steps in Lebanon.

The concentration of the French in Lebanon is rather more dangerous for themselves than it is to us.

Signed: Churchill

Political Department
Nr. 3.797/694
June 2, 1945

99. June 2, 1945   Churchill to General Paget

We do not understand what you are going to say about the interest the French are taking in Syria and in the Lebanon.

The private interests of all foreigners in Syria and Lebanon are respected.

If from a theoretical point of view we conceded certain privileges to the French in due course we are not in a position to do this from a practical point of view.

The prestige of France in Syria and in Lebanon has annoyed us very much up to now. And it is necessary to abolish it once and for all.

Signed: Churchill

Political Department
Nr. 3.798/795
June 2, 1945

100. June 3, 1945   Order by Richard Law, Parliamentary Under-Secretary of State for Foreign Affairs

Order

Try to create much ado about the names of Gen. Beynet, Humblot, etc. as far as possible in order to get them out of Syria.

Your principal task for the time being is to win the battle of propaganda. And we only can succeed in doing so by describing the French as being the aggressors and vandals in the eyes of the general public.

Signed: Law

Political Department
Nr. 3.700/699
June 3, 1945

101. June 4, 1945   Law's order

Order

It is necessary to put your hands on all administrations.

We are not going to do this by right of force but by the legitimate right to establish order.

Our political and military obligations compel us to remain firm and not to give in any relaxation.

Signed: Law

Political Department
Nr. 3.702/701
June 4, 1945

102. June 7, 1945   Law's order

Order

Do concentrate your efforts to prove that the Generals Beynet and Roget are the only guilty authors of the massacres of Damascus.

At the same time you hàve to prove that there was not a single English officer or clerk in any way connected with the disorders.

The most interesting point is to make believe that all terror has been inspired by General de Gaulle.

Signed: Law

Political Department
Nr. 3.814/709
June 7, 1945

103. June 7, 1945   Law's order

Order

In reply to your letter, dated June 6, a.C:

From a theoretical point of view: we gave our agreement to France having a privileged position in Syria and Lebanon.

To ratify this privilege it is necessary that the French succeed in getting a pact by Syria.

From a practical point of view: Syria will refuse to conclude a pact with France alone.

Signed: Law

Political Department
Nr. 3.815/710
June 7, 1945

104. June 10, 1945   Law's order

Order

I give you my permission to work against the Banque de la Syrie et du Liban.

Our efforts have to be directed towards the establishment of a national Syrian and Lebanese bank. Our money has to be detached from the French Franc and to be based on the pound sterling like all other Arab currencies.

Signed: Law

Political Department
Nr. 3.825/714
June 10, 1945

105. June 10, 1945   Law's order

Order

The declarations made by General Beynet in Beirut are wrong and without a base.

Your propaganda has to be directed towards the aim showing that the French politics has been directed against the whole Arab world. Moreover you will have to quote the atrocities done by the French in Morocco and in Algiers.

Signed: Law

Political Department
Nr. 3.826/715
June 10, 1945
Author's note: This is a response to Beynet's press conference the previous day in which he laid the blame for the crisis on British agents.

106. June 11, 1945   Law's order

<u>Order</u>

All extraordinary measures having been taken for the duration of the war remain in force until the end of the hostilities against the Japs.

As a matter of fact these measures have to be exercised in a sense advantageous to us and not to the French.

Signed: Law

Political Department
Nr. 3.829/72
June 11, 1945

107. June 10, 1945   Mardam to Wadsworth

Secret

Letter from Jamil Mardam Bey, Acting President of the Council
to Mr Wadsworth, the United States Minister in Syria

HE the Minister Plenipotentiary of the Government of the United
States of America in Damascus

Your Excellency,

Please convey to the government of the Republic the following request of the Syrian government:

All Syrians would be happy to see the American army join with the brave British army to maintain order and free the Syrians from the oppression of the French tyrant.

Such a course of action would clearly prove that Syria is not prey to the British and the Syrians have not replaced one foreign authority with another foreign authority. On the contrary, if your army were to participate with the British army in maintaining order, the spirit of this noble action taken by Great Britain and your moral support would appear in all its importance, from a political as well as a practical point of view and would allow the Syrians as well as the British to avoid the comments and the objections the French would raise that you know as well as we do.

Awaiting the generous agreement of your government, with my deepest respect.

Damascus, June 10, 1945

s/ Jamil Mardam, Minister of Foreign Affairs

Registered in the Ministry of Foreign Affairs under No. 209/II
Diplomatic correspondence – American Legation

108. June 14, 1945   Shone to Mardam

Secret

From Mr Shone
to His Excellency the Minister of Foreign Affairs, Damascus

Your Excellency,

You are no doubt aware of the serious accusations made by a French civil servant against particular British civil servants.

I do not want to intervene in an official capacity, but I ask you in the name of honesty and friendship to work, from your side, to make the truth known, so that we both can receive justice, you and us.

Yours sincerely

The Minister Plenipotentiary

June 14, 1945   S/ T. Shone

Not registered in the Ministry – Filed in the special archives

109. June 15, 1945   Mardam to Armanazi

Top secret
Coded

From Jamil Mardam Bey
to the Syrian Minister Plenipotentiary in London

I ask you to send the following, as a detailed letter, to the Ministry of Foreign Affairs:

First
The Government of the Syrian Republic thanks Great Britain for the humanitarian sentiments for which it drew criticism and attacks and which could have made its position suspect. It has put up with everything for the defense of Syrian independence with courage, independence for which it has pledged itself and which it has guaranteed.

Second
France has tried generally for twenty years to destroy the Arab movement for independence and particularly the Syrian national movement. Wherever it has met resistance, it has put it down to British encouragement, accusing the English of rousing the Syrians against them.

Third

France has assumed the habit of a policy of duplicity and blackmail in all its relations with Syria. All the statements made by its representatives for the last twenty years up to the present day are only a web of lies which have dirtied people and struck at their honor and honesty.

Fourth

The Syrian Government is not surprised to see France try, in the name of its representative, to ascribe the last Syrian independence movement and popular fury at French provocation to the wiles of Great Britain and its representatives.

Fifth

The main people the French are currently accusing are Messrs Stirling and Marsack.

The first, as the British official, has been and continues to be in continual contact with the Syrian population which he knows and which knows him and which he loves and which loves him for his sincere heart, his gentle character, his good intentions and his real desire to respect the independence and sovereignty of Syria. Mr Stirling enjoys all the support of the Syrian Government, which has not raised against him any attempt of a nature to prejudice national sovereignty, nor any activity prejudicing the independence of the country. He entered Syria with the forces of General Wilson and traveled from North to South; everywhere he made true friends, both in the city and in the desert – and, thanks to his high qualities, he succeeded in making his country popular. We think that it is not shameful for a man to be upright and honest, while the representatives of France have always acted in the opposite fashion: by allowing themselves to be corrupted, by stealing and pillaging. It is by comparison that people have seen the difference there is between Mr Stirling for example and the murderer Oliva Roget. They loved, respected and appreciated the former and detested and mistrusted the latter.

However all this predates the current events. When France rose up against us and began to foment incidents and to weave intrigues, Mr Stirling's only mistake is to have acted as the true British representative and to have lavished on those who were in touch with him – both city-dwellers and Bedouins – advice promoting calm and order. Many people have heard this advice and are disposed to testify to it if necessary. He has always told us that violence was not profitable, and that only losers began their work that way: that is what happened, praise be to God, with France.

There remains only one point on which the French can accuse Mr Stirling, following their habit of lying; it is that he distributed arms and funds to promote resistance to France. This accusation, like the other French accusations, is complete calumny. It would be true if the French could provide tangible proof relating to this, but these proofs, they do not have them at all, for Mr Stirling has not, in reality, distributed either arms or funds.

However, there is no doubt that Mr Stirling, in his capacity as a British official, has perfectly fulfilled his role, while the British security forces have taken charge of maintaining order in Syria and in Lebanon. It is this official role which has surely annoyed the French and made them mad.

Colonel Stirling's participation in all these events is entirely without foundation; he did not intervene and has not used any activity; on the contrary, when Oliva Roget was weaving his intrigues, and was preparing the troubles in Damascus, Colonel Stirling was away in Beirut; we can prove that.

We think that citing Mr Stirling's name in these events constitutes an affront to us and a distortion of our struggle against French provocation.

As for Mr Marsack, every Damascene knows the extent of his honesty and frankness. His daily contacts with the press – contacts due to the functions he fulfills – are definitely the cause of French anger, for they think that he is only working against them.

In our language we have a proverb that says, "A traitor is always afraid," and the French are afraid, not knowing whom to accuse: they believe that everyone is their enemy. In reality, they are their own enemies and enemies of every free man who loves his country.

The accusations they are making against particular English civil servants are nothing more than affronts for us and for our people.

I ask you to notify the Ministry of Foreign Affairs of this as soon as possible. Damascus, June 15, 1945

Minister of Foreign Affairs
S/ Jamil Mardam Bey

Registered in the Ministry of Foreign Affairs
No. 419 – Political reports

110. June 16, 1945   Mardam to Shone

Secret

Jamil Mardam Bey
to HE the Minister Plenipotentiary of the
Government of HM the King of Great Britain, Damascus

Your Excellency,

The Syrian Government, which is grateful to Great Britain, cannot forget that a factor exists which the French, who are enemies of the Arabs, are likely to use to exploit the position of England and Syria, that is, Palestine.

As you know, the support of Hadj Amin al-Husseini, Grand Mufti of Palestine, a hostage in their despotic hands, is such as to hit the conscience of every Arab and constitutes a certain danger as to the possibility of collaboration between the Mufti and them.

We know better than anyone HE the Mufti and his intrigues. It is for that reason that we ask His Majesty's Government to take a step aimed at taking away from the French and depriving them of a political instrument which could be used in the near or distant future.

The British Government will thus render an enormously good turn to the Arabs and to Great Britain.

As always, your devoted servant,

S/ Jamil Mardam Bey

June 16, 1945

Registered in the Ministry of Foreign Affairs
No. 202/26 – Diplomatic correspondence – British Legation

111. June 18, 1945   Mardam to Shone

Secret

HE Jamil Mardam Bey, Acting President of the Council of Ministers
to HE Mr Shone, British Minister Plenipotentiary in Damascus

Your Excellency,

We agree that at each stage of our activities we will work together, in a spirit of complete friendship, in order to create the material circumstances and a frame of mind that would provoke a popular incitement against France, which could lead to a conflict between the popular armed forces and the French forces until we could manage to chase them out.

We remain in agreement that the cooperation between your civil servants and ourselves will be complete, because total success can only be achieved if your efforts support ours.
June 18, 1945

Minister of Foreign Affairs
s/ Jamil Mardam

Registered in the Ministry of Foreign Affairs
No. 554/A – Documents

112. June 18, 1945   Shone to Mardam

Secret

From Mr Shone
to HE the Syrian Minister of Foreign Affairs, Damascus

Memorandum

I agree with the spirit of your note titled exchange of letters no. 1, which indicates your desire for complete cooperation within the framework of the cooperation defined in our agreement of June 2, 1945.
June 18, 1945

s/ Sh.

Registered in the Ministry of Foreign Affairs
No. 554 A a – Documents

113. June 19, 1945   Shone to Mardam

Secret

From Mr Shone
to Jamil Mardam Bey

To HE the Minister of Foreign Affairs, Damascus
His Majesty's Government is examining the wise desire you expressed in your letter of June 16 relating to the ex-Mufti of Palestine.
I believe we will succeed.

June 19, 1945   Yours sincerely,
                                                                      S/ Shone

Registered in the Ministry of Foreign Affairs
No. 564 – Documents

114. June 20, 1945   Mardam to Shone

Secret

From Jamil Mardam Bey
to Mr Shone
To H.E. the Minister Plenipotentiary of Great Britain, Damascus

Your Excellency,
The scheme you have referred to is not simply a scheme; it is a factor of prime importance in the Arab economy. It is for that reason that I am happy to find that you are well-disposed towards its realization.
I will enter into direct negotiations with the Iraqi Government which finds itself involved, just as we are, in order to determine our points of view and the conditions of the agreement.
I will let you know as soon as possible the outcome of our agreement so that you can notify the groups in question.

June 20, 1945   Yours sincerely,
                                                            s/ Jamil Mardam Bey

Registered in the Ministry of Foreign Affairs
No. 225/30 – Diplomatic correspondence – British Legation

115. June 24, 1945   Mardam to Shone

Secret

From Mr Jamil Mardam Bey
to HE the Minister Plenipotentiary of His British Majesty's Government,
Damascus

Your Excellency,

During the conversation we had two days ago and on which I also sent a report to the Council of Ministers, we reviewed the dangers that might surface in the near future from the spread of communist propaganda and the growing political influence of Soviet Russia.

The Syrian Council of Ministers is sure that communist Russia can neither approve of the colonialist claims nor the evil accusations that France – ruined – resorted to in order to stay in Syria. From this point of view, we are confident and untroubled that communist Russia today is only working for its own benefit. It would therefore seize any occasion to build a place in our country even to the detriment of France, its friend and ally.

This is why we do not see any inconvenience in keeping the communists in a well defined setting, despite the affection we currently display towards them with the sole aim of exploiting and using them. You know to what extent Khalid Bakdash and company were useful in the last crisis.

I wish to confirm to Your Excellency our complete willingness to eliminate the communists who number only a few and are of little importance. We will make their plans fail thanks to the same clever procedures we used against France.

As always, I remain your sincere friend

June 24, 1945

Minister of Foreign Affairs
s/ Jamil Mardam

Registered in the Ministry of Foreign Affairs of the Syrian Republic
No. 282/51 – Diplomatic correspondence – British Legation

116. June 26, 1945   Armanazi to Mardam

From Najib al-Armanazi, Minister in London
to HE the Minister of Foreign Affairs, Damascus

Colonel Stirling thanks you for having defended him so warmly. I was made to understand at the Foreign Office that your defense was more useful to the Syrian cause than anything else. The French accusations were so crass, implicating Mr Churchill among the instigators of the troubles. We all know how much Labour Party ministers could have profited from these accusations against Mr Churchill and his associates, and how our hopes would suffer if the British Labour Party came to power. These are people who, as everyone knows, attach less importance to principles than they attach to the agreement with Russia. It is common knowledge now that France is Russia's eldest daughter, having once been the Church's eldest daughter.

All the signs prove that the future of international relations is full of uncertainty. Here, in London, they do the impossible to get France on their side. Were the French to persist in their way of seeing things and insist on staying with the Soviet Union, it would be the end of them, they would be destroyed for ever, and we and the whole world would find peace; then it would be the turn of the lying Russians.

Nothing proves that the Russians will return to reason, but from today the British have made their arrangements. As for Russia, this means that the time for definitive action with France has begun; either it will align itself with British policy or its equivocal attitude will very likely drive it to its end.

All this is, from our point of view, only important in one respect: we fear that we may be the price of Anglo-French agreement.

June 26, 1945   The Minister Plenipotentiary
                                                                 S/ Najib al-Armanazi

Registered in the Ministry of Foreign Affairs
No. 288/207 – Diplomatic correspondence – London Legation

117. June 26, 1945   Shone to Mardam

Secret

From Mr Shone, Great Britain's Minister to the Levant,
to HE Jamil Mardam Bey, Minister of Foreign Affairs.

In reply to the letter you sent me today, I am pleased to learn that you are determined to grant the British citizens and companies all necessary facilities in the event that they ask to search for and exploit the mines.

I have informed my government of your present decision.

All procedures will be adhered to in order to preserve the secret nature of this decision that aims to avoid remarks or misunderstandings on such important matters.

As always, your obedient servant.

June 26, 1945

                                                                 The Minister Plenipotentiary
                                                                                S / Shone

Registered in the Syrian Ministry of Foreign Affairs
No. 293/58 – Diplomatic correspondence – British Legation

118. June 28, 1945   Syro-British meeting on equipping the Syrian army

Minutes of the Syro-British meeting
in Damascus on June 28, 1945
Minutes no. 2

HE the President of the Syrian Republic,
assisted by Jamil Mardam Bey, Acting President of the Council of Ministers and Minister of Foreign Affairs,
representing the Syrian side,

and General Sir Bernard Paget, representing the British side met in Damascus today, Thursday, June 28, 1945, and reached the following agreement:

The Government of HM the King of Great Britain represented by his military authorities pledges to deliver to the Syrian government within six months from today sufficient arms and war ammunition to equip ten thousand soldiers.

A detailed agreement will be concluded for the designation of the arms, their type and quantity. This equipment will be adapted according to the circumstances which might vary from day to day.

Its quantity could be increased.

Drawn up in Damascus on June 28, 1945

(signed)   BP.   CH.J.

Deposited in the Ministry of Foreign Affairs of the Syrian Republic
(not registered by July 1, 1945)

119. End of June, 1945   General Beynet to General de Gaulle on collaboration with the Zionist movement

General Delegation in the Levant

Beirut, end of June, 1945

Mon Général,

In the recent crisis, public opinion in the Middle East has been against us. Only the Jews of Palestine are an exception. Their concern in seeing the danger France faces in the Levant has created a consensus among them that even they themselves consider exceptional. The parallelism between a Jewish homeland in Palestine and a Christian homeland in Lebanon, which has always been advocated by the Jewish Agency, has now become everyone's leitmotif. My collaborators have been approached by the various sides, who offer their services. I have given orders for contacts to be maintained and that we consider collaborating with the Jewish Agency on a propaganda campaign, which it desires.

It appears that, at least initially, working together can only be to our benefit. It will be enough if we give a verbal reassurance, not necessarily to support the Zionist movement and its demands, but to refrain from adopting a hostile attitude, especially when it comes to the question of immigration to Palestine. The injustices and suffering of the French Jews under German occupation makes it difficult for us to take any other stand. Moreover, we could benefit on the global scale from the excellent network of information, propaganda and even political activities that the Jewish Agencies, Jewish press groups and pro-Zionist parliamentary groups are involved in. This propaganda wouldn't, at the moment, appear to be in France's interests, but in the interests of the Christians of the East. It wouldn't seek to maintain the balance of the Powers, but the rights of the minorities. We will benefit from it no less.

France's actions, interests and goals will be less obvious. In these conditions, I do not consider the contradiction, which I don't underestimate, between a Christian policy in the Middle East and an Islamic policy in North Africa, to be an obstacle.

Representatives of the Jewish Agency who are here now confirm that in the United States, Dorothy Thompson, Freda Kirchwey, Albert Einstein and Frantz Werfel will agree to plead the cause of the Christian minorities in the Middle East, and that Mr Spellman, Mr Laguardia, Mr Lehmann and Mr Myron Taylor will support them. In Great Britain, the support of Lord Strabolgi, Miss Dugdale, Miss Rathbone, M.P. and Sir Wyndham Deedes will be obtained. We can no doubt verify this through our embassies in London and Washington. In any case, I don't think it would be a bad idea for very close contacts to be maintained between our representatives and the Jewish Agency representatives in these two capitals: Mr Zaslani and Mr Linton, Dr Weizmann's secretary, in Great Britain, and Mr Nahum Goldman and Mr Eliyahu Epstein in the United States.

Furthermore, M. Shertok, who is in charge of the Jewish Agency's external affairs, will shortly be going to London. I know that he would very much like to be invited to Paris. This would be an opportunity for the French Government to go into more detail regarding the various points raised in this letter.

I didn't want to commit myself to collaborating even in a propaganda campaign with the Zionist movement before consulting with the Prime Minister. It is, in fact, a matter of general policy, on which I can only give my opinion as France's representative in the Levant: I am in favor, but I lack the necessary details in order to determine whether the disadvantages might outweigh the advantages that I outlined above.

Signed: Beynet

Author's note: The letter was read by de Gaulle

120. July 1, 1945   Shone to Mardam

From Mr Shone
to HE the Minister of Foreign Affairs of the Syrian Republic, Damascus

Memorandum

I am convinced of your wisdom and diplomatic courtesy and I believe that the moment is not well chosen to dictate conditions while we are trying to accomplish two different operations.

As far as France is concerned, our attitude consists in observing it.

As far as Russia is concerned, the interest of all of us is not to make France decide to turn forcibly to the left.

Your Excellency, this does not need high politics; these are matters which even the newspaper proprietors here have seized on. I regret seeing us constrained to play particular roles which, although seeming far from brilliant, will still give favorable results.

In any case, I am authorized by my Government to confirm to you that, just like you, it is not at all our intention to count on France for anything, even though we could pretend to.

July 1, 1945   S/ Sh.

Registered in the Ministry of Foreign Affairs
No. 582 – Documents

121. July 5, 1945   The British Legation in Damascus to Mardam

From Mr Evans of the British Legation, Damascus
to HE the President of the Council of Ministers

HE Mr Shone has asked me to notify you of the following:

"As I told you verbally, I am going to take a rest. You must know that my Government wants me to absent myself temporarily from public life in order to allow the air to clear and to prevent the French from having any more grounds for objection.

France, as you know, has always said that British civil servants have been the cause of all the misunderstandings which have occurred in Syria. For our part, we want to share with you our sincerest opinions, which is that you get on with France and reach a reasonable solution which safeguards your national interests above all.

At this moment when I am leaving Beirut for a short rest, I wish you good fortune, happiness and peace."

Unsigned note sent on July 5, 1945 by Mr Evans of the British Legation in Damascus

Registered in the Ministry of Foreign Affairs
No. 319/121 – Diplomatic correspondence – British Legation

122. July 10, 1945   Armanazi to Mardam

Secret
Coded

From the Syrian Minister in London
to HE the Minister of Foreign Affairs, Damascus

The British officials are surprised by the indifference we are displaying towards our Algerian Arab brothers.

Mr Ronald Campbell says that emancipation of the Arabs is a whole and that from now on it is necessary, for the benefit of humanity, that the Arabs, who are an important part of the human race and control the most fragile global communication routes, must not remain in this state of immobility.

The information which has come to the knowledge of the British establishes that the French savagery in Algeria was extreme, and that, in the interest of our Arab brothers in that country and even in our own interest, public opinion in our country must be directed in favor of the Algerians against France, as it is in favor of our cause.

This matter cannot be ignored.
July 10, 1945

The Minister Plenipotentiary
s/ Najib al-Armanazi

Registered in the Ministry of Foreign Affairs
No. 351/129 – Diplomatic correspondence – Syrian Legation in London

123. July 15, 1945   Atasi to Mardam

Secret
Coded

From the Syrian Minister in Paris
to HE the Minister of Foreign Affairs, Damascus

France is now more nervous than ever about the Arab League's activities. Although its leaders think that this League does not constitute a material force to fear at the moment, they note that its enlargement and future activity will be carried out at France's expense.

Extending the activities of the League towards the West will favor the growth of the germ of revolution against French colonization in Tunisia, Morocco and Algeria. This time the French will not publicly accuse the English, they will content themselves with recognizing that the existing activities in Morocco do not presage anything good.

My personal opinion is that we would benefit from these "golden" opportunities and that we should encourage those in Morocco who want to act against France. I have noticed that many people here could move actively in favor of these plans if they were provided with the necessary materials.

Were Your Excellency to judge it useful, it would be possible to encourage the Arabs to emancipate themselves from French colonial influence or to cause France problems if emancipation cannot be won in one go.

France's current activity, as you have noticed, is only aimed at showing Morocco's loyalty with regard to it. This loyalty does not deceive anyone, and people who have boarded the French cruiser – Governors, Ministers and Sultans – are only of the same category as Sheikh Taj a-Din, and only enjoy the consideration France grants them.

I eagerly await your reply.
July 15, 1945

The Minister Plenipotentiary
S/ Adnan al-Atasi

Registered in the Ministry of Foreign Affairs
No. 381/89 – Diplomatic correspondence

124. July 16, 1945   Armanazi to Mardam

Coded
Secret

From the Syrian Minister in London
to HE the Minister of Foreign Affairs, Damascus

I have learned today that Mr Yess, chief engineer in earth strata in the Anglo-Iranian petroleum company, has presented his report on petroleum resources in the Middle East to the relevant authorities.

The part of interest to us in this report is summarized by the following points which, in the opinion of certain experts, are very important for us.

<u>First</u> – There is no intention to exploit Syrian oil deposits for at least ten years. They will be content with establishing the pipeline from Iraq and from Najad only.

<u>Second</u> – The Syrian deposits are definitely richer than all those in the Middle East.

<u>Third</u> – The English and American companies want to get rid of French interests and distance them from this operation.

<u>Fourth</u> – The British Government will no longer show itself conciliatory towards France regarding its influence in the Middle East because it is thought here that French interests are not superior to those of the British who want to be the only ones with a predominant influence in the Middle East.

July 16, 1945

The Minister Plenipotentiary
s/ Najib al-Armanazi

Registered in the Ministry of Foreign Affairs
No. 382/145 – Diplomatic correspondence – London Legation

125. July 18, 1945   Mardam to President Quwatli

Secret

From HE Jamil Mardam Bey
to HE the President of the Republic

The conversation that took place between HE Mr Shone and myself can be summarized as follows:

HE thinks that it is not in Syria's interest at the moment to make any ministerial changes. It is part of the ministry's assignment to gather the results of the painful events it witnessed. Only this will make the French understand that no compromise is possible.

HE also believes that it is in our interest to show reservations towards the Russians and the claims they will soon make.

Granting a concession for an oil refinery to America will give the Russians the opportunity to make a similar claim. Mr Shone believes that the Russians have projects ready and will ask us and Lebanon to implement them.

What we should concentrate on now is taking possession of the army. Afterwards we will formulate new claims.

I noticed during my meeting with HE that nowadays he is paying less attention to the French than to the Russians.

Wednesday, July 18, 1945

The Minister of Foreign Affairs
s/ Jamil Mardam Bey

Not yet registered.

126. July 19, 1945   Qudsi to Mardam

Coded
Secret

From the Syrian Minister in Washington
to HE the Minister of Foreign Affairs, Damascus

I was summoned to the Department of State for Foreign Affairs for an urgent interview. They strongly insist that we provide them with precise information on the plans for the scheduled creation of the railway between Syria and Iraq.

Mr Crew told me, "I ask you to notify your government that American companies are disposed to undertake an operation of this sort, either in association with British companies or in competition with them!" It seems that the English are telling the Americans that this plan is purely local, that they are not connected to it, that Syria will itself take on the creation of its own track, and that Iraq and Iran will act in the same way.

Mr Crew is certain that the plan is British and not local. He asks that America take part in it, and that sufficient delays are granted to him to present his submissions. He is of the opinion that the Syrian Government is in no hurry to decide on such an operation before America is consulted.
July 19, 1945

The Minister Plenipotentiary
s/ Nazim al-Qudsi

Registered in the Ministry of Foreign Affairs
No. 384/67 – Legation correspondence

127. July 20, 1945   Solod to Mardam

Secret

From the Soviet Minister in Damascus
to the Syrian Minister of Foreign Affairs

Your Excellency,

I acknowledge receipt of your letter of July 15, 1945 which was in answer to the memorandum I sent you on July 11, 1945.

Your answer is both courteous and unclear. In reminding you of the question, I put before you the following truths:

1 The sale of land to the Jews is taking place, as you know, in a discreet way through agents.
2 The promise you gave me, that is that you would not allow the Jews – the enemies of the Arabs – to attack independence, does not in any way alter the state of affairs; most of your government partisans and even a large number of your civil servants indulge in arms trafficking which serves to kill Arabs like you.
3 I do not consider Your Excellency's response to be sufficient in this respect, because my government thinks that the current Jewish preparations for

future disorder constitute a danger which threatens not only our interests but those of all Arabs.

In putting these truths before you I do not forget that you have friends you rely on and who themselves encourage the dangers in question, that you do not want to acknowledge even though they are many and just about surround you. It is not through speeches and words that these dangers will be avoided.
Yours sincerely,
July 20, 1945

s/ D. Solod

Registered in the Ministry of Foreign Affairs
No. 403/107 – Diplomatic correspondence – Soviet Union

128. July 21, 1945   The Syrian Chargé d'Affaires in Cairo to Mardam

Secret

From Asim al-Naili, the Syrian Chargé d'Affaires in Cairo
to His Excellency the Syrian Minister of Foreign Affairs, Damascus

HE the Secretary General of the League of Arab States has asked me to notify you that a Committee of Arab notables, including a representative of the countries of the Maghreb, has just met in Cairo to discuss provocative incidents organized by the French colonizers in these sister Arab nations.

The activity of this Committee is limited to a simple exchange of views. The Secretary General asks that the Syrian Government set aside in its future budget sufficient funds to help these regions in their struggle against France, a sum in addition to the sum of fifty thousand pounds that Your Excellency so kindly sent me from the Secret Funds.

HE the Secretary General thinks that every piastre spent in helping our Algerian, Moroccan and Tunisian brothers will be amply justified by the success of the supreme aims for which we are working, the most important being to throw France out of Muslim Arab countries as it has already been thrown out of here.

I await your reply, Your Excellency.
July 21, 1945

The Chargé d'Affaires to the Syrian Legation
S/ Asim al-Naili

Registered in the Ministry of Foreign Affairs
No. 411/105 – Diplomatic correspondence

129. July 22, 1945   Armanazi to Mardam

Secret

From the Syrian Minister in London
to HE the Minister of Foreign Affairs, Damascus

Official circles in London are once again addressing the old subject of Greater Syria. It is clear that the presence of HH the Prince Regent of Iraq has put the matter on the agenda once again. One of the most well-informed journalists has confirmed to me that HH obtained the clear promise of American support in favor of this project.

The British services, in conjunction with the Foreign Office, repeat that realizing the plan for Greater Syria will increase the strength of the Arab League and will finally destroy all French hopes with regard to the intervention of this nation in the affairs of the Arab world, through the intermediary of the Maronites of Lebanon who, in Greater Syria, will only be a very small minority.

It is clear that this matter will be raised at the future meeting of the Council of the League of Arab States and that the Iraq representative will threaten to withdraw from the League if his colleagues do not agree to grant him their favors.

I believe that the affair has become serious. We must decide on our position once and for all: either we make Great Britain and America unhappy by satisfying some profiteers who want the narrow independence of Syria in its current borders, or we follow the reasonable route, which is that of Unity.
July 22, 1945

The Minister Plenipotentiary
s/ Najib al-Armanazi

Registered in the Ministry of Foreign Affairs
No. 414/93 – Diplomatic correspondence
Author's note: "British Services" usually refers to British intelligence agencies.

130. July 24, 1945   Armanazi to Mardam

Coded
Secret

From the Syrian Minister in London
to HE the Minister of Foreign Affairs, Damascus

The Maronite Patriarch's statements have raised deep concern here. The British openly think that it is necessary to destroy once and for all the Patriarch's influence and that this prelate should be subject to public attacks so that his reputation can be totally destroyed.

The Administrative Services here have told me that the reconciliation which Lebanon manifests with regard to the French may provide all the chances necessary for the Maronites and behind them the French, to create situations dangerous to the cause of the Arab nation whereas these dangers had originally been avoided.

I ask you to make the bad impression left by the Patriarch's statements disappear and to strike a mortal blow against the spies of the French.

July 24, 1945

The Minister Plenipotentiary
s/ Najib al-Armanazi

Registered in the Ministry of Foreign Affairs
No. 430/152 – Diplomatic correspondence – London Legation

131. July 25, 1945   The British Legation in Damascus to Mardam

Secret

From the Adviser to the British Legation in Damascus
to HE the Minister of Foreign Affairs, Damascus

Memorandum

My Government supports every Arab effort leading to emancipation from the colonialist yoke.

The help you give to the movement of your Arab brothers in Algeria can only be regarded serenely by any lover of liberty.

I rejoice in the link in relations uniting you with the inhabitants of North Africa when I see you supporting and helping them with deeds and in the success.
July 25, 1945

For the British Legation
s/ Young

Registered in the Ministry of Foreign Affairs
No. 649 – Documents

132. July 27, 1945   Fa'iz al-Khuri, the Syrian Minister in Moscow, to Mardam

Secret

From Fa'iz al-Khuri, the Syrian Minister in Moscow
to HE the Minister of Foreign Affairs, Damascus

My conversation today with the director of the Oriental Section at the Commissariat of Foreign Affairs has increased my incomprehension, although the following points were clarified:

First: They believe that all Arab politicians are currently in the service of British imperialism.

Second: That the current Arab leaders, despite their nationalist appearance, play the same role as capitalists in industrial Europe with regard to their own people and are only interested in their own interest.

Third: The Soviet Union is not opposed to national struggles against colonialism; that is to say it does not oppose our current struggle against France, but that it encourages it, and that it will not thwart our struggle against England tomorrow, but that it will encourage that too.

Fourth: They are convinced that we will only remove ourselves from France's blows to fall under British blows together with our Arab brothers.
Fifth: In the current circumstances it is difficult to wait for help from the Soviet Union.

Yours sincerely,
July 27, 1945

s/ Fa'iz al-Khuri

Registered in the Ministry of Foreign Affairs
No. 439/6 – Diplomatic correspondence

133. July 28, 1945   Fa'iz al-Khuri to Mardam

Secret

From Fa'iz al-Khuri, the Syrian Minister in Moscow
to HE the Minister of Foreign Affairs, Damascus

I was summoned to the Commissariat for Foreign Affairs where I was told, with great friendliness, that, for the following reasons, the current conduct of the Syrian Government was not encouraging for the establishment of a sincere collaboration profitable to our country:

"First: They believe that we are ousting the French to replace them with the English.
Second: That we are delivering our country's resources to the English (an allusion to the 'Mira' agreement)."

My interlocutor added:
"The Soviet Union will heartily support the Arabs' position against the Zionist movement which aims to take Palestine and chase them out of it. It is up to the Arabs to adopt a suitable position in defense of their threatened country."
I am sending you a summary of what was said to me.
Yours sincerely,
July 28, 1945   S/ Fa'iz al-Khuri
Registered in the Ministry of Foreign Affairs
No. 443/7 – Diplomatic correspondence

134. July 28, 1945   Qudsi to Mardam

Secret

From Nazim al-Qudsi, the Syrian Minister in Washington
to HE the Minister of Foreign Affairs, Damascus

I draw the Syrian Government's attention to the plans concerning the oil pipeline from Saudi Arabian lands to the Mediterranean Sea and to the matter of the exploitation of Syrian oil. These two matters are very clear, but both of them can constitute a grave danger for the general situation in Syria.

All the official confirmations that we receive from the political representatives of Great Britain and America must be understood as having a bearing only on the situation as it actually is. It is hard that they pledge the future, except when they encompass the future interests of Great Britain and America. The experience has in effect taught us that promises are not made forever.

My advisers and I are convinced that England and America have worries about the future. Egypt will not be, as much as Syria, Palestine, Lebanon and Iraq, the target of future international ambitions.

The Americans believe in the possibility of Russia's participation in controlling the Suez Canal, but Great Britain and America will not allow this nation to intervene in the affairs of Syria, Lebanon or Palestine, despite its current attempts which began with recognition of our independence and by sending the Patriarch Alexis on a propaganda mission.

These Powers, having obtained – or almost – France's withdrawal from Syria and Lebanon, will work to consolidate their influence in such a way as to satisfy completely the populations. But what is beyond doubt is that the inhabitants of Syria will not consent in any circumstances to a colonizing Power establishing itself with them, whatever impressions of friendship it may give. This is why the English will try to create a throne of their own in Syria, just as the Americans will try to win this throne – if it is created – over to their influence or to put a king of their choosing on it: Saudi for the Americans and Hashemite for the English.

In viewing the question from this angle, we can see that we have freed ourselves from the French epidemic only to fall into many other difficulties, which would never have been raised if we had stayed close to France.

Repentance or retreat cannot be useful in the current situation. Our independence remains a vague word. It is surrounded by all the dangers which our friends weave around us, and whose origin lies in the oil in the Arab peninsula which must be brought to the sea by the natural route of Syria. The totality of these dangers is not enough for the oil men, the Jewish danger must be added as a fundamental factor destined to weaken the whole of the Arab world.

I confirm to you that no child here is unaware that the aim of Great Britain in installing the Jews in Palestine is not so much its solicitude for this miserable people as the creation of continual difficulties for the Arab nation.

I am communicating all these dangers to you for all useful ends on the occasion of ongoing discussions between Mr Crew and Emir Faisal al-Sa'ud and of the meeting of the World Jewish Congress in London, which is arousing great interest here.

July 28, 1945

The Minister Plenipotentiary
s/ Nazim al-Qudsi

Registered in the Ministry of Foreign Affairs
No. 559 – Diplomatic reports

135. July 28, 1945   Mardam to Shone

Secret

From Jamil Mardam Bey
to HE the Minister Plenipotentiary of
HM the King of Great Britain, Damascus

Your Excellency,

The Syrian Government finds itself facing an avalanche of rumors about the likelihood of a radical change in the British position towards this Syrian independence which the Government of HM has guaranteed and which it was forced to keep recently by the force of arms.

While having complete confidence in Great Britain's good intentions with regard to the Arab cause in general and Syrian independence in particular, we find ourselves uncertain and we ask ourselves whether these last alterations which have occurred in the British ministry will influence the situation in Syria or not.

I would be happy if Your Excellency would put my mind at rest on this matter so that I may reassure the Council of Ministers who impatiently await your honorable response.

I remain, as ever, your devoted friend.

July 28, 1945

The Minister of Foreign Affairs
S/ Jamil Mardam Bey

Registered in the Ministry of Foreign Affairs
No. 444/172 – Diplomatic correspondence

136. July 30, 1945   Mardam to Armanazi

Secret
Coded

From Jamil Mardam Bey
to the Syrian Minister Plenipotentiary in London

We formally deny any agreement between Generals Paget and Beynet.

The French have left Syria and will never return; they will, God willing, leave Lebanon and will never return.

As for Patriarch Arida, he has personally denied his statement, but the truth is – as you are aware – that this miserable creature is a great schemer in the service of France. We should not be amazed by any new surprises on his part. What is important at the moment, in the interests of Syria and Lebanon, is to demolish him completely and thus rid ourselves of the head of the French fifth column.

That is the truth. Release it in any way you want.

July 30, 1945

The Minister of Foreign Affairs
S/ Jamil Mardam Bey

Not yet registered

137. July 30, 1945   Mardam to Qudsi

Top secret
Coded telegram

From Jamil Mardam Bey
to the Syrian Minister Plenipotentiary in Washington

At the request of the Council of Ministers, ask for an interview with Mr Crew and obtain answers to the following questions:

1   What is the American Government's position with regard to Jewish ambitions in Palestine?
2   What will America's position be if the White Paper is abrogated by Great Britain?
3   What will the American Government's position be if Great Britain alters its stand with regard to the Syrian cause, and if it were to reach an agreement with France at our expense?
4   We note that France will try to stay in Syria (with the agreement of Great Britain, it seems) in the name of the International Security Council. It will try to win strategic bases in the country. Will President Truman and Mr Crew give their consent to that after the promises made to us by Mr Stettinius on the final departure of the French from Syria and Lebanon?

We ask you to get precise answers swiftly.
July 30, 1945

The Minister of Foreign Affairs
S/ Jamil Mardam Bey

Not yet registered in the Ministry

138. August 1, 1945   Mardam to the Chargé d'Affaires in the Syrian Legation in Cairo

Secret
Coded

From Jamil Mardam Bey
to the Chargé d'Affaires in the Syrian Legation in Cairo

In reply to your letter no. 912/h of July 21st.

I am sending you today, through Mr Stuman, the sum of fifty thousand Syrian pounds.

I ask you to acknowledge receipt, to be very discreet and to tell me how they are being used.
August 1, 1945

The Minister of Foreign Affairs
S/ Jamil Mardam Bey

Not yet registered in the Ministry

Author's note: The money was provided by the British intelligence. Asim al-Naili, the Syrian Chargé d'Affaires in Cairo, was Mardam's closest aide and was implicated in Shahbandar's assassination in July 1940.

139. August 1, 1945   Qudsi to Mardam

Secret
Coded

From the Syrian Minister in Washington
to HE the Minister of Foreign Affairs, Damascus

Discussions are taking place now between His Highness Emir Faisal al-Sa'ud and officials of the American Department of State on various issues, particularly:

1 oil in the Arab peninsula, means of exploitation and seizure
2 extraction of metals from the peninsula
3 projects regarding irrigation and supplying the peninsula with water
4 the Jewish question
5 the plan for unity of Greater Syria
6 creating a Saudi throne in Syria.

There are three matters which interest us in these discussions. Mr Constantin Zureiq, adviser to this Legation, has, through his friends in the State Department, obtained information with regard to this which can be trusted, according to which agreement was complete in all the discussions that took place.

As for the Jewish question, the Americans are not very committed to supporting the Jewish policy, which tends towards annihilating the Arabs. They will seek to withdraw from the promises they have made with regard to the Jews.

As for the plan for Greater Syria, it is clear that HH Emir Abd al-Ilah's discussions were not crowned with success: he received very vague promises from Mr Crew.

As to the question of creating a Saudi throne in Syria, it is very likely that the Americans committed themselves verbally with Emir Faisal for him alone to become King of Syria, if the question of the throne was raised. It is clear that the Americans will not raise it themselves; it will be the English who do. At that time, the Americans and English will present their candidate. The Americans will definitely demand that a general plebiscite be held in Syria as it is at the moment and in the countries of Greater Syria.

However, the Americans do not believe that things will take this turn. There is France, and the obstacles it can create for these plans. There are also the Lebanese, who will not be in agreement, and above all the Maronites whose support will not be winnable.

What matters at the moment is that the Americans have reached an understanding with Emir Faisal to put him on the Syrian throne if there is one and that they will not accept any king other than him in any circumstances.

Yours sincerely,

August 1, 1945

The Minister Plenipotentiary

S/ Nazim al-Qudsi

Registered in the Ministry of Foreign Affairs
No. 565 – Political reports

140. August 5, 1945   Armanazi to Mardam

Secret

From the Syrian Minister in London
to HE the Minister of Foreign Affairs, Damascus

We are calling on the conscience of all Syrians and all Arabs.

The Palestinian question goes from bad to worse. The representative of world Jewry has met H.E. Attlee, who has confirmed to him that the Labour Government remains faithful to the promise it has made to the Jews.

The danger is serious. My colleague Chamoun believes that France is playing an important role in the encouragement given to the Jews against us. He thinks that if the Arabs do not undertake armed action to frighten Great Britain, the Attlee government will bow down before the Jews' demands and will grant them everything they want.

We ask you to apply strong pressure to the English, American and Russian ministers to protest against this new British policy which is sowing trouble in the Arab Orient.

August 5, 1945

The Minister Plenipotentiary

s/ Najib al-Armanazi

Registered in the Syrian Ministry of Foreign Affairs
No. 479/169 – Diplomatic correspondence

141. August 7, 1945   Armanazi to Mardam

Secret

Coded telegram

From the Syrian Minister in London
to HE the Minister of Foreign Affairs, Damascus

Great Britain will soon withdraw its troops from the whole of the Middle East.

I have not been able to find out whether this measure is a result of the Potsdam decisions or if Great Britain is applying a new policy inspired by Labour Party doctrine.

It is clear that England will start negotiations with Egypt to settle the Egyptian question anew; this should replace the Anglo-Egyptian treaty. The Egyptian Legation here is convinced that Great Britain will withdraw its forces from the country. General Spears confirmed to me that the forces of the Ninth Army will withdraw and that they will take with them all the foreign forces in the Middle East.

It is clear that the British forces will only withdraw once they have made the remnants of the French Army, which are still in the country, leave before they do.
August 7, 1945

The Minister Plenipotentiary
S/ Najib al-Armanazi

Registered in the Ministry of Foreign Affairs
No. 497/176 – Diplomatic correspondence

142. August 7, 1945   Qudsi to Mardam

Secret
Coded telegram

From the Syrian Minister in the United States
to HE the Minister of Foreign Affairs, Damascus

Mr Crew confirmed to me today that a significant change will soon appear in British policy. He believes that Great Britain will withdraw its troops from Arab countries and at the same time will ask France to withdraw its army from Syria; that matters relating to petroleum will be subject to effective revision, that is to say that oil from Arab lands will not be exploited only by Great Britain, but that an adequate share will be granted to France, to appease it; a share will also be granted to Arab countries to allow them to have modern industry and agriculture.

As to matters concerning the Jews, while refusing to express an opinion, he believes that a Jewish state will be created on a large part of Palestinian land. He asserts that it is in the interest of the Arabs to accept this solution, because it is preferable that some of the Arab countries withdraw in favor of the Jews, rather than leaving the door wide open to Jewish demands.
August 7, 1945

The Minister Plenipotentiary
s/ Nazim al-Qudsi

Registered in the Ministry of Foreign Affairs
No. 582 – Political reports

143. August 8, 1945   Qudsi to Mardam

Very urgent
Coded

From the Syrian Minister in Washington
to HE the Minister of Foreign Affairs, Damascus

I have just learned that on his return from Potsdam, President Truman discussed the question of the Orient with Dr Hitti, professor and director of the Arab Section of the Faculty at Princeton. The conversation was reported to Mr Zureiq by Dr Philippe Hitti's secretary.

President Truman, ignoring his official capacity, personally believes that those setting the policy in Syria and Lebanon are unprincipled charlatans. First, they reached an understanding, and worked, with colonizing France, then they collaborated with Fascists and the Vichy people, and then turned towards the Democrats. He adds that he does not believe that men such as the current leaders in Syria and Lebanon are working in favor of their countries; they are directly in the service of Great Britain, and are far from their people and their aspirations. To this end he cites, as an example, a film Hollywood is currently shooting about the Egyptian people titled "The Cow." The people are the cow, which the leaders milk with Great Britain. American businessmen then collaborate with the British.

President Truman is convinced that the Labour Government will adopt a new line of conduct in Syria and Lebanon, which will not be wholly hostile to France, as has occurred in the past.

What is more strange is that the President believes personally that the events which have taken place over the last few months in Syria have been a simple theatrical production the British knew how to prepare with skill, and which we Syrians have performed.

I am telling you about this reasoning which is very serious if true – and it must be – because the person who reported the conversation to us is not an idiot.
August 8, 1945

The Minister Plenipotentiary
S/ Nazim al-Qudsi

Not yet registered in the Ministry

144. August 8, 1945   Atasi to Mardam

Secret
Coded telegram

From the Syrian Minister in Paris
to HE the Minister of Foreign Affairs, Damascus

I believe that Haj Amin al-Husseini has won the favor of the French services and that in the future he will be a weapon in their hands against Great Britain.

It is true that this man has thus bought back his life, but what matters to us is that Haj Amin constitutes a redoubtable force. How dangerous will he be when he maneuvers against us and against those who exercise power in our country?
August 8, 1945   The Minister Plenipotentiary
s/ Adnan al-Atasi

Registered in the Ministry of Foreign Affairs
No. 538/119 – Diplomatic correspondence

145. August 9, 1945   Armanazi to Mardam

Secret
Coded

H.E. the Minister of Foreign Affairs, Damascus

In reply to your letter of the 2nd of this month.

The British Government is not satisfied with Mr Stirling's conduct. Our intervention in his favor has been rather detrimental.

I was able to understand that Mr Shone only supports him in appearance and that fundamentally he is against him.

All the efforts made by General Spears are fruitless, even harmful.

All we can do is to wait for the many still unclear questions to become clear.

August 9, 1945

The Minister Plenipotentiary
S/ Najib al-Armanazi

Registered in the Ministry of Foreign Affairs
No. 556/181 – Diplomatic correspondence

146. August 10, 1945   Armanazi to Mardam

Secret
Coded

HE the Minister of Foreign Affairs, Damascus

Summing up the two interviews that I had with Mr Bevin and having studied the reports by my colleagues the Arab Ministers Plenipotentiary on their contacts with him, I can give Your Excellency an account of the situation regarding our vital interests.

1 The Labour Government has not yet adopted a definite line of conduct with regard to matters in Arab lands. All that has been said so far is only commentary and supposition.
2 The rumors regarding the non-modification of British foreign policy are not correct. The Labour Government will completely overturn matters that are of prime importance.
3 Mr Bevin's tone in speaking of France is not at all like the tone of his predecessor. Mr Campbell, who is considered to be an important element in the general policy of the Foreign Office, becomes reserved after having been extreme in the support he gave us.
4 The Jews are currently playing not only with the future of Palestine but with our future too. Great dangers threaten us from their side.
5 The plan for Greater Syria has by no means been filed away.
6 Mr Bevin takes the situation in Lebanon, and Maronite fears, into consideration. He fears that difficulties may arise because of religious

rivalries which we do not want to recognize and which he does not want to forget.

7   He does not throw back on France responsibility for the events of last May, but he states that the matter requires impartial study.

In a general way, we need to employ much activity in the course of these few days, because if we refrain and if we show unconcern, the Labour politicians will take their decisions under the influence of impressions opposed to our own.

August 10, 1945   The Minister Plenipotentiary
                                                                        s/ Najib al-Armanazi

Registered in the Ministry of Foreign Affairs
No. 501– Political reports

147. August 12, 1945   Armanazi to Mardam

Secret
Coded

From HE the Syrian Minister in London
to HE the Minister of Foreign Affairs, Damascus

I discussed our position with General Spears. His opinion as a Briton is that we should remain attached to the British policy, which is the only one that will safeguard our interests; but he also thinks that we can adopt a second position of blackmail which will be very easy to maintain and which will consist of frightening the British (those in power) and making them believe that we have begun to favor others and that our attachment and our transactions will be with others.

If you think this position is reasonable, I would ask you to adopt it quickly so that it can bear fruit here.

August 12, 1945   The Minister Plenipotentiary
                                                                        s/ Najib al-Armanazi

Registered in the Ministry of Foreign Affairs
No. 564/184 – Diplomatic correspondence

148. August 14, 1945   King Ibn Sa'ud to President Quwatli

Secret

From Abd al-Aziz Ibn Abd al-Rahman al-Faisal al-Sa'ud
to HE President Shukri al-Quwatli,
may God preserve him.

Greetings and divine mercy.

It is highly regrettable that Abdullah should once again undertake his hateful attempts and busy himself in winning a crown and scepter just when dangers threaten us.

My men are sure that he is busying himself a great deal more than in the past to unify Syria under his rule, in agreement with our friends the English and in collaboration with our friend Jamil Bey. May God be witness, I have not succeeded in understanding Jamil Bey, not his ways nor his plans; may God preserve us from him.

What worries me, my dear Brother, is Abdullah and his collaboration with the Jews. You gave me to understand that he has the support of France and that the French are encouraging the Jews. For my part, I cannot believe that; the French are now weak and do not know how to manage their own affairs.

I thank you, dear Brother, for the information you sent me, but I beg you not to ignore the matter of your own Minister, Jamil Bey.

Greetings, divine mercy and blessings.

6 Holy Ramadan 1364

August 14, 1945   s/ Abd al-Aziz Ibn Abd al-Rahman

[A copy of] the letter stolen from the Saudi Legation in Damascus before reaching Shukri al-Quwatli and given to Jamil Mardam Bey by Fauzi Tello.

The thief is still not known.

149. August 15, 1945   Shone to Mardam

Secret

Private letter from Mr Shone
to HE the Minister of Foreign Affairs, Jamil Mardam Bey, Damascus

My dear friend,

I think that it is in your personal interest to withdraw. My own opinion is that you should not try too hard to remain in your position. Out of power, you will be a great force, while when you are in power, you are subject to much criticism.

My information on the direction of the deputies is not very satisfactory. It seems that we made a mistake in giving them our confidence. Now I greatly fear that a French hand is acting without our knowing whose it is.

Sabri Bey's irritation exceeds all bounds and these last few days it has evolved in a strange way. However he is not very dangerous and every new ministerial combination will not last while you are not part of it.

Yours sincerely,

August 15, 1945

S/ T. Shone

Personal, not registered with the Ministry of Foreign Affairs.

Written in English. This is the Arabic text as transmitted by the British Political Bureau.

150. August 15, 1945   Abd al-Rahman al-Azzam, Secretary General of the Arab League, to Mardam

Secret

From the Secretary General of the Arab League
to HE the Syrian Minister of Foreign Affairs, Damascus

Your Excellency,

I have, with great appreciation, received your special request regarding the convocation of the Council of the Arab League with the aim of dealing with the Palestinian question.

I have explained the matter to HE President Nuqrashi Pasha, but it seems that Ambassador Killearn made objections to HE regarding this convocation and stated that his Government had asked him to advise us to deal with this matter calmly and quietly.

You will see from the above that the British Government may:

- either not want to support us against the Jews and give us justice,
- or try – which seems likely – to deal with the matter wisely and in peace.

The Lord [Killearn] explained to HE the position of the new government regarding Syrian independence and confirmed to him that it is not the British Government's intention to abandon Syria to the French.

HE will notify the Syrian Chargé d'Affaires of the ambassador's proposals in order to convey them to you.

Greetings, mercy and divine blessings be upon you.
August 15, 1945

The Ambassador,
Secretary General of the Council of the Arab League
s/ Abd al-Rahman al-Azzam

Registered in the Ministry of Foreign Affairs
No. 581/37 – Diplomatic correspondence

151. August 15, 1945   Qudsi to Mardam

Secret
Coded telegram

From the Syrian Minister to the United States
to HE the Minister of Foreign Affairs, Damascus

The State Department has today told me of the American Government's intention to put to Syria several proposals relevant to its economic life and which will serve America at the same time. These proposals are the following:

1 – developing American teaching in Syria
2 – creating aerial routes for the global communication network and between Arab countries
3 – creating an American bank

4 – creating American factories
5 – concessions for the search for and mining of metals, especially uranium
6 – concessions for archaeological research

I was made to understand by the State Department that the American Government has already agreed with Faris al-Khuri on all these matters which will be officially presented to the Syrian Government as soon as possible.

I promised to inform you so that you could take your position with the aim of entering into negotiations and preparing a possible response.

For my part, I advise you to grant many facilities to the Americans, because their yoke is much lighter than that of Great Britain or France, God willing.

August 15, 1945

The Minister Plenipotentiary
s/ Nazim al-Qudsi

Registered in the Ministry of Foreign Affairs
No. 622 – Reports

152. August 16, 1945   Shone to Mardam

Secret

From HE Mr Shone, Minister for Great Britain
To HE the Minister of Foreign Affairs, Damascus

Your Excellency,

My Government has asked me to give you the following advice:

At the moment global Jewish influence is making the greatest of efforts to stir up universal public opinion against the British plan concerning Palestine.

HM the King's Government does not intend to alter significantly the policy outlined for Palestine. That is why it prefers that Jewish provocation should not be greeted on the Arab side with similar provocations; at the moment it is enough for the Arabs to have confidence in Great Britain's friendship and in its good and sincere intentions with regard to them.

As a result I advise you not to give free rein to Arab incitement, and not to let yourselves be drawn into the crisis which many European states – which you know and that have never wanted and will never want your best interests – are preparing.

Yours sincerely,
August 16, 1945

s/ Shone
Minister Plenipotentiary and Envoy Extraordinary
to the Government of HM the King of Great Britain

Registered in the Ministry of Foreign Affairs
No. 675 – Documents

153. August 16, 1945   Qudsi to Mardam

Secret
Coded telegram

From the Syrian Minister in the United States
to HE the Minister of Foreign Affairs, Damascus

I believe that General de Gaulle's next visit to America will define the position of that country with regard to us and will finally place America on France's side.

Humanitarian America now appears to be capitalist. We will see with our own eyes that during this whole time this country only used us as an object of barter with France and England for our business, our position and our oil.

Mr Byrnes has not hidden the fact that England wants France to be ousted from Syria in order to be able to take over at least the markets and oil resources of this country. As for the Americans, he said, they only want the civilization of Syria with whom they seek to deal. In the coming days they will busy themselves developing American universities in the East and will apportion great credit to this. In this way they will consolidate their spiritual and material influence.

Mr Byrnes is the friend of a large number of professors collaborating with Dr Zureiq. They all confirm that Mr Byrnes wishes to reach an understanding with de Gaulle at any price. He sees the interests of the small states with a purely materialistic eye. He believes that President Truman's views match those of his Foreign Minister. Thus America will have its share of influence in the politics and economy of the Middle East.

The important thing, as far as the new President and his Foreign Minister are concerned, is that they do not favor England any more than President Roosevelt did.

As a result we must wait for a change which is essential to us.
August 16, 1945

The Minister Plenipotentiary
S/ Nazim al-Qudsi

Registered in the Ministry of Foreign Affairs
No. 593/104 – Diplomatic correspondence

154. August 17, 1945   The Syrian Cabinet's secret decision on Palestine

Top Secret

Secret Decision no. 4119
The Council of Ministers of the Syrian Republic

Given the decrees of the President of the Republic on the appointment of its members

Given the constitution

Given the dangerous situation surrounding the Arab nation and its League

Decides on the following:

Only article

Each ministry will take, each according to its interest and very discreetly, the precautions and measures necessary in the eventuality of a situation of unexpected alarm between Syria and the Palestinian Jews.

Syrian policy will, in this regard, rely on the following principle:

Collaboration with Arab states, by diplomatic channels first, then by violence to respond to the aggression being prepared by the Great Powers against Palestine.

The Foreign Minister is charged with consulting the Council of the Arab League, but this does not prevent the taking of all necessary precautions. Made by the President of the Republic on August 17, 1945.

s/ Faris al-Khuri

The President of the Syrian Republic
s/ Shukri al-Quwatli

The President of the Council
s/ Faris al-Khuri

The Foreign Minister
s/ Jamil Mardam Bey

The Minister of the Interior
s/ Sabri al-Asali

The Finance Minister
s/ Naim Antaki

The Justice Minister
s/ Sa'id al-Ghazi

The Minister for Public Instruction
s/ Ahmad al-Sharabati

The Minister for Public Works
s/ Hikmat al-Hakim

The Minister of Supplies
s/ Hasan Jabara

155. August 18, 1945 King Ibn Sa'ud's message to President Truman on President Roosevelt's pledges on Palestine

Secret

From the Saudi Legation in Damascus
to HE the Syrian Minister of Foreign Affairs, Damascus

In the name of merciful God

I am sending Your Excellency the crucial passage from the letter sent by HM King Abd al-Aziz, may God preserve him, to President Truman:

"You know, Mr President, that your predecessor had made us good enough promises and had committed himself on his honor that the question of the Jews would never constitute a danger for Islam and the Arabs. Now, having come to power, you are once again opening the question: you demand for the Jews what the Jews themselves do not demand for themselves. We may therefore be forgiven if we despair of you from now on. You force us to turn to others, where we will find the attachment you reject, and to whom we will grant the advantages and concessions we had given you."

I believe, Your Excellency, that this is enough. Greetings and divine mercy. 10 Ramadan 1364 (August 18, 1945)

For the Minister Plenipotentiary
s/ Shakir al-Sama'an

Registered in the Ministry of Foreign Affairs
No. 583/27 – Diplomatic correspondence

156. August 18, 1945   Shone to Mardam

Secret

From HE Mr Shone, Minister Plenipotentiary of the British Government
to HE the Minister of Foreign Affairs, Damascus

Your Excellency, I regret seeing the crisis getting worse by the day and your personal enemies ardently attacking you, accusing you of neglecting the interests of the country and of conciliation with the French, while we were in complete agreement with the line of conduct you followed. From now on, we can – in your interest as well as ours – only adopt a new position in line with the way this situation develops.

The point on which people attack you is the plan for the unity of Syria. I regret that HE the President of the Republic is intractable on this point. I don't know if it will be possible to make him change his position and to settle the situation between you and him in a way that is satisfactory to all parties.

What matters to us today is that the Ministry being set up – whether you are part of it or not – can follow the line you adopted and show itself firmly determined to resist the French, without however provoking a crisis (which I believe we are not completely in favor of at the moment), so as to end in the retreat which we ourselves consider very necessary.

I ask you please to make the greatest effort to lessen the force of the enmity aimed at you by showing good intentions. For our part we will do our utmost to lessen the violence of this attitude if you distance yourself somewhat from the field of action.

August 18, 1945

The Minister Plenipotentiary
S/ T. Shone

Not registered
Personal letter

157. August 18, 1945 Armanazi to Mardam

Secret
Coded

From the Syrian Minister in London
to HE the Minister of Foreign Affairs, Damascus

The definitive view I can give you on Great Britain's position with regard to us is contained in these very frank words – which I heard yesterday from Mr Cadogan, whose opinion, as you know, is very important to the Ministry of Foreign Affairs,

"Great Britain will not change its policy with regard to Syria unless the Syrians change theirs."

To be certain, I asked him if there would be an understanding with Great Britain and France to our detriment. He replied to me, "Never. We will not reach an understanding with anyone which is against the independence of Arab countries."

Filled with joy, I believe that this promise is the proof that apart from the Jewish question there is nothing that can make us fearful.

August 18, 1945   The Minister Plenipotentiary
                                                 S/ Najib al-Armanazi

Registered in the Ministry of Foreign Affairs
No. 622 – Reports

158. August 19, 1945 Armanazi to Mardam

Secret
Coded telegram

From HE the Syrian Minister in London
to HE the Minister of Foreign Affairs, Damascus

HRH Emir Abd al-Ilah summarized to me his conversations with Mr Attlee and Mr Bevin.

The conversation with Mr Attlee is not important to us, but in a general way the Leader of the Labour Government shows us his goodwill and supports the Arab cause. He considers this policy to be in the tradition of Great Britain.

As for Mr Bevin, this Minister has confirmed to HRH that Great Britain will preserve with all its power the independence of Syria and Lebanon and will not allow France to harm it. He promised him that the British forces would withdraw, not after the withdrawal of French forces, but at the same time as them.

For its part, Great Britain has taken, or will take, all the measures necessary for the withdrawal of French troops.

That is a summary of the conversations which concern us.

As for the Palestinian question, HRH has learned through Mr Bevin that Great Britain would not abandon the Arabs and would not offend them with importunate solutions.

August 19, 1945   The Minister Plenipotentiary
                                                   S/ Najib al-Armanazi

Registered in the Ministry of Foreign Affairs
No. 620 – Political reports

159. August 19, 1945   Minister of the Interior Sabri al-Asali to President Quwatli and Cabinet ministers

Top secret

Report
to HE the President of the Republic,
to the Noble Council of Ministers,

Today the Director of the Sûreté Générale provided me with information and proof about the new attempts the propagandists from the House of Hashemites are making. He confirmed to me again that the Syrian higher authorities support them.

I am taking advantage of this situation to confirm to your noble Council that it is no longer possible for me to pursue my task in the atmosphere of enmity, intrigue and betrayal which sets us one against the other.

The guilty party in all this is clearly HE the Foreign Minister. HE defends himself strongly with regard to sympathy or support for the Hashemite family.

As for me, as this Government's Minister of the Interior, I am fully aware of the danger that would threaten this country if a similar line was followed. I know that it is only for a republican regime that we have given a pledge of loyalty, and I do not understand how a minister in charge, occupying the most important ministry, can plot against his government and constitution.

I place in your hands the choice of my resignation or revoking that of the person whose activities will be recognized as hostile to the republican regime.

August 19, 1945   The Minister of the Interior
                                                   S/ Sabri al-Asali

Registered
Copy in Jamil Mardam's hand

160. August 19, 1945   Atasi to Mardam

Secret
Coded

From HE the Syrian Minister in Paris
to HE the Minister of Foreign Affairs, Damascus

Our painstaking research has not given us any proof, not even a hint, that France supports the Jewish movement or provokes the Jews against us, as you have said.

The rumors reaching us from here and there deceive us. We must, if we are currently in conflict with the French, be more or less wise and not accuse innocent people.

On the contrary, I note that the French wish to reach an understanding with us; I also note that they do not like the Jews in the way you describe, and that they do not support Zionism or emigration to Palestine. The opposite of this is true: all the French politicians think that Zionism is a matter linked to Great Britain. The British, in pretending not to satisfy Jewish demands, make fun of the Arabs and deceive them.

I am serious in saying that current French policy does not plot with the Jews against us.

August 19, 1945   The Minister Plenipotentiary
                                                   S/ Adnan al-Atasi

Registered in the Ministry of Foreign Affairs
No. 619 – Political reports

161. August 20, 1945   Armanazi to Mardam

Secret
Coded

From the Syrian Minister in London
to HE the Minister of Foreign Affairs, Damascus

Here we are waiting for Emir Abdullah to come to discuss with the British Government the unification of geographic Syria and his enthronement as King of this country.

General Spears told me that King Abdullah had many opportunities to enter Damascus and be enthroned there. He confirmed to me that the last Jewish congress accepted that this Emir should be the only candidate for the future Syrian throne.

So Your Excellency will realize that our country is currently in a grave situation without us having paid enough attention to the dangers threatening us.

My loyalty towards my country and the republican regime in which I have faith makes me appreciate the danger threatening our country. Royalty in itself is not dangerous, but danger comes from what it brings with it.

I inform you of this with a heart full of bitterness.

August 20, 1945   The Minister Plenipotentiary
                                                   S/ Najib al-Armanazi

Registered in the Ministry of Foreign Affairs
No. 629 – Reports

162. August 20, 1945   The Syrian Chargé d'Affaires in Cairo to Mardam

Secret
Coded

To H.E. the Syrian Minister of Foreign Affairs, Damascus

HE Muhammad Fahmi al-Nuqrashi informed me today that Great Britain was preparing a huge plan to colonize Tripolitania, Arab Muslim land.

Under the cover of protection or friendship, Great Britain wants to lay its hand on this land and will place one of the Senussi Emirs at its head. It will give the Barka region a semblance of internal independence. France will accept a simple border change.

HE believes that this plan is very dangerous. Egypt cannot put up with having a British colony next to it. All Arabs must help each other to discuss this serious matter.

France and England have plotted for a long time against the Arab world. What HE fears is that there will now be a new plot between the two colonizing states and that Syria itself will be the prize in this agreement heavy with consequences.

August 20, 1945   The Chargé d'Affaires of the Syrian Legation in Egypt

S/ Asim al-Naili

Registered in the Ministry of Foreign Affairs
No. 639/79 – Diplomatic correspondence

163. August 20, 1945   Qudsi to Mardam

Coded

From the Syrian Minister in the United States
to HE the Syrian Minister of Foreign Affairs, Damascus

I talked to an official in the State Department who told me:

"We Americans feel sorry when we see you, the Arabs, not seeking real freedom. Your liberty does not rest in your emancipation from Great Britain, France or America, but in the liberation of your people from the yoke of its masters, the famous and wealthy. If people free themselves from the despotism of others, the quality of life will rise, production will increase, your nation will get stronger, and that is when the exploiting foreigner, French or otherwise – will be chased out.

At the moment, Great Britain has complete control in your country. It does not put up with having others than itself in your country (remember, it is Great Britain which pushes the Wafdist press to protest against the presence of an American army in Egypt).

Great Britain wants to supplant France and does not want to allow Russian influence in Syria. It will continually create ministerial crises in your country so as to weaken the position of all your governments. These, its creatures, will not be able to hold their own. Mr Wadsworth told us that the British Minister in Syria is now disposed to dismiss Jamil Mardam and replace him with someone else, having exploited him for so long."

Although I do not share the view of this American official, I am telling you anyway so that you are aware of what they are saying about us.

August 20, 1945   The Minister Plenipotentiary
S/ Nazim al-Qudsi

Registered in the Ministry of Foreign Affairs
No. 628 – Reports

164. August 20, 1945   Mardam's letter of resignation

Secret

From Jamil Mardam Bey
to   HE the President of the Republic
HE the President of the Council of Ministers

I have just found out about the letter my colleague the Minister of the Interior kindly addressed to you and in which he makes unfounded accusations against me.

I do not seek to exonerate myself, because my innocence is clear to see. Only those with evil intentions doubt it; but I beg Your Excellency to ask my colleague to provide proof and I will then be ready to account to anyone. I am convinced that there is no proof and that there are only rumors (rumors spread by lackeys of the French, enemies of this fatherland) who infiltrate government services and populist circles to reach the ears of my colleague the Minister of the Interior.

I challenge anyone to show me the weak point in the policy I have followed. I do not see anyone with the right to complain about me except for the French colonizers whom I have the honor of treating as my implacable enemy. I cannot allow or accept being accused by a colleague on simple suppositions.

Anyway, while handing you my resignation I want to provide Parliament with an explanation.

August 20, 1945   The Minister of Foreign Affairs
S/ Jamil Mardam Bey

Not registered in the Ministry

165. August 21, 1945   Shone to Mardam

Secret

To HE the Minister of Foreign Affairs, Damascus

Your Excellency,

I received your letter of today with much regret.

I am really pained that plots continue to be woven around you. Rest assured that my partners and I have used all in our power to clear this troubled atmosphere, but in vain.

I share your view: it is the plotting by our allies that has led you to this equivocal position. I am aware of the efforts they have made to this end. I have reports on the monies spent with the aim of buying the consciences of certain deputies. But rest assured that this will no longer be useful to them: this crisis – no matter how painful – will be settled in our favor.

I am pained, as I told you, but I will wait a little and hope that Your Excellency will do the same.

With my deepest respect,
August 21, 1945

Sincerely,
S/ T. Shone

Personal – not yet registered

166. August 22, 1945   Shone to President Quwatli

Secret

To HE the President of the Syrian Republic

The ex-Foreign Minister, HE Jamil Mardam Bey, had asked the British Government to send certain technical advisers to lend their support to the Syrian Government.

At the time I thought that the moment was not right for fulfilling such a request.

But my Government which I have consulted has made known to me its inclination to provide you with the requested help.

I ask you to act while waiting for me to provide the Syrian Government with the names of these advisers.

Yours sincerely,
August 22, 1945   The Minister Plenipotentiary to HM the King
s/ T. Shone

Not yet registered in the Ministry

167. August 22, 1945   Syrian Prime Minister Faris al-Khuri to Shone

Secret

To HE the British Minister Plenipotentiary, Damascus

HE the President of the Republic has shown me your kind letter.

I was deeply astonished by what you so kindly wanted to tell us about the advisers; the Syrian Government has not taken a position on these matters and the Council of Ministers has never asked the Foreign Minister to take such steps.

Your Excellency will appreciate the disappointment of the Syrian people, who have rid themselves of French advisers, when they will find themselves in the presence of English advisers, without taking into account the prejudice this will cause to the regard there is for the British.

HE the President of the Republic is wholly unaware of such an agreement, and, to speak unambiguously, the Council of Ministers has not decided anything regarding this.

Yours etc.,

August 22, 1945   The President of the Council of Ministers

s/ Faris al-Khuri

Not yet registered in the Ministry

168. August 22, 1945   Shone to Faris al-Khuri

Secret

To HE the President of the Council of Ministers, Damascus

Your Excellency,

I deeply regret that the matter of the Advisers should have taken this turn and am astonished about the way it has been raised.

HE the ex-Foreign Minister did nothing on his own initiative; he told us of the wish of the Council of Ministers.

I am sure that the Council of Ministers has taken a decision on this matter and that this was approved by you and by HE the President.

However, if you think that you must change your mind, that is another matter; as for us, we retain our position which has not changed and will not change.

Yours etc.,

August 22, 1945   The Minister Plenipotentiary to HM the

King's Government

s/ T. Shone

Not yet registered in the Ministry

169. August 22, 1945   Wadsworth's memorandum to the Syrian government

Secret

Memorandum

The Minister Plenipotentiary of the Government of the United States of America has the honor of communicating to the Syrian Government the desire of American companies producing iron and steel to explore for particular metals, especially those which fall into their area of expertise, with the exception of uranium which is present, according to them, in the Syrian desert.

The American Government fully supports these companies and asks the Syrian Government to give its agreement to searches for the metals in question. It confirms to it that these companies are ready to provide the best conditions possible to extract these primary materials.

From now this Legation gives itself the right to remind the Syrian Government that it would not be able to approve any development which would be granted to others without consulting it because from now it is ready to present the best possible offers.

I summarize this note with the two following points:

a I am ready in the name of my Government to undertake metal exploration
b I reserve the right of preference over all other candidates.

August 22, 1945   The Minister Plenipotentiary
                                                              s/ Wadsworth

Not yet registered

170. August 23, 1945   The British Legation in Damascus to the Syrian Minister of Foreign Affairs

Secret

From the British Legation
to HE the Syrian Minister of Foreign Affairs, Damascus

HE the Minister Plenipotentiary of HM the King's Government has requested me to ask the Syrian Government for details of discussions that would have taken place or that would have been taking place between it and certain states regarding development concessions for finding metals, uranium in particular.

I ask the Syrian Government, if there have been such discussions, not to make too much haste, just as I ask it to note the wish of HM the King's Government to hold discussions of this nature. I also ask it to grant us the status of preferred bidder, given that we have already expressed this request verbally and that Your Excellency has given his agreement to it.

August 23, 1945   s/ Evans

Registered in the Ministry of Foreign Affairs
No. 642/275 – Diplomatic correspondence

171. August 23, 1945   Faris al-Khuri to Shone

Secret

To HE the British Minister Plenipotentiary, Damascus

Following our verbal conversation of today, I have pleasure in confirming to you that HE the President of the Republic has decided to visit the British capital soon to be in direct contact with the relevant officials and to discuss with them possible developments in the Syrian question, particularly the special plan relating to the unification of Syria and the many difficulties it would entail.

I ask you to take note of this wish and assure you of my deep respect.

August 23, 1945   The President of the Council of Ministers
                                                            S/ Faris al-Khuri

Registered in the Ministry of Foreign Affairs
No. 660/278 – Diplomatic correspondence

172. August 24, 1945   Armanazi to the Syrian Minister of Foreign Affairs

Secret
Coded

From the Syrian Minister in London
to HE the Minister of Foreign Affairs, Damascus

Here, they are waiting and even preparing for discussions between them and the French.

What needs to be secured is that Great Britain will not backtrack, as far as we are concerned, on its position of support, but the only fear we have is that British troops will remain after French troops withdraw.

The plan for Greater Syria is still topical and I fear that the British army will busy itself supporting Hashemite ambitions in Syria.

General Spears says that Syria's interest requires that British troops do not withdraw now. I think that his proposals are based solely on British considerations, with no thought for our interest.

The situation is complex and unclear.

August 24, 1945   The Minister Plenipotentiary
                                             S/ Najib al-Armanazi

Registered in the Ministry of Foreign Affairs
No. 649/197 – Diplomatic correspondence

173. August 24, 1945   The Iraqi Minister in Damascus to President Quwatli

Secret

From the Iraqi Minister Plenipotentiary in Syria
to HE Shukri Bey Quwatli, President of the Syrian Republic

HE Nuri Pasha Sa'id has summarized to me his conversations in Europe with British officials, and the formal promises made to HE the Prince Regent.

Nuri Pasha is very optimistic about Syria's future. He is quite sure that the question of Syrian independence is one of the main topics of interest to the new ministers of the British Government. Their position will not change from that of the Conservative government and the coalition government.

For his part, HRH the Prince Regent has won the formal promise that the independence of Syria will be guaranteed, and that France will not be allowed to play its game with the Syrians again whatever changes there may be.

In bringing you this happy news I hope that I have fulfilled, for my Government and for myself, part of our task.

With my deepest respect, Your Excellency,

Damascus, August 24, 1945

S/ al-Rawi
Minister Plenipotentiary of the Government of HM the King of Iraq

Copy in the Syrian Ministry of Foreign Affairs
Not yet registered

174. August 24, 1945   Qudsi to the Syrian Minister of Foreign Affairs

Secret
Coded

From the Syrian Minister in the United States
to HE the Syrian Minister of Foreign Affairs, Damascus

Today the State Department asked me if the Syrian Government is really inclined to unite with Iraq to form a state under a Hashemite throne.

The American Government has information which establishes that the President of the Syrian Council of Ministers approves of this plan in favor of which he is working with the British Government.

As a matter of urgency, please put me in a position to provide the response asked of me.

August 24, 1945

The Minister Plenipotentiary
S/ Nazim al-Qudsi

Registered in the Syrian Ministry of Foreign Affairs
No. 651/93 – Diplomatic correspondence

175. August 24, 1945   The British Legation to Faris al-Khuri

Top secret

To HE the President of the Council of Ministers, Damascus

Your Excellency,

I have learned that the French are currently carrying out preparations with a view to attacks which may happen from one minute to the next, particularly in Aleppo.

I also learned that their Allawite and Jebel Druze supporters are beginning to show signs of activity again.

I ask you to give this the necessary attention.

August 24, 1945   For the Minister Plenipotentiary
S/ Evans

Registered in the Ministry of Foreign Affairs
No. 693/287 – Diplomatic correspondence

176. August 25, 1945   Qudsi to the Syrian Minister of Foreign Affairs

Secret
Coded

From the Syrian Minister in the United States
to HE the Minister of Foreign Affairs, Damascus

I am now certain about two matters:

1 America will support the Jewish question to the end. It is trying with all its power to make Palestine into a Jewish stronghold in the heart of the Arab world, not because it hates the Arabs and wants to thwart them, but because it fears Great Britain and does not want the English to be the only ones controlling the Arab world. It is of the opinion that the Arabs obey the English and there is no sign showing that the Arabs will one day be able to challenge Great Britain.

This point of view greatly favors the return of Libya to Italy in order to avoid it falling into the hands of Great Britain as the English hope.

2 America has adopted France's viewpoint. Its understanding with de Gaulle is not merely a matter of form or simple economics, as the English are trying to say; it is a return to reason by America and is the application of its capitalist designs on the world. Thus, France tumbles back into the embrace of capitalism, once the danger of communism there has become clear.

Here, the whole diplomatic corps believes that America's help for General de Gaulle will stretch to the point where it will allow him to establish a French, non-Communist, democratic government under his control.

When considering our general political position I ask you to take this into consideration.

August 25, 1945

The Minister Plenipotentiary
S/ Nazim al-Qudsi

Registered in the Ministry of Foreign Affairs
No. 657/94 – Legation correspondence

177. August 25, 1945   Faris al-Khuri to Qudsi

Secret

The Syrian Minister Plenipotentiary in Washington,

You can categorically deny that the President of the Syrian Council of Ministers knows this:

The Syrian Government is not responsible for the efforts made by HH Prince Abd al-Ilah and which are designed to unify Syria and Iraq nor the efforts of HH Emir Abdullah towards the realization of Greater Syria.

We ask the noble American Government not to allow itself to be impressed by baseless proposals.

August 25, 1945   The President of the Council of Ministers
s/ Faris al-Khuri

Registered in the Ministry of Foreign Affairs
No. 651/98 – Diplomatic correspondence

178. August 25, 1945   Shone to Faris al-Khuri

Secret
>   To HE the President of the Council of Ministers, Damascus

While expressing my deepest regret to you, I would like to put before the President of the Syrian Republic a request which may not please him, but which only comes from good motives.

The present atmosphere is not proving propitious for HE's journey. It is better for us to wait some time before allowing his visit to London.
>   Yours affectionately,
August 25, 1945

>   The Minister Plenipotentiary
>   S/ T. Shone

Registered in the Ministry of Foreign Affairs
No. 698-289 – Diplomatic correspondence

179. August 27, 1945   Armanazi to the Syrian Minister of Foreign Affairs

Top secret
Coded telegram
>   From the Syrian Minister in London
>   to HE the Minister of Foreign Affairs, Damascus

Colonel Stirling has left, or in the next few days will leave, London for Syria.

I understood from what he told me that his Government agrees that he can resume his past activity, that is that he can fight against all traces of France in our country.

However, the second part of his mission, which is to be feared and with regard to which we must take our position, consists in getting Emir Abdullah crowned.

So far we have collaborated with the Colonel with the aim of removing France. Now the time has come to start building: that is, in our opinion, the removal.

I feel increasingly that we will find in him a redoubtable enemy.
August 27, 1945

>   The Minister Plenipotentiary
>   S/ Najib al-Armanazi

Registered in the Ministry of Foreign Affairs
No. 662/207 – Diplomatic correspondence

180. August 28, 1945   The Governor of Aleppo to Faris al-Khuri

Secret
Coded telegram
>   To HE the President of the Council of Ministers

Your Excellency should be made aware that the telegrams addressed to HE the President of the Republic asking for the dissolution of Parliament, new elections and the formulation of a new constitution, are inspired, according to my information, by the British authorities.

I am very surprised by this scandalous intervention in our internal affairs on the part of officials of a state which is an ally and friend.

I ask you to bring to an end this campaign, in which we will find ourselves forced to proceed to arresting the plotters.

August 28, 1945   The Muhafiz of Aleppo
                                                          S/ Ihsan al-Sharif

Copy sent to the Ministry of Foreign Affairs for information

181. August 29, 1945   Atasi to the Syrian Minister of Foreign Affairs

Secret
Coded telegram

From the Syrian Minister in Paris
to HE the Minister of Foreign Affairs, Damascus

Here people think that General de Gaulle brought a lot back from his trip to America, that the unanswered questions troubling France have been settled and that France obtained American support.

What is important from our point of view is that President Truman has given his agreement, from what I understood here, for Syria to be a zone of French influence and for a Jewish state to be created in Palestine, on condition that the remainder be unified with Transjordan.

The plan for Greater Syria is not well regarded in America, France does not count at the moment, officially proclaiming its intentions with regard to Syria; it will wait to start direct negotiations with England. If the understanding between the two states were realized – it is more than likely that it will be – the united colonizers will work to implement this program.

I repeat to you that it is not reasonable to allow ourselves to be deceived by the same British maneuvers from which we suffered at the end of the last world war.

August 29, 1945   The Minister Plenipotentiary
                                                          S/ Adnan al-Atasi

Registered in the Ministry of Foreign Affairs
No. 670/107

182. September 1, 1945   The British Legation to the Syrian
Minister of Foreign Affairs

Secret
To HE the Syrian Minister of Foreign Affairs
Your Excellency,

The relevant British civil servants have informed me that certain French agents and partisans are currently trying to hinder the activities of the Syro-Iraqi oil company by carrying out attacks on its personnel and installations.

This movement, according to information in my possession, will grow in size.

As a result, I ask you to put the matter to HE the Minister of the Interior so that the Syrian side can do what is necessary; for its part, the army charged with maintaining security and order will make the necessary arrangements.

With my deep respect,

September 1, 1945   S/ Evans

Registered in the Ministry of Foreign Affairs
No. 708/292 – Diplomatic correspondence

183. September 1, 1945   Azzam to the Syrian Minister of Foreign Affairs

Secret

To HE the Syrian Minister of Foreign Affairs

Greetings. HE the Egyptian Foreign Minister addressed a memorandum to the Council of the Arab League about the future of Tripolitania. He puts before the Council the question of the complete enfranchisement of Libya after altering its borders with Egypt (the Jeraboub plain and surrounding area) and asks for a Libyan representative to be co-opted to the Council of the Arab League.

HE knows about a British plan regarding Libya which consists of extending the authority of Great Britain over this country in the form of a pact of friendship and alliance; in his opinion this constitutes a great danger not only for Libya but also for Egypt.

I need to know Your Excellency's opinion on this before putting the matter to the General Council of the League at its next session.

Yours sincerely,

September 1, 1945   The Secretary General of the Arab League
                                             S/ Abd al-Rahman al-Azzam

Registered in the Ministry of Foreign Affairs
No. 710/37 – Diplomatic correspondence

184. September 2, 1945   Armanazi to the Syrian Minister of Foreign Affairs

Secret
Coded

From the Syrian Minister in London
to HE the Minister of Foreign Affairs, Damascus

The conference of British officials concerned with the Middle East will be decisive as far as the future of Syria is concerned.

Many influential and well-informed people have reassured me about Great Britain's policy; this aims in the first place to help the Arab League. As far as

Syria and Lebanon are concerned, it aims to destroy all French influence there.

The conference of British officials, according to what people are saying, recognizes that France's position was settled in Syria. The Ministry of Foreign Affairs will therefore not worry any more about France at this juncture. Anyway, the meeting of British officials will discuss the question of Greater Syria and the monarchy.

HE the President could clarify with the British official who is with him what is being said about this plan which is currently the main focus of studies being carried out here.

It is surprising to see all the British involved with Arab policy supporting the plan for Greater Syria; but they disagree on the future king: Emir Abdullah or Emir Abd al-Ilah, or King Faisal or Emir Faisal al-Sa'ud.

September 2, 1945   The Minister Plenipotentiary
                                                            S/ Najib al-Armanazi

Registered in the Ministry of Foreign Affairs
No. 654 – Political reports

185. September 2, 1945   The British Legation to the Syrian Prime Minister

Secret

From the British Legation
to HE the President of the Council of Ministers, Damascus

Your Excellency,

I am sorry, at a time when you are negotiating a difficult situation, to inform you of an observation by the British Government and military authorities charged with maintaining security.

The many rumors circulating among the public, followed by demands to dissolve Parliament, and the trouble reigning in the Ministries, are such as to weaken the authority of power and to make the Syrian Government lose much of its administrative and political esteem, which can, as you know, only bring enormous detriment to the country.

I hope that you will make an appeal to the patriotism of the Syrian deputies and officials in order to get out of this difficult situation which threatens the Syrian machinery of government with real danger.

I ask you to regard my actions as perfectly innocent and as being only sincere advice.

Yours respectfully,

September 2, 1945   S/ Evans

Registered in the Ministry of Foreign Affairs
No. 712/294 – Diplomatic correspondence

186. September 4, 1945   Armanazi to President Quwatli

Secret

From the Syrian Minister in London
to HE the President of the Republic, Damascus

The confusion reigning in the machinery of government places us in a position of great weakness from the international point of view and prejudices Syria's reputation as to its ability to consolidate its independence.

As a result I ask Your Excellency to do all you can to prevent new clashes between the Chamber and the Government.

Mr Campbell told me today that by this confusion Syria demonstrates its lack of political maturity and the inadequacy of its leaders. In his conversation he talked of our republican regime and criticized it. Perhaps he wanted to make me understand that the monarchical regime would be better for us. He reminded me of the French experience, anarchy and the frequency of its governments and told me that the republican regime, by its nature, embodies a lack of responsibility.

I do not know what the British plans are, but I believe that their attitude with regard to us is not warm, especially after the latest doings of the Chamber. September 4, 1945

The Minister Plenipotentiary
S/ Najib al-Armanazi

Sent to the Ministry of Foreign Affairs for decoding and information
Not yet registered in the Ministry

187. September 5, 1945   Armanazi to the Syrian Prime Minister

Secret
Coded

From the Syrian Minister in London
to HE the President of the Council of Ministers, Damascus

It is believed here that Mr Blum is coming to settle the situation between Great Britain and France.

There is no disagreement, General Spears tells me, between the two states except on the Franco-German borders to the West and the question of Syria.

In London they fear (the Conservatives) that Labour will assume, in their conversations with Blum, then officially with Bidault, positions detrimental to us.

The British Conservatives reject any understanding unless it is based on the definitive withdrawal of France from Syria. Their regret is raw at the moment because they sense the gravity of the danger.

For my part, I greatly fear that Blum's steps will end in a threat with regard to us, because he does not only represent France, but also all world Jewry. The latter is not very favorable to the plan for Greater Syria (which Labour will adopt) because this plan constitutes a danger for it far more than it guarantees it a field of action.

Blum's trip is very important.
September 5, 1945

The Minister Plenipotentiary
s/ Najib al-Armanazi

Not registered

188. September 5, 1945   Qudsi to the Syrian Prime Minister

Secret
Coded

From the Syrian Minister in the United States
to HE the President of the Council of Ministers, Damascus

I paid a congratulatory visit to the new Secretary of State. He began his conversation by saying to me, "Syria, which was already an interesting country as a bridge for global communications in the past, is now an important market for us. It is from this point of view that it interests us. We do not want anything particular from it, we only want a free market there."

The conversation moving on to the present and future position of Syria, the Minister told me, "Franco-English competition has been useful to you, but you must know how to preserve these advantages. You must not rid yourselves of French domination only to fall into English hands, as you are doing at the moment."

Talking of the future, he told me, "There will be no colonization in the future, because colonization in itself is an economic procedure protected by armies and armies are no longer justified these days; the largest space will be taken by economic forces, goods, their quality and price. I do not advise you to conclude commercial treaties with anyone because nowadays exclusive commercial treaties constitute true colonization. Leave your market free to us and to others. Great Britain's design, in intervening, is to subjugate you as well as your economy, that is, it only wants to colonize you."

These views are those of the new Secretary of State. I am giving them to you for all useful ends; they express the direction of American policy with regard to us.
September 5, 1945

The Minister Plenipotentiary
S/ Nazim al-Qudsi

Registered in the Ministry of Foreign Affairs
No. 659 – Political reports

189. September 8, 1945   Syrian Minister of Foreign Affairs
Mikha'il Ilyan to Armanazi

Secret
Coded

To HE the Syrian Minister Plenipotentiary, London

HE the President of the Syrian Republic has requested me to ask you to protest to the Foreign Office about particular British officers and officials in Syria who act in favor of Emir Abdullah.

HE the President has had to put up with a great deal from this propaganda, which only tends to diminish the prestige of Syrian power and to harm the constitutional republican regime. He has also drawn the attention of the British authorities to the following question: how to coordinate the genuine help Great Britain is giving to Syrian independence and the activities of Emir Abdullah, known to be under English control?

It is no longer possible to put up with Colonel Stirling's action and the services dependent on it, and the clear support which the British Consul in Damascus gives to Emir Abdullah's propagandists.

I ask you to reply to me as soon as possible on this matter.

September 8, 1945   The Minister of Foreign Affairs
                                                              S/ Mikha'il Ilyan

Registered in the Ministry of Foreign Affairs
No. 739/304 – Diplomatic correspondence

190. September 9, 1945   Armanazi to the Syrian Minister of Foreign Affairs

Secret
Coded

                    HE the Syrian Minister of Foreign Affairs, Damascus

The conference of British officials in the Middle East is regarded as the most serious one held for a long time in the history of the Empire. The questions dealt with by this conference are huge. The future of Great Britain and the life of the Empire generally depend on it.

Here it is believed, as I indicated to you in a previous report, that the struggle and rivalry between Great Britain and America will be fierce from the point of view of the markets and economy of the Middle East. It is for these reasons that the Ministers Plenipotentiary and the British specialists will work to find appropriate ways of maintaining a British zone of economic influence in the Near and Middle East.

In addition, the struggle and rivalry will be fierce between Russia and Great Britain, as much from the economic point of view as from the point of view of political influence. The officials will examine how it may be possible to erect definitive barriers in the face of Russia and the Communist movement.

As for France, it will only count according to its inclinations; if it leans towards Russia it will finally be chased out of Syria; but if it remains within the Anglo-Saxon bloc – as people here forecast – the situation will change and a formula to maintain its influence in the Orient – within the framework of the Anglo-Saxon group – will be found.

September 9, 1945

                                                     The Minister Plenipotentiary
                                                          S/ Najib al-Armanazi

Registered in the Ministry of Foreign Affairs
No. 672 – Political reports

191. September 10, 1945   Armanazi to the Syrian Minister of Foreign Affairs

Secret
Coded

From the Syrian Minister in London
to HE the Syrian Minister of Foreign Affairs, Damascus

I have learned from well-informed sources that the conference of British officials, currently gathered at Whitehall, is discussing the following points:

1   The position of Great Britain with regard to the Arab League. Is it in Britain's interest to reinforce and support it, after the experiment in Syria and Lebanon and the annoying moves that resulted on the part of Egypt and Iraq?
2   The question of withdrawing British troops from Syria and Lebanon, then from Egypt, and the outcomes which may result from all these troubles.
3   Defining and modifying Great Britain's stand on the Franco-Syrian question. Should the policy of the Conservatives – to satisfy Syria at the expense of France – be followed, or the opposite? Is it possible to find a middle way, and what is it?
4   To find a solution to the Palestinian question. What help can the Arabs provide in order to reach this solution?
5   To take the necessary measures in the case of incidents and engagements with the Jews of Palestine.
6   To define Great Britain's definitive position with regard to France in the Orient.

These are the matters under discussion at the conference, such as I have been informed. I am sure that no decision has yet been taken on any of these matters.
September 10, 1945   The Minister Plenipotentiary
                                                        S/ Najib al-Armanazi

Registered in the Ministry of Foreign Affairs
No. 673 – Political reports

192. September 11, 1945   Armanazi to the Syrian Minister of Foreign Affairs

Secret
Coded

The Syrian Minister of Foreign Affairs, Damascus

"The British Foreign Secretary is completely unaware of activities by his civil servants intended to support Emir Abdullah Ibn Hussein's point of view in Syria.

He has not asked anyone to work against the Syrian republican regime which he has recognized and supported.

He will work to put an end to all this."

That is a summary of the statement made to me today in the British Foreign Office.

September 11, 1945   The Minister Plenipotentiary
                                                       S/ Najib al-Armanazi

Registered in the Ministry of Foreign Affairs
No. 752/310 – Diplomatic correspondence

193. September 12, 1945   King Ibn Sa'ud to President Quwatli

Secret

Coded telegram sent through the intermediary of the Saudi Legation
from King Ibn Sa'ud
to HE the President of the Syrian Republic.

King Faruq will visit us soon in Jeddah. At the moment he sees two dangerous matters on which he wants us to reach an understanding and agreement.

The first is that of Palestine and the increase in the number of Jews.

The second is that of the Hashemites.

For the Jewish Question, we are determined to do everything in our power to oppose the Jews.

The question of the Hashemites remains. King Faruq realizes the threat they constitute and, as for us, we formally reject any plan of this kind.

All I hope for at the moment is to learn your opinion on the matter quickly.

May God preserve you,

6 Shawwal 1364 (September 12, 1945)   S/ Abd al-Aziz
Not registered in the Ministry

194. September 12, 1945   Armanazi to the Syrian Prime Minister

Secret
Coded

To HE the President of the Council of Ministers, Damascus

General Spears has asked me for the Syrian Government's help in a matter of interest to him personally.

The area north of Tel Aviv in Palestine is the property of Arabs and the town of Tel Aviv is in desperate need of these lands.

The British plan for Palestine involves this area which it will certainly include in land conceded to the Jews. The General thinks that the Arabs' profit would be double if they sold this land to the Jews and if they got a good price; this if the sale takes place today, otherwise the sale will be compulsory and the price derisory.

I therefore ask you to work with our Palestinian brothers so that they ease this sale which is not detrimental to them and do not hinder it.

September 12, 1945   s// Najib al-Armanazi

Private letter wired through – not yet registered

195. September 12, 1945   Armanazi to the Syrian Minister of Foreign Affairs

Secret

Coded telegram

From the Syrian Minister in London
to HE the Syrian Minister of Foreign Affairs, Damascus

We must turn our attention to Iraqi policy, for a semblance of an alliance is operating at the moment and may crystallize between Iraq and Turkey.

Militant circles here rejoice in the steps taken by the Prince Regent of Iraq to create this bloc which will include the states of the Arab League and those of the Sa'adabad Pact.

The obstruction sought by British policy in the Middle East will be strengthened again when Egypt joins it.

In this spirit of friendship, Great Britain leaves under discussion the affairs of the Middle East and turns towards the Zionist question which it considers to be a source of danger.

On the proposal for a military, political and economic alliance between the states of the Arab League and those of the Sa'adabad Pact, Great Britain wants to establish solid friendships against the Russian danger which is on the point of greatly threatening the Mediterranean basin.

In all this, it seems to me that Great Britain will not support France and will force it to withdraw from Syria, offering it compensation in other regions, Indochina for example.

It is essential that somewhere in this plan we reinforce our internal border so that it will not disintegrate and Great Britain will not consider itself forced to neglect us and make us march despite ourselves.

September 12, 1945   The Minister Plenipotentiary
                                                               S/ Najib al-Armanazi

Registered in the Ministry of Foreign Affairs
No. 629 – Political reports

196. September 15, 1945   Qudsi to the Syrian Prime Minister

Secret

Coded

From the Syrian Minister in the United States
To the President of the Council of Ministers, Damascus

President Truman is obliged to support Jewish demands in Palestine. He advises us to be wise and accept a compromise solution for the installation in Palestine of an adequate number of Jewish émigrés.

The American Secretary of State for Foreign Affairs will strongly support the British Government, but this support will be given in response to the call by the British whose intentions coincide absolutely with American intentions regarding justice to be given to the largest possible number of Jews.

That is the declaration word-for-word which was made to me concerning the position of the Secretary of State. The American point of view is in agreement with the English point of view; it is wholly contrary to our own, and must be regarded as a mortal danger for us.

We must realize from now that the danger is in London and not in Washington.

September 15, 1945

The Minister Plenipotentiary
S/ Nazim al-Qudsi

Registered in the Ministry of Foreign Affairs
No. 693 – Political reports

197. September 15, 1945   King Ibn Sa'ud to President Quwatli

Secret

From King Ibn Sa'ud
Correspondence in code sent through the intermediary
of the Saudi Legation in Damascus
to HE the President of the Syrian Republic

Nuri al-Sa'id's activities are beginning to take a serious turn. We are unable to allow Abdullah's plots. By God, your attitude is strange. People are working for your death and you do not move. I learned that in Damascus Abdullah's propagandists are exerting themselves as much as possible. What are you waiting for? We know, as you do, who supports and controls them. Why don't you speak? God has ordered us not to be quiet when it is a matter of right, and has called someone who does not speak out a demon.

I ask you to appreciate the gravity of the situation. The anarchy reigning with you weakens any hope of success and it is sad to see that it is spreading. Can you not find a way to settle the situation instead of letting these scandals develop? Your situation pains us. It was not like this under French rule. Someone who enjoys my confidence told me that people are beginning to miss the period of French rule. Do something before your edifice falls down.

9 Shawwal 1364 (September 15, 1945)

S/ Abd al-Aziz

Not registered in the Ministry

198. September 16, 1945   President Quwatli to King Ibn Sa'ud

Secret

Coded telegram sent through the intermediary of the Saudi Legation in
Damascus
to HM the King Abd al-Aziz al-Sa'ud, Riyadh

What you so kindly said is very accurate. The Jews support Abdullah, and
the question of Palestine and the Zionist Jews is completely linked to that of
the Hashemite throne of Greater Syria.

Our delay, Your Majesty, in occupying ourselves with those working for our
downfall stems from the fact that the blue-eyed people sometimes support
these and sometimes support those.

Our unhappiness with all these infidels is great.

I beg Your Majesty to agree with HM King Faruq on a line of conduct to
save Palestine and save us from the Jews and Emir Abdullah.

I also beg you to reach an understanding with HM to make the greatest effort
with the aim of ridding Syria and Lebanon of the remaining criminal French.

10 Shawwal 1364 (September 16, 1945)

The President of the Syrian Republic

S/ Shukri al-Quwatli

Not registered in the Ministry

199. September 16, 1945   Atasi to the Syrian Prime Minister

Secret
Coded

From the Syrian Minister in Paris
to HE the President of the Syrian Council, Damascus.

I will summarize the French Government's official position for you:

1 The French Government is still insisting on maintaining its troops in Syria
   and Lebanon to oversee communication routes and to protect France's
   traditional interests in the Orient.
2 France continues to insist on intervening in general Syrian affairs, at the
   very least from the point of view of international policy.
3 France's ambitions with regard to Syrian oil are very great.
4 France wants to make the Syro-Lebanese ports into bases for its fleet.
5 The French continue to talk of their cultural interests.
6 The French continue to want to intervene in Syria and Lebanon in order
   to protect Christian denominational interests.
7 The French, having realized that Great Britain wants to get rid of them in order
   to take their place, is becoming more and more attached to Syria and Lebanon.
8 With all that, the French want to reach an understanding with Syria. They
   believe that they will succeed in all their ambitions, because Great Britain's
   interest requires that they are satisfied.

My personal opinion can only be hostile to all these ambitions. I see clearly that each of the Great Powers wants to have in Syria what France itself is seeking.

September 16, 1945   The Minister Plenipotentiary
                                                         S/ Adnan al-Atasi

Registered in the Ministry of Foreign Affairs
No. 694 – Political reports

200. September 24, 1945   Mikha'il Ilyan to Quwatli

Secret

To HE the President of the Syrian Republic

HE Mr Porter, Chargé d'Affaires to the American Legation in Damascus, visited me today and spoke to me about the following:

1 The American Government does not have any document relating to a promise made by Mr Roosevelt to King Ibn Sa'ud or to any other Arab leader on the question of Palestine.
2 The American Government cannot, at the current time, sell on credit any merchandise whatsoever originally in the possession of American troops in the Levant, but it is inclined to be conciliatory as far as prices are concerned.
3 Any American cultural plan enjoys the concern of the American Government. As a result it asks the Syrian Government to be as benevolent as possible towards the existing American schools. This benevolence alone will encourage the Americans to support the current plans for teaching and public health.
4 As for the French schools, the Syrian Government's position with regard to French institutions is a matter which concerns it alone. America will not intervene in any way in favor of the French.

September 24, 1945   The Minister of Foreign Affairs
                                                         S/ Mikha'il Ilyan

Not yet registered

201. September 24, 1945   French intelligence report on a Saudi attempt to mediate between President Quwatli and France

Beirut, September 24, 1945

Memorandum

Mr Hussein Awaini, Ibn Sa'ud's Commercial Agent in Beirut, dined in Zabadani on September 21 with the President of the Syrian Republic. He had a long conversation with the President of the Syrian Republic on this occasion.

According to Mr Awaini, Shukri Bey appeared to be very well informed about Emir Abdullah's monarchist propaganda and the role Colonel Stirling plays in this. Shukri Bey even confided to his interlocutor that he had recently summoned Mr Young to see him in order to express his astonishment to him about the monarchist activity started by the English, in particular by Colonel Stirling. At the end of the conversation, the President seems to have demanded the recall of this British officer. Apparently he later made it known that if need be he would not hesitate, despite his presidential duties, to go into the streets to fight the English.

Mr Awaini, having observed that, all in all, the English were far from being true friends and that, on the contrary, the French were not the enemies people had imagined, Shukri Bey agreed. However he added that in the current state of opinion, he did not see how he could resume contact with the French authorities.

To the remark that opinion was fluid and that Shukri Bey could perhaps meet secretly somewhere in Lebanon (at Awaini's for example) and have a frank discussion with General Beynet, Shukri Bey replied, "Yes." However, after deeper consideration of this suggestion the President preferred to leave the duty of talking to King Ibn Sa'ud concerning the situation in Syria to his interlocutor. Shukri Bey said that he was ready, if the King invited him, to go to Cairo, where, in the presence of His Majesty, he would agree to speak with an authorized French personality.

During his conversation with the President, Mr Awaini said that he had noted many times Ibn Sa'ud's wish to see the Syrians reach an understanding with France so that England would not remain alone in Arab lands. Shukri Bey seems to have decided that this view was judicious, but that unfortunately he did not see how he could come to terms with the French.

While Mr Awaini was at Shukri Bey's residence the latter called Ahmad Laham, Director of Police, and seems to have made harsh observations about the aggression which Mr Cuinet was the victim of. The President indicated to the Director of Police that he would hold him personally responsible for the non-discovery of the guilty parties. In the conversation, Shukri Bey may have put his interlocutor on guard against British meddling in this matter, in particular, against that of Abadin Husseini, the Palestinian official imposed by the English as an adviser to the Syrian police. According to Mr Awaini, the President seems to have allowed it to be understood that the British were perhaps not uninvolved in the Cuinet incident and that in any case they had an interest in seeing more such incidents.

202. September 26, 1945   Report of the Syrian Deuxième Bureau

Secret

Secret Report
to HE the Director General of the Police

I am informing you that I have received trustworthy information about General Pilleau's and HE Colonel Stirling's journey into the desert.

According to my information, Colonel Stirling talked to all the Sheikhs and Emirs of the steppe, with whom they were in touch (cf. my detailed report of yesterday) and asked them to grant their support and provide signatures in favor of the plan for unity with Transjordan, under the aegis of Emir Abdullah (descendant of the Prophet).

I have learned that large sums of money were distributed to them. Emir Fawaz alone received five thousand pounds sterling.

As for Emir Fawaz, it is established that he received money from the colonel, but I do not know how much; however, I know that he has not signed the mazbata.
September 26, 1945

The Commissioner of the Research Team
S/ Sa'id al-Nabulsi

Report sent to the Ministry of the Interior
Copy sent for information to the Ministry of Foreign Affairs

203. September 27, 1945   Mikha'il Ilyan to Armanazi

Secret
Coded

To the Syrian Minister Plenipotentiary, London

HE Nuri Pasha Sa'id has conveyed to our President formal assurances about the terms of which Turkey, in agreeing with us, neither seeks to dominate us nor to intervene in our affairs and that it is not therefore reasonable, if we cannot obtain the return of the Sanjak, to maintain hostility towards Turkey and to adopt this position of boycott at a time when we are threatened by common dangers.

The Government, before deciding anything related to this, wants to know through your channels, if the British Government currently sees any drawback to its acting as intermediary. We ask it for its guarantee for any agreement Turkey concludes with us, so that if it is broken, or in the case of territorial ambitions, it will agree to help us and remedy the situation.

Only under these conditions do we agree to reach an understanding with the Turks in whose promises we have little confidence.
September 27, 1945

The Minister of Foreign Affairs
S/ Mikha'il Ilyan

Not yet registered in the Ministry

204. End of September 1945   Nuri al-Sa'id's memorandum to Azzam

Secret

From Nuri Pasha Sa'id, ex-President of the
Iraqi Council of Ministers

MEMORANDUM
to the venerable Secretary of the Arab League

The Iraqi Government proposes to the Government of the Syrian Republic an examination of the present and future of the twenty-five million Arabs and Muslims of Morocco with a spirit of fairness and justice.

France, which has tried and continues to try to be an obstacle in the way of Syrian independence, has reduced to nothing the very foundations of existence of our Arab Moroccan brothers' spirits, and has destroyed their sacred principles, throwing them into ignorance and impoverishing them.

The only way in which they will be enfranchised lies in the swift adoption of their cause by the Arab League.

I have obtained the formal promise of the Great Powers to support the League in lending help to the Algerians, Tunisians and Moroccans to free themselves from the French yoke.

The Iraqi Government would be very happy for the question about this help to be asked and for independent, free Syria to be a support for our brothers by providing them with the desired help.

Copy marked: s/ Nuri al-Sa'id

Registered in the Ministry of Foreign Affairs
No. 729 – Documents

205. End of September 1945 Nuri al-Sa'id's memorandum on his Fertile Crescent plan

Secret

From Nuri Pasha Sa'id, ex-President of the Iraqi Council of Ministers

Memorandum

The Iraqi Government proposes to the Government of the Syrian Republic a study of the new situation from which will flow a balancing of the global political blocs, particularly in the region of "al-Hilal al-Khassib"(*).

The representative of the Iraqi Government begs the Syrian Government to examine the possibility of an understanding and a firm agreement between the states which are signatories to the Arab League pact on one hand and those of the Sa'adabad Pact on the other.

The advantages for the two parties will be in the consolidation of bases for security and peace in the Middle East and in the brotherhood between Muslims.

The Iraqi Government Representative is disposed to discuss this and to provide the necessary details.

Undated

S/ Nuri al-Sa'id

Note

* The region stretching from the Gulf of Alexandretta to the Persian Gulf. Literally the "Fertile Crescent."

Registered in the Ministry of Foreign Affairs
No. 727 – Documents

206. September 30, 1945   Qudsi to the Syrian Prime Minister

Secret
Coded

From the Syrian Minister in the USA
to the President of the Council of Ministers, Damascus

Today I became certain that Emir Abd al-Ilah and his companion Nuri Pasha Sa'id sold the bearskin before they had killed the bear.

The information in my possession establishes that Nuri Pasha came to an agreement here with the Jews to grant them all the necessary facilities to establish a Jewish state. He has officially promised them in the name of the Iraqi Government – and not in words or through the press – that a Jewish state will be created in Palestine, that they will be given the southern part of Lebanon, and that they will be permitted to maintain relations with the planned Greater Syria, relations analogous to those which currently exist between Lebanon and Syria, that is to say without customs borders or passports, or any other similar restrictions.

I do not know the sort of discussions you have had in Damascus with Nuri al-Sa'id, but I know that he is lying to you and that he is not revealing his real intentions.

September 30, 1945   The Minister Plenipotentiary
                                        S/ Nazim al-Qudsi

Registered in the Ministry of Foreign Affairs
No. 724 – Political reports

207. Early October 1945   Nuri al-Sa'id's memorandum to the Syrian government

Secret

From Nuri Pasha Sa'id, ex-President of the Iraqi Council of Ministers
Memorandum

The Iraqi Government proposes to the Government of the Syrian Republic examining with indulgence and a spirit of open-mindedness the current situation between it and the Turkish Republic with the aim of reaching a settlement.

The Government of the Turkish Republic is disposed for its part to accept an exchange of population between the Arab inhabitants remaining in Turkey or Hatay (Alexandretta) and the Turkish residents in Syria (or those of Turkish origin).

The Iraqi Government for its part will ensure the possibility of holding a plebiscite in Hatay to decide on the Syrian or Turkish fate of the Liwa.

This Syro-Turkish understanding, in favor of which the Iraqi Government proposes its mediation, is an essential factor in guaranteeing the rights of Syria and for peace in the future.

Undated   s/ Nuri al-Sa'id

Registered in the Ministry of Foreign Affairs
No. 728 – Documents

208. October 3, 1945 Qudsi to the Syrian Prime Minister

Secret
Coded

From the Syrian Minister in the USA
to HE the President of the Council of Ministers, Damascus

In accordance with your request, I have visited the Under-Secretary of State for Foreign Affairs with my fellow Arab representatives. I set out very frankly to him that the American Government's position, represented by President Truman, has been harshly rejected by the Arab world and by my Government, and that we would ask the American Government to change this position.

The reply that was categorically made to us is that the American Government has not yet openly defined its position with regard to the Palestinian question, that it does not seek to do the Arabs wrong or to oppress our brothers in Palestine, but that it pities the Jews and that it does not see any solution to their growing difficulties other than sheltering them in Palestine.

I set before him clearly and in detail our point of view. He promised me to look into the matter; he hopes to arrive at a solution which suits both the Arabs and the Jews, but he believes that this will not be possible until after the meeting of American officials in the countries of the Near and Middle East and once he has received their personal opinions. The Government will swiftly follow this up with a consultation with the British Government in order to adopt a solution which will be put to the Arabs and the Jews.

Mr Acheson has confirmed to me that he was hoping to arrive at a solution which would satisfy the two parties, if not completely, by at least fifty per cent.

October 3, 1945   The Minister Plenipotentiary
                                                        s/ Nazim al-Qudsi

Registered in the Ministry of Foreign Affairs
No. 728 – Political reports

209. October 3, 1945 King Ibn Sa'ud to President Quwatli

Secret
Coded telegram

From King Ibn Sa'ud
to his dear brother Shukri Bey Quwatli, President of the Syrian Republic

Greetings and divine mercy. Hafiz Wahba (*) tells us that he has fulfilled the mission we gave him and which consists of making the British Government understand and reminding it once again of our opposition to Abdullah's kingship. Syria belongs to none other than its inhabitants. We will accept the plan for Greater Syria if it is republican in form with Damascus as the capital; otherwise we demand a plebiscite.

All these proposals were presented by Hafiz who told us today that the English do not want to upset us, that they will reach agreement with the French to maintain the status quo in Syria and that they will proceed to new elections which will decide the situation.

That is what I have learned. I am informing you. Greetings.

27 Shawwal 1364 (October 3, 1945)

S/ Abd al-Aziz Ibn Abd al-Rahman
Faisal al-Sa'ud

Registered in the Ministry of Foreign Affairs
No. 732 – Political documents

Note

(*) Saudi Minister in London

210. October 4, 1945   Armanazi to the Syrian Minister of Foreign Affairs

Secret
Coded

From the Syrian Minister in London
to HE the Syrian Minister of Foreign Affairs, Damascus

The plan on which the British reached agreement with the French rests on the separation of the Syrian question from the Lebanese one.

Here it is now considered certain that Syria will be, by virtue of this agreement, a British zone of influence and Lebanon a French zone of influence, that is to say that each of these two Powers will see themselves granted strategic positions by the international Security Council.

As for the plan for Greater Syria, it will be restricted. After a Jewish state will have been set up in Palestine (where America and England will have the duty of exercising their sovereignty), a new state of Lebanon will be formed, with the loss of the southern part. Part of the Alawites will be annexed to it.

France will keep its share in Syrian oil.

That is a summary of the agreement as it was reported to me by certain well-informed people worthy of trust.

October 4, 1945

The Minister Plenipotentiary
S/ Najib al-Armanazi

Registered in the Ministry of Foreign Affairs
No. 729 – Political reports

211. October 5, 1945   Solod to the Syrian Minister of Foreign Affairs

Secret

From the Minister of the USSR in Syria
to HE the Syrian Minister of Foreign Affairs

<u>Note</u>

My Government has asked me to enquire of your Ministry about the efforts Nuri al-Sa'id is making and which, in addition to defense of the Palestinian question, have, I believe, a bearing on other plans which threaten security in the Middle East, and which are related to high politics.

My information regarding Mr Sa'id's plans in Syria – which are of course not on his own initiative, but for which he is authorized to act – consist of the abolition of the Syrian Republic and the establishment of a Hashemite monarchy. Does the Syrian Government know this?

As far as the formation of an Eastern Islamic bloc goes, it seems that he wants, or is asked, to work towards the creation of a cordon sanitaire around the Soviet Union. Does Syria wish to take part in that?

As for Palestine, Mr Sa'id wants to give, or is asked to give, the Jews a state at the expense of Palestine, the Arabs, Lebanese and Syrians. Does the Syrian Government know that?

In placing these truths before the Syrian Government, I would like to know if it is wholly aware of them and what its inclinations are with regard to accepting or rejecting these plans.

October 5, 1945   s/ D. Solod

Registered in the Ministry of Foreign Affairs
No. 815/42 – Diplomatic correspondence

212. October 7, 1945   King Ibn Sa'ud to President Quwatli

Coded

From King Ibn Sa'ud
to Brother Shukri bey Quwatli, President of the Syrian Republic
May God protect him

Greetings and divine mercy. Bashir (*) has told us of the plans you have to remedy your problems. On the one hand we advise you to make yourself the complcte master of Abdullah's men and on the other hand not to rush yourself, for fear that the English will bother you.

At the moment, I do not believe that the French are your enemies. Therefore avoid worrying about a danger which does not exist. The only danger for you and for us are the Jews and no one else.

Your current difficulties are due to a corrupt parliament which you must get rid of by dissolving it; but who can guarantee that in the event of dissolution, you will not have an even worse chamber? This parliament has English partisans and French partisans; but in a chamber coming from the popular vote, there will, in Bashir's opinion, be only English partisans. In that case, it will act as it sees fit and will perhaps vote for the monarchy against your wishes. You yourself will be finished.

That is my advice. Greetings.

1 Dhu al-Qa'da 1364 (October 7, 1945)

S/ Abd al-Aziz Ibn Abd al-Rahman
Faisal al-Sa'ud

Registered in the Ministry of Foreign Affairs
No. 733 – Political documents

Note

(*) Bashir Sa'adawi, Personal Adviser to the King who is spending the summer in Syria.

213. October 7, 1945   Sa'adallah al-Jabiri, the Syrian Prime Minister and Minister of Foreign Affairs, to President Quwatli

Secret

Report from Sa'adallah al-Jabiri, President of the Council
to HE the President of the Republic
and the
Noble Council of Ministers

Below is a summary of the conversation that I had today with Colonel Stirling and from which you may conclude that the letter from our Minister Plenipotentiary in London concerning the meeting of British diplomatic representatives of last month, contained some truth.

Colonel Stirling is capable of declaring, according to information that has reached him even here, that the British Government has almost completely refined the policy which the current ministry will follow in the affairs of Syria. This policy will remain a state secret, but this state secret will be revealed gradually as it is carried out in practice.

For the moment the British Government will officially refer to the Syrian Government the following matters:

"Great Britain is disposed to lending Syria its sincere aid to increase its agricultural and industrial production. It will welcome every proposition from the Syrian Government aimed at reinforcing economic and commercial relations between Syria and Great Britain, as it will also welcome every effort or proposition aimed at consolidating political relations between it and Syria."

These proposals, as Your Excellency can see, are very vague; but the resumption of discussions to conclude an Anglo-Syrian commercial agreement, Great Britain's effort to establish a special regulation for the equivalence of Syrian currency and that of other Arab countries tied to sterling by modifying the statute attaching us to the French Franc, all this constitutes proof that Great Britain is determined to move to action. It seems that it will settle economic matters before political matters. This is in complete agreement with the letter from our Minister Plenipotentiary.

October 7, 1945

The Minister of Foreign Affairs
President of the Council
S/ Sa'adallah al-Jabiri

Registered in the Ministry of Foreign Affairs
No. 733 – Political reports

214. October 7, 1945   Qudsi to Jabiri

Secret
Coded

From the Syrian Minister in the United States
to HE the Syrian Minister of Foreign Affairs

The American point of view on the Jewish question of Palestine does not rest either on encouraging the Jews or on the solicitude to give them. Here they aim to bring about a balance in the East between Great Britain and America. I heard with my own ears many American senators saying that the Arab League is only an English plaything destined to be shaken in the face of any Power that seeks an influence in Arab lands. Great Britain has used it (the League) against France. It intends to use it against the Russians if they try to reach an agreement in the Mediterranean, and against the Americans who currently have real interests in the Middle East.

Whatever efforts we make, America will try very hard to create a real Jewish position in Palestine with the aim of balancing the Arab influence in the Near East and in upsetting it permanently. The reason for this is that all the Arabs lean towards the British policy without taking the precautions necessary for adopting the appearance of justice and equity with regard to all the foreigners.

In my opinion, it is the Russians alone who will profit from this domestic fight between the Americans and the English, of which we Arabs in general and the Muslims in particular will be the victims.

I ask you to concern yourself seriously with these thorny issues.

October 7, 1945

The Minister Plenipotentiary
S/ Nazim al-Qudsi

Registered in the Ministry of Foreign Affairs
No. 734 – Political reports

215. October 7, 1945   Jabiri to Shone

Secret

From Sa'adallah al-Jabiri, President of the Council of Ministers
To HE the Minister Plenipotentiary to the Government of HM the King of
Great Britain, Damascus

Your Excellency,

The Syrian Government has received with much satisfaction your generous letter concerning the clandestine passage of Jews to Palestine. It will make sure to punish severely those Syrian officials to whom you refer, if they exist; but the Syrian security services note that this clandestine passage occurs not thanks to help from Syrian officials but, on the contrary, because of British officials who may be of Jewish origin. I can tell you, to be precise, that the name of the official, Players, is always cited in the reports which reach the Syrian Government whenever there is any activity relating to the smuggling of arms, drugs and the Jews.

For our part, we will do the necessary. I thank you for so kindly drawing my attention to all this.

Yours sincerely,
October 7, 1945

The President of the Council
The Minister of Foreign Affairs
s/ Sa'adallah al-Jabiri

Registered in the Ministry of Foreign Affairs
No. 822/342 – Diplomatic correspondence

216. October 7, 1945   Armanazi to Jabiri

Secret
Coded

From the Syrian Minister in London
to the Syrian Minister of Foreign Affairs, Damascus

Today I talked to Mr Ronald Campbell of the Foreign Office about the Palestinian question and the Jewish demands. He said to me, "The Arabs of Palestine and those of Syria cannot settle the global Zionist question by themselves, because you are small and are tiny in number; but if you Arabs were to group together, the Zionist question would settle itself." Having asked him for details, he said to me, "Why don't you unite with Iraq? Iraq and you, you would form a large body on which the Jews would founder without a trace."

I am sending you the suggestions of an official in a position of responsibility. I note that if a plan such as this were to come about, an important area would be opened to the State of Israel from the Tigris to the Sea. The Jews would no longer need to do anything other than reach an understanding among themselves and develop inside this united state. We no longer know exactly if that is the British plan for the Middle East or if the plan for Greater Syria is still Great Britain's real plan.

October 7, 1945

The Minister Plenipotentiary
S/ Najib al-Armanazi

Registered in the Ministry of Foreign Affairs
No. 732 – Political reports

217. October 8, 1945   The Syrian Legation in Baghdad to Jabiri

Secret letter

From the Syrian Legation in Baghdad
to HE the Syrian Minister of Foreign Affairs, Damascus

Your Excellency,

HRH Emir Abdullah's visit has provoked a lot of commotion here. Discussion of the plan for Syrian unity has begun once again, Emir Abdullah being the king expected for the forthcoming state.

In accordance with Your Excellency's request, I worked with the best sources in order to discover the real situation. I managed to get from Sabah bey Sa'id, Nuri al-Sa'id's son, some words which may perhaps allow us to learn the truth.

The main thing is that I have learned that the solution is no longer in the hands of Emir Abdullah and that the new plan, which has the agreement of America, England and Turkey, consists of unifying the lands of Iraq and Syria under one scepter, that of Faisal II, with Prince Abd al-Ilah as regent.

What has already been established is that everyone is currently avoiding talking about this plan, which has not been openly the subject of discussions, but which has been coldly indicated to Emir Abdullah. A lively incident on this subject took place between uncle and nephew. Nuri Pasha Sa'id has said nothing about this to anyone, but there is no doubt that he is working to surround it with a favorable atmosphere and that he will do all he can for its success.

I will inform Your Excellency of everything I find out.

With my deepest respect,

Baghdad, October 8, 1945

The Chargé d'Affaires of the Syrian Legation
s/ Baha al-Din al-Bakri

Registered in the Ministry of Foreign Affairs
No. 736 – Political reports

218. October 8, 1945   Qudsi to Jabiri

Secret
Coded

From the Syrian Minister in the USA
to HE the Syrian Minister of Foreign Affairs, Damascus

The American Government is very concerned about the Oriental bloc plan and its repercussions in Syria and the countries of the Middle East. This plan, to which you alluded in your letter of October 1, and which was explained by Nuri Pasha Sa'id is regarded as very serious from the American point of view, and as directed against the United States of America.

Here they think that Great Britain will work to preserve the friendship of the Arabs, but that this friendship is surrounded by the greatest of dangers for the Arabs themselves. When Russia clearly demonstrated its intentions of having an outlet and bases in the Mediterranean, Great Britain – with the aim of preserving its position in the Arab countries which are all still subject to its influence – only had to win their friendship and make a show of their gratitude. It seems that Great Britain had judged in advance the outcome of events and that is why it supported Syria's independence to the point where it irritated France.

Now, Great Britain's new aim is to convince the Syrians to wind up their affairs with France in a way that will satisfy both parties; which means that it will take the place of France in occupying the Arab lands it judges necessary to occupy; that is what bothers Russia and dashes our hopes.

The American Government for its part will work to make the Oriental Bloc plan fail, a plan which it considers to be a British plan directed not only against Russia, but also against America, with the aim of closing access to the Levant to its influence and economy.

October 8, 1945

The Minister Plenipotentiary
S/ Nazim al-Qudsi

Registered in the Ministry of Foreign Affairs
No. 737 – Political reports

219. October 8, 1945   Charles Dundas, head of the MI6 station in Beirut, to Jabiri

Secret

From the British Legation
to HE the Syrian Minister of Foreign Affairs, Damascus

Verbal note

HE the President of the Syrian Republic had asked HE General Paget to fix a firm date for the withdrawal of French and British forces.

As far as the withdrawal of these forces goes, this Legation notified you, in a note sent to you on September 29 last, of the decision reached by the General during his visit to London.

For the moment, I can confirm to you that the withdrawal of Allied forces, the British in particular, will depend on the ability of the Syrian army to maintain security and police the borders. This ability will become apparent in the course of the next maneuvers it carries out.

Great Britain's deepest desire is to see the Syrian army really capable of maintaining security and peace in this area of imperial communication.

October 8, 1945

For the British Legation
s/ Dundas

Registered in the Ministry of Foreign Affairs
No. 745 – Documents

220. October 9, 1945 Armanazi to Jabiri

Secret
Coded

From the Syrian Minister in London
to HE the Syrian Minister of Foreign Affairs, Damascus

I have fulfilled at the Foreign Office the mission you entrusted to me in your letter dated October 4. The replies I received are listed below:

First issue – They agree on the whole line; evacuation will definitely take place. Having asked about strategic bases I was told: it is not us who will decide on the matter, it is the five Powers. If necessity demands that bases be created by Great Britain, they will be, with no restrictions.

Second issue – HM the King's Government has not yet taken a firm decision. The matter is under discussion. Nothing will happen regarding the Palestinian question until after it has been presented to the Arab League.

Third issue – The British Government rejects all officials and any act likely to create a plan against the Republic. It is up to the Syrians alone to decide the shape of government that suits them. The British Government does not want to intervene. If a British official says the opposite, he is only expressing his personal opinion and not that of his Government.

Fourth issue – Officials here believe that the moment is not the best for discussing it.

These are the answers I was able to get. I think that they are not enough, but I am sending them to Your Excellency.

October 9, 1945   The Minister Plenipotentiary
                                                   s/ Najib al-Armanazi

Registered in the Ministry of Foreign Affairs
No. 738 – Political reports

221. October 9, 1945 Dundas to Jabiri

Secret

From the British Legation
to HE the Syrian Minister of Foreign Affairs, Damascus

Verbal memorandum

The British authorities have received from different sources many enquiries about Sheikh Amin al-Husseini, ex-Mufti of Palestine, who is now in the hands of the French authorities.

The British Government cannot impose its will on the French Government and demand his freedom, because it may be that France, in detaining him, has specific intentions which it wants to achieve by using him. However, the British Government advises the Syrian Government to raise the matter with the Council of the League. If the Council demands it, France will not find itself able to mount a refusal.

I believe that that is the shortest route to freedom for the interested party.

October 9, 1945   For the British Legation

s/ Dundas

Not yet registered

222. October 10, 1945   Armanazi to Jabiri

Secret
Coded

From the Syrian Minister in London
to HE the Syrian Minister of Foreign Affairs, Damascus

Azzam Bey has succeeded in reaching an understanding with Mssrs Attlee and Bevin to postpone the settlement of the Palestinian question.

In this period of transition, the entry of an undefined number of Jews will be authorized, but this immigration will not, under any circumstances, be very great.

At the end of this transitional period the United States of America (once it has taken the advice of its officials who are favorable to the Arabs) will have reached an understanding with England, the League of Arab States and the leaders of world Jewry about a solution based on equality between Arabs and Jews, that is that the Jews will enter Palestine until their number equals that of the Arabs.

For my part, I rejected this solution, but Azzam Bey thinks that it is not really a solution, but a basis for discussion which can be changed. He will return to Cairo to put the matter to the League of Arab States.

October 10, 1945   The Minister Plenipotentiary

s/ Najib al-Armanazi

Registered in the Ministry of Foreign Affairs
No. 740 – Political reports

223. October 10, 1945   Qudsi to Jabiri

Secret
Coded

From the Syrian Minister in the USA
to HE the Syrian Minister of Foreign Affairs, Damascus

All the information you sent me about our current position is wrong and does not rest on an accurate foundation. In London they are surely laughing at us. Our position at the moment is very serious. Great Britain is toying with us while appearing to protect our interests in Palestine. It has given its agreement to setting up a Jewish force in that country on condition that the Jews side with it and not against it, that is with it and not with America.

The plan for Greater Syria which we thought was dead is not dead; it will appear in a new shape.

The Oriental Bloc plan is a reality. Great Britain supports it and wants it. It is also supported by France, and people predict that the Americans will support it too, because their interests, despite the current competition, are with the French and the English and not with the Russians.

Our Minister Plenipotentiary in London is deceived, the English are lying to him and he believes their lies.

October 10, 1945   The Minister Plenipotentiary
                                                                            s/ Nazim al-Qudsi

Registered in the Ministry of Foreign Affairs
No. 741 – Political reports

224. October 1945   President Quwatli to Emir Abdullah

Secret

From the President of the Syrian Republic
to HRH Emir Abdullah Ibn al-Hussein, Emir of Transjordan

Your Highness,

Greetings and divine mercy. Today I must discuss frankly with you a truth which can no longer be ignored. I have discussed it verbally with brother Hassan Bey Hakim and I am sure that he will acquit himself well in the mission entrusted to him and will show you the truth as I see it.

These countries can no longer put up with divisions and splits. The enemy French are always on the lookout for these opportunities and the Christians of Lebanon are still a formidable danger to our Unity and our League. Discussion of the plan for Greater Syria which you support will take the Arab cause many steps backwards and will sow division rather than unity. The dangers it represents for the Arab League must also be considered. Opposition by one group of members among them will increase the danger.

I am convinced that Your Highness only wishes this nation good things, and that you work with good intentions and according to an idea which has its worth and honor. I beg you to study the situation once again and hope that it appears to you that we are impartial and do not act because we cling to our positions.

May God protect you and keep you for your devoted

Damascus, October 1945   S/ Shukri al-Quwatli

Not yet registered in the Ministry

225. October 18, 1945   Qudsi to Jabiri

Secret
Coded

From the Syrian Minister in the USA
to the Syrian Minister of Foreign Affairs, Damascus

Here the wind does not blow as we would like. The question of Palestine is settled. President Truman is determined to give part, or the whole, of this country to the Jews whether we like it or not. So far, all our contacts have given nothing. The only thing we Arabs could do is resist, violently resist, with arms if possible, or break off diplomatic relations, or abrogate all the American concessions: schools, businesses, including oil.

I believe that the first duty of the Syrian Government is to reach an understanding with all the Arab representatives.

October 18, 1945   The Minister Plenipotentiary
                                                    s/ Nazim al-Qudsi

Registered in the Ministry of Foreign Affairs
No. 770 – Political reports

226. October 19, 1945   The Iraqi Prime Minister to Jabiri

Secret

From the President of the Council of Iraq
to HE the President of the Council of Ministers of the Syrian Republic

Your Excellency,

Greetings. To confirm the conversation which took place earlier between HE your predecessor and me, the Royal Iraqi Government had sent to sound out in an official manner the various Arab governments who are signatories to the Arab League pact on the plan to create a unified Arab army.

The existence at the current time of such an army would virtually settle the Palestinian question; instead of Palestine being threatened by Zionist groups whose tone has been raised, the united Arab army, originating from the Arab League, would constitute a practical force to re-establish order and security in the country.

Also, the British authorities in Iraq do not see any drawback in bringing this about; on the contrary, they suggest putting these forces under their command: that is where the disagreement between them and us rests.

Your generous agreement would be an essential factor in bringing to reality this still theoretical plan.

I ask God to lend you His help in bringing about everything that is useful to the Arabs.

                                 Yours,
Baghdad, October 19, 1945   The President of the Council of Ministers
                                        s/ Hamdi al-Pachachi

Registered in the Ministry of Foreign Affairs
No. 751 – Documents

227. October 19, 1945   Qudsi to Jabiri

Secret
Coded

From the Syrian Minister in Washington
to the Syrian Minister of Foreign Affairs, Damascus

The most exact description that can be applied to President Truman is that he is more Jewish than the Jews. His plan, which I have just learned a little about, aims to establish a Jewish government in Palestine, in the shadow of which the Arabs will live instead of the Arabo-Jewish state recommended by the British White Paper.

It is clear that American diplomatic representatives, Mr Wadsworth in particular, have advised the President to avoid such a solution because of the annoying repercussions it would have on American positions in the East, but the President seems determined, despite everything, to grant a government to the Jews.

This does not however mean that President Truman is seeking to create this state from today, he seeks its realization within four years. I believe that he reached agreement on this with other countries including France. At the moment, only Great Britain, which has refused to give its agreement to the entry of one hundred thousand Jews a month, is against the plan.

I draw your attention once again to the fact that France is playing a terrible game against us. Perhaps de Gaulle wants to attract the vengeance of every Arab.

October 19, 1945   The Minister Plenipotentiary
                                          s/ Nazim al-Qudsi

Registered in the Ministry of Foreign Affairs
No. 792 – Political reports

228. October 20, 1945   Qudsi to Jabiri

Secret
Coded

From the Syrian Minister in Washington
to HE the Syrian Minister of Foreign Affairs, Damascus

The American Government wishes the Syrian Government to fall into line with the advice given below:

"It is desirable for the Syrian Government not to contribute to increasing the tension which currently exists in international relations with regard to the Middle East, and particularly with regard to the creation of an international Arab-Islamic bloc against Russia."

The Department of State for Foreign Affairs has additionally spelled out to me that efforts made by certain members of the Arab League will have unpleasant consequences for everyone.

That is what I have been asked to tell you.

October 20, 1945   The Minister Plenipotentiary
                                          s/ Nazim al-Qudsi

Registered in the Ministry of Foreign Affairs
No. 797 – Political reports

229. October 21, 1945   Yusuf Yasin, Ibn Sa'ud's political adviser, to Jabiri

Top secret

From the Political Adviser to King Ibn Sa'ud
to HE the President of the Syrian Council of Ministers

HM the King has ordered me to remind you that he advises the Syrian Government not to give its agreement in any way to the maintenance of any foreign army whatsoever.

According to HM the King's advice, Syria is not obliged to bind itself without need, and to throw itself into other greater dangers in order to avoid a simple French danger.

14 Dhu al-Qa'da 1364 (October 21, 1945)

The Head of the Political Section
s/ Yusuf Yasin

Registered in the Ministry of Foreign Affairs
No. 749 – Political documents

Author's note: In February and May 1945 the Iraqis tried to persuade Quwatli to allow their army into Syria to fight the French.

230. October 22, 1945   Shone to Jabiri

Secret

From the British Minister in Syria
to HE the Syrian Minister of Foreign Affairs, Damascus

Verbal note

HM the King's Government asks the Syrian Government to let it know its arrangements for finalizing the Syro-British agreement regarding reciprocal help to maintain security and peace in the Middle East.

October 22, 1945   s/ T. Shone

Registered in the Ministry of Foreign Affairs
No. 765 – Political documents

231. October 22, 1945   Jabiri to Shone

Secret

From HE Sa'adallah al-Jabiri
to HE the British Minister Plenipotentiary

The Syrian Government, which valued the usefulness of British intervention in favor of safeguarding its prestige and independence and for the maintenance of security and peace in the Middle East, welcomes with all its heart any discussion likely to lead to finalizing an agreement between the Syrian

Government and the Government of HM the King with the aim of providing reciprocal help in order to maintain security and peace in the Middle East.

In giving you my agreement in principle, I ask you to kindly make both sides adhere to the details of this agreement as soon as possible.
October 22, 1945

s/ S.J.

Registered in the Ministry of Foreign Affairs
No. 764 – Documents

232. October 22, 1945   Shone to Jabiri

Secret

From the Minister of Great Britain in Syria
to HE the Syrian Minister of Foreign Affairs, Damascus

Verbal note

HM the King's Government asks the Syrian Government to let it know its arrangements to finalize an equitable economic agreement, the details of which we will discuss once you have consented to be a part of the Sterling bloc.

This agreement is destined solely to provide the basis of discussions and collaboration with a view to strengthening financial and business relations between the countries of the British Empire and the Syrian Republic.

If Your Excellency gives his agreement in principle, I am prepared to discuss with him all the consequences.

At the moment the matter of importance is the agreement in principle.
October 22, 1945   s/ T. Shone

Registered in the Ministry of Foreign Affairs
No. 767 – Documents

233. October 22, 1945   Jabiri to Shone

Secret

From President Sa'adallah al-Jabiri
to HE the British Minister Plenipotentiary, Damascus

Verbal note

The Syrian Government subscribes entirely to the finalization of a financial and economic Anglo-Syrian agreement leading to complete collaboration between the States forming part of the British Empire and the Syrian Republic.

In giving you this approval in principle I ask you to start setting out the terms in this agreement with the aim of rapidly reaching the realization of a collaboration which Syria wants with all its heart.
October 22, 1945   s/ Sa'adallah al-Jabiri

Registered in the Ministry of Foreign Affairs
No. 766 – Documents

234. October 23, 1945   Jabiri to the Cabinet

Secret

To the noble Council of Ministers

During the course of my meeting with the British Minister Plenipotentiary returning from his mission, HE told me the following with regard to Palestine:

"The rumors spread by partisan groups, that is that HM's Government would give its agreement to a solution detrimental to the Arabs, are without foundation. On the contrary, the Government is seeking the best ways and means to grant the Arabs their rights and to prevent them becoming subject to any prejudice.

"HM the King's Government will consult directly with the Syrian Government on anything that could, in the future, harm the existence of Palestine and will collaborate with it."

That is the official statement made to me. I am sending it to your noble Council.

October 23, 1945   The President of the Council of Ministers
                                                         The Minister of Foreign Affairs
                                                                       S/ Sa'adallah al-Jabiri

Registered in the Ministry of Foreign Affairs
No. 768 – Documents

235. October 23, 1945   Qudsi to Jabiri

Secret
Coded

From the Syrian Minister in the USA
to HE the Syrian Minister of Foreign Affairs, Damascus

Today I was summoned to the Department of State for Foreign Affairs and I received notification of the following:

The American Government asks its friends the Arabs in general and the Syrians in particular to adopt a reasonable and thoughtful position with regard to it, removed from the tendentious positions that are apparent at the moment. America does not and will never wish any harm on the Arabs. It has not stopped working to help them fully. Its position in supporting Jewish emigration to Palestine is inspired by a higher humanitarian sentiment which is in no way designed to harm the Arabs. The American Government warns all the Arabs against certain international political maneuvers which, for set aims, are designed to show that America is the enemy of the Arabs and that another power is their only friend, while it is due to it alone that the Arabs and the Jews find themselves in the current impasse.

October 23, 1945   The Minister Plenipotentiary
                                                                         s/ Nazim al-Qudsi

Registered in the Ministry of Foreign Affairs
No. 771 – Documents

Author's note: Jabiri gave a copy of this telegram to Shone.

236. October 23, 1945   Jabiri to Armanazi

Secret
Coded

From the President of the Council of Ministers, the Minister of
Foreign Affairs
to the Syrian Minister Plenipotentiary in London

The Government, according to information received from the local British representatives favorable to our cause, is absolutely convinced that a plot is being woven against us in London between France and Great Britain.

All your reports are reassuring, but we believe that we would be wrong to remain reassured, and that it is up to us not to be content with simple statements any more; we must, rather, occupy ourselves with getting rid of the last French soldier. Great Britain, by not yet giving its official agreement to evicting the French, is following a line of conduct which is in contradiction with its earlier line of conduct.

Constantly pursue your contacts with those responsible in order to receive a rapid result.

October 23, 1945   The Minister of Foreign Affairs
                                                                        s/ Sa'adallah al-Jabiri

Registered in the Ministry of Foreign Affairs
No. 834/382 – Diplomatic correspondence

237. October 24, 1945   Armanazi to Jabiri

Coded

From the Syrian Minister in London
to HE the Syrian Minister of Foreign Affairs, Damascus

In my opinion, Abd al-Rahman bey Azzam has exceeded the responsibilities he was given.

The Syrian Government, as we know, accredited him to defend the Palestinian question. Now, it seems that he engaged in negotiations and solutions which are, at the very least, speculative, at the expense of the Arabs, between America and Great Britain, to allow Jews to enter Palestine, and to destroy the policy in the White Paper.

All the Arab countries which have accredited him to defend the Palestinian question believed that Azzam Bey would never engage in any negotiations whatsoever leading to the modification of the White Paper and the admittance of new immigrants.

In addition, the sacrifices we would consent to in recognizing the solutions Azzam Bey regards as the basis of discussion will not be of any use to us in finally settling the situation between us and France. Anyway, I have personally told him that we can make certain accommodations in Palestine should we win in Syria.

My opinion is that the Palestinian question will never be solved; it will be put off, but this delay will be a chance the Jews will benefit from with one precise detail: the abrogation of the policy in the White Paper.

October 24, 1945   The Minister Plenipotentiary
                                                           s/ Najib al-Armanazi

Registered in the Ministry of Foreign Affairs
No. 780 – Political documents

238. October 1945   Jabiri to the Cabinet

Top secret

Report to the noble Council of Ministers

The efforts being made by Nuri Pasha Sa'id must be recognized by your noble Council. We also need your advice about them.

With regard to foreign policy, the communist danger and then the French danger, are growing daily over the countries of the Middle East; the only way to preserve us from these dangers is for the Middle Eastern states to group together in an alliance or pact and to join, by ties of friendship, a great world Power, which is England. This is an undeniable fact, as you know.

With regard to the relations of the Arab states with each other, the suggested alliance or pact will give them solidity, strength and cohesion and will constitute a barrier against any ambitious or aggressive parties.

As to our particular situation, it is useful for us to do away, in any way at all, with the conflict that exists between Turkey and us, in such a way that we retain our rights over the Liwa of Alexandretta. If we do not succeed in winning all our rights, we will recover some of them. Now and at every stage we must not forget that it is the French who, without concerning themselves with our interests, have made us succumb to the problems of Alexandretta.

HE the President and I have given our agreement to Nuri Pasha Sa'id's activities, which will remain secret until a definitive agreement and an equitable ruling are reached.

The President of the Council of Ministers
The Minister of Foreign Affairs
S/ Sa'adallah al-Jabri

Registered in the Ministry of Foreign Affairs
No. 802 – Political reports

239. October 24, 1945   Jabiri to Armanazi

Secret
Coded

To the Syrian Minister Plenipotentiary in London

Please tell General Spears that we are pleased about his arrival. Confirm to him from me that his Company will receive all necessary support and favor from us. All the privileges he asks for will certainly be granted. We cannot forget the help he has given us.

However, we ask him particularly to clear our name in the eyes of world public opinion regarding the Rashid Ali incident. It is not us who made him flee, it is the French, our hateful friends, who did it.

October 24, 1945   s/ Sa'adallah al-Jabiri

Not yet registered in the Ministry

240. October 24, 1945   Armanazi to Jabiri

Secret
Coded

From the Syrian Minister in London
to the Syrian Minister of Foreign Affairs, Damascus

It is in our interest to hasten a crisis between us and France which must result in the withdrawal of the last French soldier from our country. That is what we advise our brothers and friends, as well as certain British officials (but unofficially). Serious discussions are under way with the view to reaching a final agreement between Great Britain and France. We must on the one hand pre-empt events and on the other face the whole world with the fait accompli.

I have already written to you about this. Decisions are no longer enough now; we must act.

October 24, 1945   The Minister Plenipotentiary
                                                              s/ Najib al-Armanazi

Registered in the Ministry of Foreign Affairs
No. 840/84 – Diplomatic correspondence

241. October 24, 1945   Jabiri to the Cabinet

Secret
From the President of the Council, the Minister of Foreign Affairs
to the noble Council of Ministers

The Minister Plenipotentiary of HM the King of Great Britain's Government has told me of the following:

"The British Government cannot give its agreement to the Syrian proposition aimed at unilaterally deciding on the withdrawal from Syria of foreign troops, particularly by the French army in the Levant."

As you see, this communiqué shows that matters are not progressing on the official level as we would wish, but this does not prevent me from informing you of some advice given to me by Mr Shone in his personal capacity: Syria's national interest must lead the Syrians to act in their own favor, as they understand it, without waiting for outside help.

I have the honor of putting the matter to you so that your noble Council can take the decision it thinks fit.

October 24, 1945   The President of the Council of Ministers
                                                    Sa'adallah al-Jabiri

Registered in the Ministry of Foreign Affairs
No. 804 – Reports

242. October 26, 1945   Yasin to Jabiri

Top secret

From King Ibn Sa'ud's political adviser
to HE the Minister of Foreign Affairs, Damascus

(Care of the Saudi delegation in Damascus)

I have presented what you so kindly told me to HM the King.

A certain number of Arab political representatives have already talked to HM about this matter. The same is true of the British delegate.

I can reassure Your Excellency: HM the King is determined to abrogate all the American concessions if American policy persists, as it does now, in supporting the Jews.

                                                    The Head of the Political Section
19 Dhu al-Qa'dah   S/Yusuf Yasin
(October 26, 1945)

Registered in the Ministry of Foreign Affairs
No. 752 – Political documents

243. October 26, 1945   Shone to Jabiri

Top secret

From the British Minister in Syria
to HE the Minister of Foreign Affairs, Damascus

I am deeply grateful to you for the letter from the Syrian Minister Plenipotentiary, dated October 23, 1945 which you so kindly showed me and which your generosity has allowed me to forward to my Government on condition that it remain secret and confidential, because this is a twisting of the rules of diplomatic action.

This I promise you, just as I promise you in the name of my Government to safeguard completely the rights of the Arabs regarding the question of Palestine. Thus we will have in practice given the lie to any assertion that is not innocent.

Your Excellency, please accept my sincerest regards.

October 26, 1945   The Minister Plenipotentiary
                                          of HM his British Majesty's Government
                                                            s/ T. Shone

Registered in the Ministry of Foreign Affairs
No. 782 – Documents

244. October 26, 1945   Shone to Jabiri

Top secret

From the Minister of Great Britain in Syria
to HE the Syrian Minister of Foreign Affairs, Damascus

I thank Your Excellency for the confidence placed in me. I also thank you for all your efforts with HM King Abd al-Aziz's Government relating to the abrogation of American concessions concerning the oil companies.

I believe that you are sincerely and certainly helping the Arab cause in this way. You can thus be sure of my Government's permanent support for everything that will be useful for the success and good of the Syrian and Arab cause.

Yours etc.,
October 26, 1945

s/ T. Shone

Registered in the Ministry of Foreign Affairs
No. 783 – Documents

245. October 26, 1945   Jabiri to Atasi

Secret
Coded

From H.E. Sa'adallah al-Jabiri
to the Syrian Minister Plenipotentiary, Paris

Please contact Haj Amin al-Husseini and make him understand that HE the President thinks that it is in his interest to seek refuge with King Abd al-Aziz; let him try, from his side, to persuade the French that it is preferable for them and for him that they help him reach the King.

Great Britain is in agreement with this solution; we are too, because it is in everyone's interest that Haj Amin should not be in the hands of the French who will soon try to exploit this.

October 26, 1945   The Minister of Foreign Affairs
s/ Sa'adallah al-Jabiri

Registered in the Ministry of Foreign Affairs
No. 823/176 – Diplomatic correspondence

246. October 27, 1945   Armanazi to Jabiri

Secret

From the Syrian Minister in London
to the Syrian Minister of Foreign Affairs, Damascus

Once again, the British Government thinks that the time is not right for the President of the Republic's visit to London.

Officials here do not see any comparison between Emir Abdullah's visit to London and that of HE because the Emir will discuss the plan to modify the

Transjordanian treaty, and the obtaining of a statement from Great Britain regarding the independence of Transjordan. However, this will not prevent HH from discussing the plan for Greater Syria which he favors and for which he is working.

In addition, here they think that the efforts made at the moment between the Arab capitals, with the intention of holding a meeting between the Arab kings and presidents, are not opportune at the moment.

October 27, 1945   The Minister Plenipotentiary
                                                         s/ Najib al-Armanazi

Registered in the Ministry of Foreign Affairs
No. 791– Political reports

247. October 27, 1945   Jabiri to Qudsi

Secret
Coded

From HE Sa'adallah al-Jabiri
to the Syrian Minister Plenipotentiary in Washington

Please inform the relevant authority that the Syrian Government asks the American Government to act prudently in adopting an official stand regarding the Palestinian cause.

The Syrian Government is resolved to intervene openly against any aggressive Jewish move with regard to the Arabs. From now on it is also resolved to adopt, with regard to any foreign government which helps the Jews and intervenes against the interests of the Arabs in Palestine, a position of economic boycott at first, followed by a political one.

I am thus notifying you of a decision taken by the Council of Ministers.

October 27, 1945   The President of the Council of Ministers
                                                         s/ Sa'adallah al-Jabiri

Not yet registered

248. November 1, 1945   Qudsi to Jabiri

Secret
Coded

From the Syrian Minister in the United States
to HE the Syrian Minister of Foreign Affairs, Damascus

Today I was summoned to the Department of State for Foreign Affairs, where the interim official discussed with me, with great frankness, our position with regard to Great Britain and America. He told me that Syria was committing suicide in persisting in its dubious line of conduct; it has hardly shaken off the French Mandate and now it is rushing towards British protection. The American Department of State thinks that everything proves that Great Britain has imposed its authority on Syria and that the latter accepts the influence of monopolistic British capitalism, although its interest demands that it deals only with the state that would give it real help and would provide it with the best conditions.

The creation in the Orient of a British supply committee, encompassing Syria in its zone of action, distances our country from the profits of free competition in the world market and prevents us from profiting from any economic change. Great Britain demands in effect strategic positions out of which it also wants to create zones of economic influence. The United States did not give their agreement to Syrian independence for fun but acted very seriously. At the current time, Syria is invited not to bend to any foreign economic, political or military authority. It is only then that it will be able to count on the complete help of the Americans.

A while ago, I sent you a similar objection. I am now sending you this one and I attach some importance to knowing what you intend to do.

November 1, 1945   The Minister Plenipotentiary
S/ Nazim al-Qudsi

Registered in the Ministry of Foreign Affairs
No. 865/242 – Diplomatic correspondence

249. November 4, 1945   Jabiri to Armanazi

Secret
Coded

From the President of the Council, the Minister of Foreign Affairs
to the Syrian Minister Plenipotentiary, London

Rashid Ali arrived in Syria in French military attire. He disembarked at Beirut or Rayak from a French aeroplane. Then he went to Palmyra with the French intermediary. It is up to our friends to insist on this point and to show the Government and the British people how the French lend their help to the enemies of the British nation. We hope that General Spears will succeed better than the first time in his new campaign. We possess documents that prove the above. We know that practically we will not succeed in putting our hands on Rashid Ali, but it is enough that we make his escape a matter which could draw the attention of the British people to France and to the reality of its intentions.

November 4, 1945   The Minister of Foreign Affairs
s/ Sa'adallah al-Jabiri

Registered in the Ministry of Foreign Affairs
No. 885/406 – Diplomatic correspondence

250. November 4, 1945   Jabiri to Shone

Secret

From the President of the Council, the Syrian Minister of Foreign Affairs
to HE the Minister Plenipotentiary of His British Majesty, Damascus

Your Excellency,

The future of Sheikh Amin al-Husseini, ex-Mufti of Palestine, is of interest to HE the President of the Republic and myself.

I have already written to Your Excellency, and I renew my request to remind the honorable British Government that Haj Amin has never been an enemy of Great Britain, but that he loves his country and that he is a patriot of the first order. He has never willingly collaborated with the Germans.

What matters to the Syrian Government is that he should not, under any circumstances, remain in the hands of the French authorities, who will wrong him or exploit his presence among them, as they have done in many similar situations with a large number of Arab leaders.

I hope to have a satisfactory result and be able to congratulate myself about his release, even if this is due to the intervention of the British Government, which has always accustomed the Arabs to its acts of kindness.

With my deepest respect,

November 4, 1945   The Minister of Foreign Affairs
                                                        s/ Sa'adallah al-Jabiri

Registered in the Syrian Ministry of Foreign Affairs
No. 887/407 – Diplomatic correspondence

251. November 4, 1945   Qudsi to Jabiri

Secret
Coded

From the Syrian Minister to the United States
to HE the Syrian Minister of Foreign Affairs, Damascus

Strikes in the Arab lands have not roused any interest in political circles. On the contrary, a general feeling is beginning to emerge among those responsible for policy, according to which they are persuaded that we have no motive against France, that we are not democrats and that our intentions are like those of the Nazis.

It is regrettable that the violent propaganda war unleashed here by the Jews against the Arabs, as well as the French propaganda, has made our position wholly critical. We are not, in the eyes of the Americans, a nation defending itself, we are only Nazis, we think and act in a spirit of brutal racism.

I draw your attention to this propaganda campaign and I believe that we have so far had to suffer greatly from it. It is up to the propaganda services created here and in London to direct their actions from now on, not only against the Jews but also against France the colonizer and against Great Britain which dominates the Arab world and which wants to toy with it.

November 4, 1945   The Minister Plenipotentiary
                                                        s/ Nazim al-Qudsi

Registered in the Ministry of Foreign Affairs
No. 824 – Political reports

252. November 5, 1945   Qudsi to Jabiri

Secret
Coded

> To the Syrian Minister of Foreign Affairs, Damascus

I was summoned for a second time to the State Department. Two issues were put before me, the first being the Palestinian question, and the second, the British grip on the general policy for the Arab states.

The American Government's point of view, as far as Palestine is concerned, is summarized thus: fairness requires that the Jews be given what was promised to them. America has agreed with Great Britain with the aim of asserting this right; in other words, justice will prevail.

As far as British influence is concerned, the American Government asks, "Did we recognize your independence just for you to put yourselves in the hands of Great Britain?" Having reminded them that Great Britain delivered us from French oppression, they said to me, "Is that deliverance? They freed you in order to use you themselves. Great Britain, under the pretext of delivering you from the French, wants to annex you. We will not allow feudal Syrians to sell their country to Great Britain."

In any case, I can no longer represent Syria here and I do not understand the point of my presence. The Syrian Government's policies do not take account of any of the advice I freely provide. The danger in which we find ourselves does not allow the Government to ignore to this extent the reports and information I send you.

November 5, 1945   The Minister Plenipotentiary
                                                                              s/ Nazim al-Qudsi

Registered in the Ministry of Foreign Affairs
No. 830 – Political reports

253. November 5, 1945   The Syrian Legation in Cairo to Azzam

Secret

> From the adviser to the Syrian Legation in Cairo
> <u>Verbal report</u>
> Plan for a united Arab army

What follows has been relayed to Azzam Bey.

The general defense interest requires the creation of a united Arab army, provided with the most modern of engineering machinery. All the Arab states will participate through voluntary recruitment, or compulsory service, in the formation of these units. Each of the States will contribute to its expenses according to its financial capabilities. Great Britain, for its part, will provide its help to this army's technical and administrative sections and will provide everything necessary to turn it into a powerful instrument of defense.

November 5, 1945   s/ Asim al-Naili

Registered in the Ministry of Foreign Affairs
No. 828 – Reports

254. November 7, 1945   Constantin Zureiq, Counselor to the Syrian Legation in Washington, to Jabiri

Secret
Coded

From the Syrian Legation in Washington
to HE the Syrian Minister of Foreign Affairs, Damascus

The American Government is surprised by the position the Arabs are adopting towards it, in relation to the Palestinian question. In the whole of this affair, America sees only humanitarian work and this is the basis on which it has made promises to the Jews; but the British have a different position, and the American Government expresses surprise that the Arabs consider it to be the only ones showing them hostility and threatening them with the Jews.

First of all, they say, the Balfour promise is British, not American.

Second, Great Britain wishes to exploit the Arab-Jewish conflict because it is the only way for it to remain in Palestine, to dominate all the Arab countries.

The American Government strongly desires to find a friendly settlement between the Arabs and the Jews, but it is convinced that the British colonial authorities will do everything to prevent that, as Great Britain wishes for incidents to worsen in Palestine and for disorder, where blood is spilled, to take place.

Our interest, as far as I can see, is to find a definitive settlement, to work for the withdrawal of Great Britain from Syria and Palestine and for the plan the American Government will put forward concerning the definitive settlement of the Near East question.

I believe that such a plan would win the agreement of all the states, except of course Great Britain.

November 7, 1945   For the Minister Plenipotentiary
                                                          s/ Constantin Zureiq

Registered in the Ministry of Foreign Affairs
No. 833 – Political reports

255. November 9, 1945   Jabiri to Shone

Secret

From HE the Syrian Minister of Foreign Affairs
to HE the Minister Plenipotentiary of Great Britain, Damascus

Your Excellency,

It has been proved that among Syrian citizens there was only one person to help Rashid Ali al-Gaylani during his sojourn in Syria. I cited his name as well as the conditions for his participation: it was Mr Mamduh al-Midani.

We are inclined to pursue legal avenues with regard to him as well as with regard to all those whose participation in this regrettable incident can be established.

Yours sincerely,

November 9, 1945   The Minister of Foreign Affairs
                                                              s/ Sa'adallah al-Jabiri

Registered in the Ministry of Foreign Affairs
No. 916/421 – Diplomatic correspondence

256. November 12, 1945   Jabiri to Armanazi

Secret
Coded

From the President of the Council, the Minister of Foreign Affairs
to the Syrian Minister Plenipotentiary in London

Announce in the name of this Government that it is not our intention to allow the British army to leave Syria before the total withdrawal of the French.

As for the Lebanese Government, our current position with regard to it is extremely prudent. We are no longer very trusting, for the Lebanese have started to show, once again, their fears of Great Britain and their liking for France.

Sheikh Bishara in person has not hidden from us that he is the subject of continual pressure and that he cannot demand the withdrawal of the British army which is far more numerous that the French army, and which, at the moment, does not constitute any danger for them.

This reversal matters from our point of view. We hope that a ministerial reversal will occur in Lebanon and that Riyad Bey returns to power, because he alone is a guarantee. We have, until now, made great efforts to bring about an understanding between him and his opponents from the Independence Party. We hope to succeed. Only in his return lies the solution to all these troubles in which we find ourselves.

Reassure the British Government about all this and show it that the situation is such as we see it and as I have explained it to you.

November 12, 1945   The Minister of Foreign Affairs
                                                              s/ Sa'adallah al-Jabiri

Registered in the Ministry of Foreign Affairs
No. 931/425 – Diplomatic correspondence

257. November 12, 1945   Jabiri to Shone

Top secret

From the President of the Council, the Minister of Foreign Affairs
to HE the British Minister Plenipotentiary, Damascus

The information I have and which is based on official reports proves that the Soviet Legation has so far made contact with a large number of Kurdish leaders in the various regions of the Syrian Republic.

In drawing Your Excellency's attention to this I know that you are perfectly aware of what is happening and that your specialized departments are not unaware of the maneuvers that are being prepared despite our willingness and yours.

However, the duty that I have towards you brings me to remind you that the Syrian Government, rightly concerned about the consequences of this Soviet activity, can only continue to reject all these activities and inform you of the inability in which we find ourselves of taking any measures whatsoever against this Legation. It invites you, in your capacity as the official responsible for maintaining security and peace in this country, to take the measures you judge fitting.

The Syrian Government gives its agreement in advance to whatever you decide.

November 12, 1945   The President of the Council of Ministers
                                                              s/ Sa'adallah al-Jabiri

Registered in the Ministry of Foreign Affairs
No. 935/427 – Diplomatic correspondence

258. November 26, 1945   Shone to Jabiri

Secret

From the Minister of Great Britain in Syria
to HE the Syrian Minister of Foreign Affairs, Damascus

<u>Verbal note</u>

For whatever reason I ask Your Excellency to confirm to me officially the verbal conversation that took place between us yesterday.

Personally, I cannot force my Government to follow a particular piece of advice. You yourself know the good feelings I have towards Syria, its emancipation, and the total withdrawal of the French.

With the aim of proving to my Government the accuracy of your views, which I can only approve from my personal point of view, I ask you to inform me of your position regarding French pretentions so that I can communicate them in my turn to my Government.

I hope with all my heart that my efforts supported by yours will be joined in order to protect independent Syria.

November 26, 1945   s/ T. Shone

Registered in the Ministry of Foreign Affairs
No. 831 – Documents

259. November 30, 1945   Mardam, the Syrian envoy to the Council of the Arab League in Cairo, to Jabiri

Top secret

From Jamil Mardam Bey, Syrian Representative to the Council of the
Arab League
To HE the President of the Council of Ministers, Damascus

Today I met Lord Killearn, who set before me the following truths:

The British Government regrets that the Arab governments of Syria as well as Egypt do not wholly understand the reality of British intentions when it comes to answering favorably and positively British requests, whose only aim is the defense of the Middle East and its populations against the dangers that are approaching by the day. All these dangers come, as we know, from Russia, which has opened a mouth it does not want to close. The British Government, in asking us to conclude a commercial treaty and an aeronautical treaty, like finding a practical way of having us admitted to the Sterling bloc, seeks our interest before its own. It compares our hesitant position with regard to England to that of the states of Central Europe at the beginning of the Nazi movement. If these small states had realized the reality of the situation and the dangers involved and had known how to behave at the required time, at Great Britain's side, without allowing themselves to be swept along by this idea of a narrow independence which strangled them and which the Germans were able to exploit, they would not have undergone the fate they suffered.

The Lord thinks that the danger for us will not be long delayed and that Great Britain is forced to act either with us or against us because the Middle East constitutes a danger point in the life of the Empire and that it will not leave it to the mercy of the communists whose actions seem more serious by the day.

I ask you to put this before HE the President very soon.

November 30, 1945   The Minister Plenipotentiary
                                                            s/ Jamil Mardam Bey

Registered in the Ministry of Foreign Affairs
No. 891– Political reports

260. December 2, 1945 Jabiri to Solod

Secret

From the President of the Council, the Syrian Minister of Foreign Affairs
    to HE the Minister Plenipotentiary of the USSR, Damascus

Your Excellency,

My Government, which wishes to maintain good relations with your Legation, finds itself forced to draw your attention in the friendliest way possible to the protests it has received from international Arab and non-Arab sources.

These protests indicate that your Legation has recently encouraged determined intrigues among the Kurds of northern Syria.

Also, the Syrian security services have noted special activity to which certain Kurdish and Armenian communist elements, in permanent contact with officials in your Legation in Damascus, have devoted themselves.

I can forgive all this agitation, but ask Your Excellency to stipulate now that certain of its Legation officials be more respectful of the position and complete neutrality of this country.

Yours etc.,

December 2, 1945   The Syrian Minister of Foreign Affairs

s/ Sa'adallah al-Jabiri

Registered in the Ministry of Foreign Affairs

No. 1038/74 – Diplomatic correspondence

261. December 4, 1945   Mardam to Jabiri

Secret

Coded

From the Syrian Minister in Cairo
to HE the Syrian Minister of Foreign Affairs, Damascus

The British Government thinks, as Abd al-Fattah Omaro Pasha has stated, that the Palestinian question can only have one solution: international oversight by the four following states: America, France, Great Britain and the Soviet Union.

It is likely that a local army comprising Arabs and Jews will be created.

The Arabs must know the position of each of these four states.

Great Britain will be with us all down the line.

As for America, its position is not known; it will be rather conservative but the danger for the Arabs rests with France, which supports the Jews. Russia only wants to encourage the Arabs insofar as it suits them.

The proposal for oversight, as we have learned, was at the insistence of Russia and America, and accepted by Great Britain.

There is however a hope of distancing France, unless there are secret agreements between the English and the French. Here it seems that these agreements exist, because it has been established that the French Government follows Great Britain in everything and that is why it tries to give it laughable reparation.

The situation, if it is in truth like this, will entail continual crises. Only the English will lose by it. I will seize the first opportunity here to make my views known to them.

December 4, 1945   s/ Jamil Mardam Bey

Registered in the Ministry of Foreign Affairs

No. 906 – Political reports

262. December 6, 1945   Shone to Jabiri

Secret

From the Minister of Great Britain in Syria
To H.E. the President of the Council of Ministers, Damascus

Verbal note

I was delighted, as was my Government, by HE the President of the Republic's statement on Syria's acceptance of the noble mediation proposed by HM King Abd al-Aziz al-Sa'ud with the aim of settling the misunderstanding which has existed for a long time between Syria and its Turkish neighbors.

HM's Government would be happy to see the states of the Middle East coming to an understanding and forming a bloc. It is on this understanding and on this bloc that it hopes to rely in order to distance many of the dangers threatening it, and to settle current and future difficulties.

I hope that the good efforts used in this way will be crowned with success, not only for the return to an understanding and Arabo-Turkish friendship, but also for political, economic and military collaboration which would be beneficial both to the Arab states and to the Turkish state, which constitutes an important factor in the life of the Middle East.

My Government, for its part, promises to work sincerely for the realization of this goal.

December 6, 1945

s/ T. Shone

Registered in the Ministry of Foreign Affairs
No. 857 – Documents

263. December 8, 1945   Shone to Jabiri

Secret

From the Minister of Great Britain in Syria
to HE the President of the Council of Ministers
The Syrian Minister of Foreign Affairs, Damascus

Your Excellency,

The Turkish Government has asked us through diplomatic channels for our intervention in the removal of the Kurdish leaders from the Turkish border and the reduction in the activities of Kurdish and Armenian extremists within Syrian territories.

This legation had already written to you about this. We are confirming it to you today and we are informing you that the authorities charged with military security will intervene in the matter of Syrian nationals who are working to upset good Syro-Turkish neighborly relations.

I believe that at the moment you share our opinion which is designed only to maintain peace and security, and to deflect from Syria the threat of trouble which is currently being fostered in certain regions of the Middle East.

With my deepest respect,

December 8, 1945

s/ T.Shone
Minister Plenipotentiary

Registered in the Ministry of Foreign Affairs
No. 1094/466 – Diplomatic correspondence

264. December 10, 1945   Jabiri to Mardam

Secret
Coded

From the President of the Syrian Council, the Foreign Minister
to the Syrian Minister Plenipotentiary, Cairo

I am sending you the decision taken today by the Council of Ministers.

The Council of Ministers believes that the proposition inclined to associate Syria with other Arab countries in a common pact with the states allied by Sa'adabad's pact is not to be retained.

The Council of Ministers, having examined the practical value of this pact in the past and the current and future dangers threatening the states which are part of it, thinks that Syria would be embarking on a great adventure without any possibility of benefiting from it.

In addition, Syria will decide, in the near or distant future, if it is really threatened by the Soviet Union with one of the dangers foreseen in Nuri Pasha's plan.

These are all the reasons why the Syrian Government exercises its right to an absolute rejection of this plan.
December 10, 1945

The Minister of Foreign Affairs
S/ Sa'adallah al-Jabiri

Registered in the Ministry of Foreign Affairs
No. 1099/312 – Diplomatic correspondence

265. December 13, 1945   Jabiri to Mardam

Secret
Coded

From the President of the Council, the Syrian Foreign Minister
to The Syrian Minister Plenipotentiary, Cairo

Have received detailed information on the new "Sykes-Picot" agreement.

Mr Shone suggests that we act according to our interest with regard to this agreement which does not secure us anything good, but as the responsible person, he is constrained to advise us to accept it and adopt it.

We want to know if Lord Killearn's opinion is the same. What do you advise us? Should we rest assured regarding the proposals attributed to him, or is it an intrigue?

I would like to receive your opinion as soon as possible.
December 13, 1945

The Minister of Foreign Affairs
S/ Sa'adallah al-Jabiri

Registered in the Ministry of Foreign Affairs
No. 1107/314 – Diplomatic correspondence

266. December 14, 1945   Armanazi to Jabiri

Secret
Coded

From the Syrian Minister in London
to HE the Syrian Minister of Foreign Affairs, Damascus

Mr Bevin's conversation with me, which was very brief, did not enlighten me about the statement he has made. He assured me once again that Syrian independence would not suffer any harm, that the interests of Great Britain and France will no longer be competing and that withdrawal will take place. However, there is a matter of which the Syrians must absolutely take account, that is that the international Security Council will proceed to the designation of strategic points, of which some will be in Syria and Lebanon, but it cannot yet say formally which states they will be in.

Mr Bevin states that it is in Syria's and Lebanon's interests to work from now on in perfect accord with Great Britain and France and that these two states will work to encourage economic development and to safeguard the prestige of the Syrians.

To draw the conversation to a close, he said to me, "Tell your Government that I have made an honorable commitment to maintain Syrian independence; our agreement with France consolidates and strengthens this independence which will in no way suffer."

That is a summary of the conversation. As you see, it is not very clear and sheds no light on the confused points to which you wanted an answer.

December 14, 1945   The Minister Plenipotentiary
                                                     s/ Najib al-Armanazi

Registered in the Ministry of Foreign Affairs
No. 933 – Political reports

267. December 14, 1945   Mardam to Jabiri

Top secret
Coded

From the Syrian Minister in Cairo
to the Syrian Minister of Foreign Affairs, Damascus

The encouragement you received earlier is a secret of great value because it represents the true British aid policy which the current government is fighting; it represents more exactly the policy of our friends and of all those who show a real and sincere sympathy towards our cause and who do not speculate about the Arab nation with the aim of pleasing France. What you imagine about the British official, whatever his inclination, that is whether he bends and carries out the instructions of his Government, whichever party the latter belongs to, is neither fair nor likely. If our friend is forced, by reason of his official functions, to apply a fixed policy, he may later work either for the success of this policy, if it matches his view, or for its failure if it does not. So we can rest easy about what HE asks of you, and we can regard it as sincere – like all Lord Killearn's officials here, from the lowest civil servant, who wish for the failure of the policy of the Franco-British agreement concluded at our expense. This policy will only fail if we and our friends collaborate.

This important action will have to be carried out from our side in all its phases with precision, energy and tact.

December 14, 1945   S/ Jamil Mardam Bey

Registered in the Ministry of Foreign Affairs
No. 935 – Political reports

268. December 15, 1945   The Syrian and Lebanese Presidents' agreement

Secret

Meeting in Aley

HE Sheikh Bishara al- Khuri, President of the Republic of Lebanon, and HE Mr Shukri al-Quwatli, President of the Syrian Republic met today, Saturday December 15, 1945, in Aley and in the presence of the Presidents of the Syrian and Lebanese councils and qualified officials have agreed on the following:

1 Syrian and Lebanese officials will submit the Franco-British agreement to the Council of the Arab League with the aim of determining whether this agreement harms Syrian and Lebanese independence and to arrange the necessary measures likely to give sufficient help to the two states.
2 Officials in the two states will be charged with making contact with the American and Soviet governments – if necessary – with the aim of asking for their intervention for the abrogation of this dangerous agreement, or its limitation and the destruction of the colonial plan it contains.

The two governments are in perfect agreement to grant full support and to demonstrate the sincerest friendship to the state which will, in the current dangerous situation, give its help to Syria and Lebanon.

Drawn up in Aley on December 15, 1945

s/ Bishara Khalil al-Khuri
s/ Shukri al-Quwatli

Registered in the Ministry of Foreign Affairs
No. 872 – Documents

269. December 15, 1945   Zureiq to Jabiri

Secret
Coded

From the Syrian Chargé d'Affaires in Washington
to HE the Syrian Minister of Foreign Affairs, Damascus

In reality, the American Government does not give our questions serious consideration. They know that recognition of our independence by the English is similar to the recognition of Egyptian independence, that is, purely formal, illusory recognition. That is why, when I asked a deputy in foreign affairs what the position of his country and government was with regard to the new Franco-British agreement, he said to me, "What will you give us?"

He explained his proposals to me, saying, "Is the Syrian Government inclined to grant concessions to American companies for oil exploitation?" I replied, "But then what of the promises made to us? What of the agreements? What of the United Nations agreement?"

In broad outline, the only answer I could get is that in reality America knew about the consultations and negotiations which resulted in this agreement. It does not want to intervene and impose its opinion, not having any interest in it, especially when France is inclined to believe that the Americans are impeding its renaissance.

Finally, he advised me thus: "My friend, don't torment yourself so much. I am not talking to you now in an official capacity, but as a friend. Tell your government to reach agreement with France. Don't be influenced by the diplomatic representatives who talk a lot and who come and go, making a show of their importance and their power to you. Your country, whether you like it or not, is an object of competition between the Soviet Union and Great Britain and its friends. Choose whichever you like."

That is the response I was able to get.

December 15, 1945   For the Minister Plenipotentiary

Registered in the Ministry of Foreign Affairs
No. 939 – Political reports

270. December 15, 1945   Armanazi to Jabiri

Secret
Coded

From the Syrian Minister in London
to HE the Syrian Minister of Foreign Affairs, Damascus

Let it be brought to the Syrian Government's attention that any action threatening security in the East will be repressed with force. Any attack committed against French individuals or institutions will be answered with force. The final outcome of the Syrian Government's position will be the dissolution of the cabinet and an invitation to the people to form a new plebiscite.

That is what I was given to understand so as to send it to you in written form.

December 15, 1945   The Minister Plenipotentiary
                                                      s/ Najib al-Armanazi

Registered in the Ministry of Foreign Affairs
No. 942 – Political reports

271. December 15, 1945   Mardam to Jabiri

Secret
Coded

From the Syrian Minister in Cairo
to HE the Syrian Minister of Foreign Affairs, Damascus

I do not believe that at the moment Mr Shone can do anything for us. His Government's policy has been fixed and we only have one hope: the Soviets. The Government of the Soviet Union will not help us "gratis et pro Deo" and would not be useful to us, even if it tried to help us.

Mr Smart confirms to me that he would like to help us from the bottom of his heart, because like us he does not think it is in his nation's interest to collaborate with France at our expense; but he does not see a way to help us and Mr Shone will not change the situation whatever we do.

We must learn to steel our nerves.
December 15, 1945

s/ Jamil Mardam Bey

Registered in the Ministry of Foreign Affairs
No. 953 – Political reports

272. December 16, 1945   Shone to Jabiri

Top secret

From the Minister of Great Britain in the Levant

Verbal note

The British Government would regard with great satisfaction any solution to the Syrian question resting on the basis of the unification of Syria, Transjordan and Arab Palestine.

December 16, 1945   s/ T. Shone

Registered in the Ministry of Foreign Affairs
No. 895 – Documents

273. December 17, 1945   Shone to Jabiri

Secret

Verbal note

To clarify the verbal note of yesterday, HM the King's Government does not consider that Palestine in its current state is wholly Arab. An important part remains Jewish from the racial, religious and cultural viewpoint, and it is useful that it remains so from the political point of view too.

December 17, 1945   s/ T. Shone

Registered in the Ministry of Foreign Affairs
No. 898 – Documents

274. December 17, 1945   Shone to Jabiri

Secret

Verbal note

To confirm the verbal note presented yesterday, the Government of HM the King considers that the regions in question constitute a strategic and economic unity and that it is useful in their interest to bring about political unity.
December 17, 1945   s/ T. Shone

Registered in the Ministry of Foreign Affairs
No. 897 – Documents

275. December 17, 1945   Zureiq to Jabiri

Secret
Coded

From the Syrian Chargé d'Affaires in Washington
to HE the Syrian Minister of Foreign Affairs, Damascus

The American Government asks us to adopt a forceful and harsh position with regard to the Franco-English agreement and to raise the maximum discussion, turmoil and difficulties in relation to it.

It promises to intervene when the crisis reaches its most critical point.
December 17, 1945   The Chargé d'Affaires
                                                                       s/ Constantin Zureiq

Registered in the Syrian Foreign Ministry
No. 994 – Political reports

276. December 18, 1945   Zureiq to Jabiri

Secret
Coded

From the Syrian Chargé d'Affaires in Washington
to HE the Syrian Minister of Foreign Affairs, Damascus

The American Government has communicated to me its agreement on the following important points, that is:

– The American Government agrees to grant Syria military supplies to equip the Syrian army, as well as a long-term loan for a sum not exceeding a hundred million dollars, on condition that the Syrian Parliament agrees. Negotiations to this effect will begin soon. That is why it wants to know Syria's real needs in forming its army.

– It has also agreed to help the national Syrian economy by granting it commercial and industrial loans which will be covered in the long-term, on condition that the Syrian Government guarantees these loans and that the Syrian Parliament approves them.

December 18, 1945   The Chargé d'Affaires
                                                    s/ Constantin Zureiq

Registered in the Syrian Foreign Ministry
No. 995 – Political reports

277. December 19, 1945   King Ibn Sa'ud to President Quwatli

Secret
Coded

From King Ibn Sa'ud
through the intermediary of the Saudi Legation in Damascus

To my Dear Brother, Shukri Bey Quwatli, may God preserve him.

Greetings – I ask you to pay attention to Emir Abdullah's people and to their new activities following the promulgation of the Franco-British agreement. As for us, we are expecting a surprise from Abdullah. The English are encouraging him to carry out acts of which God alone knows the outcome.

As far as the agreement goes, I think that an understanding with France is today the best of things. The English reached an understanding with the French. It is up to you now to reach an understanding with them. If you do not do it, they will reach an understanding with others (than you).

You say to me that you rely on the advice of the United Nations. We both realize its sterility. It is therefore preferable for you and for us that the agreement with the French should take place with people like you rather than be with others.

We are wholly inclined to support you in everything you seek.

Greetings and divine mercy.

14 Muharram 1365
December 19, 1945   s/ Abd al-Aziz Ibn Abd al-Rahman

Registered in the Ministry of Foreign Affairs
No. 882 – Documents

278. December 22, 1945   Solod to Jabiri

Secret

From the Minister of the USSR in Syria
to the President of the Council of Ministers
the Syrian Minister of Foreign Affairs, Damascus

Your Excellency,

My Government wishes to know if the Government of the Syrian Republic has entered into discussion or agreements of a political or economic nature with the British Government.

Great Britain, in adopting the line it has adopted since the Franco-British agreement, whose appendices are still unknown, has arrogated to itself rights determined with regard to Syria and Lebanon. It goes without saying that it only attributed these rights to itself because the two Syrian and Lebanese governments have granted it privileges allowing it to act in this way.

I rcfcr in particular to the exchange of letters which took place between you and the British Government following the events of last May.

I am notifying you in the name of my Government that we will not intervene in favor of Syria unless we know that our intervention is opportune and that it will not be regarded as undesirable at a time when you have granted the British Government rights which allow it to adopt the line that it has adopted towards you.

Yours respectfully,

December 22, 1945   The Minister Plenipotentiary
                                                                 s/ D. Solod

Registered in the Ministry of Foreign Affairs
No. 991 – Political reports

279. December 23, 1945   Jabiri to the American Chargé d'Affaires in Damascus

Secret

To HE the Chargé d'Affaires of the
American Legation, Damascus

I ask you to kindly use all your efforts to have granted to us the necessary terms in order to import materiel for the army.

Some hurdles are financial in nature. I believe that the American authorities want to show themselves as conciliatory with regard to the pressing needs of the Syrian Army.

Concerning the armaments for the sale of which agreement was reached with the Syrian Government, I am ready to sign this agreement at any time you choose. I have, from now on, Syrian experts who will need to collaborate with your experts in drawing up the terms of the agreement.

Yours,

December 23, 1945   The Minister of Foreign Affairs
                                                                 s/ Sa'adallah al-Jabiri

Registered in the Ministry of Foreign Affairs
No. 1171/271 – Diplomatic correspondence

280. December 23, 1945   Jabiri to Wadsworth

Secret

To HE the American Minister Plenipotentiary, Damascus

LIST

The minimum Syrian requirements are as follows:

Summer and winter effects and shoes for a force of not less than 40,000
One hundred fighter planes
Fifty bombardiers
Fifty transport planes
Fifty training planes
Sufficient cannon to arm two light and two heavy batteries, and four mountain cannons
A tank division
Two thousand transport vehicles
Two thousand armored vehicles
Two thousand machine guns
Fifty thousand rifles
Ten thousand revolvers

December 23, 1945   The Minister of Foreign Affairs
                                                S/ Sa'adallah al-Jabiri

Registered in the Ministry of Foreign Affairs
No. 1172/272 – Diplomatic correspondence

281. December 23, 1945   Jabiri to the American Chargé d'Affaires in Damascus

Secret

To HE the Chargé d'Affaires of the
American Legation, Damascus

I promise Your Excellency, in the name of the Syrian Government, that any agreement that you present us in the name of the Socony Company, accompanied by the American Government's official recommendation, designed to exploit oil in the zone colored red in the sketch map which has been sent, will be approved on the terms you have mentioned.

I still await your detailed proposals.

Yours etc.,

December 23, 1945   The Minister of Foreign Affairs
                                                s/ Sa'adallah al-Jabiri

Registered in the Ministry of Foreign Affairs
No. 1173/273 – Diplomatic correspondence

282. December 23, 1945   Armanazi to Jabiri

Secret
Coded

From the Syrian Minister in London
to the Syrian Minister of Foreign Affairs

The British Government knows nothing of Mr Shone's plans, which are the subject of the letter you sent me. His activity surely represents the tendencies of the British command in the Middle East, which seeks to preserve a strategic position in Syria and in Lebanon, and to present the British Foreign Secretary with a fait accompli. However, this department is not of this opinion and thinks that the agreements concluded recently between Great Britain and France cannot be exploited in this manner in favor of the British interest. The Foreign Secretary is determined to make this agreement work, whatever obstacles are placed before him. The essential features of the agreement itself are not known. There is no doubt that it includes secret additions which have not been and will not be published.

December 23, 1945   The Minister Plenipotentiary
                                         s/ Najib al-Armanazi

Registered in the Ministry of Foreign Affairs
No. 1006 – Political reports

283. December 23, 1945   Shone to Jabiri

Secret

From the Minister of Great Britain in Syria
to HE the Syrian Minister of Foreign Affairs

I have received this telegram from the relevant ministry; it has asked me to notify you of the content for your information:

"You can assure the two Syrian and Lebanese governments that there will be no distinction in the withdrawal of British troops from Syria and Lebanon allowing the French to remain there alone.

"Political discussions particular to France and Great Britain will not have a bearing on Syro-Lebanese independence and will not diminish it."

"HM's Government is determined to maintain these promises, which it will honor by carrying them out."

December 23, 1945   s/ T. Shone

Registered in the Ministry of Foreign Affairs
No. 891– Documents

284. December 23, 1945   Mardam to Jabiri

Secret
Coded

From the Syrian Minister in Cairo
to HE the Syrian Minister of Foreign Affairs, Damascus

Today I discussed with Mr Smart the settlement envisaged by the British for Alexandretta. He told me that the British Government was making the greatest of efforts with the aim of ensuring compensation to Syria from the East, that is from Jazira, in exchange for Alexandretta. His government is also trying to reach agreement with the Turkish Government to grant Syria a free zone in the port of Alexandretta, and to settle the long-running disputes relating to the waters of the Kouek* river.

Border changes in other regions are unthinkable, and recognizing Syrian sovereignty over the suffering Liwa is impossible.

December 23, 1945   S/ Jamil Mardam Bey

Registered in the Ministry of Foreign Affairs
No. 1030 – Political reports

Note
*River in Aleppo whose source is in Turkey

285. December 24, 1945   Jabiri to the Cabinet

Top Secret
                              To the noble Council of Ministers

The following communication is the result of my last conversation with the British Minister Plenipotentiary:

"His Majesty's Government has decided, whatever the situation may be, to execute the last Franco-British agreement. It advises the Syrian Government not to follow a different course."

So, as you can see, this communication is forceful and harsh.

I expressed my deep regret to the Minister Plenipotentiary for the tone used with us.

December 24, 1945   The Minister of Foreign Affairs
                                                    S/ Sa'adallah al-Jabiri

Not yet registered

286. December 24, 1945   Jabiri to the Cabinet

Top secret
                              To the noble Council of Ministers

Mr Shone has just officially notified me of a British memorandum.

He transmitted it to me faithfully in his capacity as diplomatic representative, but in his capacity as a personal friend, he found himself constrained to advise us to persevere energetically in our position of firmness and has warned us to beware all weakness by saying, "It is possible to bring about an entente with the help of a procedure different to that one, if we ourselves know how to impose our will."

These words in my opinion greatly illuminate this (official) memorandum. They allow us to understand it and to interpret it within the framework of the facts, and not only according to the official framework.

December 24, 1945   The Minister of Foreign Affairs
                                              s/ Sa'adallah al-Jabiri
Registered in the Ministry of Foreign Affairs
No. 904 – Documents

287. December 24, 1945   Mardam to Jabiri

Secret
Coded

From the Syrian Minister in Cairo
to HE the Syrian Minister of Foreign Affairs, Damascus

Lord Killearn visited me today to clarify the proposals they presented about our conflict with the Turks. He believes that the British Government is determined to put an end to this dispute. The understanding between us and the Turks is necessary in the interests of our common defense.

The Liwa of Alexandretta cannot return to Syria.

Syria will be able to profit from the oil from new regions.

Creating a Kurdish bloc in the Syrian North-East would form an obstacle to the Russians who covet the North of Syria.

The proposals presented to us today were made in an officious, but not definitive, manner, but they express London's point of view. It is to be hoped that the Syrian Government will give its agreement to them with the required speed, so that it will then be possible to consider Syria and Turkey as forming a common defensive unity.

December 24, 1945   S/ Jamil Mardam Bey
Registered in the Ministry of Foreign Affairs
No. 1031– Political reports

288. December 24, 1945   Shone to Jabiri

Secret

From the Minister of Great Britain to the Government of the
Syrian Republic
to HE the President of the Council of Ministers
the Syrian Minister of Foreign Affairs, Damascus

Your Excellency,

The discussions which took place between Lord Killearn and HE Jamil Mardam Bey, although personal for the time being, nevertheless represent a point of view which satisfies my Government. The latter currently considers them useful to a settling of the far from satisfying situation that exists at the moment between Syria and Turkey, which both enjoy a certain friendship with it.

I have been tasked with asking Your Excellency our definitive point of view on these proposals, which are presented by the Turkish representative.

I await your reply.
December 24, 1945   Very sincerely,
                                                    T. Shone

Registered in the Ministry of Foreign Affairs
No. 903 – Documents

289. December 25, 1945   President Quwatli to King Ibn Sa'ud

Secret
Coded

From the President of the Syrian Republic
to HM King Abd al-Aziz al-Sa'ud, Mecca
via the Saudi Legation

Your Highness and my illustrious brother,

Greetings. Our position with regard to the agreement between the two colonizing states can only be what it is. We oppose this agreement with all our might. To guarantee the interests of our country, which is only pursuing the aim of ejecting the foreigners, we will make the greatest of efforts with the aim of exploiting every difference between the French and the British. The British military authorities, who think that it is their duty, in order to ensure the protection of British troops, that France should not be in charge of any military situation or position, have encouraged us in this view, because they fear the French and their communism a great deal.

In the current situation, the British Foreign Secretary cannot and will not be able to undertake any action against the advice of British experts who consider that the safety of the whole of the Middle East rests on their freedom of action and defense of this important strategic zone. They have confirmed this to us openly and have stressed that our opposition to the plan could only cause its setback by reinforcing their arguments and by favoring their vision. So, remain calm and be persuaded that this generous country has a God who protects it. Goodbye.

December 25, 1945   Your sincere brother
                                                  s/ Shukri al-Quwatli

A copy for information to Foreign Affairs
Not registered in the Ministry

290. December 26, 1945   The American Chargé d'Affaires in Damascus to Jabiri

Secret

From the USA Legation
to HE the Minister of Foreign Affairs

I ask you to treat with complete discretion our discussions on providing the clothing and arms needed by the Syrian army until the agreement is brought to reality between us.

Knowledge by any foreign body of these negotiations would hinder our success and delay it. That is what in my heart I do not wish for.

December 26, 1945   The Chargé d'Affaires of the American Legation

s/ illegible

Registered in the Ministry of Foreign Affairs
No. 1185/275 – Diplomatic correspondence

291. December 26, 1945   Armanazi to Jabiri

Secret
Coded

From the Syrian Minister in London
to HE the Syrian Minister of Foreign Affairs

The British Government views with a highly suspicious eye the activities of the movements called "patriotic" which, in essence, are designed to combat the British position in the Arab East.

Secret agents – British as well as French – cannot represent the true direction of the British Government. I was placed before a precise reality: these are the officials of the Intelligence Service who belong to the clan of Conservatives who create political obstacles for the British Labour Government.

That is why it would be better for us to avoid being deceived, and not to give in to the fire of our patriotism, which will not lead us to any result, as the British Government is determined to end the situation with Syria through an agreement with France, whose friendship it cannot do without.

December 26, 1945   The Minister Plenipotentiary

s/ Najib al-Armanazi

Registered in the Ministry of Foreign Affairs
No. 1012 – Political reports

292. December 27, 1945   Mardam to Jabiri

Secret
Coded

From the Syrian Minister in Cairo
to HE the Syrian Minister of Foreign Affairs, Damascus

I am sending you the text of the comments made by Mr... and Lord Killearn during a conversation I had with them about the Franco-British agreement.

"We are surprised by the disquiet which those in Syria and Lebanon show towards the Franco-British agreement. Since its beginnings, this agreement has only been a farce. In reality Mr Bevin was joking with Mr Bidault when he signed this wretched agreement with him."

I believe no one is more competent than these two men to form a definitive opinion about it.

December 27, 1945   s/ Jamil Mardam Bey

Registered in the Ministry of Foreign Affairs
No. 1017 – Political reports

293. December 28, 1945   Armanazi to Jabiri

Secret
Coded

From the Syrian Minister in London
to HE the Syrian Minister of Foreign Affairs

The British Government does not share the view of the Middle East Command in its interpretation of the special agreement relating to withdrawal. The (Syrian) Government must be aware that the British army will withdraw and that only French troops will remain in Lebanon, whatever statements have been or will be made. We must not allow ourselves to be deceived by maneuvers currently taking place between the French and the British. The latter are naturally inclined to create certain obstacles with the aim of lessening the effects of the agreement they concluded with France.

December 28, 1945   The Minister Plenipotentiary
                                                          s/ Najib al-Armanazi

Registered in the Ministry of Foreign Affairs
No. 1014 – Political reports

294. December 29, 1945   Shone to Jabiri

Secret

From the Minister of Great Britain in Damascus
to HE the Syrian Minister of Foreign Affairs

Your Excellency,

The staff of British army, in deciding the retreat from Syria of their security personnel, do not intend to replace them in any way with secret personnel. They seek to carry out a withdrawal plan about which they have reached an understanding with France, and to place their troops in a zone they are seeking to agree with the French command.

However, a reserve force must be mentioned: British security personnel may find themselves obliged to return and intervene once again in everything concerning or prejudicing the British armed forces.

It is understood that this intervention would not be carried out against the Syrians who, we are sure, will know how to demonstrate their loyalty with regard to the British forces, but against those who would disturb security and order. Anyway, this intervention, were it to happen in the future, would be of a secret and limited nature, and would be carried out with the collaboration of the Syrian authorities who, I believe, would look on it favorably.

December 29, 1945   Yours sincerely,
                                                          s/ T. Shone
                                                Minster Plenipotentiary

Registered in the Ministry of Foreign Affairs
No. 917 – Documents

295. December 30, 1945   The Chargé d'Affaires of the Soviet Legation to Jabiri

Secret

From the Chargé d'Affaires of the Soviet Legation in Damascus
To HE the Syrian Minister of Foreign Affairs, Damascus

Your Excellency,

Following the verbal note I gave you about the future of the Liwa of Alexandretta, its current situation and the future that the Government of the Soviet Union wants for it, I draw your attention to the activities of nationalist Kurdish elements on the future they want for themselves and on the desire for unity, progress and emancipation the Soviet Union is formulating for them.

Right now I can give the Syrian Government the assurance that these elements, which are dispersed among a number of states and which enjoy the Soviet Union's sympathy, will never adopt a position unsatisfactory to the Government and people of Syria.

Thus, I will have unequivocally expressed to you, from now, the reality of our intentions.

December 30, 1945   Yours sincerely,
                                      The Chargé d'Affaires of the Soviet Legation
                                                        s/ Cherniagin

Registered in the Ministry of Foreign Affairs
No. 10 a – Documents

296. January 1, 1946   President Quwatli to Cabinet members

Secret

From the President of the Syrian Republic
to the noble Council of Ministers

The mission of General Clayton, head of the special section of Arab Middle Eastern affairs, has two aims:

First: to convince us that Syrian unity will come about;

Second: to seek an understanding between Syria and Turkey.

For the understanding with Turkey we have confirmed to him that we have given our agreement and that we want it within the limits of the British memorandum that has been presented to us.

As for unity, he presents us with two plans:

– Syrian unity including Syria, Transjordan and part of Palestine with a plebiscite on the nature of the regime and on the choice of king if the regime is a monarchy.

– Arab unity including Iraq, Syria, Transjordan and part of Palestine. Then the king would be Faisal (King of Iraq) and there would be three guardians to the throne. Laws, rules, armies etc., would be unified.

Having highlighted our clear will for independence and having asked his opinion on France's attitude and the agreement concluded with it, he said, "This is not under discussion; when you want unity everything will be settled with France."

Our replies were negative, but were tied to Great Britain's attitude towards us by comparison with France. If Great Britain attained the removal of French troops from Syria and Lebanon it will then be possible for us to discuss the plan he has presented. Before that, any discussion is impossible.

January 1, 1946   The President of the Syrian Republic
                                                              S/ Shukri al-Quwatli

Registered in the Ministry of Foreign Affairs
No. 1032 – Political reports

297. January 2, 1946   Jabiri to the Cabinet

Top Secret

The Council of Ministers of the Syrian Republic
to the Minister of National Defense

Give quick verbal orders.

Order any military authority under your command to pursue the bloodthirsty Oliva Roget and proceed to his arrest if he enters Syrian land.

The Council of Ministers gives you permission to shoot to carry out this order and will bear the consequences of this action.

January 2, 1946   For the Council of Ministers of the Syrian Republic
                                                              s/ Sa'adallah al-Jabiri

Copy for information – to the Ministry of Foreign Affairs
Not registered

298. January 3, 1946   The Chargé d'Affaires of the Soviet Legation to Jabiri

Secret

From the Chargé d'Affaires of the Soviet Legation in Damascus
to HE the Syrian Minister of Foreign Affairs, Damascust

Verbal memorandum

In the name of its Government, this legation had told the Syrian Government of the strong sympathy it had towards its demands for independence and the desire it had to support it and to give it complete support in everything to do with its development and its social progress.

My Government would be happy to see the Syrian Government officially requesting help, not only politically but also militarily and economically.

This is why my Government has asked me to indicate to it the wishes of the Syrian Government, its desire for this help and the conditions it puts on it.

January 3, 1946   For the Soviet Legation
                                                        s/ Cherniagin

Registered in the Ministry of Foreign Affairs
No. 926 – Documents

299. January 3, 1946   Zureiq to Jabiri

Secret
Coded

From the Syrian Chargé d'Affaires in the USA
to HE the Syrian Minister of Foreign Affairs, Damascus

I was called today to see Mr Byrnes. He confirmed to me his Government's respect with regard to Syrian independence. He promised me all the necessary help on condition that the Syrians remain firm in their courageous and dignified position for the defense of their independence, and that they refuse to accept the fait accompli stemming from the Anglo-French agreement. Mr Byrnes does not doubt that this agreement does not conform to the spirit of the San Francisco pact.

January 3, 1946   The Chargé d'Affaires
                                                        s/ Constantin Zureiq

Registered in the Ministry of Foreign Affairs
No. 921 – Political documents

300. January 3, 1946   Armanazi to Jabiri

Secret

From the Syrian Minister in London
to the Syrian Minister of Foreign Affairs, Damascus

The Moscow Conference has made it possible for the British Government to determine clearly that the Middle East constitutes the objective of Russian ambitions.

You will note that the British Government is going to use unheard of efforts to bring communism to an end. In each Arab country all politicians who have the slightest sympathy for the Soviets will be removed from power. All individuals whose actions do not fit with British interests will be distanced from political action.

From now on, and for a long time to come, our country will be the campaign ground for a silent battle between these two sides.

I am alerting you from now against any measures that would not correspond with these British intentions which can no longer be discussed, because of the higher interests of British policy.

January 3, 1946   s/ Najib al-Armanazi

Registered in the Ministry of Foreign Affairs
No. 1043 – Political reports

301. January 4, 1946   The Chargé d'Affaires of the American Legation to Jabiri

Secret

From the Chargé d'Affaires of the Legation of the USA in Damascus
to HE the Syrian Minister of Foreign Affairs, Damascus

Your Excellency,

This Legation had set before you the outcome of conversations that took place between the Minister of the Syrian National Economy and the American mission presided over by Mr Well.

The Minister of the National Economy had given his agreement in principle to setting up global American lines of communication with bases in Syria. The following day, however, this department sent an official letter to the mission informing it of its inclination to engage in discussions and to examine the propositions the mission would present it.

But these hurdles had been crossed and the agreement of the Ministry given. This Legation is therefore greatly astonished by this change which, we have no doubt, is more political than economic in nature.

The discussions that took place between us about the help my Government would give the Syrian Republic, on the loan and provision of military equipment we promised to the Syrian army, all that can only be considered as a whole, the implementation of which cannot be countenanced except within the framework of what is due to us and of what we are owed.

I ask you in advance to act on this.

Respectfully,

January 4, 1946   The Chargé d'Affaires of the
                                                        American Legation
                                                            s/ illegible

Registered in the Ministry of Foreign Affairs
No. 1190/282 – Diplomatic correspondence

302. January 4, 1946   Jabiri to Solod

Secret

From the President of the Council, the Minister of Foreign Affairs
to HE the Minister Plenipotentiary of the USSR, Damascus

Verbal memorandum

I studied with interest your verbal memorandum about the Soviet Government's concern with regard to our demands for independence and its desire to help us.

What matters to me is to know the motive and point of your wish to help us. Is it to achieve political or economic influence? Or, as one says here, for the love of God, something we cannot conceive of anyone?

Also, we are bound by the ties of gratitude with regard to Great Britain.

America, as you also know, does not hide its willingness to help us.

We are in a position to be able to accept all these offers if we can respond to them in the same manner, but that would become impossible if each Great Power was seeking to help us only to make its own political order, its businesses and other privileges, triumph. That is the way in which I see the possibility of help between you and us. What I ask first of all is to know what pushes you to propose this help.

January 4, 1946   s/ Sa'adallah al-Jabiri

Registered in the Ministry of Foreign Affairs
No. 927 – Documents

303. January 5, 1946   The Egyptian Prime Minister to the Syrian Prime Minister

Secret

From the President of the Council of Ministers of the Kingdom of Egypt
to HE the President of the Council of Ministers of the Syrian
Republic, Damascus

Your Excellency,

An unclear future awaits the Muslim states and common dangers threaten them. I believe that it is Egypt's duty to intervene in any misunderstanding arising between two brothers, two neighbors and two friends when understanding is needed in the interests of the Muslim brotherhood.

It has reached me through a reliable source that Great Britain has intervened in different ways to regulate the Arab-Turkish conflict. First, I think that intervention by Great Britain would not have come about if this Power did not intend to gain something: the port of Alexandretta. I imagine that it is dangerous for Syria itself that this important port should be taken from Turkey to fall into the hands of Great Britain.

All I am asking at the moment is that you accept the intervention of the Egyptian Government or refer the whole matter to the Council of the Arab League. If that happens, the British danger would first be dissipated and Syria would draw benefits that it could not obtain through British intervention. In such a case, the League could rely on the complete help of Russia, America and even France. We would then be able to grant control of Alexandretta to a common Turkish-Arab Committee (or the League would be represented and not only Syria).

I have put the matter to His Majesty the King. My proposal drew his utmost praise.

In anticipation of your generous reply, please accept my sincerest good wishes,

January 5, 1946   S/ Muhammad Fahmi al-Nuqrashi
President of the Council of Ministers

Registered in the Ministry of Foreign Affairs
No. 929

304. January 5, 1946   Armanazi to Jabiri

Secret
Coded

From the Syrian Minister in London
to the Syrian Minister of Foreign Affairs, Damascus

The United States Government, by its repeated efforts in different Arab lands, provokes British Government fears. The men at the Foreign Office think that it is forcing them into an illegitimate and unacceptable competition which will not benefit either Great Britain or America itself.

The first of these fears is due to the ambitions the American authorities have sown in Emir Faisal al-Sa'ud's head and which will lead to a sure split in the Saudi Arabian state. When this split, which Great Britain does not want, occurs, the American authorities will intervene to protect their interests and impose their influence, not only in the Arab peninsula but in the whole of the Middle East.

The diplomats in charge of this in London ask that the Syrian Government, in the person of HE the President, intervene in the matter to convince King Abd al-Aziz to do something. Great Britain has, from its end, entered into contact with King Faruq who will personally discuss it with King Abd al-Aziz. There is the safety of the holy places and the possibility of action on the part of the Hashemites. There is even a possibility that France itself will side with America when it knows that Great Britain is fighting its position in our country.

His Excellency's intervention is essential. A serious crisis threatens the whole Arab world.

January 5, 1946   The Minister Plenipotentiary
S/ Najib al-Armanazi

Registered in the Ministry of Foreign Affairs
No. 1052 – Political reports

305. January 5, 1946   Jabiri to Mardam

Top secret
Coded

The Syrian Minister Plenipotentiary in Cairo

We must strongly deny the Soviet report to which Reuter's alludes. This report will be useful to us as long as we deny it. British hatred of us will thus be avoided. As long as we deny it the latter will seek to satisfy us. They will ruin us if they know that we have tried to play with the Russians. The Minister of the Soviet Union thinks that our point of view is justified and completely supports our position.
January 5, 1946

The Minister of Foreign Affairs
s/ Sa'adallah al-Jabiri

Registered in the Ministry of Foreign Affairs
No. 1194/362 – Diplomatic correspondence

306. January 5, 1946   Armanazi to Jabiri

Secret
Coded

From the Syrian Minister Plenipotentiary in London
to HE the Syrian Minister of Foreign Affairs, Damascus

Mr Bevin has notified me of the following:
"The rumor circulating about a demand made at the last Moscow Conference by HM the King's representative designed to distance the Arab states from the next peace conference is not true. It is the Soviet representative who officially made this demand.

Also, Mr Bevin regrets the bad interpretation adopted by those who see a plot woven against Syria and its independence in the last Franco-British agreement.

He confirmed to me that Great Britain has decided to apply this agreement in spirit and following the text. It is concerned with good relations with France just as it is concerned with the friendship of the Arabs, who must realize that an extremist, national spirit no longer has a place in this century which demands closer collaboration between humanitarian groups."

In my opinion, these remarks that I am sending you in writing are full of threats and warnings.
January 5, 1946

The Minister Plenipotentiary
s/ Najib al-Armanazi

Registered in the Syrian Ministry of Foreign Affairs
No. 924 – Documents

307. January 6, 1946   Jabiri to Shone

Secret

From the President of the Council, the Minister of Foreign Affairs
to HE the British Minister Plenipotentiary, Damascus

Your Excellency,
The discussions between the Ministry of National Economy and the American Mission are reaching an advanced stage. The Ministry has promised to

give the Mission all the necessary help as it promised to grant the asked-for concession. Any delay in this area would put us in a very difficult situation with regard to the American Legation. We fear that this would practically provide a reason for suspending discussions relating to the American aid which has been promised to us.

We find ourselves completely unable to delay the grant of the concession, for that would definitely delay the provision of aid which we ourselves and our army need.

January 6, 1946   The Syrian Minister of Foreign Affairs
                                                              s/ Sa'adallah al-Jabiri

Registered in the Ministry of Foreign Affairs
No. 1197/520 – Diplomatic correspondence

308. January 7, 1946   Jabiri to President Quwatli

Secret
                          To HE the President of the Syrian Republic
                              To the Noble Council of Ministers

I submit to you the verbal note which the Chargé d'Affaires of the British Legation gave me today.

From reading it, it appears that our situation is critical. The British military and Mr Shone himself confirm to us that the time is right to undertake acts likely to end our relations with France; on the other hand, they officially remind us that these acts are harmful to us.

In submitting the matter to you, I believe that the British are only acting in this way to deceive us and create a crisis that would lead to a reversal by taking as a pretext attacks on security and attacks against the French.

As a result I ask your noble Council to take whatever decision it thinks fit.

January 7, 1946   The Minister of Foreign Affairs
                                                              s/ Sa'adallah al-Jabiri

Not yet registered

309. January 8, 1946   Jabiri to the Cabinet

Secret
                From the President of the Council, the Minister of Foreign Affairs
                              to the Noble Council of Ministers

During a visit he paid me today the representative of the British Legation informed me of what a large number of French civilians are discreetly circulating in various Syrian towns.

Mr Evans thinks that those in charge of Syrian security should show some action in pursuing these people and in delivering them to the British authorities.

Of course the aim of all this is to arouse public opinion once again against the French danger which shows itself from one day to the next.

The British representative believes that Great Britain's good intentions towards Syrian independence will not be enough if we ourselves do not demonstrate enough harshness and force in pursuing those who act in the service and interests of France.

I invite your noble Council to take the necessary measures to combat this danger.

January 8, 1946   The Minister of Foreign Affairs
                                                   S/ Sa'adallah al-Jabiri

Registered in the Ministry of Foreign Affairs
No. 1061– Political reports

310. January 9, 1946   Armanazi to Jabiri

Secret
Coded

From the Syrian Minister in London
to the Syrian Minister of Foreign Affairs, Damascus

The Foreign Secretary has confirmed to us, through Mr Bevin, that Great Britain would not withdraw its troops from Syria and Lebanon, leaving France in Lebanon. It is clear that withdrawing from these two countries will happen with both the British and French armies.

January 9, 1946   The Minister Plenipotentiary
                                                   s/ Najib al-Armanazi

Registered in the Ministry of Foreign Affairs
No. 935 – Documents

311. January 9, 1946   Atasi to Jabiri

Secret
Coded

From the Syrian Minister in Paris
to the Syrian Minister of Foreign Affairs, Damascus

Allow me to tell you that all the statements made to you by the British are lies. The agreement between Great Britain and France is final and clear.

British forces will withdraw and French troops will stay in Lebanon for the time being. Incidents currently taking place against the French and the continual attacks, of which they are victims, are factors they will exploit against us. The English will help them in this. These aggressive acts, whatever they are, will give the French the chance to challenge us by saying that we are working to upset security. At that point I can be unambiguous: you will see the English, givers of false promises, repudiate these promises.

I put these truths before you and ask you to reflect seriously on the road we are taking.

January 9, 1946   The Minister Plenipotentiary
                                                   s/ Adnan al-Atasi

Registered in the Ministry of Foreign Affairs
No. 1064 – Political reports

312. January 9, 1946   Zureiq to Jabiri

Secret
Coded

From the Syrian Chargé d'Affaires in the United States
to HE the Syrian Minister of Foreign Affairs, Damascus

The American Government has changed its mind and has decided to intervene openly in the affairs of the Middle East, but also against Great Britain as well as against France. This time it does not want to accept the Anglo-French agreement or even want to recognize it. It will announce this publicly. The reasons which can be ascribed to this change of direction are the strong pressure which we, and the American authorities in contact with Syria, have applied. The Department of State was convinced that its interests, not only in Syria, but in the whole of the Middle East, would be threatened if a position of agreement and sharing between England and France was reborn, and that America would gain nothing.

King Abd al-Aziz's objection, and his intervention regarding the agreement and Palestine, has greatly helped clarify these points. King Abd al-Aziz will receive satisfaction regarding his particular demands in favor of Syria. As for those concerning Palestine, they will not meet with encouragement.

The important thing in all this is that America should have finally decided not to abandon the Syrian and Lebanese question and to realize its ambitions in the two countries, although it has not so far fixed them, and has not, as far as I know, communicated them to either France or England.

January 9, 1946   The Chargé d'Affaires
                                                               S/ Constantin Zureiq

Registered in the Ministry of Foreign Affairs
No. 1066 – Political reports

313. January 10, 1946   Jabiri to Mardam

Secret
Coded

From the President of the Council, the Syrian Minister of Foreign Affairs
to the Syrian Minister Plenipotentiary, Cairo

His Excellency the President thinks that King Ibn Sa'ud's visit to Cairo is starting to be the subject of extended comments. The Iraqi Delegate told him yesterday that this visit and the agreements resulting from it will be the final nail in the Arab League's coffin. This is how Iraq and Transjordan think that Egypt and the Hejaz will destroy Arab unity and will prevent the consolidation of efforts by states which have joined the League.

For our part we think that our hostility towards the Jews has begun to take a serious turn and that French intervention is once again a very serious possibility. Great Britain and France could not do anything in Syria except when the Arabs were in disagreement.

All we are asking of you at the moment is that you busy yourself in combating this situation. Talk openly to King Ibn Sa'ud about the matter and demonstrate the Hashemites' fears to him. Be careful that HM does not think that we are working for anything other than for the unity threatened by Iraqi fears, which we have been unable to dispel and which will lead us into a conflict when Philippe (*) is not merely at the door but inside the house itself.

January 10, 1946   The Minister of Foreign Affairs
                                                           Sa'adallah al-Jabiri

Registered in the Ministry of Foreign Affairs
No. 1209 – Diplomatic correspondence

Note

(*) France

314. January 10, 1946   Armanazi to Jabiri

Secret
Coded

From the Syrian Minister in London
to HE the Minister of Foreign Affairs, Damascus

You must make the greatest effort to be sure of the Lebanese Government's position with regard to the Franco-English agreement. What we know here is that the Lebanese Government, and the President of the Republic himself, do not hold the same position as we do. They are inclined to reach an understanding with France with conditions they deem reasonable. As for us, we know that as far as France is concerned, we have a negative position right down the line. What would our position be if the Lebanese were to stretch out a rope in the middle of the road?

The British Government believes that Lebanon does not support all our views. It thinks that our extremism is not justified, particularly in political matters, where one should be ready to talk unless one wants to impose one's will by force, and the British laugh whenever they mention force in connection with us.

January 10, 1946   The Minister Plenipotentiary
                                                           s/ Najib al-Armanazi

Registered in the Ministry of Foreign Affairs
No. 1069 – Political reports

Author's note: The British warning came after General Beynet persuaded Christian leaders, especially in the Maronite Church, to support France's continued presence in Lebanon.

315. January 11, 1946   Mardam to Jabiri

Secret
Coded

From the Syrian Minister in Cairo
to the Syrian Minister of Foreign Affairs, Damascus

HM King Abd al-Aziz has informed me that he talked to HM Faruq today about the Syro-Lebanese question. The two monarchs agreed to use maximum efforts to combat colonizing France and stop the realization of the Judeo-British scheme which aims to unite Syria under Emir Abdullah's command.

This agreement between the two kings and its publication as an official declaration will force France to withdraw definitively. It will also present Great Britain with a reality it will be unable to change. It is true that such a step will disunite the Arab League, but what is the use of this League which has only caused us and other Arabs harm?

Iraq is thus invited today to finally renounce its old ambitions of swallowing Syria. The agreement between these two kings will help us from now on to pass a milestone on the road to our freedom.

January 11, 1946   S/ Jamil Mardam Bey

Not yet registered

316. January 11, 1946   Mardam to Jabiri

Secret
Coded

From the Syrian Minister in Cairo
to the Syrian Minister of Foreign Affairs, Damascus

It is quite clear that the Saudi and Egyptian kings will present the British Government with two memoranda concerning the efforts being made by certain British officials in Syria, Transjordan and Baghdad with the aim of perfecting the plan for Greater Syria or uniting Transjordan with Iraq.

The two kings have decided to combat, at any price, the Hashemite family's plans. If they were to see in the British Government a desire to continue supporting the Hashemites and countering Saudi-Egyptian interests, the two Saudi and Egyptian Governments will have recourse, not to arbitration by the Arab League, but to Russian and American intervention and perhaps France too. In this way, the influences and global balance in Arab lands will evolve. I believe that Kings Abd al-Aziz and Faruq will not turn to this solution because of its seriousness, but they want to make it into a threat for the British who seem to be seriously decided in favor of the plan for Greater Syria or for unity.

I hope that the two kings will act in a considered way. For my part, I have fulfilled my duty and expressed my opinion, which is to see them keeping their sang-froid and not worrying about Iraqi-Transjordanian activity. This cannot, effectively, have serious consequences unless we, the Syrians, are in favor, which, as everyone knows, is impossible.

January 11, 1945   The Minister Plenipotentiary
                                                          S/ Jamil Mardam Bey

Registered in the Ministry of Foreign Affairs
No. 1071 – Political reports

317. January 12, 1946   Jabiri to Armanazi

Secret
Coded

From the President of the Council, the Syrian Minister of Foreign Affairs
to the Syrian Minister Plenipotentiary in London

Please inform the Ministry of Foreign Affairs that the Syrian Government is fully satisfied with the conduct of British diplomatic representatives in Syria and would not sanction in any way changing them or changing some of them. On the contrary, the Syrian Government believes that such a move would cause a misunderstanding between us.

In addition, the Syrian Government cannot allow any contact with France from its side before the effective withdrawal of French military forces, not only from Syria but also from Lebanon. We believe, in effect, that maintaining these forces in Syria and Lebanon directly threatens Syrian independence.

January 12, 1946   The Minister of Foreign Affairs
                                                          s/ Sa'adallah al-Jabiri

Not yet registered

318. April 4, 1946   General Beynet in support of secret Franco-Zionist collaboration

For Franco-Zionist collaboration

Mr Moshe Shertok, head of the Political Bureau of the Jewish Agency, intends to go to Paris during a trip he is currently undertaking in Europe. He will seek a chance to present to the Quai d'Orsay the Zionist organization's views on some problems which concern the French Ministry of Foreign Affairs as much as the Zionist movement, and he hopes to find the basis for collaboration in certain areas.

This is the thesis the Zionists are setting out to justify collaboration:

First, they underline the fact that they are fully aware of how concern to manage the susceptibilities of its Muslim Empire imposes on France great caution regarding the Palestinian problem. They understand that this caution expresses itself, in an official arena, as a position of neutrality. It is not a question here of seeking France's support for Zionist demands.

Further, the Zionists clearly see that official collaboration, whatever it is, or even too frequent, indiscreet contact, would be incompatible with the position of neutrality that France thinks it must adopt. For their part, the Zionists maintain with the British Mandatory Power and the Arab Muslim world relations that require much prudence from them too.

This said, the Zionists think that effective but secret collaboration over acts of French and Zionist policy will assert itself where French and Zionist interests are identical, and above all where only a coordination of efforts can offer some chance of effective action.

Since 1941, the Zionists have taken part in carrying out a plan which aimed to bring about the union of the "Arab World" subject to the exclusive influence of Great Britain. This plan included the removal of France from the Levant. In the absence of political conditions, in the Arab countries, favoring the positive tendency towards unity, the builders of Arab Union turned the attention of all these countries towards Palestine, and it is around the idea of the struggle against Zionism that the Arab League was formed.

North African agitators who today seek the support of this League in Cairo do not fail to appreciate the role that anti-Zionism plays as an element in the rapprochement between all Arab Muslims. Once the Palestinian question is dealt with, they anticipate using the same formulae and reuniting the same sympathies for the benefit of a crusade against French positions in North Africa.

It matters little, from the point of view that concerns us, if the organizers of the Arab League have drawn the advantages they were counting on. It is only too clear that the plan has succeeded in its destructive elements and particularly as far as eliminating direct French influence in the Levant.

The Zionists have always had an interest in Lebanon. Not, as pan-Arab propaganda would have us believe, because they nurse territorial ambitions over it, but because it seemed as though Christian Lebanon ought to have been a natural ally against the assault of Arab Muslim nationalism. From the Lebanese side, the notion of solidarity of Lebano-Zionist interests has always existed among all those who, until the arrival of the 1943 government, were considered to be the defenders of the Lebanese idea against that of Syrian unity. Today the Christian elements who dream of resuming the struggle for the Lebanese idea are again turning their sights to Zionism.

To the Zionists it has always seemed essential that a Christian Lebanon should be a counterpart of a Jewish Palestine, a Lebanon which would be Christian not by virtue of the presence (more than dubious) of a Christian majority among its inhabitants, but by virtue of the official recognition of its nature as a home for the Christians of the Middle East. The Zionists have always considered it as clear that maintaining traditional relations between Lebanon and France was the necessary condition for the existence of such a home.

After the withdrawal, France will maintain a very important moral position in Lebanon, based on the Christian element in the country, and which the Arab nationalist element – internally as well as externally – will try to destroy in order to hasten assimilation in Lebanon by the pan-Arab body. France cannot think of compromising its vital interests in North Africa by setting itself up, even on the diplomatic level, as the exclusive champion of the Lebanese Christians. But nor can it abandon the positions of prestige it has held in Lebanon without its prestige in North Africa being deeply shaken, or renounce exercising all influence in a center where the cultural influence over the Arab world is significant. France will therefore be led, without allowing itself to be reduced to direct intervention – and after having thoroughly convinced Lebanese public opinion that the era of direct intervention belongs to the past – into entering into a coalition with forces which, internally as well as externally, will try to reinforce the struggle of Christian Lebanon to maintain its traditional ties with the West.

Deprived of all external direction, Christian Lebanon will not be able to resist the mounting tide of Arabism; it will be led, by one compromise after another, to lose – in the most favorable of cases – all individuality.

It is not however by the intervention of a nucleus of Lebanese Christians that the resistance movement may be able to benefit from external support capable of organizing it.

Four strands will converge on the same target: that of France, that of the Zionists, that of the Church and that of the nucleus of Christian resistance. With regard to the Church's future action, it is enough to say here that the Vatican does not seem at all hostile to a collaboration with the Zionists and to the idea of a Jewish national home consolidating the position of a Christian home.

By acting separately, the external supports risk not only not being able to confront the common adversary, they may also act at cross-purposes. It is not enough that the agreement exists regarding the intended result; there must also be agreement about the means to bring it about. It would, for example, be deplorable to see two or three resistance movements forming, each with a secret leader and fighting among themselves. In addition, it is clear that the French, the Zionists and the clergy have access to means of action which will work hard in very different areas and which are likely to complement one another.

The envisaged collaboration could play out within a very wide framework. It would be enough for there to be an agreement in principle, maintenance of a discreet link, exchange of information and, at regular intervals, common decisions on certain points of policy to follow. The very subjects of this coalition, the Lebanese Christians, would be able to remain ignorant of the agreement of their protectors.

It is clear that Franco-Zionist collaboration could intervene in many other areas than that of the Levant, without ever having to reveal itself in the daylight: a study of the development of political, social, cultural and economic movements in the Middle East, North African policy, international propaganda.

319. June 7, 1946   Musa al-Alami to the ex-Mufti Amin al-Husseini in Paris

Beirut, June 7, 1946

Information

Report from Musa Alami to the Grand Mufti in Paris

(not word-for-word – very good source)

1 I have noticed that the Arab League (and Egypt in particular) does not in any way want the Palestine affair to be put before the Security Council or before the UN Assembly. The reasons given for this by the states of the Arab League are as follows:

   a   By the fact of having recourse to the UN, they are not sure of winning the majority of votes on the Council, because the Anglo-Saxons form a majority there.

   b   The states of the Arab League do not want to assume a position hostile to the English in favor of the Russians.

2 The states of the Arab League, which are nothing more than a British creation, by adopting this line of conduct, carry out English directives to the letter.

3 In fact, the states of the Arab League have agreed to limit their demands to two points:

   a   the cessation of Jewish immigration,

   b   the installation of a local Judeo-Arab administration under British mandate.

4 It is important to the Arab League that the Palestinian problem be solved by it, that Jamal Husseini is not one of the negotiators with the British except as a secondary member and that finally it should be said that the Arab League succeeded in fixing the final fate of Palestine.

5 The leaders of the Arab League and particularly behind them Riyad al-Sulh and Nuri Pasha Sa'id are strongly opposed to the return of the Mufti before the Palestinian problem has been finally settled by the Arab League.

6 Jamil Mardam, Riyad al-Sulh and Nuri Pasha Sa'id have succeeded in forming the Palestinian bloc which will dispute prestige and prerogatives with the Husseini bloc. This new bloc (the supreme Arab front) will follow a tactic cloaked in a more extremist form than the Husseini committee, in order to weaken the prestige of the latter in the eyes of nationalist Arab opinion. It is only with this aim that this new bloc will be formed and will pretend to act so that the Palestinian question can be put before the UN.

7 The Supreme Arab Committee has held back from replying officially to the Russian overtures made by Solod and which consist of bringing the Palestinian question before the Security Council. Solod has however explicitly confirmed to me that Soviet diplomacy would succeed in not leaving the fate of Palestine to be decided by the Jews and Anglo-Saxons alone. This proposition has had no response from me, I put it before you so that you will have the greatest of latitude in acting and can show me the line to follow.

***

Finally the essential part of the said report consists of a detailed account of the armed forces in Arab countries which are ready to come to your aid and to take part in any insurrection unleashed in Palestine. Jamal Husseini is very optimistic about the outcome of this undertaking. He says that the Russians are inclined to support this movement with money and arms. He says that he has already had discussions about this with Solod and that the latter promised, on the part of his Government, to exploit the fact diplomatically, but on condition that the Arab masses in neighboring countries take part in this act of insurrection.

320. October 4 (or 14), 1946   King Faruq to President Quwatli

Top secret

Copy

His Excellency Shukri bey Quwatli, may God protect him

May the benediction, mercy and blessings of Allah be upon you.

I am informing you that the Turkish Government has asked me to intervene to persuade Syria to forget its fears and mistrust with regard to its neighbors the Turks and to conclude an agreement of good neighborliness with them in view of their reciprocal interests and advantages, according to their way of putting it.

As I knew the legitimate rights of the Syrians, my reply was that Syria was ready, without intervention, to come to an understanding and to cooperate on condition that its rights are preserved, that the wrong it has undergone is recognized and that which was torn from it is returned.

The Turks, to my mind, are at long last inclined to satisfy the rights that you have, on condition that you do not show any negligence or let-up, no matter the power of the pressure the British bring to bear on you.

I wish, on this occasion, to tell you that Syria is a piece of us ourselves and that if we are keen to see the satisfaction of its rights, it is because for us it is a duty vis-à-vis men who are our brothers in religion, language and nationality.

Greetings   Sincerely,
                                                                                                    Faruq

Written in Abadin, October (4 or 14), 1946
Registered in the Syrian Foreign Ministry
No. 1301 – Political documents

321. November 2, 1946   King Ibn Sa'ud to President Quwatli

Top secret

HE President Shukri Quwatli, may God preserve him in life

May peace and God's mercy be with you.

The British Minister Plenipotentiary has informed me that his Government has no intention of creating a throne in Damascus for Abdullah and that the relevant British civil servants in the Middle East have not been asked by their government to bring about the state of Greater Syria, that their action is purely personal and that the British Government has given the necessary instructions for them to conform to them and not to embark on scheming which is beyond the scope of their prerogatives. The British Government understands that my friendship for it is a necessity for peace in the East and it will not destroy this friendship by creating a throne for Abdullah who provokes us. The Minister believes that it is you who is the cause of the current poor situation and that Abdullah is negotiating at your expense with the Turks who currently see in him a close friend, who can guarantee them, as well as Great Britain, the friendship of the inhabitants of Syria and Iraq, while you yourself refuse to shake the hand the Turks are holding out to you. In our opinion that represents a chronic threat for us as well as for you; it is also a clear example of the pressure you are under. I hope that you will not allow yourself to be affected by it. I have written in this way to my "brother" Faruq – may God preserve him – so that he can give us all the help possible.

Abd al-Aziz

November 2, 1946

Registered in the Syrian Ministry of Foreign Affairs
No. 1303 – Political documents

322. November 3, 1946   General Spears to Jabiri

Top secret

> HE Sa'adallah Bey Jabiri, President of the Council, Minister of
> Foreign Affairs – via the British Legation

I doubly regret the sentiments which I am persuaded are not noble and which the Syrians have shown towards me.

I am convinced that such hostile sentiments can only come from people who you and I know act according to French suggestions and want to see me as an enemy.

I also regret the rumors according to which I am supposedly a Jew as is my wife, and would work in the service of Zionism to separate you from your Arab brothers.

I am also regretful because I cannot change my position with regard to Haj Amin al-Husseini who, I am convinced, currently serves France more than he serves his own country.

I regret all that in the first instance.

In the second instance, I regret your hardly reasonable position with which you threaten to break agreements we have agreed upon, seeming to forget that Great Britain is not so weak that it can be treated in such a way.

I send you this letter full of regret, hoping that you will consider the exact circumstances in which you and I find ourselves.

I also hope that you will accept my deepest respect.

Spears

November 3, 1946
Registered in the Ministry of Foreign Affairs
No. 3314/1132B – Diplomatic correspondence

323. November 3, 1946   President Bishara al-Khuri to President Quwatli

Top secret

HE President Shukri al-Quwatli

The British Chargé d'Affaires has just visited me and asked me with insistence to inform you that his Government regards the act of bringing the matter of the Syro-Turkish dispute to the Council of the League as a bad move likely to unsettle the peace in the Near East, and that his Government sees it as an unfriendly gesture which makes all those who do it and who take part in it fully responsible.

My view is that you should quickly request the withdrawal of this complaint and insist on it because this discussion will only lead to dangers for you and for us.

November 3, 1946   Bishara Khalil al-Khuri

Registered in the Syrian Ministry of Foreign Affairs
No. 3313L/540 – Diplomatic correspondence

324. November 3, 1946   President Quwatli to King Faruq

Top secret

His Majesty King Faruq I, may God preserve him

Your Majesty,

I read your noble address with tears in my eyes and I thank God for giving Syria a champion and a helper it can have recourse to and who defends both it and its rights.

The Turks, my Lord, have evil designs with regard to us and whatever the changes in the situation, the spirit of oppression and domination rules them. All their dreams are of the restoration of the Ottoman Empire, but weakness is what restrains them: injustice is buried in their soul; strength reveals it, weakness hides it.

The Turks want at all costs to reach agreement with us and the English want us to do it, but what is the use for us Arabs, and especially for us Syrians? Absolutely nothing unless becoming a millstone, losing Alexandretta and losing our unknown future. I thank you, in the name of all Syrians for your noble defense of our legitimate rights. Syria only sees danger to itself from its old oppressors, Turks and French. God preserve it from concluding an agreement with one of them. God preserve you as champion and Treasure of the Arabs.

November 3, 1946   Shukri al-Quwatli

Registered in the Ministry of Foreign Affairs
No. 1305 – Documents

325. November 12, 1946   Solod's memorandum

Top secret

Report

My government considers it important to remind you that the policy of mistrust that the Syrian Government is following with regard to the Soviet Union is wholly unjustified. Many proposals made by this legation have been subject to non-receipt or total silence by you.

Today I come to remind you that the policy of pressure, oppression and stifling liberties, to which irresponsible British civil servants encourage the Syrian Minister of the Interior, such a policy, I say, can only bring you disappointment, something that the Soviet Union does not wish on you.

I come to give you this advice, although I know in advance that you are not prepared to listen to it; but I am fulfilling my duty which the good we wish for you tells me to do.

November 12, 1946

D. Solod

Registered
No. 1312 – Documents

326. November 12, 1946   Jabiri to the Saudi Minister in Damascus

Top secret

His Excellency the Minister Plenipotentiary
of the
Kingdom of Saudi Arabia

Your Excellency,

Please convey to his august Majesty the King, the Syrian Government's impressions regarding the Palestine question and tell him what it thinks about this at the moment.

The Syrian Government is convinced that the Palestine question, as well as Jewish demands, is, fundamentally, the result of French encouragement which wants to undermine the basis of Arab issues. Through information received and statements heard we know for a fact that France is the support which firmly props up the Jews and encourages them in all areas of activity and in all circumstances. In this way it wants to try to return to the East to resume its previous guardianship of the Arabs and chase them out.

That is why we want you to remind His Majesty that the Palestine question must not be detached from questions which, in the same light, involve us vis-à-vis France. Quite to the contrary, the Syrian Government believes that it is not possible to consider the Palestine question fully except in connection with other issues of the Arab West.

I would ask you to solicit His Majesty's opinion, which the Syrian Government would like to know before presenting the matter to the Council of the League.

Yours sincerely,

Your devoted
Sa'adallah al-Jabiri
President of the Council and Minister of Foreign Affairs
Damascus, November 12, 1946
Registered in the Ministry of Foreign Affairs
No. 3327/127 - I – Diplomatic correspondence

327. November 14, 1946   Armanazi to Jabiri

Top secret

The Syrian Minister of Foreign Affairs, Damascus

I can summarize the following outcomes from a conversation I had yesterday with a British representative:

We will tire ourselves and we will tire others if we seem to forget the reality facing Great Britain; it is that it cannot do without Turkey and that it is forced to help it and to strengthen it, just as it is forced to keep a strong military base on the Suez Canal.

Here they reproach us with not understanding the need which makes them resort to the speedy conclusion of an Arab-Turkish agreement, while they are convinced that the Egyptians do not want to understand the reality of factors forcing Great Britain to keep a war footing. It is our lack of understanding with regard to this fact that makes certain British representatives encourage King Abdullah just as it makes the British support Sidqi Pasha in Egypt. From this, it will appear to you that the problem for the British is not a simple matter; it has been mapped out: that we fall in step with them completely or they will go without us, overwhelming the land from end to end.

Once again I suggest to you that you yourself have contact with the Americans, the French and the Russians; maybe we can exploit their position with regard to us against the English. This is our last hope.
November 14, 1946

The Minister Plenipotentiary
Najib al-Armanazi
Registered in the Ministry of Foreign Affairs
No. 3330B/1141 – Diplomatic correspondence

328. November 14, 1946   King Ibn Sa'ud to President Quwatli

Top secret

To His Excellency the President of the Syrian Republic – Damascus
(through the intermediary of the Saudi Legation in Damascus)

We have informed the British Minister Plenipotentiary that we will under no circumstances give our consent to a plan to divide Palestine.

We have also informed him of the surprise (?) caused by the certainty reached by us that it is British agents and individuals who are working to create disorder and unrest in Syria and to shake the stability of the Government and create a throne for Abdullah there.

We have also given him clearly to understand that, if that is really their true ambition, these maneuvers will remain unsuccessful and that if they are only a pretense, they would not know how to induce Arab countries to preserve their friendship with England. We have added that Syria would not agree to be the victim by abandoning Alexandretta to the Turks and resigning themselves to the arrival of Abdullah. He promised to give me a prompt answer.

Abd al-Aziz Ibn Rahman al-Sa'ud

November 14, 1946

Registered in the Syrian Ministry of Foreign Affairs
No. 1315 M – Diplomatic documents

329. November 15, 1946   President Quwatli to King Faruq

Top secret

His Majesty the venerable King Faruq I
May God protect him.

Your Majesty,

I have recently given Jamil Mardam Bey the honor of telling you our preferences regarding the negotiations for Egyptian Sudan and Tripoli (Libya).

Although a respected enemy because of our relations with Great Britain is opposed to you, your eminent government will not forsake the peaceful happiness of its tribes even if Sudan does not hold great interest for Egypt. In addition, the Arab authorities have placed under your high patronage the region of Tripoli whose independence you must defend, as well as the limits of the furthest Arab West in the face of French oppression.

The heart of the Arabs today turns to Your Majesty, for if the Sudan affair hardly affects Egypt, Great Britain takes not account of the fact that one million Arabs live in Tripoli under your authority.

Also, I hope that you will inform me, my Lord, of all whom this matter interests and that you will succeed in bringing British policy, despite its opposition, to recognize the established situation.

May God guide your hand and protect you for your devoted

Shukri al-Quwatli

November 15, 1946
Not registered in the Ministry

330. November 17, 1946   Jabiri to Armanazi

Top secret

The Syrian Minister Plenipotentiary, London

The Syrian Government appreciates your valuable comments. But we must recognize that we can do nothing to oppose the British and we can only resist them with one force, that of the people.

The mob is against us; they use the Druze and the opposition and we can only answer them with the procedure they use with us; that has effectively started; for the policy of strikes and demonstrations must now come to an end in our interest, not against our interest.

Your opinion is to be taken into consideration with regard to an agreement with the Americans, but we cannot draw any benefit from France for, apart from France no longer having any worth in the international arena, we reject, with regard to ourselves, any relations with France. As for the Russians, I believe that no one can benefit from them, it is, quite the opposite, they who profit from others at their expense.

I assure you once again that the best we can do is to persuade the British that it is neither in their interest nor in ours to achieve what they are threatening, that King Abdullah will not serve their interests because it is us and us alone who are their true friends.

November 17, 1946

The Minister of Foreign Affairs
Sa'adallah al-Jabiri

Registered in the Ministry of Foreign Affairs
No. 333B/1146 – Diplomatic correspondence

331. November 18, 1946   Armanazi to Jabiri

Top secret

The Syrian Minister of Foreign Affairs, Damascus

I informed the relevant party of the discussions Faris Bey had, the answers you stipulated and the tenor of the letter you sent me. Full of warmth and sorrow this anyway expresses my own convictions exactly. We were greatly pleased by the honorable position you adopted as regards Syro-British friendship.

I have been assured that our fears are unfounded, that British policy is not two-faced. The Labour Government thinks that the Syro-British friendship would not run any risks and that King Abdullah's demands involve only him. They also added that if there are British politicians who give their support to this sovereign, they are not however part of the Labour Party now in power and responsible for general British policy.

I thank you for having made known these conversations in good time. We would like to be informed of subjects broached there.

The Minister Plenipotentiary
Najib al-Armanazi

November 18, 1946

Registered in the Syrian Ministry of Foreign Affairs
No. 1304 – Diplomatic reports

332. November 20, 1946   Jabiri in Cairo to the Acting Minister of Foreign Affairs

Top secret

The Syrian Legation in Cairo
to the Acting Syrian Minister of Foreign Affairs

I think that we should not do anything at the moment. We really do not know the true intentions of the English. Yesterday I had a warning from Mr Bowker who told me that the current situation in Syria is "confused" (in French in the text).

I therefore suggest that you act with extreme prudence and use all your efforts to avoid conflict with the opposition. Really, at the moment, any incident would cause us irreparable damage. Our current situation is extremely delicate and serious. ... (an incomprehensible nine-word sentence) ... Also, we should realize that the political aims of Great Britain and the position it means to adopt remain unclear. So let the opposition shout; if it wants to withdraw from the House, let it withdraw! As for these dogs, we must hasten to give them the money they want, to guarantee their silence and avoid them creating difficulties for us.

Sa'adallah al-Jabiri

November 20, 1946

Registered in the Syrian Ministry of Foreign Affairs
No. 3,373/886Q – Diplomatic dispatch

333. November 1946   Nuri al-Sa'id to the Turkish President Ismet İnönü

Top secret

His Excellency President Ismet İnönü

The Iraqi Government must, for the moment, despite its desire to see a royal Syrian government established and facing the possibility of seeing the problem of the government of the Syrian Republic in its current state resolved, study with a degree of reserve all the proposals you have made to it regarding the question of the Turkish-Syrian borders and particularly as far as the regions of Aleppo and Qamishli are concerned.

The greatest difficulty really rests with this claim you have made and which is the annexation of Aleppo to Turkey. But I can assure you, with authority that your claim regarding the border at Qamishli can be accepted from now, so long as it does not exceed in depth the adjustments imposed on the borders of [18]70, as regards fortified land in relation to the current borders.

So I must also now obtain an assurance that the lands for which you accept cession to Syria are the equivalent of lands you are demanding. And you will indicate the detail of the matter to me.

S/Nuri al-Sa'id

Registered in the Syrian Ministry of Foreign Affairs
No. 1378/5 – Documents

334. November 1946   Turkish-Iraqi agreement from summer 1945

Top secret
Summary of the Turkish-Iraqi agreement concluded in the course of the summer of 1945
(by Tawfiq Pasha al-Suwaidi, ex-President of the Iraqi Council, who has given this document to the Syrian Ministry of Foreign Affairs).

The agreement essentially consists of two protocols and an exchange of letters, *all secret.*
Protocol No. 1

The Iraqi and Turkish governments commit themselves to resisting jointly any threat to which the other is subject. This mutual help will automatically come into play. Each of the contracting parties will provide the other with indispensable help, assistance and facilities.

For its part, the Turkish Government promises to put its political influence to the service of the plans of Iraq, whose ambition is to guarantee the direction of the Arab nation and to establish its full sovereignty over Syria and Transjordan by establishing Hashemite domination in these two countries.

S/ Tawfiq al-Suwaidi

Registered in the Syrian Ministry of Foreign Affairs
No. 1,002 – Diplomatic documents

335. November 22, 1946   Zureiq to Jabiri

Top secret
Coded

To the Syrian Minister of Foreign Affairs, Damascus

His Majesty King Abd al-Aziz has informed the Department of State that he is inclined to grant America extended privileges if it agrees to renounce its demands in favor of the Jews in the Palestinian question.

Negotiations will soon take place between Saudi Arabia and America for granting this country the concession to build a Saudi port.

His Highness Emir Faisal gave me to understand that Great Britain had warned him about adopting such a policy but that His Majesty his father is inclined towards a complete understanding with America, even if he thus has to disappoint the British.

The King has, in effect, become convinced that it is only thanks to an agreement with America that one can hope to tear Palestine from the clutches of the Jews.

King Abd al-Aziz no longer has complete confidence in the importance of Great Britain in the international arena; also, he no longer thinks that he can depend on another European Power now that France has practically ceased to exist and that it is only a worthless thing in world politics.

As for the Soviet Union, King Ibn Sa'ud does not like to hear talk of it. For all these reasons, he deliberately turns to America and grants it everything it asks for.

November 22, 1946   S/ Constantin Zureiq
                                                        Minister Plenipotentiary

Registered in the Syrian Ministry of Foreign Affairs
No. 1315M – Political reports

336. November 26, 1946   Egyptian Prime Minister, Isma'il Sidqi, to Mardam

Top secret

His Excellency the Minister Plenipotentiary of the
Syrian Republic in Cairo

His Majesty the revered King has commanded me to give the Government of the Syrian Republic a summary of the declarations he made on the Turkish affair at the last meeting. He is persuaded of the need for your current Government to benefit from it.

His Majesty invited the Turkish Minister Plenipotentiary, despite Arab concerns with regard to this pact concluded between Iraq and Turkey. His Majesty emphasized that this agreement connects the pact with the Arab League pact. The Arab League, in effect, as the Turks know, considers it important that Arab and Turk live in harmony, without repelling or killing each other in the Middle East, and that Turkish-Arab relations can result in friendlier relations between the Arabs themselves. But the policy of one friend is not enough; that of all the Arabs with the Turks is necessary.

As for His Majesty's opinion on King Abd al-Aziz's position, overt indifference or hatred towards the Turks, it is that the Arab countries do not prepare for an eventual rivalry between the Hashemite and Saudi dynasties; the attachment of the Turks to such a union of dynasties can only increase the difficulties of succession and thus weaken Arab countries. So, Turkey, clearly, wants real unity and not domestic infighting.

His Majesty thinks that the fact of a solemn alliance is a deceitful affair and that the alliance between Turkey and the Arab countries will not be able to be subordinated to the pressure exerted by British policy on these countries, especially as regards to Turkish-Syrian differences.

That is why His Majesty suggests his mediation.

Such is, largely and briefly, the position of which I was to make Your Excellency aware.
November 26, 1946

The President of the Egyptian Ministry
Sidqi

Registered in the Syrian Ministry of Foreign Affairs
No. 1317 – Documents

337. November 28, 1946   The Syrian Minister in Ankara to the Syrian Ministry of Foreign Affairs

Top Secret

The Syrian Ministry of Foreign Affairs, Damascus

The atmosphere here is becoming more and more somber, and although Russia is not openly applying pressure, the pressure on the Turks continues and with some force. The English encourage the Turks each day in a new way and the latter refuse to concede anything to Russia.

On the other hand, what is certain is that they refuse to recognize that we have any claims on Alexandretta.

I am convinced that our interest now forces us to reach an understanding, even if it were with the Russians, to preserve our rights, as long as our friends the English refuse to help us, for in fact they would leave Alexandretta with the lion's share.

The Soviet ambassador here has, in conversations with me, expressed the desire of the Soviet Government to persuade the Arabs that no danger threatens them from their side and that the Moscow Government is inclined and even wants to help us take back from Turkey the rights it has snatched from us with the help of France and England.

I am convinced that an intention from this side will never be detrimental and that if it cannot be used to persuade the English of our importance, it can, however, not do us any harm.
November 28, 1946   The Minister Plenipotentiary in Turkey

Registered in the Syrian Ministry of Foreign Affairs
No. 1325 – Political reports

338. November 28, 1946   The Saudi Minister in Damascus to the Syrian Acting Prime Minister

Top secret

His Excellency the Acting President of the Council of Ministers – Damascus

There is no point in this Legation reminding Your Excellency that His Majesty King Abd al-Aziz readily agrees to the obligation of not abandoning his Arab brothers of Palestine and not passively accepting the plan designed to reject them.

But His Majesty still wants to draw the Syrian Government's attention to the fact that the Palestine question is not, in his opinion, the work of France. Universal Zionism does not rely on France in the first instance, and French conduct vis-à-vis the Arabs, which you refer to in your letter, is not considered in any way wise, for France is not the only power to oppress the Arabs. Many other influences come into play, which we know and which you know, and which have been the subject of friendly conversations between His Majesty and His Excellency the President of the Republic.

In addition, the current situation requires that one does not see hostility on the part of France towards the Arab question and His Majesty does not want to remind you that good relations with France have, several times, avoided the causes of conflict in Syria. But at this time His Majesty does not want others to attribute to him audacious and bold sentiments such as those you set before him in your letter.

Please take note of all this and let me know what you think.

Yours very sincerely,
Damascus, November 28, 1946

From: Ibn Za'id
Minister Plenipotentiary of
the Kingdom of Saudi Arabia

Registered in the Syrian Ministry of Foreign Affairs
No. 3375/133 – Diplomatic correspondence

339. November 28, 1946   The British Chargé d'Affaires to President Quwatli

Top secret

Memorandum presented in person on November 28, 1946
to the President of the Syrian Republic
by the British Chargé d'Affaires

My government has learned that certain members of the current Syrian government intend to busy themselves giving credit to the rumor that some British representatives are striving to weaken the position of this government.

My government has given me instructions to strongly deny these rumors. It desires that I remind His Excellency the President of the Syrian Republic that Syria is undergoing a delicate experimental period and that such startling accusations would not discharge them from responsibility for mistakes which its leaders are currently making.

The discontent of the Druze and of Sultan Pasha has reasons that are well known. The rumor going around the Syrian Parliament is surely provoked by the ministers' absence of democratic spirit. Some of them in effect do not want to face their responsibilities.

My Government asks His Excellency the President of the Republic to remind his Ministers that they must respect their duties and assume their responsibilities before delivering attacks on the friends of their country.

The reputation Great Britain has acquired by ardently defending the cause of Syrian independence would be reduced to nothing by propaganda with a new tone.

My Government expects radical action. It expects the name of Great Britain to be left out of the partisan propaganda circulating in Syria.

November 28, 1946

Registered in the Ministry of Foreign Affairs

No. 1421 – Documents

340. November 29, 1946   Jabiri in Cairo to the Syrian Minister of Foreign Affairs

Top secret

The Syrian Legation in Cairo
To the Syrian Minister of Foreign Affairs,
locum tenens

The insolence with which the Friend of the Arabs, General Clayton, received me today was beyond a joke.

He was not bothered about laughing at all our efforts, saying,

"You are playing around (like children), you don't know what you want or where you are going." I was unable to hold a conversation with him; in fact, he seemed to have only one aim, which was to get me angry. I remained calm and replied,

"I have nothing to do with you. I represent an independent country; you yourself are the agent of a friendly power, but for me you are not its representative, so I cannot recognize you."

He shot back, "You will know me well enough once I'm in Damascus." In reality, I could not know where this conversation was leading; it seems that he unveiled his whole plan during the course of a conversation he had with him, to our friend Jamil whom he immediately sent to you.

November 29, 1946

Sa'adallah al-Jabiri

Registered in the Syrian Ministry of Foreign Affairs

No. 1322 – Diplomatic reports

341. November 29, 1946   Jabiri to the Iraqi representative in the Arab League

Top secret

To His Excellency the President of the Assembly of the League
representing the Royal Government of Iraq
Through the intermediary of the Syrian Legation in Cairo

I have just now received your letter. I must express to you my deep regrets regarding my language which I tried, in vain, to moderate, such was the passion behind it.

Syria will never accept that a single inch of its territory should be subject to bargaining. I have told you clearly that King Abdullah, be he king or emir, will never penetrate our country and that it will stay a republic forever. If it were absolutely indispensable that Transjordan be reunited with Syria, it could only be considered as a Muhafazat dependent on our Government. So there would be neither king nor emir.

The simplest solution for us would be that we withdraw from the League, but we all know that our departure would entail the dissolution of this organization, for we are the only independent Arab state that is not oppressed by either military occupation or foreign privilege. Please inform the interested parties of this point of view.

Greetings,
Sa'adallah al-Jabiri

November 29, 1946

Registered in the Syrian Ministry of Foreign Affairs
No. 3375/887 – Diplomatic correspondence

342. November 29, 1946   President Quwatli to the British Minister in Damascus

Top secret
His Excellency the Minister Plenipotentiary of Great Britain – Damascus
The Syrian Government presents in advance its welcome to [Field] Marshal Montgomery if he visits Syria.

While confirming to you the friendship and perfect agreement which exists between our two countries, I am using this occasion to inform you that Syria considers that it is an unbreakable part of the Arab countries that surround it and that its strategy will always be based on the principle of common defense with its Arab neighbors.

Subject to this, please express to Marshal Montgomery once again the confidence we have in his wisdom for the establishment of all the arrangements he thinks necessary for the defense of Syria.

With greatest sincerity,

The President of the Syrian Republic
Shukri al-Quwatli

November 29, 1946
Registered in the Syrian Ministry of Foreign Affairs
No. 1.349 – Diplomatic documents

343. November 29, 1946   Zureiq to the Syrian Minister of Foreign Affairs

Top secret
Coded
To the Syrian Minister of Foreign Affairs – Damascus

I informed the State Department of the terms of your despatch.

The reply I received was not as precise as we had asked for. It is however, in my opinion, reassuring for the time being. This is the tenor:

"The State Department does not officially recognize the existence of the plan for Greater Syria. However it does not deny that it has been informed of the general outlines of this plan.

"Although this matter was originally developed by others and the idea has undergone considerable development, it is linked to the division of Palestine into two Jewish and Arab areas."

"The State Department will not make known its position regarding this plan. It is however inclined to examine it with the British Government which it is close to, and to spread to a large degree the exchange of views to the Arab governments who are the principal interested parties."

"The State Department thinks that the present time is not the most favorable for examining this important plan. It is of the opinion that its examination should be postponed for some time."

November 29, 1946   The Minister Plenipotentiary
                                                       Constantin Zureiq

Registered in the Syrian Ministry of Foreign Affairs
No. 1337 – Political reports

344. November 29, 1946   Jabiri's letter of resignation to President Quwatli

Top secret

<u>His Excellency the President of the Syrian Republic</u>
(Letter delivered by Naim al-Antaki)

My dear brother, my President,

After expressing my respectful greetings, I have the honor of informing you that my strength no longer allows me to put up with the considerable pressure being applied on me from different sides. So, I think I must withdraw from power to allow you to confer the presidency of the government on someone else. The continual threats to which I am subject on the part of the men from Great Britain lead me to believe that this power is settled on bringing about the plan for Syria which we all know about and that all those insincere promises which were made to us have been blown away by the wind.

The Council of the League can indeed throw a veil over the question of Greater Syria – it is however all that it has done; the plan does not exist any less. The British, I understand too well, will lead it to its conclusion under the guise of a popular movement and they will give us the treatment which we gave the French.

At the time when I am preparing myself to leave power and its responsibilities, I believe that it is incumbent on us to seek to benefit from Russian and American influences.

Anyway, I leave it to your wisdom.

S/ Sa'adallah al-Jabiri

November 29, 1946
Registered in the Syrian Foreign Ministry
No. 1336 – Documents

345. December 1, 1946   Armanazi to President Quwatli

Top secret
Telegram

HE the President of the Syrian Republic

The British Foreign Office hopes that Your Excellency will be good enough to consider the reality of the current situation in Syria as well as the regrettable effects and consequences it may entail for Syro-British relations.

British policy never aimed to bring about the plan for Greater Syria and the accusations made by members of the Syrian Ministry against Great Britain are very regrettable.

In the same way, British policy has never wanted to destroy the independence of Syria, and has contributed all its energies to establishing it.

That is why Mr Sa'adallah Jabiri's position must be revised for it does not conform to a true spirit of friendship.

The British Foreign Office regards HE Jamil Mardam Bey as the strongest Syrian who may be able to radically redress the situation.

December 1, 1946   The Minister Plenipotentiary
                                                                          Najib al-Armanazi

Not registered in the Ministry

346. December 2, 1946   Report of the head of the Syrian Deuxième Bureau

Report I

From the Chief of General Staff of the Syrian army to His Excellency the National Defense Minister to be brought to the attention of the Ministry of Foreign Affairs.

Report of the head of the Deuxième Bureau

The information drawn up by Captain 202, currently operating in Turkey as no. 28, has been sent to you with this. It can be summarized thus:

1 The Turkish Government has indeed swiftly signed an agreement with Iraq stipulating that the Turks will, in future, no longer take part in any offensive and that the forces of Iraq and Transjordan will have the option of standing up to Syria for the unification of this region.

2 The Turkish Government gives its consent in advance to Iraq regarding any Hashemite government that could arise in Syria under the aegis of Transjordan or Iraq.

3 The most dangerous issue is that the author foresees the creation of a common defense committee of Turkish and Iraqi officers for the preparation of all the plans for the defense of Turkey and Iraq in the common interest of the two countries.

And next week I will send Your Excellency the terms of the special agreement on Alexandretta and the ratification documents which have been signed for Iraq by Nuri al-Sa'id and for Turkey by President Inönü.

December 2, 1946   Signature
                                    Seal of General Staff, War, of the Syrian Army

Registered in the Syrian Ministry of Foreign Affairs
No. 1355 – Official reports

347. December 2, 1946   The Syrian Minister in Ankara to the Syrian Ministry of Foreign Affairs

Top secret
Coded
                    The Syrian Ministry of Foreign Affairs, Damascus

The Turkish Government, despairing of being able to conclude an agreement with us, has finally turned to Iraq, Transjordan and the international Jewish coterie which acts at the moment in close agreement with the two countries.

Nuri Pasha Sa'id who enjoys a not negligible influence here has finally promised Turkey, in the name of King Abdullah that he would recognize the annexation of Alexandretta and that he would come to an understanding with Turkey in order to adopt a common line of defense.

For all these reasons, I am in a position to inform you that the Turks are no longer interested in us and that they no longer wish to negotiate with us.

For my part, I can only attribute this change in position to the British who, it seems, have made the Turks understand that this understanding with us would only be necessary if they did not reach an agreement with King Abdullah. The Turks do not hesitate to maintain now that the Syrian regime is far from being stable.

December 2, 1946   The Minister Plenipotentiary
                                                          Ihsan al-Sharif

Registered in the Syrian Ministry of Foreign Affairs
No. 1341 – Diplomatic reports

348. December 2, 1946   Armanazi to the Syrian Ministry of Foreign Affairs

Top secret
Coded
                    The Syrian Ministry of Foreign Affairs, Damascus

I have been asked to inform you of the following:

The British Government regards with sympathy the Egyptian nationalist movement, however it asks of its Arab friends to understand precisely the spirit of the reservations which new demands impose on it which became apparent after the defeat of the Axis. It hopes that Arab governments will understand that Great Britain only desires happiness for Egypt and its people. However that does not mean that His Majesty's Government is disposed to grant Egypt absolute rights over the Sudanese people whose situation can give the impression that it is part of the Arab League.

The British Government would rejoice to see the Syrian government admitting its point of view and using its influence with the Egyptian individuals who doubt Great Britain's peaceful and just intentions.

December 2, 1946

Najib al-Armanazi
Minister Plenipotentiary

Registered in the Syrian Ministry of Foreign Affairs
No. 1356 – Diplomatic documents

349. December 2, 1946   British Legation in Damascus to the Syrian government

Top secret

Memorandum

His Majesty's Government asks the Syrian Government to note that the statements by Mr Bevin are based on the conviction that the conclusion of an alliance between the various Arab powers and Turkey, either through the Arab League or independent of this organization, can be considered an element likely to contribute efficiently to maintaining peace in the Middle East.

December 2, 1946

Signed: seal of the British Legation in Syria

Registered in the Syrian Ministry of Foreign Affairs
No. 1355 – Documents

350. December 4, 1946   Zureiq to the Syrian Minister of Foreign Affairs

Top secret
Coded

To the Syrian Minister of Foreign Affairs, Damascus

The lawyer, Mr Habib Bourguiba, has visited me, I gave him the sum of 20,000 dollars that Your Excellency had had sent to me. He is determined to put his country's cause in the hands of America alone. In reality he can have no confidence in British promises. He has told me what he intends to say to the Americans. This is the essence:

The Arabs in his country wish to liberate themselves from France at any price. When they will have succeeded in chasing them out of their country, they will be disposed to grant America all the privileges and all the facilities it desires. Bourguiba, on the other hand, expects America to put at its disposal, from now, its cultural and political influence to help it in the light of opinion against France. He also expects the Americans to provide the necessary aid to undertake the liberation revolt which he deems essential.

I will telegraph you the outcome of these conversations with the relevant circles.

December 4, 1946   Constantin Zureiq
                                                    Minister Plenipotentiary

Registered in the Syrian Ministry of Foreign Affairs
No. 1349 – Political reports

351. December 7, 1946   Armanazi to Quwatli

Top secret
                    HE the President of the Syrian Republic, Damascus

The British Government is very unfavorably impressed by the position (three illegible words) assumed by Sa'adallah Bey. It is a pity that he is not a man more like Jamil Mardam Bey who is at Foreign Affairs, at a time when so much skill and caution is necessary for Syria, in particular with these sensitive suggestions.

My interlocutors insist that detailed exchanges of opinion should take place concerning the correspondence exchanged between General Spears and Sa'a-dallah al-Jabiri. They think that while Sa'adallah Bey's way of thinking predominates at the Ministry of Foreign Affairs it will be very difficult to reach an agreement either with Turkey or with the Arab governments. They say openly that Sa'adallah Bey has clearly shown that he wants to fight France, but that he is incapable of reaching a positive result with anyone at all.

It wants a swift reply.
December 7, 1946

                                                        Najib al-Armanazi

Not yet registered

352. December 7, 1946   President Quwatli to Jabiri after his resignation

Top secret
            HE Sa'adallah al-Jabiri, President of the Syrian Council, Cairo
            (delivered by HE Edmond Homsi, Syrian Finance Minister)

My dear friend,

The crisis has taken a regrettable turn. Sultan al-Atrash has once again started to threaten and the fire is smoldering in Jebel. As for the Bedouins,

Abu Hunaik – (in other words, General Glubb) – has distributed more than two million Syrian pounds to them to enable them to march against us. However we know how to react to smother the fire before it takes hold. But what really worries us is Parliament, the proposals circulating there and the calumnies of the deputies. This is why it is said that the ministers have fled, your friend Emir Adel at their head.

The current situation requires a quick response from us and forces us to seek extended help. I think we must form a new Ministry, a Ministry that will aim to push public opinion in a new direction. I think Jamil Mardam Bey is capable of this.

The only thing that we would fear at the moment is that the English heighten their propaganda against us; the situation would then become even more difficult.

I would like you to tell me frankly if you would be inclined to form a Ministry with a popular appeal or if, on the other hand, you want me to give the job to our friend Jamil.

Please let me know soon.

Greetings,

S/ Shukri al-Quwatli

December 7, 1946
Not registered

353. December 11, 1946   Zureiq to the Syrian Minister of Foreign Affairs

Top secret

The Syrian Minister of Foreign Affairs

Foreign Affairs here is very interested in the various types of activity related to British policy in Transjordan.

As far as Egypt is concerned, it is thought here that the British will decide to use force and that in Palestine they will also have recourse to violence. The only thing feared in political circles here is that Great Britain and France should reach agreement about this. There is also a question of new aspirations currently manifesting themselves in Tunis, Marrakesh and Algiers. But the fears are more connected to the new economic interests in Syria and Lebanon, which the diplomatic machine is following closely.

The men here familiar with foreign policy think that Great Britain has, through its representatives, perfect knowledge of Arab policy and in particular of the League of Arab countries. It is said that this League is largely guided by British interests too which govern their representatives, already known for their sympathy towards Great Britain. In addition, the attachment of Great Britain to the plan for Greater Syria and its realization by King Abdullah is explained here by the fact that it became aware that as the Arabs are fighting each other it will gain for itself a greater influence over all of us.

The Americans, from what it seems here, only want to safeguard their material interests and, in this way, their political influence, because they have taken the same route as France in Syria and Lebanon. In the East, they avoid anything that is not of material or commercial interest and, for this reason, they closely observe every detail of British policy.

The Minister Plenipotentiary
Constantin Zureiq

December 11, 1946
Registered in the Syrian Ministry of Foreign Affairs
No. 1381 – Political reports

354. December 11, 1946   Jabiri in Cairo to President Quwatli

Top secret

The Acting Syrian Minister of Foreign Affairs
to HE the President of the Republic

The British Minister Plenipotentiary in Cairo, Mr Bowker asked me to go to see him. He immediately asked me not to insist to the League regarding the demands I presented on the subject of North Africa.

England attaches great importance to our showing proof of moderation in our intervention. Its position does not allow it at the moment to meet all the obligations which would be imposed on it if the French were to lose their temper and turn to acts inspired by their usual stupidity.

The Minister however states that he does not see any objection with Arab governments supporting liberation movements and giving them enough help. Quite the contrary, this help is even necessary in the current circumstances, the question of North Africa still being at the beginning.

He also adds that he would be disposed – or rather his government would be disposed – to revise without delay if the political situation in France got worse, in other words if the communist danger became more threatening. At the moment, nothing would stand in the way of effective help being provided. As a result, I think it is advisable to modify our attitude towards this completely.

December 11, 1946   S/ Sa'adallah al-Jabiri

Not yet registered

355. December 11, 1946   King Ibn Sa'ud to President Quwatli

Top secret

HE President Shukri al-Quwatli, Damascus
(through the intermediary of the Saudi Legation)

During a conversation with our son Faisal, Mr Bevin did not hide his desire to resolve the Palestinian question on the basis of a division into three areas. He added:

"I know that your father will not be in agreement and that he will oppose any plan proposed by us, because he believes that increasing the size of King Abdullah's possessions would be detrimental to him. He invites me to think about sovereignty for the whole of the peninsula, including Yemen and the British protectorates; he thinks in effect that the balance would be restored if, at the same time as a Hashemite state in the north, a Saudi state were formed in the south."

I ask you to let me know if you would eventually be in agreement with the formation of a Greater Syria under a republican regime. As far as we are concerned, we know that Yemen is ready to join with us if we want it to and that respect for the treaties we have signed leads us to delay and to seeking a solution willingly. Also we must first take a general position on the matter of knowing whether we will recognize a Jewish state or not.

Your brother,

Abd al-Aziz Abd al-Rahman al-Faisal

17 Muharram 1365 (December 11, 1946)

Not registered in the Ministry of Foreign Affairs

356. December 12, 1946   Letter from Nuri al-Sa'id to the Turkish President, obtained by the Syrian Deuxième Bureau

Report I

From the Chief of the General Staff of the Syrian Army to His Excellency the National Defense Minister to be brought to the attention of the Syrian Ministry of Foreign Affairs.

Report from the head of the Deuxième Bureau – No. 3712/210 dated December 12, 1946

The points from the Iraqi-Turkish convention relevant to Syria have been dealt with in five pieces of correspondence. They have been sent from Baghdad by Lieutenant A.K.

Letter No. I:

Arabic text – His Excellency President Ismet Inönü.

I ask you please to take into consideration that the Iraqi Government, fully aware of the situation, recognizes, for the present and the future, the definitive attribution of Alexandretta to Turkey. It does not think, and is not aware, that a demand has been prepared for the future; in the past was it a government administrative division? It also points out to us that the Syrian government is not at all favorable to the establishment of the royal regime of the Hashemites.

This matter, together with requests for arbitration or even asking its opinion, has already been settled.

S/ Nuri al-Sa'id

Registered in the Ministry of Foreign Affairs

No. 1378/I – Documents

357. December 12, 1946   President Bishara al-Khuri to President Quwatli

Top secret

His Excellency the most honorable President Shukri Bey Quwatli

Friendliest greetings, for health etc.

I have indeed received your two noble letters of bitterness and affliction. I also take God as witness, knowing the depth of your heart, knowing your greatness of spirit, but what is in the hand is a burden, but you well know that a bird in the hand is worth two in the bush.

For our rapprochement with the Turks, it involves only commercial agreements and is only intended for Lebanese goods. We must conform to it all down the line, and as for me in particular, I cannot follow another path, given everything that interests the English in the matters relating to the borders and all sorts of things. Since I have concerned myself with public affairs, they threaten me all the time with taking their help away from me.

As for the Jews, don't be fearful: we have not compromised ourselves in any way with them and I am convinced that they themselves do not wish to have an agreement with us. What could have appeared to suggest this way of thinking, is only appeasement given to the Maronite Patriarch whose ardor to defend them you know.

So you see that there is nothing that justifies your worries or nervousness.

For the fourth matter, I hope that the Syrian people, whose noble qualities we appreciate and which the people themselves maintain, will obtain satisfaction and break free from their shackles.

For my part, I hope to be able to talk to you soon in person at a meeting about everything that worries you. I also hope that God will keep you in good health.

Bishara Khalil al-Khuri
December 12, 1946   President of the Lebanese Republic

Registered in the Syrian Ministry of Foreign Affairs
No. 1376 – Political documents

358. December, 1946   The Syrian Chargé d'Affaires in Paris to the Syrian Ministry of Foreign Affairs

Top secret
Coded

The Syrian Ministry of Foreign Affairs, Damascus
(via the Syrian Legation in London)

What the British Legation told you is false, both in general and in the details; it is a piece of inexact and tendentious information whose clear aim is to increase the tension between France and the Arab world.

France has not signed any agreement with the Jews; help such as you mention only exists in the minds of the liars who have dreamed it up.

It is true that there are Jews among French politicians but that does not mean that there is an agreement such as you mention. Our painstaking enquiry has not brought us any proof of what you mention. As for the help the Jews find here, it goes without saying and no one should be surprised. For my part, I cannot draw any conclusion from it. The influence the Jews have here is anyway too small for the British to be able to make us believe in it.

I am also able to inform you of an evident truth: it is that the Jews of France do not want the continuation of wrongs done to Palestine. On the contrary, they wish that those of theirs who have moved there should establish good relations with the Arabs – a desire that the British clearly do not share.

I can definitely confirm that what has been said about such a supposed agreement is quite without foundation. France is neither the center of Jewish emigration nor the Jewish arsenal.

The Chargé d'Affaires
Shaker al-Ar

Registered in the Syrian Ministry of Foreign Affairs
No. 1464 – Diplomatic reports

359. December 12, 1946   Armanazi to President Quwatli

Top secret

HE the President of the Republic

British circles see in Jamil Bey the only politician who can pull the country out of the crisis in which it is mired at the moment because of Sa'adallah Bey's mistakes. Personally I believe that the direction in which British policy is pushing us is very dangerous. As we all know, Jamil Mardam, even if he denies any collusion with Nuri al-Sa'id, is however anyway acting in concert with him. But each of them pretends to have opposite opinions to the other.

Personally I believe that at the moment two people in the Arab world have been won over by Great Britain; they are Nuri Pasha and Jamil Mardam Bey. I fear that British policy is now about to enjoy the fruits of the efforts it made by following its well-known line regarding the unification of Syria under a Hashemite throne. You are familiar with the modalities of the agreement which arose between Jamil and Nuri, an agreement they both deny, but which I think is in force more than ever.

December 12, 1946   The Minister Plenipotentiary
Najib al-Armanazi

Not registered in the Ministry

360. December 14, 1946   Faris al-Khuri in Washington to President Quwatli

Top secret

HE the President of the Syrian Republic, Damascus
through the intermediary of the Syrian Legation in Washington

In a conversation I had today with Mr Bevin in the presence of Byrnes, Bevin talked about the question of the Arab Orient and the position of the Egyptians faced with a policy which he would like to be one of complete understanding and friendship with Egypt. Then suddenly he turned to Syria and said to me straight out, "And Syria's oil?" I replied, "It is in your hands." And he continued, "But peace is hardly on the right track in the Orient." I replied, "The question of the Jews is what stops the establishment of peace. For us, we put the Jewish question on one side of the scales and the Arab countries' oil on the other." That is when Byrnes said, "Will you come to an understanding with us if we go along with you in the matter of Palestine?" I said to him, "In the name of the Syrian Government, I propose a bargain to you – we give you half our oil and you, you chase out the Jews."

Bevin began to laugh and added, "This suggestion is good but will we be the only ones for the second part?" I said to him, "Here, there is a third condition: remove France from us." He replied, "We have already reached agreement on this." I added, "And before starting the discussion, you were of our opinion." "Yes," he said. I said to him again, "It is not a matter of reaching an agreement only for us to give and for you to receive."

On that matter, they have asked me to send you our discussion, which I have done.

December 14, 1946   S/ Faris al-Khuri

Not yet registered

361. December 17, 1946   King Ibn Sa'ud to President Quwatli

HE and brother, Shukri Bey al-Quwatli, President of the Syrian Republic
c/o the Minister Plenipotentiary of Saudi Arabia, Damascus

May you be blessed with good health and with the mercy and blessing of Allah.

We have made great efforts to work out a development in British policy with regard to you. And the British Minister Plenipotentiary demonstrates to us the necessity which drives them to return to the ambitions of the Hashemites and to join them at the conference for the settlement of all causes of conflict which arise between us.

The wish is to confound the intimate association of the British and American representatives by pursuing our interest. It is also desirable that we join together and give the Hashemites our confidence. But on what basis, in what way and under the protection of what guide for them? Well said in all frankness.

Anyway what we know is that the Americans and the English, having distanced France from the East, in reality want to make security and peace reign in all the regions in such a way as to draw a benefit for themselves. And the agreements which they will be able to establish will be dictated by the imperative of the question of oil, it is there only, that for you, lies the sincerity of the proposal.

I am writing to you about this to ask your opinion, knowing the straightforwardness of your intentions and to know if they have made similar proposals to you, my brother.

23 Muharram 1365   S/ Abd al-Aziz Abd al-Rahman al-Faisal al-Sa'ud
December 17, 1946
Not registered in the Ministry of Foreign Affairs

362. December 20, 1946   President Quwatli to unknown recipient

Top secret
Telegram sent through the intermediary of the Saudi Legation in Damascus

Your most noble Highness,

I have received your noble letter: the best of friendly countries invites us to reach an understanding with King Abdullah, and with Abd al-Ilah. They hope that we will meet in a conference in Yemen or Baghdad and say that you must take part because of the different choices there are. Our response relies on the differences between us. Abdullah intends to place Syria under his protection, which we cannot accept from this country. A mutual understanding with them, just as they are preparing to tear us apart, is not possible; and you can easily see that we will have no affection and friendship unless they stay inside their borders.

But it seems to me that it is not possible to reach this point. In effect the Americans and the British are following a very advanced Jewish policy and, what is confirmed to us, day after day, by the reports sent by our ministers, the Jews have indeed put their safety in the hands of Abdullah and Abd al-Ilah. These two have accepted with a light heart and without conditions, because of the support confronting the Arab people. Which makes us, who fight for the reign of Abdullah, see that the Jews can draw from the Arab people whatever suits them, because of the egoistical Hashemite machinations.

It is the same abroad, for the Turks are playing for high stakes in this matter, guaranteeing their help to the Hashemites, having treated with them very advantageously, in placing the Arab people in their hands.

The passion for domination, leading in our view to the subjugation of the whole Arab people, is what emboldens the Americans and the English who, today, have already reached an agreement to share our riches among themselves. This is our information at the moment; I will send you the outcome in two days' time. And I hope that God will carefully guard for us your support.

Damascus, 26 Muharram 1366
December 20, 1946
                                                          S/ Shukri al-Quwatli

Not registered in the Ministry of Foreign Affairs

363. December 20, 1946   Acting Minister of Foreign Affairs to the Syrian Legation in Cairo

Top secret

Instructions

The Syrian Legation – Cairo

Please ask for an urgent meeting with His Excellency the President of the Council and inform him of the following:

The Syrian Government has recently learned that His Excellency Sheikh Bishara al-Khuri has once again started discussions with the Turks about a plan for a pact inspired by the Turkish-Iraqi pact. The President and his ministers have not told the Syrian Government about these discussions which are one of the state secrets in Lebanon. The effect of a pact of this nature would be the complete removal of Lebanon from the common political cadre in which it found itself with Syria, and to separate it from us. We would therefore be forgiven if we had recourse to similar measures, which would allow us to protect our general economic and political interests from dangers which we fear.

Lebanon, showing to us its antipathy in such a clear manner, demonstrates that it feels a deep aversion towards the Syrian Republic whose leaders have however done the impossible to protect its independence and sovereignty.

His Excellency the President hopes that the Egyptian Government will intervene as arbiter between the two parties. This is in reality the only way to make the Lebanese understand that Syrian policy does not differ from that of Egypt or the Kingdom of Saudi Arabia.

The Acting Minister of Foreign Affairs
Khaled al-Azm

December 20, 1946

Registered in the Syrian Ministry of Foreign Affairs
No. 3389/694 Q – Diplomatic despatch

364. December 20, 1946   Jabiri to General Spears

Top secret

HE General Sir Edward Spears

I am confirming to you in writing the outcome of our conversation, that the Syrian Government which I represent no longer has any intention of signing any separate agreement with any power whatsoever. It wants, however, to sign general agreements within the framework of the UN.

As a result, the communications that were exchanged between us last October have lost their value unless they are included in international agreements which would no longer be limited only to the British and Syrian governments and which the Arab nations would also be part of at the same time.

December 20, 1946   S/ Sa'adallah al-Jabiri

Registered in the Syrian Ministry of Foreign Affairs
No. 1364 – Documents

365. December, 1946   From the Governor of the Jazira province to the Prime Minister

Top secret
Confidential

HE the Muhafiz of Jazira
to HE the President of the Council

Your Excellency,

For 20 days the Turkish-Syrian border has been lined with Turkish troops. According to information from our services, these concentrations on the borders of these Muhafazat number about 20,000 men. Here we are worried about this collection of Turkish troops who are engaged in digging trenches along the whole length of the border, without being able to learn the reason for this activity.

Yesterday I was in touch with the Turkish Governor of Nardin and asked him what all this meant. He replied to me,

"We fear that the Kurds of Syria or those of Turkey who have taken refuge there will cause trouble."

I think we should attach a very great importance to this concentration of troops on our borders, because of the rumors which accompany them in this province. People are saying in effect that the English have left the hands of the Turkish and Iraqi Governments free and that they have promised the first some of the oil from the Syrian Jazira.

The atmosphere in which we live here is very difficult. The strangest thing is that the Turks are distributing considerable funds to individuals and to partisans they have here but that we have not yet been able to catch any of these agents, even though what I am suggesting is well established. Please let me know your orders.

The Muhafiz of Jazira
Abd al-Kader al-Midani

Registered in the Syrian Ministry of Foreign Affairs
No. 1323 – Political reports

366. December, 1946   President Inönü to King Abdullah

Top secret

Letter 1
His Hashemite Majesty King Abdullah Ibn al-Hussein I

The Government of the Republic of Turkey, for the greatest good of all, will ensure its protection of the legal regime of the Arab Hashemite kingdom. And I remind you, in the name of the Government of the Republic of Turkey, that we are the first speedily to recognize you as the legal king of Syria, as soon as the moment comes. You also know that we hope for your entry into Damascus soon, God willing.

Signature
Ismet Inönü

Delivered by the Russian Legation
Registered in the Syrian Ministry of Foreign Affairs
No. 1427 – Documents

367. December, 1946   King Abdullah to President Inönü

Top secret

Letter 3
HE President Ismet Inönü

I wish to inform you that I fully approve the constitution of the Defense Committee as you have proposed it and which includes the three members: the Turks, the British and the Arabs. I sincerely hope that this committee will make it possible for justice to reign and, through a spirit of mutual help and harmonious understanding between its members, the establishment of peace in our countries.

S/ Abdullah

Forwarded by the Russian Legation
Registered in the Syrian Ministry of Foreign Affairs
No, 1429 – Documents

368. December, 1946   Agreement between President Inönü and King Abdullah

Top secret

Secret agreement

For the Hashemite Arab King – His Majesty King Abdullah Ibn al-Hussein
For the Government of the Republic of Turkey – His Excellency President
Ismet Inönü

A lasting peace will reign between the Hashemite Arab King and the Turkish nation, based on a spirit of brotherly trust to safeguard the common interests of the two parties.

The Government of the Republic of Turkey will use all possible means to establish the sovereignty of the Hashemite Arab King in the territories of Syria, Lebanon and Transjordan with their current borders which will be united.

The unification of these countries will be guaranteed under the protection of the Hashemite dynasty. The Turkish Government will find support, both political and economic, under the rule of Transjordan.

The two parties must consult each other and help each other as brothers regarding anything of importance to the two parties and neither one more than the other will be able to take a decision to conclude an agreement without the consent of the other party when there is a matter that concerns both at the same time.

Signature
Ismet Inönü
Abdullah

Given by the Soviet Legation
Registered in the Syrian Ministry of Foreign Affairs
No. 1426 – Documents

369. December 21, 1946   Armanazi to the Syrian Minister of Foreign Affairs

The Syrian Minister of Foreign Affairs

The important issue preoccupying the British Government at the moment is the military agreement which was presented to you through the intermediaries of General Clayton and General Spears.

I am certain that General Clayton will return to Damascus once again to exert new pressure, given the importance of this agreement which Great Britain regards as an important policy element in future relations in the whole of the Near East.

The British Government does not want publicity about this agreement and it will not be asked of us to join to it in any way at all, Turkey with France so that our agreement with Great Britain will be settled quickly. It is only designed to stop the main arrangements in the eventuality of a sudden war.

That is why it seems to me that our services must quickly examine an essential matter like this one on which the whole of our existence and all our future depends.

December 21, 1946

The Minister Plenipotentiary
Najib al-Armanazi

Registered in the Syrian Ministry of Foreign Affairs
No. 1394 – Political reports

370. January 17, 1947   Armanazi to the Syrian Ministry of Foreign Affairs

The Syrian Ministry of Foreign Affairs, Damascus

British politicians fear above all a Franco-Jewish agreement and they are convinced, here, that France itself is conducting a skewed policy with them and that Socialist-Communist intrigues will not allow the reaching of a sincere agreement between France and Great Britain. And this agreement, if it is ever signed, will not have any real importance, for France was for a long time before on an equal footing with Great Britain, in the event of a global conflict with the Soviet Union. For all these reasons, they are convinced that France, which has been unable to maintain its position in the Middle East, would shake hands with the devil himself to stop Great Britain signing as the more important party. They admit that if there is agreement with the Jews, already accomplished or possible, the help that France will provide to the Jews will be powerful, even if the modalities remain secret.

Also, they are very closely watching the two French legations in Damascus and Beirut, because they are in areas favorable to Jewish activity. The British spy on everything that happens, fearing that the French Consulates, with their money, will come to the aid of the Jewish rabbis but, so far, nothing tangible has confirmed this.

The leaders here force us to register these realities in order to know what view of them we should take: as enemies who only want to hunt and intimidate us.

January 17, 1947   The Minister Plenipotentiary
Najib al-Armanazi

Registered in the Syrian Ministry of Foreign Affairs
No. 1462 – Secret report

371. May 3, 1947   Soviet Legation to Prime Minister Jamil Mardam

Top secret

Memorandum

My government has asked me to inform you that it regards favorably the efforts the Syrian government is making to encourage the Arab liberation movement in North Africa. As a fundamental principle it has to approve all independence activity in these countries and is disposed to recognize it as timely.

But it draws the attention of the Syrian government to the mistake it would make if it allowed itself to be led by the encouragement of the British and the Americans who have no other aim than to install themselves in place of France. The promises made to the Sultan of Morocco thus arouse deep suspicions.

My Government has asked me to assure you that the liberation of North Africa will in itself be considered a happy event and that it is also ready to give all the help necessary to bring it about.

But it still fears that the Arab liberation movement in North Africa may transform itself into creating colonialist dangers.

I have been charged with contacting you to assure you of all of that.

May 3, 1947

Signature
Legation of the Soviet Union

Commentary in Jamil Mardam Bey's hand.

A new Russian lie: they want to lead us bit by bit to understanding the reality of the facts, they want to make North Africa into an object of barter like Palestine.

Registered in the Syrian Ministry of Foreign Affairs
No. 1699 – Political documents

372. May 3, 1947   Shaker al-Asi, Syrian Chargé d'Affaires in Cairo to Mardam

Top secret

Shaker al-Asi

Briefing letter

The Syrian Minister of Foreign Affairs

The only danger facing us in the action with our brothers, the Arabs of North Africa, is the absence of agreement between them on anything, and I believe that the French knew very well how to sow division among them in such a way that it is impossible for any of them to work with the others.

In the conversations that took place between me and the representatives of other Arab lands, I saw that each works in his own way and cooperates with others. So, the fact is that we attribute a great weight to the representatives from Algeria, although they are people who do not have great influence. Also our actions are directed in many ways and success, as it seems to me, is doubtful in all arenas at once.

For all these reasons, I think that at present sending some officer from the Syrian Intelligence Service is an unnecessary assumption. Also, providing the movement with funds is difficult for us. As for arms, they are distributed there freely and it would be possible to get them at very low prices when any armed movement starts.

In my opinion the important thing would be a complete understanding between the Arab countries on the mode of action in North Africa. I believe that the Egyptian action is very disorganized and that it would be necessary for there to be coordination between all our actions there. As for the Iraqis, as you know, they talk a lot and act little, thus the duty will fall on us alone and we must prepare for it before undertaking any action whatsoever.

Also, I imagine that we should contemplate a budget which does not at present fall below a million pounds.

As for the radio which was sent there, it will remain unable to work from here unless we send the necessary technicians, as, so far, we have not been able to find an Algerian one we could rely on.

May 3, 1947   The Chargé d'Affaires
                                                                          Shaker al-Asi

Registered in the Syrian Ministry of Foreign Affairs
No. 2805 – Political reports

373. May 3, 1947   Armanazi to Mardam

Top secret

The Syrian Minister of Foreign Affairs, Damascus

Camille Chamoun's plan is now clear to me after having been unclear and I am convinced that he played us for a long time; now it appears that he works for King Abdullah and the English policy which is preparing the plan for Greater Syria.

Camille Chamoun has received the promise of having the Presidency of the Republic from Great Britain. It is a settled thing, for his success and that of the party he works with in the elections is a sure thing and Sheikh Bishara's return is impossible, whatever he may think, for the plan requires the presence in Lebanon of a President who is a paid man and there is none more so than Camille Chamoun.

Lebanon will separate from us and will become loyal to King Abdullah, that also is decided, while it has for a time pretended to be friends with us.

As for King Abdullah, from his side, he mocks the Maronite Patriarch and thus Lebanon in its totality will find itself against us given that Riyad al-Sulh is there.

As for the role played by Riyad, as I understand it is twofold, for he will act to calm the fury of the French who, it seems, Great Britain does not want to provoke in such circumstances. On the one hand, he can make a mockery of them and persuade them that Lebanon must be free and independent and he can at the same time deny it as much as he wants, and all with the agreement of the English themselves.

I believe that the dangers are beginning to bite.

May 3, 1947

The Minister
Najib al-Armanazi

Registered in the Syrian Ministry of Foreign Affairs
No. 2807 – Political reports

374. May 4, 1947   King Faruq to President Quwatli

Top secret

From Faruq I, King of Egypt, by the grace of God, to HE President
Shukri al-Quwatli

May the blessings and mercy of Allah be upon us.

The President of our Council of Ministers has today informed me of a secret conversation which took place between him and the Syrian Chargé d'Affaires about the passage of a certain number of Syrians from North Africa going from Syria to Tunisia and from there to Algeria or Morocco.

He told me that reports from the Egyptian services indicate that the French are perfectly well aware of the doings and actions of these people. So he has taken an urgent decision to detain these people and send them back to their point of departure. And personally I find the occasion favorable for restating to Your Excellency my opinion and that of my government on the position that should be taken towards France.

Currently there is no cause for conflict between the Arab countries and France, but we have a strong sympathy for the legitimate demands for freedom made by our brothers, the Arabs of North Africa, but we must now ask ourselves whether, were we to use all our forces to help them, we would win the freedom of these countries or if another influence would replace that of France.

I am convinced and I hope you will be convinced with me that Great Britain and America have huge ambitions in these countries; so, the colonialists are like the wild wolves of the Russian forest, they tear each other apart and it is enough for us here, as far as it concerns us, to deal with Great Britain and America.

My Government and I consider that the moment has not yet come to intervene in this direct way in the affairs of North Africa and in this spirit, we must ask you to forgive us as we cannot provide any aid of a violent nature although we will work with you with all our strength to help our North African brothers to struggle peacefully to win the largest possible number of rights and freedoms.

May the Lord preserve you for your faithful

Faruq

May 4, 1947
Registered in the Syrian Ministry of Foreign Affairs
No. 1701– Political documents

375. May 5, 1947   Azzam to Mardam

To the Syrian Minister of Foreign Affairs, Damascus
through the intermediary of the Syrian Legation in America.

I have just received a personal letter from HM the Sultan of Morocco in which he sets out for me the reality of the situation in his country. His people are demanding national rule and he cannot openly assume this rule against France. He can support this movement and help this rule. That is wisdom personified. He explains to us that this rule would be facilitated if we succeeded in persuading Emir Abd al-Karim al-Khattabi to act, but the latter has promised France to remain calm. In addition, he is in French hands and he should be rescued.

I have sent HM Faruq a rousing appeal and I do not know what HM's reply will be, if it will be refusal or acceptance. If he decides to refuse, I hope that Syria will take on the matter. I am persuaded that it is still in the first rank with these generous gestures. Mr Cadogan has replied to me personally that Emir Abd al-Karim's flight would be a wise response to the Mufti's flight and His Majesty's Government is not of a different opinion; it is in agreement and will support whatever will save Abd al-Karim from French oppression.
May 5, 1947

The Secretary General of the Arab League
Abd al-Rahman al-Azzam

Registered in the Syrian Ministry of Foreign Affairs
No. 1717 – Political documents

376. May 5, 1947   King Abdullah to the Sultan of Morocco, Muhammad V

Top secret

> To our revered brother, descendant of the Sharifs, leader of the pure, branch of the Oriental tree, HM the Sultan of Morocco. May God protect him and give him life.

May health, mercy and the blessings of Allah be with you.

I received your noble letter, and remained dazzled before a good odor and the intelligence of its content. God leads you by the hand towards the happiness of this noble people.

I bring you big news that a British person of great importance has asked me to give you; it is that the Government of HM the King of Great Britain sees in you the only man worthy of ruling over the whole of the Arab Maghreb and that, if there is a decisive victory with Allah's permission, he will not treat you as King only of Morocco, but will extend your sovereign rule over all the countries of the Maghreb, including Algeria and Tunisia.

I pray God that he guides your hand to exalt the dignity of the Arabs and Islam.

I also hope that you will redouble the ambition and distrust with regard to individuals in your court in the pay of foreigners, enemies of the motherland and religion.

May health, mercy and the blessings of Allah be on you.

4 Jumada al-Awwal 1366   Your affectionate brother,
May 5, 1947   Abdullah

Letter stolen from the Council (Diwan) of King Abdullah in Amman
Registered in the Syrian Ministry of Foreign Affairs
No. 1703– Political documents

Note: This letter is one of the six exchanged between King Abdullah and the Sultan of Morocco.

377. May 6, 1947   Armanazi to Mardam

Top secret

> The Syrian Minister of Foreign Affairs, Damascus

Mr Bevin summoned me and asked me to inform you of the following:

"Under the personal pressure of President Truman I ask the Syrian Government to give its agreement to the pipeline route, and the passage of Saudi oil and also ask it to give its agreement to allowing the outlet to be in Lebanon and not in Syria."

This was his statement ... Then he set out for me the British point of view on the matter in a few words, "So Lebanon will finally be rid of France."

Of course, he did not explain the meaning of his words to me. But the information I have been able to obtain here is that Great Britain was decided on placing the oil outlet in Syria and not in Lebanon, because it was counting on our friendship and because it was placing its hopes on the plan for Greater Syria which would make Syria into an instrument to its liking and because, in addition, it believed that Lebanon was a region where French influence could find a foothold.

The result that it now has before it is that America has definitively put its hand on Lebanon while it abandons us to the mercy of British policy. I believe that for us it is the most dangerous stage to pass through, for King Abdullah's plan now becomes possible if America favors him to satisfy the demands of the Jews and of Great Britain.

My opinion is that we should look to Russia, as the situation is extremely difficult.

May 6, 1947

The Minister Plenipotentiary
Najib al-Armanazi

Registered in the Syrian Ministry of Foreign Affairs
No. 2816 – Political reports

378. May 6, 1947   Shaker al-Asi, Syrian Chargé d'Affaires in Cairo, to Mardam

Top secret

The Syrian Minister of Foreign Affairs

Briefing letter.

I have gratefully received the sum of fifty thousand pounds. I sent it through a secure intermediary to Haj Messali and I now have the receipt.

At the moment it is not the need for money or arms that is being felt and despite the constraints which the French place him under, el Haj is personally patient and firm and he considers that what should most hold our attention is that Arab problems should all be brought together before the Security Council – the presence of France in the Arab Maghreb and the presence of England in Egypt, Iraq and Transjordan. He also considers it essential to organize a general congress in which all Arabs would participate to decide the future of the Arabs.

El Haj Messali, from this point of view, is influenced by communist thought; he is convinced that Great Britain and America will help the Arabs take the place of France and anyway he does not want to change French sovereignty for another sovereign power (as happens in Syria in my opinion).

As for the Sultan of Morocco, he sent me a letter last week in which he says that there are great hopes of arriving at sensible results with the French there and he adds that the latter are beginning to feel the existence of a danger which threatens them and that this is why they want to arrive at an arrangement with him without our intervention. So, I am convinced that any arrangement that the Moroccans reach would be in their interest, for I am sure that soon we will unleash a new assault after we have restated the question of Palestine to ourselves.

I am convinced that it is necessary for the President of the Republic to establish direct contact with the Sultan. I greatly admire the Sultan of Morocco for he is an intelligent man and he can pretend to be loyal to France and act despite the group of traitors who surround him.

May 6, 1947
The Chargé d'Affaires
Shaker al-Asi

Registered in the Syrian Foreign Ministry
No. 2815 – Political reports

379. May 7, 1947 Armanazi to Mardam

Top secret

The Syrian Minister of Foreign Affairs, Damascus

The British Government regards with extreme distrust the secret attempts the French Government is making to draw closer to Yemen.

You probably know that any such foreign meddling now to strengthen Yemen and prop up Imam Yahya would completely reverse the balance in the Arab peninsula.

The principle we must not lose sight of is the expulsion of France from Arab lands, and it is regrettable, with regard to information which has reached me, that Imam Yahya should have recourse to France to support his position.

Secret conversations took place there between the French and the Imam; the British know nothing about them and are very worried. King Abd al-Aziz, despite British warnings, does not appreciate the importance of the matter; he does not believe that France could do anything for the Imam and he has replied to the British Minister that France is free to maintain friendly relations with Imam Yahya and that the latter is equally free to maintain friendly relations with the Soviet Union. It seems that recently the Imam has been able to contact King Abd al-Aziz and calm his apprehensions completely. The British Government hopes that we will intervene quickly in the matter and the fact that France is concerning itself once again with Arab lands greatly worries and concerns it and they draw the attention of Your Excellency personally to this.

May 7, 1947

The Minister
Najib al-Armanazi

380. May 7, 1947 Zureiq to Mardam

Top secret

The Minister of Foreign Affairs, Damascus

Professor Philip Hitti told me what I am now sending you in summary:

All the opinions we have been able to trust for the last four months concerning the existence of an understanding between British and American officials on Middle Eastern oil and the future of political and economic positions in this region are not complete.

The topics on which Byrnes and Bevin agreed in their conversations in Paris or America will perhaps now be disavowed by the two parties, in such a way that one can say that a serious conflict will erupt between these two parties, a secret and terrible conflict before which we must remain alert and on our guard, for it will touch our lives and our destiny.

President Truman has categorically asked Bevin not to intervene in the matter of Arabian oil and not to encourage us to persist in our opposition to its passage.[1]

Then he refused to enter into negotiations with the British, touching on the possibility of giving a share in the same oil and I learned today that America is demanding a direct interest in Transjordanian and Syrian oil.

From the point of view of political influence, the Secretary of State for Foreign Affairs, who is the primary person in a position of responsibility, told me that he would not recognize the influence of any state in our country, that no one has the right to demand any privileges whatsoever there. He assured me also that America would consider the liberty and independence of Syria as something inviolable, above all bartering and all discussion, that no one other than its people would decide the future of Syria and that the country's regime returns to the people alone.

I am convinced, after all that, that the British have often bluffed us with their agreements with the Americans which I note were imaginary or that the Americans are enfranchising themselves from them for reasons we don't know.

May 7, 1947   The Minister Plenipotentiary
                                                        Constantin Zureiq

Registered in the Syrian Ministry of Foreign Affairs
No. 2821– Political reports

Note

1   Translator's note: This no doubt refers to the route of the pipeline.

381. May 8, 1947   Mardam to Armanazi

Top secret

The Syrian Minister in London

Rest assured that the French Legation in Damascus is closely supervised: its staff will be unable to undertake any action likely to harm us.

As for the content of the advice officials in the Foreign Office gave us, I am convinced that its intention is to hide their intentions, for, it is quite clear to us that from now on the French are completely incapable of doing anything in Syria. For, as you know, they do not know their lines of action; they begin with culture, cinema, religious schools and all that is simply "small beer" (unimportant). But our English friends warn us of the French intrigues towards the Bedouins and the Druze and the truth is that it is they themselves who incite them against us. Well, at the moment, we cannot subdue them for fear of the English who protect them, and if they served the French now we would not hesitate for a minute to subdue them.

The reply you will give to the Foreign Office is that we thank them for their directives and advice which we will take into consideration.

But the thing we would like you to make them take note of is that we do not want the Legation of Great Britain to be more important than the French Legation, because it is important to us to bring an end to this foreign Legation movement in our country and when we want to have contact with a foreign Power we have our Ministers Plenipotentiary there.

The fact is that insulting France no longer worries people here, because they are now convinced that all those who attack the French are simply instruments of the English, so the Syrian government wants to make people understand that it is not a British tactic, but that must not stop us observing French activity and ending any movement by France in our country.

May 8, 1947   The Minister of Foreign Affairs
                                                              Jamil Mardam Bey

Registered in the Ministry of Foreign Affairs
No. 2695 – Diplomatic correspondence

382. May 8, 1947   President Quwatli to King Faruq

Top secret

HM King Faruq I

May health, mercy and the blessings of Allah be with you.

I sorrowfully regret reminding Your Majesty on a personal level, as a friend, the dangers that will be provoked by the accommodating position of the Egyptian Government with the French Legation in Cairo, which has now become a source of considerable danger threatening not only Syria and Lebanon but Egypt itself.

The documents the Chargé d'Affaires will bring you will prove to Your Majesty that the French Legation in Cairo is today a source of problems for us and that up till now it has also given considerable help to Jewish terrorists.

One could turn a blind eye to all that if there was not the question of French intervention in the affairs of Arab lands and in their futures and in particular in Yemen, something which we all distrust with all our hearts and of which we fear the consequences. The information we have clearly shows that France has colonialist ambitions fixed on Yemen. It is a serious matter for the interests of the Arab countries and which also influences the projects and programs which King Abd al-Aziz has shown you, as he knows that the French center of action is not now Cairo.

For all these reasons I call the attention of Your Majesty to the importance of the matter, hoping that you will wish to give your directives to the venerable

Egyptian Government so that it can quickly enter into negotiations with the representatives of significant Arab countries in order to take the necessary measures.

May 8, 1947   The President of the Republic
                                                                          Shukri al-Quwatli

Registered in the Syrian Ministry of Foreign Affairs
No. 1704 – Political documents

Telegram written in the Palace of the Republic on May 3. The Foreign Minister objected to its being sent, but then gave in to the insistence of the President of the Republic and it was sent on May 8.

383. May 10, 1947   Armanazi to Mardam

Top secret
                         The Syrian Minister of Foreign Affairs, Damascus

While giving our support to Arab nationalist movements in North Africa and despite the aid we have given to strengthen individuals fighting against France, I am of the opinion, and it is currently the opinion of the British Government, that any recourse to armed force and therefore to revolt and insurrection are not useful and would indeed be harmful for us all.

France's current position is shaky and we must seize the moment before the establishment of a strong government in France, but the British Government thinks that the French regime is threatened with weakness for a long time and that it will be difficult for France to shake off its current decline for five years at least and circumstances will remain good for us, even after a long time. In addition, starting a revolt now would probably condemn the current regime and would entail the formation of a strong government which would have recourse to violence, and I was given to understand that Great Britain and America are not disposed to support us in such circumstances as they have done in Syria.

We fear, on the other hand, that the communists will seize the opportunity and will throw themselves into furious action, which is what England fears, for the Communist movement in North Africa is active and strong and the Arab nationalists of this country cannot act alone without the communists. For all these reasons, I am of the opinion that we should limit our current activities to pursuing peaceful actions and to pressuring France as far as possible in order to obtain conditions and rights wider than they are at present.

Liberating North Africa means we must go through many stages and we must now pass through the stage of obtaining reforms and when these are realized, which will be a great victory for us, we will be able to make new demands; then the planned liberation movement will be strong if it has recourse to armed force to finally chase France from Arab lands.

May 10, 1947   The Minister Plenipotentiary
                                                                          Najib al-Armanazi

Registered in the Syrian Ministry of Foreign Affairs
No. 2830 – Political reports

384. May 15, 1947   Armanazi to President Quwatli

Top secret

Through the Syrian Ministry of Foreign Affairs
to HE the President of the Republic, Damascus

I was summoned to Foreign Affairs and requested to ask you to intervene
to get a swift response from King Faruq about the earlier plan concerning
Tripolitania. The Foreign Office again confirms, as it confirmed to the Egyptian
Ambassador here, that it is disposed to provide genuine help to establish the
sovereignty of the King of Egypt over Libya on condition that he gives his
agreement to two proposed conditions which are: the final settlement of the
Sudan question and the recognition of Great Britain's privileged position in
Tripolitania. Concluding an agreement on this matter is in the interest of
Egypt itself from all points of view, for in this way Egypt would gain in Sudan
and in Libya something it could not even dream of. Also, the Arab point of
view would gain considerably by suppressing the barrier imposed between the
Arab countries and the countries of the Maghreb which remain under French
influence and which we are wholly unable to liberate completely if they are
not our neighbors.

The plan as Your Excellency sees requires determination and patriotism,
qualities that King Faruq has, without counting on the fact that he is in
agreement with these aims.

The intervention of King Abd al-Aziz with Faruq was not, it seems, serious
and now the British Government hopes that King Faruq will take into consideration the general situation of the Arab lands as well as the hopes of the
Arabs of North Africa for freedom, the Communist danger which seeks to
penetrate the Mediterranean and the ambitions of America which wants to
place a strong hand on affairs in Arab lands. If he reflects on all this, he will
find that it is essential for him to reach agreement with Great Britain, and
soon, so as to find a solution to the problem of Libya.

I await your reply,

May 15, 1947

The Minister
Najib al-Armanazi

Registered in the Syrian Ministry of Foreign Affairs
No. 1725 – Political documents

385. May 15, 1947   King Faruq to President Quwatli

Top secret
Urgent telegram

With blessed greetings for HE the President of the Syrian Republic,
Mr Shukri al-Quwatli.

I received with great interest Your Excellency's telegram. French activity in Egypt is very limited so far as cultural and commercial matters go, and our government has not, so far, identified any political activity in them.

As for its intervention in Yemen, it is something we cannot prevent, for the understanding between Yemen and France did not take place in our country. It seems that Imam Yahya is fully aware of King Abd al-Aziz's intentions and, to come to his aid, he finds none other than the Soviet Union and France, for Great Britain and America have resolved to help it (that means King Abd al-Aziz) the day his movement starts.

France, in spite of everything, is loved by the Egyptians and it is difficult for us to reproach the French for anything with their current correct attitude.

As for the help they give the Jews, we blame them for their official support, but we must remember the reach of the Jews' capitalist influence and the large number of French, Jewish politicians.

The matter that now deserves our attention is not making France a declared enemy of the Arab League, especially while we are asking it to leave North Africa. I believe that it is enough that the Arabs now keep the friendship of France to confront Great Britain and America, for there is no doubt that Russian aid to the Arabs is imaginary and anything that the Arabs will now undertake openly against France will be a mistake and we must limit ourselves now to organizing secret actions against it and behaving with great friendliness towards the French as far as necessary in these dangerous circumstances.

Yours sincerely,

Faruq

Telegram received on May 15, 1947

Registered in the Ministry of Foreign Affairs
No. 1714 – Political documents

386. May 16, 1947   Mardam to President Quwatli

Top secret

Report

From the President of the Council of Ministers to HE President Shukri al-Quwatli, President of the Syrian Republic.

Today I spoke frankly, as requested by Your Excellency, with Mr Riyad al-Sulh about the unclear position he has recently adopted vis-à-vis France and the strong sympathy he shows Haj Amin, although he knows that Haj Amin has become, in relation to us, an ally and friend of France.

I told him frankly the opinion of all our brothers concerning his attitude and his reply to all these statements was categorical, confirming to me that the matter was beyond him, that it was the English themselves who had pressured him about the understanding with Camille Chamoun. Then, he thinks that he must keep a line of retreat for himself through a good understanding with both the French and the Russians, knowing that that would not displease the English, but will be done with their knowledge and agreement.

For, giving France a chance to reestablish its presence in Lebanon is unthinkable; he is only playing a role and is certain of ultimate success.

As for his friendliness with regard to Haj Amin, it is very natural, for it alone will win him great popularity in Lebanon. In addition helping Haj Amin is an overwhelming need and he adds that the English do not regard Haj Amin with a hostile eye at all and picturing him as a man who collaborates with France and with them is without foundation.

I am convinced that it is unnecessary to make the situation worse between Riyad Bey and us. I have no doubts about him and it would be pure imagination to believe that he is satisfied with France when in reality he is playing the role he told me about himself. I trust him.

May 16, 1947   The President of the Council
                                                        Jamil Mardam Bey

Registered in the Syrian Ministry of Foreign Affairs
No. 2843 – Political reports

387. May 23, 1947   King Faruq to President Quwatli

Top secret

HE Shukri al-Quwatli

Greetings and regards. It is really sad that someone should want to doubt the intentions of those close to him; for me you are above all suspicion and doubt and your affection for us is above all other considerations, but it seems that your Minister in London does not want to appreciate the situation the British want to surround the Arabs with.

Your Excellency is aware of the steps taken here by the Tripolitans to unite Tripolitania with Egypt, as well as the end result, the oppression and terror it brings from Great Britain.

So, it is not reasonable to brandish the name of France in all circumstances to exploit the difficulties the English endure. Although France is not loved here, we will not allow ourselves to slide into the tide of British interests in the name of resistance to France and if Great Britain is settled on making France disappear from North Africa, it only has to do it itself, enough of the twists and turns and games it is playing with us and others.

All their intentions consist in weakening our position as far as Sudan is concerned and they want to direct our wishes to other things. Also, they want to exploit our name and the crown of our ancestors at the same time in order to establish their sovereignty over Tripolitania, using us as a cover for their colonialist ambitions and that is what we absolutely refuse to countenance. Also, they would like us to work to light the fire in North Africa and to distance France. It is something we would like and which we shall all force ourselves to do, but in the interests of the Arabs and not in the interest of Great Britain which considers itself the guardian of the Arabs.

I hope that your Minister will take our brief reply to them and know we accept sovereignty over Tripolitania on certain conditions, the most important and first being that Great Britain must recognize the rightness and true basis of our position with regard to the question of Sudan.

We will not study the problem of Tripolitania before settling the one regarding the Sudan.

With my sincerest respect,

May 23, 1947

Your faithful

Faruq

Registered in the Syrian Ministry of Foreign Affairs
No. 1728 – Political documents

388. May 28, 1947   Mardam to Armanazi

Top secret

The Syrian Minister Plenipotentiary, Damascus

Give the Ministry of Foreign Affairs the opinion we expressed today to the British Minister Plenipotentiary.

From now on, we will meet with force every intervention by King Abdullah in Syrian affairs and any referendum is impossible; the only referendum that will take place is the next election to the Chamber of Deputies.

Syria has made known to the Kingdom of Saudi Arabia and the Egyptian Government the dangerous situation King Abdullah creates around it, and has asked for their help in the case of armed Hashemite aggression against Syria; it has received a reassuring response from these two countries.

Make it known in our name to the Ministry of Foreign Affairs that this cold war of nerves will have absolutely no point and that it is unthinkable that Syria will renounce its independence.

The Syrian Government, in keeping secret with steadfastness this terrible maneuvering King Abdullah is undertaking, in agreement with the Zionists, well understands that the ruin of the Arab front will only harm the Palestinian cause in the East and the cause of our North African brothers; we want to do the impossible to avoid the belief that this imposing edifice called the Arab League will crumble, this edifice for which we want to do the impossible to maintain its existence as a symbol that King Abdullah wants to bring down.

Frankness forces us to remind the British Government that action to bring about Greater Syria will not guarantee either King Abdullah or Great Britain what they want; on the contrary, the only result will be that the French will succeed in implanting themselves once again in Lebanon and that the Soviets will intervene directly in the affairs of the Arab world and will place their hand on it, so, it is a terrible danger for Great Britain for it will thus harm itself and us.

May 28, 1947   The Syrian Minister of Foreign Affairs
                                                        Jamil Mardam Bey
Registered in the Syrian Ministry of Foreign Affairs
no. 4963
   2354 – Diplomatic correspondence

389. May 28, 1947   Armanazi to Mardam

Top secret
                      The Syrian Ministry of Foreign Affairs, Damascus
Supporting General Clayton is something which surpasses the imagination;
the British Ministry of Foreign Affairs has been completely forced into
accepting him because the Intelligence Services have categorically refused to
remove him from Egypt and have given him carte blanche to direct the vast
program he aims to complete.

In my enquiries I have arrived at the conclusion that General Clayton is
busy acting in two directions, the first being the plan for Greater Syria and
the second attaching Libya to the British Government through one procedure
or another.

The plan for Greater Syria, as General Spears sees it, is now up for discussion more than at any time in the past and he is persuaded that it is possible to reach a reasonable settlement between us and King Abdullah. Do you
want him to intervene quickly before his intervention becomes useless?
Please give me your answer quickly.
May 28, 1947   The Minister
                                                          Najib al-Armanazi

Registered in the Syrian Ministry of Foreign Affairs
No. 2873 – Political reports

390. May 29, 1947   Faris al-Khuri to Mardam

Top secret
                          The Syrian Ministry of Foreign Affairs

I draw this Ministry's attention to the strong antagonism which currently
exists between the British and American policies concerning Arabia and the
mining both countries are seeking to carry out in Yemen in particular.

So, while the circumstances of this antagonism remain hidden as if unimportant, our attention remains divided; we imagine that Arabia is menaced by
the Communist danger which seeks to camouflage itself in Yemen in many
ways, but in reality, it is this that has no importance because communism
would not be able to take hold with the Arabs and the Muslims, or it is
threatened by French intervention in the affairs of Yemen while France is
condemned to remain a second-rate country and cannot present any danger,
in particular for Yemen, as its internal conditions would not allow it to do

anything, even something insignificant, unless we imagine that people like Adnan Tarcici can do anything for it, but he is only one of the regular English agents. For all these reasons I think that we must not worry ourselves about what can be said about France's and Russia's ambitions towards Yemen and that the important thing in reality is the antagonism between the English and the Americans which is in effect an aspect of the general conflict between the two countries regarding all Arab lands. From now on we must consider that the English will seek to mine the land under American procedures and that they will not leave Ibn Sa'ud's hands free in Yemen, (as up to now they greatly desired to do it progressively) unless they are sure that the latter will remain their man and not America's. So, it is quite unclear to them at the moment, for it is common knowledge that Imam Yahya's sympathy is with the Hashemites, from which we can rest assured that any privilege granted to the Russians or to France will have no value while Imam Yahya is alive. And if he dies or a revolution starts in his country, the English keep his son ready to succeed him and serve them from now on.

I believe that the only conclusion that we can draw from this account is that we must warn King Abd al-Aziz against allowing himself to be led by the Americans, for everything leads me to think that from now on England only sees King Abd al-Aziz with one good eye and that he must be prepared for unpleasant incidents.

May 29, 1947

Faris al-Khuri
Permanent Syrian Representative to the Security Council

Registered in the Syrian Ministry of Foreign Affairs
No. 2877 – Political reports

391. June 2, 1947   The Soviet Legation to President Quwatli

Top secret

Memorandum

My Government asks the Syrian Government to take note of the fact that it does not give its agreement to the maneuvers that King Abdullah is carrying out for avowed colonialist principles.

At this time when the threat of these maneuvers has become a constant, my Government feels itself inclined to provide the necessary aid to protect and safeguard Syrian independence.

My Government considers that the current situation as a whole in Syria, which is the basis of security in the Middle East, is a fact that must be respected and guaranteed.

The information I have allows me to confirm the existence of a continuing plot directed by British military officials under the command of King Abdullah and in complete agreement with the Iraqi and Turkish governments.

A complaint lodged with the Security Council by the Syrian Government would be viewed favorably and this would then win the complete support of my Government. We are also disposed to provide material aid as well as military experts should the Syrian Government so wish.

June 2, 1947   Seal of the Soviet Legation
                                                                    Damascus

Oral memorandum given by the Soviet Minister to the President of the Syrian Republic.
Registered in the Syrian Ministry of Foreign Affairs
No. 1734 – Political documents

392. June 3, 1947   Report by the head of the Syrian Sûreté Générale

Top secret

From the Minister of National Defense
and the Minister of the Interior
to the Council of Ministers
Secret report

In accordance with its request, I present your honorable Council with the summary of our specialized services' reports on the general results of the new Lebanese situation.

The last Lebanese elections were on the whole a true reflection of the international antagonism which includes Lebanon and divides the Lebanese and which we fear seeing repeated in the same way in our country in a manner that would not allow it to say that there is national sovereignty and independence there.

Russia acted through the intermediary of the Communist Party and France through the intermediary of its avowed partisans, and England and America also acted with all their power. Mr Camille Chamoun, who is the first person the English rely on has succeeded. Mr Riyad al-Sulh, whose position I cannot define exactly as he is with the English as well as with the Americans, and with the French as well as the Communists, has also succeeded.

The interest the Americans have shown in the Lebanese elections was astonishing in its way, but this control has not been able to change anything in the conduct of the elections in which, undoubtedly, the friends of England succeeded in such a way that we can say that the British influence did not shrink but on the contrary was confirmed and strengthened.

The failure of the Communists was crushing, as well as that of the pro-French group, and the field stayed free for the British and American secret agents to lead along important Lebanese men and make them take the bait one after the other. Thus the future of Lebanon will rest to a certain extent on the success of Great Britain and America in winning the Lebanese to their cause.

The Lebanese question has now opened before us the question of the four cazas and, without taking into account external political conditions, I can confirm, with regard to purely internal conditions, that the problem of the annexation and return to Syria of the four cazas can, perhaps now more than at any other time in the past, be the object of our concern by reason of the possibility of certain success it offers us, with regard to the wishes of the inhabitants which are becoming clearer and clearer and merit serious attention as well as quick action on our part.
June 3, 1947

The Director of the Sûreté Générale
For the Ministry of Defense Deuxième Bureau
Signature

The Director General of the Interior of the Syrian Republic
Nashua al-Ayubi

Registered in the Syrian Ministry of Foreign Affairs
No. 2887 – Political reports

393. June 3, 1947   Armanazi to Mardam

Top secret

The Syrian Minister of Foreign Affairs

British circles are very agitated by the last position adopted by Riyad Bey. Their secret agents are sure that there is an agreement there concluded between Riyad and the Americans. They do not yet know the aims of this agreement, but they are certain it is not to their advantage and General Spears would like you to make him understand indirectly that Great Britain is not powerless to settle its accounts with anyone at all and that if Riyad can mock all the countries separately or together, Great Britain would not be an object of derision for him. They want him to understand that he has responsibilities with regard to them and that Great Britain has not expelled France from Syria and Lebanon for men like Riyad to come and facilitate the Americans' arrival and chase out Great Britain.

The substance of these words must be reported and said to Sheikh Bishara al-Khuri who must know that Great Britain is not yet dead.

That is what they ask us to tell him, and as the messenger, I only need to pass it on.

Personally, I believe that the role Riyad is playing is useful to us because in fact he will greatly weaken King Abdullah's power and ruin the British plan of action which, we feel strongly, is directed against us.
June 3, 1947

The Minister
Najib al-Armanazi

Registered in the Syrian Ministry of Foreign Affairs
No. 2886 – Political reports

394. June 3, 1947 Mardam to Bevin

Top secret

From the Syrian Legation in London
to HE the British Foreign Secretary

Dear Minister,

For the seventh time I call Your Excellency's attention to the intrigues of British officers who have the upper hand over the army of Transjordan from where aggression is directed against Syria and Syrian independence.

What makes the situation even more delicate is that the plot organized against Syria is welcomed by all the British officials in the Near East.

Neither the Syrian government, nor the Syrian people, would ever have thought that Great Britain had helped Syria drive France out so that British sovereignty could replace French sovereignty in Syria, for Transjordan and King Abdullah, as is well understood, are working to achieve British sovereignty and British interests and no more.

To prove our good intentions, I place before Your Excellency the Soviet memorandum which was presented to us and to which we have so far refused to reply.

But if the British Government were to push us to despair, we would have recourse to any foreign aid whatsoever to safeguard our independence which, today, is threatened more than at any other time in the past.

I hope that you will want to undertake an act that will put an end to the state of extreme tension which, in the Middle East, creates a man with illegitimate appetites who acts with the acknowledged inspiration and advice of the British.

Yours sincerely,
June 3, 1947

The President of the Council
The Minister of Foreign Affairs
Jamil Mardam Bey

395. June 6, 1947 Mardam to President Quwatli

Top secret

HE the President of the Syrian Republic

The Abdelkrim affair has created an atmosphere of intense tension for the Egyptian Government and I heard King Faruq talking bitterly in the following way: "Abdelkrim will be a source of difficulty for us since the Egyptian Government put its hand on a letter addressed by King Abdullah to Abdelkrim inviting him to establish himself in Transjordan from where it would be possible to arrange to convey him to North Africa."

Here the atmosphere is extremely troubled as far as Abdelkrim is concerned, for the honor of the Egyptian Government no longer allows it to deliver Abdelkrim to France and at the same time the Egyptians fear that

France will resolve to kill or capture Abdelkrim through the intermediary of its many spies in Egypt. What makes the situation even more difficult is that Abdelkrim will no longer be anything other than a plaything in the hands of his Maghrebian compatriots who act mostly at the prompting of the Sultan of Morocco, who is at the same time for and against France and I believe that he will only be sincere with the Hashemites and their English masters.

I do not know who will benefit from Abdelkrim's flight and I believe that Egypt will suffer much wrong from his actions. Nuqrashi told me, "France was an old friend for Egypt, and we have finally lost this friendship." They fear encountering France's opposition to their complaint against Great Britain before the Security Council.

As for us, I believe that a move to insurrection in North Africa would only benefit us if it had a popular Arab nature which neither the Sultan, the Hashemites, nor lastly the English could exploit.

King Faruq has expressed his opinion well in the conversation we had, saying: "We contributed to giving the French policy a violent kick, but who will benefit?" He is convinced that Great Britain played us all and exploited us in its own interest and won on all fronts simultaneously.

But what I admire in King Faruq is that he plays his role very well even when he feels that he is losing.

June 6, 1947

The Minister of Foreign Affairs
Jamil Mardam Bey

Registered in the Syrian Ministry of Foreign Affairs
No. 2892 – Political reports

396. May 11, 1948   Intelligence Report by the French Military Attaché in Beirut

Beirut, May 11, 1948
French Legation in Lebanon
Military, Naval and Air Attaché

Intelligence Report no. 68

It appears that the resolve of the Arab states regarding the struggle over Palestine has grown stronger over the last few days.

They have suddenly realized their considerable loss of prestige in the entire world if they abandon Palestine to the Jewish enterprise after so much ranting.

They would prefer risking a military defeat rather than inaction, which they consider to be a disgrace.

All the states have decided on an extensive military effort with quick and massive action, whatever the price, against the Jewish state itself, hoping that a sudden and violent strike, using all the means available to the Arabs, would lead to a favorable outcome before the Jews, under vigorous attack in the vital areas of their territory, would have time to rally and organize themselves.

Arab military circles rely on the lack of heavy weapons (artillery, tanks) and war planes on the Jewish side, for the success of the operation.

The beginning of action is planned for May 15, and it appears that 1) the first main objective of the regular armies will be Tel Aviv itself, and 2) the Arabs have considered the aerial bombardment of this city.

The region of Tel Aviv will be the goal of the Egyptian army. (Knowing the Arabs, we can't rule out, without making any guesses, that not many of them would be prepared for a blitzkrieg.)

The following numbers can be anticipated (their reinforcement has already been studied for Egypt and Syria):

Egypt:	1 armored brigade	
	1 mobile infantry brigade	
	1 artillery regiment	
	3 groups of bombers	from 8,000 to 10,000 men
Iraq:	1 armored brigade	
	1 mobile infantry brigade	
	3 artillery batteries	
	1 aviation group	from 6,000 to 8,000 men
Transjordan:	Arab Legion	5,000 men
Syria:	2 or 3 battalions	
	3 artillery batteries	
	Tanks (about 40)	
	Airplanes	3,000 men
Lebanon	2 battalions	
	Various other elements	2,000 men

The Egyptian troops will be gathering at al-Arish. The British oppose their crossing the Palestinian border before May 15.

The Iraqi troops are concentrated in Mafraq, the Syrian troops in Kuneitra.

The Lebanese troops, already in place on the Lebanese-Palestinian border, don't appear to have to take an active part in the operations, but to make only some demonstration intended to hold back a part of the Zionist strength.

The removal of Ismail Pasha Safwat from his post as Commander of the Arab forces must have been motivated by his refusal to acquiesce in the British orders concerning the future progression of operations in Palestine, notably the question of Haifa, which Safwat wanted to attack and take over. The British opposed this, wanting to keep the port for the evacuation of their troops. Safwat protested. Abdullah and the Iraqi Regent gave in to the British demands. Safwat was removed from office and replaced by the Iraqi Division General, Nur a-Din Mahmmud, the Regent's man, whose compliance with the British is well-known.

The American Government's proposal – conveyed a few days ago to the Arab states and consisting of extending the British mandate over Palestine by ten days in order to facilitate an agreement between the Arabs and Jews – would have been accepted, it appears, straightaway by Azzam Pasha, Riyad al-Sulh, Jamil Mardam and Haj Amin al-Husseini, but rejected by King Abdullah. The others, even if they didn't want to, would then agree with him, in the present circumstances – not wanting to appear less enthusiastic defenders of an Arab Palestine than the Hashemite sovereign.

Certain circles in Damascus fear the consequences, after May 16, of the USSR's recognition of the establishment of the Jewish state and the immediate conclusion of a Judeo-Soviet treaty, on the positions of the Americans and the British vis-à-vis the Jewish state.

Bibliography

Archive Sources

France

I Archives Nationales, Paris (AN)
Archives du Général de Gaulle, Série AG, Papiers des Chefs d'Etat
Papiers de Georges Bidault
Papiers de Georges Catroux
II Ministère des Affaires Etrangères, Paris (MAE)
Série K – Syrie et Liban, 1944-1952
Papiers d'Agents – René Massigli Papers
III Centre des Archives Diplomatiques, Nantes (CADN)
Fonds Beyrouth – Syrie et Liban
IV Service Historique de l'Armée, Vincennes (SHA)
Série 4H Levant
Série 7NN – Fonds de Moscou (Moscow): Les archives des services militaires
Série Q – Secrétariat général de la défense nationale (SGDN)
Série S – Etat-major des armées (EMA)
Série T – Etat-major de l'armée de terre (EMAT)
Fonds privés – Général Paul Beynet (1K230)
Dossier personnel du Général Fernand François Oliva Roget (13Yd 725)

Great Britain

The National Archives, London (TNA)
FO371 Foreign Office: General Correspondence
FO226 Foreign Office: Consulate Beirut
Middle East Centre, St. Antony's College, Oxford (MEC) – Spears Papers

Israel

Central Zionist Archives, Jerusalem (CZA)
Haganah Archives, Tel Aviv (HA)
Ben-Gurion Archives, Sede Boqer (BGA)

Published Documents

Israel State Archives, Yogev, Gedalia (ed.), *Political and Diplomatic Documents, Vol.1, December 1947–May 1948* (Jerusalem, 1979)

Rashid, Ibrahim al- (ed.), *Documents on the History of Saudi Arabia*, Vol. V, Part II (Salisbury, N.C.: Documentary Publications, 1980)

Iraqi Parliamentary Committee on the War in Palestine, *Behind the Curtain* (Tel Aviv: Israel Defense Forces Publications, 1954) translated into Hebrew by Shmuel Segev

Secondary Sources

Aid, Matthew M. and Cees Wiebes (eds.), *Secrets of Signals Intelligence during the Cold War and Beyond* (London: Frank Cass, 2001)

Albord, Maurice, *L'Armée Française et les Etats du Levant, 1936-1946* (PhD dissertation, University of Paris X – Nanterre, 1998)

Aldrich, Richard J., "Imperial Rivalry: British and American Intelligence in Asia, 1942-46," *Intelligence and National Security*, 3(1), 1988, pp.5-55

Aldrich, Richard J., *The Hidden Hand: Britain, America and Cold War Secret Intelligence* (New York: The Overlook Press, 2001)

Aldrich, Richard J., "Policing the Past: Official History, Secrecy and British Intelligence since 1945," *English Historical Review*, CXIX(483), 2004, pp.922-53

Aldrich, Richard J. (ed.), *British Intelligence, Strategy and the Cold War, 1945-51* (Abingdon: Routledge, 1992)

Aldrich, Richard J. and Michael F. Hopkins (eds.), *Intelligence, Defence and Diplomacy: British Policy in the Post-War World* (London: Frank Cass, 1994)

Andrew, Christopher, *For the President's Eyes Only: Secret Intelligence and the American Presidency from Washington to Bush* (New York: Harper Perennial, 1996)

Andrew, Christopher, *The Defence of the Realm: The Authorized History of MI5* (London: Allen Lane, 2009)

Andrew, Christopher and David Dilks (eds.), *The Missing Dimension: Governments and Intelligence Communities in the Twentieth Century* (Champaign: University of Illinois Press, 1985)

Andrew, Christopher and Jeremy Noakes (eds.), *Intelligence and International Relations, 1900-1945* (Exeter: University of Exeter Press, 1987)

Anglim, Simon, "MI(R), G(R) and British Covert Operations, 1939-42," *Intelligence and National Security*, 20(4), 2005, pp.631-53

Avon, Earl of, *The Eden Memoirs: The Reckoning* (London: Cassel, 1965)

Balfour-Paul, Glen, *The End of the Empire in the Middle East* (Cambridge: Cambridge University Press, 1991)

Barr, James, *A Line in the Sand: The Anglo-French Struggle for the Middle East, 1914-1948* (London: W.W. Norton & Co., 2011)

Becker, Anja, "The Spy Who Couln't Possibly be French: Espionage (and) Culture in France," *The Journal of Intelligence History*, 1(1), 2001, pp.66-87

Beevor, Antony and Artemis Cooper, *Paris after the Liberation, 1944-1949* (London: Hamish Hamilton, 1994)

Bell, Philip M.H., "La Grande-Bretagne, de Gaulle et les Français libres, 1940-1944: Un bienfait oublié?" *Espoir*, Revue de l'Institut Charles de Gaulle (Paris: Plon), no.71, 1990, pp.27-35

Bernert, Philippe, *Roger Wybot et la Bataille pour la D.S.T.* (Paris: Presses de la Cité, 1975)

Bernert, Philippe, *SDECE, Service 7: L'extraordinaire Histoire du Colonel Le Roy-Finville et de ses Clandestins* (Paris: Presses de la Cité, 1980)

Bidault, Georges, *Resistance: The political autobiography of Georges Bidault* (London: Weidenfeld and Nicolson, 1967)

Birdwood, Lord, *Nuri As-Said: A Study in Arab Leadership* (London: Cassel, 1959)

Bloch, Jonathan and Patrick Fitzgerald, *British Intelligence and Covert Action: Africa, Middle East and Europe since 1945* (Dingle, Co. Kerry: Brandon Books, 1984)

Borden, Mary, *Journey Down a Blind Alley* (London: Hutchinson & Co., 1947)

Bowyer Bell, J., "Assassination in International Politics: Lord Moyne, Count Bernadotte, and the Lehi," *International Studies Quarterly*, 16(1), 1972, pp.59-82

Brown, L. Carl, and Matthew S. Gordon, (eds.), *Franco-Arab Encounters: Studies in Memory of David C. Gordon* (Beirut: American University of Beirut, 1996)

Bullock, Alan, *Ernest Bevin: Foreign Secretary, 1945-1951* (London: Heinemann, 1983)

Catroux, General, *Dans la Bataille de Méditerranée* (Paris: René Juillard, 1949)

Chair, Somerset de, *The Golden Carpet* (London: Faber and Faber, 1944)

Chaitani, Youssef N., *Syro-Lebanese Cooperation or Integration? Bilateral Relations, 1943-1950* (PhD dissertation, University of London, Birkbeck College, 2004)

Chamoun, Camille, *Crise au Moyen-Orient* (Paris: Gallimard, 1963)

Charters, David A., "British Intelligence in the Palestine Campaign, 1945-47," *Intelligence and National Security*, 6(1), 1991, pp.115-40

Chavkin, Jonathan S., *British Intelligence and the Zionist, South African, and Australian Intelligence Communities during and after the Second World War* (PhD dissertation, University of Cambridge, 2009)

Clarke, Dudley, *Seven Assignments* (London: Jonathan Cape, 1949)

Cohen, Michael J. and Martin Kolinsky (eds.), *Demise of the British Empire in the Middle East: Britain's Response to Nationalist Movements, 1943-55* (London: Frank Cass, 1998)

Cohen-Shany, Shmuel, *Paris Operation: Intelligence and Quiet Diplomacy in a New State* (Tel Aviv: Ramot Publishing, Tel Aviv University, 1994) (in Hebrew)

Cooper, Artemis, *Cairo in the War, 1939-1945* (London: Hamish Hamilton, 1989)

Cooper, Duff, *Old Men Forget: The Autobiography of Duff Cooper* (London: Rupert Hart-Davis, 1953)

Copeland, Miles, *The Game of Nations: The Amorality of Power Politics* (New York: Simon & Schuster, 1970)

Cradock, Percy, *Know Your Enemy: How the Joint Intelligence Committee Saw the World* (London: John Murray, 2002)

Dalloz, Jacques, *Georges Bidault: Biographie Politique* (Paris: L'Harmattan, 1992)

Davet, Michel-Christian, *La Double Affaire de Syrie* (Paris: Fayard, 1967)

Davies, Philip H.J., "From Special Operations to Special Political Action: The 'Rump SOE' and SIS Post-War Covert Action Capability 1945-1977," *Intelligence and National Security*, 15(3), 2000, pp.55-76

Davies, Philip H.J., *MI6 and the Machinery of Spying* (London: Frank Cass, 2004)

Dawn, C.E., *The Project of Greater Syria* (unpublished PhD dissertation, Princeton University, 1948)

Deacon, Richard, *The French Secret Service* (London: Grafton Books, 1990)

Dilks, David (ed.), *The Diaries of Sir Alexander Cadogan, 1938-1945* (New York: G.P. Putnam's Sons, 1972)

Doran, Michael, *Pan-Arabism before Nasser: Egyptian Power Politics and the Palestine Question* (Oxford: Oxford University Press, 1999)

Dorril, Stephen, *MI6: Inside the Covert World of Her Majesty's Secret Intelligence Service* (New York: The Free Press, 2000)

Dovey, H.O., "The Middle East Intelligence Centre," *Intelligence and National Security*, 4(4),1989, pp.800-12

Dovey, H.O., "Security in Syria, 1941-45," *Intelligence and National Security*, 6(2), 1991, pp.418-46

Dovey, H.O., "Maunsell and Mure," *Intelligence and National Sec*urity, 8(1), 1993, pp.60-77

Dovey, H.O., "The Intelligence War in Turkey," *Intelligence and National Security*, 9 (1), 1994, pp.59-87

Egremont, Max, *Under Two Flags: The Life of Major General Sir Edward Spears* (London: Phoenix Giant, 1997)

Eisenberg, Laura Zittrain, *My Enemy's Enemy: Lebanon in the Early Zionist Imagination, 1900-1948* (Detroit: Wayne State University Press, 1994)

Elath, Eliahu, *San Francisco Diary* (Tel Aviv: Dvir, 1971) (in Hebrew)

Eshed, Haggai, *Reuven Shiloah: The Man Behind the Mossad* (London: Frank Cass, 2005)

Evans, Trefor E. (ed.), *The Killearn Diaries, 1934-1946* (London: Sidgwick & Jackson, 1972)

Faligot, Roger and Pascal Krop, *La Piscine: Les services secrets Français, 1944-1984* (Paris: Editions du Seuil, 1985)

Forcade, Olivier, *La République Secrète: histoire des services spéciaux Français de 1918 à 1939* (Paris: Nouveau Monde, 2008)

French, David, *The British Way in Counter-Insurgency, 1945-1967* (Oxford: Oxford University Press, 2011)

Fry, Michael G. and Itamar Rabinovich, *Despatches from Damascus: Gilbert MacKereth and British Policy in the Levant, 1933-1939* (Jerusalem: Tel Aviv University, Daf-Chen Press, Ltd., 1985)

Garder, Michel, *La Guerre Secrète des Services Spéciaux Français, 1935-1945* (Paris: Plon, 1967)

Garnett, David, *The Secret History of PWE: The Political Warfare Executive, 1939-1945* (London: St. Ermin's Press, 2002)

Gauché, Général, *Le Deuxième Bureau au travail, 1935-1940* (Paris: Lavauzelle, 2002)

Gaulle, Charles de, *Lettres, notes et carnets, Juin 1943–Mai 1945* (Paris: Plon, 1983)

Gaulle, Charles de, *The Complete War Memoirs of Charles de Gaulle* (New York: Carroll & Graf Publishers, Inc., 1998)

Gaunson, A.B., *The Anglo-French Clash in Lebanon and Syria, 1940-45* (New York: St. Martin's Press, 1987)

Gershoni, Israel (ed.), *Arab Responses to Fascism and Nazism, 1933-1945* (Austin: University of Texas Press, 2014)

Gilad, Zrubavel, *Secret Shield: Activities of the Jewish Underground in World War II* (Jerusalem: Jewish Agency Publishing House, 1948) (in Hebrew)

Glubb, John B., *A Soldier with the Arabs* (London: Hodder and Stoughton, 1957)

Gomaa, Ahmed M., *The Foundation of the League of Arab States* (London: Longman, 1977)

Gorst, Anthony and W. Scott Lucas, "The Other Collusion: Operation Straggle and Anglo-American Intervention in Syria, 1955-56," *Intelligence and National Security*, 4(3), 1989, pp.576-95

Graves, Philip P. (ed.), *Memoirs of King Abdullah of Transjordan* (London: Jonathan Cape, 1950)

Grob-Fitzgibbon, Benjamin, *Imperial Endgame: Britain's Dirty Wars and the End of Empire* (New York: Palgrave Macmillan, 2011)

Halliday, Fred, *The Middle East in International Relations: Power, Politics and Ideology* (Cambridge: Cambridge University Press, 2005)

Hamdi, Walid M.S., *Rashid Ali Al-Gailani and the Nationalist Movement in Iraq, 1939-1941* (London: Darf Publishers Ltd., 1987)

Harouvi, Eldad, *Palestine Investigated: The Story of the Palestine C.I.D., 1920-1948* (Kochav Yair: Porat Publishing, 2011) (in Hebrew)

Harvey, John (ed.), *The War Diaries of Oliver Harvey* (London: Collins, 1978)

Hastedt, Glenn P. (ed.), *Controlling Intelligence* (Abingdon: Frank Cass, 2005)

Hinsley, F.H. and C.A.G. Simkins, *British Intelligence in the Second World War: Volume Four: Security and Counter-Intelligence* (London: HMSO, 1990)

Horowitz, David, *State in the Making* (New York: Alfred A. Knopf, 1953)

Hourani, Albert H., *Syria and Lebanon: A Political Essay* (The Royal Institute of International Affairs, London: Oxford University Press, 1946)

Hourani, Cecil A., "The Arab League in Perspective," *The Middle East Journal*, 1(2), 1947, pp.125-36

Jeffery, Keith, *MI6: The History of the Secret Intelligence Service, 1909-1949* (London: Bloomsbury, 2010)

Johnson, Loch K. (ed.), *Strategic Intelligence Vol.1: Understanding the Hidden Side of Government* (Westport: Praeger Security International, 2007)

Johnson, Loch K. (ed.), *Strategic Intelligence Vol.2: The Intelligence Cycle: The Flow of Secret Information from Overseas to the Highest Councils of Government* (Westport: Praeger Security International, 2007)

Johnson, Loch K. (ed.), *Strategic Intelligence Vol.3: Covert Action: Behind the Veils of Secret Foreign Policy* (Westport: Praeger Security International, 2007)

Johnson, Loch K. (ed.), *Strategic Intelligence Vol. 4: Counter-intelligence and Counter-terrorism: Defending the Nation Against Hostile Forces* (Westport: Praeger Security International, 2007)

Johnson, Loch K. (ed.), *Strategic Intelligence Vol. 5: Intelligence and Accountability: Safeguards Against the Abuse of Power* (Westport: Praeger Security International, 2007)

Kaplan, Robert D., *The Arabists: The Romance of an American Elite* (New York: The Free Press, 1995)

Keay, John, *Sowing the Wind: The Mismanagement of the Middle East 1900-1960* (London: John Murray, 2003)

Kedourie, Elie, *The Chatham House Version and Other Middle-Eastern Studies* (London: Weidenfeld and Nicolson, 1970)

Kelley, Saul, "A Succession of Crises: SOE in the Middle East, 1940-45," *Intelligence and National Security*, 20(1), 2005, pp.121-46

Kersaudy, François, *Churchill and de Gaulle* (New York: Atheneum, 1982)

Khuri, Bishara al-, *Haqa'iq lubnaniyya, Vol.2* (Beirut: 1960) (in Arabic)

Kimche, Jon, *Seven Fallen Pillars: The Middle East, 1915-1950* (London: Secker and Warburg, 1950)

Kimche, Jon and David Kimche, *Both Sides of the Hill: Britain and the Palestine War* (London: Secker & Warburg, 1960)

King Abdallah of Jordan, *My Memoirs Completed* (London: Longman, 1978)

Kirk, George, *The Middle East in the War* (Oxford: Oxford University Press, 1954)

Kirkbride, Alec S., *A Crackle of Thorns: Experiences in the Middle East* (London: John Murray, 1956)

Laffargue, André, *Le Général Dentz: Paris 1940 – Syrie 1941* (Paris: Les Iles d'Or, 1954)

Landis, Joshua, "Syria and the Palestine War: Fighting King Abdullah's 'Greater Syrian Plan'," in Rogan, Eugene L. and Avi Shlaim (eds.), *The War for Palestine* (Cambridge: Cambridge University Press, 2007), pp.176-203

Langhorne, Richard (ed.), *Diplomacy and Intelligence During the Second World War* (Cambridge: Cambridge University Press, 1985)

Laurent, Sébastien, "The Free French Secret Services: Intelligence and the Politics of Republican Legitimacy," *Intelligence and National Security*, 15(4), 2000, pp.19-41

Lawrence, T.E., *Seven Pillars of Wisdom* (New York: Penguin Books, 1977)

Lefen, Asa, *The SHAY: The Roots of the Israeli Intelligence Community* (Tel Aviv: Ministry of Defense Publications, 1997) (in Hebrew)

Lenczowski, George, *The Middle East in World Affairs* (Ithaca: Cornell University Press, 1958)

Lerner, Henri, *Catroux* (Paris: Albin Michel, 1990)

Little, Douglas, "Cold War and Covert Action: The United States and Syria, 1945-1958," *The Middle East Journal*, 44(1), 1990, pp.51-75

Longrigg, Stephen H., and Frank Stoakes, *Iraq* (London: Ernest Benn Ltd., 1958)

Longrigg, Stephen H., *Oil in the Middle East* (Oxford: Oxford University Press, 1961)

Longrigg, Stephen H., *Syria and Lebanon under French Mandate* (Beirut: Oxford University Press, 1968)

Louis, Wm. Roger, *The British Empire in the Middle East, 1945-1951: Arab Nationalism, the United States, and Post-war Imperialism* (Oxford: Oxford University Press, 1985)

Lyttelton, Oliver, *Lord Chandos: An Unexpected View from the Summit* (New York: New American Library, 1963)

Mackenzie, W.J.M., *The Secret History of SOE: The Special Operations Executive, 1940-1945* (London: St. Ermin's Press, 2000)

Maddy-Weitzman, Bruce, *The Crystallization of the Arab State System, 1945-1954* (Syracuse: Syracuse University Press, 1993)

Magan, William, *Middle Eastern Approaches: Experiences and Travels of an Intelligence Officer, 1939-1948* (Norwich: Michael Russell Publishing, 2001)

Major, Patrick and Christopher R. Moran (eds.), *Spooked: Britain, Empire and Intelligence since 1945* (Newcastle upon Tyne: Cambridge Scholars Publishing, 2009)

Marck, David de Young de la, *Free French and British Intelligence Relations, 1940-1944* (PhD dissertation, University of Cambridge, 2000)

Marck, David de Young de la, "De Gaulle, Colonel Passy and British Intelligence, 1940-2," *Intelligence and National Security*, 18(1), 2003, pp.21-40

Mardam, Salma, *Syria's Quest for Independence* (Reading: Ithaca Press, 1994)

Massigli, René, *Une Comédie des Erreurs 1943-1956: Souvenirs et Réflexions sur une Étape de la Construction Européenne* (Paris: Plon, 1978)

McGowan, Marcia Phillips, "'A Nearer Approach to the Truth': Mary Borden's *Journey Down a Blind Alley*," *War, Literature and The Arts*, 16(1-2), 2004, pp.198-216

McLoughlin, Leslie J., *Nest of Spies … ?: The History of MECAS* (London: Alhani, 1994)

McLoughlin, Leslie J., *In a Sea of Knowledge: British Arabists in the Twentieth Century* (Reading: Ithaca Press, 2002)

Miller, Rory, *Divided Against Zion: Anti-Zionist Opposition in Britain to a Jewish State in Palestine, 1945-1948* (London: Frank Cass, 2000)

Milstein, Uri, *History of the War of Independence: The First Month* (Lanham, MD: University Press of America, 1997)

Mizrahi, Jean-David, *Genèse de l'Etat mandataire: Service de Renseignements et Bandes Armées en Syrie at au Liban dans les Années 1920* (Paris: Publications de la Sorbonne, 2003)

Mockler, Anthony, *Our Enemies the French: Being an Account of the War Fought Between the French and the British, Syria 1941* (London: Leo Cooper, 1976)

Monroe, Elizabeth, *The Mediterranean in Politics* (London: Oxford University Press, 1938)

Monroe, Elizabeth, "Mr. Bevin's Arab Policy," in Hourani, Albert (ed.), *Middle Eastern Affairs* (2), St. Antony Papers, No.11 (Carbondale, Illinois: Southern Illinois University Press, 1961)

Monroe, Elizabeth, *Britain's Moment in the Middle East, 1914-1956* (London: University Paperbacks, Methuen & Co. Ltd., 1965)

Mott-Radclyffe, Charles, *Foreign Body in the Eye: A Memoir of the Foreign Service Old and New* (London: Leo Cooper, 1975)

Murphy, Christopher J., "SOE's Foreign Currency Transactions," *Intelligence and National Security*, 20(1), 2005, pp.191-208

Navarre, Henri, *Le Service de Renseignements, 1871-1944* (Paris: Plon, 1978)

Nicolson, Nigel (ed.), *Volume II of the Diaries and Letters of Harold Nicolson: The War Years, 1939-1945* (New York: Atheneum, 1967)

Ovendale, Ritchie, *Britain, the United States and the Transfer of Power in the Middle East, 1945-1962* (London: Leicester University Press, 1996)

Oxford Dictionary of National Biography (Oxford: Oxford University Press, 2004)

Pearse, Richard, *Three Years in the Levant* (London: Macmillan, 1949)

Peterson, Maurice, *Both Sides of the Curtain: An Autobiography* (London: Constable and Co., 1950)

Pinkus, Benjamin, *From Ambivalence to a Tacit Alliance: Israel, France and French Jewry, 1947-1957* (Sede Boqer: Ben-Gurion University of the Negev Press, 2005) (in Hebrew)

Pipes, Daniel, *Greater Syria* (Oxford: Oxford University Press, 1990)

Porath, Yehoshua, *In Search of Arab Unity, 1930-1945* (London: Frank Cass, 1986)

Puaux, Gabriel, *Deux Années au Levant: Souvenirs de Syrie et du Liban, 1939-1940* (Paris: Hachette, 1952)

Qadi, Atif al-, *Qimmat Radwa* (Yanbu', 2008) (in Arabic)

Qawuqji, Fauzi al-, "Memoirs, 1948, Part I," *Journal of Palestinian Studies*, 2(1), 1971, pp.27-58

Rabinovich, Itamar, *The Road Not Taken: Early Arab-Israeli Negotiations* (Jerusalem: Keter Publishing, 1991)

Ranfurly, Countess of, *To War with Whitaker: The Wartime Diaries of the Countess of Ranfurly, 1939-1945* (London: Heinemann, 1994)

Rathmell, Andrew, *Secret War in the Middle East: The Covert Struggle of Syria, 1949-1961* (London: I.B. Tauris, 1995)

Rathmell, Andrew, "Copeland and Za'im: Re-evaluating the Evidence," *Intelligence and National Security*, 11(1), 1996, pp.89-105

Rivlin, Gershon and Elhanan Orren (eds.), *Ben-Gurion's War Diary* Vol. I, (Tel Aviv: Ministry of Defense Publishing, 1982) (in Hebrew)

Roosevelt, Kermit, *Arabs, Oil and History: The Story of the Middle East* (London: Victor Gollancz Ltd., 1949)

Roshwald, Aviel, *Estranged Bedfellows: Britain and France in the Middle East During the Second World War* (Oxford: Oxford University Press, 1990)

Rubin, Barry, *The Great Powers in the Middle East, 1941-1947: The Road to the Cold War* (London: Frank Cass, 1980)

Rubin, Barry, *Istanbul Intrigues* (New York: McGraw-Hill, 1989)

Said, Edward W., *Orientalism* (London: Penguin Books, 1978)

Sasson, Eliyahu, *On the Road to Peace: Letters and Conversations* (Tel Aviv: Am Oved, 1978) (in Hebrew)

Satia, Priya, "The Defense of Inhumanity: Air Control and the British Idea of Arabia," *The American Historical Review*, 111(1), 2006, pp.16-51

Satia, Priya, *Spies in Arabia: The Great War and the Cultural Foundations of Britain's Covert Empire in the Middle East* (New York: Oxford University Press, 2008)

Schillo, Frédérique, *La Politique française à l'égard d'Israël, 1946-1959* (Brussels: André Versaille Editeur, 2012)

Scott, Len, "Secret Intelligence, Covert Action and Clandestine Diplomacy," *Intelligence and National Security*, 19(2), 2004, pp.322-41

Seale, Patrick, *The Struggle for Syria: A Study of Post-War Arab Politics, 1945-1958* (Oxford: Oxford University Press, 1965)

Seale, Patrick, *The Struggle for Arab Independence: Riad el-Solh and the Makers of the Modern Middle East* (Cambridge: Cambridge University Press, 2010)

Sheffy, Yigal, *British Military Intelligence in the Palestine Campaign, 1914-1918* (London: Routledge, 1998)

Shelley, Adam B., *British Intelligence in the Middle East, 1939-1946* (PhD dissertation, University of Cambridge, 2007)

Sirrs, Owen L., *A History of the Egyptian Intelligence Service: A History of the Mukhabarat, 1910-2009* (Abingdon: Routledge, 2010)

Spears, Edward, *Assignment to Catastrophe: Vol. 1: Prelude to Dunkirk, July 1939-May 1940*, and *Vol. 2: The Fall of France* (London: William Heinemann Ltd., 1954)

Spears, Edward, *Fulfilment of a Mission: The Spears Mission to Syria and Lebanon, 1941-1944* (London: Leo Cooper, 1977)

Stafford, David, *Churchill and Secret Service* (New York: The Overlook Press, 1998)

Stark, Freya, *East is West* (London: John Murray, 1945)

Stark, Freya, *Dust in the Lion's Paw: Autobiography 1939-1946* (London: John Murray, 1961)

Stirling, Walter F., *Safety Last* (London: Hollis and Carter, 1953)

Sweet-Escott, B., *Baker Street Irregular* (London: Methuen & Co Ltd, 1965)

Sykes, Christopher, *Four Studies in Loyalty* (London: Collins, 1946)

Tamkin, Nicholas, *Britain, Turkey and the Soviet Union, 1940-45: Strategy, Diplomacy and Intelligence in the Eastern Mediterranean* (London: Palgrave Macmillan, 2009)

Tempest, Paul (ed.), *The Arabists of Shemlan: Volume 1, MECAS Memoirs 1944-78* (London: Stacey International, 2006)

Thomas, Martin, "France in British Signals Intelligence, 1939-1945," *French History*, 14(1), 2000, pp.41-66

Thomas, Martin, "French Intelligence-Gathering in the Syrian Mandate, 1920-40," *Middle Eastern Studies*, 38(1), 2002, pp.1-32

Thomas, Martin, *Empires of Intelligence: Security Services and Colonial Disorder after 1914* (Berkeley: University of California Press, 2008)

Vaughan, James R., "'A Certain Idea of Britain': British Cultural Diplomacy in the Middle East, 1945-57," *Contemporary British History*, 19(2), 2005, pp.151-68

Walton, Calder, *Empire of Secrets: British Intelligence, the Cold War and the Twilight of Empire* (London: Harper Press, 2013)

Warburg, Gabriel, "Lampson's Ultimatum to Faruq, 4 February 1942," *Middle Eastern Studies*, 11(1), 1975, pp.24-32

West, Nigel, *MI6: British Secret Intelligence Operations, 1909-1945* (New York: Random House, 1983)

West, Nigel, *The Sigint Secrets: The Signals Intelligence War, 1900 to Today* (New York: Quill, William Morrow, 1988)

Westrate, Bruce, *The Arab Bureau: British Policy in the Middle East, 1916-1920* (Philadelphia: University of Pennsylvania Press, 2003)

Wichart, Stefanie K., *Intervention: Britain, Egypt, and Iraq During World War II* (PhD dissertation, University of Texas at Austin, 2007)

Wight, Martin, *Power Politics* (London: Penguin Books, 1978)

Wilmington, Martin W., *The Middle East Supply Centre* (London: University of London Press, 1972)

Wilson, Lord, *Eight Years Overseas, 1939-1947* (Hutchinson, London, 1951)

Woodhouse, Roger, *British Policy towards France, 1945-51* (London: Macmillan, 1995)

Wylie, Neville (ed.), *The Politics and Strategy of Clandestine War: Special Operations Executive, 1940-1946* (Abingdon: Routledge, 2007)

Yapp, M.E. (ed.), *Politics and Diplomacy in Egypt: The Diaries of Sir Miles Lampson, 1935-1937* (London: Oxford University Press, 1997)

Young, John Wilson, "The Foreign Office and the Departure of General de Gaulle, June 1945–January 1946," *The Historical Journal*, 25(1), 1982, pp.209-16

Zamir, Meir, *The Formation of Modern Lebanon* (Ithaca: Cornell University Press, 1988)

Zamir, Meir, *Lebanon's Quest: The Road to Statehood, 1926-1939* (London: I.B. Tauris, 1997)

Zamir, Meir, "An Intimate Alliance: The Joint Struggle of General Edward Spears and Riad al-Sulh to Oust France from Lebanon, 1942–1944," *Middle Eastern Studies*, 41(6), 2005, pp.811-32

Zamir, Meir, "De Gaulle and the Question of Syria and Lebanon During the Second World War," *Middle Eastern Studies*, 43(5), 2007, pp.675-708

Zamir, Meir, "BID for Altalena: France's Covert Action in the 1948 War in Palestine," *Middle Eastern Studies*, 46(1), 2010, pp.17-58

Zamir, Meir, "The 'Missing Dimension': Britain's Secret War Against France in Syria and Lebanon, 1942-45 – Part II," *Middle Eastern Studies*, 46(6), 2010, pp.791-899

Zamir, Meir, "Against the Tide: The Secret Alliance Between the Syrian National Bloc Leaders and Great Britain, 1941-1942," in Gershoni, Israel (ed.), *Arab Responses to Fascism and Nazism, 1933-1945* (Austin: University of Texas Press, 2014)

Zamir, Meir, "Espionage and the Zionist Endeavor," *Jerusalem Post*, November 21, 2008

Zisser, Eyal, *Lebanon: The Challenge of Independence* (London: I.B. Tauris, 2000)

Index

Note: The Documents are referenced in the index with the letter 'd', for example 204d5 would denote page 204 Document number 5. The notes sections in the book are referenced in the index with a letter 'n', for example 161n122 would denote page 161 note 122.

Section de Centralisation de Renseignements (SCR) 51
Service de Renseignement (SR) 54; Egypt 57; Iraq 57; main characters 54–7; role in French Middle East politics 56; Transjordan 57; Vichy collaboration 70
Shertok (Sharett), Moshe xi, 149, 120d25, 299d119, 409d318
Shone, Terence 18, 227d29, 252d54, 291d108, 302d125, 369–70d241, 382d265, 386d271, 392–93d286, 404d308; agreement with Quwatli 283–86d94; *see also* Jabiri; Mardam
Sidqi, Isma'il 40, 179, 417d327, 442d336
signals intelligence (sigint) 22, 47n47, 65, 88n33
Smart, Walter 38–9, 245–46d42; CPA 39, 240d38, 241d39, 386d271, 391–92d284; diplomatic career 39; Hashemite Greater Syria 40; indirect control of Egyptian politics 39–40; ousting France from Syria 246d43, 247d44; Pan-Arabist-Egyptian policy 29, 38–40
Solod, Daniel 140–42, 273–74d79, 412–13d319; *see also* Soviet Union
Soviet Union 4, 207d9, 226d28, 306d132; Anglo-Soviet rivalry 14, 265–66d71, 399–400d300; Middle East ambitions 399–400d300; perceived threat 123; recognition of Syria's independence 207–8d9, 209d11, 265d70, 273–75d79, 276d81, 398–99d298; Syrian Kurds, relationship with 378d257, 379–80d360; Solod 141, 218d21, 219d22, 262–63d67; support against Zionist movement 307d133
Spears, Edward 3; anti-French crusade 48n65, 53, 78–9, 86-7n7; 97–9; Bevin-Bidault agreement 32–3; Churchill 25–6, 30–1, 78–9, 95, 97–8, 104; the 'Club' 6; conflict with Catroux 75; efforts to oust France 3–4, 29, 30–3; financial interests 342–43d194, 368–69d239, 414d322; Lebanese constitutional crisis 94–7, 98; Lebanese independence 75–6, 460d393; Mardam and 209d10, 316d147; Quwatli, relationship with, 260d64; SOE 24–25, 31–2; Spears Mission, 31; Syrian crisis 122–23; Syrian Unity

261d65, 262d66, 325d161, 338d187, 457–58d389
Spears Mission 31, 34, 51, 77–8, 80, 85–6, 91n69, 104, 110
Special Operations Executive (SOE) 22, 31–2; Axis forces and 24; foundation 23; Sharq al-Adna 24; special political operations 24–5; Stay-Behind Plans 24
Stark, Freya 6, 21
Stirling, Walter F. 24, 33, 315d145; Bevin-Bidault agreement 35–6; efforts to oust France 29, 334d179; manipulation of inter-Arab politics 34, 48n68, 340d189, 354d213; Oliva Roget and 35, 155n35; resignation of Jabiri 36; SOE 33–4; support of Hashemite Greater Syria 35–6, 348d202; *see also* Arabists; Barazi; Syrian crisis
Suez Canal 9, 57, 59, 63, 176, 263d67, 266d72, 308d134, 417d327
Sulh, Riyad al- 15, 18, 57, 65, 82–4, 65, 91n69, 164, 177–79, 272d77, 412d319, 445d373, 459d392, 460d393; anti-French campaign 96–7, 454d386; Khuri and 85; Lebanese constitutional crisis 19, 32, 94–7; Maronites 112, 136–37; Transjordan 263d68; *see also* Clayton; Lebanon
Sûreté Générale 54, 324d159
Sûreté Nationale 54
Sykes-Picot Agreement 8, 18, 166, 382d265
Syria 3–11, 199d1; anti-British feeling 68–9, 395d291, 404d308, 424d339; Arab Unity and 204d5, 211–12d13; British control 128–30, 237d35, 328–29d167, 329d168, 372–73d248, 375d252; British zone of influence 352d210; conflict with Iraq 125, 214–15d16, 215d17; economic development 318–19d151; elections 1943 93, 94–5; French mandate 227d29, 236–38d35; French military occupation 125–28, 332d175, 345d199, 377d256, 391d283; French undercover activities 112–13, 268d74, 404–5d309; government indecision 126–27, 338d186; Lebanon, relationship with 384d268; North Africa 445–46d374; oil exploitation 252d52, 252d53, 256d58; Palestinian question 320–21d154, 416d326;

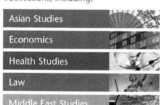